THE GUINNESS

1999

BOOK OF RECORDS

GUINNESS PUBLISHING

British Library cataloguing-in-Publication Data
A catalogue record for this book is available from the British Library
ISBN 0-85112-070-9

Managing Editor
Nic Kynaston

Editor
Rhonda Carrier

Assistant Editors
Hephzibah Anderson
and Georgie Naumann

Picture Editor
Gregory King

Consultant Editor
Elizabeth Wyse

Proof Reader
Debra Clapson

Index
Sue Harper

Designers
Lesley Horowitz
and Dominic Sinesio
at Office, NYC

Assistant Designers
Garry Waller
and Robert Hackett

Mac Operator
Tamsin Pender

Cover
Ron Callow at Design 23
and Office, NYC

Page Production
Catherine Bonifassi

Pre Production Manager
Patricia Langton

Fulfilment
Mary Hill
and Cathryn Harker

Director of Records Research
Mark Young

Keeper of the Records
Clive Carpenter

Research
Jane Bolton, Shelley Flacks, John Hansen, Della Howes, Stewart Newport, Antonia Short, Kim Stram

Correspondence
Amanda Brooks

Production Director
Chris Lingard

Colour Origination
Rival Colour

Printing and Binding
Printer Industria Grafica, S.A., Barcelona

Paper
Printed on woodfree, chlorine free and acid free paper

Publishing Director
Ian Castello-Cortes

Managing Director
Christopher Irwin

Abbreviations and measurements

The Guinness Book of Records uses both metric and imperial measurements (imperial in brackets). The only exception to this rule is for some scientific data, where metric measurements only are universally accepted, and for some sports data.

All currency values are shown in dollars with the sterling equivalent in brackets except when transactions took place in the United Kingdom, when this is reversed. Where a specific date is given the exchange rate is calculated according to the currency values that were in operation at the time. Where only a year date is given the exchange rate is calculated from December of that year. The billion conversion is one thousand million.

Accreditation

Guinness Publishing Ltd has a very thorough accreditation system for records verification. However, whilst every effort is made to ensure accuracy, Guinness Publishing Ltd cannot be held responsible for any errors contained in this work. Feedback from our readers on any points of accuracy is always welcomed.

General Warning

Attempting to break records or set new records can be dangerous. Appropriate advice should be taken first and all record attempts are undertaken entirely at the participant's risk. In no circumstances will Guinness Publishing Ltd have any liability for death or injury suffered in any record attempts. Guinness Publishing Ltd has complete discretion over whether or not to include any particular records in the book.

THE GUINNESS

1999

BOOK OF RECORDS

GUINNESS PUBLISHING

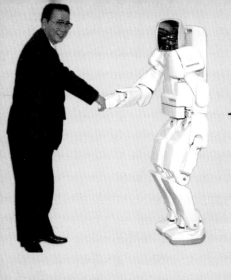

introduction

The *Guinness Book of Records* that you have in your hands is part of a global phenomenon. Many countries including Brazil, the Czech Republic, Denmark, Finland, France, Germany, Greece, Hungary, Italy, the Netherlands, Norway, Poland, Romania, Russia, Sweden and much of Latin America, as well as the United Kingdom and the USA, have contributed to what we believe is the most exciting *Guinness Book of Records* ever.

Our transatlantic research teams, based in London and Stamford, Connecticut, have brought you not only the latest records, but also whole new categories that reflect the true state of the record-breaking world in 1999. We have even more hi-tech and computer records than last year. There are new music and fashion sections and lots more on stars and celebrities. We also celebrate the achievements of the unique Guinness record-breakers in our section 'Extraordinary People', which features many new records and personalities but also some old favourites surpassing their own extraordinary standards.

Most of you are keen sports fans, and we hope you will like our new Sports Reference section, which begins on page 304. This lists important world records in a quick-access format. You will find the traditional sports section between pages 250 and 303. We are particularly thrilled to have added paralympics records on pages 266 and 267; the sheer determination and excellence of the achievers in this section really captures that special *Guinness Book of Records* spirit.

The records that really stand out this year? As ever it is hard to chose, but Richard Noble's breaking of the land speed record (page 158), the amazing success of the film *Titanic* (page 209) and the winning of an eighth gold medal at the Nagano Olympic Games by Nordic skier Bjørn Dæhlie (page 276), making him the most successful individual in the history of the Winter Olympics, really did amaze everyone.

Finally, remember that we are always in search of new record-breakers. See pages 334 and 335 on how to compete for a record and how you too could become an accredited Guinness record-holder. You never know — you may even see yourself in *The Guinness Book of Records* one day!

contents

①

②

③

1 ▪ Fame
010 Hollywood
012 Movie Stars
014 TV Stars
016 Sports Superstars
018 Pop Stars
020 Supermodels
022 Diana and Royalty
024 Celebrity Icons
026 World Leaders
028 Benefits, Charities and Parties

2 ▪ Money & Big Business
032 Wealth
034 Valuable Stuff
036 Going, Going, Gone
038 Gambling
040 Shopping
042 Brand Names
044 Advertising
046 World Markets
048 Company Power
050 Business Tycoons
052 High Earners

3 ▪ Extraordinary People
056 Collections
058 Fans and Followers
060 Food and Drink I
062 Food and Drink II
064 Achievers I
066 Achievers II
068 Teamwork
070 Early Starters
072 Golden Oldies
074 Players and Games
076 Driving and Riding
078 Epic Journeys I
080 Epic Journeys II

4 ▪ Extraordinary Lives
084 Crime
086 Punishment
088 Hoaxes and Confidence Tricks
090 Religions, Rites and Cults
092 Great Escapes

5 ▪ The Body
096 Big and Small
098 Body Parts
100 Bodily Phenomena
102 Life
104 Death and Disease
106 Medical Extremes
108 Body Transformation I
110 Body Transformation II
112 Body Art

6 ▪ The Natural World
116 Largest and Smallest Mammals
118 Mammal Lifestyle
120 Fish
122 Water Creatures
124 Reptiles and Dinosaurs
126 Birds
128 Spiders and Scorpions
130 Insects and Creepy Crawlies
132 Parasites
134 Animal Attack
136 Endangered and New Species
138 Pets
140 Trees and Plants
142 Dangerous and Strange Plantlife
144 Genetics
146 Amazing Earth
148 The Universe
150 Weird Science

⑦

⑧

⑨

hollywood

RICHEST HOLLYWOOD SCHOOL

Beverly Hills High School is the wealthiest school in Hollywood. The school is set in a 10.5-ha (26-acre) site on Lasky Drive. Established in 1928, the school's revenue from its own oil wells has underwritten its lavish sporting facilities, which include the famous gym-over-a-swimming-pool featured in the Frank Capra movie *It's a Wonderful Life* (USA, 1946). The school is used by many Hollywood parents, and famous former pupils have included Richard Dreyfuss, Carrie Fisher, Nic Cage and Richard Chamberlain. The school depicted in the TV series *Beverly Hills 90210* is not the real Beverly Hills High School.

MOST MARRIED HOLLYWOOD STARS

Actors Stan Laurel, Mickey Rooney, Lana Turner, Georgia Holt and Zsa Zsa Gabor have all been married a total of eight times. Elizabeth Taylor has also married eight times to date, but has only had seven different husbands: she married Richard Burton twice.

MOST JAILED HOLLYWOOD STAR

Errol Flynn, the star of *The Adventures of Robin Hood* (USA, 1938) and *They Died with Their Boots On* (USA, 1941) was jailed more often than any other Hollywood star. In the 1920s he was sentenced to two weeks in prison in New Guinea for hitting a man who had addressed him by his surname without the prefix 'Mr'. In 1929 he was charged with murder, but was acquitted when the prosecution failed to produce a body. He was jailed in 1933 in Somaliland (now Somalia) for hitting a customs officer, and a few years later he stamped on the instep of a policeman who had forced his car off the road in New York, USA, and demanded his autograph in an allegedly menacing manner. He was thrown into a cell for the night.

BIGGEST HOLLYWOOD RIVALRY

Peter Sellers and Orson Welles disliked each other so intensely that when they had to play a major scene together at the gaming table in *Casino Royale* (GB, 1967) they acted the scene on different days, each performing to a double.

MOST VALUABLE HOLLYWOOD LEGS

Actress Cyd Charisse, who starred in *Brigadoon* (USA, 1954) and *Singin' in the Rain* (USA, 1952), had an insurance policy for the sum of $5 million (£1.24 million) accepted on her legs. This outdid Betty Grable, who had been dubbed 'the Girl with the Million Dollar Legs' when she insured hers for the sum of $1.25 million (£444,840) c. 1940.

MOST FAMILY MEMBERS TO LEAVE MARK ON HOLLYWOOD BOULEVARD

Kirk Douglas, the star of *The Vikings* (USA, 1958) and *Spartacus* (USA, 1960), became the first member of his family to leave his mark on Hollywood Boulevard, Los Angeles, USA, when his footprints were set in stone in 1962. His son Michael, who has starred in *Fatal Attraction* (USA, 1987) and *Basic Instinct* (USA, 1992), was invited to leave his mark in Sept 1997. Their hand- and footprints now sit side by side, making the Douglases the first ever family to have two generations of prints in cement. Between them, Kirk and Michael have starred in more than 100 films.

MOST ENDURING HOLLYWOOD STAR

Lillian Gish made her acting debut in *An Unseen Enemy* (USA, 1912) and her last film, *The Whales of August* (USA, 1987), was made 75 years later.

BIGGEST HOLLYWOOD CEMETERY

Forest Lawn Memorial Park in Glendale, Hollywood, covers 135 ha (300 acres) and has three churches. Its celebrity graves include those of Walt Disney, Errol Flynn, Nat King Cole, Clark Gable and Jean Harlow.

MOST EXPENSIVE HOLLYWOOD HOTEL

The Beverly Hills Hotel on Sunset Boulevard, nicknamed 'The Pink Palace', is the most expensive hotel in Hollywood and one of the most expensive hotels in the world. A visual and social landmark in Hollywood, it was the location for many of the scenes in *Pretty Woman* (USA, 1990), which starred Richard Gere and Julia Roberts. Its top suites cost $3,300 (£2,000) a night.

MOST *LIFE* COVERS

Elizabeth Taylor has been on the cover of *Life* magazine a total of 11 times, more than any other Hollywood star. Liz began her film career at the age of 10 in 1942, with *There's One Born Every Minute*. She won two Oscars, for *Butterfield 8* (USA, 1960) and *Who's Afraid of Virginia Woolf* (USA, 1966), and was the first actress to earn $1 million (£357,105) for a picture, for *Cleopatra* in 1963.

LARGEST HOLLYWOOD HOME

The Manor on Mapleton Drive, Hollywood, was built for Aaron Spelling. The largest home in Hollywood, it occupies 3,390 m² (36,500 ft²) on a 6,040-m² (65,000-ft²) plot of land. The estate includes a doll museum, four bars, three kitchens, a gymnasium, a theatre, eight two-car garages, an Olympic-size swimming pool, a bowling alley, a skating rink, six formal gardens, 12 fountains and a room in which to wrap gifts. Spelling is the producer of a number of TV series, including *Beverly Hills 90210*, which stars his daughter Tori (pictured right, third from left).

HOLLYWOOD STREET WITH THE MOST CELEBRITY HOMES

Mulholland Drive, the long thoroughfare that forms the dividing line between the San Fernando valley and Los Angeles proper, is lined with expensive houses. The stretch where the drive passes the edge of Beverly Hills and Bel-Air has been nicknamed 'Bad Boy Drive', because it housed the estates of famous one-time party-givers Jack Nicholson, Warren Beatty and Marlon Brando.

RICHEST HOLLYWOOD PET

Screen legend Ava Gardner's beloved corgi Morgan Gardner was left a monthly salary and his own limousine and maid when the star passed away in 1990. He lived off his inheritance for seven years in a Hollywood mansion before passing away at the age of 15 in March 1997. Morgan, who had been given to Ava by her third husband Frank Sinatra, was buried in the backyard of the actress' friend Gregory Peck. Morgan's death was mourned by *Hello!* magazine.

MOST POPULAR HOLLYWOOD DIET DESIGNERS

PhD nutritionist Tony Perrone has customized diets for stars such as Demi Moore, Denzel Washington and Robin Williams, while Carrie Latt Wiatt of Diet Designs delivers low-fat meals to the doors of Jennifer Aniston, Ben Stiler and Neve Campbell. David Kelmenson and Steven Kates of the Brentwood training studios have been known to race their motorcycles to the Ivy and Spago restaurants to assist clients in ordering meals. Rob Parr, another diet guru, invented a pregnancy work-out that has helped re-shape stars such as Demi Moore and Tatum O'Neal.

MOST HOLLYWOOD MARRIAGES

Born in Hungary in either 1917, 1918 or 1919 (the real date remains a mystery), Zsa Zsa Gabor has had roles in a number of films and is famous for her succession of wealthy husbands. Her first marriage, reputedly when she was 13, was to Burhan Belge, a Turkish diplomat. After fleeing to the USA, she married, in swift succession, Texan hotel magnate Conrad Hilton, British actor George Sanders (who later married Zsa Zsa's sister Magda), businessmen Herbert Hunter and Joshua Cosden Jr, and Barbie Doll creator Jack Ryan. Her seventh husband was the lawyer Michael O'Hara, who had dealt with her divorce from Ryan. In 1982 Zsa Zsa claimed that her eight-day marriage to Felipe De Alba, whom she wed at sea, was invalid, as she was still technically married to O'Hara. Her longest marriage to date was to official husband No. 8, Prince Frederick von Anhalt, who she married in 1986 and divorced in 1998. Zsa Zsa, whose movie career highlights have included *Moulin Rouge* (USA/France, 1952), *The Girl in the Kremlin* (USA, 1957), in which she was bald, and *A Nightmare on Elm Street 3: Dream Warriors* (USA, 1987), has also been romantically linked with John F. Kennedy, Henry Kissinger, Mario Lanza, Sean Connery, Richard Burton and Frank Sinatra.

movie stars

MOST DEVOTED METHOD ACTORS

Daniel Day Lewis is said to have spent many nights without sleep in a mock jail cell in order to prepare for his role in *In the Name of the Father* (Ire/GB/USA, 1993), while for *Last of the Mohicans* (USA, 1992) he went on survival camp, where he learnt to track and kill animals and make canoes from trees.

Nicolas Cage had two teeth removed without painkillers for his part in *Vampire's Kiss* (USA, 1988). He also ate six live cockroaches to make the scene "really shock".

MOST WEIGHT GAINED FOR A FILM APPEARANCE

Robert De Niro gained a total of 27.21 kg (60 lb) for his role as the heavyweight boxer Jake La Motta in the classic movie *Raging Bull* (USA, 1980).

MOST WEIGHT LOST FOR FILM APPEARANCES

Gary Oldman's efforts to lose weight to play the punk star Sid Vicious in *Sid and Nancy* (GB, 1986) were so successful that the British actor ended up in hospital, where he was treated for malnutrition.

Jennifer Jason Leigh slimmed down to 39 kg (6 st 2 lb) for her role as an anorexic teenager in the TV movie *The Best Little Girl in the World* (USA, 1981).

GREATEST AGE SPAN PORTRAYED BY AN ACTOR IN ONE FILM

Dustin Hoffman was 33 years old when he played the title role in *Little Big Man* (USA, 1970) from the age of 17 to 121.

MOST SUCCESSFUL NUDE DOUBLE

Shelly Michelle has appeared on screen for many of Hollywood's most famous females. She doubled for Julia Roberts in *Pretty Woman* (USA, 1990) and Kim Basinger in *My Stepmother is an Alien* (USA, 1988) and *Final Analysis* (USA, 1992). She also claims to have doubled for Barbra Streisand and Madonna.

MOST PC MOVIE CONTRACT

Comic actor Robin Williams is famous for demanding the most politically-correct film contracts on record: each one prohibits commercial tie-ins connected with alcohol, tobacco, weapons, toys of violence, soft drinks and junk food.

MOST COSTLY LATE ATTENDANCE

Eddie Murphy's habitual lateness allegedly cost the producers of *Boomerang* (USA, 1992) more than $1 million (£568,180).

HIGHEST INSURANCE QUOTE

Robert Downey Jr was reputedly working uninsured on *The Gingerbread Man* (USA, 1998). The premium would have cost $1.4 million (£840,000) on a film with a budget of less than $42 million (£25 million).

MOST LEADING ROLES

John Wayne was in 153 films from *The Drop Kick* (USA, 1927) to *The Shootist* (USA, 1976). In all but 11 he played the lead.

MOST SUCCESSFUL ACTOR-TURNED-POLITICIAN

Ronald Reagan, who starred in *Bedtime for Bonzo* in 1951, was elected Governor of California in 1966 and 1970 and became US president in 1980.

LONGEST SCREEN CAREER

Curt Bois made his debut in *Der Fidele Bauer* (Germany, 1908) at the age of eight and his final film appearance in Wim Wenders' *Wings of Desire* (Germany, 1988).

LONGEST SCREEN PARTNERSHIPS

The Indian superstars Prem Nazir and Sheela had played opposite each other in a total of 130 movies by 1975.

The longest Hollywood partnership (excluding performers billed together solely in 'series' films) was 15 films, by husband-and-wife team Charles Bronson and Jill Ireland from 1968 to 1986.

BIGGEST SCREEN FAMILY

There have been four generations of screen actors in the Redgrave family, from Roy Redgrave, who made his screen debut in 1911, through Sir Michael Redgrave and his daughters Vanessa and Lynn and son Corin, to Vanessa's daughters Joely and Natasha and Corin's daughter Jemma.

YOUNGEST NO. 1 BOX-OFFICE STAR

Shirley Temple was seven years old when she became the No. 1 star at the box office in 1935.

HIGHEST-PAID CHILD PERFORMER

Macaulay Culkin was paid $1 million (£568,180) for *My Girl* (USA, 1991), when he was 11 years old. He was subsequently paid $5 million (£2.8 million) plus 5% gross for *Home Alone II: Lost in New York* (USA, 1992) and a reputed $8 million (£5.2 million) for *Richie Rich* (USA, 1994).

YOUNGEST OSCAR-WINNERS

Tatum O'Neal was 10 years old when she was voted Best Supporting Actress for *Paper Moon* (USA, 1973).

MOST BEST ACTOR AWARDS

Jack Nicholson, who has won Best Actor Academy Awards for *One Flew Over the Cuckoo's Nest* (USA, 1975) and *As Good as It Gets* (USA, 1997), is one of seven actors who have won the award twice. In 1998 ABC News ranked the star, who dropped out of school and grew up believing his grandmother was his mother and his mother was his sister, as one of the most powerful people in Hollywood today. In total he has had 11 Oscar nominations for Best Actor and Best Supporting Actor. The other actors who have won the Best Actor award twice are Spencer Tracy for *Captain Courageous* (USA, 1937) and *Boys Town* (USA, 1938), Fredric March for *Dr Jekyll and Mr Hyde* (USA, 1932) and *The Best Years of Our Lives* (USA, 1946), Gary Cooper for *Sergeant York* (USA, 1941) and *High Noon* (USA, 1952), Marlon Brando for *On the Waterfront* (USA, 1954) and *The Godfather* (USA, 1972), Dustin Hoffman for *Kramer vs. Kramer* (USA, 1979) and *Rain Man* (USA, 1988) and Tom Hanks for *Philadelphia* (USA, 1993) and *Forrest Gump* (USA, 1994).

Shirley Temple was awarded an honorary Oscar at the age of five for achievements in 1934.

OLDEST OSCAR-WINNER

Jessica Tandy won the Best Actress award for *Driving Miss Daisy* in 1990, at the age of 80.

MOST BEST ACTRESS AWARDS

Katharine Hepburn won four Oscars, for *Morning Glory* (USA, 1933), *Guess Who's Coming to Dinner* (USA, 1967), *The Lion in Winter* (GB, 1968) and *On Golden Pond* (USA, 1981). She also had the longest award-winning career, spanning 48 years.

MOST OSCAR NOMINATIONS WITHOUT AN AWARD

Richard Burton received six nominations, for *My Cousin Rachel* (USA, 1952), *The Robe* (USA, 1953), *The Spy Who Came in from the Cold* (GB, 1965), *Who's Afraid of Virginia Woolf* (USA, 1966), *Anne of the Thousand Days* (GB, 1970) and *Equus* (GB, 1977), but never won an award.

MOST APPEARANCES AS HOST AT THE OSCARS

Bob Hope hosted the Academy Awards a record 13 times: in 1940 (the second half of the show), 1945, 1946, 1953, 1955, 1958, 1959, 1960, 1966, 1967, 1968, 1975 and 1978.

SHORTEST ADULT ACTOR IN FILMS

Tamara de Treaux, who played the title role in *ET: the Extra-Terrestrial* (USA, 1982), was 78 cm (2 ft 7 in tall).

SHORTEST ACTOR IN LEAD ROLE

Paratrooper and black belt martial arts exponent Weng Weng, the star of *Agent 00* (Philippines, 1981) and *For Your Height Only* (Philippines, 1984), was 86 cm (2 ft 9 in) tall.

SHORTEST ACTOR IN LEADING ROLES TODAY

Danny DeVito, who starred opposite Arnold Schwarzenegger in *Twins* (USA, 1988), is 1.52 m (5 ft) in height.

SHORTEST ACTOR TO ACHIEVE HOLLYWOOD CELEBRITY STATUS

Billy Barty, who founded The Little People of America Inc. and is the only dwarf to have been honoured in the Hollywood Walk of Fame, is 1.14 m (3 ft 9 in) tall. Barty has appeared in approximately 150 films.

SHORTEST ACTRESS IN MAJOR ROLE

Linda Hunt, who won an Oscar for her role as a Eurasian cameraman in *The Year of Living Dangerously* (Australia, 1982), is 1.44 m (4 ft 9 in) tall.

TALLEST MALE STAR

Christopher Lee, veteran of horror films such as *Dracula* (GB, 1958), is the tallest major star today, at 1.95 m (6 ft 5 in) in height.

TALLEST LEADING LADIES

Margaux Hemingway, Brigitte Nielsen, Sigourney Weaver and Geena Davis are all 1.83 m (6 ft) tall.

MOST GENEROUSLY PROPORTIONED LEADING LADY

Chesty Morgan, the star of *Deadly Weapons* (USA, 1974), had a 1.85-m (73-in) chest.

EXPENSIVE ACTRESSES

With a current asking price of $12.5 million (£7.5 million) per film, Demi Moore is one of the most expensive actresses in the world today. Born Demetria Guynes in 1962, Moore began her acting career at the age of 20, when she became a regular on the TV show *General Hospital*. She now has 26 films under her belt. In 1987 she was married to fellow film star Bruce Willis by the singer Little Richard.

BIGGEST BREACH OF CONTRACT AWARD

In 1991 Kim Basinger pulled out of the movie *Boxing Helena* four weeks before the start of filming, a move that resulted in her bankruptcy in 1993, when a jury ordered her to pay $8.1 million (£5.1 million) to the movie's producer for breach of contract. An appeal court subsequently threw out that ruling. In a subsequent compromise Basinger paid an undisclosed amount to the producer.

tv stars

MOST POPULAR CULT TV STARS

Gillian Anderson, who stars as Agent Scully in the US sci-fi series *The X-Files*, is one of the most popular TV stars of the 1990s. Pictured left with her co-star, David Duchovny, Anderson was voted the world's sexiest woman in 1996 by more than 10,000 *FHM* magazine readers. She earns $58,000 (£35,000) per episode and in June 1997 signed a $6.6-million (£4-million) deal to star in a movie of the hit series.

HIGHEST-PAID TV ACTOR

Jerry Seinfeld, the star of the US sitcom *Seinfeld*, is the most highly-paid television star and the richest male TV actor in the world, with an estimated total worth of $94 million (£58.75 million). His 1997 earnings were estimated at $66 million (£41.25 million).

HIGHEST-PAID NEWS PRESENTER

Christiane Amanpour, the frontline reporter for CNN and CBS, became the world's most highly paid news presenter after an unprecedented bidding war between US networks. The foreign correspondent signed a $2-million (£1.25-million) deal with NBC, a $1.5-million (£937,000) deal with CNN and a $500,000 (£312,500) deal for CBS' *60 Minutes*. She had made her name covering the Bosnian and Gulf wars.

HIGHEST-PAID TV COOK

The British cook Delia Smith is reputed to have amassed a £24-million ($38.4-million) fortune, making her joint 837th richest person in the United Kingdom. The chef has hosted six hit television series and written more than 13 accompanying books.

MOST WATCHED MALE TV STAR

George Clooney, who plays paediatrician Doug Ross in the popular US hospital drama *ER*, is the most watched male television star in the world. He is reputed to earn $147,200 (£92,000) for each episode of the show, which had an average of 20.78 million viewers per episode in the USA and 3.45 million viewers in the United Kingdom in the 1996/97 season. Clooney has also made his mark in the film world, alongside Quentin Tarantino, Harvey Keitel and Juliette Lewis in *From Dusk Til Dawn* (USA, 1996), with Michelle Pfeiffer in *One Fine Day* (USA, 1996) and with Uma Thurman and Alicia Silverstone in *Batman and Robin* (USA, 1997).

MOST WATCHED FEMALE TV STAR

Brooke Shields is the star of the US show *Suddenly Susan*, which had viewing figures of about 20.09 million in its 1996/97 season — the world's highest ratings for a show with a female star. Shields first made her name in *The Blue Lagoon* (USA, 1980), at the age of 15.

MOST WATCHED TELEVISION PRESENTER IN GERMANY

Thomas Gottschalk currently hosts Germany's top-rating show *Wetten Daß (I Bet That...)*, in which guest celebrities are asked to bet on whether the contestants will succeed in record attempts. Viewing figures exceeded 71 million in 1997 and the programme receives 23% of the total audience share. Gottschalk, Germany's most popular personality, has also appeared in many other TV shows and a great number of national advertising campaigns.

MOST POPULAR TV STAR IN THE NETHERLANDS

Henny Huisman holds the largest audience share in the Netherlands with the show *SurpriseShowFin*. The show aims to make people's dreams come true. Huisman began his career as a DJ, and got his break in TV with *The Playback Show*, where candidates impersonated their favourite performers.

MOST WATCHED TELEVISION STAR IN FRANCE

News presenter Patrick Poivre d'Arvor is watched by more viewers than any other French television personality. On 2 Dec 1997 his news show *TF1 20 hrs* had a record 15.02 million viewers across the country. The star receives extensive press attention and in April 1996 he was the victim of *L'entarteur* — the Belgian 'Pieman', Noel Godin — who also pelted Bill Gates with custard pies in Feb 1998.

HIGHEST-PAID FEMALE TV STAR

Talk show hostess Oprah Winfrey, who earned $104 million (£65 million) in 1997, is the richest television entertainer in the world, with an estimated total worth of $201 million (£126 million), according to *Forbes* magazine. She is due to receive $130 million (£81 million) for her talk show alone — which has been rated the No.1 television talk show for 11 seasons in a row and been awarded 30 Emmys — for the TV season 1999/2000. Oprah, who is now 44 years old, landed her first broadcasting job at the age of 19 in 1973. In 1976 she was hired to host Baltimore's WJZ-TV chat show, *People Are Talking*, and in 1984 moved to Chicago to host *A.M. Chicago*. In 1985 she starred in Steven Spielberg's *The Color Purple* (USA), for which she received an Oscar nomination for Best Supporting Actress. *A.M. Chicago*, now titled *The Oprah Winfrey Show*, was relaunched in 1986 and Oprah, having established Harpo Productions, went on to buy the programme outright from Capital Cities/ABC. In 1998 a group of Texas cattlemen filed suit against the star, claiming that she had defamed the beef industry by making comments about 'mad cow disease' on her show. Oprah won the case.

FASTEST TELEVISION DEAL
On 20 June 1997 the US production company King World signed actress/comedienne Roseanne Barr — the star of the hit series *Roseanne* from 1988 to 1997 — for a new 'talk show'. Five days later the show had been cleared for air by five major television stations, and the next day it had been accepted by a further two stations. The enthusiasm for the show was said to be "unprecedented in television history".

MOST WATCHED FEMALE PRESENTER IN THE UNITED KINGDOM
Cilla Black, who hosts the popular British dating show *Blind Date*, is currently the most viewed television presenter in the United Kingdom. The show, which has been running since 1984, had an average of 9.1 million viewers per show in the 1997/98 season. In 1997 Cilla received an OBE (Order of the British Empire) from Queen Elizabeth II for her services to British entertainment.

MOST WATCHED MALE PRESENTER IN THE UNITED KINGDOM
Michael Aspel's *This Is Your Life*, which celebrates the careers of celebrities, won an average audience of 10 million viewers in the United Kingdom for the 1998 series.

MOST WATCHED TELEVISION STAR IN RUSSIA
Valdis Pelsh, the star of the music show *Uguday Melodiyu* (*Guess the Melody*), is Russia's most popular television personality. The show, which is shown six times a week (three original broadcasts and three morning repeats) receives up to 56% of the total audience share in Russia.

MOST WATCHED TV STAR IN BRAZIL
Regina Duarte, who has been appearing on Brazilian television for more than 33 years and has appeared in many Brazilian soap operas (*telenovelas*), is Brazil's most popular and prolific TV star. She is nicknamed 'Namoradinha do Brasil' ('Brazil's Girlfriend').

MOST WATCHED TELEVISION PRESENTER IN JAPAN
George Tokoro, who currently appears in two of Japan's top shows, *Ichiokuninn no Daihitsumon* and *Tokoro-san no Kaitaishinasho*, is the nation's most popular television star. *Ichiokuninn no Daihitsumon* is a road show in which Tokoro and his guests taste famous local dishes from different villages all over the country, while *Tokoro-san no Kaitaishinasho* deals with thematic historical issues. Tokoro is also a comedian and singer and has appeared in a number of national TV ads.

MOST MONEY REFUSED PER EPISODE
In Dec 1997 comedian Jerry Seinfeld turned down the highest personal contract in television history. NBC, the network producers of his show *Seinfeld*, had offered the star $5 million (£3 million) per episode to continue one of the most popular shows in the USA. A third of the USA's population of 263 million tuned in to watch the final episode, which was aired in May 1998, and all-day and all-night Seinfeld parties took place across the country. One-minute commercials during the 75-minute episode cost advertisers more than $1.66 million (£1 million).

sports superstars

FASTEST $1 MILLION BY GOLFER

In 1996 US golfer Tiger Woods broke Ernie Els' record for the fewest events played to earn $1 million (£625,000). Woods, a 20-year-old, needed only nine pro starts. By the end of his debut season, he had won five tournaments and earned more than $2 million (£1.25 million). He was the highest-earning golfer of 1997 and the second highest-paid endorser in sport, collecting $2.1 million (£1.3 million) in salary and winnings and $24 million (£15 million) in endorsements. In 1997 Woods signed a $40-million (£25.3-million) contract with Nike, who planned to bring out a new Woods apparel line in spring 1998. Other endorsers include American Express, Rolex and Japanese company Asahi.

LARGEST SPORTS SPONSORSHIP

Michael Jordan, the legendary point guard for the US basketball team the Chicago Bulls, is reputed to earn $12 million (£7.5 million) a year from his deal with sports manufacturer Nike and is said to have been paid more than $100 million (£62.5 million) in total from Nike during his career.

LARGEST SPORTS CONTRACTS

In 1997 the US basketball hoopsters Shaquille O'Neal, Alonzo Mourning and Juwan Howard all signed deals worth more than $100 million (£62.5 million) – the first nine-figure contracts in sports history.

HIGHEST EARNINGS IN A YEAR

In 1996 the US boxer Mike Tyson earned a record $75 million (£46 million) from three fights. In doing so, he made more money in one year than any other athlete in history. In 1986 Tyson had become the youngest boxing heavyweight world champion of all time when he beat fellow US boxer Trevor Berbick to win the WBC version at Las Vegas, Nevada, USA, at the age of 20 years 144 days. He added the WBA title to his achievements with his victory over James 'Bonecrusher' Smith on 7 March 1987, at the age of 20 years 249 days, and he became Universal Champion on 2 Aug 1987, when he beat Tony Tucker of the USA for the IBF title.

HIGHEST CAREER EARNINGS BY A SPORTSMAN

Michael Jordan has earned more money during his eight-year basketball career than any other sportsman in history. Now aged 34, Jordan earned a total of $30 million (£18.25 million), plus a further $47 million ($29 million) in endorsements, making him the highest-paid sportsman for the fifth time in six years. By 1998 his career earnings had exceeded $300 million (£187.5 million).

HIGHEST CAREER EARNINGS BY SPORTSWOMEN

In April 1998 US tennis player Martina Navrátilová continued to hold the record for the highest career earnings of any sportswoman, despite having retired from her 14-year career on the tennis circuit in 1994. She had earned $20.34 million (£12.71 million) from prize money alone, and had won a world record 167 singles tournaments and 165 doubles titles.

The German tennis star Steffi Graf had earned a total of $20.18 million (£12.62 million) from prize money by April 1998. It is estimated that by the end of the 1998 season, she will have exceeded Navrátilová's career earnings. However, Navrátilová will continue to hold the record if endorsements and sponsorship deals are included in total career earnings.

HIGHEST-EARNING TENNIS PLAYER

By April 1998 US tennis player Pete Sampras' career earnings from prize money alone totalled $32.3 million (£20.2 million). In 1997 he was paid $8 million (£5 million) for his biggest endorsement deals, with Nike and Wilson. Sampras also holds the men's record for earnings in a season, at $6.5 million (£4.06 million) in 1997.

HIGHEST-EARNING FORMULA 1 DRIVER

In 1996 the German driver Michael Schumacher was paid a

HIGHEST-EARNING FOOTBALLER

The Brazilian footballer Ronaldo Luis Nazario de Lima, known simply as Ronaldo, made a $28.8-million (£18-million) transfer from Spain's Barcelona to Inter Milan of Italy at the age of just 20 in 1997, and now earns more than $160,000 (£100,000) a week, making him the world's richest footballer. He is seen here during the unveiling of a Pirelli advertising campaign, which shows the Brazilian star with his arms outstretched over the Rio de Janeiro landscape. Ronaldo had been a member of the winning Brazilian squad in the 1994 World Cup and won a bronze medal with the Brazilian Olympic team in 1996. When he joined Inter Milan, the team's season ticket sales rose by 40%. In 1998 Inter Milan won the UEFA Cup, with Ronaldo scoring the third goal in a 3–0 victory over fellow Italians Lazio. At the age of just 22 Ronaldo is already being compared to the greatest record $25 million (£15.6 million) to drive for Ferrari's Formula 1 team. This is the highest salary in the history of Formula 1. Schumacher's total earnings in 1997 have been estimated at $35 million (£22 million), including salary and winnings, as well as endorsements.

HIGHEST-EARNING GOLFERS

The highest all-time career earnings on the US PGA circuit is $11.91 million (£7.44 million), by Australia's Greg Norman between 1976 and 1997.

The season's record on the US PGA circuit is $2.1 million (£1.3 million), by US player Tiger Woods in 1997.

Hale Irwin (USA) won a record-breaking $2.34 million (£1.46 million) on the US Seniors PGA Tour in 1997.

Nick Faldo (GB) won a record £1.56 million ($2.74 million) worldwide in 1992.

The record for the highest ever career earnings by a golfer is $8.58 million (£5.36 million), by Bernhard Langer of Germany from 1976 to 1997.

The record career earnings for a woman golfer is $5.97 million (£3.73 million), by Betsy King (USA) from 1977 to 1997.

The record season's earnings by a woman golfer is $1.24 million (£772,993), by Annika Sorenstam of Sweden in 1997.

Colin Montgomerie (GB) won a season's record of £875,146 ($1.37 million) in European Order of Merit tournaments in 1996.

OLDEST HIGH-EARNING SPORTSMAN

In 1997 the 68-year-old US golfer Arnold Palmer earned a total of $16.1 million (£10 million) from salary, winnings and endorsements, making him the 12th highest-earner in sport. Palmer, who was the first golfer to win more than $1 million (£625,000) on the PGA tour, still plays on the PGA Senior Tour.

MOST SUCCESSFUL MUSICAL CAREER BY A SPORTSMAN

Shaquille O'Neal, hoopster for the Los Angeles Lakers, also has a highly successful music career. He released his debut album, *Shaq Diesel* (1993), when he was 21, and in 1997 his record label Twism (The World is Mine) formed a joint venture with A&M Records to produce a fourth album.

YOUNGEST SPORTSWOMAN TO EARN £1 MILLION

In 1997, at 16 years of age, the Swiss tennis star Martina Hingis became the youngest sportswoman ever to earn $1 million (£610,426). By April 1997 the No. 1 player had earned $3 million (£1.87 million), and by Sept of that year, in the space of six months, she had achieved 37 successive victories. The only woman in the history of the Open era to have started a year on better form was Steffi Graf (Germany), who had 45 successive wins in 1987. Hingis became the first woman to surpass $4 million (£2.5 million) in earnings over the course of a single season. In addition to prize money, her sponsorship deals are worth an estimated $5 million (£3.1 million) a year. In 1997 she set a season's winnings record of $3.4 million (£2.12 million).

MOST MAGAZINE COVERS

Michael Jordan appeared on the cover of *Sports Illustrated*, the sports magazine with a weekly readership of 23 million, for the 42nd time on 16 Feb 1998. The previous record was 34, by boxer Muhammed Ali.

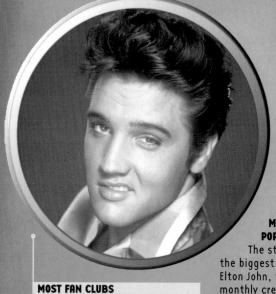

pop stars

MOST FAN CLUBS
There are more than 480 active Elvis Presley fan clubs worldwide – more than for any other star. This is particularly astonishing in view of the fact that Elvis did not record in other languages, except for a few soundtrack songs, and only once performed in concert outside the USA, in Canada, in 1957.

HIGHEST-EARNING POP GROUP
The Beatles are the wealthiest musical entertainers of all time. In 1997 their earnings were estimated at £41.5 million ($68 million). The Beatles formed in 1960 and had their first hit with *Love Me Do* in 1962. After disbanding in 1970, the 'fab four' – Paul McCartney, John Lennon, Ringo Starr and George Harrison – all pursued solo careers.

MOST VALUABLE POP STAR ON THE STOCK MARKET
David Bowie commands an estimated fortune of £150 million ($250 million). In 1997 Bowie raised £33 million ($55 million) through the issue of bonds, which he sold to Prudential Insurance. Other stars allegedly following suit include members of the Rolling Stones.

MOST SHOPAHOLIC POP STAR
The star who confesses to the biggest shopping sprees is Elton John, whose average monthly credit card bill is about £250,000 ($413,000). His most memorable bills have included £38,000 ($63,000) for a month's purchases at the florist's department of Bloomingdales, New York, USA, and £200,000 ($330,000) for a single visit to jeweller Theo Fennell in London, UK.

LARGEST PRIZE DONATIONS TO A CHARITY BY POP STARS
In 1996 Pulp, fronted by Jarvis Cocker, won the Mercury Prize for music over the favourites Oasis, and donated their £25,000 ($41,000) cheque to the War Child charity. Other Mercury prizewinners who have made sizeable donations to charity include Suede in 1993, M People in 1994 and the 1997 winner Roni Size, who gave most of his prize money to a community project in Bristol, UK.

MOST PROMOTIONS FOR AN ALBUM BY A POP STAR
Promotions for Michael Jackson's album *HIStory* (1995) included a 9.1-m-high (30-ft) inflated statue of the star on top of Tower Records in Hollywood, USA, a huge sign in Times Square, New York, and another statue floated on a barge down the River Thames in London, UK. Jackson's record company Sony spent $40 million (£24.25 million) on the launch of the album in the USA, the United Kingdom, Italy, Australia, Japan, South Africa and the Netherlands.

BIGGEST LEGAL BATTLE OVER A RECORD CONTRACT
George Michael fought a nine-month court battle during 1993 and 1994 in an attempt to end his contract with Sony Music. He lost the case, which cost him an estimated £3 million ($1.96 million), the contract was eventually bought out by US company Dreamworks.

MOST PRODUCT ENDORSEMENTS BY A POP GROUP IN A YEAR
The Spice Girls hold the record for the greatest number of promotions by a group in any one year, with 10 different advertisers in 1997. They included Sony Play Station, Mercedes, and a $1-million (£625,000) deal with Pepsi, which involved 40,000 Pepsi drinkers being flown to Istanbul, Turkey, for a Spice Girls concert and after-show party.

MOST PAID TO POP STAR FOR ADVERTISING RIGHTS
Microsoft paid the Rolling Stones $8 million (£4.85 million) to feature their hit *Start Me Up* in its *Windows' 95* campaign.

BIGGEST ADVERTISING DEAL TO BE TURNED DOWN
The record for the largest sum of money ever rejected by a pop star for an advertising deal is $12 million (£7.32 million), by Bruce Springsteen in 1987. The sum had been offered by US car manufacturer Chrysler for the use of Springsteen's *Born in the USA* in a car commercial.

MOST APPEARANCES ON THE COVER OF *ROLLING STONE* MAGAZINE
Rolling Stones frontman Mick Jagger has appeared on the cover of *Rolling Stone* magazine a total of 15 times. He first featured on the cover of the 50th issue on 10 Aug 1968, and his most recent appearance was with Keith Richards on 11 Dec 1997 (issue 775).

MOST CAMEO ROLES IN A POP FILM
The Spice Girls' film *Spiceworld – the Movie* (UK, 1997) featured a larger cameo cast than any other pop film, with appearances by Meatloaf, Roger Moore, Stephen Fry, Michael Barrymore, Richard Briers and Elvis Costello.

MOST MONEY RAISED IN A SECOND-HAND CLOTHES SALE
Elton John's infamous wardrobe has had to be cleared many times due to its overwhelming size. The star's last two second-hand sales made a total of £530,000 ($875,000) for the Elton John AIDS Foundation and he once had to rent a shop to sell off more than 10,000 outfits, which were estimated to have originally cost c. £2.5 million ($4.13 million). The Stage Costume and Memorabilia section of Elton's 1988 sale at Sotheby's, London, UK, which included personal possessions as well as clothes, raised £421,185 ($758,133) at auction.

HIGHEST PRICES PAID FOR POP STAR CLOTHING
The most expensive item of clothing formerly owned by John Lennon is an afghan coat that he wore on the cover of the Beatles' *Magical Mystery Tour* album in 1967. It was bought for £34,999 ($57,750) in 1997 on behalf of the star's son Julian Lennon.

STAR COUPLE
Whitney Houston and Bobby Brown are one of the world's most successful pop star couples. Houston, the daughter of a gospel/soul singer Cissy Houston and cousin of Dionne Warwick, spent her early teens modelling for *Vogue* and *Glamour* and was signed to the Arista label at the age of 19. In 1992 she achieved popular acclaim for her role in *The Bodyguard* alongside Kevin Costner, as well as for her best-selling soundtrack to the film. Her cover of Dolly Parton's *I Will Always Love You* for the album stayed at the top of the US singles chart for an unprecedented 14 weeks. The same year Houston married Bobby Brown, an R&B star who had first achieved pop success with his singles *Don't Be Cruel* and *My Prerogative* in 1988, the latter giving him his first No. 1. During 1988 and 1989 he had five singles in the US Top 10. The couple have had one child, and Houston has received the Outstanding Career Achievement award at the Soul Train Music Awards.

The most ever paid for an item of clothing belonging to Madonna is £12,100 ($19,360), for a corset designed by Jean Paul Gaultier and sold at Christie's, London, UK, in May 1994.

The most expensive item of clothing to have belonged to ♀ (The Artist formerly known as Prince) is a complete stage costume that sold for £12,100 ($20,570) at Christie's, London, UK, in Dec 1991.

The most expensive piece of Michael Jackson clothing is a white rhinestone glove, which sold for £16,500 ($28,050) in Dec 1991.

MOST VALUABLE SONG LYRICS

Paul McCartney's hand-written lyrics for the Beatles' *Getting Better* sold for £161,000 ($257,600) in Sept 1995.

MOST POPULAR POP STAR HOTEL

The Chelsea Hotel in the Chelsea district of New York, USA, was opened in 1884 as a co-operative apartment block and was converted into a hotel in 1905. It became a haven for writers and artists almost immediately. The French actress Sarah Bernhardt set its eccentric tone by sleeping there in a coffin, and subsequent guests have included musicians Frank Zappa, Jimi Hendrix, Iggy Pop, Bob Dylan and Janis Joplin. It achieved notoriety in 1978, when Sex Pistols star Sid Vicious killed his 20-year-old girlfriend Nancy Spungen in room 100.

MOST GRAMMYS WON IN A YEAR

The most Grammy awards won in a single year is eight, by Michael Jackson in 1984. Jackson was born on 29 Aug 1958 in Gary, Indiana, USA, and began his career as a child star in his older brothers' band, the Jackson Five. He launched his solo career in 1979 with *Off The Wall*, and three years later released *Thriller*, which sold more than 48 million copies worldwide.

MADONNA

Born Madonna Louise Ciccone in Rochester, Michigan, USA, on 16 Aug 1958, the self-styled 'queen of controversy' has sold 100 million records worldwide and had almost 50 hit records. Madonna's major breakthrough came in 1984 with *Like A Virgin*. She has also enjoyed box-office success as an actress, most memorably in *Desperately Seeking Susan* (1985) and *Evita* (1996).

super models

MOST MAGAZINE COVERS

German model Claudia Schiffer was spotted in a disco in her native country when she was 17 and has not stopped working since. She has appeared on a record 550 magazine covers, including *Vanity Fair*, despite the latter's editorial line against featuring models on its covers.

BIGGEST COSMETICS CONTRACT

In 1993 Claudia Schiffer signed the biggest ever cosmetics contract when she was offered

BIGGEST SUPERMODEL

Sophie Dahl, the granddaughter of British author Roald Dahl, was discovered by fashion editor Isabella Blow, who thought the size-16 (US size-14) beauty — whose statistics are 102-76-102 cm (40-30-40 in) — looked like a *Playboy* bunny. Sophie has worked with top photographers such as David Bailey, appeared in *Vanity Fair* and modelled at big shows such as Nina Ricci. Her agency Storm have asked her not to lose any weight.

the sum of $6 million (£4 million) to become the face of Revlon. Claudia has done campaigns for all the big fashion houses and is a particular favourite of Karl Lagerfeld. She has produced her own fitness video and made her movie debut in 1998 with *The Blackout*. She co-owns the Fashion Cafe with fellow supermodels Naomi Campbell and Christy Turlington.

LONGEST CONTRACT

Christy Turlington from the USA has represented Calvin Klein for almost 10 years — a record in the industry. The groundbreaking model has twice

clinched big deals without signing exclusivity contracts. She gave up the international catwalks in 1995 and now works for Max Mara and Calvin Klein, among others.

TOP-PAYING CATWALK SHOWS

One of the main forces behind the supermodel phenomenon was the late Italian designer Gianni Versace, who is reputed to have paid the top models as much as $50,000 (£30,000) for a half-hour show in the late 1980s and early 1990s on the proviso that they would only appear in his show that season. This is said to have created the elite group of girls — Christy Turlington, Naomi Campbell and Linda Evangelista — who dominated fashion magazines in the early 1990s.

YOUNGEST SUPERMODEL TO WIN A MAJOR COSMETICS CONTRACT

Nikki Taylor was 13 when she won $500,000 (£295,000) in a 'Fresh Faces' contest run by a top New York model agency in 1989 — the most any girl who has gone on to become a supermodel has won in a contest of this kind. She went on to sign a deal with L'Oreal for Cover Girl, making her

SHORTEST SUPERMODEL

Kate Moss was discovered by Storm's Sarah Doukas at JFK airport, New York, USA, in 1990. At just over 1.69 m (5 ft 6 in) in height, she seemed an unlikely choice, but she went on to revolutionize modelling, making way for a new type of model and a new trend called 'grunge'. The first big designer to use her was Calvin Klein, with whom she signed a $2-million (more than £1.1-million) contract in 1991.

HIGHEST HEELS

The British supermodel Naomi Campbell was discovered by Elite scout Beth Boldt while she was shopping in Covent Garden, London, and has not looked back since appearing on the cover of French *Vogue* in 1990. She is now one of the most successful models in the world and has been featured on numerous magazine covers. In 1993 Naomi hit the headlines when she fell off her 30-cm-high (12-in) platform shoes and twisted her ankle at the Vivienne Westwood 'Anglomania' catwalk show (pictured below). The mock snakeskin lace-ups that she wore are now on show in a specially-made glass case at the Victoria and Albert Museum, London. Naomi's numerous high-profile boyfriends have included actors Robert de Niro and Sylvester Stallone, boxer Mike Tyson, bassist Adam Clayton of rock group U2 and the flamenco dancer Joaquín Cortés. Now an international celebrity, she has released an album, *Baby Woman*, and published a novel, *Swan*. She has also appeared in the movies *Miami Rhapsody*, *Invasion of Privacy* and *Girl Six* and co-owns the Fashion Cafe in London. In Nov 1993 she left her agency Elite New York and was subsequently signed up by Ford.

the youngest girl ever to win a major cosmetics contract. At 16 she became a self-made millionaire with her own company, Nikki Inc, and now has her own lawyer, accountant, manager and publicist.

MOST DRAMATIC CAREER CHANGE

Before being booked by Select agency, Jayne Windsor was a 21-year-old single mother of two working in a factory in Newcastle, UK. She now earns $200 (£120) an hour working for top magazines, including *Elle*, *Vogue* and *Harpers and Queen*.

LONGEST-LEGGED SUPERMODEL

Of all the supermodels, German model Nadja Auerman has the longest legs, at 1.14 m (45 in). She shot to fame in 1993, when the fashion world rejected grunge in favour of glamour. By 1994 she had begun to appear on the cover of *Harper's Bazaar* and US and British *Vogue*.

OLDEST SUPERMODEL

At 34, Canadian model Linda Evangelista is the world's oldest catwalk supermodel. According to her agency Elite, she is still offered many assignments. Linda's success may be partly due to her famed ability to transform herself: in 1990 she claimed that she spent all of her free time colouring her hair. Linda is also responsible for the most famous supermodel quote: "We don't get out of bed for less than $10,000 a day."

YOUNGEST CURRENT SUPERMODEL

Model Karen Elson has taken the fashion world by storm since being discovered by a scout in Manchester, UK, at the age of 15. Now 18, she is the youngest supermodel working today, and has been the star of many prestigious campaigns, including Christian Lacroix, Hermes and Comme des Garçons.

LONGEST SUPERMODEL CAREER

Christy Turlington has been modelling for a longer period of time than any other supermodel since being discovered at the age of 13 in her school holidays. Christy began modelling full-time at the age of 17, in 1987. By 1988 she was the face of Eternity perfume and had secured a deal with Maybelline worth $800,000 (more than £440,000) for 12 days' work.

MOST SUCCESSFUL AGENCIES

Elite agency has a record 35 supermodels on its books, including Claudia Schiffer, Cindy Crawford, Christy Turlington and Amber Valetta, and bills more than $100 million (£60 million) in modelling fees every year. Set up by John Casablanca in Paris, France, in 1971, it now has offices in a further 23 cities worldwide, including New York, Milan, Munich, London and Tokyo.

Ford, which is run by Eileen Ford, has had more supermodels on its books for longer periods of time than any other agency. Its greatest successes have included Christy Turlington and Jerry Hall.

HIGHEST-PAID SUPERMODEL

US supermodel Cindy Crawford began modelling at the age of 17 and now earns an estimated $12 million (£7.2million) a year — more than any other model. In 1989 she was paid $600,000 (£360,000) by Revlon for just 20 days' work. Cindy has now diversified her career: she hosted the MTV *House of Style* show and made a fitness video that sold 2 million copies within one month of its release.

TALLEST SUPERMODEL

Australian-born supermodel Elle MacPherson is 1.85 m (6 ft 1 in) tall and is known as 'the Body' because her dimensions — 91-61-89 cm (36-24-35 in) — are regarded as perfect. Elle, who made her screen debut in *Sirens* (1994), is now pursuing an acting career. She owns one of Australia's most popular lingerie lines, which has an estimated annual turnover of $30 million (£18.75 million).

diana and royalty

Diana
Princess of Wales Memorial Fund

The monies generated for the fund by this lottery will go to the charities and charitable causes which were close to the Princess' heart.

£1 20p FROM THE SALE OF EACH TICKET PLUS ALL FURTHER PROCESS AFTER PRIZES AND EXPENSES GO TO THE DIANA PRINCESS OF WALES MEMORIAL FUND.

TOP PRIZE £25,000
ALL WINS OF £25,000 WILL BE MATCHED IN IDENTICAL DONATIONS TO THE DIANA PRINCESS OF WALES MEMORIAL FUND

BIGGEST TV AUDIENCE

More people watched the funeral of Diana, Princess of Wales, on 6 Sept 1997 than any other TV broadcast. The global audience was estimated at 2.5 billion.

MOST PHOTOGRAPHED WOMAN OF THE 1990S

It is impossible to know exactly how many photographs were taken of Diana during her short life, but she was undoubtedly the most photographed woman of the last 15 years. Not even Grace Kelly or Jackie Kennedy caught the media's attention to the same extent. Photos taken of Diana and Dodi Al Fayed on holiday off the island of Sardinia shortly before their deaths sold for up to $210,000 (£127,000), and Mario Brenna, the photographer, stood to make up to $3 million (£1.8 million) worldwide from their sale.

BIGGEST-SELLING SINGLE

Candle In The Wind, a song originally about Marilyn Monroe composed by Elton John and Bernie Taupin in 1973, was re-written as a tribute to Diana. It was performed by Elton at her

MOST WATCHED WEDDING

On 29 July 1981 approximately 750 million people in 74 countries tuned in to a live broadcast of Diana and Prince Charles' wedding at St Paul's Cathedral, London, UK. The estimated earnings from mementos relating to the wedding exceeded £650 million ($1 billion). The wedding dress, designed by Elizabeth and David Emmanuel, is displayed at the exhibition commemorating Diana at Althorp, Northants, UK.

funeral and recorded later that day. On 19 Dec 1997 the singer was presented with a disc commemorating 33 million sales of *Candle in The Wind 1997/Something About the Way You Look Tonight*. The first single to top the chart in almost every country, it had earned more than 140 platinum discs around the world and became the biggest- and fastest-selling single ever in many countries by the end of 1997.

MOST EXPENSIVE LYRICS

In Feb 1998 the autographed lyrics to *Candle In The Wind 1997* sold for $400,000 (£240,963) to the Lund Foundation for Children, which was founded by Walt Disney's daughter Sharon Disney-Lund. Consisting of three handwritten pages and a printed version, they are the world's most valuable contemporary lyrics.

MOST EXPENSIVE DRESSES SOLD AT AUCTION

The record for the most valuable auctioned dress is $200,000 (£134,000), for a blue silk and velvet gown owned by Diana and sold at Christie's, New York, USA, on 26 June 1997. The dress, one of a selection sold by Diana to raise money for British and US AIDS charities, was the one she wore when she danced with John Travolta at the White House, Washington DC, USA, in 1985. The previous record for a garment sold at auction was £87,000 ($145,000), for the white suit worn by Travolta in *Saturday Night Fever* (USA, 1977).

At a charity auction in Boston, Massachusetts, USA, in Sept 1997, an anonymous buyer paid $200,000 (£121,000) for a black velvet gown worn by Diana to a London premiere in 1985. It had originally sold for $36,000 (£21,800) at the auction of Diana's dresses at Christie's, New York, USA, the previous June.

MOST EXPENSIVE 20TH-CENTURY PRINTED BOOK AT AUCTION

Christie's leather-bound limited edition of the catalogue of Diana's dresses sold for £50,000 ($83,000) to Firoz Kassam, head of the Holiday Inn hotel chain in Asia, at the Grosvenor House Hotel, Mayfair, London, UK, on 4 Oct 1997.

BIGGEST FLOWER SHRINE

Between 1 and 8 Sept 1997 an estimated 5 million bouquets of flowers weighing 10,000–15,000 tonnes were laid in memory of Diana at Buckingham Palace, St James's Palace and Diana's home Kensington Palace (seen left) in London, UK, forming the world's biggest ever known flower shrine. Diana, together with her friend Dodi Al Fayed and their driver Henri Paul, died after a car crash at the Pont de l'Alma in Paris, France, on 31 Aug 1997, and her body was sent back to London 16 hours after the accident. Mourners began to lay flowers at the palaces as soon as the news of the tragic event broke, and a total of 43 books were filled with messages of condolence from the public at St James's Palace alone, with hundreds more filled around the world, although it had initially been thought that four books would suffice. On 9 Sept, three days after her funeral, Diana's brother Earl Spencer and the rest of her family made an appeal to the public to stop laying flowers at her ancestral home, Althorp Park, Northants, and to contribute the money that they would have spent on blooms to some of Diana's favourite charities. Most of the flowers that were laid at the gates of Althorp were eventually taken by boat to the island in the park's grounds where she was buried, and were placed around her grave. The others were given to hospitals.

LANDMINE AWARENESS

In Jan 1997 Diana made a high-profile visit to Huambo in central Angola, one of the most densely-mined areas in a country with one of the worst landmine problems in the world. Diana was briefed by the British mine-sweeping organization Halo Trust. On 18 Sept 1997 a ban on anti-personnel landmines was signed in Oslo, Norway, by more than 100 countries. The USA, China, Russia, Pakistan and India refused to sign up.

BIGGEST MEMORABILIA INDUSTRY

By Dec 1997 the Diana memorabilia industry was worth $240 million (£145 million) worldwide. An estimated 25,000 products, official and unofficial, bear Diana's image or signature, including ashtrays, rose bushes and dolls (above). There are c. 36,000 Internet sites linked to Diana memorabilia and her estate receives up to 200 applications a day from prospective manufacturers.

MOST VALUABLE PLAYING CARD

A Queen of Hearts card signed by Diana in Nov 1995 for air hostess Sheila Berkley-White was due to fetch up to $83,215 (£50,000) at auction in New York, USA, on 4 June 1998 but was sold before the auction, and is thought to have fetched the expected price.

MOST CONDOLENCES EXPRESSED VIA THE NET

A record 350,000 people left messages of condolence for Diana at the official memorial website of the British monarchy. The latter is also the most popular royal website: in the month after Diana's death about 14 million people visited it.

GREATEST NUMBER OF ROYALS KILLED IN AN ACCIDENT

Seven members of the royal family of Hesse (Ernst Ludwig, the last Grand Duke of Hesse, and his wife, son, daughter-in-law and three grandchildren) died in an air crash at Ostende, Belgium, on 16 Nov 1937.

GREATEST NUMBER OF ROYALS KILLED IN A REVOLUTION

Between 1918 and 1919 a record 15 members of the Russian imperial family were killed by the Bolsheviks during the Russian Revolution, including Tsar Nicholas II, the Tsarina Alexandra, their five children and seven other members of the family. There are continuing claims that at least one of the tsar's children escaped the massacre of the immediate imperial family at Yekaterinburg.

MOST STATE ROLES HELD BY A MODERN ROYAL

King Norodom Sihanouk of Cambodia was king from 1941 to 1955, prime minister from 1955 to 1966, head of state and regent from 1960 to 1970, head of the government-in-exile in 1970, president in 1976, president-in-exile from 1982 to 1988, head of the government-in-exile from 1989 to 1991, president of the National Council in 1991 and head of state from 1991 to 1993. In 1993 he was restored as king.

OLDEST ROYAL FAMILY

The present Japanese imperial family is descended from Jimmu, who is said to have ascended the throne on 11 Feb 660 BC.

RICHEST ROYAL FAMILY

Saudi Arabia's Saudi dynasty is the richest royal family. In 1998 King Fahd and the Saudi princes had an estimated personal wealth of $32.2 billion (£19.37 billion).

QUEEN OF HEARTS

On 1 July 1997, on her 36th birthday, Diana attended a centenary gala honouring the Tate Gallery in London, UK. It was the first time Diana had socialized with members of the royal family since her divorce. She was dressed in a black Jacques Azagury beaded evening gown, with the Queen Mary diamond and emerald necklace, which she famously once wore as a headband to dance with her ex-husband Prince Charles.

BIGGEST ROYAL FAMILY

There are more than 4,200 royal princes and more than 40,000 other relatives in the Saudi royal family.

MOST ROYAL SIBLINGS

King Mswati III of Swaziland has 600 siblings, as his father King Sobhuza II had 112 wives.

MOST POP HITS BY A ROYAL

Princess Stephanie of Monaco has had several pop records in the charts around the world. Her biggest hit was *Comme un Ouragan* (1985). She has also been a designer and model.

LONGEST ROYAL JOURNEY

In 1985 Prince Abdul aziz al–Saud, a nephew of King Fahd of Saudi Arabia, flew more than 2.9 million km (1.8 million miles) on *Discovery STS 51G*. His space trip lasted 7 days 1 hour 48 min.

celebrity icons

MOST VISITED GRAVE SITE
Graceland, the former home and final resting place of Elvis Presley, receives over 700,000 visitors annually from all over the world — more than any other grave site. The record for the greatest number of visitors to Graceland in one year is 753,962, in 1995.

MOST MOURNERS TO ATTEND AN OPEN CASKET IN ONE DAY
On 17 Aug 1977 about 75,000 mourning fans attempted to visit Elvis's open casket and an estimated 10,000 to 20,000 people actually made it inside

the foyer of Graceland. On the same day a total of 3,166 floral wreaths were sent to Graceland by fans and celebrities.

MOST FAMOUS ROBBERY OF A CELEBRITY GRAVE
In March 1978 the body of the silent movie star Charlie Chaplin was stolen from its grave in Vevey, Switzerland. The graverobbers, Roman Wardas and Gantcho Ganev, demanded a $133,240 (£69,407) ransom for Chaplin's body, but were arrested a short distance away from the cemetery.

MOST ROCK STARS TO DIE IN A SINGLE DISASTER
Rock stars Ritchie Valens, Buddy Holly and 'The Big Bopper' Richardson were flying in the same aeroplane when it crashed

MOST POSTERS OF A MALE ICON SOLD
James Dean, the star of *East of Eden* (USA, 1955) and *Rebel Without a Cause* (USA, 1955), died in a car accident at the age of 24 in 1955, but his legend lives on. In the last six years alone, Cartell International have sold more than 17,500 posters of James Dean.

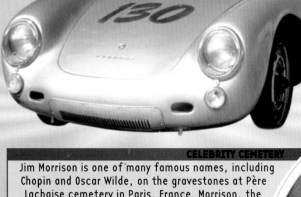

on 3 Feb 1959, killing all three. The stars had chartered the plane in order to avoid the weather conditions that were making overland travel difficult. Valens reportedly obtained a seat on the plane by the toss of a coin.

BIGGEST GAP BETWEEN ARTIST'S DEATH AND A NO. 1 HIT
Words of Love by Buddy Holly (& The Crickets) set the record for the longest interval between an artist's death and a No. 1 hit when it reached the top of the UK album chart in Feb 1993, 34 years after Holly's death.

MOST ALBUMS SOLD IN A DAY
On 17 Aug 1977, the day after his death, Elvis sold in excess of 20 million albums — more than any other artist in a single day.

ROCK CONTROVERSY
In the most controversial music documentary of recent times, the suicide of Kurt Cobain — the lead singer of Seattle grunge band Nirvana — came under question. Award-winning journalist Nick Broomfield unveiled new witnesses claiming to have been offered money to kill Cobain. The star's widow Courtney Love, who appeared in the documentary, has now had the film banned, but this has only increased the media's interest in it.

MOST POSTHUMOUS NO. 1s IN SUCCESSION
Former Beatle John Lennon, who was shot dead in New York, USA, on 8 Dec 1980, had three No. 1 hit singles in the following two months. *(Just like) Starting Over* was the first on 20 Dec, followed by *Imagine* on 10 Jan and *Woman* on 7 Feb.

LONGEST SPELLS IN THE UK AND US ALBUM CHARTS
Frank Sinatra's album *My Way* was on the British chart in June 1998, almost 40 years after his *Come Fly with Me* featured on the first ever British chart, in Nov 1958. The singer also holds the record for the longest Top 20 album career in the USA: his first chart entry in the rock era was *In The Wee Small Hours*, which entered on 28 May 1955, and his

CELEBRITY CEMETERY
Jim Morrison is one of many famous names, including Chopin and Oscar Wilde, on the gravestones at Père Lachaise cemetery in Paris, France. Morrison, the lead singer with the Doors, was found dead in the bath of a Paris hotel room at the age of 27 on 3 July 1971. An autopsy was never performed, and the death certificate stated that he had died as a result of heart failure. Since his burial at Père Lachaise, thousands of people have visited Morrison's grave and some relatives of other people buried in the cemetery have petitioned for his removal, because many visitors write graffiti on the headstones and drop litter. In any case, the lease on Morrison's plot is due to expire in 2001, and it is rumoured that his body will be moved to Los Angeles, USA.

most recent was *Duets II*, on 31 Dec 1994. Sinatra died on 20 May 1998. Mourners at his funeral included his ex-wife Mia Farrow, former First Lady Nancy Reagan, singers Bob Dylan, Tony Bennett and Liza Minnelli, actors Jack Lemmon, Jack Nicholson and Sophia Loren, and a host of other US celebrities.

YOUNGEST CELEBRITY TO DIE OF AN OVERDOSE

River Phoenix was 23 years old when he collapsed in 1993 outside Hollywood nightclub the Viper Room, which is owned by his fellow actor Johnny Depp. River was an avid environmentalist and at one time campaigned against the use of drugs. It was thought that the pressures of an excessive workload and his increasing fame were factors in his death. Phoenix's career highlights include *Stand By Me* (USA, 1986) and *My Own Private Idaho* (USA, 1991).

BIGGEST AUSTRALIAN ROCK ICON

Michael Hutchence, the lead singer of rock band *INXS*, died in a hotel room in Sydney, NSW, Australia, on 21 Nov 1997, aged 37. After an accident in 1992 left him robbed of his senses of taste and smell, he was reportedly prone to bouts of depression, and it was this tendency that was later blamed by some for the resulting verdict of suicide. *INXS* had been preparing to embark on their 20th anniversary tour.

MOST POSTERS OF A FEMALE ICON SOLD

Marilyn Monroe has featured on a record number of posters: since 1992 Cartell International have sold more than 37,500 posters of the star worldwide. Marilyn will also be among the first stars to have her DNA extracted, if Californian-based company Stargene has its way. It plans to extract the DNA of famous Americans, including George Washington.

MOST FAMOUS PUNK ROCK MURDER

On 11 Oct 1978 Nancy Spungen was murdered by her boyfriend Sid Vicious, the bass player of the Sex Pistols, in the Chelsea Hotel, New York, USA. Four months later Vicious committed suicide by overdose. He left a poem to his 'departed love', ending with the words:

"I don't want to live this life if I can't live for you." The events were later made into a film, *Sid and Nancy* (GB, 1986), starring Gary Oldman and Chloe Webb and featuring Courtney Love.

world leaders

HIGHEST-PAID WORLD LEADER
Ryutaro Hashimoto, who was the prime minister of Japan until 1998, had an annual salary of $343,000 (£232,000), including monthly allowances and bonuses. Many national leaders have a higher salary than the Japanese premier, but this includes perks and other sources of income.

MOST PRESIDENTIAL PALACES
Saddam Hussein, who has been the president of Iraq since 1979, has eight main palaces containing a total of 1,058 buildings, as well as a number of other minor residences throughout Iraq. His palace in Babylon, 88 km (55 miles) south of Baghdad, is built alongside the remains of the palace of Nebuchanezzar II (630–562 BC), and every brick is stamped with the legend 'The Leader, Saddam Hussein, Victor of Allah'. Further palaces are currently under construction in Baghdad and in Saddam's home town Tikrit.

MOST EXPENSIVE PRESIDENTIAL INAUGURATION
The inauguration of the US president in Washington DC, which takes place every fourth year, is the most expensive in the world. The most expensive ever US presidential inauguration was that of George Bush in 1989, which cost a total of $30 million (£18.9 million).

BIGGEST GATHERING OF WORLD LEADERS
A Special Commemorative Meeting of the General Assembly was held at United Nations Headquarters in New York, USA, in Oct 1995, to celebrate the 50th anniversary of the UN. It was addressed by 128 heads of state and heads of government.

PRESIDENT WHO HAS SPENT THE LEAST TIME IN HIS COUNTRY
Valdus Adamkus, who became president of Lithuania in 1998, returned to the republic in 1997 after living in Chicago, Illinois, USA, for more than 50 years, where he was Midwest chief of the US Environmental Protection Agency (EPA). His opponents say he speaks Lithuanian with an American accent.

MOST RELUCTANT PRESIDENT
Kim Jong-Il has been head of state of the Democratic People's Republic of Korea (North Korea) since the death of his father in 1994. By June 1998 Kim had not formally taken on the title of president, although he had assumed the most powerful post in the land: leader of the Korean Workers' Party.

MOST ACCESSIBLE PRIME MINISTER
With the exception of the leaders of some 'micro-states', the most accessible head of government is the Danish premier Poul Nyrup Rasmussen, whose home phone number is in the public domain. Rasmussen often personally answers telephone queries from Danish citizens. Openness in government in Denmark extends to the sovereign — any citizen may request a personal audience with Queen Margrethe II.

BIGGEST SOCIAL CLIMB TO THE PRESIDENCY
Kocheril Raman Narayanan was inaugurated as the 10th president of India in July 1997, despite having been born with the rank of 'untouchable' (the lowest social caste in India) and suffering extreme poverty. Caste discrimination was made illegal in 1947 but has not disappeared from Indian society.

MOST LITERARY PRESIDENT
The leader with the greatest literary reputation is Vaclav Havel, a Czech playwright and poet whose works were banned for 20 years after the 1968 Soviet invasion. He became president of Czechoslovakia in 1989 and president of the Czech Republic in 1993.

PRESIDENT WITH MOST FAMILY MEMBERS IN POWER
Until 1995 Barzan Ibrahim, a half-brother of Iraqi president Saddam Hussein, was ambassador to the UN and controlled much of the family fortune. Another of Saddam's half-brothers, Watban Ibrahim, was minister of the interior, and a third half-brother, Sabaoni Ibrahim, was chief of general security. Saddam's son-in-law Saddam Kamal Hussein was commander of the presidential guard until he fled to Jordan in 1995, and his sons, Udday and Qusay, hold various state and other offices. The latter was head of security services but was replaced by one of Saddam's in-laws.

HIGHEST PERSONAL MAJORITIES
The highest personal majority for a politician was 4.73 million, for Boris Yeltsin, the people's deputy candidate for Moscow, in the parliamentary elections in the Soviet Union in March 1989. He received 5.12 million votes out of the 5.72 million cast in the Moscow constituency. His closest rival received 392,633 votes.

Benazir Bhutto achieved 98.48% of the poll in the Larkana-III constituency at the 1990 general election in

MOST SUBSTANTIAL WORLD LEADER
Helmut Kohl, left of picture, has been the Federal German chancellor since 1982. At 1.93 m (6 ft 4 in) in height and with an average weight of 120 kg (almost 19 st), he is the most substantial world leader. Kohl's weight fluctuates considerably and he has been known to weigh considerably more than 120 kg at times, but has shed weight at health clinics. His healthy appetite is renowned and his wife, Hannelore, has published a book called *A Culinary Voyage Through Germany*, which features some of the Chancellor's favourite food, which features many hearty meat and cream dishes but also some low-calorie platters such as Paderborn Carrot Salad. Kohl is pictured here with Tony Blair, who became the first British prime minister to give a live video interview over the internet on 29 April 1998. Interviewer Sir David Frost chose from more than 700 questions which were sent into the 10 Downing Street website before the interview. Tony Blair said he believed information had a huge potential to give the people more say in the way that their country is run.

Pakistan, with 94,462 votes. The next highest candidate obtained 718 votes.

LONGEST TIME IN POWER
Fidel Castro became prime minister of Cuba in July 1959 and has been president of Cuba and head of state and head of government since 3 Dec 1976.

LONGEST SPEECH BY A POLITICIAN
Chief Mangosuthu Buthelezi, the leader of the Inkatha Freedom Party and South African home affairs minister, spoke for an average of $2^1/_2$ hours on 11 of the 18 days of the KwaZulu legislative assembly in 1993.

YOUNGEST PRESIDENT
The youngest republican head of state is Lt. Yaya Jammeh, who became president of the

MOST HOSPITALIZED PRESIDENT
Boris Yeltsin, the president of the Russian Federation since 1991, has had nine known hospital stays, some of them emergency admissions, during his term of office, but has surpassed the average age attained by Russian males, 58, by more than nine years.

provisional council and head of state of the Gambia at the age of 29 on 26 July 1994 and was elected president at the age of 31 on 27 Sept 1996.

YOUNGEST PRIME MINISTER
The youngest head of government is Dr Mario Frick, who became prime minister of Liechtenstein at the age of 28 on 15 Dec 1993.

OLDEST PRESIDENT
Rafael Caldera became president of Venezuela at the age of 76 in 1993. He had previously served as president from 1969 to 1974.

When he leaves office in Feb 1999, the oldest republican head of state will be 82-year-old Kiro Gligorov, president of The Former Yugoslav Republic of Macedonia.

OLDEST PRIME MINISTER
Sirimavo Bandaranaike became the Sri Lankan prime minister at the age of 78 in 1994. When she first became premier in 1960, she was the world's first woman prime minister. Her daughter Chandrika Bandaranaike Kumaratunga is the republic's president.

BIGGEST PRESIDENTIAL STAFF
The republican head of state with the biggest staff is the US president Bill Clinton, seen here with the highest-paid world leader, Japanese prime minister Ryutaro Hashimoto. There are probably more than 1,000 employees at the White House, including domestic staff, caterers, groundspeople, security personnel and interns. Some of this number also work for Hillary Rodham Clinton, the First Lady.

benefits, charities and parties

MOST SECURITY AT A HOLLYWOOD WEDDING

Elizabeth Taylor's eighth wedding ceremony was expected to attract about 1,000 journalists to Michael Jackson's estate at Neverland valley, California, USA, in 1991. As a result the 1,093-ha (2,700-acre) site was guarded by some of the tightest security the world has ever seen. Eighty security guards worked with mounted police and secret service bodyguards to watch for intruders, and red and white balloons were floated 165 m (541 ft) above the estate to keep helicopters from filming. Despite all the security a parachutist with a video camera managed to land at the wedding, but was immediately arrested. Taylor married former construction worker Larry Fortensky. She wore a yellow chiffon Valentino dress that reportedly cost $20,000 (£12,000) and the official wedding photographs taken by Herb Ritts were sold exclusively to *Hello!* magazine. In 1996 she filed for divorce.

NEURO-SPINAL RESEARCH

On 1 Feb 1998 Christopher Reeve (seen above with his wife and son) hosted Hollywood's biggest fundraiser in aid of neuro-spinal research. The event raised $256,000 (£160,000), and was attended by more than 1,000 guests, including Robin Williams, Jane Seymour and Glenn Close. In May 1995 Reeve, the star of *Superman* (GB, 1978), was involved in a riding accident that left him wheelchair-bound.

MOST MONEY RAISED BY A BIRTHDAY FUNDRAISER

Elizabeth Taylor's 65th birthday party, which was held in Hollywood, Los Angeles, USA, on 15 Feb 1997, raised a total of $1 million (£625,000) for AIDS causes. The party was attended by a host of celebrities, including Michael Jackson, Dennis Hopper, Shirley MacLaine, Cher, Roseanne Barr, Patti LaBelle and Madonna.

BIGGEST TELETHON

The Jerry Lewis 'Stars Across America' Muscular Dystrophy Association Labor Day Telethon reached 27.6 million US homes and 75 million US viewers in 1997. Its audience figures rank with those of the World Series and the Academy Awards. The 21½-hour live extravaganza is broadcast from CBS Television City in Hollywood and carried by about 200 'Love Network' TV stations. Hosted by actor and producer Jerry Lewis, it was first broadcast by a station in New York in 1966 and was the first televised fundraising event of its kind to raise more than $1 million (£358,012). In 1997 it raised a record $50.47 million (£30.81 million) in pledges and contributions. The most raised by a British TV fundraiser is £17.01 million ($27.87 million), by Comic Relief in 1997. Comic Relief is held every year in aid of a variety of causes and has raised a total of £140 million ($233 million) over six years.

MOST MONEY RAISED BY A WAR RELIEF BENEFIT

Pavarotti's two concerts for the War Child charity, which supports child victims of war across the world, raised $863,915 (£553,189). Held in Modena, Italy, on 12 Sept 1995 and 20 June 1996, the concerts also included artists such as Eric Clapton, Brian Eno and Sheryl Crow. U2's Bono wrote *Miss Sarajevo* for the 1995 show.

BIGGEST ROCK BENEFIT

Live Aid was the first ever simultaneous rock concert with satellite links between two countries. The 17-hour concert took place at Wembley Stadium, London, UK, and JFK Stadium, Philadelphia, USA, on 13 July 1985 and was attended by 150,000 people (80,000 people in Philadelphia and 70,000 in London). More than 1.6 billion people around the world watched satellite broadcasts of the event. Organized by the British charity Band Aid, which was masterminded by musicians Bob Geldof (seen centre left, with Pete Townsend and Paul McCartney) and Midge Ure, it raised £51.36 million ($80 million) for the Ethiopian Famine Relief Fund and has raised more than £37.5 million ($60 million) since then. Included in the star-studded line-up were Queen, U2, Elvis Costello, INXS, Sting, Phil Collins, the Beach Boys, Elton John, Mick Jagger and Tina Turner. In the finale all the musicians got up on the stage and sang *Do They Know It's Christmas*, the single that reached No. 1 in the United Kingdom in Christmas 1984, selling 6 million copies and raising about £5.14 million ($8 million) for famine relief.

BIGGEST ANNUAL PARTIES AT BUCKINGHAM PALACE

The garden parties held by the British Royal Family are attended by more than 30,000 people a year. At least three have been held every year since the 1860s, and each party is attended by approximately 8,000 people. At a typical garden party, which is attended by the Queen, the Duke of Edinburgh and other members of the Royal Family, about 27,000 cups of tea, 20,000 sandwiches and 20,000 slices of cake are consumed.

BIGGEST REGULAR SIT-DOWN DINNER AT BUCKINGHAM PALACE

On the occasion of an incoming state visit – such as the visit of the Emperor of Japan in June 1998 – Queen Elizabeth II holds a state banquet in honour of the visitor. The dinners, which are generally attended by up to 140 people, usually take place twice a year and are the biggest formal dinners regularly held at the palace. The annual gathering of the ambassadors from all countries that are accredited by the Court of St James has a guest list of 1,500 people, and is the biggest drinks reception held at Buckingham Palace.

BIGGEST WHITE HOUSE EVENT

The annual Easter Egg Roll, which is held on the front lawn of the White House on the Monday after Easter, is the biggest celebration held at the presidential dwelling. On 31 March 1997 it was attended by a record 29,000 people.

BIGGEST PARTY IN LAS VEGAS

The first annual Frank Sinatra Las Vegas Celebrity Golf Classic was held in Las Vegas, Nevada, USA, from 28 to 31 May 1998, as a tribute to Sinatra who had died on 15 May. The proceeds went to the Barbara Sinatra Children's Center in Rancho Mirage, California, founded to counsel abused children, and to Opportunity Village, Las Vegas. The tribute was the biggest party ever held in Las Vegas, with the golf tournament alone attracting an estimated 10,000 spectators. Guests at the black-tie gala included Gregory Peck, Robert de Niro, Leslie Nielson, Jack Lemmon, and Dina Merrill. Among the Honorary Chairs of the tournament were Bruce Springsteen, Brooke Shields, Andre Agassi, and the Aga Khan.

MOST SUCCESSFUL FUND-RAISER FOR EJAF

A musical event held on 8 Feb 1997 raised $900,000 (£549,384) for the Elton John Aids Foundation (EJAF). Elton John gave a concert with Jessye Norman and Luciano Pavarotti, and an auction was held with prizes including dinner with Cindy Crawford and tennis lessons with Andre Agassi. Billy Joel and Whoopi Goldberg were among the guests.

MOST LAVISH BIRTHDAY PARTY

On 13 July 1996 Sir Muda Hassanal Bolkiah Mu'izzaddin Waddaulah, the Sultan of Brunei and formerly the richest man in the world, put on the world's most lavish ever party. The attractions included a funfair, which was later donated to the people of Brunei. The party cost a total of $27.2 million (£17 million), $16 million (£10 million) of which was spent on three pop concerts by Michael Jackson.

BIGGEST ROCK BENEFIT FOR AIDS

A concert held in memory of Freddie Mercury (left), the rock star who died of AIDS in Nov 1991, was held at Wembley Stadium, London, UK, on 20 April 1992. The event was attended by approximately 75,000 people and was estimated to have reached close to 1 billion people in more than 70 countries. The event raised a total of £20 million ($25 million) for AIDS causes, and featured artists such as U2, Elton John, Queen, Guns 'N' Roses and Liza Minnelli. Freddie Mercury was the lead singer of the rock group Queen, whose hits included *Bohemian Rhapsody* (1975) and *We Are The Champions* (1977).

money.
a big business

wealth

RICHEST MAN
Bill Gates, the 42-year-old chairman and co-founder of Microsoft Corporation, has a net worth of $39.8 billion (£24.3 billion). His wealth now exceeds that of the Sultan of Brunei, whose fortune is estimated to be $38 billion (£23.1 billion).

RICHEST WOMAN
Liliane Bettencourt is the daughter of L'Oreal's founder. As an heiress to the fortune of the cosmetics empire, she has a net worth of $8.4 billion (£5.1 billion).

RICHEST TEENAGER
Prince Abdul Aziz Bin Fahd of Saudi Arabia was given $300 million (£183 million) in 1987, when he was 14. His father, the king, had heard that he was spending more than his already generous allowance.

YOUNGEST MULTI-BILLIONAIRE
Athina Onassis Roussel, the granddaughter of shipping magnate Aristotle Onassis, inherited an estimated $5-billion (£3.04-billion) empire and the Greek island of Skorpios in 1988, at the age of three. She will have control of the fortune in 2003 when she is 18.

RICHEST DICTATOR
Iraqi dictator Saddam Hussein is worth $5 billion (£8 billion). His wealth is reputed to be the result of his son's monopoly of smuggling in the country.

MOST EXPENSIVE HOUSES
In 1997 Wong Kwan, chairman of Pearl Oriental Holdings, bought

MOST EXPENSIVE LUXURY LINER
The world's most expensive luxury liner, *The World of ResidenSea*, is due to be launched in the year 2000. Of its 250 ocean-going apartments, which are currently on sale for $1.3–5.8 million (£800,000–3.5 million), the most covetable will be the 199.92-m² (2,152-ft²) three-bedroom, three-bathroom penthouses. The 304-m (1000-ft) ship, which is being produced by a German shipyard, is expected to cost $529.7 million (£323 million), and will be the most luxurious ever built: there will be 500 staff to cater to guests' whims, as well as seven restaurants, bars, a cinema, a casino, a nightclub, a Roman spa, a house of worship, a library, museums, a business service centre with secretaries, and a licensed stock and bond broker. On the top three of the 15 decks there will be shops, a supermarket, a swimming pool, a retractable marina for water sports, a golf academy with driving ranges and putting greens, a tennis court and a helipad. *The World of ResidenSea* will follow the Sun so that it will always be summer on board. Passengers will stop off at major events such as the Sydney 2000 Olympics and the Monte Carlo Grand Prix, and will celebrate the millenium with a two-day stop on the International Date Line.

RICHEST MEN
The richest man for many years was the Sultan of Brunei (seen above, centre) This year his fortune has been exceeded by that of Bill Gates, but the latter's wealth fluctuates according to the value of Microsoft shares, and the gap between their fortunes is at times minimal.

two properties in the Skyhigh development, Hong Kong, for $70.2 million (£42.8 million) and $48.9 million (£29.8 million). Another property was reported to have sold for $98.88 million (£61.8 million). At $2,863/ft² (£19,257/m²) it was then the world's most expensive house.

Bill Gates' house in Seattle, USA, was appraised by the King County assessors at $53,392,000 (£32.3 million). Gates claims that it is worth $30.3 million (£18.5 million).

MOST EXPENSIVE ISLANDS
The 161,88-ha (40,000-acre) island of Niihau, Hawaii, is the largest privately owned island in the USA and has been valued at $100 million (£60 million). It is owned by the Robinson family.

The most expensive island currently on the market is D'Arros in the Seychelles. The atoll, which covers 242.8 ha (600 acres) and has a private lagoon, an airstrip and three homes, can be bought for $21 million (£12.8 million).

MOST LUXURIOUS PRIVATE JET
The $35-million (£21.3-million) *Gulfstream V*, the highest-flying passenger aircraft after Concorde and the fastest long-range executive jet, can fly 6,500 nautical miles at almost the speed of sound. If fitted with customized extras, its value increases to $40 million (£24.4 million). Passengers have included Diana, Princess of Wales, and Dodi Al-Fayed.

MOST EXPENSIVE YACHT
The *Prince Abdul Aziz*, which belongs to the Saudi Arabian royal family and was built in 1984 at a cost of $109 million (£66.46 million), is believed to be the world's most expensive yacht. It is also the world's largest yacht, with a crew of 60, a complex underwater surveillance system and a swimming pool that converts into a dance floor.

GREATEST PHILANTHROPIST
US tycoon Charles 'Chuck' Feeney has given away almost all of his $4.1 billion (£2.5 billion) fortune, owns neither a car nor a house and wears a $16 (£10) wristwatch. The 66-year-old's wealth comes from the duty-free empire that he co-founded and sold to Moet & Chandon. Most of his money has gone into education and research in Ireland, with £3 million ($5 million) put aside for personal living expenses.

LARGEST BEQUESTS
In 1997 the US media tycoon Ted Turner pledged $1 billion (£600 million) to United Nations causes, which include anti-landmine and refugee aid programmes.

In 1991 publishing tycoon Walter Annenberg announced his intention to leave his $1 billion (£600-million) collection of art works to the Metropolitan Museum of Art in New York, USA.

BIGGEST DIVORCE SETTLEMENTS
The world's largest ever publicly declared divorce settlement amounted to £500 million ($874 million) plus property. It was secured in 1982 by the lawyers of Soraya Khashoggi from her husband Adnan, a Saudi entrepreneur and property owner. In 1997 the US mobile phone pioneer Craig McCaw gave his ex-wife Wendy c.$463 million (£282.6 million) in stock plus $19 million (£11.6 million) in real estate. The settlement was so large that the US Securities and Exchange Commission was notified of the stock transfers.

BIGGEST 1990S ROCK HEIRESS
Lisa Marie Presley, Elvis' daughter, seen here with her former husband Michael Jackson, has inherited $130 million (£79.3 million). She received $38 million (£23.2 million) on her 30th birthday in 1997, and the rest in instalments. When Elvis died his estate faced liquidation, but it has since been turned into one of the world's most successful merchandising enterprises.

valuable stuff

MOST VALUABLE JEWELLERY

The largest jewellery auction was the sale of the Duchess of Windsor's collection at Sotheby's, Geneva, Switzerland, on 3 April 1987. It fetched $53 million (£31.4 million).

The most expensive ring was a 13.49-carat Fancy Deep Blue diamond ring bought for $7.5 million (£4.7 million) by an Asian buyer at Christie's, New York, USA, in April 1995. It was the highest price ever paid for a blue diamond per carat.

The costliest diamond per carat was a 0.95-carat fancy purplish-red stone sold at Christie's, New York, USA, in 1987. It fetched $926,315.79 (£548,375.43).

The highest price paid for a diamond was $16.55 million (£10.5 million), for a 100.10-carat pear-shaped 'D' Flawless diamond sold at Sotheby's, Geneva, Switzerland, on 17 May 1995. It was purchased by Sheikh Ahmed Fitaihi for his chain of jewellery shops in Saudi Arabia.

The highest known price paid for a rough diamond was $9.8 million (£5.8 million), for a 255.10-carat stone from Guinea, bought by the William Goldberg Diamond Corporation with the Chow Tai Fook Jewellery Co. Ltd in 1989.

The highest price paid for a ruby is $4.6 million (£2.9 million), for a 32.08-carat ruby and diamond ring made by Chaumet in Paris, France, and sold at Sotheby's, New York, USA, in 1989.

MOST EXPENSIVE CUE

A cue incorporating an 18-diamond tube mounted in 14-carat gold was designed by Joe Gold Cognoscenti Cues, USA, and is worth $22,000 (£13,253). It was produced for nine months to Sept 1997. The cue is the most elaborate ever designed by Joe Gold, and was delivered to a Mr Keith Walton when finished.

The highest-priced ruby per carat is $227,300 (£130,767), for a ring with a stone weighing 15.97-carats sold at Sotheby's, New York, USA, on 18 Oct 1988.

The highest price paid for a single emerald is $2.1 million (£1.3 million), for a 19.77-carat emerald and diamond ring made by Cartier in 1958. It sold at Sotheby's, Geneva, Switzerland, in April 1987.

The top price paid for a sapphire is $2.8 million (£1.6 million), for a 62.02-carat step-cut stone sold as a sapphire and diamond ring at Sotheby's, St Moritz, Switzerland, on 20 Feb 1988.

The world's highest-priced pearl is the egg-shaped 15.13-g (302$^{7}/_{10}$-grain) La Régente. Formerly part of the French crown jewels, it sold for a record-breaking $864,280 (£457,533) at Christie's, Geneva, Switzerland, on 12 May 1988.

The record price paid per carat for an emerald is $107,569 (£63,680), for the 19.77-carat diamond and emerald ring that sold for $2.13 million (£1.32 million) at Sotheby's, Geneva, Switzerland, on 2 April 1987.

MOST EXPENSIVE BOX

A Cartier jewelled vanity case set with a fragment of ancient Egyptian steel was sold at Christie's, New York, USA, for a record sum of $189,000 (£127,651) in Nov 1993.

MOST VALUABLE FABERGE EGG

Fabergé, jeweller to the Russian Imperial family, created about 56 Imperial eggs between 1885 and 1917. The most valuable is the Imperial Winter Egg, made of solid rock crystal and embellished with more than 3,000 diamonds. In Nov 1994 it sold at Christie's, Geneva, Switzerland, for $5,587,308 (£3,560,539). The most valuable Easter Egg (above) sold at Sotheby's, New York, USA, for £1,375,000 ($2,141,563) in 1985.

MOST EXPENSIVE BILLIARD TABLE

The Golden Fleece has been valued at $100,000 (£60,240), making it the most expensive billiard table on sale in the world. The carved table, which is covered in 23-carat gold leaf and protected with a special aged varnish, is the only one of its kind. It was designed and built by husband and wife team Andee and Gil Atkisson, who own one of the world's leading billiard table companies.

MOST VALUABLE MISSING ART TREASURE

The Amber Room, which consisted of intricately carved amber panels and richly decorated chairs, tables and amber ornaments, was presented to Catherine the Great of Russia by Frederick William I of Prussia in 1716 and installed in the Catherine Palace at Tsarskoye Selo near St Petersburg, Russia. Described as 'the eighth wonder of the world', it was at the top of Hitler's trophy list during WWII. Before the German invasion he carefully plotted the dismantling of the room, but was thwarted by the Russians, who buried the delicate panels in the palace garden. However, Hitler seconded hundreds of troops to dig them up and had them shipped to Königsberg castle, East Prussia (now Kaliningrad, Russia). In 1945 the room was put into storage because the Russian army was advancing, and it subsequently disappeared. A single panel surfaced in Germany in 1997, fostering hopes of rebuilding the room. Meanwhile, 22 Russian craftsmen are painstakingly recreating the room from photographs taken before the war. A total of 60 tonnes of amber are being used, at a cost of $164 million (£100 million). Work began in 1982 and will not be complete for at least 15 years.

MOST EXPENSIVE WATCHES

The most paid for a watch is $3.15 million (£1.86 million), for a Patek Philippe 'Calibre '89' with 1,728 separate parts, at Habsburg Feldman, Geneva, Switzerland, on 9 April 1989.

The highest price ever paid for a wristwatch is $1.78 million (£1.14 million), for a Patek Philippe 'Calatrava' 1939 that was auctioned at Antiquorum, Geneva, Switzerland, on 20 April 1996.

The most expensive wristwatches currently on sale are Abraham-Louis Breguet 18-carat-gold watches, with tourbillon, perpetual calendar, minute-repeater and retrograde date. Only 10 have been made. Each one costs $450,000 (£271,084).

The most expensive Rolex in the world is an extremely rare 'Oyster Perpetual' that was sold for the sum of $83,220 (£50,132) by Antiquorum in Geneva, Switzerland, in April 1997. The 18-carat yellow gold and diamond gentleman's wristwatch is waterproof and self-winding.

MOST EXPENSIVE LUGGAGE

A complete set of Louis Vuitton luggage, including an armoire trunk, a wardrobe trunk, a steamer trunk, four matching suitcases, a hat box, a cruiser bag and a jewellery case, costs a total of $601,340 (£362,253), making it the world's most expensive luggage.

MOST EXPENSIVE SHOES

Emperor Field Marshall Jean Feeder Bokassa of the Central African Empire (now Republic) commissioned a pair of pearl-studded shoes costing a record $85,000 (£48,571) from the House of Berluti, Paris, France, for his self-coronation in 1977.

MOST EXPENSIVE WEDDING DRESS

A wedding outfit created by Hélène Gainville with jewels by Alexander Reza is estimated to be worth $7,301,587.20 (£4,269,934). The dress, which is embroidered with diamonds and mounted on platinum, was unveiled in Paris, France, on 23 March 1989.

MOST EXPENSIVE CIGARS

On 16 Nov 1997 an Asian buyer paid a record £9,890 ($16,560) each for 25 Trinidad cigars made by the Cuban National Factory. The sale took place at Christie's, London, UK.

MOST EXPENSIVE SURGICAL INSTRUMENT

A record sum of $34,848 (£23,368) was paid for a 19th-century German mechanical chainsaw sold at Christie's, London, UK, in Aug 1993.

MOST EXPENSIVE SKULL

The skull of Swedish philosopher and theologian Emanuel Swedenborg was purchased in London, UK, by the Royal Swedish Academy of Sciences for £5,500 ($10,668) on 6 March 1978.

MOST EXPENSIVE MONOPOLY SET

An exclusive $2-million (£1.12-million) Monopoly set was created by the jeweller Sidney Mobell, San Francisco, USA, in 1988. The board is made from 23-carat gold and the dice have 42 full cut diamonds for spots.

MOST EXPENSIVE PHONE CARD

The highest price known to have been paid for a telephone card is $49,462 (£28,000), for the first card ever issued in Japan, which sold in Jan 1992.

MOST EXPENSIVE FOUNTAIN PEN

A Japanese collector paid a record sum of $218,007 (£122,677) in Feb 1988 for the 'Anémone' fountain pen, which was made by French company Réden. The pen was encrusted with a total of 600 precious stones, including emeralds, amethysts, rubies, sapphires and onyx, and took a team of skilled craftsmen more than a year to complete.

MOST EXPENSIVE LETTER SIGNED BY A LIVING PERSON

The record sum of $12,500 (£5,375) was paid at the Hamilton Galleries in New York, USA, on 22 Jan 1981 for a two-page signed letter from the former US president Ronald Reagan. The letter, which was undated, praised the singer and actor Frank Sinatra. It is the most expensive letter to have been signed by a person who is still alive today.

MOST EXPENSIVE TAPES

In 1997 the US government paid $28 million (£17 million) to the estate of former president Richard Nixon for the Watergate tape recordings, which forced him from office in 1974 by proving that he had plotted to cover up the bugging of the Democratic Party HQ. They are now in the US National Archives.

MOST EXPENSIVE FILM SCRIPT

Clark Gable's script for *Gone With The Wind* (USA, 1939) sold for $244,500 (£147,289) in Dec 1996 at Christie's, New York, USA.

MOST EXPENSIVE OSCAR

Clark Gable's Academy Award for *It Happened One Night* (USA, 1934) sold for $607,500 (£365,963) at Christie's, New York, USA, in Dec 1996.

MOST EXPENSIVE SLICE OF CAKE

In Feb 1998 a piece of cake left over from the wedding of the Duke and Duchess of Windsor sold at Sotheby's, New York, USA, for $29,900 (£18,231) to the Californian entrepreneur Benjamin Yim and his wife Amanda. The cake, which was part of the Windsor collection auction, had only been expected to fetch a maximum of $1,000 (£602) at the sale.

going, going, gone

MOST EXPENSIVE MOVIE POSTER
The poster from Universal Studio's 1932 film *The Mummy* sold for a record $453,000 (£276,523) at Sotheby's, New York, USA, in March 1997. The poster, which features the film's star Boris Karloff, went for more than twice the previous record of $198,000 (£123,750). There are only two known copies of *The Mummy* poster in existence.

MOST VALUABLE PIECES OF OTHER PLANETS
A tiny piece of Martian meteorite fetched $7,333 (£4,583) — more than 1,000 times its weight in gold — at Phillips, New York, USA, in May 1998. The rock, which measures 2 x 2 x 4 mm ($^7/_{100}$ x $^7/_{100}$ x $^3/_{20}$ in) and weighs 0.28 g ($^9/_{1,000}$ oz), was found in Brazil in 1958 and was expected to sell for $1,600–3,200 (£1,000–2,000). Known as the Governador Valadares, it is the most valuable of the 12 Martian meteorites discovered on Earth.

Sotheby's sold 0.33 g ($^1/_{100}$ oz or less than two carats) of rock from the Moon for $442,000 (£283,000) in 1996. A total of 363 kg (800 lb) of lunar rock exists on Earth, compared to 41 kg (90 lb) of Martian rock.

MOST IMPORTANT SCIENTIFIC THEORY SOLD AT AUCTION
Albert Einstein's *Theory of Relativity*, which was written in 1913 in collaboration with Michele Besso and proposed to account for the constant speed of light, sold for $398,500 (£249,026) at Christie's, New York, USA, in 1996. The 51-page manuscript of the most important document in modern science had an asking price of $250,000–350,000 (£156,000–218,000). Einstein went on to formulate his general theory of relativity in 1919.

MOST EXPENSIVE TOBACCO TIN
The tobacco tin in which John Lennon kept his cigarette papers fetched £5,400 ($8,453) at a sale of Beatles memorabilia at Christie's, London, UK, in Sept 1995. The 27-cm-high (11-in) leather covered pot, which was bought by a British fan, had been expected to fetch £300–400 ($475–634). Cynthia Lennon, the star's first wife, provided the items for the sale.

MOST EXPENSIVE BIRTH CERTIFICATE
Sir Paul McCartney's birth certificate sold for $84,146 (£52,591) in a Bonhams auction conducted simultaneously in Tokyo, Japan, and London, UK, in March 1997. The pre-sale estimate was $13,000 (£8,125). The certificate, which was originally sold by McCartney's stepmother after the death of his father, was put on the market by a Californian record collector and bought by an anonymous London buyer.

MOST EXPENSIVE TELEGRAM
The highest price ever paid for a telegram is $68,500 (£45,900), for a telegram sent by Soviet premier Nikita Khrushchev to Yuri Gagarin on 12 April 1961 congratulating him for becoming the first man in Space. It was bought by Alberto Bolaffi of Turin, Italy, at Sotheby's, New York, USA, on 11 Dec 1993.

MOST PAID FOR PRESIDENTIAL UNDERWEAR
Two pairs of John F. Kennedy's long johns were bought for $3,450 (£2,156) by Richard Wilson (left) at Guernsey's, New York, USA, in March 1998. Wilson runs a mail order business selling unusual celebrity memorabilia. He plans to display the former president's underwear alongside Marilyn Monroe's slip and knickers. Many of the items in the auction were part of Robert White's 100,000-strong Kennedy collection, left to him in 1995 by Kennedy's secretary Evelyn Lincoln, who saved almost everything to do with Kennedy or his family. The sunglasses that Kennedy was wearing on the day he was shot went for $46,000 (£28,750) and a plastic comb that probably cost about 25c (15p) sold for $1,265 (£790).

MOST EXPENSIVE SHOES SOLD AT AUCTION
The red slippers worn by Judy Garland when she played Dorothy in *The Wizard of Oz* (USA, 1939) sold for $165,000 (£90,000) at Christie's, New York, USA, on 2 June 1988. The shoes belonged to Roberta Baumann, who had won them in a competition in 1940, and were bought by Anthony Landini. At the time it was a record price for any item worn in a movie.

MOST EXPENSIVE DINKY TOY
In 1994 a collector paid £12,650 ($20,312) for a 1937 Dinky Bentalls store delivery van.

MOST EXPENSIVE BUBBLE CAR
In March 1997 the British entrepreneur Peter de Savary paid £24,150 ($38,640) for a three-wheeled German-built 1962 Messerschmitt KR 200 'Bubble Top' — a record for any Messerschmitt car. The 191cc two-seater was expected to sell for £8,000 ($12,800). De Savary, a former Americas Cup yachtsman who once owned Land's End and John O'Groats, UK, also paid record prices for a 1962 Trojan 200 and a 1959 Goggomobil T400, the world's smallest limousine. They were put up for auction at Christie's, London, UK, by Canadian bubble-gum magnate Bruce Weiner.

MOST EXPENSIVE RACING CAR MEMORABILIA
A pair of overalls worn by Brazilian racing driver Ayrton Senna, who died in a high speed crash at the 1994 San Marino Grand Prix, sold at Sotheby's, London, UK, in Dec 1996 for £25,300 ($42,140). Senna had worn the overalls in his first

Formula 1 race for the Toleman team in Monaco in 1984. A pair of gloves worn by Senna during the 1987 season went for £2,530 ($4,048) and a race helmet he wore in 1982 fetched £28,750 ($46,000). The latter was bought by British fan Peter Radcliffe, the overalls and gloves by anonymous bidders.

MOST EXPENSIVE WORLD CUP REPLICA
A World Cup 'decoy' trophy sold for £254,500 ($407,200) — 12 times the estimated price — at Sotheby's, London, UK, in July 1997. The gold painted trophy, a replica of the one won by England in 1966, was ordered by the Football Association after the real cup was stolen in 1966. For two years it was passed off as the genuine Jules Rimet trophy and was protected by security guards to keep up the pretence for the public. The original was later found by a dog called Pickles in London, UK.

MOST EXPENSIVE CRICKET BAT
A cricket bat used by W. G. Grace in 1868 sold for £26,450 ($43,100) in London, UK, in May 1998.

MOST PAID FOR A BARK PAINTING
An Aboriginal bark painting from the late 1960s sold for a record

$18,400 (£11,500) to an art collector in Sydney, NSW, Australia, in 1996. The artist Yarawala, who died in 1970, was admired by Picasso.

MOST PAID FOR AN ABORIGINAL SCULPTURE
A large Tiwi figure carved by Aurangamirri sold for $20,700 (£12,937) in Sydney, NSW, Australia, in 1996, to an Australian collector.

MOST EXPENSIVE TEDDY BEAR
A 1904 Steiff bear called *Teddy Girl* was sold to Japanese businessman Yoshihiro Sekiguchi for £110,000 ($171,523) at Christie's, London, UK, in Dec 1994. It is now in a Japanese museum. The previous record was £55,100 ($86,589) for a c. 1920 Steiff brown bear at Sotheby's, London, UK, in Sept 1989.

MOST EXPENSIVE STUFFED DOG
The stuffed body of Toto the dog, who starred alongside Judy Garland in *The Wizard of Oz* (USA, 1939), sold for £2,300 ($3,680) at auction in 1996.

MOST VALUABLE FILM PROP
A statuette used in *The Maltese Falcon* (USA, 1941) sold for $398,500 (£265,666) at Christie's, New York, USA, in 1994.

MOST EXPENSIVE CARTOON POSTER
A poster for Walt Disney's film short *Alice's Day At Sea* (USA, 1924) sold for a record £23,100 ($34,273) at Christie's, London, UK, in April 1994.

MOST PAID FOR A FILM COSTUME
The white polyester suit worn by John Travolta in *Saturday Night Fever* (USA, 1977) was sold for $145,500 (£92,500) in June 1995. The pre-sale estimate was between $30,000 and $50,000 (£18,928–31,547).

BOXING MEMORABILIA
The calf-length white robe worn by Muhammad Ali when he beat George Foreman in their 'Rumble in the Jungle' world heavyweight title fight in Zaïre (now Congo) in 1974 sold for $140,000 (£85,000) — a record for boxing memorabilia — at Christie's, Los Angeles, USA, in Oct 1997. A pair of gloves (below) worn by Ali for a fight against Zora Folley in 1967 sold for a record $29,900 (£18,680). The buyers were anonymous.

gambling

BIGGEST POKER TOURNAMENT
The World Poker Series, which was won by Stu Unger (above right) in 1997, is the largest poker tournament in the world. The annual event began in 1970 at Binion's Horseshoe, Las Vegas, USA, and the total prize money won since then now exceeds $117 million (£70.3 million). The tournament offers a $1-million (£600,900) prize for the winner as well as a $10,000 (£6,024) buy-in.

BIGGEST GAMBLING WIN
The biggest ever individual gambling win was $111.24 million (£74.1 million), by Leslie Robbins and Colleen DeVries of Fond du Lac, Wisconsin, USA, in the Powerball lottery draw on 7 July 1993. They will each receive an annual net sum of $1.5 million (£892,857) over the next 20 years.

LARGEST LOTTERY JACKPOT
The biggest ever jackpot for any lottery in the world was $118.8 million (£71.3 million) in California, USA, on 17 April 1991. There were 10 winners.

BIGGEST MEGABUCKS JACKPOT
The Nevada Megabucks progressive slot jackpot passed the $15-million (just over £9-million) mark in April 1998 and will be the largest slot jackpot in history when it is hit. The current record stands at $12.51 million (£7.6 million), which was won by Suzanne Henley in Las Vegas in April 1997.

BIGGEST VIDEO POKER JACKPOT
In April 1998 a grandmother from San Antonio, USA, hit a jackpot of $839,306.92 (£508,670) on the Five Duck Frenzy™ at the Las Vegas Club, Las Vegas, Nevada, USA.

BIGGEST GAMBLERS
Australia has a greater number of gamblers than any other country, and on average an Australian bets in excess of $2,700 (£1,626) a year — three times more than a US citizen.

BIGGEST HIGH ROLLER
The world's largest high roller or 'whale' (the term for people who bet huge amounts at casinos) is the Australian media tycoon Kerry Packer, who has an estimated personal fortune of $1.5 billion (£0.9 billion).

BIGGEST SLOT MACHINE JACKPOT
The largest amount ever won on a 'one-armed bandit' is $12.51 million (£7.6 million), by Suzanne Henley on a Megabucks machine at the New York–New York Hotel and Casino, Las Vegas, on 14 April 1997. Henley, who was 46 at the time, said she "just had a feeling" about the poker machine, which for major prizes is linked to 746 others. She waited for more than an hour to play it.

Packer is guaranteed an instant $20-million (£12-million) line of credit at any casino that is prepared to admit him. In 1997 he purchased his own casino

BIGGEST LOTTERY
Spain's government-run lottery El Gordo ('The Fat One') is the biggest in the world, awarding more prize money and offering 800% better odds of winning (one in six) than any other lottery. Winning ticket holders are seen here celebrating after their numbers came up. El Gordo awarded $1.2 billion (£0.72 billion) in Dec 1997, with a grand prize of $270 million (£162.6 million). Its largest ever cash jackpot was $236 million (£142 million). The next biggest lotteries in terms of average pool size are the Florida state lottery, at $14 million (£8.4 million), the Australian government lottery, at $10 million (£6 million), the German state lottery, at $6.5 million (£3.9 million), the New York state lottery, USA, and the French national lottery, both at $6 million (£3.6 million). Of these, the biggest jackpot prize has been $7 million (£4.2 million), on the Florida state lottery. The United Kingdom's National Lottery is one of the world's newest: it began on 1994 — 168 years after the last lottery was allowed in the country. The typical jackpot prize is £2 million ($3.33 million) and the chance of winning the jackpot is one in 14 million.

in Australia after two Las Vegas casinos lost $22 million (£13.2 million) to him. He also won the sum of $26 million (£15.6 million) in seven hands of blackjack at the MGM Grand Casino, Las Vegas, USA. His favourite bet is $1 million (£600,000).

BIGGEST CASINO

Foxwoods Resort casino in Connecticut, USA, is the largest in the world, with a gaming area covering 17,900 m² (192,670 ft²) and a total of 3,854 slot machines, 234 gaming tables and 3,500 bingo seats.

HIGHEST CASINO

The Stratosphere Hotel Casino in Las Vegas is the highest casino in the world. The 350-m-high (1,149-ft), 100-storey tower, which opened in April 1996 at a cost of about $550 million (£331 million), is the tallest free-standing observation tower in the USA. It is 47.5 m (156 ft) taller than the Eiffel Tower in Paris, France. The casino covers 9,300 m² (100,000 ft²) and has more than 2,000 slot and video poker machines.

BIGGEST POT IN POKER

In 1996 Huck Seed, a poker professional from Las Vegas, won a pot of $2.3 million (£1.4 million) from Dr Bruce Van Horn of Ada, Oklahoma, USA — the largest in the history of the game. Seed went on to win the World Series Poker Title.

BIGGEST HOUSE IN BINGO

The largest ever house in bingo sessions was 15,756, at the Canadian National Exhibition, Toronto, on 19 Aug 1983. Staged by the Variety Club of Ontario, Canada, the competition offered total prize money of $202,872 (£132,710) with a record one-game payout of $81,084 (£53,149).

BIGGEST BOOKMAKER

The world's largest bookmaker is Ladbrokes, which has more than 2,460 offtrack betting units in the United Kingdom,

74 in the Republic of Ireland, 474 in Belgium, six in the USA, and seven in Argentina.

LONGEST ODDS EVER OFFERED

In 1996 bookmakers William Hill offered odds of 15 million to one on Screaming Lord Sutch of the Monster Raving Loony Party becoming British prime minister — longer odds than they offer for Elvis Presley crashing a UFO into the Loch Ness Monster (14 million to one). Lord Sutch has been a familiar face on the political scene since 1963 and is the UK's longest-serving political leader.

BIGGEST HORSERACING PAYOUT

The largest horseracing payout was $1,627,084 (£988,211), to Anthony Speelman and Nicholas Cowan (UK) on a $64 (£39.25) nine-horse accumulator at Santa Anita racecourse, California, USA, in 1987. After tax, the pair's total winnings amounted to $406,768 (£249,550).

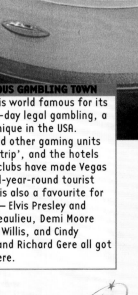

MOST FAMOUS GAMBLING TOWN

Las Vegas is world famous for its 24-hour-a-day legal gambling, a feature unique in the USA. Casinos and other gaming units line the 'Strip', and the hotels and nightclubs have made Vegas a major all-year-round tourist resort. It is also a favourite for weddings — Elvis Presley and Priscilla Beaulieu, Demi Moore and Bruce Willis, and Cindy Crawford and Richard Gere all got married here.

shopping

BIGGEST DEPARTMENT STORE

At 198,500 m² (2.15 million ft²), the largest department store by area is Macy's. The shop's 11-storey building occupies an entire block in Herald Square, New York, USA. Macy's also has a chain of department stores across the USA and was one of the first major retailers to place stores in shopping malls. The firm's red star trademark derives from a tattoo borne by its founder, Rowland Macy.

and a total of 1,100 shops and restaurants, making it the world's biggest subterranean shopping complex.

BIGGEST WHOLESALERS

The world's biggest wholesale merchandise mart is the Dallas Market Center, Texas, USA, which has a floor area of almost 641,000 m² (6.9 million ft²) and houses about 2,580 permanent showrooms displaying the merchandise of more than 50,000 manufacturers.

BIGGEST RETAILING FIRM

Wal-Mart Stores, Inc., which was founded by Sam Walton in Bentonville, Arkansas, USA, in 1962, had a net income of $2.74 billion (£1.8 billion) by 31 Jan 1996. By June 1998 it had had total sales of $117.9 billion (£71.02 billion) and 3,487 retail locations worldwide with 800,000 employees.

MOST SHOPS

On 28 Jan 1996 the Woolworth Corporation of New York, USA, had 8,178 retail stores worldwide — the most that any company has ever had. The company's founder, Frank Winfield Woolworth, opened his first shop, The Great Five Cent Store, in Utica, New York, USA, in 1879. Woolworth no longer trades in the USA.

MOST SHOPPERS AT ONE DEPARTMENT STORE

The most visitors to a single department store on one day is an estimated 1.07 million, to the Nextage Shanghai, China, on 20 Dec 1995.

MOST MALLS IN ONE COUNTRY

The USA has more shopping malls (which are defined as enclosed, climate-controlled environments typically anchored by at least one major full-line department store with an area of more than 37,160 m² or 400,000 ft²) than any other country, with a total of 1,897 to date. If they are added to the number of grocery-, drug- or discount-anchored centres (which are generally of open-air design), the total number of shopping centres is 42,048.

LONGEST MALL

The longest shopping mall in the world is located inside the £40-million ($64-million) shopping centre in Milton Keynes, Bucks, UK. The mall is 720 m (2,360 ft) in length.

BIGGEST RETAIL SPACE

The Del Amo Fashion Center in Torrance, California, USA, is the biggest retail centre in the world in terms of square metres of space, covering a total of 278,700 m² (3 million ft²).

BIGGEST OPEN-AIR SHOPPING CENTRE

Ala Moana Center in Honolulu, Hawaii, USA, has more than 200 shops over a 20-ha (50-acre) site, making it the world's largest open-air shopping centre. It is visited by more than 56 million shoppers every year.

BIGGEST UNDERGROUND SHOPPING COMPLEX

The Toronto Underground in Canada has more than 9.65 km (6 miles) of shopping arcades

FIRST SUPERMARKET ART GALLERY

From 9 Dec 1997 to 10 Jan 1998 — for a period of five weeks — Leclerc supermarket at Le Cannet near Cannes on the French Riviera installed an art gallery in its aisles in an effort to boost a local art market that had been in decline for a considerable time. A total of 17 artists from the region had their work on display and received all profits from the sales. The supermarket did not take any commission. Some of the artists were present in the 'art gallery' to explain their works to potential buyers. During the trial period visitors to the supermarket could fill their shopping trolleys with paintings, sculptures and lithographs, all of which were shrink-wrapped and labelled for price scanners. The 1,700 pieces of art ranged in price from $14 (£8.50) to $4,167 (£2,525) and were aimed at the supermarket's wealthier customers. By the end of the five weeks the supermarket had sold 185 pieces for a total of $5,553 (£3,423). Yvon Guidez, one of the artists and a promoter of the scheme, said that art should be open to everyone and treated in the same way as consumer items such as washing-up powder or soft drinks. One of his works, a bronze sculpture entitled *Octave Auguste*, was bought by a French shopper for $2,500 (£1,515).

BIGGEST SHOPPING CENTRE

The West Edmonton Mall in Alberta, Canada, was opened in 1981 and completed four years later. The mall is the size of 110 soccer pitches, covers an area of 483,000 m² (5.2 million ft²) on a 49-ha (121-acre) site, and houses more than 800 stores and services, as well as 11 major department stores. It serves approximately 20 million customers annually and provides parking for 20,000 vehicles. A water park, golf course, ice rink and chapel can all be found inside the mall.

BIGGEST DUTY FREE SHOP

The world's biggest duty free shop will be opened by the Indonesian tourist operator PT Sona Topas in Bali in late 1998. It will bring the total number of duty free shops on the island to 22. PT Sona Topas currently accounts for 60% of Indonesia's duty free market and has prime locations in every major international airport worldwide.

BIGGEST DUTY FREE CENTRE

Heathrow Airport, London, UK, is currently the biggest duty free centre in the world in terms of revenue, which amounted to $585.2 million (£365.75 million) in 1996. Honolulu Airport, USA, is second, with $425.8 million (£266.12 million), followed by Hong Kong, China, with $380 million (£237.5 million). It is predicted that the new Chek Lap Kok airport in Hong Kong will overtake all three of these airports to become the most lucrative duty free shopping area in the world.

BIGGEST TOYSHOP CHAIN

Toys 'R' Us, which has its headquarters in Paramus, New Jersey, USA, has a total of 1,000 stores and 4 million m² (43 million ft²) of retail space worldwide. The largest single Toys 'R' Us store is the branch in Birmingham, W Midlands, UK, at 6,040 m² (65,000 ft²).

GREATEST SALES PER UNIT AREA

The record for the greatest sales based on square metres of selling space is held by Richer Sounds plc, the hi-fi retail chain. Its sales at London Bridge Walk, UK, reached a peak of £1,630 m² ($26,380 ft²) for the year ending 31 Jan 1994.

MOST EXPENSIVE SHOP SPACE

Oxford Street in London, UK, is the most expensive place in the world in which to rent shop space. The price of hiring the equivalent floor area of a wastepaper basket there has jumped by 25% to £500 ($800).

BIGGEST JUMBLE SALES

The record for the greatest amount of money raised at a one-day sale is $214,085.99 (£142,723.93), at the 62nd one-day jumble sale that was organized by the Winnetka Congregational Church, Illinois, USA, in May 1994.

The White Elephant Sale at the Cleveland Convention Center, Ohio, USA, raised $427,935.21 (£285,785.50) over two days from 18 to 19 Oct 1983.

HIGHEST CREDIT CARD TRANSACTION

In 1995 Eli Broad, an art collector from Los Angeles, California, USA, purchased Roy Lichtenstein's painting *I...I'm Sorry* (1965–66) for the sum of $2.5 million (£1.6 million), paying for it by American Express. The highest Amex transaction to date, it earned Broad a total of 2.5 million air miles.

MOST CREDIT CARDS

Walter Cavanagh from Santa Clara, California, USA, has a total of 1,397 different credit cards, which together are worth more than $1.65 million (£1 million) in credit. He keeps his collection in the world's longest wallet, which is 76.2 m (250 ft) in length and weighs 17.49 kg (38 lb 8 oz).

BIGGEST PURCHASER OF HAUTE-COUTURE

Mouna al-Ayoub, the ex-wife of Nasser al-Rashid, the consultant to the Saudi royal family, spends more money on haute-couture than anybody else in the world. Al-Ayoub's most expensive purchase to date was a $160,000 (£100,000) gold embroidered dress from Chanel.

brand names

MOST VALUABLE BRAND NAME
The most valuable brand name in the world today is Coca-Cola, which was worth $48 billion (£29 billion) in 1997. Coca-Cola is also considered by many people to be the most famous brand name in the world and the brand name with the strongest global advertising image. Its share value has increased from $4 billion (£1.97 billion) in 1981 to more than $150 billion (£74 billion) today.

MOST POPULAR SPORTS BRAND
Nike is the top sports goods group, with a global market share of 35%, and the biggest shoe manufacturer in the world. It is worth $6.16 billion (£3.7 billion). In 1998 it signed an eight-year sponsorship deal with the US Soccer Federation worth $120 million (£74 million). It has also put up $1 billion (£602 million) to sponsor leading sportspeople and teams around the world, in a marketing battle with its rival Adidas. Tiger Woods, Michael Jordan and John McEnroe are some of its sponsored celebrities. The Nike 'swoosh', now so recognizable that sports stars do not need to wear anything else on their vests to identify

their sponsor, was created by a designer in Oregon, USA, for $35 (£22) in 1971.

MOST EXPENSIVE RE-BRANDING OF AN AIRLINE
In 1997 British Airways, the biggest international carrier in the world, underwent a £60 million ($98-million) facelift in the biggest ever relaunch of its kind. British Airways' previous symbol, the Union Jack flag, was replaced by African paintings of jackals, Japanese wave designs and other ethnically inspired works of art. Payment to artists, lawyers and design consultancies accounted for about £2 million ($3.2 million) of the total sum, and a similar amount was spent on a satellite broadcast to 63 countries of the unveiling ceremony at Heathrow airport, UK. Other launch events included a flotilla of barges in Thailand, with sails displaying the new images.

BIGGEST BRAND CONSULTANCY
In 1997 Interbrand, which branded the anti-depressant drug Prozac, merged with design business Newell and Sorrell, who had overhauled British Airways' image, to create the world's biggest brand consultancy. The combined business, which has an annual turnover of $33.2 million

(£20 million), is owned by the US advertising agency Omnicom and employs a total of 600 people worldwide.

MOST SUCCESSFUL BRAND AGENCY
Set up in 1981, Dentsu Young and Rubicam is the world's largest advertising resource. In 1996 it was worth $1,930 million (£1,236 million). An alliance between Dentsu, the largest agency in Japan, and Young and Rubicam, the biggest US agency, Dentsu Young and Rubicam has 19 offices in 12 countries in Asia and 341 offices worldwide. Its main accounts include AT&T, Cadbury Schweppes, Kraft Foods, Colgate–Palmolive, Ericsson, Fuji–Xerox, Nike, Philip Morris, Sony and United Airlines.

BIGGEST BRAND SPONSORSHIP DEAL
In 1996 Nike signed a record $400-million (£256-million) deal with the Brazilian football team. It gives Nike the right to arrange a series of international soccer fixtures over 10 years with the team as part of the group's expansion into sports sponsorship.

MOST VALUABLE COLLECTIBLE BRANDS
Old Nike, Puma and Adidas trainers are being included for

TOP SOFT DRINKS BRAND
The world's most popular soft drinks brand by volume sales is Coca-Cola, which had a 43.9% share of the $54.7-billion (£33.4-billion) US carbonated drinks market in 1997. Its closest rival, Pepsi, has 30.9% of the market. Coca-Cola sales in the USA in 1996 indicate a consumption of 207.5 litres (46 gallons) per person.

BIGGEST BRAND FORGERY
Financial losses created by counterfeiting operations amount to 5–7% of world trade, or $250–$350 billion (£150.2–£210.3 billion). From 1990 to 1995, world trade grew by 47% and the counterfeiting trade grew by 150%, and in 1995–96 British customs officers busted a total of 81 counterfeiting consignments, compared with just 12 the previous year. The world's top producer of counterfeit products is Turkey, followed by China, Thailand, Italy and Colombia. According to the Service de Statistiques Industrielles, 60% of the world's counterfeited goods end up for sale in the European Union, with France receiving 25% of them. In the USA the most common form of piracy, according to the Motion Picture Association of America (MPAA), is the 'back to back' copying of videos, but the industry is more affected by organized and sophisticated duplication facilities that have the ability to produce hundreds of thousands of copies a year. Worldwide video piracy currently costs US motion picture companies $2.5 billion (£1.5 billion) a year in lost revenues. The music industry also loses vast sums each year through piracy. Pictured here, a consignment of pirated videos is crushed by steam-roller in Bangkok, Thailand.

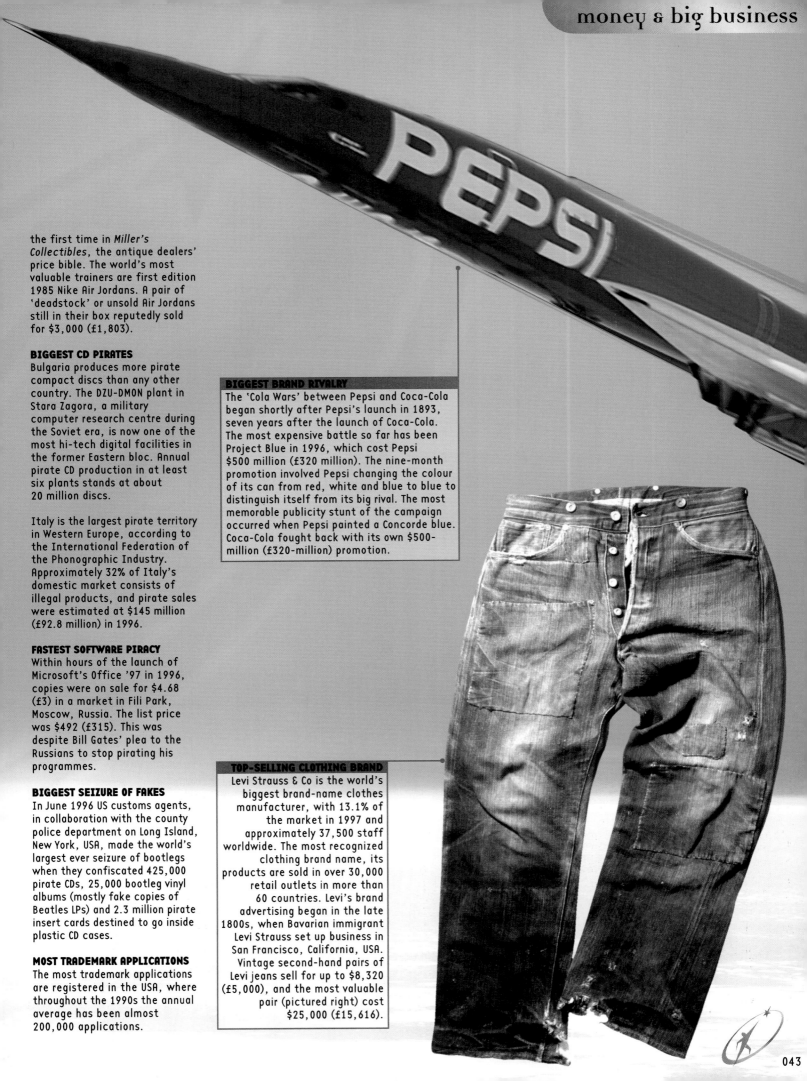

the first time in *Miller's Collectibles*, the antique dealers' price bible. The world's most valuable trainers are first edition 1985 Nike Air Jordans. A pair of 'deadstock' or unsold Air Jordans still in their box reputedly sold for $3,000 (£1,803).

BIGGEST CD PIRATES

Bulgaria produces more pirate compact discs than any other country. The DZU-DMON plant in Stara Zagora, a military computer research centre during the Soviet era, is now one of the most hi-tech digital facilities in the former Eastern bloc. Annual pirate CD production in at least six plants stands at about 20 million discs.

Italy is the largest pirate territory in Western Europe, according to the International Federation of the Phonographic Industry. Approximately 32% of Italy's domestic market consists of illegal products, and pirate sales were estimated at $145 million (£92.8 million) in 1996.

FASTEST SOFTWARE PIRACY

Within hours of the launch of Microsoft's Office '97 in 1996, copies were on sale for $4.68 (£3) in a market in Fili Park, Moscow, Russia. The list price was $492 (£315). This was despite Bill Gates' plea to the Russians to stop pirating his programmes.

BIGGEST SEIZURE OF FAKES

In June 1996 US customs agents, in collaboration with the county police department on Long Island, New York, USA, made the world's largest ever seizure of bootlegs when they confiscated 425,000 pirate CDs, 25,000 bootleg vinyl albums (mostly fake copies of Beatles LPs) and 2.3 million pirate insert cards destined to go inside plastic CD cases.

MOST TRADEMARK APPLICATIONS

The most trademark applications are registered in the USA, where throughout the 1990s the annual average has been almost 200,000 applications.

BIGGEST BRAND RIVALRY

The 'Cola Wars' between Pepsi and Coca-Cola began shortly after Pepsi's launch in 1893, seven years after the launch of Coca-Cola. The most expensive battle so far has been Project Blue in 1996, which cost Pepsi $500 million (£320 million). The nine-month promotion involved Pepsi changing the colour of its can from red, white and blue to blue to distinguish itself from its big rival. The most memorable publicity stunt of the campaign occurred when Pepsi painted a Concorde blue. Coca-Cola fought back with its own $500-million (£320-million) promotion.

TOP-SELLING CLOTHING BRAND

Levi Strauss & Co is the world's biggest brand-name clothes manufacturer, with 13.1% of the market in 1997 and approximately 37,500 staff worldwide. The most recognized clothing brand name, its products are sold in over 30,000 retail outlets in more than 60 countries. Levi's brand advertising began in the late 1800s, when Bavarian immigrant Levi Strauss set up business in San Francisco, California, USA. Vintage second-hand pairs of Levi jeans sell for up to $8,320 (£5,000), and the most valuable pair (pictured right) cost $25,000 (£15,616).

advertising

MOST EXPENSIVE TV ADVERT

A commercial for the computer manufacturer Apple Macintosh cost a total of $600,000 (£360,000) to produce and $1 million (£600,000) to show. Produced by Ridley Scott, the director of *Blade Runner* (USA, 1982), the advertisement's impact was so great and the recall among viewers so high that it is believed to be one of the most cost-effective commercials ever made. Based on the novel *1984* by George Orwell, the ad was shown only once, in 1984.

FASTEST PRODUCTION OF AN ADVERT

A television ad for Reebok's InstaPUMP shoes was created, filmed and aired during Super Bowl XXVII at the Atlanta Georgia Dome, USA, on 31 Jan 1993. Filming took place up to the beginning of the fourth quarter of play, editing began in the middle of the third quarter and the finished product was aired during the break at the two-minute warning of the fourth quarter. The commercial starred Emmitt Smith of the Dallas Cowboys and lasted for 30 seconds.

SHORTEST ADVERT

An advert lasting four frames (there are 30 frames in a second) was aired on KING-TV's *Evening Magazine* on 29 Nov 1993. The ad, which was for Bon Marché's Frango sweets, cost $3,780 (£2,500).

MOST EXPENSIVE COMMERCIAL BREAK

The US TV network NBC raked in $2 million (£1.25 million) for a 30-second spot during the final episode of the top-rating show *Seinfeld* on 14 May 1998. The sitcom was regularly No. 1 in the Nielsen ratings, with audiences of about 20 million, but it was estimated that there were more than 40 million viewers for the last show. Half-minute spots during regular episodes cost $575,000 (£359,375) in 1998 — $15,000 (£9,375) more than *Seinfeld*'s closest rival *ER*.

LONGEST ADVERTISING MESSAGE

Yellow Pages, the British phone directory, created the world's longest advertising message on a London Underground train in Feb 1997. The train was painted with brightly-coloured images on the outside to reflect the different services covered by the directory, while the interior was refurbished with Yellow Pages liveried upholstery. The ad cost £1 million ($1.6 million).

MOST CELEBRITIES IN AN ADVERT

Reebok's 90-second ad *Field of Dreams*, which ran on British TV in 1996, starred 22 celebrities, including singer Tom Jones, film director Richard Attenborough, opera singer José Carreras and ex-football star George Best. The stars had to imagine they were Ryan Giggs, the Manchester United star sponsored by Reebok.

MOST LUCRATIVE AD CONTRACT

In April 1997 the US golfer Tiger Woods landed the most lucrative advertising and sponsorship contract in history after winning the US Masters at the age of 21. Nike signed up the new star for a $40-million (£25.3-million) five-year deal involving product endorsement and appearances in adverts. Experts estimate that Woods will be able to generate around $1 billion (£625,000) in other endorsement deals, making him the most valuable human billboard ever.

TOP-SELLING SINGLE FROM AN AD

In Dec 1995 Levi's *Planet*, a 60-second pan-European TV and cinema ad promoting Women's Fit 501 jeans, used the song *Spaceman* by British band Babylon Zoo, which had been released in Sept 1995 but failed to chart. The remix for the commercial was released as a single in Jan 1996 and went straight to No. 1 in the UK charts. It stayed there for five weeks, selling 420,000 copies in its first week.

RUSSIAN SPACE ADVERTISING

Milk in Space, a commercial advertising a brand of Israeli long-life milk, was filmed aboard the Russian orbiting station *Mir* on 25 July 1997 and portrays a cosmonaut who longs for the taste of fresh milk while in Space. The advert, which shows the space station commander Vasily Tsibliyev swallowing floating milk bubbles squeezed out of a Hebrew-lettered carton and singing the praises of the product in Russian, was shot one month after an accident on board involving Alexander Lazutkin, *Mir*'s flight engineer. The milk and other cargo were delivered into orbit by the *Progress* space shuttle. The Russians are reputed to have charged the Israeli GITAM/BBDO advertising agency $450,000 (£281,250) for the 90-second ad, which was shown on Israeli television for the first time on 20 Aug 1997. It was the second advertisement that Russia had filmed in Space: in 1996 two *Mir* cosmonauts were filmed with an outsize replica of Pepsi's blue can during a space walk.

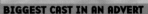

MOST INNOVATIVE AD DEAL
In Aug 1995 Microsoft tied up a ground-breaking deal with British newspaper *The Times* to promote its new operating software package Windows '95. For the first time in its 210-year history, the paper was given away for free, at Microsoft's expense. In exchange for sponsoring the edition and matching its cover price revenue, Microsoft had a near monopoly on all premium advertising space and distributed a 28-page supplement for free with the paper's increased 1.5 million print run.

MOST COMMERCIALS MADE BY A CELEBRITY FOR ONE ADVERTISER
Between May 1994 and Dec 1996 British actor Bob Hoskins made 55 TV commercials, rising to 94 different cut-downs and adaptations, for British telecommunications giant BT. His slogan 'It's good to talk' reached No. 1 in Adwatch, the weekly survey on advertising recall carried out for the British trade magazine *Marketing* soon after the campaign broke, and remained unchallenged in the top spot for 14 months.

MOST AWARDS WON BY AN INTERNATIONAL COMMERCIAL
The Levi 501 jeans *Drugstore* TV advert won 33 awards in 1995.

MOST ADVERTS IN ONE EVENING
All 17 versions of a Castlemaine XXXX commercial were shown on the first night of Granada Sky Broadcasting, UK, on 1 Oct 1996.

BIGGEST ADVERTISER
Detergent giant Procter and Gamble, which manufactures global brands such as Daz, Fairy Liquid and Ariel, was the leading national advertiser in the USA in 1996, spending a total of $2.62 billion (£1.68 billion). It is also the leading TV advertiser in a number of Western European countries (including Germany, the Netherlands and all the Scandinavian states), and spent $2.56 billion (£1.62 billion) on non-US advertising in 1995.

BIGGEST AD CAMPAIGN BY A FIRM
The 1996 campaign for AT&T telephone services cost parent company AT&T Corporation $474 million (£296.25 million).

LARGEST ADVERTISING NATION
In 1996 the USA spent more than $63.81 billion (£39.88 billion) on advertising and promotion. Japan, in second place, has an annual advertising expenditure just one-third that of the USA.

FASTEST-GROWING AD MARKET
Russia had a record-breaking 94% year-on-year increase in 1996, according to *World Advertising Trends 1998*. The survey, which examines advertising expenditure from 86 countries, found that seven of the world's highest-growing markets are in Eastern Europe.

BIGGEST CAST IN AN ADVERT
Saatchi and Saatchi's 60-second ad *Global*, for British Airways, was filmed in Utah, USA, in Oct 1989 and starred 6,300 people in coloured track-suits. Shot from the air, the cast assembled in different configurations to create giant images of an ear, an eye, a pair of lips and finally a whole face and a globe. It took 350 people to create the lips, 410 to make the ear and about 2,000 to make the face.

MOST CONTROVERSIAL ADVERTS
The Benetton advertisement featuring a new born baby, which was run in the UK in 1991, prompted more than 800 complaints to the Advertising Standards Authority. Also in the UK, the series of Wonderbra advertisements starring the model Eva Herzigova (pictured left) was the subject of 100 complaints and was even reputed to be distracting male drivers and causing car crashes.

world markets

MOST RURAL ECONOMY
Somalia has the most rural economy in the world, with an estimated 65% of its GDP generated by agriculture. Its two major crops are bananas and sugar cane. About two-thirds of the labour force are either nomadic herdsmen or subsistence farmers. Much of Somalia's infrastructure has been destroyed by a civil war that began in 1991, and famine has been widespread, although it has been partially alleviated by $47.1 million (£28.3 million) worth of international aid.

product (GDP) per capita in 1996 was Switzerland, with $43,233 (£28,533). Luxembourg came second with $42,298 (£27,916) and Japan was third with $40,726 (£26,878).

BIGGEST GNP
The country with the largest gross national product (GNP) in the world is the USA, with an estimated $7,300.2 billion (£4,456.2 billion) for 1997.

BIGGEST BALANCE OF PAYMENTS SURPLUS
Japan had a $131.5-billion (£85-billion) surplus in 1993.

BIGGEST BALANCE OF PAYMENTS DEFICIT
The USA reported a record deficit of $167.1 billion (£102 billion) for the 1987 calendar year.

OLDEST STOCK EXCHANGE
The Stock Exchange in Amsterdam, Netherlands, was founded in the Oude Zijds Kapel in 1602 for dealings in printed shares of the United East India Company of the Netherlands.

BIGGEST TRADING LOSSES
In 1996 Sumitomo Corporation of Japan revealed that they had suffered losses of $2.6 billion (£1.7 billion) due to unauthorized dealings over 10 years on the London Metal Exchange by one of their top traders.

BIGGEST PERSONAL LOSS OF STOCKS IN ONE DAY
The highest known personal paper losses on stock values were incurred by Ray Kroc,

the former chairman of McDonald's Corporation, on 8 July 1974. They amounted to $65 million (£28.3 million).

HIGHEST SHARE VALUE
On 22 April 1992 a single share in Moeara Enim Petroleum Corporation was worth a record $89,032 (£50,586).

BIGGEST FLOTATION
The privatization of Japan's Nippon Telegraph and Telephones in 1986 had an initial public offering of $12.4 billion (£8.45 billion) — the biggest ever.

BIGGEST BROKERAGES
In 1997 Merrill Lynch and Company had an annual revenue of $31,731 million (£19,832 million).

The Institutional Network of Instinet Corp, which began operating in 1969, became the world's largest computerized brokerage when it was purchased by Reuters in 1987. In 1997 it had a volume of over 110 million shares per day trading via more than 55,000 terminals.

BIGGEST FINANCIAL SECTORS
Singapore and the United Kingdom have the largest financial sectors of any nations, representing 27% of their gross domestic product.

RICHEST COUNTRIES
According to OECD (Organization for Economic and Commercial Development), the country with the highest gross domestic

MOST INDUSTRIAL ECONOMY
Belarus has the most industrial economy, with a total of 45% of its GDP coming from manufacturing industry.

HIGHEST TAXATION
The highest rate of income tax in Denmark is 68%, but a net wealth tax of 1% can result in a tax of more than 100% on income in extreme situations.

LOWEST TAXATION
The sovereign countries with the lowest income tax are Bahrain and Qatar, where the rate is nil, regardless of income.

HIGHEST INFLATION
The world's worst inflation occurred in Hungary in June 1946, when the 1931 gold pengó was valued at 130 million trillion (1.3×10^{20}) paper pengós. Notes were issued for 'Egymillárd billió' (1,000 trillion or 10^{21}) pengós on 3 June and withdrawn on 11 July. Vouchers for 1 billion trillion (10^{27}) pengós were issued for taxation payment only.

On 6 Nov 1923 there were 400,338,326,350,700,000,000 German marks in circulation — taking the level of inflation to 755,700 million times the level of 1913.

BIGGEST STOCK EXCHANGE
At the end of Dec 1996 more than 2,900 companies had stock listed on the New York Stock Exchange (NYSE), and more than 180 billion shares worth a total of $9.2 trillion (£5.9 trillion) were available for trading on the exchange, giving Wall Street the world's biggest market capitalization. The NYSE also holds the record for the largest ever trading volume, at $3.1 trillion (£8,237 billion) in 1995. This compares with $1,640 billion (£1,045 billion) for London and $1,400 billion (£891 billion) for the Federation of Germany Stock Exchanges. The NYSE has its origins in a meeting of 24 men beneath a tree on what is now Wall Street in 1792. It was formalized as the New York Stock and Exchange Board in 1817 and took its present name in 1863. It is now threatened with a 'bug' that has the potential to paralyze trading: when New York's Dow Jones Industrial average reaches 10,000, which it is predicted to do in the near future, it will be illegible to much of the software used to monitor share activity, and in a similar manner to the millennium bug, the figure 10,000 will be read as 1,000 or 0,000. This could cause electronic trading systems to dump stock, which may result in a global stock market crash.

LOWEST MODERN INFLATION
The Seychelles had deflation in 1995, when the CPI (consumer price index) fell by 1.28%.

MOST WORTHLESS CURRENCY
In May 1998 there were 257,128 Angolan kwanza to the US dollar (428,375 to the British pound).

BIGGEST FOREIGN AID DONOR
The largest foreign aid donor in 1996, in terms of Official Development Assistance, was Japan, with aid amounting to $14,489 million (£9,562 million).

Denmark has the highest ratio of Official Development Assistance to GNP, at 0.96% in 1996.

HIGHEST EDUCATION BUDGET
Canada and Finland spend 7.3% of their GDP on education (public and private expenditure).

LOWEST EDUCATION BUDGET
The OECD country spending the least on education is Turkey, which allocates 3.3% of its GDP.

EXPANSION AND DECLINE
The GNP of Thailand grew by an average of 9.8% a year in the decade ending 1995, making it the most rapidly expanding economy in the world in the early 1990s. By 1998 it was decreasing by 0.4% a year, and the fastest-growing country was Uganda, with a 10% growth rate. In the decade ending 1995 Armenia's GNP decreased by a record average of 12.9% a year.

HIGHEST HEALTH BUDGET
The USA is the country with the highest health expenditure as a percentage of gross domestic product. In 1995, the last year for which comparable figures are available, US health expenditure totalled 14.2% of GDP.

BIGGEST GOLD RESERVES
The US Treasury had approximately 7.43 billion g (262 million fine oz) of gold in 1996, which would have been worth $100 billion (£62.5 billion) at the June 1996 price of £245 per 31 g ($382 per fine oz). The US Bullion Depository at Fort Knox, 48 km (30 miles) south-west of Louisville, Kentucky, USA, has been the principal federal depository of US gold since Dec 1936, and 4.17 billion g (147 million fine oz) are currently stored there. Gold's peak price was $850 (£365) on 21 Jan 1980.

BIGGEST MINT
The largest mint in the world is the US Treasury, which was built on Independence Mall, Philadelphia, Pennsylvania, between 1965 and 1969 and covers an area of 4.7 ha (11.5 acres). The Treasury used to have an annual production capacity of 15 billion coins and now produces 12 billion coins a year. One high-speed stamping machine called Graebner Press is capable of producing coins at a rate of 42,000 per hour. The highest-ever production was 19,519,253,440 coins, in the fiscal year 1995. The Denver Mint also set a record for coin production by a single facility, with more than 10.3 billion coins in the fiscal year 1995.

SMALLEST MINT
The smallest issuing mint in the world belongs to the Sovereign Military Order of Malta, in the City of Rome. Its single-press mint is housed in a small room.

POOREST COUNTRIES
Pictured right, a woman from Mozambique carries water on her head. For most of the 1990s Mozambique and Rwanda had the lowest GDP per capita in the world, according to the World Bank. In 1996 GDP per capita in Rwanda was less than $80 (£60), which represented a decrease on the previous year. Mozambique is now experiencing economic growth and in 1996 had a GDP per capita of $133 (£71).

company power

BIGGEST MEDIA CORPORATION

Walter Elias Disney had $40 (£9) to his name when he began his company, Walt Disney, in 1923. His first commission, about a little girl called Alice, was the start of what is now the world's largest entertainment empire. The Walt Disney Company had total assets of $37.77 billion (£22.89 billion) in 1997 and a turnover of $22.473 billion (£13.504 billion). This compares with Viacom, the world's second largest media corporation, which had a turnover of $13.2 billion (£8 billion) that year. *Steamboat Willie* (USA, 1928), Disney's first film with a soundtrack, was an immediate success, and since then 35 feature films have been released. Disney also has a host of theme parks, the latest addition being Animal Kingdom, Florida, USA.

MOST EXPENSIVE COMPANY BUILDING

The headquarters of the Hong Kong Shanghai Bank is the world's most expensive building. Built from 1982 to 1985, it cost $645.4 million (£388.8 million) to construct, while the land that it was built on cost c. $387 million (£233.2 million). The 52-storey, 178.8-m-tall (586.6-ft) building has a total of 23 express lifts and 63 escalators (the most escalators in any building in the world). Its air-conditioning and flushing water systems use pumped-in seawater.

MOST EXPENSIVE OFFICE LOCATIONS

The highest-ever office rents were in central Tokyo, Japan, in June 1991. Prime spaces there were at a peak of $2,357/m² or $219/ft² (£418/m² or £127.20/ft²).

Quoted rents for prime space in the central business district of Bombay (Mumbai), India, in Jan 1997 were $1,539/m² or $143/ft² (£931/m² or £86.50/ft²) a year. Total occupation costs (including property taxes and service charges) were $1,679/m² or $156/ft² (£1,017/m² or £94.50/ft²) for a three-year lease. These costs were 31% higher than in Hong Kong, the world's second most expensive location.

BIGGEST ANNUAL PROFIT

The largest ever net profit by a corporation in 12 months was $7.6 billion (£4.1 billion), by American Telephone and Telegraph Company (now AT&T Corporation) from 1 Oct 1981 to 30 Sept 1982.

BIGGEST ANNUAL SALES

In 1995 General Motors Corporation of Detroit, Michigan, USA, had record annual sales of $168.8 billion (£102 billion).

BIGGEST COMPANY REVENUES

In 1996 the Japanese trading company Mitsubishi Corporation had revenues of $184,365.2 million (£121,677.1 million).

HIGHEST MARKET VALUE OF A COMPANY

General Electric of Fairfield, Connecticut, USA, has the highest aggregate market value of any corporation in the world. In May 1995 it was valued at $152.3 billion (£92.3 billion).

BIGGEST RAILWAY COMPANY

The East Japan Railway Company had revenues of $25.63 billion (£16.9 billion) in 1996, making it the world's largest railway company. The Japanese railway network, which began in 1872, is believed to be one of the safest and most efficient in the world. It has more than 20,000 km (12,500 miles) of track and runs an average of 25,000 trains a day. In 1964 certain main lines, amounting to just under 15% of the entire Japanese rail system, were revolutionized by the introduction of the *Shinkansen* or bullet train, which has been known to reach a speed of 443 km/h (275 mph). Here an ASAMA bullet train is seen crossing a bridge over the Chikuma River in Ueda City, Nagano prefecture, in Oct 1997. It was part of a brand new train service linking Nagano, the location of the 1998 Winter Olympics, and Tokyo.

BIGGEST RESTAURANT CHAIN

The largest global food service retailer is McDonald's, which opened its first fast food outlet in Des Plaines, Illinois, USA, in 1955. By the end of 1997 McDonald's operated more than 21,000 restaurants in 101 countries around the world. Global revenue in 1997 exceeded $10.7 billion (£6.4 billion). Here two workers install a sign at a new McDonald's in Beijing, China.

HIGHEST AGM ATTENDANCE
A total of 20,109 shareholders attended the Annual General Meeting of American Telephone and Telegraph Company (now AT&T Corporation) in April 1961.

BIGGEST MERGER
The biggest ever industrial merger was between the motor companies Daimler-Benz and Chrysler. Announced in May 1998, it created a company worth $92 billion (£55.3 billion).

BIGGEST TAKE-OVER BID
The highest bid in a corporate take-over was $21 billion (£12 billion), for the tobacco, food and beverage company RJR Nabisco Inc. by Wall Street leveraged-buyout firm Kohlberg Kravis Roberts. The latter offered $90 (£50) a share on 24 Oct 1988. By 1 Dec the By 1 Dec the shares had reached $109 (£60) making an aggregate of $25 billion (£14 billion).

BIGGEST SINGLE CASH BEQUEST
The Ford Foundation of New York, USA, announced a bequest of $500 million (£300 million) to a total of 4,157 educational and other institutions in Dec 1995.

BIGGEST CORPORATE BANKRUPTCY
The world's biggest ever corporate bankruptcy in terms of assets amounted to $35.9 billion (£21.9 billion). The bankruptcy was filed by the petroleum company Texaco in 1987.

BIGGEST COMPANIES
The US Ford Motor Company, the multi-national motor manufacturer, is the biggest company in the world today in terms of assets. In 1997, its total assets were valued at $222.14 billion (£133.12 billion).

The biggest company in terms of the number of employees is the US Postal Service, which employed more than 887,600 people in 1997.

The world's biggest company in terms of profits is the Royal Dutch Shell Group, a jointly-owned Anglo-Dutch petroleum refining company. In 1997 it had profits of $8.89 billion (£5.35 billion).

The biggest manufacturing company in terms of revenues and employees is the General Motors Corporation, which has a global workforce of 647,000. In 1997 the company's revenues were $168.39 billion (£101.44 billion) and it had assets of $222.14 billion (£133.12 billion). The company announced a profit of $4.96 billion (£3 billion) for the year.

BIGGEST BANKS
The biggest bank in the world today in terms of the number of branches is the State Bank of India, which had a record 12,947 outlets and total assets of $42 billion (£26.3 billion) on 31 March 1996.

The world's largest bank by equity is the British-based HSBC Holdings. In 1996 it had $25.8 billion (£16.12 billion) of equity.

The biggest commercial bank by assets is the Bank of Tokyo-Mitsubishi, Japan. In July 1997 it had assets of $692.3 billion (£409.91 billion).

The world's biggest international investment bank is Morgan Stanley, Dean Witter, Discover & Co., which has a market capitalization of $21 billion (£13 billion).

The biggest multilateral development bank in the world is the International Bank for Reconstruction and Development, known as the World Bank. Based in Washington DC, USA, the bank had total assets of $168.7 billion (£107 billion) for the 1995 fiscal year.

BIGGEST EMPLOYER
The largest commercial or utility employer in the world is Indian Railways, which had more than 1 million regular employees in 1997.

BIGGEST PUBLISHING COMPANY
The largest publishing and printing company in the world is Bertelsmann AG of Germany. In 1997 the company's total revenue was $14.73 billion (£9.2 billion).

BIGGEST PC COMPANY
Compaq Computer Corp. of Houston, Texas, USA, is the world's biggest manufacturer of personal computers. In 1997 its revenues rose by more than 30% to $24.6 billion (£14.8 billion) and its profits climbed 36% to $1.9 billion (£1.15 billion).

BIGGEST TELECOMMUNICATIONS COMPANY
Nippon Telegraph and Telephone Corporation of Japan had revenues of $78.32 billion (£47.18 billion) in 1997.

BIGGEST PETROLEUM COMPANY
The largest petroleum company is Anglo-Dutch Royal Dutch Shell Group, based in the Netherlands. In 1997 it had a total revenue of $128.17 billion (£80.1 billion).

BIGGEST AEROSPACE GROUP
McDonnell Douglas Corp., the world's biggest military aircraft maker, and Boeing Co., the world's biggest commercial aircraft maker, merged in 1996 to form the largest aerospace group in the world. The group's total annual revenues are approximately $35 billion (£23 billion).

BIGGEST AIRLINE
AMR Corporation, based in Fort Worth, Texas, USA, whose major subsiduary is American Airlines,

BIGGEST BEVERAGE COMPANY
The Coca-Cola Company had revenues of $18,018 million (£11,900 million) in 1996, making it the biggest beverage company in the world. The picture above shows spectators gathering to see the world's largest replica Coca-Cola bottle surrounded by fireworks at the Showcase Mall on the Strip, Las Vegas, USA, in July 1997. The display was part of the opening of the Coca-Cola Museum.

had a total revenue of $17.75 billion (£11.1 billion) for the year 1997, making it the largest airline in the world today.

BIGGEST FOOD COMPANY
Unilever N.V./Unilever Plc is the biggest food company in the world. It is also the world's biggest ice cream maker, with more than 50% of the ice cream market in several European countries. Its brands include Cornetto, Viennetta and Magnum. The company is also the world leader in prestige fragrances, including Calvin Klein perfume.

BIGGEST DAIRY FARM
Al Safi dairy farm near Al Kharj, Saudi Arabia, covers 3,500 ha (8,600 acres).

BIGGEST BREWER
The biggest brewing organization is Anheuser-Busch Inc. of Missouri, USA. In 1995 it sold 10.27 billion litres (2.26 billion gal) of beer.

business tycoons

Rupert Murdoch (pictured with his eldest son Lachlan), the global magnate, is one of the world's most powerful businessmen and successful entrepreneurs. The son of Sir Keith Murdoch, the late editor of the Australian newspaper the *Melbourne Herald*, Murdoch was born in 1931 and was running his first newspaper, the *Adelaide Herald*, by the age of 23. An Oxford graduate, he expanded into the United Kingdom with the daily newspapers *The Sun* and *The Times*. Today he is chairman of News Corporation Ltd and Fox Broadcasting Company, which he took over in 1985. His communications empire News Corporation is worth about $26 billion (£16.25 billion). In 1985 Murdoch renounced his Australian nationality and became a naturalized US citizen in order to comply with US laws that prohibit foreigners from owning US television stations. He is now the largest owner of TV stations in the USA, and in terms of his global reach and the diversity of his interests he is the most powerful media tycoon in history. Lachlan Murdoch is widely tipped to take over News Corporation.

GREATEST EVER TYCOON

The legendary oilman John D. Rockefeller founded the Standard Oil company of Ohio, USA, with his brother William in 1870. By the time of his death in 1937, Rockefeller had amassed a $1.4-billion (£283-million) fortune at a time when the GNP of the USA was just $90 billion (£18 billion). This makes him the richest US citizen ever, with a wealth amounting to $\frac{1}{65}$th of the wealth of the entire country. As a comparison, Bill Gates' fortune only amounts to $\frac{1}{213}$th of the USA's GNP today. On this basis, Rockefeller can be seen as the greatest tycoon in the history of the world.

RICHEST BUSINESSMAN

William H. Gates III, the chairman and CEO of Microsoft Corporation, is the richest man in the world, according to *Forbes* magazine, with an estimated fortune of $39.8 billion (£24.3 billion). The *New York Times* predicts that if Microsoft's value continues to grow at its current rate, Bill Gates will become the world's first dollar trillionaire by the age of 48. In 1997, his net worth grew by an average of $400 million

(£250 million) a week, and his personal holdings are now worth twice the gross domestic product of Sri Lanka. His wealth that year increased by $21.3 billion (£13.3 billion) — more than the total wealth of the second richest businessman, Warren Buffet. In a single morning in 1996, a jump in price of Microsoft stock increased Gates' worth by $2 billion (£1.3 billion).

RICHEST BUSINESSWOMEN

Barbara Cox Anthony and Anne Cox Chambers are the world's richest businesswomen, with a combined fortune of $10 billion (£6.25 billion). Their father James Cox, a poor farm boy and school drop-out, built Cox Enterprises, a major media empire. By the time of his death in 1947, it owned seven newspapers, three TV stations and several radio stations. Aged 74 and 77 respectively, the sisters have 98% control of the empire, which now comprises 16 daily newspapers, cable systems with 3.3 million subscribers, cable programming investments and radio and terrestrial TV stations. They also own Manheim auctions, the world's biggest car auctioneer.

RICHEST SELF-MADE WOMAN IN THE USA

Pam Lopker, the founder of the US software company QAD, is worth an estimated $425 million (£265 million).

RICHEST BUSINESS FAMILY

According to *Forbes*, the richest business family in the world today is the Walton family from

the USA. The empire's founder Sam Walton opened his first 'small-town discount store' in Arkansas, USA, in 1962. Today Wal-Mart is the largest US retailer, with 2,750 stores. It also has a further 250 stores in six other countries. Wal-Mart Corporation is reputed to be a huge spender on information technology, with storage capacity second only to the US government. Sam Walton's widow Helen and their three sons and one daughter have a combined fortune of $35 billion (£21.8 billion).

RICHEST BUSINESSMEN IN HONG KONG

Brothers Walter, Thomas and Raymond Kwok, the real estate magnates, are worth $13.3 billion (£8.3 billion).

RICHEST BUSINESSMAN IN TAIWAN

Taiwan's richest businessman is the insurance and financial services broker Tsai Wan-lin, who, with his family, is worth $8.3 billion (£5.2 billion).

BIGGEST CHARITABLE DONOR, UK

John Paul Getty II, the oil heir and reclusive son of the late John Paul Getty (once the richest man in the world), has distributed at least £120 million ($192 million) of his estimated £1-billion ($1.6-billion) personal fortune to a number of British causes, making him the country's single biggest charitable donor. During the 1980s Getty's £20-million ($31.14-million) donation to the British Film Institute enabled thousands of old movies to be saved from destruction. He also gave £50 million ($77.85 million) to the National Gallery, London, UK, and has helped to keep several rare works of art in the United Kingdom, including pieces that were going to be sold to his father's museum in California, USA. In 1986 the 65-year-old billionaire philanthropist was awarded an honorary KBE for his charitable efforts, and in 1997 he was granted British citizenship. Sir Paul, as he is now known, moved to the United Kingdom in 1972 after the death of his second wife. His father had removed him from a post in one of the family businesses, and he lived off the income from his grandmother's trust.

RICHEST BUSINESSMAN IN KOREA

Businessman Chung Ju Yung made his money from diversified enterprises, and together with his family is worth $6.1 billion (£3.8 billion).

BIGGEST EUROPEAN BANKRUPTCY

In 1991 Robert Maxwell died in mysterious circumstances soon after it was discovered that he had taken assets from the Maxwell Communications Works Pension Scheme. His company, Maxwell Communications, became the subject of Europe's largest ever bankruptcy when it collapsed in Dec 1992. It had previously had assets of $6.35 billion (£3.68 billion).

RICHEST TAX EXILES IN THE UK

Billionaire brothers Hans and Gad Rausing, who made their fortune with the Tetra-Pak packaging company, are among the wealthiest British residents today. They are the richest tax exiles currently living in the United Kingdom, having left their native Sweden in the 1980s in order to avoid its notoriously high taxes. Hans Rausing's personal fortune is estimated at $4.8 billion (£3 billion).

MOST RECLUSIVE TYCOON

Considered the most reclusive tycoon ever, the film director and aviator Howard Hughes died on a flight to Houston, USA, in 1976. Obsessively secretive, Hughes was once contracted by the CIA to build a giant spy station on the ocean bed. In the 1970s he received the largest cash settlement ever paid to an individual when he received $546 million (£248.7 million) for his holdings in the airline TWA.

BIGGEST CHARITABLE DONATIONS BY BUSINESSMEN

John D. Rockefeller gave away $500 million (£101 million), worth around $14.1 billion (£8.8 billion) today, by the time of his death in 1937.

During his lifetime and through legacies made in his will, Andrew Carnegie, the Scottish-born steel magnate, gave away the equivalent of $3.5 billion (£2.1 billion) in today's money. Among the causes to benefit from his interest were libraries, the Carnegie Peace Fund, and Carnegie Hall, New York, USA.

David Packard, co-founder of the printer giant Hewlett-Packard, gave away more than $5 billion (£3 billion) — most of his life earnings — before he died on 26 March 1996.

GREATEST PERSONAL FINANCIAL RECOVERY

In 1989 Donald Trump owned two casinos, an airline (the Trump Shuttle), buildings in New York, USA (including Trump Tower), and an 85-m (280-ft) yacht, as well as other property worth an estimated $1.7 billion (£1 billion). The onset of the recession, and the slumping property market of the late 1980s, pushed his businesses into $8.8 billion (£5.6 billion) of debt, $975 million (£613 million) of which was personally guaranteed by Trump himself. He became the world's greatest bankrupt individual as a result. His assets have now crept up to $2.5 billion (£1.56 billion), which includes a reported $500 million (£312 million) in cash, making his long struggle the greatest personal financial recovery in history. Today he owns Trump International Hotel and Tower — hailed as "the Most Important New Address in the World" — as well as a host of other properties.

MOST POWERFUL PRIVATE ART COLLECTOR IN THE UK

Charles Saatchi is considered to be the most powerful private art collector in the United Kingdom today, with a collection believed to number more than 800 works. Only an estimated 5% of Saatchi's collection, which includes works by Damien Hirst, has been shown in public; the rest is stockpiled unseen in a warehouse. He has been buying modern art for almost 30 years.

SPORTING BILLIONAIRE

In 1976 wealthy philanthropist Ted Turner diversified his business interests by acquiring the Atlanta Braves baseball team, and the following year his company, Turner Broadcasting Systems, Inc., acquired a limited partnership in the Atlanta Hawks. In 1985 Turner deepened his sporting associations by initiating the Goodwill Games.

high earners

VIRGIN EMPIRE

Richard Branson was the 14th richest man in the United Kingdom in 1998 according to the *Sunday Times*, with a fortune estimated at £1.7 billion ($2.8 billion). He left school at 16 to launch a student magazine, and founded a record label, Virgin Records, in 1973. Today the Virgin empire includes an airline, a rail service, jeans, cola, pensions and a bridal company.

HIGHEST-EARNING CHIEF EXECUTIVES

In 1997 Millard Drexler, the chief executive officer (CEO) of the clothing company Gap, earned $104.8 million (£64 million).

Stephen C. Hilbert, the chief executive of Conesco, earned $277 million (£174 million) over the five-year period 1992–96. He founded the construction company in 1979 with a loan of $10,000 (£6,289), and it is now worth $7 billion (£4.2 billion).

HIGHEST-EARNING BANK HEAD

John Reed of Citicorp earned $46 million (£29.5 million) in 1996, and $70 million (£43 million) in total over the last five years.

HIGHEST-EARNING LAWYER

In 1995, when *Forbes* magazine published its most recent survey of the best-paid lawyers, William Lerach earned a record $7 million (£4.5 million). At the time he was running the office of Melvyn Weiss' firm in San Diego, USA, specializing in shareholder class-action suits.

HIGHEST-EARNING POLITICIAN

Boris Berezovsky, deputy chief of the Russian security council, is worth $4.05 billion (£2.81 billion). A wealthy businessman before he became a politician, he claims to have made his money from oil, cars and the media.

HIGHEST-EARNING HONG KONG BUSINESSMAN

Manual Pangilinan, head of the First Pacific National Bank, received a record salary of $14.34 million (£8.96 million) in 1997.

HIGHEST-EARNING HONG KONG BUSINESSWOMAN

Nina Wang is said by *Forbes* magazine to be worth $7 billion (£4.2 billion).

She took over the Chinachem real estate empire, considered the largest private landholder in Hong Kong, after her husband was kidnapped and disappeared, and is now widely regarded as Asia's most powerful businesswoman. The Chinachem Group's 108-storey 'Nina Tower' in Hong Kong, one of the world's tallest buildings, is named after her.

HIGHEST-EARNING JAPANESE BUSINESSMAN

Yoshiaki Tsutsumi, a real estate and transport mogul, is worth about $8 billion (£5 billion). Once the world's richest businessman, he owns over 40 golf courses in Japan and was a major force behind the country's successful bid for the 1998 Winter Olympics.

HIGHEST-EARNING PUBLISHING EXECUTIVE

The Australian-born media baron Rupert Murdoch is currently worth $2.8 billion (£1.75 billion). He owns 36% of the national press in the United Kingdom, 20th Century Fox in the USA and the US TV network Fox, and has newspaper, magazine and book interests worldwide.

HIGHEST-EARNING FILM EXECUTIVE

Michael Eisner, the chairman and CEO of the Walt Disney Company, earned $8.65 million (£5.4 million) in 1996. He is the third highest-paid chief executive of the last five years, with total earnings of $236 million (£147.5 million).

HIGHEST-EARNING TV EXECUTIVE

Ted Turner, founder of Cable News Network and Vice Chairman of Time Warner Inc., is worth about $3.2 billion (£2 billion). He is married to fitness queen and actress Jane Fonda.

HIGHEST-PAID SCREENWRITERS

Shane Black sold the script for *The Long Kiss Goodnight* (USA, 1996) to New Line Cinema for $4 million (£2.4 million). His girlfriend came up with the idea and he gave her a cheque for $20,000 (£12,048) before starting to write.

RICHEST CHIEF EXECUTIVE

Microsoft's Bill Gates is the wealthiest chief executive in the world, with $28 billion (£17.5 billion), or 23.67%, of Microsoft stock. Born in 1958, Gates began his software career at the age of 13 and later dropped out of Harvard University, USA, to concentrate on his fledgling company. On 4 Feb 1998 he became the latest victim of *L'entarteur* or Pieman, the Belgian social critic Noel Godin, who is notorious for throwing custard pies at the rich and famous. Pieman's victims have included French philosopher Bernard Henri-Lévy and film director Jean-Luc Godard. Gates was hit by four pies as he entered a government building in Brussels, Belgium, to give a speech on education. Pieman escaped, but his two apprentices were held in custody. He eventually came forward to confess to his crime but Gates did not press charges.

Hungarian-born Joe Eszterhas has written 13 screenplays, including *Flashdance* (USA, 1983), *Basic Instinct* (USA, 1992) and *Showgirls* (USA, 1995). He is Hollywood's highest-paid screenwriter and his scripts now sell for at least $1 million (£625,000).

Michael Crichton, the co-writer of *Jurassic Park* (USA, 1993) and originator of TV series *ER*, earned $65 million (£40 million) in 1997.

HIGHEST-EARNING DIRECTOR

Steven Spielberg, director of such films as *E.T.: the Extra-Terrestrial* (USA, 1982) and *Amistad* (USA, 1997) earned $283 million (£170 million) in 1997, making him the world's highest-earning director. George Lucas, the director of *Star Wars* (USA, 1977) followed with $249 million (£150 million).

HIGHEST-EARNING COMEDIAN

Forbes magazine estimated that the highest-earning comedian in 1997 was Robin Williams, with $53 million (£32 million). Much of Williams' earnings come from his film company Blue Wolf Productions, which made $431 million (£260 million) from *Mrs Doubtfire* (USA, 1993).

HIGHEST-EARNING WRITER

Mary Higgins Clark began writing to support her five children. Her first suspense novel, *Where Are the Children?* (1992), brought her $100,000 (£62,500) in royalties. In 1996 she signed a contract with Simon and Schuster giving her $12 million (£7.5 million) for each of three novels — almost double the amount paid to John Grisham and Stephen King.

HIGHEST-EARNING ARTIST

LeRoy Neiman from New York, USA, is famous for painting athletes, jet-setters and celebrities, including Michael Jordan, Frank Sinatra, Liza Minnelli, Robert Kennedy Jr and Princess Grace of Monaco. He produces about 1,000 pieces a year and his original paintings sell for between $20,000 (£12,500) and $500,000 (£312,500).

BIGGEST BONUS

Lawrence Coss, the CEO of Green Tree Financial Corporation, which finances mobile homes, reaped a bonus of $102 million (£68 million) in 1996, the highest ever reported in *Forbes'* annual executive pay surveys. The bonus was almost a quarter of the size of his salary, and took his total earnings over the last five years to $216 million (£144 million), of which $95 million (£59 million) was in stock.

HIGHEST-EARNING OPERA STAR

Italian opera superstar Luciano Pavarotti is said to earn $16 million (£10 million) a year.

HIGHEST-EARNING MAGICIAN

US illusionist David Copperfield is the world's most successful magician today, earning $45 million (£28 million) in 1997.

MOST SUCCESSFUL INVESTOR

The 67-year-old US investor Warren Buffet has made $23.2 billion (£14.5 billion) playing the stock market.

HIGHEST OPTION GAIN

In 1997 Andrew Grove of Intel had the highest option gain of any chief executive, at $95 million (£59.4 million).

BIGGEST GOLDEN HANDSHAKE

A record golden handshake of $53.8 million (£30.7 million) was given to F. Ross Johnson when he stepped down as chairman of RJR Nabisco in Feb 1989.

HIGHEST SALARY

Hungarian-born George Soros earned at least $1.1 billion (£770 million) in 1993, according to *Financial World*'s list of the highest-paid individuals on Wall Street. His company, Soros Fund Management, is principle advisor to the Quantum Group, which includes Quantum Fund N.V., the fund with the best performance record in the world.

HIGHEST FEES

Harry D. Schultz, an investment consultant who lives in Monte Carlo, Monaco and Zürich, Switzerland, charges $2,400 (£1,500) for a standard one-hour consultation on weekdays and $3,400 (£2,125) at weekends.

HIGHEST LECTURE FEES

In June 1986 Dr Ronald Dante was paid the sum of $3.08 million (£2.1 million) for lecturing students on hypnotherapy at a two-day course in Chicago, Illinois, USA.

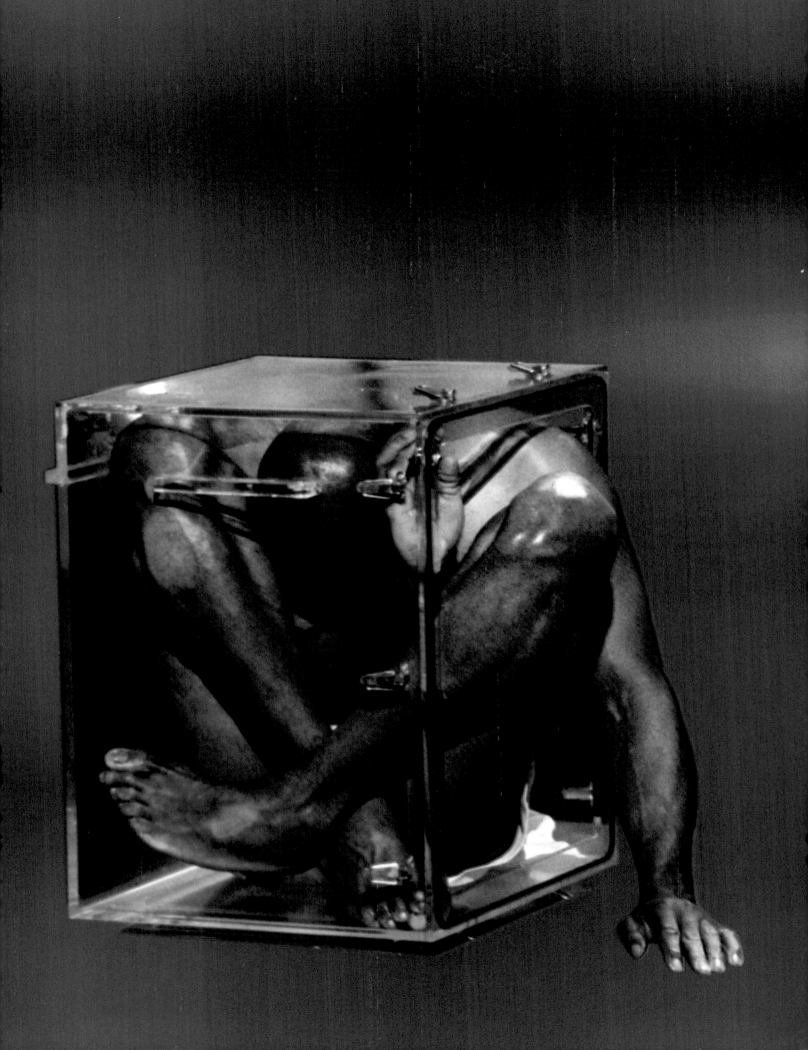

extraordinary *people*

collections

BIGGEST FAMOUS HAIR COLLECTION

John Reznikoff from Stamford, Connecticut, USA, collects the hair of long-dead celebrities. Some of the most famous hair in his 100-strong collection, which is insured for $1 million (£600,900), once belonged to Abraham Lincoln, John F. Kennedy, Marilyn Monroe and Elvis Presley.

BIGGEST COLLECTION OF ROYAL PHOTOGRAPHS

In 14 years of travels throughout the United Kingdom and Europe, Julia McCarthy-Fox of Worthing, W Sussex, UK, has taken 30,000 photographs of the British Royal Family. Now 33 years old, she used to work flexi-time in order to arrange her life around royal events. Julia's husband Sam has the world's biggest marble collection (see far right).

BIGGEST UNDERWEAR COLLECTIONS

Imelda Marcos, the former First Lady of the Philippines, had 500 black bras (one of which was bullet-proof), 200 Marks and Spencers girdles and 1,000 packets of unopened tights in her palace wardrobe, as well as about 3,000 pairs of shoes.

Robert Corlett and Mary Ann King from Glasgow, UK, started collecting 1970s nylon underpants after finding a signed pair of Engelberg Humperdinck's pants in an Engelberg Humperdinck record cover two years ago. They now have more than 200 pairs, including 30 psychedelic pairs. They have received pants from all over Europe since displaying their collection in their shop Mr Ben Vintage Clothing.

BIGGEST SHOE COLLECTION

Sonja Bata of Toronto, Canada, has collected 10,000 pairs of shoes over a period of 50 years. While her family firm Bata sold the world low-cost footwear, Sonja bought the shoes that their customers discarded. She has set up a museum in Toronto to house her collection, which includes Queen Victoria's dancing slippers, John Lennon's Beatle boots and Napoleon's socks.

BIGGEST COLLECTION OF SWATCH WATCHES

Fiorenzo Barindelli of Cesano Maderno in Milan, Italy, has amassed 3,562 Swatch watches since he started his collection in 1983. It includes every watch documented in the Swatch catalogue, as well as some prototypes and special edition pieces. He plans to open a Swatch museum in the year 2000.

BIGGEST BARBIE DOLL COLLECTION

Tony Mattia from Brighton, E Sussex, UK, has about half of all the Barbie doll models produced since 1959 and many versions of Barbie's boyfriend, Ken. He changes the dolls' costumes once a month and spends hours brushing their hair. The collection grew so large that he had to move to a larger flat.

BIGGEST MOUSETRAP COLLECTION

Reinhard Hellwig of Meerbusch, North Rhine Westphalia, Germany, has collected 2,334 mousetraps from a total of 66 countries since he first became interested in them in 1964. The most unusual mousetrap in his collection is currently a replica of a 5,000-year-old trap crafted from clay – one of the earliest known examples. As well as being an avid collector, Hellwig has also managed to acquire more than 6,300 patents on mousetraps over the years.

BIGGEST COLLECTION OF GNOMES AND PIXIES

Since 1978 Anne Atkin from North Devon, UK, has collected a record 2,010 gnomes and pixies, all of whom live on her 1.61-ha (4-acre) Gnome Reserve. Atkin's collection has been seen by more than 25,000 visitors over the past 18 years.

BIGGEST LIGHTBULB COLLECTION

US collector Hugh Hicks has amassed approximately 60,000 different lightbulbs since childhood. Included in his collection is the world's largest lightbulb, which is 1.2 m (4 ft) in height, and the smallest lightbulb, a pinpoint used to inspect missile parts.

BIGGEST JET FIGHTER COLLECTION

Michel Pont, a winemaker and collector who lives in Savigny-Les-Beaune in Burgundy, France, has a personal collection of 100 jet fighters, ranging from British *Vampires* to Russian *MiGs*. Pont first started collecting jet fighters in 1986, having collected motorbikes since 1958 and cars since 1970. By Jan 1998 the 66-year-old had accumulated 70 different jet fighters, 500 motorcycles and a series of crimson *Abarth* race cars. His rarest jet is a Dassault *Mirage 4*, the aircraft that carries French nuclear weapons, with the oldest being a 1949 Dassault *Ouragan*. Although the planes' exteriors are in perfect condition and are cleaned twice a year, some are no longer in working order. Pont, who has never flown a plane and has given up motorcycling, has opened his collection to the public by setting up a museum at his home, the 14th-century Château de Savigny-Les-Beaune that he bought 20 years ago. As well as viewing the collection, the estimated 30,000 visitors a year can also sample the Burgundy wines of which Pont produces around 275,000 bottles a year.

BIGGEST BANKNOTE COLLECTION

Israel Gerber from Ashdod in Israel began collecting banknotes in 1962 and now has notes from 215 different countries and territories. There are an estimated 4,000 banknote collectors worldwide. In 1993 the second £1 note ever issued in the United Kingdom fetched a record £52,000 ($78,078) at auction. It is not only rare notes that are valuable: a note with an error, such as an image that has been printed back to front, may also command a high price.

BIGGEST MARBLE COLLECTION

Over the past 45 years printer Sam McCarthy-Fox from Worthing, W Sussex, UK, has built up a collection of 40,000 marbles. His record-breaking collection includes antique marbles as well as modern glass and fibre-optic marbles made from semi-precious stones. McCarthy-Fox, who is now 53 years old, spends much of his free time polishing his marbles in his loft. He also helps organize international marble-playing championships.

BIGGEST COLLECTION OF CHAMBER POTS

Manfred Klauda from Germany has collected a total of 9,400 chamber pots, the earliest of which dates back to the 16th century. His record-breaking collection can be viewed at the Zentrum für Aussergewöhnliche Museum in Munich, Germany.

BIGGEST COLLECTION OF AEROPLANE SICKBAGS

Nick Vermeulen from Wormerveer in the Netherlands had built up a record-breaking collection of 2,112 different aeroplane sickbags from a total of 470 airlines by May 1997.

BIGGEST PLASTER COLLECTION

Brian Viner from London, UK, has collected about 3,750 unused sticking plasters of many different colours, styles, shapes and sizes.

BIGGEST HANDCUFF COLLECTION

Chris Gower from Dorset, UK, has amassed 412 pairs of handcuffs since he began collecting in 1968, at the age of 15. His interest in handcuffs arose from a fascination with escapology.

BIGGEST COLLECTION OF PARKING METERS

In 1989 Lotta Sjölin from Solna in Sweden began collecting different disused parking meters from local authorities all over the world. By July 1996 her collection contained a record 292 meters.

BIGGEST CLOVER COLLECTION

Over five months in 1995, George Kaminski single-handedly collected a total of 13,382 four-leaf clovers during his recreation time in the prison yard at the State Correctional Institution, Pennsylvania, USA. He also found 1,336 five-leaf, 78 six-leaf and six seven-leaf clovers in the same 2-ha (5-acre) area. The collection had to be sent home to Kaminski's sister, since the US Bureau of Corrections policy states that no inmate is allowed to collect anything for any reason.

BIGGEST BUBBLEGUM COLLECTION

Thomas and Volker Martins of Freiburg, Germany, have collected 1,712 packs of bubblegum since 1992.

BIGGEST NUT CRACKER COLLECTION

Jürgen Löschner from Neuhausen, Germany, has collected about 2,200 nut crackers since 1966. They are all housed at his Nut Cracker Museum.

BIGGEST COLLECTION OF TEABAG LABELS

Since 1992 Felix Rotter from Erkrath in Germany has collected 5,681 teabag labels.

fans and followers

BIGGEST SCI-FI FOLLOWING

Star Trek premiered in 1966 and now has an unprecedented following. The TV series can be seen in more than 100 countries, and a 'Trekker' convention takes place somewhere almost every weekend. There are more than 350 *Star Trek* sites on the net and about 500 fan publications. After more than 400,000 requests from fans, NASA named one of its space shuttles *Enterprise*.

MOST ARDENT FILM WATCHERS

Sal Piro, the president of the US *Rocky Horror Show* fan club, has seen *The Rocky Horror Picture Show* (GB, 1975) about 1,000 times. *The Rocky Horror Show*, the stage show on which the film is based, was written by

Richard O'Brien and opened at the Royal Court Theatre, London, UK, in 1973. It rapidly crossed from cult status to the mainstream, and today it has played in all the major European countries as well as Australia and the Far East. The film is still showing in more than 100 cinemas in the USA. Many of its fans dress up as their favourite characters when they watch the film.

Gwilym Hughes of Gwynedd, Wales, UK, saw his first film in 1953, while he was in hospital. He keeps a diary of all the films he has seen and had logged a total of 22,990 films by 28 Feb 1997. Most of the films he now watches are on video.

MOST POPULAR DOLL

On 13 May 1998 a group of Barbie fans hit the streets of Westchester, Los Angeles, USA, in a campaign to have their idol depicted on a stamp as part of the US Postal Service's 20th Century Commemorative Stamp Program. In April 1998 it had been announced that 'Barbie Steps Out' was among 30 subjects that would compete by popular vote to appear on stamps depicting the 1960s. Barbie, whose full name is Barbara Millicent Roberts, was 'born' on 9 March 1958 and since then has become one of the world's most talked about women. It has been estimated that a typical girl between the ages of three and 10 owns an average of 10 Barbie dolls. The world's love affair with the doll, which is made by Mattel, has spawned thousands of fan clubs, and a number of Barbie conventions take place across the globe every year. In 1995 the first Internet Barbie Collector's convention, Cybervention, was held in Seattle, USA. In 1976, during Bicentennial celebrations, some Barbie dolls were placed in sealed time capsules to be opened in 2076.

MOST ARDENT THEATRE-GOERS

Dr H. Howard Hughes, Prof. Emeritus of Texas Wesleyan College, Fort Worth, USA, attended a record 6,136 shows from 1956 to 1987.

Edward Sutro saw a record 3,000 first-night productions in his native United Kingdom from 1916 to 1956 and possibly more than 5,000 shows in his 60 years of theatre-going.

TOP TRAINSPOTTER

Bill Curtis from Clacton-on-Sea, Essex, UK, is the world champion trainspotter, or 'gricer' (after Richard Grice, the first champion, who held the title from 1896 to 1931). Curtis' sightings include about 60,000 locomotives, 11,200 electric units and 8,300 diesel units over 40 years in a number of different countries.

TOP BIRDSPOTTERS

Phoebe Snetsinger from Webster Groves, Missouri, USA, has spotted 8,040 of the 9,700 known bird species since 1965. She has now seen 82% of the world's species, all of the families on the official list and more than 90% of the genera.

The greatest number of bird species spotted in a 24-hour period is 342, by Kenyan spotters Terry Stevenson, John Fanshawe and Andy Roberts on the second

day of Birdwatch Kenya '86, which took place from 29 to 30 Nov 1986.

MOST BIRDS RINGED

Between 1953 and 26 Feb 1997 Óskar J. Sigurósson, principal bird-ringer of the Icelandic Institute of Natural History and lighthouse keeper at Stórhöfôi on Heimay in the Westmann Islands, ringed 65,243 birds.

MOST AERIALS PHOTOGRAPHED

David Neal from Kent, UK, has spent 10 years photographing aerials in his native country. By Jan 1998 the 22-year-old had taken more than 3,000 photos of 524 different types of aerial. His ambition is to photograph every aerial mast in the United Kingdom — approximately 10,000 in total. David used to record his sightings of electricity pylons but now finds aerials more 'majestic'.

MOST PUBS VISITED

Bruce Masters of Flitwick, Beds, UK, has visited 29,203 pubs and 1,568 other drinking establishments since 1960, drinking local beer wherever it was available.

MOST IMPERSONATED ICON

There are estimated to be more than 48,000 Elvis impersonators worldwide. In 1988 the First Presleyterian Church of Elvis the Divine was formed in the USA. In London, UK, Paul Chan entertains customers at his Gracelands Palace restaurant with his Elvis impressions. Known as 'the Chinese Elvis', Chan has even changed his middle name to his hero's by deed poll. Seen here are two impersonators at an Elvis convention in the USA.

MOST RESTAURANTS DINED IN

Fred Magel from Chicago, Illinois, USA, dined out a record 46,000 times in 60 countries during his 50 years as a restaurant grader. Magel claimed that the restaurant that served the biggest helpings was Zehnder's Hotel, Frankenmuth, Michigan, USA. His favourite dishes were South African rock lobster and mousse of fresh English strawberries.

MOST CHRISTMAS CARDS SENT

The record for the greatest number of personal Christmas cards ever sent out is believed to be 62,824, by Werner Erhard from San Francisco, California, USA, in Dec 1975.

MOST LETTERS WRITTEN

Uichi Noda, the former deputy minister of the treasury and minister of construction in Japan, wrote 1,307 letters to his bedridden wife Mitsu during his overseas trips from July 1961 until her death in March 1985. They have been published in 25 volumes totalling 12,404 pages and more than 5 million characters.

MOST LETTERS TO AN EDITOR

David Green from Pembrokeshire, UK, had his 143rd letter printed in the main correspondence columns of *The Times* on 21 April 1998. His most productive year was 1972, with 12.

LONGEST-KEPT DIARY

Col. Ernest Loftus from Harare, Zimbabwe, began writing his daily diary at the age of 12 on 4 May 1896 and continued it until his death aged 103 years 178 days on 7 July 1987.

GREATEST *STAR WARS* TRIBUTE

In 1998 a group of friends from California, USA, made a 10-minute film depicting scenes that are only mentioned in *Star Wars* (USA, 1977). *Troops*, which was directed by Kevin Rubio, shows the death of Luke Skywalker's Aunt Beru and Uncle Owen, which inspired his mission to save the galaxy. It has its own website (www.theforce.net), and fans are said to include *Stars Wars* director George Lucas and Mark Hamill, who played Luke.

food and drink 1

FASTEST YARD OF ALE

Peter Dowdeswell of Northants, UK, drank a yard of ale (1.42 litres or 2½ pints) in five seconds in May 1975.

BIGGEST WINE TASTING

In 1986 about 4,000 tasters consumed 9,360 bottles of wine at a tasting sponsored by TV station KQED in California, USA.

MOST MEAT EATEN AT A BARBECUE

In 1996 21.7 tonnes of meat and 22 tonnes of chicken were cooked and eaten in eight hours at the Lancaster Sertoma Club's Chicken Bar-B-Que, Pennsylvania, USA.

GREATEST TRENCHERMAN

In 1963 Edward Miller ate 28 pullets, weighing 907 g (2 lb) each, in one sitting at Trader Vic's, San Francisco, California, USA.

FASTEST EGG EATERS

In 1984 Peter Dowdeswell ate 13 raw eggs in one second.

In 1987 John Kenmuir ate 14 cooked eggs in 14.42 seconds.

FASTEST KIPPER EATER

Reg Morris filleted and ate 27 kippers in 16 min 52.66 sec at Walsall, W Midlands, UK, in 1988.

FASTEST FRANKFURTER EATER

Reg Morris ate 30 frankfurters in 64 seconds in Burntwood, Staffs, UK, in Dec 1986.

FASTEST SAUSAGE MEAT EATER

Reg Morris ate 2.72 kg (6 lb) of sausage meat in 3 min 10 sec at Walsall, W Midlands, UK, in 1986.

FASTEST SPAGHETTI EATER

In 1986 Peter Dowdeswell ate 91.44 m (100 yd) of spaghetti in 12.02 seconds at Halesown, W Midlands, UK.

FASTEST PICKLED ONION EATER

Pat Donahue ate 91 pickled onions in 1 min 8 sec at Victoria, British Columbia, Canada, in 1978.

FASTEST BANANA EATER

Dr Ronald Alkana ate 17 bananas, each with an edible weight of at least 128 g (4½ oz), in two minutes at the University of California, Irvine, USA, in 1973.

FASTEST LEMON EATER

In 1979 Bobby Kempf of Virginia, USA, ate three lemons, including skin and pips, in 15.3 seconds.

FASTEST GRAPE EATER

Jim Ellis of Montrose, Michigan, USA, ate 1.39 kg (3 lb 1 oz) of grapes in 34.6 seconds in 1976.

FASTEST ICE CREAM EATER

Tony Dowdeswell ate 1.53 kg (3 lb 6 oz) of unmelted ice cream in 31.67 seconds in New York, USA, in July 1986.

FASTEST NOODLE MAKER

Simon Sang Koon Sung made 8,192 strings from one piece of dough in 59.29 seconds at the Singapore Food Festival in 1994.

FASTEST ONION PEELERS

In July 1980 Alan St. Jean peeled 22.67 kg (50 lb) of onions in 3 min 18 sec in Connecticut, USA.

In Oct 1980, under new rules stipulating that a minimum of 50 onions have to be peeled, Alfonso Salvo of Pennsylvania, USA, peeled 22.67 kg (50 lb) of onions (52 onions) in 5 min 23 sec.

FASTEST OYSTER OPENER

Mike Racz opened 100 oysters in 2 min 20.07 sec at Invercargill, New Zealand, on 16 July 1990.

FASTEST PANCAKE TOSSER

Ralf Laue from Germany tossed a pancake 416 times in 2 minutes at Linz, Austria, in 1997.

BIGGEST HAMBURGER

In 1989 a 2.5-tonne hamburger was made at Outagamie County Fairgrounds, Wisconsin, USA.

LONGEST KEBAB

An 880.6-m-long (2,889-ft 3-in) kebab was made by the West Yorkshire Family Service Units, the Trade Association of Asian Restaurant Owners and National Power at Bradford, W Yorks, UK, on 19 June 1994.

LONGEST SALAMI

In 1992 a record-breaking 20.95-m-long (68-ft 9-in) salami was made by A/S Svindlands at Pølsefabrikk, Norway.

LONGEST SAUSAGE

A 46.3-km-long (28-mile 1,354-yd) continuous sausage was made by M & M Meat Shops and J. M. Schneider Inc. at Kitchener, Ontario, Canada, in April 1995.

LONGEST BRATWURST

A 3.1-km (1-mile 1,630-yd) bratwurst was made at Jena, Thuringia, Germany, in 1994.

BIGGEST LASAGNE

A 21.33 x 2.13-m (70 x 7-ft) lasagne was made by the Food Bank for Monterey County at Salinas, California, USA, in 1993.

BIGGEST PIZZA

A pizza measuring 37.4 m (122 ft 8 in) in diameter was made at Norwood Hypermarket, South Africa, on 8 Dec 1990.

BIGGEST QUICHE LORRAINE

The world's biggest ever quiche lorraine was baked in Paris, France, in Nov 1997 by chef Alain Marcotullio and a team of 30 cooks. Its preparation took more than 16 hours. The 4.87-m-wide (16-ft) quiche contained, among other ingredients, 1,298 eggs, 71 kg (156 lb) of bacon and 119 litres (31 gal) of milk. A standard-size quiche lorraine requires just three eggs, eight slices of bacon and ½ cup of milk. Here Claude Dejean, dressed as an 18th-century custodian, beats a drum to celebrate the completion of the quiche.

BIGGEST PAELLA
Juan Carlos Galbis and a team of helpers made a paella measuring 20 m (65 ft 7 in) in diameter at Valencia, Spain, in March 1992. It was eaten by 100,000 people.

BIGGEST OMELETTE
In 1994 representatives of Swatch cooked a 128.5-m^2 (1,383-ft^2) omelette containing a total of 160,000 eggs at Yokohama, Japan.

BIGGEST CHINESE DUMPLING
In 1997 the Hong Kong Union of Chinese Food and Culture Ltd and the Southern District Committee made a Chinese dumpling weighing 480 kg (1,058 lb 6¼ oz) for the celebration of Hong Kong being returned to China.

BIGGEST PANCAKE
A 3-tonne pancake with a diameter of 15.01 m (49 ft 3 in) was flipped in Manchester, UK, in Aug 1994 during celebrations to mark the 150th anniversary of the Co-operative movement.

TALLEST CAKE
In Aug 1997 Network Television Marketing Ltd created a 32-m-tall (105-ft), 105-tier cake in Faisalabad, Pakistan.

LONGEST APPLE STRUDEL
A 1.674-km (1-mile 2,211-yd) apple strudel was made on 26 May 1994 in Karlsruhe, Germany.

BIGGEST CHERRY PIE
In 1990 a 17.11-tonne cherry pie with a diameter of 6.1 m (20 ft) was baked by the Oliver Rotary Club, British Columbia, Canada.

BIGGEST SWEET
In 1997 a 2.31-tonne Turkish Delight was made by Bahattin, Bulent and Ediz Pektuzun at Real Turkish Delight, NSW, Australia.

BIGGEST COCKTAIL
A 25,963-litre (5,711-gal) Juicy Duce was made at the Buderim Tavern, Queensland, Australia, in

BIGGEST FOOD FAIR
Gudrun and Lena, promoters of the 'Green Week' fair in Berlin, Germany, bite into a giant pretzel in front of the Brandenburg Gate. The fair is the biggest food and agriculture fair in the world today. In 1998 it was attended by exhibitors from more than 60 countries. Germany is also home to the biggest ever apple strudel and the longest bratwurst.

1996. It contained 100 litres (22 gal) each of rum, scotch, gin, bourbon, ouzo and brandy, 4,000 litres (880 gal) of vodka, 1,800 litres (396 gal) of orange juice, 4 tonnes of ice, 400 watermelons, 400 oranges and 400 lemons.

BIGGEST MILK SHAKE
A 16,400-litre (3,607-gal) strawberry shake was made by Age Concern East Cheshire and Lancashire Dairies at Macclesfield, UK, in 1996.

food and drink II

MOST EXPENSIVE MEAL PER HEAD

In Sept 1997 three diners at Le Gavroche, London, UK, spent £13,091.20 ($20,945.92) on one meal. Only £216.20 ($345.60) went on food: cigars and spirits accounted for £845 ($1,384) and the remaining £12,030 ($19,248) went on six bottles of wine. The most expensive bottle, a 1985 Romanee Conti costing £4,950 ($7,920), proved 'a bit young' so they gave it to the restaurant staff. The diners began with a 1949 Krug champagne at £560 ($896) and followed it with fine clarets and burgundies: a 1985 DRC Montrachet at £1,400 ($2,240), a 1954 Haut Brion at £2,100 ($3,360), a 1967 Château D'Yquem at £1,070 ($1,712) and a 1961 Château Latour at £1,950 ($3,120).

MOST EXPENSIVE BOTTLE OF WINE

In Dec 1985 £105,000 ($136,248) was paid for a bottle of 1787 Château Lafite claret at Christie's, London, UK. It was engraved with the initials of Thomas Jefferson, the third US president. In 1986 its cork, dried out by exhibition lights, slipped, spoiling the wine.

MOST EXPENSIVE GLASS OF WINE

A record $1,453 (£982) was paid for the first glass of Beaujolais Nouveau 1993 released in Beaune (from Maison Jaffelin), Burgundy, France. It was bought by Robert Denby at Pickwick's, a British pub in Beaune, on 18 Nov 1993.

MOST EXPENSIVE SPIRITS

The most expensive spirit on sale is Springbank 1919 Malt Whisky, a bottle of which costs £6,750 including VAT ($10,800) at Fortnum & Mason in London, UK.

The highest price paid for a spirit at auction was $79,552 (£45,200), for a bottle of 50-year-old Glenfiddich whisky. It was sold to an anonymous Italian businessman at a charity auction in Milan, Italy, in 1992.

MOST EXPENSIVE STEAK

The most expensive steak comes from Wagyu cattle, which have been bred around the Japanese city of Kobe for centuries. The herds have a remarkable genetic purity and the cows are treated like royalty, regularly rubbed down with saké and fed huge amounts of beer. They are extremely docile animals and their stress-free life is said to explain the quality of their flesh. Since the Japanese will not export any cattle for breeding, Kobe beef is rarely available, and costs about $160/lb (£45.36/kg).

MOST EXPENSIVE FISH

Sushi chefs pay phenomenal prices for giant bluefin tuna. In Jan 1992 a 324-kg (715-lb) bluefin sold for the sum of $83,500 (£50,301) – almost $117/lb (£30/kg) – in Tokyo, Japan. The tuna was reduced to 2,400 servings of sushi for wealthy diners at $75 (£45) per serving. The estimated takings from this one fish were $180,000 (£108,433).

MOST EXPENSIVE CAVIAR

The most expensive caviar in the world is Almas caviar, the yellow eggs from an albino beluga sturgeon, which sells for $1,000/1³/₄ oz (£625/50 g).

MOST EXPENSIVE MUSSELS

The world's most expensive mussel is the Percebes barnacle, at $176/lb (£50/kg). Known as the 'truffle of the seas', the barnacles need a lot of oxygen to survive and so attach themselves to rocks where waves are most violent and the water is very aerated. They live in the uninhabited Sisargas Islands off Spain, where fishermen risk their lives to catch them. Deaths and casualties are commonplace. Once the shellfish reach a restaurant, they are boiled alive and served up with a garlic sauce. They are so highly prized that a festival, the Fiesta de Los Percebes, is held in their honour.

MOST EXPENSIVE SPICES

Prices for wild ginseng (the root of *Panax quinquefolium*) from China's Chan Pak mountain area were as high as $23,000/oz (£310,489/g) in Hong Kong in Nov 1979. Total annual shipments of the spice — which is thought by many to be an aphrodisiac — from Jilin Province do not exceed 4 kg (140 oz).

MOST EXPENSIVE TRUFFLE

Guy Monier, the owner of the Truffle House in Paris, France, displays a giant 1.14-kg (2.5-lb) black truffle. Found by a dog in Tricastin, southern France, in Dec 1997, it was worth an estimated $1,500 (£916). The world's most expensive truffle is *Tuber magmatum pico*, a rare white truffle found in Alba, Italy, wich sells for $8,820/lb (£2,500/kg). Scientists are unable to cultivate the fungus, which can only be found by trained pigs or dogs.

The most expensive widely-used spice is saffron, made from the dried stigmas of *Crocus sotivus*. It costs $4/^{11}/$_{500}$ oz (£2.50/625 mg).

HOTTEST SPICE

A single dried gram (^{3}/$_{100}$ oz) of Red 'Savina' Habanero (1994 special), developed by GNS Spices of Walnut, California, USA, can produce detectable 'heat' in 577 kg (1,272 lb) of bland sauce.

MOST EXPENSIVE CHILLI

The most expensive chilli is served by Chasen's of West Hollywood, USA, and costs £46.16/kg ($16.75 for ^{1}/$_2$ lb). Liz Taylor had some flown to her when she was filming *Cleopatra* (USA, 1963).

MOST EXPENSIVE FRUIT

In 1977 restaurateur Leslie Cooke paid £530 ($906) for 453 g (1 lb) of strawberries at an auction in Dublin, Republic of Ireland.

BIGGEST PUB

Germany is renowned for its production and consumption of beer, most notably at the Oktoberfest held each year in Munich. Munich is also home to the Mathäser, the world's biggest pub, which sells 48,000 litres (84,470 pints) of beer every day.

MOST METAL EATEN

Michel Lotito of Grenoble, France, is known as Monsieur Mangetout ('Mr Eat-everything') and has been eating metal and glass since 1959. Gastroenterologists who have x-rayed his stomach have described his ability to consume up to 900-g (2-lb) of metal a day as unique. Mangetout's diet since 1966 has included 18 bicycles, 15 supermarket trolleys, seven TV sets, six chandeliers, two beds, a pair of skis, a Cessna light aircraft, a computer and a coffin (including handles). He cuts up the objects with an electric power saw to make bite-sized chunks and instead of chewing the 'food' swallows the metal like a pill – something that would normally prove fatal and should never be attempted. He first became aware of his ability when a glass from which he was drinking broke one day. He started chewing the fragments, found that he could swallow them, and began eating glass and metal as a party trick. Now he makes a living from his act and has a resistance to pain that is 10 times stronger than a normal person's. By Oct 1997 the 47-year-old had eaten nearly eight tonnes of metal in his 22-year career but said that bananas and hard-boiled eggs make him sick.

MOST EXPENSIVE COFFEE

The Indonesian coffee Kopi Luwak sells for $75/^{1}/$_4$ lb (£21.26/^{1}/$_4$ kg), partly because of its rarity but also because of the way it is processed: the beans from which it is made are ingested by a small tree-dwelling animal called the *Paradoxurus* before being extracted from the excreta of the animals and made into Kopi Luwak.

BIGGEST RESTAURANT

Mang Gorn Luang (The Royal Dragon) in Bangkok, Thailand, has 1,200 staff and can seat 5,000 customers. The 541 waiters wear roller skates to serve up to 3,000 dishes an hour in the 1.6-ha (4-acre) service area.

LONGEST LUNCH TABLE

In March 1998 a team of caterers set places for more than 15,000 guests to eat at the longest continuous table. The table stretched over 5 km (3 miles) along the newly-built Vasco da Gama bridge in Lisbon, Portugal – Europe's longest bridge, at 18 km (11 miles). The organizers of the event had to hire 200 buses to transport the diners to their seats.

GREATEST DISPLAYS OF STRENGTH

Grant Edwards of Sydney, NSW, Australia, single-handedly pulled a 201-tonne train a distance of 36.8 m (120 ft 9 in) along a rail track at the NSW Rail Transport Museum, Thirlmere, Australia, on 4 April 1996.

Juraj Barbaric single-handedly pulled a 360-tonne train a record distance of 7.7 m (25 ft 3 in) along a rail track at Kosice, Slovakia, on 25 May 1996.

Khalil Oghaby from Iran lifted an elephant off the ground using a harness and platform weighing approximately 2 tonnes at Gerry Cottle's Circus, UK, in 1975.

Yuri Scherbina, a powerjuggler from Ukraine, threw a 16-kg (35-lb 4½-oz) weightball from hand to hand 100 times on the eastern summit of Mount Elbrus (at an altitude of 4,200 m or 13,800 ft) in July 1995.

GREATEST LIFT USING TEETH

Walter Arfeuille of Ieper-Vlamertinge, Belgium, lifted weights totalling 281.5 kg (620 lb 10 oz) a distance of 17 cm (6¾ in) off the ground with his teeth in Paris, France, on 31 March 1990.

GREATEST PULL USING TEETH

Robert Galstyan of Masis, Armenia, pulled two railway wagons a distance of 7 m (23 ft) along a rail track with his teeth at Shcherbinka, Moscow, Russia, on 21 July 1992. The wagons were coupled together and had a total combined weight of 219,175 kg (483,198 lb).

GREATEST DISPLAY OF LUNG POWER

On 26 Sept 1994 Nicholas Mason of Cheadle, Greater Manchester, UK, inflated a standard 1,000-g (35-oz) meteorological balloon to a diameter of 2.44 m (8 ft) in a time of 45 min 2.5 sec for BBC TV's *Record Breakers* show.

FASTEST BEER KEG LIFTER

Tom Gaskin lifted a keg of beer above his head a total of 902 times in six hours at Liska House, Newry, Northern Ireland, on 26 Oct 1996. The keg weighed 62.5 kg (137 lb 8 oz).

FASTEST INVERTED SPRINTER

On 19 Feb 1994 Mark Kenny of Norwood, Massachusetts, USA, completed a 50-m (164-ft) sprint on his hands in a record time of 16.93 seconds.

FASTEST YODELLER

Thomas Scholl from Munich, Germany, achieved 22 tones (15 falsetto) in one second on 9 Feb 1992.

FASTEST DRUMMER

Rory Blackwell from Starcross, Devon, UK, played a total of 400 separate drums in a time of 16.2 seconds on 29 May 1995.

HIGHEST CHAIR BALANCER

Henrys is a chair balancer who has performed his act all over the world, including over the Grand Canyon, USA, and in Moscow, Russia. He balances on just two legs of a dining chair under which are two ordinary household glasses. He is seen here over the edge of L'Aiguille du Midi at 3,842 m (12,604 ft) in altitude, (above) and over the River Meuse (below), both in France.

PULLING FEATS

David Huxley single-handedly pulled a 187-tonne Qantas Boeing 747-400 a distance of 91 m (298 ft 6 in) across the tarmac at Sydney Airport, NSW, Australia, on 15 Oct 1997, beating his previous record of 54.7 m (179 ft 6 in). Huxley has also pulled the 105-tonne Concorde for a distance of 143 m (469 ft 2 in), and the 387-tonne HMAV *Bounty* for a distance of 25 m (82 ft).

FASTEST SHAVERS

The record for the most people shaved with a cut-throat razor in 60 minutes is 278, by Tom Rodden of Chatham, Kent, UK, on 10 Nov 1993 for BBC TV's *Record Breakers* show. Averaging 12.9 seconds per face, he drew blood seven times.

The record for the greatest number of people shaved with a safety razor in 60 minutes is 1,994, by Denny Rowe at Herne Bay, Kent, UK, on 19 June 1988. He took an average of 1.8 seconds per volunteer and drew blood four times.

FASTEST HAIRCUTTER

The most haircuts given in an hour is 18, by Trevor Mitchell at the Wembley Conference Centre, London, UK, on 27 Oct 1996, meeting guidelines set down by the Organisation Artistique Internationale de la Coiffure. During this attempt he completed one haircut in a record time of 2 min 20 sec.

FASTEST SHEEP SHEARERS

The record for hand shearing is 390 lambs in eight hours, by Deanne Sarre of Pingrup at Yealering, Western Australia, on 1 Oct 1989.

The men's record for hand shearing is 353 lambs in nine hours, by Peter Casserly of Christchurch, New Zealand, on 13 Feb 1976.

FASTEST TALKERS

The world's fastest talkers are Steve Woodmore from Kent, UK, Sean Shannon from Canada (pictured right) and Steve Briers from Pembrokeshire, UK. Woodmore spoke 595 words in 56.01 seconds (equal to 637.4 words per minute) on British TV show *Motor Mouth* on 22 Sept 1990. He trains by choosing a passage from a book and reciting it over and over again until it becomes second nature. He usually only practises the evening before a speaking event, but if his record is broken he trains for up to six weeks to win it back. Shannon recited Hamlet's soliloquy 'To be or not to be' (260 words) in a time of 23.8 seconds (equal to 655 words per minute) at Edinburgh, UK, on 30 Aug 1995. He realized that he had a talent while he was still a child, when people would ask him to slow down because they could not understand what he was saying. Now he only practises for a few minutes a day: if he does more, the speech becomes impossible to keep together. Briers recited the lyrics of Queen's album *A Night at the Opera* backwards in 9 min 58.44 sec on 6 Feb 1990. The world's fastest backwards talker, he locks himself up in his room until he has learnt his speeches, sometimes training for four hours a day.

The highest ever speed for solo machine-shearing in one working day (nine hours) is 805 lambs, by Alan MacDonald at Waitnaguru, New Zealand, on 20 Dec 1990. This works out at an average of 89.4 sheep per hour.

FASTEST TREE TOPPER

Guy German ascended a 30.5-m-tall (100-ft) spar pole and sawed off the top, which had a circumference of 1 m (3 ft 4 in), in a record time of 53.35 seconds at Albany, Oregon, USA, on 3 July 1989.

FASTEST WIFE-CARRIER

Jouni Jussila carried his wife Tiina over the World Wife-Carrying Championship course — a 235-m-long (771-ft) obstacle course that includes chest-high water and two wooden stiles — in a record time of 1 min 5 sec in 1997. It was the Jussilas' fifth success in the annual contest, which is held in Sonkajärvi, Finland. The winner takes home litres of beer equivalent to the weight of his partner, who need not be his wife but must be over the age of 17 and wear a crash helmet.

FASTEST COCONUT TREE CLIMBER

The annual Coconut Tree Climbing Competition held at Sukana Park, Fiji, is a local tradition that has become an international event, and organizers have had to standardize the length of the climb. The fastest time in which a 9-m-tall (29-ft 6-in) coconut tree has been climbed barefoot is 4.88 seconds, by Fuatai Solo of Western Samoa (now Samoa) in Sukana Park, on 22 Aug 1980. After being declared the winner for the third time running, Fuatai climbed the tree again, clutching the prize money of $100 (£43) in his mouth.

achievers II

MOST PLATES FLASHED
Albert Lucas (USA), flashed eight plates in 1993. He also juggled eight plates in 1997, equalling the record that was reputedly set by Enrico Rastelli (Italy) in the 1920s. 'Flashed' means that the number of catches made at least equals the number of objects, while 'juggled' requires double the number of catches.

LONGEST BUBBLE
Alan McKay of Wellington, New Zealand, created a 32-m-long (105-ft) bubble on 9 Aug 1996. He used a bubble wand, washing-up liquid, glycerine and water.

BIGGEST BUBBLE-GUM BUBBLE
The greatest reported diameter of a bubble-gum bubble is 58.4 cm (23 in). It was blown by Susan Montgomery Williams of Fresno, California, USA, at the ABC-TV studios in New York, USA, on 19 July 1994.

LARGEST BUBBLE WALL
Fan-Yang of Mississauga, Ontario, Canada, created a 47.7-m (156-ft) bubble wall with an area of about 376.1 m^2 (4,000 ft^2) at the Kingdome Pavilion, Seattle, Washington, USA, on 11 Aug 1997. The bubble stayed up continuously for between 5 and 10 seconds.

MOST MOSQUITOES KILLED
The most mosquitoes ever killed in the five-minute world mosquito killing championships held yearly in Finland is 21, by Henri Pellonpää in 1995.

LONGEST EGG THROW
Johnny Dell Foley threw a fresh hen's egg a distance of 98.51 m (323 ft 2 in) without breaking it on 12 Nov 1978 at Jewett, Texas, USA. The egg was caught by Keith Thomas.

LONGEST FLYING DISC THROWS
The World Flying Disc Federation distance record for men is 200.01 m (656 ft 2 in), by Scott Stokely (US) on 14 May 1995 at Fort Collins, Colorado, USA.

The official Flying Disc distance record for women is 136.31 m (447 ft 3 in), by Anni Kreml (USA) at Fort Collins, Colorado, USA, on 21 Aug 1994.

LONGEST GUMBOOT THROWS
A size 8 (US size 8½) Challenger Dunlop boot was thrown a record 63.98 m (209 ft 9 in) by Teppo Luoma at Hämeenlinna, Finland, on 12 Oct 1996.

The women's record for throwing a size 8 (US size 8½) Challenger Dunlop boot is 40.87 m (134 ft 1 in), by Sari Tirkkonen at Turku, Finland, on 19 April 1996.

LONGEST COW PAT THROW
The greatest distance that a cow pat has been thrown under the 'non-sphericalization and 100% organic' rule is 81.1 m (266 ft), by Steve Urner at the Mountain Festival, Tehachapi, California, USA, on 14 Aug 1981.

LONGEST SPEAR THROW
The furthest that a spear has been thrown using an atlatl, a hand-held device that fits onto it, is 258.63 m (848 ft 6½ in), by David Engvall at Aurora, Colorado, USA, on 15 July 1995.

LONGEST SPITS
The greatest recorded distance that a cherry stone has been spat is 28.98 m (95 ft 1 in), by Horst Ortmann at Langenthal, Germany, on 27 Aug 1994.

David O'Dell of Apple Valley, California, USA, spat a tobacco wad a record distance of 15.07 m (49 ft 5½ in) at the 19th World Tobacco Spitting Championships at Calico Ghost Town, California, in March 1994.

The greatest distance that a water-melon seed has been spat is 22.91 m (75 ft 2 in), by Jason Schayot at De Leon, Texas, USA, on 12 Aug 1995.

GREATEST GRAPE CATCH
The greatest ever distance at which a grape thrown from level ground has been caught in the mouth is 99.82 m (327 ft 6 in), by Paul Tavilla at East Boston, Massachusetts, USA, on 27 May 1991. The grape was thrown by James Deady.

LONGEST CRAWLS
Over 15 months to 9 March 1985, Jagdish Chander crawled a distance of 1,400 km (870 miles) from Aligarh to Jamma, India, in order to appease his revered Hindu goddess, Mata.

The longest ever continuous voluntary crawl, keeping at least one knee in unbroken contact with the ground, was 50.6 km (31 miles 880 yd) by Peter McKinlay and John Murrie from 28 to 29 March 1992. They covered 115 laps of an athletics track at Falkirk, Scotland, UK.

LONGEST DANCE
The greatest distance ever danced by one person is 37.367 km (23 miles 385 yd), by David Meenan, who tap-danced for 6 hr 12 min 53 sec at Red Bank, New Jersey, USA, on 30 June 1996.

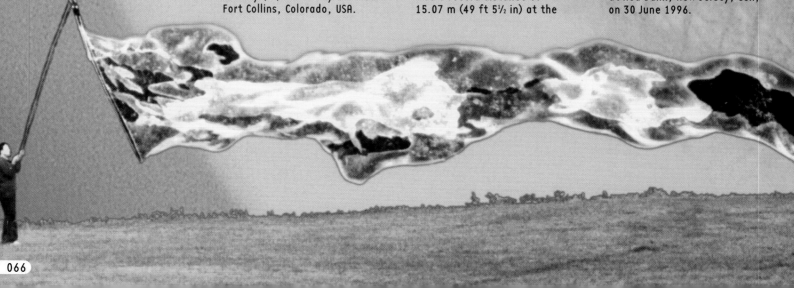

MOST EGGS BALANCED

The most eggs balanced on end simultaneously on a flat surface by one person is 210, by Kenneth Epperson of Monroe, Georgia, USA, on 23 Sept 1990. The most eggs simultaneously balanced by a group is 467, by a class at Bayfield School, Colorado, USA, on 20 March 1986, the vernal equinox. The picture left shows eight-year-old Malik Shabazz Pizzarro and urban park ranger June Yoo balancing eggs on a wall in Central Park, New York, USA, as part of a vernal equinox celebration in March 1997. It has long been thought that it is possible to balance raw eggs on their end on the first day of spring, although astronomers argued that there is no reason for this. In 1996 they were proved right by Science Alliance, who demonstrated that if an egg balances on an equinox day it will balance on any other day.

LONGEST TIME SPENT BALANCING ON ONE FOOT

Amresh Kumar Jha balanced on one foot for a record time of 71 hr 40 min at Bihar, India, from 13 to 16 Sept 1995. He did not rest his disengaged foot on the standing foot or use any object for support or balance at any point.

LONGEST PERIOD WITHOUT MOVING

Radhey Shyam Prajapati (India) stood motionless for a record 18 hr 5 min 50 sec at Gandhi Bhawan, Bhopal, India, from 25 to 26 Jan 1996.

LONGEST STATIC WALL SIT

Rajkumar Chakraborty (India) stayed in an unsupported sitting position against a wall for a time of 11 hr 5 min at Panposh Sports Hostel, Rourkela, India, on 22 April 1994.

LONGEST TIME CAMPING OUT

The silent Indian *fakir* Mastram Bapu ('contented father') remained on the same spot by the roadside in the village of Chitra for a total of 22 years from 1960 to 1982.

LONGEST TIME SPENT IN A TREE

Bungkas went up a palm tree in the Indonesian village of Bengkes in 1970 and has been there ever since, living in a nest that he made from branches and leaves. Repeated efforts to persuade him to come down have failed.

CHINESE CIRCUS

Balancing and juggling acts date back to the Middle Ages in Europe, Asia and Africa, but Chinese circus in particular is renowned for its balancing acts. The Chinese State Circus, which was put together by Philip Gandey, is an animal-free circus which has dazzled audiences worldwide with its daring high wire and trapeze acts, massive human pyramids, plate balancing and acrobatics.

LONGEST RIDE IN ARMOUR

The longest known ride while wearing armour is 334.7 km (208 miles), by Dick Brown from Edinburgh to Dumfries, UK, in 1989. His total riding time was 35 hr 25 min.

LONGEST BACKWARDS UNICYCLE

Ashrita Furman (USA) rode backwards for a distance of 85.56 km (53 miles 299 yd) at Forest Park, Queens, New York, USA, on 16 Sept 1994.

MOST BOOMERANGS CAUGHT

Lawrence West from Basingstoke, Hants, UK, threw, and caught, a boomerang 20 times in one minute at the Indoor Boomerang Throwing Competition held on BBC TV's *Tomorrow's World* on 20 March 1998.

MOST RINGS JUGGLED

A record-breaking 11 rings were juggled by Albert Petrovski of the USSR in 1963 (not fully substantiated), Eugene Belaur of the USSR in 1968 and Sergei Ignatov of the USSR in 1973 (not fully substantiated).

MOST FLAMING TORCHES JUGGLED

Anthony Gatto (USA) juggled seven flaming torches in 1989.

MOST DOMINOES STACKED

Ralf Laue of Leipzig, Germany, successfully stacked 529 dominoes on a single supporting domino on 26 June 1997 at the Ramada Hotel, Linz, Austria.

FASTEST BED MAKER

The fastest time for one person to make a bed is 28.2 seconds, by Wendy Wall of Sydney, NSW, Australia, on 30 Nov 1978.

teamwork

BIGGEST DANCE
An estimated 72,000 people took part in a Chicken Dance during the Canfield Fair, Ohio, USA, on 1 Sept 1996.

BIGGEST TAP DANCE
A record-breaking 6,654 people tap danced outside Macy's department store in New York, USA, on 18 Aug 1996.

BIGGEST LINE DANCE
On 25 Jan 1997 a total of 5,502 people took part in a country line dance held in Tamworth, NSW, Australia. They danced to Brooks and Dunn's extended play version of *Bootscooting Boogie*, which lasts for 6.28 minutes.

LONGEST CONGA
On 13 March 1988 the Miami Super Conga, held in conjunction with Calle Ocho — a Cuban-American celebration of life held in Miami, Florida, USA — consisted of 119,986 people.

LONGEST DANCING DRAGON
On 3 Nov 1996 a team of 2,431 people brought a dancing dragon to life measuring 1.9 km (1 mile 317 yds) from the end of its nose to the tip of its tail. The dragon danced for more than one minute at the Grandstand Forecourt, Shatin Horse Racecourse, Hong Kong.

BIGGEST HUMAN CENTIPEDE
On 2 Sept 1996 a 'human centipede' made up of 1,665 students from the University of Guelph, Canada, with their ankles firmly tied together, moved 30 m (98 ft 5 in) without any of them falling over.

BIGGEST SIMULTANEOUS SIGNING
The most people to have signed simultaneously is 250, signing *Somewhere Over The Rainbow* during a performance of the *Wizard of Oz* at the Swan Theatre, High Wycombe, Bucks, UK, on 9 Aug 1996.

MOST KISSING COUPLES
The greatest number of couples to have kissed in the same place at the same time was 1,420, at the University of Maine at Orono, Maine, USA, on 14 Feb 1996.

FASTEST HUMAN DEMOLITION
On 11 May 1996, 15 members of the Aurora Karate Do demolished a 10-room house in Prince Albert, Saskatchewan, Canada, with their feet and hands in 3 hr 6 min 50 sec.

FASTEST BRIDGE BUILDERS
On 3 Nov 1995 a team of British soldiers from 21 Engineer Regiment based at Nienburg, Germany, constructed a bridge across an 8-m-wide (26-ft 3-in) gap using a five-bay single-storey medium girder bridge at Hameln, Germany, in a time of 8 min 44 sec.

FASTEST CAR WASHERS
The record for the greatest number of cars to have been washed in eight hours at one location is 2,169, by a team of people led by police officers from Walsall at Aldridge Airport, W Mids, UK, on 9 June 1996.

FASTEST BEDMAKERS
The fastest time in which two people have made a bed with one blanket, two sheets, an undersheet, an uncased pillow, a counterpane and 'hospital' corners is 14 seconds, by Sharon Stringer and Michelle Benkel of the Royal Masonic Hospital, London, UK, on 26 Nov 1993.

FASTEST SHOE SHINERS
The most shoes shined by a team of four people in eight hours is 14,975, by four teenagers from the London Church of Christ at Leicester Square, London, UK, on 15 June 1996.

FASTEST CLOTHES MAKERS
On 3 Sept 1986 a team of eight people at the International Wool Secretariat Development Centre in Ilkley, W Yorks, UK, sheared a sheep and made a jumper from its wool in 2 hr 28 min 32 sec using commercial machinery.

The record for the fastest production of a three-piece suit from sheep to finished article is 1 hr 34 min 33.42 sec, by 65 members of the Melbourne College of Textiles, Victoria, Australia, on 24 June 1982. Catching and fleecing took 2 min 21 sec, and carding, spinning, weaving and tailoring occupied the remaining time.

FASTEST COAL SHOVELLERS
Brian McArdle and Rodney Spark from Middlemount, Queensland,

BIGGEST ALUMINIUM CAN REPLICA
In Dec 1997 about 40 volunteers, mostly retired construction workers, constructed a scale version of St Peter's Basilica, Rome, Italy, from more than 10 million empty aluminium cans. The model, which was one-fifth the size of the original and built mainly from bright red Coca-Cola cans, was created in aid of AIDO and AVIS charities, the Italian associations for blood and organ donation. It was 95 m (316 ft) long, 48 m (160 ft) wide and 29 m (97 ft) high with a 20-m-wide (67-ft) dome and remained in place on the outskirts of Rome for two months. The aluminium was then auctioned off, with the proceeds going to the charities, whose previous projects included can replicas of Rome's Colosseum, Verona's Roman arena and Saint Anthony's Basilica in Padua, northern Italy. The world's biggest can pyramids consisted of 6,201 empty cans built by two teams of 10 people in 30 minutes at Tamokutekihiroba Ouike Park, Tokai, Japan, on 1 Sept 1996.

BIGGEST ORCHESTRA

In April 1998 the record for the world's largest orchestra was broken by the 2,049-strong Pittsburgh Symphony Youth Orchestra at the Civic Arena, Pittsburgh, USA. It consisted of 961 string players, 458 woodwind instrument players, a 410-person brass section and 220 percussionists, recruited from more than 5,000 young hopefuls who applied through their schools and youth orchestras, or auditioned individually. The players, who were conducted by the Pittsburgh Symphony Orchestra Music Director Mariss Janson, performed the world premiere of *Music Forever* by the local composer Michael Moricz. The ambitious event was part of a community outreach and education programme by the Pittsburgh Symphony. The record was previously held by the Wolverhampton Orchestra, UK, with a total of 2,023 players.

Australia, filled a ½-tonne hopper with coal in 15.01 seconds — the record by a team of two — at the Fingal Valley Festival, Tasmania, Australia, on 5 March 1994.

FASTEST LADDER CLIMBERS

A team of 10 firefighters from the Pietermaritzburg Msunduzi Fire Services, South Africa, climbed a vertical height of 90.49 km (56 miles 401 yd) up a standard fire-service ladder in 24 hours from 14 to 15 June 1996.

MOST LITTER COLLECTORS

The record for the greatest number of volunteers to have collected litter in one place on one day is 50,405, along the coastline of California, USA, on 2 Oct 1993 in conjunction with International Coastal Cleanup.

LONGEST BUCKET CHAIN

On 5 Aug 1997 a total of 6,569 boys representing Boy Scouts of America made a fire service bucket chain which stretched for 4.18 km (2 miles 59 yd) at the National Scout Jamboree, Fort A. P. Hills, Virginia, USA. They started with 630 litres (140 gallons) and finished with 572 litres (126 gallons).

BIGGEST UNSUPPORTED CIRCLE

The greatest number of people seated without a chair in an unsupported circle was 10,323, all employees of the Nissan Motor Co., at Komazawa Stadium, Tokyo, Japan, on 23 Oct 1982.

MOST DOMINOES TOPPLED

On 2 Jan 1988, 30 students at Delft, Eindhoven and Twente Technical Universities in the Netherlands set up 1.5 million dominoes. Of these, 1,138,101 were toppled by one push and only 117,889 remained standing.

BIGGEST ROPE PULLED

A 172-m-long (564-ft 4-in) rice straw rope — the biggest made from natural materials — was pulled at the Giant Tug-of-War at the annual Naha City Festival, Okinawa, Japan, in 1995.

TALLEST SCARECROW

A 31.56-m-tall (103-ft 6¾-in) scarecrow called 'Stretch II' was constructed by the Speers family and 15 helpers at the Paris Fall Fair, Ontario, Canada, on 2 Sept 1989.

LONGEST DAISY CHAIN

On 27 May 1985 the villagers of Good Easter, Chelmsford, Essex, UK, constructed a 2.12-km-long (1 mile 3 ft) daisy chain over seven hours.

BIGGEST ORIGAMI MODEL

A paper crane with a record wing-span of 35.7 m (117 ft 2 in) was folded by residents of the district of Gunma at Maebashi, Japan, on 28 Oct 1995. The 16-m-tall (52-ft 6-in) crane took six hours to make.

LONGEST STUFFED TOY

A 508.915-m-long (556-yd) Asian dragon was created at the National Stadium, Singapore, on 28 Sept 1997 to mark the 50th anniversary of Singapore Airlines (SIA). The body of the dragon, which was made by volunteers from SIA and MINDS (Movement for the Intellectually Disabled of Singapore), was stuffed with sponge by representatives of both organizations in front of 20,000 spectators after a charity walk-a-jog that raised a total of $121,294 (£75,809) for MINDS.

TALLEST SANDCASTLE

A record-breaking 6.56-m-tall (21-ft 6-in) sandcastle was constructed by a team led by Joe Maize, George Pennock and Ted Siebert at Harrison Hot Springs, British Columbia, Canada, on 26 Sept 1993. The team used only their hands, buckets and shovels.

LONGEST KISS

Mark and Roberta Griswold from Allen Park, Michigan, USA, are pictured towards the end of a kiss that lasted a record 29 hours. They remained standing and went without rest breaks throughout the record attempt. The Griswolds were competing at the 'Breathsavers Longest Kiss Challenge Contest', held at the Harley Davidson Cafe, New York, USA, from 24 to 25 March 1998, and were awarded a trip to Paris, France.

early starters

YOUNGEST DIRECTOR, WRITER AND PRODUCER
The thriller *Lex the Wonderdog* (USA, 1972) was written, produced and directed by Sydney Ling at the age of just 13, making him the youngest-ever director of a professionally made, feature length film.

YOUNGEST HOLLYWOOD FILM PRODUCER
Steven Paul wrote, produced, directed and appeared in the romantic comedy *Falling In Love Again* (USA, 1980) — which starred Eliott Gould, Susannah York and Michelle Pfeiffer — at the age of 20, making him the youngest Hollywood producer.

YOUNGEST PERFORMER TO RECEIVE STAR BILLING
Leroy Overacker, whose screen name was Baby Leroy, starred opposite Maurice Chevalier in *Bedtime Story* (USA, 1933) at the age of six months.

YOUNGEST PERSON TO BE INCLUDED IN *WHO'S WHO*
The youngest ever entrant in *Who's Who* (excluding people who qualify for inclusion because of their hereditary title) was the concert violinist Yehudi Menuhin (now Lord Menuhin), a child prodigy who first appeared in the 1932 edition of the book at the age of 15.

YOUNGEST TO HAVE A NO. 1 HIT
Jordy (Lemoine) was four and a half years old when he reached No. 1 in the French charts with *Dur Dur d'Etre Bébé (It's Tough To Be A Baby)*. The song later entered the US Billboard chart. In Feb 1994 France's main TV channel, TF1, and RTL, the country's largest radio station, banned Jordy, saying that his parents, Claude Lemoine, a songwriter, and Patricia Lemoine, a singer, were exploiting him.

YOUNGEST GRADUATE
Michael Kearney began studying for an Associate of Science degree at Santa Rosa Junior College, California, USA, at the age of six years seven months in Sept 1990. He became the youngest graduate in June 1994, at the age of 10 years four months, when he obtained his BA in anthropology from the University of South Alabama, USA.

YOUNGEST NOBEL PRIZE WINNERS
Theodore W. Richards won the 1914 Chemistry Prize for work done when he was 23, as did Professor Sir Lawrence Bragg, the winner of the 1915 Nobel Prize for Physics.

YOUNGEST PEOPLE TO RECEIVE BRAVERY AWARDS
Kristina Stragauskaite from Skirmantiskes, Lithuania, was awarded a medal 'For Courage in Fire' when she was just four years 252 days old, after saving the lives of her younger brother and sister in a fire that broke out at their home while their parents were out in April 1989.

YOUNGEST PERSON TO VISIT BOTH POLES
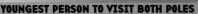
British boy Robert Schumann (seen left) went to the North Pole at the age of 10 on 6 April 1992 and the South Pole at the age of 11 on 29 Dec 1993. On the first trip he arrived and left by air, while on the second he arrived by mountain bike (having flown to within a short distance of the pole) and left by air. On 1 May 1997 eight-year-old Alicia Hempleman-Adams of Swindon, Wiltshire, UK, became the youngest person ever to visit the North Pole. Alicia flew to the pole to meet her father David, who after a 965.6-km (600-mile), 57-day journey across ice had become the first person to complete the grand slam — all four poles: magnetic and geographic, north and south — and climb the highest peak in every continent. The challenge took him 18 years to complete, and it was his third attempt at the North Pole following unsuccessful trips in 1983 and 1997.

YOUNGEST CHESS GRANDMASTER
On 22 March 1997 Etienne Bacrot of France became the youngest person to ever qualify as an International Grand Master, winning the masters tournament at Enghien-les-Bains, near Paris, France, at the age of 14 years 59 days. Etienne, who began playing chess at the age of four, beat the previous record set by Hungarian Peter Leko who won the title of Grand Master at the age of 14 years six months in 1994.

The youngest person to receive an official gallantry award was Julius Rosenberg of Winnipeg, Canada, who was awarded the Medal of Bravery in March 1994 for foiling a black bear that was attacking his three-year-old sister in Sept 1992. He was five at the time of the incident.

YOUNGEST PERSON TO MAKE A SOLO CIRCUMNAVIGATION
David Dicks of Australia was 18 years 41 days old when he completed his circumnavigation of the globe in 264 days 16 hr 49 min on 16 Nov 1996.

YOUNGEST PERSON TO MAKE A SOLO TRANSATLANTIC CROSSING
David Sanderman was 17 years 176 days old when he made a 43-day crossing in 1976.

YOUNGEST WORLD RECORD-BREAKERS
The youngest person to have ever broken a non-mechanical world record was swimmer Gertrude Ederle, who was 12 years

298 days old when she set a record for the women's 880-yd freestyle at Indianapolis, USA, on 17 Aug 1919. Her time was 13 min 19 sec.

YOUNGEST WORLD CHAMPIONS

The youngest ever successful competitor in a world title event was a French boy — whose name is not recorded — who coxed the Netherlands' Olympic pair in Paris, France, on 26 Aug 1900. The boy was not more than 10 years of age and may have been as young as seven.

Fu Mingxia from China won the women's world title for platform diving at Perth, Australia, on 4 Jan 1991, at the age of 12 years 141 days.

YOUNGEST INTERNATIONAL

The tennis player Joy Foster was eight years old when she represented Jamaica in the West Indies Championships at Port of Spain, Trinidad, in Aug 1958, making her the world's youngest ever international.

YOUNGEST PERSON TO PERFORM QUADRUPLE SOMERSAULTS

The youngest person to have achieved a quadruple somersault was 15-year-old Pak Yong Suk of North Korea's Pyongyang Circus troupe during the Monte Carlo Circus Festival, Monaco, in Feb 1997.

YOUNGEST CONSCRIPTS

In March 1976 President Francisco Macías Nguema of Equatorial Guinea decreed compulsory military service for all boys aged between seven and 14. Any parent refusing to hand over their son would be 'imprisoned or shot'.

YOUNGEST SOLDIERS

The Brazilian military hero and statesman Luís Alves de Lima e Silva, Marshall Duke of Caxias, entered his infantry regiment at the age of five in 1808.

Fernando Inchauste Montalvo, the son of a major in the Bolivian airforce, went to the front with his father on his fifth birthday during the war between Bolivia and Paraguay from 1932 to 1935. Montalvo had received military training and was subject to military discipline.

YOUNGEST JUDGE

John Payton took office as Justice of the Peace in Plano, Texas, USA, at the age of 18 years 11 months in Jan 1991.

YOUNGEST MARRIED COUPLE

In 1986 it was reported that an 11-month-old boy had been married to a three-month-old girl at Aminpur, Bangladesh. The marriage had been arranged in order to end a 20-year feud between two families.

YOUNGEST AUTOBIOGRAPHER

Drew Barrymore, a member of the famous Hollywood Barrymore family, was born on 22 Feb 1975 and co-wrote her autobiography *Little Girl Lost* in 1989, at the age of 14, making her the world's youngest published autobiographer. The star had dropped out of school and entered a rehabilitation clinic at the age of 13, after the pressures of her celebrity childhood became too much. Drew had made her screen debut at the age of 11 months, in a television commercial for Puppy Choice Dog Food, made her TV movie debut in *Suddenly Love* (USA, 1978) and achieved international stardom at the age of seven, when she starred in *E.T.: the Extra Terrestrial* (USA, 1982), the sci-fi blockbuster directed by her godfather Steven Spielberg. By the time she was 21 the actress had posed nude for an *Interview* cover and for *Playboy*, played Amy Fisher in *The Amy Fisher Story* (USA, 1993), and married and then divorced after less than two months. In 1996 she appeared in a cameo role in Wes Craven's *Scream* (USA), the top-grossing horror movie of all time. By May 1998, she had appeared in a total of 37 films for television and the big screen, and was seen most recently in *The Wedding Singer* (USA, 1998).

golden oldies

OLDEST PERSON TO HAVE A NO. 1

What a Wonderful World gave US jazz trumpeter and singer Louis Armstrong a No. 1 hit in the UK in 1968 and was No. 1 in several countries as late as 1970, when he was 69. Armstrong — whose nickname was 'Satchmo' — was almost 63 when he had his first No. 1, with *Hello Dolly!* in 1964. He had made himself known in the 1920s through his Chicago recordings with the Hot Five and the Hot Seven.

OLDEST PARACHUTISTS

Hildegarde Ferrera became the oldest ever parachutist when she made a tandem parachute jump at the age of 99 at Mokuleia, Hawaii, USA, in 1996.

The world's oldest ever male parachutist was Edward Royds-Jones, who parachuted in tandem at the age of 95 years 170 days at Dunkeswell, Devon, UK, on 2 July 1994.

Sylvia Brett became the oldest female solo parachutist at the age of 80 years 166 days. She made a jump at Cranfield, Beds, UK, on 23 Aug 1986.

OLDEST CRESTA RUN RIDER

Prince Constantin of Liechtenstein rode the Cresta Run tobogganing course at the age of 85 on 11 Feb 1997.

OLDEST TIGHTROPE WALKER

William Ivy Baldwin became the world's oldest ever tightrope walker when he crossed the South Boulder Canyon, Colorado, USA, on a 97.5-m-long (320-ft) high-wire with a 38.1-m (125-ft) drop on his 82nd birthday on 31 July 1948.

OLDEST HOT-AIR BALLOONIST

Florence Laine of New Zealand flew in a balloon at the age of 102 at Cust, New Zealand, on 26 Sept 1996.

OLDEST BOARDSAILER

Charles Ruijter of the Netherlands took up boardsailing in 1978 at the age of 63 and still sails in the lakes around Eindhoven, Netherlands, at the age of 83.

OLDEST OLYMPIC MEDALLIST

Oscar Swahn from Sweden was in the winning Running Deer shooting team at the age of 64 in 1912 and was a silver medallist in the same event in 1920, at the age of 72.

OLDEST PERSON TO HAVE VISITED BOTH POLES

Major Will Lacy from the United Kingdom travelled to the North Pole on 9 April 1990 at the age of 82 and to the South Pole on 20 Dec 1991 at the age of 84. On both trips he arrived and left by light aircraft.

OLDEST PEOPLE TO HAVE CLIMBED MT EVEREST

Spanish guitar- and violin-maker Ramón Blanco, who has lived in Venezuela since 1970, became the oldest person to ever reach the summit of Mt Everest on 7 Oct 1993, at the age of 60 years 160 days.

The oldest woman to climb Mt Everest was Yasuko Namba of Japan, at the age of 47 in 1996.

OLDEST PERSON TO FLY

Charlotte Hughes of Redcar, N Yorks, UK, was given a flight on Concorde from London, UK, to New York, USA, as a 110th birthday present in 1987. She flew again in 1992, aged 115.

OLDEST PILOTS

Burnet Patten of Victoria, Australia, obtained his flying licence on 2 May 1997 at the age of 80, making him the oldest person ever to qualify as a pilot.

LONGEST MARRIAGE IN THE USA

Paul and Mary Onesi, who are now 101 and 93 years old respectively, are seen (top picture) at their wedding in Clymer, Pennsylvania, USA, in 1917. In Jan 1998 they celebrated their 80th anniversary (bottom picture), becoming the longest-married couple in the USA today. For the past 51 years the couple, who never celebrate Valentine's Day, have lived in Niagara Falls, the USA's 'honeymoon capital'.

OLDEST PERSON IN SPACE

US senator John Glenn is set to become the oldest person ever to visit Space when he takes part in the space shuttle mission in Oct 1998. Glenn, who was born in 1921, first achieved fame in Feb 1962 when he became the first US astronaut to orbit the Earth. A former marine pilot who had served in both WWII and the Korean War, he entered politics in the 1970s and was elected Democratic senator for Ohio in 1974. Re-elected in 1984, he launched an unsuccessful campaign for the US presidency. Glenn is pictured here outside the Levette research laboratory addressing the media in his space shuttle suit, shortly before beginning NASA space shuttle training at Brooks Air Force Base Research Laboratory's centrifuge in Feb 1998. The centrifuge is used by NASA space shuttle astronauts to simulate the g-forces that are experienced by astronauts during a shuttle launch, and Glenn's training there will help to prepare him for the shuttle mission.

Clarence Cornish of Indianapolis, Indiana, USA, flew aircraft until the age of 97. He died 18 days after his last flight on 4 Dec 1995.

OLDEST WALL-OF-DEATH RIDER
The oldest rider to regularly perform in public is 71-year-old Jerry De Roye, who rides a 1927 Indian Type 101 'Scout'.

OLDEST GROOM
Harry Stevens was 103 years old when he married 84-year-old Thelma Lucas at the Caravilla Retirement Home, Wisconsin, USA, on 3 Dec 1984.

OLDEST BRIDE
Minnie Munro became the world's oldest known bride when she married Dudley Reid at the age of 102 at Point Clare, NSW, Australia, on 31 May 1991. The groom was 83.

OLDEST DIVORCED COUPLE
The highest combined age of a divorcing couple is 188, by Ida Stern (91) and her husband Simon (97) of Milwaukee, Wisconsin, USA, in Feb 1984.

LONGEST MARRIAGES
Cousins Sir Temulji Bhicaji Nariman and Lady Nariman from India were married when they were both five years old in 1853. Their marriage lasted 86 years, until Sir Temulji's death aged 91 years 11 months in 1940.

Records show Lazarus Rowe and Molly Webber, who were both born in 1725, to have married in 1743. Molly died in June 1829 at Limington, Maine, USA, after 86 years of marriage.

LONGEST ENGAGEMENT
Octavio Guillén and Adriana Martínez from Mexico finally got married in June 1969, after a 67-year engagement. Both were 82 years old when they wed.

LONGEST CAREERS
Shigechiyo Izumi, who lived to a greater age than any other man on record, began working with draught animals at a sugar mill at Isen, Tokunoshima, Japan, in 1872 and retired as a sugar-cane farmer in 1970, 98 years later, when he was 105 years old. He died aged 120 in 1986.

Johann Heinrich Karl Thieme, the sexton of Aldenburg, Germany, was a gravedigger for a record 50 years, during which time he dug 23,311 graves. In 1826 his understudy dug his grave.

NATIONAL TREASURES
Kin ('Gold') and Gin ('Silver') Kanie became Japan's most famous twins in 1992 when they celebrated their 100th birthday, prompting the mayor of their town Nagoya to call a press conference reminding people of the need to respect the elderly. Since then the twins have made a number of television appearances and advertisements and have been interviewed many times. Now 105 years old, they remain in very good health.

players and games

FASTEST BARROW RACERS
The fastest time in a 1.609-km (1-mile) wheelbarrow race is 4 min 48.51 sec, by Piet Pitzer and Jaco Erasmus at Transvalia High School, Vanderbijlpark, South Africa, on 3 Oct 1987.

FASTEST BED RACERS
The fastest time in the 3.27-km (2-mile 56-yd) Knaresborough Bed Race, UK, is 12 min 9 sec, by the Vibroplant team in June 1990.

FASTEST PANCAKE RACE
The fastest time in the annual 384-m (420-yd) pancake race held in Melbourne, Australia,

FASTEST SNAIL
The all-time record-holder at the annual World Snail Racing Championships held at Congham, Norfolk, UK, is Archie, trained by Carl Banham. His best time over the 33-cm (13-in) circular course was 2 min 20 sec.

is 59.5 seconds, by Jan Stickland on 19 Feb 1985.

FASTEST COAL CARRIER
David Jones carried a 50-kg (110-lb) bag over the 1,012.5-m (3,321-ft) course at Gawthorpe, W Yorks, UK, in a record 4 min 6 sec in April 1991.

BEST LOG ROLLER
The most International Championships won is 10, by Jubiel Wickheim of Shawnigan Lake, British Columbia, Canada, between 1956 and 1969.

FASTEST BOG SNORKELLER
Steve Madeline has won the annual World Bog Snorkelling Championship at Llanwrtyd Wells, Powys, UK, on a record two occasions, in 1989 and 1994. Contestants swim two lengths of a 60-m (196-ft 10-in) bog filled with weeds, leeches and newts.

MOST GAMES OF HOPSCOTCH
The greatest number of hopscotch games played in 24 hours is 408, by Terry Cole of London, UK, in April 1997.

BIGGEST GAME OF MUSICAL CHAIRS
The world's biggest known game of musical chairs involved a total of 8,238 people at the Anglo-Chinese School, Singapore, on 5 Aug 1989.

BIGGEST GAME OF PASS THE PARCEL
The largest game of pass the parcel involved 3,464 people removing 2,000 wrappers from a 1.5 x 0.9 x 0.9-m (5 x 3 x 3-ft) parcel in two hours at Alton Towers, Staffs, UK, on 8 Nov 1992. The event was organized by Parcelforce International and the gift, an electronic keyboard, was won by Sylvia Wilshaw.

LONGEST GIANT TOP SPIN
A team of 25 people from the Mizushima Plant of Kawasaki Steel Works in Okayama, Japan, spun a giant top 2 m (6 ft 6³⁄₄ in) in height, 2.6 m (8 ft 6¹⁄₄ in) in diameter and 360 kg (793 lb 10 oz) in weight for 1 hr 21 min 35 sec on 3 Nov 1986.

MOST YO-YO LOOPS
Eddy McDonald from Canada completed 21,663 loops with a yo-yo in three hours at Boston, Massachusetts, USA, on 14 Oct 1990. He had set a one-hour record of 8,437 loops in 1990.

BIGGEST YO-YO
A yo-yo with a diameter of 3.17 m (10 ft 4 in) and a weight of 407 kg (897 lb) was devised by J. N. Nichols (Vimto) Ltd and constructed by engineering students at Stockport College, UK. It was launched by crane from 57.5 m (187 ft) at Wythenshawe, Greater Manchester, on 1 Aug 1993 and yo-yoed about four times.

BIGGEST JIGSAW PUZZLES
The world's largest jigsaw puzzle measured 4,783 m² (51,484 ft²) and consisted of 43,924 pieces. Assembled on 8 July 1992, it was devised by Centre Socio-Culturel d'Endoume in Marseille, France.

A jigsaw puzzle consisting of a record 204,484 pieces was made by BCF Holland b.v. of Almelo, Netherlands, and assembled by students from the local Gravenvoorde School from 25 May to 1 June 1991. The completed puzzle measured 96.25 m² (1,036 ft²)

TALLEST TOY BRICK STRUCTURE
A 25.05-m-tall (82-ft 2-in) toy brick pyramid was built by a team of 800 people to commemorate the inauguration of Taiwanese president Lee Teng-hui. The tower burned down almost immediately after it was constructed in Taipei, Taiwan, in May 1996.

MOST WORLD TIDDLYWINKS TITLES
Larry Kahn (USA) won the singles title 16 times from 1983 to 1997 and the pairs title nine times between 1978 and 1997.

Geoff Myers and Andy Purvis won seven consecutive pairs titles from 1991 to 1995.

HIGHEST TIDDLYWINK JUMP
The high-jump record is 3.49 m (11 ft 5 in), by Adrian Jones, David Smith and Ed Wynn from Cambridge University Tiddlywinks Club, UK, all on 21 Oct 1989.

LONGEST TIDDLYWINK JUMP
A 9.52-m (31-ft 3-in) jump was made by Ben Soares (St Andrews Tiddlywinks Society) in Jan 1995.

CRICKET SPITTING
Every year thousands of people visit the annual Bug Bowl at Purdue University in West Lafayette, Indiana, USA. The three-day insect celebration includes a cricket-spitting contest, cockroach racing and tractor-pulling (using tiny tractors) and an insect petting zoo, and offers an insect menu including Mealworm Chow Mein and Caterpillar Crunch with Wax Worms. The Bug Bowl was founded by the university's professor of entomology Tom Turpin in 1990 as a way to stir up campus interest in entomology. Word spread and the event went public, attracting 1,500 bug-cravers in its first year. The following year the Bug Bowl was formalized, and in 1997 it was attended by more than 12,000 people. In April 1997 11-year-old Matt Criswell, seen left, competed in the first cricket-spitting contest, which proved popular with both participants and spectators. The contest was open to people of all ages, who had to spit dead crickets as far as possible, and was split into four groups: junior and senior categories for men and women. The adult women were said to be the most reluctant participants.

MOST TIDDLEWINKS POTTED

The world record for potting winks in relay is 41 in three minutes, by Patrick Barrie, Nick Inglis, Geoff Myers and Andy Purvis of the Cambridge University Tiddlywinks Club, UK, on 21 Oct 1989 and 14 Jan 1995.

FASTEST GAME OF SOLITAIRE

Stephen Twigge played a game of solitaire lasting 10 seconds, at Scissett Baths, W Yorks, UK, on 2 Aug 1991.

HIGHEST SCRABBLE SCORES

The highest competitive single turn score recorded is 392, by Dr Saladin Karl Khoshnaw at Manchester, UK, in April 1982. He laid down 'CAZIQUES', which means 'native chiefs of West Indian aborigines'.

The highest score achieved on the opening move is 124, by Sam Kantimathi at Portland, Oregon, USA, in July 1993. He laid the word 'BEZIQUE', a whist-like card game.

MOST WORLD DRAUGHTS TITLES

US draughts player Walter Hellman won a record-breaking eight world titles during his tenure as World Champion from 1948 to 1975.

MOST WORLD CHESS TITLES

The USSR won the biennial men's team title (Olympiad) a record 18 times between 1952 and 1990 and the women's team title a record 11 times between 1957 and 1986.

FEWEST GAMES LOST BY A WORLD CHESS CHAMPION

José Raúl Capablanca (Cuba) lost only 34 games out of 571 in his adult career from 1909 to 1939. He was unbeaten from 10 Feb 1916 to 21 March 1924 (63 games) and was World Champion from 1921 to 1927.

YOUNGEST WORLD CHESS CHAMPIONS

Gary Kasparov (USSR, now Russia) won the title on 9 Nov 1985 at the age of 22 years 210 days.

Maya Grigoryevna Chiburdanidze (USSR, now Georgia) won the women's title aged 17 in 1978.

SLOWEST CHESS MOVES

The slowest move played since time clocks were introduced was 2 hr 20 min, by Francisco Torres Trois on his seventh move against Luis Santos at Vigo, Spain, in 1980.

The slowest reported move in an official event before the use of time clocks is reputed to have been made by Louis Paulsen (Germany) against Paul Morphy (USA) at the first American Chess Congress, New York, on 29 Oct 1857. The game ended in a draw on move 56 after 15 hours of play, of which Paulsen used about 11 hours.

The most moves known in a Master game was 269, in the tie between Ivan Nikolic and Goran Arsovic in a tournament in Belgrade, Yugoslavia, in Feb 1989. The game lasted 20 hr 15 min.

MOST CHESS OPPONENTS

The most consecutive games played is 686 with 16 defeats, by Gert Jan Ludden (Netherlands) over 29½ hours at Gouda, Netherlands, from 24 to 25 Oct 1997.

The record for the greatest number of games to have been played simultaneously is 310, with just two defeats, by Ulf Andersson (Sweden) at Älvsjö, Sweden, from 6 to 7 Jan 1996.

FASTEST BATH TUB RACERS

Above, a replica bath tub is raced off the coast of Vancouver, Canada. The record for a 57.9-km (36-mile) bath tub race over water is 1 hr 22 min 27 sec, by Greg Mutton at the Grafton Jacaranda Festival, NSW, Australia, on 8 Nov 1987. Tubs must be no longer than 1.90 m (75 in) and must have 4.5-kW (6-hp) motors. The World Championship Bath Tub Races are held every July. Competitors race from Nanaimo on Vancouver Island across the strait to Vancouver, Canada.

The highest competitive game score is 1,049, by Phil Appleby in June 1989. His opponent scored 253, giving Appleby a record 796-point margin of victory.

The highest score in an Open tournament is 770, by Mark Landsberg (USA) at Pasadena, California, USA, on 13 June 1993.

MOST DRAUGHT OPPONENTS

The Reverend Roy White played 363 games simultaneously, and won all of them, at Leslie Thomas Junior High School, Lower Sackville, Nova Scotia, Canada, on 16 Nov 1996.

LONGEST-HELD CHESS TITLES

The record for the longest ever undisputed tenure as World Chess Champion was 26 years 337 days, by Dr Emanuel Lasker of Germany, who held the title from 1894 to 1921.

The record for the longest-held women's World Chess Championship title was set by Vera Francevna Stevenson-Menchik of Czechoslovakia (later GB), whose tenure lasted from 1927 until her death in 1944. Stevenson-Menchik successfully defended the title a record-breaking seven times.

driving and riding

HEAVIEST VOLUME OF TRAFFIC
The most heavily travelled road is Interstate 405 (San Diego Freeway) in Orange County, California, USA, which carries 331,000 vehicles a day. The 1.44-km (1,584-yd) stretch between Garden Grove Freeway and Seal Beach Boulevard has a peak-hour volume of 25,500 vehicles. The road runs through a built-up area of West Los Angeles to the beach. California has 19 million licensed drivers.

HIGHEST AUTO FLIGHT
In Feb 1998 the world famous stunt driver Brian Carson from Tarzana, California, USA, broke his own 90.8-m (298-ft) 'auto flight' record with a 96.6-m (314-ft) flight in a specially-constructed sedan, at a speed of 149.6 km/h (93 mph). The stunt took place at the Orleans Hotel and Casino in Las Vegas, USA.

FASTEST REVERSE DRIVE
The highest average speed achieved in a non-stop reverse drive exceeding 805 km (500 miles) was 58.42 km/h (36.30 mph), by John Smith, who drove a 1983 Chevrolet Caprice Classic 806.2 km (501 miles) in 13 hr 48 min at the I-94 Speedway, Fergus Falls, Minnesota, USA, on 11 Aug 1996

FASTEST SPEED REACHED ON TWO SIDE WHEELS
Göran Eliason (Sweden) achieved a record speed of 181.25 km/h (112.62 mph) over a 100-m (328-ft) flying start on the two wheels of a Volvo 850 Turbo at Såtenäs, Sweden, on 19 April 1997. Eliason set a speed record of 159.18 km/h (98.90 mph) for the flying kilometre on the same occasion.

LONGEST DRIVE ON TWO SIDE WHEELS
Bengt Norberg of Äppelbo, Sweden, drove a Mitsubishi Colt GTi-16V on two side wheels non-stop for 310.391 km (192.873 miles) in a time of 7 hr 15 min 50 sec. He also drove 44.808 km (27.842 miles) in one hour at Rattvik Horse Track, Sweden, on 24 May 1989.

LONGEST RAMP JUMP IN A CAR
The longest ever ramp jump in a car, with the car landing on its wheels and being driven on, is 70.73 m (232 ft), by Jacqueline De Creed in a 1967 Ford Mustang at Santa Pod Raceway, Beds, UK, on 3 April 1983.

LONGEST RAMP JUMPS ON MOTORCYCLES
The longest distance jumped by a man on a motorcycle is 76.5 m (251 ft), by Doug Danger (USA) on a 1991 Honda CR500 at Loudon, New Hampshire, USA, in 1991.

The longest distance ever jumped by a woman on a motorcycle is 57.9 m (190 ft 2 in), over 12 lorries, by Fiona Beale of Derby, UK, on 14 Aug 1997. She was riding a Kawasaki KX500.

LONGEST WALL OF DEATH FEAT
The greatest ever endurance feat on a wall of death was 7 hr 0 min 13 sec, by Martin Blume at Berlin, Germany, on 16 April 1983. He rode a Yamaha XS 400 over 12,000 laps on a wall with a diameter of 10 m (33 ft), averaging 45 km/h (30 mph) over the 292 km (181 miles 880 yd).

MOST PEOPLE ON ONE MOTORBIKE
The most people on one machine was 47, by the Army Corps of Brasília, Brazil, on a 1200cc Harley Davidson in Dec 1995.

BIGGEST MOTORCYCLE PYRAMID
The 'Dare Devils' team from the Signals Corps of the Indian army created a pyramid of 140 men on 11 motorcycles, without using straps, harnesses or any other aids, and travelled a distance of 200 m (218 yd) at Jabalpur, India, on 14 Feb 1996.

FASTEST MOTORCYCLE WHEELIE
The highest speed attained on a back wheel of a motorcycle is 270.04 km/h (167.8 mph), by Patrik Furstehoff (Sweden) on a Suzuki GSXR 1100 at Bruntingthorpe Proving Ground, Leics, UK, on 26 April 1994.

FURTHEST DISTANCE TRAVELLED ON A MOTORCYCLE WHEELIE
Yasuyuki Kudo covered 331 km (205 miles 1,232 yd) non-stop on the rear wheel of his Honda TLM220R motorcycle at the Japan Automobile Research Institute proving ground on 5 May 1991.

LONGEST BICYCLE WHEELIE
The longest ever bicycle wheelie lasted for 10 hr 40 min 8 sec. It was achieved by Leandro Henrique Basseto at Madaguari, Paraná, Brazil, on 2 Dec 1995.

FASTEST CARAVAN TOW
The world speed record for a caravan tow is 204.02 km/h (126.77 mph), for a Roadstar

caravan towed by a 1990 Ford EA Falcon saloon driven by Charlie Kovacs, at Mangalore Airfield, Seymour, Victoria, Australia, on 18 April 1991.

LONGEST TAXI RIDE

The longest taxi ride on record covered a distance of 34,908 km (21,691 miles) from London, UK, to Cape Town, South Africa, and back, at a cost of £40,210 ($62,908). It was made by Jeremy Levine, Mark Aylett and Carlos Arrese from 3 June to 17 Oct 1994.

LONGEST SKID MARKS

The skid marks made by the jet-powered *Spirit of America*, driven by Norman Breedlove, after the car went out of control at Bonneville Salt Flats, Utah, USA, on 15 Oct 1964, were almost 9.6 km (6 miles) long.

WORST ROAD ACCIDENT

At least 176 people died when a petrol-tanker exploded in the Salang Tunnel, Afghanistan, in Nov 1982. Western estimates put the death toll at c. 1,100.

MOST ROAD DEATHS

Latvia is the country with the highest fatality rate in road accidents, with 34.7 deaths per 100,000 of the population.

LONGEST TRAFFIC JAMS

The longest known traffic jam stretched 176 km (109 miles) from Lyon towards Paris, France, on 16 Feb 1980.

A traffic jam with a record 1.5 million cars was reported on the East–West German border on 12 April 1990.

LONGEST JOURNEY BY CAR

Since 16 Oct 1984 Emil and Liliana Schmidt from Germany have travelled a record 451,231 km (280,609 miles) through a total of 117 countries in a Toyota Landcruiser.

FASTEST DRIVE OVER SIX CONTINENTS

The fastest drive over six continents, with a total travelled distance of more than an equator's length (40,075 km or 24,901 miles), lasted 39 days 7 hr 55 min. It was achieved by Navin Kapila, Man Bahadur and Vijay Raman, who left New Delhi, India, in their Hindustan 'Contessa Classic' on 22 Nov 1992 and returned on 31 Dec 1992.

OLDEST DRIVERS

Layne Hall of Silver Creek, New York, USA, was issued with a driving licence on 15 June 1989, when, according to the date on the licence, he was 109 years old. He died the following year, but his death certificate gave his age as 105.

MOTORCYCLE JUMPING

Robbie Knievel, the son of legendary stunt man Evil Knievel, soared more than 70 m (230 ft) over 30 limousines at the Tropicana Hotel, Las Vegas, USA, in Feb 1998, reaching a speed of almost 161 km/h (100 mph). The stunt was part of a two-hour television special. The 35-year-old gained fame in 1989, when he jumped the 49-m (160-ft) fountains at Caesar's Palace, Las Vegas — a feat that nearly killed his father, who is still partially crippled from injuries he received during the attempt 21 years earlier. Robbie is now said to be planning jumps of the reflecting pool in front of the Washington Monument and of the Grand Canyon, Arizona, USA. He followed in his father's footsteps from an early age: as a nine-year-old he mounted a Harley Davidson 10cc motorcycle, and while his father watched, jumped 1.5 m (5 ft) from ramp to ramp at a practice field.

CIRCUMNAVIGATION BY CAR

The record for the first and fastest circumnavigation of the world by car, under the applicable rules in 1989 and 1991, embracing more than an equator's length of driving (40,750 km or 24,901.41 road miles), is held by Mohammed Salahuddin Choudhury and his wife Neena of Calcutta, India. The first circumnavigation took 69 days 19 hr 5 min, from 9 Sept to 17 Nov. The Choudhurys drove a Hindustan 'Contessa Classic' 1989 car, starting and finishing in Delhi, India.

epic journeys 1

FASTEST TRANSATLANTIC ROW
New Zealanders Phil Stubbs and Robert Hamill raise their national flag to celebrate breaking the transatlantic rowing record by a wide margin. The pair reached Port St. Charles, Barbados, on 22 Nov 1997, after setting out from Tenerife 41 days before. The previous record for rowing across the Atlantic was 73 days, by Britons Sean Crowley and Mike Nestor in 1986.

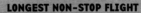

LONGEST NON-STOP FLIGHT
The longest unrefuelled non-stop flight was by Robert Ferry (USA), who flew a Hughes YOH-6A 3,561.6 km (2,213 miles 132 yd) from Culver City, California, to Ormond Beach, Florida, USA, in April 1966.

LONGEST JOURNEYS MADE BY SCHEDULED FLIGHT
The fastest round-the-world journey taking in antipodal points was by former Scottish rugby union captain David Sole, who travelled 41,709 km (25,917 miles) in a time of 64 hr 2 min from 2 to 5 May 1995.

Brother Michael Bartlett of Sandy, Beds, UK, flew around the world on scheduled flights in 58 hr 44 min in 1995, taking in the airports closest to antipodal points and covering 41,547 km (25,816 miles).

The fastest circumnavigation using scheduled flights under Fédération Aéronautique Internationale regulations was 44 hr 6 min, by David J. Springbett (UK). He travelled 37,124 km (23,068 miles) from 8 to 10 Jan 1980.

FASTEST HELICOPTER CIRCUMNAVIGATION
Ron Bower and John Williams (both USA) flew around the world in a Bell helicopter in 17 days 6 hr 14 min 25 sec in 1996.

HIGHEST ALTITUDE REACHED IN A HOT-AIR BALLOON
Per Lindstrand (GB) attained 19,811 m (64,997 ft) in a Colt 600 over Texas, USA, in 1988.

GREATEST DISTANCE BY BALLOON
In Jan 1997 Steve Fosset (USA) flew a record 16,673.81 km (10,406 miles) from St. Louis, Missouri, USA, to Sultanpur, India, as part of an aborted attempt to

fly around the world. He ascended to 7,300 m (24,000 ft), exceeded speeds of 160 km/h (100 mph) and endured storms and sub-zero temperatures in his $300,000 (£180,000) balloon *Free Spirit*.

FASTEST ATLANTIC CROSSING
The record for the fastest ever crossing of the Atlantic is 58 hr 34 min, by the 68-m (222-ft) powerboat *Destriero* in 1992.

FASTEST PACIFIC CROSSING
The fastest ever crossing from Yokohama, Japan, to Long Beach, California, USA, (a total distance of 8,960 km or 4,840 nautical miles) was 6 days 1 hr 27 min, by the 50,315-tonne container ship *Sea-Land Commerce* in 1973. Its average speed during the trip was 61.65 km/h (33.27 knots).

FASTEST TRANSATLANTIC SAILS
The record for the fastest west–east crewed sail is 6 days 13 hr 3 min 32 sec, by the 22.9-m (75-ft) catamaran sloop *Jet Services 5* between Ambrose Light Tower, USA, and Lizard Point, Cornwall, UK, from 2 to 9 June 1990. The skipper was Serge Madec (France).

The fastest west–east solo sail was 7 days 2 hr 34 min 42 sec, by the 18.3-m (60-ft) trimaran *Primagaz* between Ambrose Light Tower, USA, and Lizard Point, Cornwall, UK, from 27 June to 4 July 1994. The skipper was Laurent Bourgnon (France).

The record for the fastest ever east–west crewed sail is 9 days 8 hr 58 min 20 sec, by the trimaran *Primagaz* between Plymouth, Devon, UK, and Newport, Rhode Island, USA, from 5 to 14 June 1994. The skippers were Laurent Bourgnon (France) and Cam Lewis (USA).

The fastest ever east–west solo sail was 10 days 9 hr, by the 18.3-m (60-ft) trimaran *Fleury*

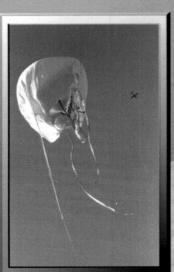

BALLOON CIRCUMNAVIGATION
The race to make the first circumnavigation of the globe by hot-air balloon is dominated by Virgin tycoon Richard Branson (seen above left with Per Lindstrand, Rory McCarthy, and his son Sam Branson), who has been involved in a variety of record-breaking attempts since 1985. In 1986 Branson crossed the Atlantic Ocean in a then record time in his boat *Virgin Atlantic Challenger 11*, and in 1987 he became the first person to cross the Atlantic in a hot-air balloon (the biggest ever flown). In 1991 he went on to set a then balloon distance record when he crossed the Pacific from Japan to northern Canada. In Jan 1997 Branson announced his intention to circumnavigate the globe in a time of 18 days in the *Virgin Global Challenger*, which was designed at the Lindstrand factory and launched in Morocco on 7 Jan 1997. The balloon ascended to its float altitude of 9,100 m (30,000 ft) within the first two hours, but the next day the crew (Branson, Lindstrand and flight engineer Alex Richie) were forced to make a dramatic landing near Bechar Military Base in a desert in north-west Algeria due to technical problems (left). The current balloon distance record is held by Steve Fosset, who flew from the USA to India in Jan 1997.

FIRST UNAIDED SOLO TREK
In Jan 1997 explorer Boerge Ousland (Norway) became the first person to ever cross Antarctica alone and unsupported. His 64-day trek began at Berkner Island and ended at Scott Base, a New Zealand station on Antarctica. During the trip Ousland towed a 180-kg (400-lb) sled loaded with his supplies and used skis and a sail to take advantage of wind currents.

Michon (IX) between Plymouth, Devon, UK, and Newport, Rhode Island, USA, from 5 to 15 June 1988. The skipper was Philippe Poupon (France).

FASTEST TRANSPACIFIC SAILS
The fastest crewed sail was 16 days 17 hr 21 min 19 sec, by the 18.3-m (60-ft) trimaran *Lakota* from Yokohama, Japan, to San Francisco, USA, from 14 to 31 Aug 1995. It was sailed by Steve Fossett and three crew (USA).

The fastest solo sail was 20 days 9 hr 52 min 59 sec, by the *Lakota* skippered by Steve Fossett (USA) between Yokohama, Japan, and San Francisco, USA, from 5 to 24 Aug 1996.

FASTEST CIRCUMNAVIGATIONS
The fastest crewed non-stop marine circumnavigation was 74 days 22 hr 17 min, by the 28-m (92-ft) catamaran *Enza*, which was sailed by Peter Blake (NZ) and Robin Knox-Johnston (GB) from Ushant, France, between 16 Jan and 1 April 1994.

The fastest solo non-stop marine circumnavigation was 109 days 8 hr 48 min, by the 18.3-m (60-ft) monohull *Ecureuil d'Aquitaine II* sailed by Titouan Lamazou (France) from Les Sables d'Olonne, France, between Nov 1989 and March 1990.

DEEPEST DIVES
The deepest ever breath-held dive was 130 m (428 ft), by Francisco 'Pipín' Ferreras (Cuba) off Cabo San Lucas, Mexico, on

10 March 1996. He was underwater for 2 min 11 sec.

The deepest ever dive with scuba (self-contained underwater breathing apparatus) was 282 m (925 ft), by Jim Bowden (USA) in the Zacaton cave, Mexico, in April 1994.

GREATEST OCEAN DESCENT
In Jan 1960 the Swiss-built US Navy bathyscaphe *Trieste,* which was manned by Dr Jacques Piccard (Switzerland) and Lt. Donald Walsh (USA), reached a record depth of 10,911 m (35,797 ft) in the Challenger Deep of the Mariana Trench in the Pacific Ocean.

LONGEST POLAR SLEDGE JOURNEY
The six-member International Trans-Antarctica Expedition sledged a record distance of 6,040 km (3,750 miles) from Seal Nunataks to Mirnyy in 220 days from 27 July 1989 to 3 March 1990.

MOTORBIKE CIRCUMNAVIGATION
British adventurer Nick Sanders completed a 32,074-km (19,930-mile) circumnavigation in a record riding time of 31 days 20 hours between 18 April and 9 June 1997. Starting and finishing in Calais, France, Sanders' trip took him through Europe, India, south-east Asia, Australia, New Zealand and North America.

LONGEST MOTORCYCLE RIDE
Emilio Scotto (Argentina) covered more than 735,000 km (457,000 miles) by motorcycle in 214 countries from 1985 to 1995.

LONGEST CYCLE JOURNEYS
Heinz Stucke (Germany) has travelled 365,000 km (226,800 miles) and visited 211 countries since Nov 1962.

Walter Stolle (Germany) cycled more than 646,960 km (402,000 miles) and visited 159 countries from 1959 to 1976.

John W. Hathaway (Canada) cycled a total of 81,430 km (50,600 miles) from 10 Nov 1974 to 6 Oct 1976, visiting every continent including Antarctica.

Laura Geoghegan and Mark Tong rode 32,248 km (20,155 miles) by tandem from London, UK, to Sydney, NSW, Australia, from 21 May 1994 to 11 Nov 1995.

Thomas Godwin (UK) covered 120,805 km (75,065 miles) in 365 days in 1939. He then rode 160,934 km (100,000 miles) in 500 days by May 1940.

Jay Aldous and Matt DeWaal (USA) cycled 22,997 km (14,290 miles) in 106 days on a round-the-world trip from This is the Place Monument, Salt Lake City, Utah, USA, in 1984.

Tal Burt (Israel) circumnavigated the world from Place du Trocadéro, Paris, France, in 77 days 14 hr in 1992. He covered 21,329 km (13,253 road miles).

epic journeys II

LONGEST SNOWMOBILE JOURNEY
John Outzen, and Carl, Denis and Andre Boucher drove snowmobiles from Anchorage, Alaska, USA, to Dartmouth, Nova Scotia, Canada, between 2 Jan and 3 March 1992, covering a record distance of 16,499.5 km (10,252 miles 528 yd) in a total of 56 riding days. Their crossing of the continent was undertaken in celebration of the 500th anniversary of Christopher Columbus' landing in North America. It was the first such journey to be made entirely on snow.

BEST-TRAVELLED PERSON
The most travelled man in the world is John D. Clouse, a lawyer from Evansville, Indiana, USA, who has visited all of the sovereign countries and all but three of the non-sovereign or other territories that existed in early 1998. His most recent trip was to the disputed Spratly Islands in 1997. John's son George began travelling at the age of 10 weeks and had accompanied him to 104 countries by his fifth birthday.

LONGEST WALKS
Arthur Blessitt from North Fort Myers, Florida, USA, has walked a total distance of 51,824 km (32,202 miles) in more than 27 years since 1969. Carrying a 3.7-m (12-ft) cross and preaching throughout his walk, he has been to all seven continents, including Antarctica.

Steven Newman of Bethel, Ohio, USA, spent four years (1 April 1983 to 1 April 1987) walking 24,959 km (15,509 miles) around the world solo, at a faster rate than Blessitt. He covered 20 countries and five continents.

LONGEST BACKWARDS-WALK
Plennie L. Wingo, then of Abilene, Texas, USA, made a 12,875-km (8,000-mile) trans-continental walk from Santa Monica, California, USA, to Istanbul, Turkey, from 15 April 1931 to 24 Oct 1932.

LONGEST BACKWARDS-RUN
Arvind Pandya of India ran backwards across the USA (from Los Angeles to New York) in a time of 107 days between 18 Aug and 3 Dec 1984, covering more than 5,000 km (3,100 miles). He also ran backwards from John O' Groats to Land's End, UK, in a time of 26 days 7 hr from 6 April to 2 May 1990, covering a total distance of 1,512 km (940 miles).

LONGEST WHEELCHAIR JOURNEY
Rick Hansen from Canada, who has been paralyzed from the waist down since a car crash in 1973, travelled a record distance of 40,075.16 km (24,901 miles 960 yd) by wheelchair over four continents and through a total of 34 countries. He started his journey in Vancouver, Canada, on 21 March 1985 and arrived back there on 22 May 1987.

GREATEST DISTANCE HITCHHIKED
Since 1972 hitchhiker Stephan Schlei of Ratingen, Germany, has obtained free rides over a total distance of 807,500 km (501,750 miles).

LONGEST HORSE-DRAWN JOURNEY
The Grant family from the United Kingdom covered a distance of more than 27,650 km (17,200 miles) during a round-the-world trip in a horse-drawn caravan. They began their journey at Vierhouten, Netherlands, on 25 Oct 1990 and returned to the UK early in 1998, after travelling through Belgium, France, Italy, Austria, northern Yugoslavia (which became Slovenia while they were there), Hungary, Russia, the Ukraine, Kazakhstan, Mongolia, China, Japan, the USA and Canada. They sold their house to finance the trip, which cost them £60,000 ($96,000) over seven years.

LONGEST UNICYCLE RIDE
Akira Matsushima from Japan unicycled 5,248 km (3,261 miles) across the USA from Newport, Oregon, to Washington DC, between 10 July and 22 Aug 1992.

LONGEST LAWNMOWER RIDE
In summer 1997 12-year-old Ryan Tripp made a 5,417-km (3,366-mile) journey by lawnmower across the USA, raising $10,400 (£6,500) for a sick baby in his town. Beginning in Salt Lake City, Utah, Ryan rode the Walker 25-hp mower along secondary roads approved by police, following a lead car driven in turn by a family friend, an aunt and uncle, and his grandparents. Ryan's father Todd followed in a pick-up truck with an equipment trailer. The mower was fitted with road tyres and had extra springs and seat padding to make the trip comfortable for Ryan, who slept in rooms donated by hotels along the route. Nineteen states and 42 days later he arrived at the US Capitol building in Washington DC, where he was welcomed by Utah senator Orrin Hatch. Soon afterwards he was asked to appear on David Letterman's *Late Show* (right). Ryan's next ambition is to make the high school basketball team, but he and his father are already looking for a new record to break.

LONGEST STILT-WALKS
The greatest distance ever covered on stilts is 4,804 km (3,008 miles), by Joe Bowen from Los Angeles, California, to Bowen, Kentucky, USA, from 20 Feb to 26 July 1980.

In 1891 Sylvain Dornon walked from Paris, France, to Moscow, Russia, on stilts in either 50 or 58 stages, covering a distance of 2,945 km (1,830 miles). He walked at a much higher speed than Joe Bowen.

LONGEST WALK ON HANDS
The greatest distance ever covered by a person walking on their hands is 1,400 km (870 miles), by Johann Hurlinger (Austria) in 1900. He walked from Vienna, Austria, to Paris, France, in a total of 55 daily 10-hour stints, averaging a speed of 2.54 km/h (1.58 mph).

LONGEST WALK ON WATER
Rémy Bricka from Paris, France, walked across the Atlantic Ocean on 4.2-m-long (13-ft 9-in) skis.

He left Tenerife, Canary Islands, on 2 April 1988 and arrived at Trinidad in the Caribbean on 31 May 1988, after covering 5,636 km (3,502 miles).

LONGEST LAND-ROW
Rob Bryant of Fort Worth, Texas, USA, covered 5,278.5 km (3,280 miles) on a land-rowing machine. He left Los Angeles, California, on 2 April 1990 and reached Washington DC on 30 July.

LONGEST LEAP-FROG
The record for the greatest distance covered while leap-frogging is 1,603.2 km (996 miles 352 yd), by 14 students from Stanford University, California, USA. They began on 16 May 1991 and stopped 244 hr 43 min later, on 26 May.

LONGEST PEDAL-BOAT JOURNEY
Kenichi Horie of Kobe, Japan, set a pedal-boating distance record of 7,500 km (4,660 miles). He left Honolulu, Hawaii, USA, on 30 Oct 1992 and arrived at Naha, Okinawa, Japan, on 17 Feb 1993.

MOST COUNTRIES TRAVELLED THROUGH IN 24 HOURS
The most countries travelled through entirely by train in 24 hours is 11, by Alison Bailey, Ian Bailey, John English and David Kellie from 1 to 2 May 1993. They started in Hungary and continued through Slovakia, the Czech Republic, Austria, Germany, Liechtenstein, Switzerland, France, Luxembourg and Belgium, and arrived in the Netherlands 22 hr 10 min after setting off.

FURTHEST PIZZA DELIVERY
Eagle Boys Dial-a-Pizza in Christchurch, New Zealand, regularly deliver pizzas to Scott Base, Antarctica, for the New Zealand Antarctic Programme team. The pizzas are cooked, packed and shipped to a military air field, where they are loaded onto a C.130 Hercules. They arrive at the base nine hours later, with re-heating instructions.

MICROLIGHTING
Britons Brian Milton (right) and his co-pilot Keith Reynolds pose for photographers in London, UK, in Jan 1998, just prior to setting out on their attempt to make the first ever circumnavigation of the globe by microlight aircraft. The pair hoped to make the journey in their GT Global flyer in a time of 80 days, over a route that included Europe, the Middle East, India, Japan and the USA.

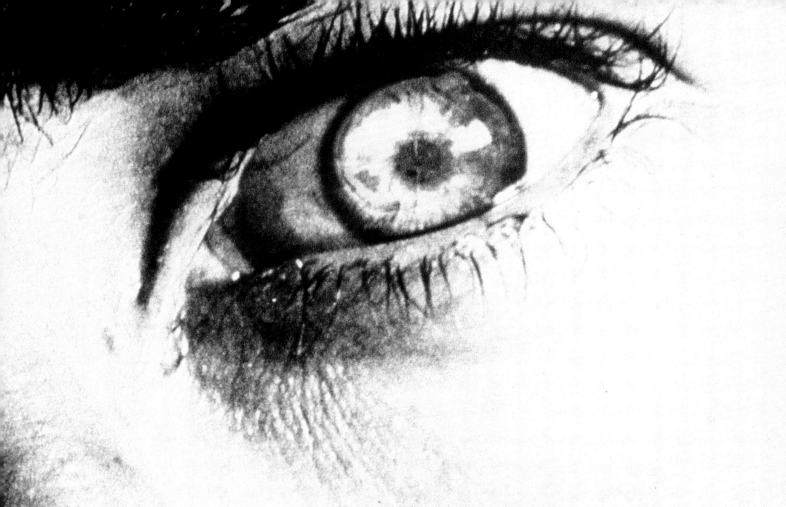

extraordinary

lives

crime

HIGHEST MURDER RATES

The country with the greatest number of murders is the USA, which has around 25,000 cases of homicide per year.

The country with the highest murder rate in proportion to its population varies from year to year, but Colombia has had a consistently high rate of 77.5 per 100,000 for the last 10 years (more than eight times higher than the US rate). It has more than 27,000 murder victims a year.

The city with the highest murder rate in proportion to its population is the Colombian capital Bogotá, where violence is the leading cause of death for individuals aged between 10 and 60. The city has about 8,600 murders per year — an average of 23 per day.

MOST PROLIFIC MURDERERS

Behram, a member of the Thuggee cult, strangled at least 931 victims with his yellow and white cloth strip or *ruhmal* in the Oudh district of India between 1790 and 1840.

The most prolific murderer of all time in the western world, and the most prolific ever female murderer, was Elizabeth Bathori.

The niece of Stephen Bathori, who became King of Poland in 1575, she is alleged to have killed more than 600 girls and young women in order to drink and bathe in their blood, ostensibly to preserve her youth. When the murders were discovered, the countess was walled up in her home, Csej Castle in Transylvania (now in Romania), from 1610 until her death in 1614.

The most prolific murderer of the 20th century was the bandit leader Teófilo 'Sparks' Rojas, who is said to have killed between 592 and 3,500 people from 1945 to his death in an ambush near Armenia, Colombia, on 22 Jan 1963.

The most prolific known serial killer of recent times was Pedro Lopez, who killed a total of 300 young girls in Colombia, Peru and Ecuador. Known as the 'Monster of the Andes', Lopez was charged on 57 counts of murder in Ecuador in 1980 and sentenced to life imprisonment.

The Mexican sisters Delfina and Maria de Jesus Gonzales, who abducted girls to work in brothels, formed the world's most prolific ever murder partnership. Known to have murdered at least 90 of their victims but suspected to have killed many more, Delfina and Maria were sentenced to 40 years' imprisonment in 1964.

The world's biggest ever mass killing carried out by one person took place in April 1982, when policeman Wou Bom-kon went on a drunken eight-hour rampage in the Kyong Sang-namdo province of South Korea. He killed a total of 57 people and wounded another 35 with 176 rounds of rifle ammunition and hand grenades, before blowing himself up with a grenade.

The world's most prolific ever murderer by poison was nurse Jane Toppan of Massachusetts, USA, who killed between 30 and 100 patients with morphine or atropine over a period of 20 years. In 1902 Toppan confessed to a total of 30 murders but claimed that they had been acts of mercy. She was committed to a mental institution.

MOST ASSASSINATION ATTEMPTS

Charles de Gaulle, who was president of France from 1958 to 1969, was the target for the greatest number of failed assassination attempts on any head of state in modern times. He is reputed to have survived a total of 31 plots against his life between 1944 and 1966.

BIGGEST CRIMINAL ORGANIZATION

The Six Great Triads of China form the largest organized crime association in the world today, with an estimated 100,000-plus members worldwide. The five Triads with headquarters in Taiwan and Hong Kong have recently been joined by the Great Circle Triad, which is based in Shanghai, China.

MOST BANKS CONTROLLED BY A CRIMINAL ORGANIZATION

The Russian *Mafiya*, which has extended into Europe and North America, controls an estimated 400 banks. This allows the organization to launder its estimated annual profits of $250 billion (£156 billion) from drug trafficking.

BIGGEST MAFIA TRIALS

In 1986 a total of 474 Mafia suspects were formally charged in Palermo, Italy. Of these, 121 had fled and had to be charged *in absentia*.

The most publicized Mafia trial in the world took place at Caltanisetta, Italy, in May 1995, when Salvatore 'Toto' Riina, the reputed head of the Sicilian Mafia and the most wanted person in Italy, went on trial with 40 other alleged mob bosses. Riina was charged with drug trafficking, extortion and 50 murders.

BIGGEST DRUGS HAUL

On 28 Sept 1989 cocaine with an estimated street value of

BIGGEST PURPORTED THEFT FROM A NATION

In 1986 the Filipino government claimed that $860.8 million (£569.5 million) had been 'salted' by the country's former president Ferdinand Marcos and his wife Imelda. The total national loss from Nov 1965 was believed to be $5–$10 billion (£3–£6 billion). The presidential couple were renowned for their extravagant lifestyle: when Corazon Aquino, Marcos' successor, opened the Malancanang Palace she found 3,000 pairs of shoes, 2,000 ball gowns, 1,000 unopened packets of tights, 200 Marks & Spencer girdles and 500 bras that had belonged to the former First Lady. When they were toppled by 'People Power' in 1986, Ferdinand and Imelda fled to Hawaii, USA, and Ferdinand died in exile in 1989. Imelda was allowed back into the Philippines in 1991, and the following year she returned again with her husband's body, which was buried there. Imelda was found guilty of corruption in 1998, shortly after an unsuccessful bid for the presidency. The conviction is subject to appeal.

$6–7 billion (£3.7–4.4 billion) was seized in a raid on a warehouse in Los Angeles, California, USA. The 20-tonne haul was prompted by a tip-off from a local resident who had complained about heavy lorry traffic and people leaving the warehouse "at odd hours and in a suspicious manner".

BIGGEST ROBBERIES

The robbery of the Reichsbank following the collapse of Germany during April and May 1945 was the world's biggest ever bank robbery. The book *Nazi Gold* estimated that the total haul would have been worth $3.34 billion (£2.5 billion) at 1984 values.

During the extreme civil disorder that took place in Beirut, Lebanon, in 1976, a guerrilla force blasted the vaults of the British Bank of the Middle East in Bab Idriss and cleared out safe-deposit boxes with contents valued by the former finance minister Lucien Dahdah at $50 million (£22 million) and by another source at an "absolute minimum" of $20 million (£9 million).

The biggest ever jewel robbery on record took place in Aug 1994, when gems with an estimated value of $46 million

VIOLENT CRIME

Despite an alleged decline in violent crime since 1994, the United States probably has the highest incidence of armed robbery in the world. More than 620,000 cases of robbery are officially recorded each year, with firearms being used in around 30% of these crimes. Firearms are used in more than 1.28 million cases of murder, rape, robbery and aggravated assault in the USA each year.

(£30 million) were stolen from the jewellery shop at the Carlton Hotel in Cannes, France, by a three-man gang. A security guard was seriously injured in the raid.

The largest object ever to have been stolen by one person was the 10,639-dwt *SS Orient Trader*, which was slashed free from Wolfe's Cove, St. Lawrence Seaway, Canada, by N. William Kennedy on 5 June 1966. The vessel drifted to a waiting blacked-out tug, thus evading a ban on any shipping movements during a violent wildcat waterfront strike. It then set sail for Spain.

BIGGEST RANSOMS

A hall full of gold and silver worth a total of $1.6 billion (£1 billion) at today's values was paid to the Spanish conquistador Francisco Pizarro at Cajamarca, Peru, for the release of Atahualpa, the last Inca emperor, in the 16th century.

In 1975 the record sum of $57.7 million (£26 million) was paid to the left-wing urban guerrilla group Montoneros for the release of brothers Jorge and Juan Born, of the family firm Bunge and Born, in Buenos Aires, Argentina.

BIGGEST BANK FRAUD

In 1989 the Banca Nazionale del Lavoro, Italy, admitted that it had been defrauded of a huge amount of funds when its branch in Atlanta, Georgia, USA, made unauthorized loan commitments to Iraq. The loss was subsequently estimated to be about $5 billion (£3 billion).

BIGGEST BANKNOTE FORGERY

The German Third Reich's forging operation during WWII involved more than £130 million ($216 million) in counterfeit British notes, produced by 140 prisoners at Sachsenhausen concentration camp.

BIGGEST WHITE-COLLAR CRIME

In Feb 1997 the copper trader Yasuo Hamanaka pleaded guilty to fraud and forgery in connection with illicit trading that had cost Sumitomo, Japan's largest trading company, an estimated $2.6 billion (£1.58 billion) over a 10-year period of unauthorized transactions. The case recalled two other trading scandals that hit the Daiwa Bank, Japan, and Barings Bank, UK, both in 1995.

punishment

CAPITAL PUNISHMENT
The electric chair as a method of execution was thought up by Dr Albert Southwick in 1881. Southwick, a US dentist, believed that it would be a painless and humane method of killing criminals, and told a senator friend of his, who thought that it would be a good replacement for hanging. The state of New York was the first to introduce electrocution, in 1888, and the following year the world's first Electrical Execution law was passed. The first ever person to be killed in the electric chair was William Lelmer, who had murdered his lover Matilda with an axe. Between 1891 and 1963 a further 614 inmates were executed in the Sing Sing electric chair. The death penalty has now been abolished in half of the countries of the world: 97 countries in total still employ it.

LARGEST PRISONS
The largest known prison in modern times was the State Prison of Southern Michigan, USA, which had a peak maximum capacity of 6,500 inmates.

Kresty Prison in St Petersburg, Russia, houses between 6,000 and 6,500 inmates.

MOST EXPENSIVE PRISONS
The most expensive civil prison to maintain was Alcatraz in San Francisco Bay, California, USA. Nicknamed 'the Rock', it became a federal maximum security prison in 1933 and was closed by the government in 1963, when the annual cost of running and maintaining it had risen to double that of any other prison in the USA.

The most expensive prisons on record today (figures are not kept in all countries) are US maximum security prisons, where the 'cost per bed' exceeds $155,000 (£92,000) a year or $425 (£252) a day.

MOST PRISONERS
Some human-rights organizations have estimated that there are currently approximately 20 million prisoners in China (1,658 per 100,000 people), but this figure has never been officially acknowledged.

The highest prison population per capita among countries for which statistics are available is in the USA, which has 1.75 million prisoners, or one person in every 147 of the US population.

FEWEST PRISONERS
Slovenia has less than 500 prisoners in a population of almost 2 million. Few offenders are jailed: community service, probation and similar schemes are employed where possible.

MOST OVERCROWDED PRISONS
The most overcrowded prisons today are in the former Soviet republic of Turkmenistan, where several prisoners died of suffocation in overcrowded cells in 1996 and 1997.

The number of people detained in the Central African state of Rwanda is so great that many prisoners are held in tents and former warehouses.

MOST RAPID MODERN INCREASE IN THE PRISON POPULATION
The number of convicted detainees in Italy doubled to 55,000 between 1990 and 1995.

MOST PRISONERS AWAITING TRIAL
In 1997 more than 35,000 people were awaiting trial in Nigerian jails. Some had been detained for more than 10 years.

MOST EXECUTIONS
China exercises the death penalty more than any other country: in 1996 about 2,200 of the 2,930-plus executions worldwide took place in China.

MOST PEOPLE HANGED
The record for the greatest number of people hanged from one gallows was set by William Duly, who executed 38 Sioux Indians outside Mankato, Minnesota, USA, in Dec 1862.

A Nazi *feldkommandant* simultaneously hanged a total of 50 Greek resistance men as a reprisal measure in Athens, Greece, on 22 July 1944.

MOST LEGAL HANGINGS SURVIVED
Joseph Samuel was sentenced to death for murder in Sydney, NSW, Australia, in 1803, and survived three attempts to execute him. The first attempt failed when the rope broke, the second attempt misfired when the replacement rope stretched so much that Samuel's feet touched the ground and the third attempt was aborted when the second replacement rope broke. Samuel was reprieved.

John Lee escaped execution three times at Exeter, Devon, UK, in 1885: the trap-door failed to open on each attempt.

MOST FAMOUS POLITICAL PRISONER
Nelson Mandela and Bill Clinton are seen in the cell on Robben Island where Nelson spent more than 27 years in prison. In the 1980s Mandela was often described as 'the world's most famous political prisoner'. He was, however, one of many national leaders who have been political prisoners. Kim Dae Jung, president of South Korea, was detained by a previous military regime, as was Argentinian president Carlos Menem. Among the East European leaders detained during the Communist era are presidents Vaclav Havel (of the Czech Republic) and Arpad Goncz (of Hungary).

MOST WITCHES BURNED
At least 1,500 alleged witches were burnt at the stake in less than a decade in the towns of Wurzburg and Bamberg, Germany, in the mid 17th century.

A total of 133 witches were burnt in one day at Quedlinburg near Leipzig, Saxony, Germany, in 1589.

MOST PRISONERS ON DEATH ROW
In 1996 there were more than 3,150 prisoners on death row in the 39 US states in which the death penalty is exercised.

LONGEST TIME ON DEATH ROW
Sadamichi Hirasawa from Japan was convicted of poisoning bank employees with potassium cyanide in order to steal $370 (£100) in 1948. He died in Sendai Prison, Japan, aged 94, after 39 years on death row.

LONGEST SENTENCES
Chamoy Thipyaso and seven of her associates were each jailed for 141,078 years by the Bangkok Criminal Court, Thailand, on 27 July 1989. They were found guilty of swindling the public.

A 384,912-year sentence was demanded at the prosecution of Gabriel March Grandos at Palma de Majorca, Spain, on 11 March 1972. The former postman had failed to deliver 42,768 letters.

The longest sentence ever imposed on a mass murderer was 21 consecutive life sentences and 12 death sentences, for John Gacy, who killed 33 boys and young men between 1972 and 1978. He was sentenced by a jury in Chicago, Illinois, USA, in March 1980 and executed in May 1994.

LONGEST TIME SERVED
Paul Geidel was convicted of second-degree murder at the age of 17 in Sept 1911 and released from the Fishkill Correctional Facility, Beacon, New York, USA, at the age of 85, in 1980. Geidel, who first refused parole in 1974, had served 68 years 245 days.

LONGEST-SERVING PRISONER OF CONSCIENCE
Kim Sung-myun served 43 years 10 months in Seoul, South Korea, after being arrested in 1951 for supporting North Korea.

OLDEST PRISONER
Bill Wallace spent the last 63 years of his life in Aradale Psychiatric Hospital at Ararat, Victoria, Australia, after shooting a man dead in Dec 1925. He died in 1989, aged 107.

BIGGEST JAILBREAK
On 11 Feb 1979 approximately 11,000 inmates of Gasr prison, Tehran, Iran, took advantage of an attempt to rescue two US prisoners and the Islamic revolution to make history's largest ever jailbreak.

LONGEST ESCAPE BY A RECAPTURED PRISONER
In 1923 Leonard Fristoe escaped from Nevada State Prison, USA, where he had been jailed for killing two sheriff's deputies in 1920. He was turned in by his son at the age of 77 in 1969, after almost 46 years of freedom.

MOST ARRESTS
By April 1988 Tommy Johns from Queensland, Australia, had been convicted for drunkenness almost 3,000 times since 1957.

BIGGEST ARREST
The biggest known mass arrest in a democratic country occurred when 15,617 demonstrators were rounded up by South Korean police in July 1988 to ensure security prior to the Olympic Games in Seoul.

BIGGEST FINE
The sum of $650 million (£335 million) was imposed on the US securities house Drexel Burnham Lambert in 1988 for insider trading. Of this $300 million (£164 million) was direct fines; the balance was to be put into an account to satisfy claims of parties that could prove they were defrauded by Drexel's actions.

HIGHEST FINE ON ONE PERSON
The highest fine imposed on an individual was $200 million (£112 million), in settlement of a criminal racketeering and securities fraud suit brought by the US government against Michael Milken in 1990. Originally 98 counts were filed against Milken, but 92 were dropped in exchange for Milken's plea of guilty. Milken also agreed to settle civil charges filed by the Securities and Exchange Commission. He was released from a 10-year prison sentence in Jan 1993. In addition he received three years on probation and 5,400 hours of community service.

hoaxes and confidence tricks

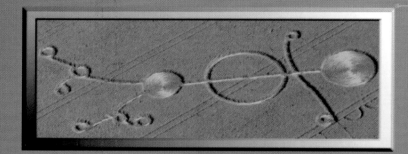

BIGGEST PANIC CAUSED BY A RADIO PLAY

Orson Welles' radio play *War of the Worlds*, based on H. G. Wells' novel chronicling a Martian invasion of Earth, caused unintentional mass hysteria in the USA when it was broadcast on 30 Oct 1938. Several million listeners who tuned in late missed the introduction and caught what they believed were a series of special radio bulletins describing the alien events. Some listeners, mostly from New York and New Jersey, panicked and fled their homes. The public reaction sparked research into the phenomenon of mass hysteria.

LONGEST HOAXES

Huge footprints discovered on a beach in Clearwater, Florida, USA, in 1948 were believed to belong to a giant penguin until 1988, when a reporter at the *St. Petersburg Times* managed to get the hoaxer to confess. The latter still owned the three-toed feet that were made out of concrete.

In 1912 the reported discovery of a half-human, half-primate skull in the village of Piltdown, Sussex, UK, caused worldwide controversy. Scientists thought that 'Piltdown Man' might be the 'missing link' between ape and man and may be 1 million years old. In 1952 it emerged that a 200-year old human skull had been joined to an orang utan's jaw. *Sherlock Holmes* creator Sir Arthur Conan Doyle was one of those accused of the hoax.

MOST FAMOUS SUSPECTED HOAXES

Big Foot, a giant ape-like creature reputed to walk on its hind legs and live in dense forested regions of the USA, is said to be 1.8–3 m (6–10 ft) tall and weigh 320–1,135 kg (50 st–178 st 8 lb). On 20 Oct 1967 Roger Patterson shot a film that apparently shows Big Foot at Bluff Creek, northern California,

CROP CIRCLES

The depressions in fields known as crop circles were first widely reported in the 1970s, and more than 9,000 have now been sighted, mostly in the UK, USA and Germany. Some people claim that they are caused by alien spacecraft or vortexes; others believe they are hoaxes or the result of unusual weather conditions. In 1991 two British men claimed to have been producing circles since 1978.

but sceptics believe that it was a man in a gorilla suit. There have been hundreds of sightings and several photographs have been taken but their authenticity is still doubted. Along with crop circles and the Roswell Incident, Big Foot is the most famous suspected hoax.

BIGGEST POLITICAL HOAX

In 1967 the book *Report From Iron Mountain* — supposedly a secret US government document examining the drawbacks of world peace — caused worldwide controversy by claiming that war creates vital social and economic controls. It suggested deliberate environmental pollution, modern forms of slavery and birth control and the addition of drugs to food and water supplies to maintain control if peace broke out. Author Leonard Lewin admitted that it was a hoax in 1972, after it had been translated into 15 languages and had fooled many prominent intellectuals.

In 1972 it was claimed that a primitive tribe, the Tasadays, had been discovered in the Mindanao rainforest of the Philippines. The tribe was said to be on the verge of extinction and to have had no previous contact with the modern world. Anthropologists later discovered that the Filipino cultural minister Manuel Elizalde had hired a group of local people to pose as the tribe in order to boost the government's claim to be protecting minorities.

BIGGEST INTERNET HOAX

The original *Good Times* virus hoax started in Nov 1994 and is still circulating on the internet today. It relies on people to pass it along rather than spreading from one computer to another by itself. The hoax claims that the virus is sent via e-mail and erases hard drives, and the hoaxers falsely allege that the US Federal Communications Commission have released a warning about it.

BIGGEST JOURNALISTIC HOAX

The Great Moon Hoax of 1835 is the most famous and enduring newspaper hoax. A series of articles describing the discovery of life on the Moon was printed in the *New York Sun* from 25 Aug onwards. Details included the

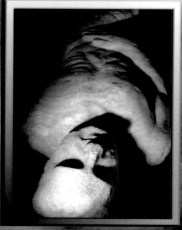

BIGGEST LAWSUIT FOR A HOAX

In 1868 archaeologist George Hull of Binghamton in New York, USA, had a giant carved from gypsum shipped from Chicago to Cardiff, New York, USA, and buried on his cousin's farm. He had been planning the elaborate hoax for two years. Hull had the giant carved as if he had suffered great pain during death and the end result was slightly twisted in agony, with the giant's right hand clutching his stomach. The giant was carved down to the finest of details: it had toenails, nostrils and sex organs, and even realistic looking skin pores that were created with a needlepoint mallet. A year later, on 15 Oct 1869, workers 'discovered' it and it became an instant tourist attraction. It was believed to be either a real fossilized giant or an ancient statue. The circus founder P. T. Barnum offered to buy it from its new owner for $50,000 (£9,400) but was turned down, so he built his own and claimed that he had bought the original. A lawsuit ensued, with each owner claiming the other's giant was a fake. It came to an end when Hull confessed that the Cardiff Giant was a hoax too.

existence of furry, winged men resembling bats and a temple built from sapphires and gold. The articles, supposedly written by eminent British astronomer Sir John Herschel, so intrigued the public that the *New York Sun* claimed what was then the world's largest newspaper circulation of 19,360. Rival editors were panicked into reprinting the articles and Edgar Allan Poe stopped work on *The Strange Adventures of Hans Pfaall* because he felt he had been outdone. On 16 Sept the stories were revealed as false.

BIGGEST DIARIES HOAX
In 1983 British newspaper *The S. Times* fell victim to the biggest hoax in post-war newspaper history when it published the 'Hitler Diaries'. The German weekly magazine *Stern* and the US magazine *Newsweek* were also deceived and published the forgeries. It was later discovered that the diaries were the work of German hoaxer Konrad Kujau, who had also faked some Hitler poetry. The first person to declare the diaries a fraud was the British journalist and historian David Irving, but he then changed his mind

and claimed that they were authentic, days before they were proved fake.

MOST SUCCESSFUL ART HOAXES
In 1936 the little-known Dutch artist Han van Meegeren began painting his first forgery with the aim of proving the ignorance of art critics. Seven others followed, all passed off as the works of Vermeer and de Hooch, and they sold for more than $2.25 million (£523,256). Van Meegeren lived a lavish lifestyle and had bought a mansion in the south of France and 50 houses by his eventual arrest. In Oct 1947 he was sentenced to a year in prison after being convicted of forging signatures rather than paintings, but died in Dec 1947.

BIGGEST FILM HOAX
The New Zealand film *Forgotten Silver* (1995) was alleged to be a documentary about a forgotten pioneer of cinema, Colin McKenzie. Its director Peter Jackson, who also made the successful film *Heavenly Creatures*

(New Zealand, 1994) created the hoax as a satire on the number of historical documentaries made for the centenary of cinema. The story chronicles how McKenzie invented a motion picture camera in 1900 when he was 12, produced his own film stock from raw eggs, discovered how to make colour film stock from a type of berry in 1911, and finally filmed his own death in 1937. The film sparked complaints from deceived viewers when shown on New Zealand TV in 1995.

BIGGEST PHOTOGRAPHIC HOAX
In July 1917, 15-year-old Elsie Wright took photographs of her cousin Frances with a group of fairies dancing in front of her in woodland near Cottingley, W Yorkshire, UK. Photographic experts could not explain how such images had been taken by the girls. On 17 March 1983 — 66 years later – Frances confessed that the fairies had been cut out and painted by Elsie, then held in place by hatpins.

BIGGEST BIZARRE PHENOMENA HOAX
In 1974 Ronald DeFeo murdered his mother, father, two brothers and two sisters at their home in Amityville, Long Island, USA. The house's subsequent owners, George and Kathy Lutz, soon claimed that ghosts drove them away,

and in 1977 a book was published based on their accounts of bizarre phenomena corresponding to the slaughter. A film was made in 1979. The Lutz's story was soon exposed as a hoax, but a further seven novels and films based on the 'Amityville Horror' were released.

BIGGEST PARANORMAL HOAX
From 1983 to 1987 thousands of people believed that they saw a 61–305-m-long (200–1,000-ft), boomerang-shaped UFO covered in multicoloured lights in Hudson Valley, New York, USA. In 1987 the phenomena was exposed as a giant hoax by a science magazine: a group of pilots known as the 'Stormville Flyers' had been flying in formation and attached lights to their craft, making them look like a huge UFO. When they switched the lights off the 'ship' seemed to disappear.

THE ROSWELL INCIDENT
In 1947 an officer of Roswell Army Air Field, New Mexico, USA, issued an unauthorized press release stating that the army had gained possession of a flying disc. This was later denied by the US Air Force office. Years of controversy over whether aliens landed has followed. A 1997 report by the US military stated the 'bodies' found were dummies from a test aircraft. Roswell now has a museum devoted to UFOs. Pictured here is a model of an alien from the museum.

religions rites and cults

BIGGEST SUICIDE BY POISONING
The biggest ever mass suicide in peacetime took place on 18 Nov 1978, when 913 members of the People's Temple cult died after drinking a soft drink, Kool Aid, mixed with cyanide at Jonestown near Port Kaituma, Guyana. The tragedy took place after bizarre rehearsals of mass suicide staged by the cult leader Jim Jones, who had fled San Francisco, USA, together with 900 followers after accusations of financial irregularities. Jones was found to have died of a gunshot wound.

LONGEST PERIOD OF STIGMATISM
Padre Pio (Francesco Forguione), a devout Italian Capuchin friar, bore the stigmata (the wounds received by Christ on the Cross) from 1918 until his death in 1968. They were seen by thousands of pilgrims.

FURTHEST REINCARNATION OF A BUDDHIST LAMA
Following the death of lama Thubten Teshe, the leader of the Buddhists of Mongolia, in 1984, his reincarnated successor, Osel Hita Torres, was found more than 8,000 km away (5,000 miles) in Spain. Torres, who was born in 1985, is the son of Catholic converts to Buddhism.

LONGEST SIEGE INVOLVING A RELIGIOUS CULT
The armed stand-off at Mount Carmel Center, Waco, Texas, USA, by US Federal agents lasted from 23 Feb to 19 April 1993. The compound was the HQ of the Branch Dravidians, led by self-styled messiah David Koresh (real name Vernon Howell). The cult was stockpiling arms and ammunition. Four agents were shot dead during an initial gun battle, leading the Federal forces to lay siege to the compound. On 19 April the buildings went up in flames, and about 80 cult members died, including Koresh. Some of the corpses had gunshot wounds. It is not known how the fire started nor whether the deaths were the result of a suicide pact or mass murder.

MOST MURDEROUS RELIGIOUS SECT
Members of India's Thuggee cult, a secret society devoted to Kali, the Hindu goddess of death and destruction, are estimated to have ritually strangled more than 2 million people in 300 years. The cult was wiped out during the British Raj in the 19th century, when more than 4,000 members were put on trial. Most were hanged or jailed.

MOST HUMAN SACRIFICES IN A RELIGIOUS CEREMONY
The most human sacrifices made at a single ceremony is believed to have been the 20,000 people killed by Aztec priests at the dedication of the Great Temple (Teocalli) at Tenochtitlan (now Mexico City) to the war-god Huitzilpochtli in 1486.

MOST WITNESSES TO A MODERN-DAY RELIGIOUS APPARITION
About 70,000 people saw the Sun 'dance' in the sky during the sixth and last apparition of the Virgin Mary to three children at Fatima, Portugal, on 13 Oct 1915. The globe seemed to fall and rise in a circular motion. The Fatima apparitions have been officially recognized by the Roman Catholic Church.

MOST RECENT RECOGNIZED APPARITION OF THE VIRGIN MARY
An apparition at the cave of Betania, Cau, Venezuela, has been seen by Maria Esperanza Medrano Bianchini at intervals since March 1976, and has also been witnessed by hundreds of other people. It was recognized by the Roman Catholic Church in 1987.

MOST RECENTLY DISCOVERED RELIC OF THE BUDDHA
In 1981 a box containing ashes of the Buddha was found at Yunju, 75 km (47 miles) from Beijing, China. The ashes were divided into eight lots on the Buddha's death c.483 BC in Kusinārā (now Kasia), India, and sent to different parts of Asia for safe-keeping.

MOST INACCESSIBLE RELIC
A relic believed by the Ethiopian Orthodox Church to be the Ark of the Covenant is guarded by one priest in a chapel in Axum, Ethiopia. The guardian, the only person allowed to see the relic or be in its presence, cannot leave the chapel area ever again, and must appoint a successor before his death.

MOST HINDU PILGRIMS
Every three years, millions of people gather at India's Kumbha Mela, the largest Hindu festival in the world. According to myth, the son of the Hindu god Indra was chased by demons for a pot of Ambrosia (the food of the gods) and spilled the nectar at four sites — Nasiik, Ujjain, Haridwar and Prayag. The 1½-month-long Kumbha Mela is held at the four sites in rotation, but the biggest event takes place at Prayag ('place of purification') every 12 years. On 30 Jan 1995, during a 'half' Kumbha Mela in Prayag, a record 20 million pilgrims bathed in the cold waters at the confluence of the Ganges and Jumna rivers — a ritual which they believe will absolve them of all sins. An estimated 200,000 people an hour had entered Prayag the day before the festival. The pilgrims began bathing soon after midnight, and by 10am an estimated 15 million people had been in the water and another 5 million were waiting their turn. The next Prayag Mela will take place in 2001.

MOST FEMALE-DOMINATED RELIGIOUS SECT
Dianic Wicca, a neo-pagan movement, worships a monotheistic goddess and has female-only covens. The feminist witchcraft sect was founded in California, USA, in the 1920s.

MOST MALE-DOMINATED SOCIETY
Mount Athos, a 336-km^2 (129-mile^2) autonomous republic within Greece, bars all females, including domestic animals and birds, and women are not allowed to approach its shores by boat. The republic is occupied by 20 Orthodox monasteries and their dependencies.

MOST COMPLETE MODERN PURDAH
Since the Taliban movement took the capital of Afghanistan, Kabul, in 1996, Afghan women have to wear a loose garment hiding their body and face, with a cotton grill covering the eyes.

MOST THREATENED MAJOR RELIGION
Parseism, a religion of the Indian subcontinent, encourages neither intermarriage nor conversion. Its dwindling numbers are now estimated at no more than 120,000.

BIGGEST WEDDING CEREMONIES
Blessing '97 saw 30,000 couples re-dedicate their marriages at RFK Stadium, Washington DC, USA, in Nov 1997. The ceremony was carried out by the Holy Spirit Association for the Unification of World Christianity, founded by the Reverend Sung Myung Moon and his wife Dr Hak Ja Han Moon. In 1995 Moon married a record 35,000 couples in the Olympic Stadium in Seoul, South Korea, and a further 325,000 via a satellite link.

FASTEST-GROWING CHURCH TODAY
The Kimbanguist Church was founded in the Democratic Republic of Congo (ex-Zaire) by Baptist student Simon Kimbangu in 1959. By 1996 the Church, which is a member of the World Council of Churches, had more than 6.5 million members.

BIGGEST RADIO AUDIENCE FOR A REGULAR RELIGIOUS BROADCAST
Decision Hour, a religious radio show that has been broadcast regularly since 1957 by the US Baptist evangelist Billy Graham, attracts an average audience of 20 million people.

BIGGEST RELIGION WITHOUT ANY RITES
The Baha'i faith, which is practised by approximately 6 million people in more than 70 countries worldwide, has no ceremonies, no sacraments and no clergy. The religion, which emphasizes the importance of all religion and the spiritual unity of humanity, developed through the teaching of two Iranian visionaries in the 19th century.

SMALLEST CHRISTIAN SECT
The Sabbathday Lake community of Shakers in Maine, USA, currently has seven members, making it the smallest surviving Christian sect. The Shakers, formally known as the United Society of Believers in Christ's Second Appearing, were founded in England in 1747 and taken to the New World by Ann Lee, known as Mother Ann, in 1774. The followers of the religion, who formed the first communistic settlement in the USA, claimed they had been 'commissioned by Almighty God to preach the everlasting Gospel to America'.

MOST PROLIFIC CRYING STATUE
In April 1998 a statue brought from the Marian shrine of Medjurorje, Bosnia, was thought to be weeping blood at Sant Marti church, Mora, Catalonia, Spain, but was declared a hoax by local Roman Catholic authorities. The most prolific crying religious statue was a 40-cm-high (15-in) plaster of the Virgin Mary brought from the same shrine by a curate from Civitavecchia, Italy, in 1994. The statue appeared to cry tears of blood on 14 days between 2 Feb 1995 and 17 March 1995. One manifestation was witnessed by the diocesan bishop.

MOST CHRISTIAN PILGRIMS
The House of the Virgin Mary at Loretto, Italy, and the basilica of St Antony at Padua, Italy, both receive about 3.5 million pilgrims a year – more than three times the number who visit Lourdes, France, each year.

MOST MUSLIM PILGRIMS
The annual Muslim pilgrimage (*hajj*) to Mecca, Saudi Arabia, attracts an average of 2 million people a year.

great escapes

MOST LABOUR CAMP ESCAPES
Tatyana Mikhailovna Russanova, a former Soviet citizen who now lives in Haifa, Israel, escaped from Stalinist labour camps in the former Soviet Union a total of 15 times between 1943 and 1954. She was recaptured and sentenced 14 times. All of the escapes are judicially recognized by independent Russian lawyers, but only nine of them are recognized by Soviet Supreme Court officials.

LONGEST FALL SURVIVED WITHOUT A PARACHUTE
On 26 Jan 1972 Vesna Vulovic, an air hostess from Yugoslavia, survived a fall from a record-breaking height of 10.16 km (6 miles 551 yd) when the DC-9 airliner in which she was travelling blew up over Srbska Kamenice, Czechoslovakia (now Czech Republic).

LONGEST UPWARDS FALL SURVIVED
In May 1993 Didier Dahran, who was making his third parachute jump at Boulac, France, was sucked into a freak cyclone current. The reading on his altimeter shot up from 304 m to 7,620 m (1,000 ft to 25,000 ft) before jamming at its maximum. Two hours after his jump, at the kind of altitude that is usually only reached by jet airliners, Dahran's rectangular parachute collapsed in the thin atmosphere, sending him hurtling towards the ground. He launched his emergency parachute and passed out, landing 48.3 km (30 miles) from where he had jumped.

HIGHEST WAVE RIDDEN
On 3 April 1868 a Hawaiian man called Holua rode a tsunami "perhaps 50 ft" (15.24 m) in height in order to save his life when it struck Minole, Hawaii.

MOST LIGHTNING STRIKES SURVIVED
The only person to have been struck by lightning seven times was Roy Sullivan, a former park ranger from Virginia, USA. In 1942 Sullivan lost a big toe nail after being struck, in 1969 he lost his eyebrows, in July 1970 his left shoulder was seared, in April 1972 his hair caught fire, in Aug 1973 his hair caught fire again and his legs were seared, in June 1976 his ankle was injured and in June 1977 he received chest and stomach burns. In Sept 1983 he committed suicide, reportedly after being rejected in love.

LONGEST TIME SURVIVED IN ROOM WITH SUB-ZERO TEMPERATURES
In Jan 1997 Dale Powitsky from Dayton, Ohio, USA, was loading sides of beef into a cold room when the heavy steel door slammed behind him, trapping him inside for two days. To lessen the danger of freezing to death, Powitsky collected the labels from the animal carcasses and set fire to them with his cigarette lighter. He then cut pieces of fat off the carcasses and melted them before dripping the liquid fat onto a pad made from asbestos-lagging from the freezer pipes. This allowed him to generate just enough heat to keep himself alive.

LONGEST DESERT SURVIVAL
A Mexican man survived for a record eight days in the desert in temperatures of 39°C (102°F). Equipped with only 7.6 litres (2 gallons) of water, he travelled 56.3 km (35 miles) on horseback until his horse died and then walked 161 km (100 miles) to reach help. When he was finally found he had gone blind and deaf and lost 25% of his body weight. His hair had turned completely grey.

DEEPEST UNDERWATER ESCAPES
The record for the deepest underwater rescue is 480 m (1,575 ft), by Roger Chapman and Roger Mallinson, who were trapped in *Pisces III* for 76 hours when it sank 240 km (150 miles) south-east of Cork, Republic of Ireland, on 29 Aug 1973. The vessel was hauled to the surface by the cable ship *John Cabot* after work by *Pisces V*, *Pisces II* and the remote-control recovery vessel *Curv* (Controlled Underwater Recovery Vehicle) on 1 Sept.

The greatest depth from which an escape has been made without any kind of equipment is 68.6 m (225 ft), by Richard Slater from the rammed submersible *Nekton Beta* off Catalina Island, California, USA, on 28 Sept 1970.

The record for the deepest escape with equipment is 183 m (601 ft), by Norman Cooke and Hamish Jones from the submarine *HMS Otus* in Bjørnefjorden, off Bergen, Norway, during a naval exercise on 22 July 1987. The men were wearing standard suits with built-in lifejackets, which allow air expanding during the ascent to pass into a hood over the escapee's head.

LONGEST SURVIVAL UNDERWATER WITHOUT EQUIPMENT
In 1991 Michael Proudfoot was investigating a sunken naval cruiser around Baja California, Mexico, when he smashed his scuba regulator and lost all air. Unable to make it back to the ship's hull, Proudfoot found a big bubble of air trapped in the ship's galley and a tea-urn almost full of fresh water. By rationing the water, breathing shallowly and eating sea urchins he stayed alive for two days until he was rescued.

YOUNGEST SURVIVOR OF THE *TITANIC*
Millvina Dean was eight weeks old when the *Titanic* struck an iceberg and sank on 14 April 1912. Although she was travelling third class, Millvina survived, along with her mother

LUCKIEST PLANE ESCAPE
On 9 April 1998 a *Cessna 150* became entangled in power lines and was left hanging by one wheel when its pilot aborted landing and veered sharply about 183 m (200 yd) from the control tower at Boeing Field near Seattle, USA. Authorities immediately cut off electricity in the power lines. The pilot, 47-year-old crane operator Mike Warren, remained in the cockpit — which was hanging upside down halfway between two power poles about 18 m (60 ft) above a main road — for four hours before he was rescued by firefighters. The rescuers gave the uninjured pilot a harness through a window of the plane. He put it on, released his seatbelt and exited from the cockpit window feet first. He then slid down the underside of the plane's left wing into the bucket of a cherry-picker. The plane, which had only suffered a bent propeller, was then lowered to the ground in a harness.

and her 18-month-old brother. Her father, Bert, was among the 1,517 passengers who were never seen again.

BIGGEST RESCUE WITHOUT LOSS OF LIFE

All 2,689 people aboard the *Susan B. Anthony* survived when the ship sank off Normandy, France, on 7 June 1944.

LONGEST PERIODS SURVIVED ON RAFTS

The longest known survival by one person on a raft is 133 days, by Poon Lim of the British Merchant Navy after his ship, the *SS Ben Lomond*, was torpedoed in the Atlantic 910 km (565 miles) west of St Paul's Rocks at 11.45 am on 23 Nov 1942. He was picked up by a fishing boat off Salinópolis, Brazil, on 5 April 1943, and was able to walk ashore.

The record for the longest known survival by two people on a raft is 177 days, by fishermen Tabwai

ANDES CRASH

In 1972 a plane flying from Uruguay to Chile crashed into the Andes, killing 16 of the 45 passengers. For 10 days the survivors starved in temperatures as low as 17.5°C (-40°F), finally having to resort to eating the flesh of the dead. A further 13 people died, either from their injuries or in an avalanche. Rescue came 72 days later, when two of the survivors travelled more than 80 km (50 miles) in eight days to find help.

Mikaie and Arenta Tebeitabu from the island of Nikunau in Kiribati. The pair, together with another man, were caught in a cyclone shortly after setting out on a trip in their 4-m-long (13-ft) open dinghy on 17 Nov 1991 and were found washed ashore in Western Samoa (now Samoa) — 1,800 km (1,100 miles) away — on 11 May 1992. The third man died a few days before they reached Western Samoa.

MOST UNSUCCESSFUL SUICIDE PACT

In March 1996 Taiwanese newly-weds Huang Pin-jen and Chang Shu-mei made a suicide pact when their parents refused to sanction their marriage, but went on to survive four suicide attempts, including hanging, driving their car off a cliff and leaping from the top of a 12-storey building. They stopped trying when their parents agreed to reconsider their position.

MOST PEOPLE RESCUED BY ONE DOG

The most famous canine rescuer of all time is Barry, a St Bernard who saved more than 40 people during his 12-year career in the Swiss Alps. His best known rescue was that of a boy who lay half frozen under an avalanche in which his mother had died. Barry spread himself across the boy's body to warm him and licked the child's face to wake him up, before carrying him back to the nearest house.

LONGEST PERIOD SURVIVED IN AN UNDERGROUND CAVERN

Bats are generally seen as sinister creatures, but speleologist George Du Prisne owes his life to them. In 1983 he was exploring caves in Wisconsin, USA, when he fell into an underground river and was sucked down a water siphon into a cavern. Rescuers abandoned their search after four days, but Du Prisne was alive, surviving on fish and algae scraped from the walls. Determined to escape, he unravelled orange yarn from his jersey and tied it to the legs of a dozen bats. Residents of a nearby town saw the bats and he was saved 13 days later.

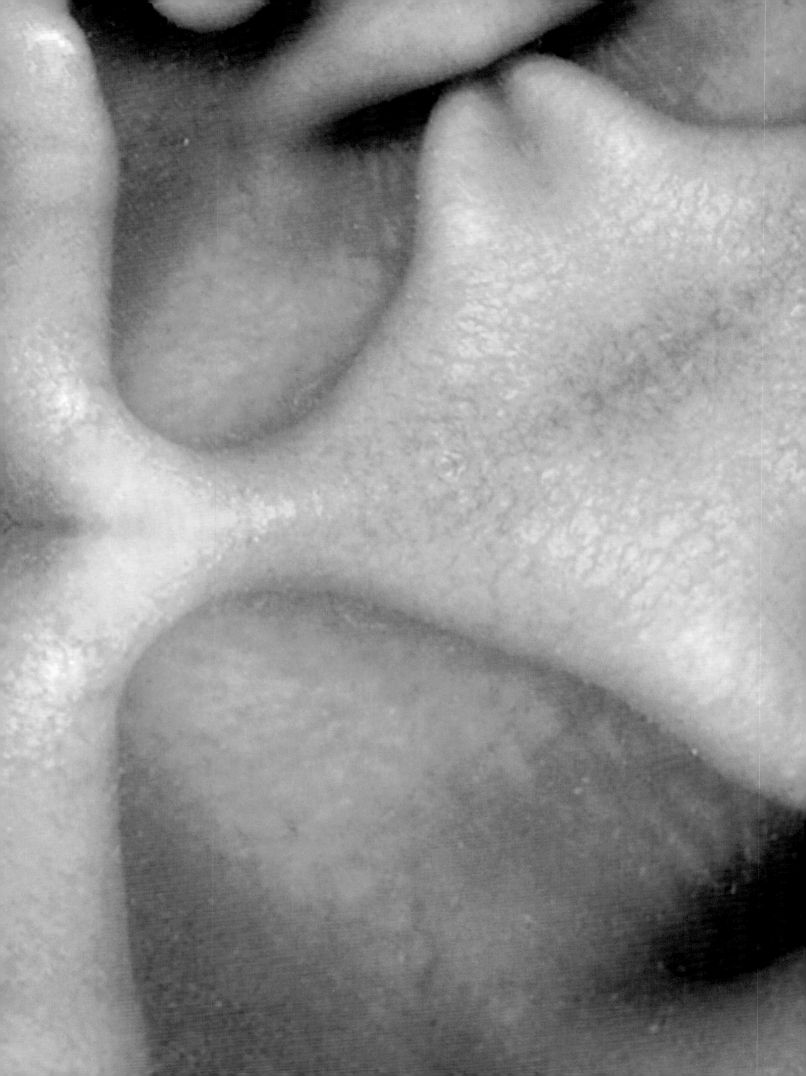

the *body*

big and small

TALLEST TRIBE
The world's tallest major tribe is the Tutsi (also known as the Watussi) of Rwanda and Burundi, Central Africa. Young adult males average 1.83 m (6 ft).

SMALLEST TRIBE
The smallest pygmies are the Mbutsi of Congo (ex-Zaïre), who have an average height of 1.37 m (4 ft 6 in) for men and 1.35 m (4 ft 5 in) for women. Some groups average only 1.32 m (4 ft 4 in) for men and 1.24 m (4 ft 1 in) for women. Pygmy children are not significantly shorter than other children but they do not grow in adolescence because they produce a limited amount of the hormone IGF (insulin-like growth factor).

TALLEST PEOPLE
The tallest ever person for whom there is irrefutable evidence was Robert Wadlow (USA), who was 2.72 m (8 ft 11¹/₁₀ in) tall with an arm-span of 2.88 m (9 ft 5³/₄ in) when he was last measured in 1940, shortly before his death. He would probably have just exceeded 2.74 m (9 ft) in height had he survived for another year.

The tallest man in the USA is Manute Bol, who is 2.31 m (7 ft 6³/₄ in) tall and was born in 1962 in Sudan. He is a naturalized US citizen, and played professional basketball for the Philadelphia 76ers and other teams.

The tallest living British man is Christopher Greener, who is 2.29 m (7 ft 6¹/₄ in) tall.

The tallest woman ever was Zeng Jinlian of Yujiang village in the Bright Moon Commune, Hunan Province, China. Her height was 2.48 m (8 ft 1³/₄ in) when she died in 1982 (assuming normal spinal curvature: she had severe curvature of the spine).

The tallest living woman is Sandy Allen (USA), who is currently 2.317 m (7 ft 7¹/₄ in) in height. Her abnormal growth began soon after birth and by the age of 10 she stood 1.905 m (6 ft 3 in) tall. She weighs 209.5 kg (33 st).

The tallest married couple were Anna Hanen Swan of Nova Scotia, Canada, and Martin van Buren Bates of Kentucky, USA, who stood 2.27 m (7 ft 5¹/₂ in) and 2.2 m (7 ft 2¹/₂ in) respectively when they married in 1871.

The tallest male twins in the world are Michael and James Lanier of Troy, Michigan, USA, who were born in 1969 and are both 2.235 m (7 ft 4 in) in height. Their sister Jennifer is 1.57 m (5 ft 2 in) tall.

The tallest female twins are Heather and Heidi Burge from Palos Verdes, California, USA. Born in 1971, they are both 1.95 m (6 ft 4³/₄ in) tall.

SHORTEST PEOPLE
The shortest female was Pauline Musters, who measured 30 cm (1 ft) at birth in Ossendrecht, Netherlands, in 1876 and at the age of nine was 55 cm (1 ft 9³/₄ in) tall. A post mortem examination after her death from pneumonia with meningitis at the age of 19 in New York, USA, showed her to be exactly 61 cm (2 ft) in height (there was some elongation after death).

The shortest living female is Madge Bester of Johannesburg, South Africa, at 65 cm (2 ft 1¹/₂ in). She suffers from *Osteogenesis imperfecta*, which results in brittle bones and other deformities of the skeleton.

The shortest twins were Matyus and Béla Matina of Budapest, Hungary (later the USA), who were both 76 cm (2 ft 6 in) tall.

The shortest living twins are John and Greg Rice of West Palm Beach, Florida, USA, who are both 86.3 cm (2 ft 10 in) tall.

MOST VARIABLE STATURE
Adam Rainer (Austria) was 1.18 m (3 ft 10¹/₂ in) tall at the age of 21 but started growing at a rapid rate and by the age of 32 was 2.18 m (7 ft 1³/₄ in). He became so weak as a result that he was bedridden for the rest of his life. At his death aged 51 in 1950, he was 2.34 m (7 ft 8 in) tall.

MOST DISSIMILAR COUPLE
When 94-cm-tall (3-ft 1-in) Natalie Lucius married 1.885-m (6-ft 2-in) Fabien Pretou at Seyssinet-Pariset, France, in 1990 there was a record height difference of 94.5 cm (3 ft 1 in) between bride and groom.

HEAVIEST PEOPLE
The heaviest person in medical history was Jon Minnoch from Bainbridge Island, Washington State, USA, who was 1.85 m (6 ft 1 in) in height and weighed more than 635 kg (100 st) when he was rushed to hospital suffering from heart and respiratory failure in 1978.

The heaviest man alive in the world today is T. J. Albert Jackson from Canton, Mississippi, USA, who weighs 404 kg (63 st 9 lb) and measures 3.05 m (120 in) around the chest, 2.94 m (116 in) around

FATTEST MAN CONTEST
'Big is Beautiful' is a motto dear to the males of Sudan's Dinka tribe, who compete each year to earn the title of 'fattest man'. With an unstable future and no other material way of showing their wealth, obesity is a status symbol — it proves that a tribesman has enough money to keep a large herd of cattle and as a result is able to fatten up on the milk, which is traditionally mixed with cows' urine before it is drunk. Not only does a larger appearance set the men above their peers and ensure respect, it also makes them more attractive to the opposite sex. Dinka women choose their husbands according to their size. The Dinkas are famous not only for their traditions: one of the most successful supermodels in the world was born to this tribe. Alek Wek was brought up in a mud hut with the Dinka tribe before making her career in London, UK. She has now appeared on a number of magazine covers, including *Elle*, and earns an average of £10,000 ($16,600) a day. Alek has not forgotten her roots, however, and while she watches her weight for the catwalk she makes sure to send money back to her relatives to help them keep their weight up and their traditions strong.

the waist, 1.78 m (70 in) around the thighs and 75 cm (29½ in) around the neck.

The heaviest ever woman is Rosalie Bradford (USA), who is reported to have registered a peak weight of 544 kg (85 st) in Jan 1987, before beginning a strict diet after developing congestive heart failure.

The world's heaviest twins were Billy and Benny McCrary, alias the McGuires, from Hendersonville, North Carolina, USA. Normal in size until they were six years old, Billy and Benny weighed in at 337 kg (53 st 1 lb) and 328 kg (51 st 9 lb) respectively in Nov 1978, when each had a waist measurement of 2.13 m (7 ft). As professional tag wrestling performers they were billed at weights of up to 349 kg (55 st).

LIGHTEST PERSON
Lucia Xarate, a 67-cm-tall (26½-in) dwarf from San Carlos, Mexico, weighed just 2.13 kg (4.7 lb) at the age of 17. She had increased to 5.9 kg (13 lb) by her 20th birthday.

SMALLEST WAISTS
The smallest waist of a person of normal height was 33 cm (1 ft 1 in), for Ethel Granger of Peterborough, Cambs, UK. She reduced from a natural 56 cm (1 ft 10 in) between 1929 and 1939.

The 19th-century French actress Mlle Polaire (Emile Marie Bouchand) also claimed a waist measurement of 33 cm (1 ft 1 in).

HEAVIEST SINGLE BIRTH
Anna Bates (Canada) gave birth to a 10.8-kg (23-lb 12-oz) boy in Seville, Ohio, USA, in 1879.

LIGHTEST SINGLE BIRTHS
A premature baby girl weighing 280 g (9 9/10 oz) is reported to have been born at the Loyola University Medical Center, Illinois, USA, on 27 June 1989.

SHORTEST TWINS
At 86 cm (2 ft 10 in) John and Greg Rice, seen here appearing in the hit US television show *Guinness World Records™: Primetime*, are the world's smallest twins. Being short has not stopped them from becoming hugely successful. They made their fortunes as real estate speculators in Florida, USA, in the 1970s, and now own and run a multi-million dollar motivational speaking company called Think Big which organizes seminars on creative problem solving. In addition the pair produce, write and even star in commercials for their clients.

The lowest definite birthweight recorded for a surviving infant is 283 g (10 oz), for Marian Taggart (née Chapman), who was born six weeks premature in Tyne & Wear, UK, in 1938. The 30-cm-long (12-in) child was nursed by Dr D. A. Shearer, who fed her hourly for the first 30 hours with brandy, glucose and water through a fountain-pen filler.

SHORTEST PERSON EVER
The shortest ever mature human of whom there is independent evidence was Gul Mohammed of New Delhi, India. In 1990 he was 57 cm (1 ft 10½ in) in height and weighed 17 kg (2 st 9½ lb). He died aged 36 in 1997, of a heart attack after a long struggle with asthma and bronchitis. Mohammed had a lifelong dislike of children, who sometimes bullied and robbed him. He also had a great fear of cats and dogs due to his size.

LARGEST WAIST
Walter Hudson (USA) had a 3.02-m (9-ft 11-in) waist in 1987. His typical daily snack intake was 12 doughnuts, 10 packets of crisps, two giant pizzas or eight Chinese takeaways, and half a cake.

Holy Bible

body parts

OLDEST HUMAN CELLS
Pictured above is a scan of the human body. Cells taken from the body of Henrietta Lacks were missing a chromosome, which means they can live indefinitely, and are still alive in laboratories more than 40 years after her death. Scientists hope these cells may one day help in a cure for cancer.

HIGHEST-INSURED BODY
British glamour model Suzanne Mizzi's 86-61-86-cm (34-24-34-in) body has been insured by a fashion firm for the sum of £10 million ($16.6 million). This includes £5 million ($8.3 million) for her face, £1 million ($1.66 million) for her arms, £1 million ($1.66 million) for her behind, £1 million ($1.66 million) for her legs and £2 million ($3.32 million) for her breasts. The premiums cost £35,000 ($58,100) a year. One condition of the policy is that Mizzi must not get pregnant for a period of three years. She is also banned from hot-air ballooning, standing on football terraces and 'immoral behaviour'.

HIGHEST-INSURED LEGS
Former *Riverdance* star Michael Flatley, now performing in *Lord of the Dance*, has had his legs insured for £25 million ($40 million). He is currently the world's highest-paid dancer.

HIGHEST-INSURED FEET
Charlie Chaplin, the most popular comedian of Hollywood's silent era, had his feet insured for $150,000 (£33,497) in the 1920s. A splay-footed walk was the trademark of Chaplin's character the Tramp.

HIGHEST-INSURED HANDS
Rolling Stones guitarist Keith Richards has had his left (guitar-playing) hand insured for £1 million ($1.6 million).

British boxer Nigel Benn, the former super middleweight world champion nicknamed the 'Dark Destroyer', had his fists insured for £10 million (£16.6 million) in the 1990s.

In 1939 Fleischer Studios in Hollywood, USA, took out an insurance policy for $185,000 (£41,480) with Lloyd's of London, UK, to cover the hands of the 116 animators working on the full-length cartoon *Mr Bug Goes To Town* (USA, 1941).

HIGHEST-INSURED FACES
Hollywood screen stars Rudolph Valentino, Douglas Fairbanks and Mary Pickford all had their faces insured in the early 1920s, the latter for $1 million (£273,149). The actors were all taking advantage of the 'scarred face' policy that had recently been introduced by the Los Angeles underwriter Arthur Stebbins.

Silent screen star John Bunny insured his comical face for $100,000 (£20,550) in 1911. The first major comedian of US cinema, Bunny made a total of 260 short films known as 'Bunnygraphs', 'Bunnyfinches' and 'Bunnyfinchgraphs' between 1910 and 1914.

HIGHEST-INSURED NECK
Hollywood star Kathleen Key, whose 19 films included *College Days* (USA, 1926) and *North of Hudson Bay* (USA, 1923), had her neck insured for $25,000 (£5,177) in the mid 1920s.

MOST CONTROVERSIAL MEDICAL EXHIBITION
Body World: a Look into the Human Body, an exhibition of dissected, skinless human bodies, opened at the State Museum for Technology and Labour at Manheim, Germany, in Oct 1997. Despite causing controversy among many local people, who thought that the display of human limbs and organs — which included lungs infected by cancer — was undignified, the show was an enormous success, with people queuing for up to three hours to get in. It has been estimated that more than 200,000 people saw the show, which was put on by Professor Gunther Von Hagens of the University of Heidelberg and first shown in Japan in 1996, where it attracted 1 million visitors. Hagens is responsible for developing the 'Plastination technique', the process by which dead bodies are put into cold acetone to get rid of water, which is replaced by molten plastics. The plastic then turns hard, making the bodies and body parts shine. The bodies were those of people who had donated their remains to science.

HIGHEST-INSURED EYES
In the 1920s Ben Turpin, the cross-eyed Hollywood film and vaudeville actor whose 114 films included early Keystone Cops comedies, paid the sum of $100,000 (£21,126) to insure against his eyes ever uncrossing.

In 1918, at the peak of her career, the actress Clara Kimball Young, often described as the most beautiful woman in the world, insured her large eyes for $150,000 (£31,479).

HIGHEST-INSURED TEETH
The British entertainer Ken Dodd has insured his trademark buck teeth — the result of a schoolboy cycling accident — for £4 million ($6.6 million). The insurers prohibit him from eating seaside rock and riding a motorbike, and insist that he brushes his teeth at least three times a day. They have also said they would not pay out a claim from an accident involving a fracas in a pub.

HIGHEST-INSURED NOSE
Jimmy Durante, who starred in *It's A Mad Mad Mad Mad World* (USA, 1963) and *Billy Rose's Jumbo* (USA, 1962), had the most famous nose in Hollywood. Nicknamed 'Da Schnozz', he had it insured for $100,000 (£20,395) in the mid 1930s.

HIGHEST-INSURED VOICES
The US pop group En Vogue, one of the most successful all-girl groups ever, have insured their voices for a total of $6.4 million (£4 million).

US rock star Bruce Springsteen, whose multi-platinum album *Born in the USA* (1984) is one of the biggest-selling records in history, has insured his voice for $5.6 million (£3.5 million).

MOST VALUABLE PENIS
Napoleon Bonaparte's penis was removed at autopsy by a team of French and Belgian doctors and first put up for auction at Christie's auctioneers in 1972. About 2.5 cm (1 in) long and listed as 'a small dried up object', it failed to get the

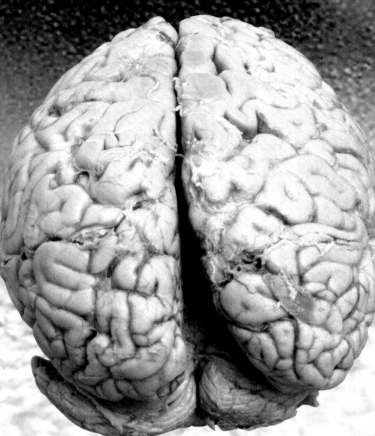

reserve price. It was bought five years later by a US urologist for $3,800 (£2,262).

MOST VALUABLE HAIR

In 1988 a lock of Horatio Nelson's hair sold for £5,575 ($9,475) to a bookseller in Cirencester, UK.

In 1994 two collectors paid Sotheby's, London, UK, the sum of £4,000 ($6,000) for a 10-cm (4-in) lock of Beethoven's hair, said to have been cut off by the composer's father in 1827. The buyers wanted to have it DNA-tested to confirm reports that the composer had African blood and suffered from syphilis.

MOST EXPENSIVE BEARD HAIRS

Hairs pulled from the beard of Henri IV of France in 1793, when his tomb was profaned, were sold for $122 (£78) in Paris, France, in 1994.

MOST VALUABLE TOOTH

In 1816 a tooth belonging to Sir Isaac Newton sold for £730 ($3,785) in London, UK. It was purchased by a nobleman who had it set in a ring.

STRANGEST BODY PART KEPT AS A KEEPSAKE

Joni Mabe of Athens, Georgia, USA, owns one of Elvis Presley's warts as part of her Elvis memorabilia collection.

MOST BIZARRE USE FOR A BODY PART

King Charles I's fourth cervical vertebra was stolen by a surgeon during an autopsy and fashioned into a salt cellar. The novelist Sir Walter Scott used it at dinner parties for 30 years until Queen Victoria found out and demanded its return to St George's Chapel, Windsor, Berks, UK.

MOST ARTIFICIAL JOINTS

US woman Norma Wickwire, who has rheumatoid arthritis, had eight of her 10 major joints replaced from 1976 to 1989.

HEAVIEST AND LIGHTEST BRAINS

The world's heaviest known brain weighed 2.3 kg (5 lb 1^{1}/$_{10}$ oz) and belonged to a 30-year-old male. It was reported by Dr Mandybur of the Department of Pathology and Laboratory Medicine at the University of Cincinnati, Ohio, USA, in Dec 1992. The lightest 'normal' or non-atrophied brain on record weighed 680 g (1 lb 8 oz). It belonged to Daniel Lyon, who died at the age of 46 in New York, USA, in 1907. He was just over 1.50 m (5 ft) tall and weighed 66 kg (10 st 5 lb).

BIGGEST FEET

Excluding cases of elephantiasis, the biggest feet of any living person are those of Matthew McGrory from Westchester, Pennsylvania, USA, seen here in scenes from the hit US TV show *Guinness World Records™: Primetime*. He wears UK size 28 (US size 28^{1}/$_{2}$) shoes. McGrory is 25 years old and stands 2.29 m (7 ft 6 in) tall. His shoes are specially made for him by Converse, and his socks are knitted by his mother, Maureen McGrory-Lacey.

BIGGEST GALLBLADDER

The world's biggest gallbladder weighed 10.4 kg (23 lb) and was removed from a 69-year-old woman by Professor Bimal C. Ghosh at the National Naval Medical Center in Bethesda, Maryland, USA, on 15 March 1989. The patient recovered and left the hospital 10 days later.

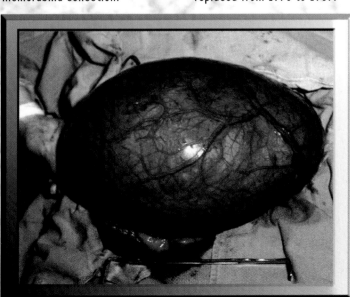

bodily *phenomena*

LONGEST-LIVING SIAMESE TWINS

Chang and Eng Bunker, the famous conjoined twins from Siam (now Thailand), were born on 11 May 1811, married sisters Sarah and Adelaide Yates of Wilkes County, North Carolina, USA, and fathered 22 children between them. They died within three hours of each other at the age of 63 on 17 Jan 1874. The pair, who were never separated because it was thought that to do so would endanger both their lives, earned their living in the USA as a circus attraction in the Barnum and Bailey Circus.

Millie and Christine McCoy were born into slavery in North Carolina, USA, on 11 July 1851 and sold several times. They became very successful in showbusiness under the title of 'Two-Headed Lady' or 'Two-Headed Nightingale'. In 1900 the pair, who were never separated, retired. They died aged 61 in 1912.

MOST SUCCESSFUL SIAMESE TWIN OF MODERN TIMES

Andy Garcia, the US actor who has starred in films such as *The Godfather, Part 3* (USA, 1994) and *Things to Do in Denver When You're Dead* (USA, 1995), was born with his twin attached to his shoulder in Cuba in 1956. The twin was no bigger than a tennis ball and was removed by surgeons minutes after birth.

LONGEST UNDISCOVERED TWIN

In July 1997 a foetus was discovered in the abdomen of 16-year-old Hisham Ragab of Egypt, who had been complaining of stomach pains. A swollen sac found pressing against his kidneys turned out to be Hisham's 18-cm-long (7-in), 2-kg (4-lb 6-oz) identical twin. The foetus, which had been growing inside him, had lived to the age of 32 or 33 weeks.

LONGEST HUMAN TAIL

In 1889 *Scientific American* described a 12-year-old Moi boy from Thailand who had a soft tail almost 30 cm (1 ft) in length. In ancient literature there are many reports of adult men and women with 15–17-cm (6–7-in) tails. Today they are removed at birth.

FASTEST-GROWING HUMAN TAIL

In 1901 Ross Granville Harrison of Johns Hopkins University, Maryland, USA, described a child whose tail grew at an alarming rate. By the time the boy was six months old his tail, which was covered by normal skin with muscular strands but without a bone, was 7.6 cm (3 in) long. When he sneezed or coughed his tail would wag or contract.

LONGEST-LIVING TWO-HEADED PERSON

The Two-Headed Boy of Bengal was born in 1783 and died of a cobra bite at the age of four. His two heads, each of which had its own brain, were the same size and were covered with black hair at their junction. When the boy cried or smiled the features of the upper head were not always affected and their movements were thought to be reflex.

HAIRIEST WOMAN

Julia Pastrana, who was born into an Indian tribe in Mexico in 1834, was covered in hair apart from her eyes. She was exhibited to the public in the USA, Canada and Europe in the 1850s and mummified on her death during childbirth in 1860. In 1964 Marco Ferreri made *La Donna Scimmia* (*The Ape Woman*) based on her life. Julia's mummy was exhibited in Norway and Denmark in the 1970s before mysteriously vanishing. It was found in 1990.

LONGEST BEARDS

Hans Langseth had a record-breaking 5.33-m-long (17½-ft) beard at the time of his death in Kensett, Iowa, USA, in 1927. The beard was presented to the Smithsonian Institute in Washington DC in 1967.

Janice Deveree from Bracken County, Kentucky, USA, had a 36-cm (14-in) beard in 1884 — the longest of any 'bearded lady'.

LONGEST MOUSTACHE

Kalyan Ramji Sain of India began growing a moustache in 1976. In July 1993 it had a total span of 3.39 m (11 ft 11 in).

MOST FINGERS AND TOES

A baby boy was found to have 14 fingers and 15 toes at an inquest held in London, UK, in Sept 1921.

LEAST TOES

Some members of the Wadomo tribe of Zimbabwe and the Kalanga tribe of Botswana have only two toes.

MOST EXTREME SIAMESE TWINS

Dicephales tetrabrachius dipus twins have two heads, four arms and two legs. The only fully documented case is that of Masha and Dasha Krivoshlyapovy (below), who were born in the USSR in 1950. They had three legs (one vestigial) at birth. The earliest successful separation of Siamese twins was performed on *xiphopagus* girls (twins joined at the sternum) by Dr Jac S. Geller in Ohio, USA, in 1952.

MOST BREASTS

The greatest number of distinct breasts is believed to have been 10. Between 1878 and 1898 a total of 930 cases of multiple breasts were reported.

MOST SETS OF TEETH

In 1896 'Lison's case', describing a woman who grew a fourth set of teeth, was published in France.

MOST EXTREMES CASES OF COMPULSIVE SWALLOWING

In 1927 a 42-year-old woman complaining of 'slight abdominal pain' was found by doctors at Ontario Hospital, Canada, to have 2,533 objects, including 947 bent pins, in her stomach.

The heaviest object to have been extracted from a human stomach is a 2.35-kg (5-lb 3-oz) hairball, from a 20-year-old British woman on 30 March 1895.

MOST EXTREME CASE OF MUNCHAUSEN'S SYNDROME

British man William McIlroy had the most extreme known case of Munchausen's syndrome, an incurable condition characterized by a constant desire for medical treatment. In 50 years McIlroy had 400 operations and stayed at 100 hospitals under 22 aliases. The estimated cost of his treatment up to 1979, when he retired to an old people's home, was £2.5 million ($5.3 million).

MOST FAMOUS WIND BREAKER

Joseph Pujol, better known as Le Petomane, was born in France in 1857 and discovered at an early age that he had an amazing talent involving breaking wind. He perfected his skill and eventually put on shows in which he played tunes and imitated noises by breaking wind. When he died in 1945, the Sorbonne offered his family $4,940 (£1,226) to examine his body. They refused.

LONGEST FINGERNAILS

Frances Redmond, pictured right, has the longest fingernails in the USA. They have grown to 48 cm in 12 years. The world's longest fingernails are those of Shridhar Chillal of India, who last cut his fingernails in 1952. At the end of March 1997 the nails of his left hand, from the thumb to the little finger, were 1.4 m (55 in), 1.09 m (43 in), 1.17 m (46 in), 1.25 m (49 in) and 1.22 m (48 in) long.

LONGEST HAIR

Hu Saelao, an 85-year-old tribesman from Chiang Mai province, Thailand, is one of several people claiming to have the world's longest hair. It is a tradition in this part of Thailand for men to have very long hair. Saelao has not cut his hair for more than 70 years and it is now 5.15 m (16 ft 10 in) long. The dispute will be settled on the hit US TV show *Guinness World Records™: Primetime.*

life

OLDEST PEOPLE

The greatest fully authenticated age to which a human being has ever lived is 122 years 164 days, by Jeanne Calment (France). She died on 4 Aug 1997.

The greatest age to which any man has lived is 120 years 237 days, by Shigechiyo Izumi of Isen, Tokunoshima, Japan. He was recorded as a six-year-old in Japan's first census of 1871 and worked until he was 105. He died of pneumonia in 1986.

The oldest ever twins were Eli Shadrack and John Meshak Phipps, who were born on 14 Feb 1803 at Affington, Virginia, USA. Eli died first, at the age of 108 in 1911.

The longest-lived triplets on record were Faith, Hope and Charity Cardwell, who were born on 18 May 1899 at Elm Mott, Texas, USA.

The first case of four siblings being centenarians occurred on 2 April 1984 when Lili Parsons from Teignmouth, Devon, UK, reached her 100th birthday.

MOST DESCENDANTS

The last Sharifian Emperor of Morocco, Moulay Ismail, is reputed to have fathered a total of 525 sons and 342 daughters by 1703 and produced a 700th son in 1721.

Samuel S. Mast of Fryburg, Pennsylvania, USA, had 824 living descendants (11 children, 97 grandchildren, 634 great-grandchildren and 82 great-great-grandchildren) when he died aged 96 on 15 Oct 1992.

MOST LIVING ASCENDANTS

Megan Austin from Bar Harbor, Maine, USA, had a complete set of grandparents and great-grandparents and five great-

great-grandparents (a total of 19 direct ascendants) when she was born in 1982 .

LONGEST FAMILY TREE

The lineage of the Chinese philosopher K'ung Ch'iu or Confucius (551–479 BC) can be traced back further than that of any other family. K'ung Ch'iu's great-great-great-great grandfather K'ung Chia is known from the 8th century BC. Seven of K'ung Chia's 86th lineal descendants are alive today.

MOST LIVING GENERATIONS OF ONE FAMILY

Augusta Bunge from Wisconsin, USA, became a great-great-great-great-grandmother on 21 Jan 1989, when her great-great-great-granddaughter gave birth to a son, Christopher Bollig. Augusta was born in 1879.

YOUNGEST LIVING GREAT-GREAT-GREAT GRANDMOTHER

Harriet Holmes of Newfoundland, Canada, was a record 88 years 50 days old when she became a great-great-great-grandmother on 8 March 1987.

OLDEST MOTHERS

Rosanna Dalla Corta of Viterbo, Italy, is reported to have given birth to a baby boy at the age of 63 in 1994. She had received fertility treatment.

Arceli Keh is also said to have been 63 when she gave birth at the University of Southern California, USA, in 1996. She too had received fertility treatment.

MOST PROLIFIC MOTHERS

The greatest officially recorded number of children born to one mother is 69, to the wife of Feodor Vassilyev, a peasant from Shuya, Russia. In a total of 27 confinements between 1725 and 1765 she gave birth to 16 pairs of twins, seven sets of triplets and four sets of quadruplets (the greatest number of multiple births in one family). Only two of the children failed to survive their infancy.

The world's most prolific living mother is believed to be Leontina Albina from San Antonio, Chile, who produced her 55th and last child in 1981. Her husband states that they were married in

OLDEST PEOPLE

The title of world's oldest person may be one of the most coveted of all but the many claims to it are usually fraught with difficulty and controversy. Amm Atwa Moussa, a former fisherman from Egypt, claims to be 150. In evidence, Moussa (pictured being bathed by one of his 39 grandchildren) states that he was married to his first wife for 60 years prior to a further four marriages and says that he can recall fleeing with his family in 1869 to avoid being forced to work on the Suez Canal. Another contender is the USA's Maggie Barnes, who claimed to be six months older than Marie Meilleur, who held the record for oldest living person from Aug 1997 to April 1998. Neither claimant has documents to prove their date of birth. The minimum *Guinness Book of Records* criteria are a birth certificate, together with proof that it is that of the individual concerned rather than that of a relative, evidence from census and proof of the person's age at a major event in their life. People who live to be 100 are called centenarians, while those who live to 110 are super centenarians. Of the former there are approximately 20,000 in the USA alone, and according to demographers the number of people who live to at least 100 is increasing all the time. Perhaps the most famous super centenarian of all was French woman Jeanne Calment, who died aged 122 in 1997, after outliving 17 national presidents. Jeanne was renowned for having taken up fencing at the age of 85.

Argentina in 1943 and had five sets of triplets (all boys) before moving to Chile.

MOST CONFINEMENTS

Elizabeth Greenhille of Abbots Langley, Herts, UK, is reported to have had a total of 39 children (32 daughters and seven sons) in a record 38 confinements. She died in 1681.

LARGEST PREGNANCY

In 1971 Dr Gennaro Montanino from Rome, Italy, claimed to have removed the foetuses of 10 girls and five boys from the womb of a 35-year-old woman after four months of the pregnancy. A fertility drug was responsible for this unique instance of quindecaplets.

MOST CHILDREN PRODUCED IN A SINGLE BIRTH

A record 10 children (two males and eight females) are reported to have been born at Bacacai, Brazil, on 22 April 1946. Reports of 10 children in one birth were also received from Spain in 1924 and China in 1936.

The record for the greatest fully authenticated number of children ever produced in one birth is nine, to Geraldine Brodrick at the Royal Hospital for Women, Sydney, NSW, Australia, on 13 June 1971. None of the five boys and four girls lived for more than six days. The birth of nine children was also reported in Philadelphia, Pennsylvania, USA, in 1971 and in Bagerhat, Bangladesh, in 1977. No children survived in either case.

LONGEST INTERVAL BETWEEN THE BIRTH OF TWINS

Peggy Lynn of Huntingdon, Pennsylvania, USA, gave birth to a baby girl, Hanna, at the Geisinger Medical Center, Danville, Pennsylvania, USA, on 11 Nov 1995. She gave birth to Hanna's twin Eric 84 days later, on 2 Feb 1996.

WORLD'S BIGGEST BABIES

In Sept 1996 17-month-old Zack Strenkert, one of the largest babies in the world, made an appearance on *The Jerry Springer Show* with his parents Chris and Laurie from Goshen, New York, USA. He weighed in at an astonishing 31.75 kg (5 st) — the weight reached by boys at any age between six and 14. Zack's elder brother Andrew weighed 55 kg (5 st 9 lb) at the age of seven.

SHORTEST INTERVAL BETWEEN THE BIRTH OF TWO CHILDREN

The record for the shortest interval between the birth of two children in separate confinements is 209 days, to Margaret Blake of Luton, Beds, UK, who gave birth to Conor on 27 March 1995 and Bunty on 23 Oct 1995.

LONGEST INTERVAL BETWEEN THE BIRTH OF TWO CHILDREN

The record for the longest interval between the birth of two children to one mother is 41 years, to Elizabeth Buttle of Carmarthenshire, UK, who gave birth to a daughter, Belinda, in 1956, and a son, Joseph, on 20 Nov 1997, when she was 60.

MOST PREMATURE BABY

James Gill was born 128 days premature to Brenda and James Gill in Ottawa, Ontario, Canada, on 20 May 1987. He weighed 624 g (1 lb 6 oz) — about the same as 12 hens' eggs.

OLDEST LIVING PERSON

The greatest fully authenticated age of any person alive today is 119, by Sarah Knauss, seen here with her great-great-great grandson. She was born on 24 Sept 1880 in Hollywood, a small mining village which is now part of Hazelton, Pennsylvania, USA, and now lives in a nursing home in Allentown, Pennsylvania. Six generations of her family celebrated her 119th birthday with her.

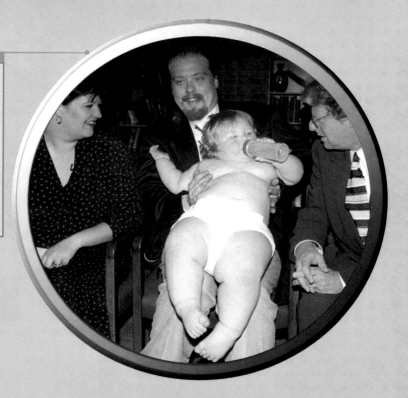

death and disease

MOST HIV INFECTIONS
Above, the HIV virus (in red) is shown attacking a T-cell. According to the UN AIDS Report of 25 Nov 1997, India holds the record for the country most affected by the disease, with between 3 and 5 million HIV positive people. The World Health Organization (WHO) calculates that 20 million people – more than the total population of Australia and New Zealand – are infected with HIV worldwide.

DEADLIEST BUG
The bacterium *Yersinia pestis* caused the death of 25 million people in 14th-century Europe. Transmitted by fleas and rats, it causes bubonic plague, the symptoms of which include fever, headache and chills.

DEADLIEST DISEASES
The AIDS virus (Acquired Immune Deficiency Syndrome) and rabies encephalitis, a viral infection of the central nervous system, are universally considered to be fatal.

Lassa fever, a condition caused by a rare West African virus, has a mortality rate of more than 50%. Marburg fever (Green Monkey disease) and Ebola fever also have very high death rates.

Cholera has killed approximately 20 million people in India since 1900. Death rates can be up to 50% in untreated outbreaks.

Yellow fever is an increasingly rare mosquito-borne infection prevalent in the Caribbean, Brazil and on the west coast of Africa. Some reports suggest yellow fever kills as many as 90% of those infected.

MOST URGENT HEALTH PROBLEM
According to a 1996 report by the WHO, tuberculosis (TB) is spreading rapidly and will kill more than 30 million people worldwide between 1996 and 2005 if this spread continues at the present rate. One-third of people with HIV die from TB.

BIGGEST KILLER OF WOMEN
Tuberculosis (TB) has now become the single biggest killer of women globally. It has been estimated that a third of all women in Asia are infected with it.

MOST DEVASTATING PANDEMIC
The pneumonic form of plague (bacterial infection) killed about 25% of the population of Europe and approximately 75 million people worldwide during the Black Death of 1347–51. Between one-eighth and two-thirds of infected people are estimated to have died of the disease.

MOST KILLED BY INFLUENZA
A record 21,640,000 people worldwide died of influenza between 1918 and 1919.

DEADLIEST MALARIAL INFECTION
Plasmodium falciparum causes malignant tertian malaria, which can affect the brain. It causes fits, coma or even sudden death.

MOST KILLED BY INFECTION
The West African island-republic of Sao Tome and Principe has a record 241 deaths per annum through infectious diseases for every 100,000 people.

NEWEST INFECTIOUS DISEASE
The most recently discovered disease that infects humans is

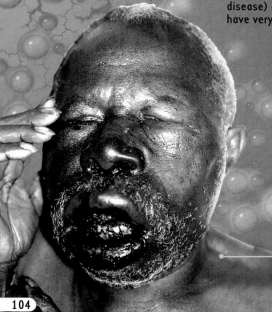

WORST FLESH-EATING BUG
Necrotising fascilitis, the extremely rare disease dubbed the 'flesh-eating bug' by the British press in May 1994 after a number of outbreaks, has been around since WWI and is the world's most dangerous flesh-eating disease. It is caused by Streptococcus type A bacteria multiplying under a person's skin to form a mixture of toxins that attacks the tissue and leaves gangrene in its wake. The only cure is surgical removal of the damaged area. Sufferers report wounds that gush cloudy, bloody-orange fluid, temperatures of up to 40° C (104° F), delirious fevers, oozing pus, purple skin, open holes up to 15 cm (6 in) deep and flesh that falls off in their hands in pieces. Those with a weakened immune system are thought to be most at risk, but it is feasible that a healthy person could contract it. However, new research has shown that injections of a blood product containing immunoglobulins pooled from many people seems to reduce deaths from the disease.

a new type of Creutzfeld Jacob Disease (CJD) which leads to dementia and death. It is probably caused by a piece of protein passed on by cattle suffering from bovine spongiform encephalitis (BSE).

MOST RESURGENT DISEASE
The deterioration in health services and medical supplies following the collapse of the Soviet Union in 1991 has been a major factor in the spread of diphtheria. The International Red Cross estimates that there were 150,000–200,000 cases in the countries of the former USSR in 1997. This compares with 2,000 cases in the Soviet Union in 1991.

COUNTRY WITH THE MOST RESURGENT DISEASES
According to the WHO, Russia is facing a resurgence of diseases, including diphtheria, cholera and tuberculosis. Contagious diseases have made a dramatic comeback in all the countries of the former Soviet Union since 1991, but the problem is greatest in Russia.

MOST COMMON DISEASE
Caused by a group of rhinoviruses of which there are at least 180 types, the cold is almost universal: only those who live in small, isolated communities or on the frozen wastes of Antarctica escape it. There are at least 40 different viruses, either airborne or transmitted by direct contact.

LEADING CAUSE OF DEATH
Diseases of the heart and blood vessels account for more than 50% of all deaths in industrialized nations. The most prevalent direct causes of death are heart attacks and strokes.

HIGHEST CANCER TOLLS
Guernsey, Channel Islands, has a record 314 deaths a year per 100,000 people from cancer. Hungary has 313 deaths from cancer per annum per 100,000 people — the highest rate for a sovereign country.

LOWEST CANCER TOLL
The Former Yugoslav Republic of Macedonia has just six deaths from cancer per annum per 100,000 people.

GREATEST NUMBER OF SUFFERERS FROM ALZHEIMER'S DISEASE
The USA has nearly 4 million sufferers from Alzheimer's disease, the highest number in any country. This degenerative disease leads to confusion and forgetfulness and threatens one person in 20 over the age of 65 in the USA. Among the most well known sufferers is former US president Ronald Reagan.

HIGHEST PERCENTAGE OF POPULATION WITH DEFECTIVE VISION
Around 40% of the population of Japan require glasses or contact lenses.

GREATEST NUMBER OF CARRIERS OF HEPATITIS B
There are 110 million carriers of hepatitis B in China, out of an estimated world total of 350 million. Hepatitis B is found in blood and body fluids, and causes inflammation of the liver.

GREATEST INCIDENCE OF LEPROSY
The country with the most cases of leprosy is Brazil, with 160,000 cases per annum; that is, 10.2 people per 100,000 of the population.

WORST EBOLA TOLL
The highest known toll for an Ebola haemorrhage fever outbreak is 232 fatalities out of 296 possible cases, in the Democratic Republic of Congo (ex-Zaire) in 1995. The disease causes massive bleeding and throws the body into shock.

BIGGEST CREMATION
The world's largest mass cremation took place at a temple in Samut Sakorn province, Thailand, when tonnes of bones and 21,347 skulls were cremated in Dec 1997 to mark the end of urban burials in Bangkok. The bones and skulls represent unclaimed remains from a former Chinese cemetery in the Thai capital.

medical extremes

MOST PILLS TAKEN

The record for the greatest number of pills known to have been taken by one patient is 565,939, by C. H. A. Kilner of Bindura, Zimbabwe, between 9 June 1967 and 19 June 1988. This works out at an average of 73 tablets per day. It is estimated that if all the pills he had taken were laid out end to end they would form an unbroken line 3.39 km (2 miles 186 yd) long.

LONGEST COMA

Elaine Esposito from Tarpon Springs, Florida, USA, fell into a coma at the age of six, after an appendectomy on 6 Aug 1941. She died at the age of 43 years 357 days on 25 Nov 1978, after remaining unconscious for 37 years 111 days.

LATEST POST MORTEM BIRTH

On 5 July 1983 a baby girl was delivered from a woman who had been brain-dead for 84 days at Roanoke, Virginia, USA.

LONGEST TIME SPENT IN AN IRON LUNG

Jame Firwell from Chichester, W. Sussex, UK, has been using a negative pressure respirator since May 1946.

John Prestwich from Kings Langley, Herts, UK, has been dependent on a respirator since 24 Nov 1955.

LONGEST-LASTING TRACHEOSTOMY

Winifred Campbell from Wanstead, London, UK, breathed through a silver tube in her throat for a record-breaking 86 years. She died in 1992.

LONGEST CARDIAC ARREST

On 7 Dec 1987 fisherman Jan Egil Refsdahl suffered a cardiac arrest lasting a record four hours after falling overboard in the freezing cold waters off Bergen, Norway. Refsdahl was rushed to Haukeland hospital when his body temperature fell to 24°C (75°F) and his heart stopped beating, but he went on to make a complete recovery after being hooked up to a heart-lung machine.

OLDEST PERSON TO UNDERGO AN OPERATION

The oldest person ever to have been operated on was James Henry Brett Jr, who underwent a hip operation in Houston, Texas, USA, at the age of 111 years 105 days on 7 Nov 1960.

BIGGEST BLOOD TRANSFUSION

Warren Jyrich, a 50-year-old haemophiliac, required a record 2,400 donor units of blood — the equivalent of 1,080 litres (285³/₁₆ gal) — during open-heart surgery at the Michael Reese Hospital, Chicago, Illinois, USA, in Dec 1970.

HIGHEST BLOOD SUGAR LEVEL

Jonathan Place of Mashpee, Maryland, USA, had a blood sugar level 17 times above average while still conscious in Feb 1997.

HIGHEST BODY TEMPERATURE

On 10 July 1980 — a day when the temperature reached 32.2°C (90°F) with 44% humidity — 52-year-old Willie Jones was admitted to Grady Memorial Hospital, Atlanta, Georgia, USA, with heatstroke and found to have a body temperature of 46.5°C (115.7°F) — the highest on record. He was discharged after 24 days.

LOWEST BODY TEMPERATURE

The lowest authenticated body temperature was a rectal temperature of 14.2°C (57.5°F) registered by two-year-old Karlee Kosolofski of Regina, Saskatchewan, Canada, on 23 Feb 1994. Karlee, who had been accidentally locked outside her home for six hours in a temperature of -22°C (-8°F), suffered frostbite and had to have her left leg amputated above the knee, but made a full recovery. Some people have died of hypothermia with body temperatures of 35°C (95°F).

LONGEST HICCOUGHING FIT

Charles Osborne from Anthon, Iowa, USA, began hiccoughing in 1922, while he was trying to weigh a hog before slaughtering it, and continued until Feb 1990. He was unable to find a cure but led a normal life, marrying twice and fathering eight children.

LONGEST SNEEZING FIT

Donna Griffiths from Pershore, Hereford & Worcester, UK, started sneezing at the age of 12 on 13 Jan 1981 and sneezed an estimated 1 million times in the following year. She did not have a sneeze-free day until 16 Sept 1983.

OLDEST KIDNEY DONOR AND RECIPIENT

In Dec 1995 78-year-old Victoria Whybrew became the oldest kidney donor on record when she donated one of her kidneys to her 77-year-old husband Robert, who is now the oldest kidney recipient on record with the US United Network for Organ Sharing. The couple, pictured left, had been married for 49 years when the exchange took place at the San Francisco Medical Center, California, USA. In May 1998 two couples took part in a medical first by swapping kidneys at the Beilinson Hospital in Petach Tikva, outside Tel Aviv, Israel. Yosef Chillag, a Jewish man, needed a new kidney but his wife Victoria was not a good match. Victoria did match Suham Hamash, an Arab woman from a village in northern Israel, and Suham's husband Youssef turned out to be the right match for Yosef. In operations lasting six hours, doctors removed the kidneys from the spouses and transplanted them into the other two. The Chillags, who are in their sixties, and the Hamashs, who are in their fifties, were the first people to take part in the computerized kidney cross-swap programme at Beilinson Hospital. The programme is aimed at reducing the three to four year wait for kidney transplants in Israel.

LOUDEST SNORER

Kåre Walkert of Kumala, Sweden, who suffers from the breathing disorder apnea, recorded peak noise levels of 93 dBA while sleeping at the Örebro Regional Hospital, Sweden, in May 1993.

LONGEST DREAM

The longest known period of REM sleep (the rapid eye movements that characterize dream sleep) lasted 3 hours 8 minutes. It was achieved by David Powell at the Puget Sound Sleep Disorder Center, Seattle, Washington, USA, on 29 April 1994.

HIGHEST G FORCES BORNE

On 13 July 1977 British racing driver David Purley survived a deceleration from 173 km/h (108 mph) to zero within a distance of 66 cm (2 ft 2 in) during a crash at Silverstone racetrack, Northants, UK. He endured 179.8 G, suffered 29 fractures and three dislocations, and his heart stopped six times.

LARGEST TUMOUR

A tumour weighing 137.6 kg (21 st 61 lb) and 1 m (3 ft) in diameter was removed intact from a 34-year-old woman's abdomen in Oct 1991. It had been growing for eight years according to Dr Kate O'Hanlan of Stanford University, California, USA, seen here preparing to remove it in a clip from the hit US TV show *Guinness World Records™: Primetime*.

The highest voluntarily-endured G value was 82.6 G, for a time of 0.04 seconds, by Eli Beeding Jr. on a water-braked rocket sled at Holloman Air Force Base, New Mexico, USA, on 16 May 1958. Beeding was subsequently hospitalized for three days.

LONGEST PERIOD SURVIVED UNDERWATER

In 1986 two-year-old Michelle Funk from Salt Lake City, Utah, USA, made a full recovery after spending 1 hr 6 min underwater. She had fallen into a creek.

HIGHEST DRY-AIR TEMPERATURES BORNE

In US Air Force experiments carried out in 1960, the highest dry-air temperature endured by naked men was 205°C (400°F), while heavily clothed men could bear temperatures of up to 260°C (500°F). By comparison, a bearable temperature in a sauna is about 140°C (284°F).

LONGEST PERIOD SURVIVED WITHOUT FOOD AND WATER

Andreas Mihavecz of Bregenz, Austria, lived for a record-breaking 18 days without food and water after being put into a holding cell in a local government building in Höchst by the police on 1 April 1979 and then being totally forgotten about. The 18-year-old, who had been a passenger in a crashed car, was discovered close to death on 18 April 1979.

MOST INJECTIONS RECEIVED

Samuel Davidson from Glasgow, UK, has had at least 78,900 insulin injections since the age of 11 in 1923. Insulin lets the body absorb sugar and is taken by people with diabetes, which develops when the body does not produce enough insulin or utilize it properly. It was discovered by Canadian Frederick Banting and first used on humans in 1922. Before insulin, diabetes was usually fatal.

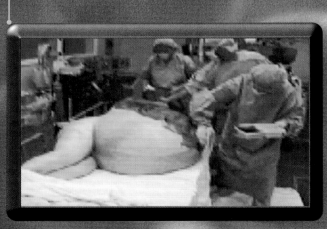

body
transformation 1

MOST PLASTIC SURGERY FOR ART
Since May 1990 Orlan, a French performance artist whose most recent work is herself, has undergone a series of plastic surgical operations to transform herself into a new being, *The Reincarnation of Saint Orlan*, modelled on Venus, Diana, Europa, Psyche and Mona Lisa. Orlan has been exhibited worldwide and is supported by the French Ministry of Culture. Her video *New York Omnipresence* shows implants being sewn into her temples.

MOST WEIGHT GAINED
Doris James from San Francisco, California, USA, is alleged to have gained 147 kg (23 st 3 lb) in the 12 months before her death in Aug 1965, aged 38, when she weighed 306 kg (48 st 3 lb). She was 1.57 m (5 ft 2 in) tall.

The greatest weight gain by a man was 89 kg (14 st) in seven days, by Jon Minnoch (USA), the heaviest person in medical history, in Oct 1981.

Arthur Knorr of the USA gained 133 kg (21 st) in the six months prior to his death in 1960.

MOST WEIGHT LOST
Jon Minnoch reduced from 635 kg (100 st) to 216 kg (34 st) in the 16 months to July 1979.

The greatest weight loss by a woman is 416 kg (65 st 7lb), by Rosalie Bradford (USA), the heaviest ever woman, when she reduced from 544 kg (85 st) in Jan 1987 to 128 kg (20 st) in Feb 1994.

In 1984 Ron Allen sweated off 9.7 kg (1 st 7½ lb) of his weight of 113 kg (17 st 1 lb) in 24 hours in Nashville, Tennessee, USA.

MOST PLASTIC SURGERY
Cindy Jackson has spent $99,600 (£60,000) on 27 operations over a period of nine years. Born on a pig farm in Ohio, USA, 42-year-old Jackson has had three full facelifts, two nose operations, knee, abdomen and jawline surgery, thigh liposuction, breast reduction and augmentation, and semi-permanent make-up. Her look is based on Leonardo Da Vinci's theory of a classically proportioned face. Dubbed the 'human Barbie Doll', Cindy is now the director of the London-based Cosmetic Surgery Network.

MOST DOUBLES CREATED BY PLASTIC SURGERY
The Russian dictator Stalin was reportedly so paranoid that he employed several doubles to lessen the likelihood of being assassinated. The lookalikes, who had plastic surgery to resemble him, are said to have attended most state funerals, and Stalin's own guards often failed to tell the difference.

MOST PLASTIC SURGERY UNDERGONE BY A CRIMINAL
Drug baron Richie Ramos had an extra 16 months of freedom from the FBI after plastic surgery. The 27-year-old boss of an immense drugs empire in Philadelphia, USA, Ramos had five bullet-wound scars removed and the skin on his fingertips changed, in addition to work on his 'bull-like chest, flabby waist and fleshy face'. The operations cost a total of $74,900 (£45,000). Ramos is now serving 30 years after confessing.

MOST DRAMATIC CHANGE UNDERGONE FOR ART
Former British photographer Della Grace has undergone a self-transformation through the use of male hormone injections. Now Del La Grace, she has a beard and a deep husky voice. The procedure is irreversible.

MOST FAMOUS SEX CHANGE
In 1953 Christine Jorgensen, a former male GI from the Bronx, New York, USA, made headlines when she had a sex change. Part of it was done in Casablanca, Morocco — then the sex change capital of the world — and part of it was carried out in Denmark. Christine's 1967 autobiography inspired other transsexuals.

OLDEST SEX CHANGE
The greatest age at which a person is known to have had sex change surgery is 74. According to the American Educational Gender Information Service it is common for individuals to change gender roles at retirement age.

YOUNGEST SEX CHANGE
Neonates are frequently born with ambiguous genitalia, and doctors often decide whether they are to be raised as boys or girls. Sometimes their genitals are operated on in infancy to match the doctors' selections. The most famous instance of this was the John/Joan case in which John, one of a pair of identical twin boys, suffered an accident during circumcision at the age of about six months and was raised as a girl, Joan. Joan was never very happy as a girl, and in her late teen years, when she discovered what had happened to her, became John again.

LONGEST NECKS
The women of the Padaung or Kareni tribe of Myanmar (Burma) extend their necks by putting copper coils around them. The maximum recorded length is 40 cm (15¾ in), and a Padaung woman of marriageable age will have had her neck extended by an average of 25 cm (9⁴/₅ in). Worn in an increasing number from the age of five or six, the coils can reach 9 kg (20 lb) in weight.

HEAVIEST BREASTS

Eve Lolo Ferrari from Grasse, Alpes-Maritimes, France, has one of the world's biggest chests. She has undergone a total of 18 operations – five for her face and 13 for the rest of her body – and currently takes a size 130 F (57 F) bra. Each of her breasts weighs 3 kg (6 lb 2 oz). 'Lolo', who lives in Cannes, France, starred in *Camping Cosmos* (Belgium, 1996) and has released a single.

MOST SEX CHANGES

It is estimated that there are around 12,000 surgeons in the USA who carry out sex change operations, making it the sex change capital of the world. (It has been suggested that Thailand leads the field, and there is great demand for operations in Asia, but no figures are available.)

BIGGEST COMPENSATION PAYOUT FOR BREAST IMPLANT CLAIMS

In Aug 1997 the Dow Corning Corporation, USA, offered $2.4 billion (£1.5 billion) to 200,000 women who claimed that their health had been ruined by breast implants. The women blamed leaking silicone for pain, fatigue and a flu-like syndrome.

MOST EXPENSIVE WIG

The toupee worn by actor Sean Connery in the James Bond movie *Never Say Never Again* (GB, 1983) cost Warner Bros. the record sum of $52,000 (£34,000). The film company decided that a full head of hair was necessary for the portrayal of Bond as envisaged by Ian Fleming, the character's creator.

MOST BEAUTY QUEENS PRODUCED

Venezuela is seen as the beauty queen factory of the world — over the last 20 years Venezuelan women have won a total of 10 top international beauty contests, a record unmatched by any other country, and of the last 18 Miss Universes, four have been from Venezuela. Aspiring beauty queens attend schools such as the Miss Venezuela Academy, where they work out in the gym, answer pageant questions, practise catwalk modelling for a gruelling 16 hours a day and sometimes undergo plastic surgery over a period of six months. The most successful beauty school in the world is Miss Venezuela Organization, which also attracts potential beauty queens from Brazil, Colombia, Bolivia and the Dominican Republic. The average cost of training a beauty queen in Venezuela, where poverty affects 70–80% of the population, is $60,000 (£36,000), but the beauty contests are as popular with the public as important sporting events, with 90% of the Venezuelan population — approximately 21 million people — tuning in. The shows themselves cost $7–8 million (£4.2–4.8 million) to put on.

MOST EXPENSIVE HAIRCUT

In 1993 the US president Bill Clinton went under the scissors of Monsieur Christophe, a top Beverly Hills stylist, while sitting in the plane *Air Force One* on the tarmac at Los Angeles airport, USA. The full cost of his 'runway trim', taking into account delays caused to other aircraft, was estimated at more than $83,000 (£50,000).

MOST TEETH BLEACHED

Dr Ronald Goldstein and colleagues at his practice have bleached more than 100,000 teeth in the USA over the last 40 years. One of the first dentists to ever bleach teeth, Goldstein's book *Change Your Smile* has been translated into six languages and been read by more people than any other book on cosmetic dentistry.

BIGGEST BICEPS
The right biceps of Denis Sester of Bloomington, Minnesota, USA, measure 77.8 cm (30⅝ in) when cold. He began building his biceps when he started wrestling pigs on his parents' farm as a teenager.

GREATEST STRONGMEN
Iceland's Magnus Ver Magnusson won the World's Strongest Man contest four times, in 1991, 1994, 1995 and 1996, becoming only the second man (after Bill Kazmaier of the USA) to win three years in a row. He began powerlifting in 1984 and won senior titles in Europe in 1989 and 1990. He also won the World Muscle Power Championship in 1995. Born in 1963, he is 1.87 m (6 ft 2 in) tall, weighs 130.18 kg (20 st 7 lb) and has a chest measurement of 1.3 m (51 in). He now owns Magnus' Gym, Reykjavik, Iceland.

Jon Pall Sigmarsson from Iceland also won the World's Strongest Man contest four times, in 1984, 1986, 1988 and 1990. Sigmarsson, who weighed 133 kg (21 st) and had a 1.44-m (57-in) chest, dominated the WSM competition in the mid and late 1980s and won five World Muscle Power titles. He died of a heart attack while weightlifting in 1993.

MOST MR OLYMPIA TITLES
Lee Haney of South Carolina, USA, won the Mr Olympia contest eight times from 1984 to 1991.

MOST CONSECUTIVE MR OLYMPIA TITLES
Dorian Yates from Staffs, UK, won five Mr Olympia contests in a row from 1992 to 1997.

MOST IFBB PRO WINS
Vince Taylor of Pembroke Pines, Florida, USA, has had a record 19 wins from competitions all over the world recognized by the International Federation of Body Building (IFBB). He won the Masters Olympia for those aged 40 and over in 1996 and 1997.

MOST ARNOLD CLASSICS (FORMERLY MEN'S PRO WORLD) TITLES
Ken 'Flex' Wheeler, nicknamed the 'Sultan of Symmetry', won the 'triple crown' (the Ironman, the Arnold Classic and the San Jose Classic) in 1997 and the Arnold Classic in 1993, 1997 and 1998. He has been training since the age of 15.

MOST SUCCESSFUL FORMER BODYBUILDERS
Along with Arnold Schwarzenegger, Lou Ferrigno of California, USA — the only man in history to win the Mr Universe title two years in succession — is the most successful former bodybuilder. Ferrigno starred in *The Incredible Hulk* from 1978 to 1982 and has since appeared in a succession of TV shows, plays and films, including *Hercules* (USA, 1983) and *The Adventures of Hercules* (USA, 1985). He is 1.95 m (6 ft 5 in) tall and weighs (21 st 6 lb).

MOST SUCCESSFUL PERSONAL TRAINERS
Jake Steinfeld has trained Steven Spielberg, Harrison Ford and Priscilla Presley and heads a multi-million-dollar fitness empire which includes a cable television network FiT TV — the world's only 24-hour fitness channel — a national magazine, home videos and branded equipment and merchandise. In three years, Los Angeles-based Body by Jake Enterprises sold more than $250 million (£156 million) in licenced products through infomercials.

Radu Teodorescu, known as the 'Grand Master' of exercise, has been a personal trainer for more than 20 years and his clientele has included Candice Bergen, John Kennedy Jr. and Matthew Broderick. Voted 'Toughest Trainer In Town' by *New York* magazine, Radu has featured in more than 400 magazine articles and created Cindy Crawford's multi-million-selling fitness video *Shape Your Body Workout*.

Ray Kybartas from Chicago, USA, began as a fitness consultant to entertainment attorneys in the 1970s and has since worked with

BODYBUILDING MECCA
Venice Beach, the beachfront between the *Baywatch* sands at Santa Monica and Marina del Rey, California, attracts up to 175,000 visitors every weekend. One of its most famous spots is Muscle Beach, an open-air gym where bodybuilders pump iron (left). The original Muscle Beach in Santa Monica was closed in 1959. A small group of weightlifters was working out at a facility known as 'The Pen' in neighbouring Venice, and this became the new Muscle Beach in the 1960s. It is now the world's most famous bodybuilding venue. The most successful bodybuilding empire is the Weider Corporation, a group of companies that sell more than 100 bodybuilding and fitness products. It is run by Canadian brothers Joe and Ben Weider, often seen as the pioneers of bodybuilding. In the 1960s Ben established the International Federation of Bodybuilding, which has 150 member countries and promotes Mr Olympia. Their magazine *Muscle & Fitness* has 1.7 million readers, and they also publish *Shape, Men's Fitness* and *Flex*, which, together with vitamin and food supplements, have sales of almost $1 billion (£625 million) in 60 countries.

MOST FAMOUS FORMER BODYBUILDER
Austrian-born Arnold Schwarzenegger, who is pictured here with Lou Ferrigno, has won 13 world titles (seven Mr Olympia titles, five Mr Universe titles and one Mr World title). He has been producing bodybuilding contests for 20 years, and in 1989 set up the Arnold Classic. During President Bush's administration he was Chairman of the President's Council on Fitness and Sport and since 1979 has been International Weight Training Coach for the Special Olympics. He is now one of the world's biggest box office draws, with movies such as *The Terminator* (USA, 1984), *Terminator 2: Judgment Day* (USA, 1991), *Total Recall* (USA, 1990), *True Lies* (USA, 1994) and *Batman and Robin* (USA, 1997) under his belt. In 1993 the US National Association of Theater Owners named him 'International Star of the Decade'.

Tatum O'Neal and Sean Penn, who asked him to help him gain 13 kg (2 st 2 lb) in three months for *At Close Range* (USA, 1985). This led Kybartas to a job with Madonna, and he is now one of Hollywood's most sought-after trainers.

BIGGEST-SELLING FITNESS VIDEO
Supermodel Cindy Crawford was the star and executive producer of the *Cindy Crawford/Shape Your Body Workout*, which topped the Billboard Health and Fitness chart for several years after its release in Oct 1992 and has sold more than 10 million copies worldwide to date.

BIGGEST CHAIN OF GYMS
Gold's Gym opened in Venice, California, USA, in 1965 and became internationally famous when it featured in *Pumping Iron* (USA, 1975), with up-and-coming stars Arnold Schwarzenegger and Lou Ferrigno. It is now the world's biggest international gym chain, with more than 500 centres. It has many star clients, including Charlie Sheen, Richard Dreyfuss, Janet Jackson, Carrie Fisher, Jodie Foster and Hulk Hogan, and boasts its own Motion Picture and TV Division.

BIGGEST CHEST
Isaac Nesser (pictured below) of Greensburg, Pennsylvania, USA, has a record muscular chest measurement of 1.88 m (6 ft 2 1/16 in). He has been lifting weights since he was eight years old and has worked out every day for the past 20 years. His routine includes bench-pressing 254 kg (560 lb) in a series of repetitions and curling 136-kg (300-lb) barbells in a similar series.

MS OLYMPIA
Right, a contestant flexes her muscles for the Ms Olympia contest, which began in 1980. US bodybuilder Cory Everson won the competition a record six times from 1984 to 1989. She is now the star of her own TV show, *Gotta Sweat*, and has produced successful fitness books and videos. The most consecutive titles is five, by Lenda Murray (USA) between 1990 and 1994.

body art

MOST INDIVIDUAL TATTOOS
Bernie Moeller of Pennsylvania, USA, had had his body covered by a record total of 14,006 individual tattoos by 3 April 1997. Moeller's tattoos have made him a popular guest at various outdoor events and he has made several television appearances. In 1996 he was interviewed by Ron Reagan Jr., son of the former US president Ronald Reagan, and he was also present at the world's biggest tattoo and piercing contest, at the Astroland Amusement Park, New York, USA.

MOST PIERCED MAN
Alex Lambrecht has acquired a total of 137 piercings with a combined weight of approximately 0.5 kg (1 lb 2 oz) over a period of 40 years, making him the most pierced man in the world. At an average of $83 (£50) a time, Lambrecht's piercings would have cost him $11,400 (£6,850) had he not done them himself. Most of them are on his face but more than 50 are intimate.

MOST TATTOOED WOMAN
The world's most tattooed woman is the strip artiste 'Krystyne Kolorful' from Alberta, Canada. Krystyne's 'suit' of tattoos covers 95% of her entire body and took a total of 10 years to complete.

OLDEST TATTOOS
Ötzi, the world's oldest preserved human body, has 15 tattoos. He was found in a glacier near the Ötz Valley, Italy, in 1991 and is believed to be 5,300 years old and to have died at the age of 40. Ötzi has a series of blue parallel lines covering his lower spine, as well as stripes across his right ankle and a tattoo of a cross behind his right knee.

Two Egyptian mummies dating back to 2160–1994 BC have abstract patterns of dots and dashes on their bodies. The tattoos were probably believed to offer protection from evil spirits.

MOST INFLUENTIAL BODY ARTIST
Body artist Fakir Mustafar from Aberdeen, South Dakota, USA, is internationally renowned for his 50 years of research into primitive body decoration and his exploration of modern body modifications. The 68-year-old's work has been featured in a number of films, television programmes and books and has been a major catalyst behind the recent revival of body piercing, branding and body sculpting. Mustafar co-developed the body piercing techniques that are used today and is the director of Fakir Body Piercing & Branding Intensives, which are licenced by the state of California and are the only courses of their kind in the world.

MOST FAMOUS TATTOOED BODY ARTISTS
Enigma, an American circus star from Jim Rose's circus, has had his entire body covered in jigsaw-puzzle tattoos. He also has horns, a tail and porcupine quills, which were implanted into his body using coral. Real bone is growing around the implants and the horns on his head are growing at the rate of 3.8 cm (1¹/₂ in) a year. Enigma achieved TV stardom in 1995, when he appeared in an episode of *The X-Files* alongside David Duchovny and Gillian Anderson.

Michael Wilson, who died in 1996, was known as the 'Illustrated Man' because of the tattoos that covered 90% of his body. In the 1980s Wilson left his native California, USA, after tattooists there refused to colour his face. He moved to New York and made a living exhibiting himself as the 'Illustrated Man' at the famous Coney Island Circus Sideshow, where he became one of the most popular attractions. Wilson gradually covered almost his entire body with tattoos.

MOST BODY PARTS ADDED FOR ART
Stelarc, a performance artist based in Australia, has a third robotic hand which is operated by muscle stimulation from his real arm. Stelarc's work, which is based on the belief that the human body has become obsolete, explores the concept of the body and its relationship with technology. His latest project involves the grafting of an extra ear next to his existing right ear. It will be constructed by stretching his skin over an ear-shaped plastic scaffold. The second ear will not be able to hear, but the artist will be able to make it talk electronically using a sound chip, as he wants to make it "whisper sweet nothings into the other ear".

MOST COMMON FORM OF BODY ART
Tattooing is an ancient form of body art that is found all over the world, including among the native peoples of Borneo, Polynesia, Thailand, New Zealand, Burma and parts of Asia and Africa. The Gauls and the

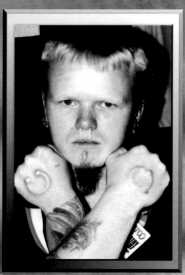

MOST SUCCESSFUL THREE-DIMENSIONAL BODY ARTIST
Steve Haworth, who is based at Haworth Tech Company Body Adornments, Phoenix, USA, is widely acknowledged as the world's leading 3-D artist working in the medium of human flesh. Haworth specializes in sub-dermal and trans-dermal implants and practises piercing, laser-cautery branding and near-surgical art. He first started designing medical equipment at the age of 18 and in 1989 began producing body jewellery. Examples of his work, which is revolutionizing the worlds of body modification and modern art, include the implantation of 11 rows of beads that look like backbone vertebrae into a friend's forearm and the placing of a Mohawk made from steel spikes into a man's forehead. The artist has performed between 150 and 175 bead implants — which are generally easier to remove than they are to insert — on approximately 130 individuals. Haworth also creates sub-cutaneous horns for foreheads for about $600 (£375) and has worked on the famous circus star Enigma. He is apprehensive about doing work on the back of the hand (pictured left) because of a possible loss of sensation to some of the tissue, but has completed eight pieces without any problems.

Teutonic peoples practised tattooing, as did the Greeks, the Romans and the Iberians, who preceded the Celts in the British Isles. One of the world's most beautiful and complex forms of tattooing was practised by the ancient Horis from Japan, whose decorations were made to look almost three-dimensional through design, colour and the use of shade and light.

LONGEST EARS

The men and women from the Suya tribe in Africa wear large discs of wood in their ears in order to elongate them. When they take the discs out, they wrap their dangling ear lobes around their ears.

MOST POINTED HEADS

Head shaping was practised by the Greeks, the Romans, Native Americans and Africans, as well as by certain groups in Europe during prehistoric times. The head-shaping process began in a person's infancy, when the head is still soft and malleable enough to be changed. The skull was either tightly bound with a piece of cloth or the baby was placed into a cradle that had a specially shaped wooden headboard. The elongated head that resulted from these processes was deemed both beautiful and refined.

FLATTEST NOSES

In New Guinea people often insert feathers, small shells and tusks through a hole in their noses in order to flatten them out and render them more attractive. Certain Polynesian groups go so far as to break their noses in order to make them flatter.

SMALLEST FEET

The Chinese custom of foot binding dates back to the Sung dynasty (960–976 BC), when it arose in imitation of an imperial concubine who was required to dance with her feet bound. By the 12th century, when a girl turned three, eight of her toes were broken and her feet were bound with cloth strips to prevent them from growing any larger than 10 cm ($3^9/_{10}$ in). The art of foot binding ceased in the 20th century with the end of the imperial dynasties and the influence of western fashion. Studies showed that it caused severe lifelong disabilities for millions of Chinese women.

GREATEST COVERAGE BY TATTOOS

Tom Leppard, a retired soldier who lives alone on the Isle of Skye, UK, has had a record 99.9% of his body tattooed with a leopard skin design. His body is now covered with dark spots whilst the skin between them is tattooed saffron yellow. The only parts of Leppard's body that remain free of tattoos are the insides of his ears and the skin between his toes.

MOST PIERCED WOMAN

By 31 Jan 1998, just one year after getting her first piercing, Grace Martin from Edinburgh, UK, had 290 piercings over her entire body.

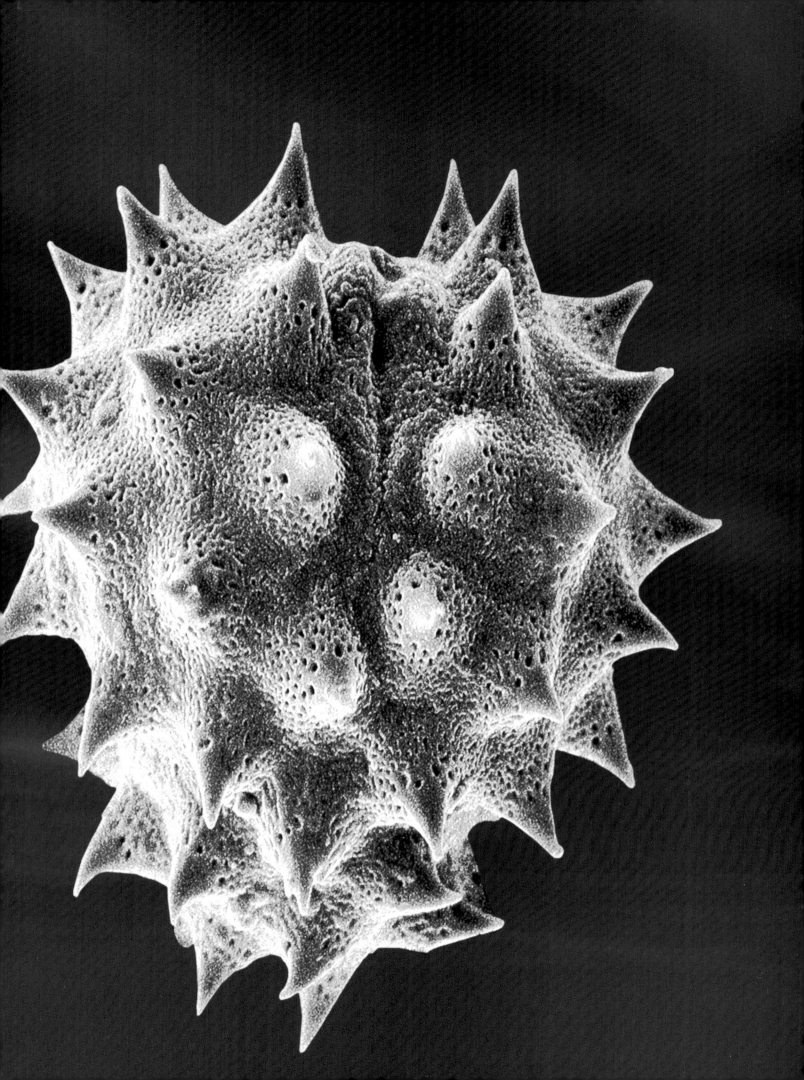

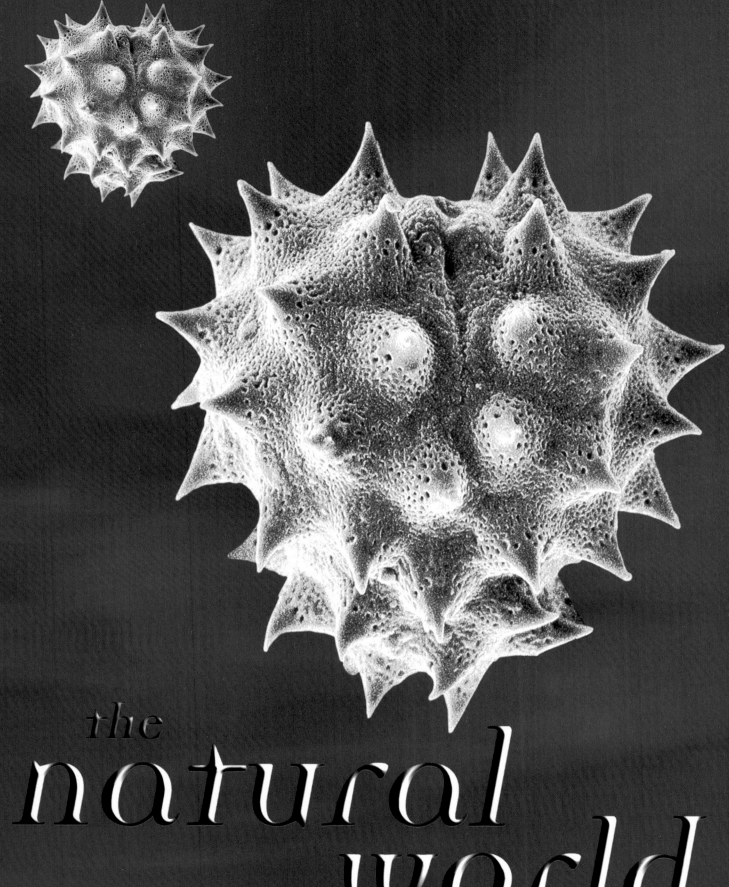

the natural world

largest and smallest
mammals

HEAVIEST LION
Confined mostly to sub-Saharan Africa, lions feed on large herbivores such as wildebeest, zebra and antelope, with most of the hunting carried out by females on a co-operative basis. The heaviest wild African lion (*Panthera leo*) on record weighed 313 kg (690 lb). It was shot near Hectorspruit, Transvaal, South Africa, in 1936.

LARGEST ANIMAL
The blue whale (*Balaenoptera musculus*) begins life as an ovum weighing a fraction of a milligram and grows to an average weight of 26 tonnes by the age of 12 months. Newborn calves weigh up to 3 tonnes.

HEAVIEST MAMMAL
A 190-tonne, 27.6-m-long (90-ft 6-in) female blue whale was caught in the Southern Ocean in 1947.

LARGEST LAND MAMMAL
The male African bush elephant (*Loxodonta africana africana*) is 3–3.7 m (9 ft 10 in–12 ft 2 in) tall at the shoulder and can weigh between 4 and 7 tonnes. The largest specimen on record was a bull shot in Mucosso, Angola, in 1974. The creature had an estimated standing height of about 3.96 m (13 ft) and is thought to have weighed 12.24 tonnes.

HEAVIEST CARNIVORE
A polar bear weighing an estimated 900 kg (2,000 lb) was shot in the Chukchi Sea, Alaska, USA, in 1960, and is the heaviest known land mammal in the world. It was said to measure 3.5 m (11 ft 3 in) from nose to tail over its body contours, 1.5 m (4 ft 10 in) around the body and 43 cm (1 ft 5 in) around the paws.

LARGEST CARNIVOROUS MAMMAL
Adult male polar bears (*Ursus maritimus*) often weigh 400–600 kg (880–1,320 lb) and have a nose-to-tail length of 2.4–2.6 m (7 ft 11 in–8 ft 6 in). Male Kodiak bears (*Ursus arctos middendorffi*) are usually shorter but more robustly built.

LONGEST MAMMAL
A 33.58-m-long (110-ft 2½-in) female blue whale was landed at Grytviken, South Georgia, in the South Atlantic in 1909.

LARGEST TOOTHED MAMMAL
The 5-m-long (16-ft 5-in) lower jaw of a male sperm whale (*Physeter macrocephalus*) estimated to have been almost 25.6 m (84 ft) long is on show in the Natural History Museum in London, UK. The longest officially measured specimen was a 20.7-m (67-ft 11-in) male captured off the Kurile Islands in the north-west Pacific in 1950.

LARGEST RODENT
The capybara (*Hydrochoerus hydrochaeris*) of northern South America has a head-and-body length of 1–1.3 m (3¼–4½ ft) and can weigh up to 79 kg (174 lb). One cage-fat specimen weighed 113 kg (250 lb).

LARGEST MARSUPIAL
The male red kangaroo (*Macropus rufus*) of Australia is up to 1.8 m (5 ft 11 in) tall and 2.85 m (9 ft 4 in) long (including the tail). Exceptional specimens have weighed 90 kg (198 lb).

TALLEST PRIMATE
The tallest wild gorilla on record was a mountain bull that was shot in the eastern Congo (ex-Zaïre) in 1938. It measured 1.95 m (6 ft 5 in) from the top of the crest to the heel.

HEAVIEST PRIMATE
The heaviest gorilla kept in captivity was a male of the N'gagi mountain sub-species who

died in San Diego Zoo, California, USA, in 1944. Weighing 310 kg (683 lb) at its heaviest in 1943, it was 1.72 m (5 ft 7¾ in) tall and boasted a record chest measurement of 1.98 m (6 ft 6 in).

LARGEST PINNIPED
Male southern elephant seals (*Mirounga leonina*) from the sub-Antarctic islands average 5 m (16 ft 6in) in length from the tip of the inflated snout to the tips of the outstretched tail flippers, have a maximum girth of 3.7 m (12 ft) and weigh 2,000–3,500 kg (4,400–7,720 lb). The largest accurately measured specimen was a bull weighing at least 4 tonnes. Measuring 6.5 m (21 ft 4 in) after the blubber had been stripped off its skin, its original length was estimated at 6.85 m (22 ft 6 in). It was killed in the South Atlantic at Possession Bay, South Georgia, in 1913.

SMALLEST MAMMAL
The bumblebee or Kitti's hog-nosed bat (*Craseonycteris thonglongyai*), which is confined to about 21 limestone caves on the Kwae Noi River, Kanchanaburi Province, south-west Thailand, has a body no bigger than that of a large bumble-bee, a head-and-body length of 2.9–3.3 cm (1⁷/₅₀–1³/₁₀ in) and a wingspan of about 13–14.5 cm (5¹/₁₀–5⁷/₁₀ in). It weighs 1.7–2.0 g (³/₅–⁷/₁₀ oz).

SMALLEST NON-FLYING MAMMAL
Savi's white-toothed pygmy shrew, also called the Etruscan shrew (*Suncus etruscus*), has a head-and-body length of 35–48 mm (1²/₅–1⁴/₅ in), a tail length of 25–30 mm (⁴⁹/₅₀–1¹⁷/₁₀₀ in) and weighs 1.5–2.5 g (¹³/₂₅–²²/₂₅ oz).

SMALLEST FELINE CARNIVORE
The rusty-spotted cat (*Prionailurus rubiginosus*), which lives in southern India and Sri Lanka, has a head-and-body length of 35–48 cm (13²/₅–18⁹/₁₀ in) and a tail length of 15–25 cm (5⁹/₁₀–9⁴/₅ in). The average weight of a female is 1.1 kg (2 lb 7 oz).

LARGEST FELINE CARNIVORE
The male Siberian tiger (*Panthera tigris altaica*) averages 3.15 m (10 ft 4 in) in length from the nose to the tip of the extended tail, stands 0.99–1.07 m (3 ft 3 in–3 ft 6 in) at the shoulder and weighs about 265 kg (585 lb). The world's largest feline carnivore, it faces a bleak future: of the 100,000 tigers alive a century ago there remain just 400 Siberian tigers, 3,000 Bengal tigers, 1,000 Indo-Chinese tigers and around 20 Sumatran tigers today. The latter are expected to become extinct in the near future, following the Bali tiger, which became the first tiger to die out in 1940, and the Caspian tiger, which disappeared in the 1970s. Tigers are endangered through hunting and the loss of natural habitat. Despite classification as an endangered species by the World Conservation Union (IUCN) and protection by the convention on International Trade in Endangered Species, 180 tigers were killed between 1991 and 1996. This led to the formation of several conservation groups, including the Tiger Trust, and Tuskforce in the United Kingdom. Together with the World Wide Fund for Nature these have helped to slow the killing of tigers: it is estimated that 20 tigers were killed in 1996 and 1997.

SMALLEST RODENT

The northern pygmy mouse (*Baiomys taylori*) from Arizona and Texas, USA, and Mexico and the Baluchistan pygmy jerboa (*Salpingotulus michaelis*) from Pakistan are probably the world's smallest rodents. Both have a head-and-body length of as little as 3.6 cm (1²/₅ in) and a tail length of 7.2 cm (2⁴/₅ in).

SMALLEST MARSUPIAL

The two main contenders for the title of smallest marsupial are the rare long-tailed planigale (*Planigale ingrami*) of northern Australia and the pilbara ningaui (*Ningaui timealeyi*) of north-western Australia. The first has a head-and-body length of 5.5–6.3 cm (2¹⁷/₁₀₀-2¹²/₂₅ in) and a tail length of 5.7–6 cm (2¹/₄–2⁹/₂₅ in), and weighs

3.9–4.5 g (2¹/₅–2¹/₂ dram). The ninguai has a head-and-body length of 4.6–5.7 cm (1⁴/₅–2¹/₄ in) and a tail length of 5.9–7.9 cm (2¹/₃–3¹/₁₀ in), and weighs 2–9.4 g (⁷/₁₀₀–¹/₃ oz).

SMALLEST PRIMATE

The smallest true primate (excluding tree shrews, which are normally classified separately) is the pygmy mouse lemur (*Microcebus myoxinus*) from Madagascar. Its head-and-body length is about 6.2 cm (2²/₅ in), its tail is 13.6 cm (5²/₅ in) long and it weighs around 30.6 g (1¹/₁₀ oz).

SMALLEST PINNIPED

Female Galapagos fur seals (*Arctocephalus galapagoensis*) average 1.2 m (3 ft 11 in) in length and weigh about 27 kg (60 lb).

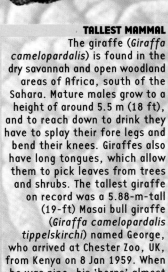

TALLEST MAMMAL

The giraffe (*Giraffa camelopardalis*) is found in the dry savannah and open woodland areas of Africa, south of the Sahara. Mature males grow to a height of around 5.5 m (18 ft), and to reach down to drink they have to splay their fore legs and bend their knees. Giraffes also have long tongues, which allow them to pick leaves from trees and shrubs. The tallest giraffe on record was a 5.88-m-tall (19-ft) Masai bull giraffe (*Giraffa camelopardalis tippelskirchi*) named George, who arrived at Chester Zoo, UK, from Kenya on 8 Jan 1959. When he was nine, his 'horns' almost grazed the roof of the 6.1-m-high (20-ft) Giraffe House. George died in 1969.

OLDEST GORILLA

Gul Gul was believed to be the world's oldest male gorilla when he died at the estimated age of 44 in Ueno Zoo, Tokyo, Japan, in 1988. There are a total of three sub-species of gorilla – males measure around 1.7 m (5 ft 7 in) when standing and weigh about 150 kg (331 lb); females are considerably smaller, weighing on average 80 kg (176 lb). The male eastern lowland gorilla (*Gorilla gorilla graueri*) from the eastern Congo (ex-Zaïre) is the largest of all primates. It has a bipedal standing height of up to 1.75 m (5 ft 9 in) and can weigh as much as 163.4 kg (360 lb).

mammal lifestyle

FATTIEST DIET

In spring and early summer the diet of the polar bear (*Ursus maritimus*) consists largely of recently weaned ringed seal pups, which have a fat content of up to 50%. When the seals are in plentiful supply the bears feed only on the fat below the skin, leaving the rest of the carcass untouched.

FASTEST LAND MAMMALS

Over a short distance (up to 550 m or 600 yd) on level ground, the cheetah (*Acinonyx jubatus*) has a probable maximum speed of about 100 km/h (60 mph).

The pronghorn antelope (*Antilocapra americana*) sustains a speed of 56 km/h (35 mph) for 6 km (4 miles), 67 km/h (42 mph) for 1.6 km (1 mile) and 88.5 km/h (55 mph) for 0.8 km (½ mile), and is the fastest land animal over long distances.

FASTEST MARINE MAMMALS

In 1958 a bull killer whale (*Orcinus orca*) estimated to be 6.1–7.6 m (20–25 ft) in length was timed swimming at a speed of 55.5 km/h (34½ mph) in the eastern North Pacific. Similar speeds have been reported for Dall's porpoise (*Phocoenoides dalli*) during short bursts.

SLOWEST MAMMAL

The slowest mammal is the three-toed sloth from tropical South America (*Bradypus tridactylus*), which has an average ground speed of between 1.8 and 2.4 m (6 and 8 ft) per minute, or 0.1–0.16 km/h ($^7/_{100}$–$^1/_{10}$ mph). In the trees it can accelerate to 4.6 m (15 ft) per minute, or 0.27 km/h ($^{17}/_{100}$ mph).

DEEPEST DIVES

In 1969 a bull sperm whale (*Physeter macrocephalus*) surfaced from a 1-hr 52-min dive 160 km (100 miles) south of Durban, South Africa, where the water is known to exceed a depth of 3,193 m (10,473 ft) for a radius of 48–64 km (30–40 miles). Inside its stomach were two small sharks of a type found only on the sea floor. The sharks had been swallowed about an hour earlier, which suggests that sperm whales can descend more than 3,000 m (9,800 ft) when seeking food and that they are limited by time rather than water pressure.

The deepest authenticated dive was 2,000 m (6,500 ft) and lasted for 1 hr 13 min. It was made by a bull sperm whale off the coast of Dominica in the Caribbean in 1991.

MOST DANGEROUS LOVE LIFE

The male brown antechinus (*Antechinus stuartii*), a marsupial mouse native to eastern Australia, has an insatiable sexual appetite. Every year the entire adult male population of the species goes on a rampage for two weeks in a bid to mate with as many females as possible. The mice are so busy chasing females and fighting off rivals that they do not have time to eat, and die within days from starvation, ulcers or infection.

BIGGEST EYES

The Tarsier (pictured below), is one of the world's smallest primates, and lives in the forests of Borneo, Sumatra and the Philippines. Tarsiers have a maximum body length of 16 cm (6⅓ in) and a 27-cm (10½-in) tail. Their eyes are so enormous they would be equivalent to grapefruit-sized eyes in a human being, and are the only primates, along with animals from the *Galago* genus, able to turn their heads through 180° in each direction. Galagos, known as bush babies, share this large eye to body ratio, and can be found in sub-Saharan African forests.

MOST SUCCESSFUL NON-NATIVE MAMMAL

The brown rat (*Rattus norvegicus*) has spread from its original habitat in Mongolia and Kazakhstan and can now be found almost everywhere. It is estimated that the number of rats in the world today is roughly equal to the number of humans (approximately 5.3 billion) but will increase more rapidly in the future. One 1993 British survey estimates that rat infestations in large towns have increased by 43% in 20 years. Rats spread a number of serious diseases, including bubonic plague and leptospirosis, but control of the creatures is difficult for several reasons, especially their staggering rate of reproduction: the female common rat (*Rattus rattus*) starts to mate when she is just two or three months old and can reproduce all year round, giving birth to litters of 10–12 babies. Rats are also extremely adaptable and can live off anything, from fast food to faeces. When an epidemic of the pneumonic plague broke out in India in 1994, killing at least 60 people, thousands of dead rats from Bombay and surrounding areas were brought in daily to the Haffkine Institute and about 150 dissected and tested for the disease. Here a government employee is pictured inspecting part of the day's collection of rats.

MOST FERTILE MAMMAL
The field mouse (genus *Apodemus*) can produce up to seven litters of 4–12 young (occasionally more) a year in favourable conditions. The mice would overrun entire continents within decades were it not for disease, predators and lack of food, which kill most of them within a few months.

MOST STERILE MAMMAL
In a colony of sand or naked mole rats (*Heterocephalus glaber*) every male can breed, but all the females except the 'queen' are sterile workers whose job is to care for the young and dig tunnels.

MOST VULNERABLE YOUNG
The smaller dasyurids (Australian carnivorous marsupials) have a precarious start to life because the females have six teats but give birth to 12 or more young. Once the first six babies have reached the teats and hang on, the rest of the brood die.

EARLIEST PREGNANCY
The female true lemming (*Lemmus lemmus*) can get pregnant at the age of just 14 days, and give birth 16–23 days later. One lemming couple was reported to have produced eight litters in 167 days, after which the male died.

MOST DOMINANT FEMALES
Female hyenas of the family *Hyaenide* and female common squirrel monkeys (*Saimiri sciureus*) are larger and more aggressive than their mates.

BRAVEST MAMMAL
The ratel or honey badger (*Mellivora capensis*) will defend itself against animals of any size. Its tough skin is impervious to bee stings, porcupine quills and most snakebites. It is also so loose that if the creature is held by the scruff of the neck it can turn inside its skin and bite the attacker until it lets go.

MOST TIME SPENT EATING
Apart from ungulates such as cattle, the mammals that spend the most time eating are probably weasels (genus *Mustela*). Their long, thin bodies lose a great deal of heat, so they have to consume protein- and fat-rich food ceaselessly. They require 100 times more energy per gram of body weight than an elephant.

FUSSIEST EATER
The koala (*Phascolarctos cinereus*) of eastern Australia feeds almost exclusively on eucalyptus leaves. It browses regularly on about six of the 500 species and selects certain individual trees and leaves in preference to others, sometimes sifting through up to 9 kg (20 lb) of leaves a day to find the 0.5 kg (1¼ lb) that it needs.

MOST MEAGRE DIET
The dromedary or Arabian camel (*Camelus dromedarius*) can lose up to a quarter of its body fluid without suffering dehydration or overheating and can survive on the most meagre diet, drawing upon a large fat reserve in its hump for sustenance.

SHARPEST HEARING
Ultrasonic echolocation gives bats the most acute hearing of any terrestrial animal. Some can hear frequencies as high as 120–250 kHz (the human limit is almost 20 kHz).

LOUDEST SOUND
Low-frequency pulses made by fin whales (*Balaenoptera physalus*) and blue whales (*B. musculus*) to communicate with each other have been measured at up to 188 decibels — the loudest sound by a living source.

LARGEST COLONY
A colony of black-tailed prairie dogs (*Cynomys ludovicianus*) found in 1901 contained about 400 million individuals and was estimated to cover 61,400 km² (24,000 miles²) — almost the size of the Republic of Ireland.

HIGHEST RODENT DENSITY
A colony of house mice (*Mus musculus*) discovered in the dry bed of Buena Vista Lake, Kern County, California, USA, in 1926 and 1927, contained a total of 205,000 creatures per hectare (83,000 per acre).

BEST BUILDER
The North American beaver (*Castor canadensis*) is the best mammalian builder (as opposed to excavator), constructing dams that are typically 5–30 m (16–96 ft) long.

MOST EXPERT TOOL USER
Chimpanzees (*Pan troglodytes*) have developed tool use and simple tool-making to a higher level than any other mammal except humans: they use straw and twigs to extract termites; branches to investigate out-of-reach objects; stones to hammer open hard-shelled nuts; pointed sticks to prise pieces of nut from shells; and leaves as cloths to remove dirt from their bodies and as sponges to obtain water.

BIGGEST METHANE PRODUCER
Domestic cows emit about 48 kg (105 lb) of methane a year, and annual bovine emissions of the gas exceed 62,000 million kg (136,000 million lb). As a result, the level of methane in the atmosphere is increasing eight times faster than carbon dioxide levels.

SLEEPIEST MAMMALS
Certain species of armadillo (Dasypodidae), together with opossums (Didelphidae) and sloths (Bradypodidae and Megalonychidae) are the world's sleepiest mammals. They can spend as much as 80% of their lives sleeping or dozing. This efficient use of energy is due to their rather low body temperatures, their slow metabolic rates and their low-quality plant diet. As a result, they move slowly, have small territories and seldom venture far. Armadillos inhabit much of South and Central America and parts of the southern USA and the West Indies.

fish

BIGGEST PREDATORY FISH
Adult rare great white sharks (*Carcharodon carcharias*) average 4.3–4.6 m (14–15 ft) in length and weigh approximately 520–770 kg (1,150–1,700 lb). There has been circumstantial evidence to suggest that some specimens grow to more than 6 m (20 ft) in length.

Arapaima gigas of South America is reported to grow to 4.5 m (14 ft 9 in) in length but weighs only 200 kg (440 lb).

In the 19th century there were several reports of 4.6-m-long (15-ft), 336-kg (720-lb) European catfish or wels (*Silurus glanis*) in Russia. Today any

GENDER DIFFERENCE
A dwarf male anglerfish is seen permanently attached to the female. The dwarf anglerfish is one of four out of the 210 anglerfish species in which the male is unusually small. What is extraordinary about these four species is that the male attaches himself, by biting, to the female. The male's mouth fuses to the skin of his mate, and the bloodstreams of the two fish become connected.The male is then totally dependent upon the female for nourishment.

BIGGEST FRESHWATER FISH
The rare pla buk or pa beuk (*Pangasianodon gigas*), which lives mainly in the Mekong River basin, and *Pangasius sanitwongse*, which is generally found in the Chao Phraya River basin, are said to grow to 3 m (9 ft 10¼ in) in length and attain a weight of 300 kg (669 lb).

specimen over 1.83 m (6 ft) long and 90 kg (200 lb) in weight is considered large.

SMALLEST FISH
The dwarf goby (*Trimmatom nanus*) of the Indo-Pacific is the shortest known vertebrate. The average length of a male specimen is 8.6 mm ($^{34}/_{100}$ in).

SMALLEST FRESHWATER FISH
The shortest and lightest freshwater fish in the world is the dwarf pygmy goby (*Pandaka pygmaea*), an almost transparent species found in the streams and lakes of Luzon, Philippines. Males are 7.5–9.9 mm ($^1/_3$–$^2/_5$ in) long and weigh 4–5 mg ($^3/_{50}$–$^2/_{25}$ grains).

SMALLEST COMMERCIAL FISH
Male specimens of the endangered sinarapan (*Mistichthys luzonensis*), a goby found only in Lake Buhi on Luzon in the Philippines, are just 1–1.3 cm ($^{39}/_{100}$–$^{51}/_{100}$ in) long. One dried 454-g (1-lb) fishcake would contain about 70,000 of them.

LIGHTEST FISH
The lightest vertebrate is the dwarf goby (*Schindleria praematurus*), which weighs only 2 mg ($^3/_{100}$ grains) and is 12–19 mm ($^1/_2$–$^3/_4$ in) in length.

FASTEST FISH
The cosmopolitan sailfish (*Istiophorus platypterus*) is considered to be the fastest fish over short distances. In speed trials that were carried out at the Long Key Fishing Camp in Florida, USA, one sailfish took out 91 m (300 ft) of line in a time of 3 seconds. This is equivalent to a speed of 109 km/h (68 mph).

SLOWEST FISH
There are about 30 species of sea horse (family Syngnathidae), and all are very slow swimmers. The only parts which can be moved rapidly are the pectoral fins on either side of the back of the head, and the dorsal fin along the back. The fish propels itself forward in an erect posture by waving its dorsal fin. In still water, some of the smaller species such as the dwarf sea horse (*Hippocampus zosterae*) probably never exceed 0.016 km/h (0.001 mph). Sea horses are incapable of swimming against the current and cling to plants to avoid being swept away.

LONGEST MIGRATION
The longest known straight-line distance covered by a fish is 9,335 km (5,800 miles), by a bluefin tuna (*Thunnus thynnus*) dart-tagged off Baja California, Mexico, in 1958. It was caught 483 km (300 miles) south of Tokyo, Japan, in 1963. Its weight had increased from 16 kg (35 lb) to 121 kg (267 lb).

LONGEST JOURNEY BY A FRESHWATER FISH
The European eel (*Anguilla anguilla*) spends between seven and 15 years in freshwater before setting out for the species' spawning grounds in the Sargasso Sea, a journey that may take it overland from landlocked waters to the Atlantic. The journey covers 4,800–6,400 km (3,000–4,000 miles) and takes about six months.

DEEPEST-LIVING FISH
The deepest-living vertebrates are believed to be ophidiids of the genus *Bassogigas*. A specimen was recovered from a depth of 8,300 m (27,230 ft), in the Puerto Rico Trench in the Atlantic in 1970.

HIGHEST-LIVING FISH
The Tibetan loach (Cobitidae) is found at an altitude of 5,200 m (17,056 ft) in the Himalayas — higher than any other fish.

OLDEST FISH
A female European eel (*Anguilla anguilla*) named Putte was reported to be 88 years old when she died in the aquarium of Hälsingborg Museum in Sweden in 1948. She was believed to have been born in 1860 in the Sargasso Sea, North Atlantic, and was caught in a river as a three-year-old elver.

BIGGEST FISH

The rare plankton-feeding whale shark (*Rhincodon typus*), which is found in warmer areas of the Atlantic, Pacific and Indian oceans, is the largest fish in the world. The first specimen to have been scientifically examined was harpooned in Table Bay, South Africa, in 1828. Since then many have been sighted but few have been examined. The largest on scientific record was captured off Baba Island, near Karachi, Pakistan, in Nov 1949. It was 12.65 m (41 ft 6 in) long and 7 m (23 ft) around the thickest part of the body and weighed an estimated 15–21 tonnes. Despite its size, the whale shark poses very little risk to humans, although some specimens have been known to ram boats that they have mistaken for rival sharks. Its diet consists of plankton and small fish, which it strains from the upper waters of tropical and subtropical seas by lying motionless beneath the surface.

SHORTEST-LIVED FISH

Some killifish species of the family Cyprinodontidae, found in Africa, the Americas, Asia and warmer parts of Europe, normally live for about eight months.

MOST ELECTRIC FISH

The electric eel or paroque (*Electrophorus electricus*), which is related to the piranha, can be up to 1.8 m (6 ft) long and lives in Brazil and the Guianas. Live from head to tail, its electrical apparatus consists of two pairs of longitudinal organs which can release a shock of up to 650 volts. This force, which is used to immobilize prey, is strong enough to light an electric bulb or stun an adult human.

LONGEST FIN

All three species of thresher shark (family Alopiidae) have a huge scythe-shaped caudal fin (tail fin) which is roughly as long as the body itself. The largest and commonest species, *Alopias vulpinus*, found worldwide in temperate and tropical seas, may grow to a length of 6 m (19 ft 8 in), of which almost 3 m (9 ft 10 in) consists of the upper tail fin. It is thought that the tail is used to herd and stun schools of fish ready for eating.

LARGEST EGG

The largest whale shark (*Rhincodon typhus*) egg on record measured 30.5 x 14 x 8.9 cm (12 x 5½ x 3½ in) and contained a live 35-cm-long (13⁴/₅-in) embryo. The specimen, which was found in 1953 in the Gulf of Mexico, may have been aborted.

MOST EGGS

The ocean sunfish (*Mola mola*) produces up to 30 million eggs, each about 1.3 mm (¹/₂₀ in) in diameter, at a single spawning.

FEWEST EGGS

The mouth-brooding cichlid *Tropheus moorii* of Lake Tanganyika, East Africa, produces a maximum of seven eggs during normal reproduction.

MOST VALUABLE FISH

A 1,227-kg (2,706-lb) female Russian sturgeon (*Huso huso*) caught in the River Tikhaya Sosna in 1924 yielded 245 kg (540 lb) of best-quality caviar, which would be worth $315,135 (£189,350) on today's market.

A prizewinning ginrin showa koi from Japan sold for about $87,445 (£50,000) in 1982. In 1986 it was acquired for an undisclosed sum by the Kent Koi Centre, UK, where it died five months later. It has since been stuffed and mounted.

MOST ABUNDANT FISH

The 6.4-cm-long (2½-in) deep-sea bristlemouth (*Cyclothone microdon*) has an almost worldwide distribution.

NEWEST LAND-LIVING FISH

Phreatobius walkeri, a worm-like species of trichomycterid catfish, was found in Brazil in the mid-1980s. It lives a fully terrestrial life among leaf litter on river banks and when it is placed into water jumps back out again.

LONGEST SURVIVAL OUT OF WATER

The six species of lung fish (Lepidosirenidae, Protopteride and Ceratodidae families)

FISH TEETH

The fangtooth anoplogaster bares its sharp fangs, which, like the teeth of all fish, are used not for chewing, but primarily for the capture of prey or the collection of plant food. The larger members of the shark subclasses Selachii and Elasmobranchii have the biggest teeth.

live in freshwater swamps that can dry out for months or even years at a time. Two of the four species found in Africa can live for up to four years in dormant positions in burrows in the ground, abandoning gill breathing in favour of their air-breathing lungs, and secreting a mucus to form a moisture-saving cocoon around their bodies.

water creatures

BIGGEST ANIMAL STRUCTURE
The Great Barrier Reef off Queensland, Australia, is the largest structure built by living creatures. It measures 2,027 km (1,260 mile) long, and covers an area of about 207,000 km² (80,000 miles²). Made up of billions of dead and living stony corals, the reef is estimated to have taken a total of 600 million years to accrete.

BIGGEST ANIMAL EYE
The world's largest invertebrate, the Atlantic giant squid, has the largest eye of any animal, living or extinct. A record-breaking specimen found in Thimble Tickle Bay, Newfoundland, Canada, in 1878 had eyes estimated to have been 50 cm (20 in) in diameter.

BIGGEST AMPHIBIAN
The world's largest amphibian is the Chinese giant salamander (*Andrias davidianus*), which lives in north-eastern, central and southern China. The largest was found in Hunan Province, and was 1.8 m (5 ft 11 in) long and weighed 65 kg (143 lb).

BIGGEST FROG
The African goliath frog (*Conraua goliath*) is the largest known frog. A specimen captured on the River Sanaga, Cameroon, in 1989, had a snout-to-vent length of 36.83 cm (1 ft 2½ in) and an overall length of 87.63 cm (2 ft 10½ in) with its legs extended. It weighed 3.66 kg (8 lb 1 oz).

LONGEST FROG LEAP
The longest triple jump by a frog is 10.3 m (33 ft 5½ in), made by a South African sharp-nosed frog (*Ptychadena oxyrhynchus*) called Santjie, at a frog derby at Lurula Natal Spa, KwaZulu-Natal, South Africa, in 1977.

SMALLEST AMPHIBIAN
The Cuban frog *Eleutherodactylus limbatus* is the world's smallest amphibian. When fully grown it is 8.5–12 mm (¹⁷⁄₅₀ –½ in) long from snout to vent.

BIGGEST TOAD
The cane or marine toad (*Bufo marinus*) of tropical South America and Queensland, Australia, weighs 450 g (1 lb). The largest specimen on record was called Prinsen and was owned by Håkan Forsberg of Sweden. In 1991 it weighed 2.65 kg (5 lb 13½ oz) and was 53.9 cm (1 ft 9¼ in) long when fully extended.

SMALLEST TOAD
The largest specimen of the African sub-species *Bufo taitanus beiranus* was just 2.4 cm (¹⁵⁄₁₆ in) long.

SMALLEST NEWT/SALAMANDER
The lungless salamander from Mexico (*Bolitoglossa mexicana*) has a maximum length of about 2.54 cm (1 in), including its tail.

LARGEST CRUSTACEAN
The largest crustacean in the world is the taka-ashi-gani or giant spider crab (*Macrocheira kaempferi*). One specimen had a claw-span of 3.7 m (12 ft 1½ in) and weighed 18.6 kg (41 lb).

HEAVIEST MARINE CRUSTACEAN
An American or North Atlantic lobster (*Homarus americanus*) weighing 20.14 kg (44 lb 6 oz) and measuring 1.06 m (3 ft 6 in) from the end of the tail-fan to the tip of the largest claw was caught off Nova Scotia, Canada, in 1977. It was later sold to a restaurant in New York, USA.

BIGGEST FRESHWATER CRUSTACEAN
The crayfish or crawfish (*Astacopsis gouldi*), found in the streams of Tasmania, Australia, can be up to 61 cm (2 ft) long and weighs as much as 4.1 kg (9 lb). A specimen caught at Bridport in 1934 was reported to weigh 6.35 kg (14 lb) and was 73.6 cm (29 in) long.

BIGGEST CRUSTACEAN SWARM
A swarm of krill (*Euphausia superba*) estimated to weigh up to 10 million tonnes was tracked by US scientists off Antarctica in March 1981. It was the largest concentration of crustaceans ever seen.

BIGGEST JELLYFISH
In 1870 an Arctic giant jellyfish (*Cyanea capillata arctica*) was washed up in Massachusetts Bay, USA, from the north-western Atlantic, with a bell diameter of 2.28 m (7 ft 6 in) and tentacles 36.5 m long (120 ft).

BIGGEST CLAM
The marine giant clam *Tridacna gigas*, found off the Indo-

FROG SIZE
The green leaf frog belongs to the family Hylidae, the second largest frog family. There are a total of 2,660 species of frog, ranging in length from 8.5 mm (⅓ in) for *Eleutherodactylus limbatus* to 36.83 cm (14 ½ in) for a *Conrava goliath* or African goliath frog.

GIANT CRABS
The annual Crabfest at Chandlers Restaurant in Seattle, USA, runs for six weeks between March and May, and offers crab-lovers a choice of 35 dishes, from chilled crabs and crab quiche to crab ice cream. Prior to the feast, four chefs scour the world for the finest crabs, including 16-kg (35-lb) giant Tasmanian crabs from Australia with 1.3–3.2-kg (3–7-lb) claws as big as human arms, and Arkansas king crabs, which are reputed to be the tastiest in the world. The prized giant Tasmanian crabs cost $36.95/lb (£48.94/kg). The restaurant, which normally sells 726 kg (1,600 lb) of crab in six weeks, serves up about 4,536 kg (10,000 lb) a week during the Crabfest and makes an extra $30,000–47,000 (£18,026–28,240). In 1998 a team of celebrities cracked and judged the first crabs for taste, texture and quality.

Pacific coral reefs has the largest bivalve shell. One 1.15 m (3 ft 9¼ in) long, 333-kg (734-lb) specimen was found off Ishigaki Island, Okinawa, Japan, in 1956. It probably weighed just over 340 kg (750 lb) when alive.

LARGEST MARINE GASTROPOD

A trumpet or baler conch (*Syrinx aruanus*) found off Australia in 1979 had a 77.2-cm-long (30²/₅-in) shell and a girth of up to 1.01 m (39¾ in). It weighed nearly 18 kg (40 lb) when alive.

BIGGEST OYSTER

A common oyster (*Ostrea goulis*) found at Arisaig, UK, in 1997 weighed 828.4 g (1 lb 13 oz) and had a maximum width of 16.5–18.56 cm (6½–6¾ in).

BIGGEST SPONGE

The barrel-shaped loggerhead sponge (*Spheciospongia vesparium*), which lives in the West Indies and the waters off Florida, USA, is up to 1.05 m (3 ft 6 in) in height and 91 cm (3 ft) in diameter.

HEAVIEST SPONGE

A wool sponge (*Hippospongia canaliculatta*) collected off the Bahamas in 1909 weighed between 36 and 41 kg (80–90 lb) and measured 1.83 m (6 ft) in circumference.

SMALLEST SPONGE

Leucosolenia blanca is just 3 mm tall (¹¹/₁₀₀ in) when fully grown.

BIGGEST STARFISH

A specimen of the very fragile brisingid *Midgardia xandaros* found in the Gulf of Mexico in 1968 was 1.38 m (4 ft 6 in) long from tip to tip. Its disc was only 2.6 cm (¹¹/₅₀ in) in diameter.

SMALLEST STARFISH

The asterinid sea star *Patiriella parvivipara,* discovered on the west coast of the Eyre peninsula, South Australia, in 1975, had a maximum radius of 4.7 mm (⁹/₅₀ in) and a diameter of less than 9 mm (⁷/₂₀ in).

GREATEST SIZE DIFFERENCE

Females of the marine worm *Bonellia viridis* are 10–100 cm (4–40 in) long, including the extendable proboscis, while males are only around 1–3 mm (¹/₂₅–³/₂₅ in) long. The females are thus thousands of times heavier than their mates.

MOST PATERNAL AMPHIBIAN

The 7.6-cm-long (3-in) male West European midwife toad *Alytes obstetricans* fertilizes the string of eggs that the female has laid — which can be up to 0.9–1.2 m (3–4 ft) long — and winds it around his thighs. He carries the eggs around for up to four weeks until they are ready to hatch, at which point he swims into suitable water and releases the tadpoles.

GREATEST REGENERATION

The sponges (Porifera) are able to regrow from tiny fragments of their former selves, and even if one of them is forced through a fine-meshed silk gauze, the separate fragments can reform into a full-sized sponge.

DEEPEST-LIVING SPONGE

Some sponges of the class Hexactinellida have been recovered from depths of up to 29.000 ft (8.500 m).

DEEPEST-LIVING STARFISH

A specimen of the species *Porcellanaster ivanovi* was collected from a depth of 7,584 m (24,881 ft) by the Soviet research ship *Vityaz* in the Mariana Trench in the west Pacific c. 1962.

LARGEST INVERTEBRATE

The Atlantic giant squid (*Architeuthis dux*) is the largest known invertebrate. The heaviest ever discovered ran aground in Thimble Tickle Bay, Newfoundland, Canada, on 2 Nov 1878. It had a body length of 6.1 m (20 ft) and one tentacle was 10.7 m (35 ft) long.

reptiles and dinosaurs

SNAKE ATTACK AND DEFENCE
Snakes evolved from lizard ancestors 120 million years ago and have become extremely successful hunters, suffocating or biting their prey to death or killing them with their venom. Snakes' heads are specially adapted for eating large animals: they have a number of extra joints that allow the skull to dislocate so that the snake can swallow large prey whole. These prey can sometimes be several times the normal diameter of the snake's mouth. Here, a black timber rattlesnake devours a field mouse. Rattlesnakes use their 'rattles' to warn off other animals without recourse to venom. The rattle is made from dead scales that brush against one another when the snake vibrates its tail.

BIGGEST REPTILE
The longest known estuarine or saltwater crocodile (*Crocodylus porosus*) measures 7 m (23 ft) and lives in the Bhitarkanika Wildlife Sanctuary, Orissa, India. There are several reports of 10-m-long (33-ft) specimens, but they are not substantiated.

SMALLEST CROCODILIAN
Female dwarf caimans (*Paleosuchus palpebrosus*) from northern South America rarely exceed 1.2 m (4 ft) in length, and males are usually not more than 1.5 m (4 ft 11 in) long.

LONGEST LIZARD
The Salvadori or Papuan monitor (*Varanus salvadorii*) from Papua New Guinea can attain a length of up to 4.75 m (15 ft 7 in). Its tail accounts for almost 70% of this length.

SMALLEST LIZARD
Sphaerodactylus parthenopion, a gecko indigenous to Virgin Gorda, British Virgin Islands, West Indies, is known from just 15 specimens. The three largest among some pregnant females found in 1964 were 1.8 cm (⁷/₁₆ in) long from snout to vent.

LONGEST SNAKE
The reticulated python (*Python reticulatus*) of South east Asia often exceeds 6.25 m (20 ft 6 in) in length. A specimen shot in 1912 in Celebes, Indonesia, was recorded as measuring 10 m (32 ft 9½ in) long.

SHORTEST SNAKES
The thread snake (*Leptotyphlops bilineata*) is extremely rare, and the longest known specimen was just 10.8 cm (4¼ in). The snake's body could have fitted into the lead hole in a standard pencil. Another snake, the Brahminy blindsnake (*Rhamphotyphlops braminus*), from the tropics, is less than 10.8 cm (4¼ in) long.

BIGGEST CHELONIAN
The biggest chelonian, the leatherback turtle (*Dermochelys coriacea*), averages 1.83–2.13 m (6–7 ft) from the tip of the beak to the end of the tail and about 2.13 m (7 ft) across the front flippers and weighs up to 450 kg (1,000 lb). The largest known was a male found dead on the beach at Harlech, Gwynedd, UK, in 1988. It measured 2.91 m (9 ft 5½ in) in total length over the carapace and 2.77 m (9 ft) across the front flippers, and weighed 961.1 kg (2,120 lb).

BIGGEST TORTOISE
The largest living tortoise is a Galapagos tortoise (*Geochelone elephantopos elephantopos*) known as Goliath, which has lived at the Life Fellowship Bird Sanctuary, Sessner, Florida, USA, since 1960. It is 1.35 m (53⁵/₈ in) long, 1.02 m (40½ in) wide and weighs 385 kg (849 lb).

SMALLEST CHELONIANS
The speckled sape tortoise or speckled padloper (*Homotopus signatus*) has a total shell length of just 6–9.6 cm (2.3–3.7 in).

SNAKE EATING
A vendor in Ho Chi Minh City, Vietnam, tries to attract customers to buy a 5-m-long (16-ft) python. Snake venom is believed to help fight cancer and snakes are considered a culinary delicacy in a number of Asian countries. In Indonesia, the government is now discouraging snake eating as it is endangering certain species. To make your own snake dish, try the recipe below, though if you can't find rattlesnake, chicken will do!

GRILLED RATTLESNAKE CHINESE STYLE
1 fresh rattlesnake
⅓ cup soy sauce
¼ cup fresh lime juice
⅓ cup mirin or 2 tbsp sweet sherry
Combine the soy sauce, lime juice and mirin or sherry. Add the snake and marinate for at least two hours. Prepare a fire in a charcoal grill. Remove the snake from the marinade and keep the marinade. Thread the snake onto bamboo skewers and grill over medium or hot coals, basting frequently with the marinade for about five minutes until tender.

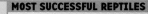

Pictured left is an emerald swift lizard. Lizards are the most successful living group of reptiles, with 3,100 species compared with snakes, which are the second most successful group and have 2,000 species. Lizards are also the most diverse group of living reptiles in terms of size and shape, and range in total body length from small lizards such as geckos, measuring about 3 cm (1¹/₅ in), to monitor lizards of 4.75 m (15 ft). Different species move at different speeds, depending on where they live – those native to desert regions are generally the fastest, and all are able to accelerate rapidly.

The smallest marine turtle in the world is the Atlantic ridley (*Lepidochelys kempii*), which has a shell length of 50–70 cm (20–28 in) and a maximum weight of 80 kg (176 lb).

OLDEST CHELONIAN
A Madagascar radiated tortoise (*Astrochelys radiata*) called Tui Malila was presented by Captain Cook to the Tonga royal family in either 1773 or 1777. It was at least 188 years old when it died in 1965.

DEEPEST CHELONIAN DIVE
In 1987 a leatherback turtle fitted with a pressure-sensitive recording device was reported to have reached a depth of 1,200 m (3,973 ft) off the Virgin Islands, West Indies.

FASTEST REPTILES
The highest speed attained by a reptile in water is recorded as 35 km/h (22 mph), by a scared Pacific leatherback turtle.

The highest speed measured for a reptile on land is 34.9 km/h (21⁷/₁₀ mph), attained by a spiny-tailed iguana (*Ctenosaura*) from Costa Rica.

FASTEST SNAKE
The fastest land snake is thought to be the aggressive black mamba (*Dendroaspis polylepis*) of eastern tropical Africa, which is capable of speeds as high as 16–19 km/h (10–12 mph) in short bursts over level ground.

FASTEST DINOSAURS
Dinosaur trackways discovered in the Morrison formation, Texas, USA — which dates from the Late Jurassic period — indicate that a carnivorous dinosaur had been moving at 40 km/h (25 mph).

The large-brained, 100-kg (220-lb) *Dromiceiomimus* ('emu mimic lizard') of the Late Cretaceous period from Alberta, Canada, could probably outsprint an ostrich, which can move at more than 60 km/h (37 mph).

BIGGEST HERBIVOROUS DINOSAUR
The world's largest ever land animals were sauropod dinosaurs, a group of long necked, long-tailed, four-legged plant eaters that lumbered around most of the world during the Jurassic and Cretaceous periods, 208–65 million years ago. The largest specimen was 40 m (131 ft) long and would have weighed up to 100 tonnes.

SMALLEST DINOSAUR
Compsognathus (meaning 'pretty jaw'), a chicken-sized dinosaur from southern Germany and south-east France was 60 cm (23 in) long from the snout to the tip of the tail and weighed approximately 3 kg (6 lb 8 oz).

BIGGEST DINOSAUR FOOTPRINTS
In 1932, the 1.36-m-long (53½-in), 81-cm-wide (32-in) footprints of a bipedal hadrosaurid (meaning 'duckbill') were discovered in Salt Lake City, Utah, USA, while other reports from Colorado and Utah refer to 0.95–1-m-wide (37–40-in) footprints. Prints attributed to the hind feet of the largest brachiosaurids are also up to 1 m (40 in) wide.

BIGGEST DINOSAUR CLAWS
The therizinosaurids ('scythe lizards'), which lived in the Nemegt Basin, Mongolia, in the Late Cretaceous period, had the largest claws of any known animal. Claws of *Therizinosaurus cheloniformis* were up to 91 cm (36 in) along the outer curve.

BIGGEST DINOSAUR SKULL
The long-frilled *Torosaurus* ('piercing lizard'), a ceratopsid, had the largest skull of any known land animal. The 7.6-m-long (25-ft), 8-tonne herbivore's skull was up to 3 m (9 ft 10 in) long (including the fringe) and weighed as much as 2 tonnes.

STUPIDEST DINOSAUR
Stegosaurus (meaning 'plated lizard'), which roamed across Colorado, Oklahoma, Utah and Wyoming, USA, about 150 million years ago, was up to 9 m (30 ft) long but had a walnut-sized brain weighing 70 g (2½ oz). This is equal to 0.002 of 1% of its estimated bodyweight of 3.3 tonnes (compared with 0.06 of 1% for an elephant and 1.88% for a human).

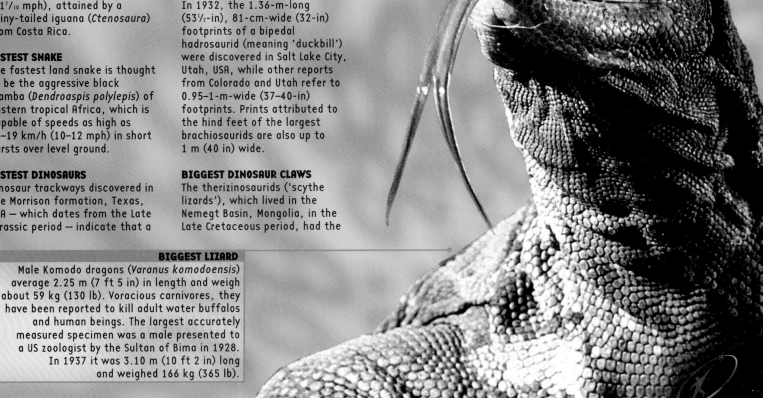

BIGGEST LIZARD
Male Komodo dragons (*Varanus komodoensis*) average 2.25 m (7 ft 5 in) in length and weigh about 59 kg (130 lb). Voracious carnivores, they have been reported to kill adult water buffalos and human beings. The largest accurately measured specimen was a male presented to a US zoologist by the Sultan of Bima in 1928. In 1937 it was 3.10 m (10 ft 2 in) long and weighed 166 kg (365 lb).

birds

SMALLEST BIRD

Male bee hummingbirds (*Mellisuga helenae*), which live in Cuba, weigh 1.6 g (0.056 oz) and are 5.7 cm (2¼ in) in length. The bill and tail account for half of this length.

SMALLEST BIRDS OF PREY

The black-legged falconet (*Microhierax fringillarius*) of South-east Asia and the white-fronted or Bornean falconet (*M. latifrons*) of north-western Borneo both have an average length of 14–15 cm (5½–6 in), including a 5-cm (2-in) tail, and weigh approximately 35 g (1¼ oz).

TALLEST FLYING BIRDS

The largest cranes (family Gruidae) can be almost 2 m (6 ft 6 in) tall.

HEAVIEST FLYING BIRDS

The Kori bustard or paauw (*Ardeotis kori*) of north-east and southern Africa and the great bustard (*Otis tarda*) of Europe and Asia weigh about 18–19 kg (40–42 lb). There is a report of a 21-kg (46-lb 4-oz) male great bustard shot in north-eastern China. It was too heavy to fly.

HEAVIEST BIRDS OF PREY

Andean condors (*Vultur gryphus*) are the heaviest species of bird of prey. Males weigh 9–12 kg (20–27 lb) and have a wing-span of at least 3 m (10 ft).

A male California condor (*Gymnogyps californianus*) preserved in the California Academy of Sciences, USA, is said to weigh 14.1 kg (31 lb). The species rarely exceeds 10.4 kg (23 lb) in weight.

LONGEST FEATHERS

The phoenix fowl or Yokohama chicken (a strain of the red junglefowl *Gallus gallus*) is bred in Japan for ornamental purposes. A rooster with a 10.6-m (34-ft 9½-in) tail covert was reported in 1972.

LONGEST BILLS

The bill of the Australian pelican (*Pelicanus conspicillatus*) is 34–47 cm (13–18½ in) long.

The longest beak in relation to body length is that of the sword-billed hummingbird (*Ensifera ensifera*) of the Andes. At 10.2 cm (4 in), the beak is longer than the bird's body (excluding the tail).

BIGGEST EYES

The ostrich has the largest eyes of any land animal. Each eye can be up to 5 cm (2 in) in diameter.

MOST AIRBORNE BIRD

The sooty tern (*Sterna fuscata*) leaves the nesting grounds as a youngster and remains aloft for 3–10 years, settling on water from time to time. It returns to land to breed as an adult.

LONGEST FLIGHT

A common tern (*Sterna hirundo*) that was banded in June 1996 in Finland was recaptured alive 26,000 km (16,250 miles) away at Rotamah Island, Victoria, Australia, in Jan 1997. It had travelled at a rate of 200 km (125 miles) a day.

SLOWEST-FLYING BIRDS

Both the American woodcock (*Scolopax minor*) and the Eurasian woodcock (*S. rusticola*) have been timed flying at 8 km/h (5 mph) without stalling during courtship displays.

SLOWEST WING-BEAT

The slowest wing-beats recorded during true level flight averaged one per second. They were by several species of the New World vulture (family Cathartidae).

BIGGEST EVER WING-SPAN

The South American teratoron (*Argentavis magnificens*), which existed 6–8 million years ago, had an estimated wing-span of 7.6 m (25 ft).

FASTEST FLYING BIRD

The peregrine falcon (*Falco peregrinus*) is the fastest living creature, reaching speeds of at least 200 km/h (124 mph) and possibly as much as 270 km/h (168 mph) when swooping from great heights during territorial displays or while catching prey birds in mid-air.

FASTEST WING-BEAT

The horned sungem (*Heliactin cornuta*), a hummingbird from South America, beats its wings 90 times a second.

FASTEST LAND BIRD

Despite its bulk, the ostrich can run at speeds of up to 72 km/h (45 mph) if necessary.

HIGHEST-FLYING BIRDS

A Ruppell's vulture (*Gyps rueppellii*) collided with a commercial aircraft over Abidjan, Ivory Coast, at an altitude of 11,300 m (37,000 ft) in Nov 1973. The impact damaged one of the aircraft's engines but the plane landed safely. The species is rarely seen above 6,000 m (20,000 ft).

In 1967 about 30 whooper swans (*Cygnus cygnus*) were spotted at an altitude of just over 8,230 m (27,000 ft) by an airline pilot over the Western Isles, UK. They were flying from Iceland to Loch Foyle on the Northern Ireland/Republic of Ireland border. Their altitude was confirmed by air traffic control.

LONGEST STRIDE

The stride of an ostrich may exceed 7 m (23 ft) in length when the bird is sprinting.

HIGHEST G-FORCE BORNE

The beak of the red-headed woodpecker (*Melanerpes erythrocephalus*) hits the bark of a tree with an impact velocity of 20.9 km/h (13 mph), subjecting the bird's brain to a deceleration of approximately 10 g when its head snaps back. Other woodpeckers may experience an even higher g-force.

MOST FOOD CONSUMED

Hummingbirds (family Trochilidae) require at least half their own body weight in food (mainly nectar and tiny insects) every

BIGGEST BIRD

The largest and strongest living bird is the North African ostrich (*Struthio camelus camelus*). Males can be up to 2.75 m (9 ft) tall and weigh 156.5 kg (345 lb), and when fully grown they have one of the most advanced immune systems of any animal. South Africa was the first country to see the commercial potential of ostrich products — the creatures are prized not only for their large soft white feathers and their meat but also for their skins, which are made into the strongest commercially available leather in the world. Ostrich farming is believed to have begun in the Karoo and Eastern Cape c. 1863. By 1910 there were more than 20,000 domesticated ostriches in the country and by 1913 ostrich feathers were the fourth most important South African export product. Demand began to dry up soon afterwards but there was an ostrich revival in the 1920s when farmers started to produce *biltong* (dried strips of ostrich meat) commercially. Ostrich farming is now practised in 50 countries and is especially popular in South Africa, Algeria, Australia, France and the USA. It has saved ostriches from becoming an endangered species: there are currently about 1.75 million worldwide.

single day. With the possible exception of shrews, they have the highest metabolic rate of any known animal.

STRANGEST DIET

An ostrich living at London Zoo, UK, was found to have swallowed an alarm clock, a roll of film, a handkerchief, a 91-cm-long (3-ft) piece of rope, a cycle valve, a pencil, three gloves, a comb, part of a gold necklace, a collar stud, a Belgian franc, four halfpennies and two farthings.

LONGEST FAST

The male emperor penguin (*Aptenodytes forsteri*) spends several months without feeding on the frozen wastes of the Antarctic sea ice: it travels overland from the sea to the breeding colony, courts the female, incubates the egg for 62–67 days, waits for the female to return and travels back to the open sea, going without food for up to 134 days.

LARGEST PREY

The largest wild animal known to have been killed and carried away by a bird was a 7-kg (15-lb) male red howler monkey killed by a harpy eagle (*Harpia harpyja*) in Manu National Park, Peru, in 1990. The harpy eagle is considered the world's most powerful bird of prey, although it weighs only 9 kg (20 lb).

KEENEST VISION

The peregrine falcon (*Falco peregrinus*) is believed to be able to spot a pigeon from a distance of more than 8 km (5 miles) under ideal conditions.

BIGGEST NESTS

The incubation mounds built by the mallee fowl (*Leipoa ocellata*) of Australia are up to 4.57 m (15 ft) tall and 10.6 m (35 ft) wide. A nest site is estimated to weigh 300 tonnes.

A 2.9-m-wide (9-ft 6-in), 6-m-deep (20-ft) nest was built by a pair of bald eagles (*Haliaeetus leucocephalus*), and possibly by their successors, close to St. Petersburg, Florida, USA. When examined in 1963, it was estimated to weigh in excess of 2 tonnes.

SMALLEST NESTS

The vervain hummingbird (*Mellisuga minima*) builds a nest about half the size of a walnut shell. The deeper but narrower nest of the bee hummingbird (*M. helenae*) is thimble-sized.

BIGGEST EGGS

The extinct giant elephant bird (*Aepyornis maximus*) laid 33-cm-long (1-ft) eggs with a liquid capacity of 8.5 litres (2¼ gals) — the equivalent of seven ostrich eggs and more than 12,000 hummingbird eggs.

The ostrich egg is 15–20 cm (6–8 in) long, 10–15 cm (4–6 in) in diameter and weighs 1.0–1.78 kg (2 lb 3 oz–3 lb 14 oz). It is equal in volume to 24 hens' eggs. The shell is 1.5 mm ($^3/_{50}$ in) thick but can support the weight of an adult human. The largest on record was laid in 1988 by a two-year-old northern/southern hybrid (*Struthio c. camelus x S. c. australis*) at the Kibbutz Ha'on collective farm, Israel. It weighed 2.3 kg (5 lb 2 oz).

SMALLEST EGG

The smallest known birds' eggs were two vervain hummingbird (*Mellisuga minima*) eggs less than 1 cm ($^{39}/_{100}$ in) long. They weighed 0.365 g (0.0128 oz) and 0.375 g (0.0132 oz).

MOST ABUNDANT BIRD

The red-billed quelea (*Quelea quelea*) of Africa has an estimated adult breeding population of 1.5 billion. The slaughter of at least 200 million of them each year has no impact on this number.

BOSSIEST BIRD

The kea (*Nestor notabilis*) from New Zealand is the only bird known to have a society in which the higher-status individuals force others to work for them.

SMELLIEST BIRD

The South American hoatzin (*Opisthocomus hoazin*) has an odour similar to cow manure. Colombians call it *pava hedionda* ('stinking pheasant'). The cause of the smell is believed to be a combination of its diet of green leaves and its specialized digestive system, which involves a kind of foregut fermentation.

LARGEST CURRENT WING-SPAN

The wandering albatross (*Diomedea exulans*) has the largest wing-span of any living bird. As a result it is an expert glider and is capable of remaining in the air without beating its wings for several hours at a time. The largest known specimen was an extremely old male with a 3.63-m (11-ft 11-in) wing-span. It was caught in the Tasman Sea in Sept 1965.

LARGE FLOCKS

Flamingoes, with their long necks and legs, have a height range of 0.9–1.5 m (3–5 ft) and are the biggest bird to form large flocks. Of the four species, the lesser flamingo (*Phoeniconaias minor*) of eastern and southern Africa has been seen in flocks of several million birds, particularly in the Great Lakes of eastern Africa.

spiders and scorpions

BIGGEST SPIDER
The goliath bird-eating spider (*Theraphosa leblondi*), which is found mostly in the coastal rainforests of Surinam, Guyana and French Guiana, is the world's largest known spider. A male specimen found in Venezuela in 1965 had a leg-span of 28 cm (11 in) and was big enough to cover a dinner plate.

HEAVIEST SPIDER
Female bird-eating spiders are more heavily built than the males. A 122.2-g (4^{3}/$_{10}$-oz) female captured in Surinam in 1985, had a maximum leg-span of 26.7 cm (10½ in) and 2.5-cm (1-in) fangs.

SMALLEST SPIDER
Patu marplesi of the family Symphytognathidae from Samoa is the world's smallest known spider. A male found in 1965 was 0.43 mm (^{17}/$_{1000}$ in) long overall — about the size of one of the full stops on this page.

LONGEST SPIDER FANGS
The bird-eating spider *Theraphosa leblondi* has fangs that are up to 1.2 cm (½ in) long.

BIGGEST SIZE DIFFERENCE
In some species of the golden orb-web spider (genus *Nephila*), which are found all over the tropical and temperate world, females are almost 1,000 times heavier than their mates. The males are smaller than the females' normal prey in order to avoid being eaten by them.

FASTEST SPIDERS
The long-legged sun spiders (order Solifugae) of the arid semi-desert regions of Africa and the Middle East can reach speeds of over 16 km/h (10 mph).

NOISIEST SPIDERS
In courtship the male European buzzing spider (*Anyphaena accentuata*) produces a buzzing sound audible to the human ear. Produced by the spider vibrating his abdomen rapidly against a leaf, the sound cannot be heard by the female: she can only detect it through vibrations.

The male *Lycosa gulosa*, once known as the purring spider, taps his palps and abdomen on leaves to make a purring sound.

MOST SOCIABLE SPIDER
Several thousand members of both sexes of the South African species *Anelosimus eximus* cohabit peaceably on webs that are more than 1 m (3 ft) across.

MOST MATERNAL SPIDER
In many spider species the maternal relationship ends when the eggs are laid, and the mother never sees her young. *Theridion sisyphium* females, however, feed their young with liquid from their own mouths. When they are a few days old, the infants begin to share their mother's prey and as they grow older they help her to hunt. The relationship comes to an end when the mother dies, and is eaten by her offspring.

LARGEST WEBS
The golden silk spider is one of around 50 species of the genus *Nephila*, found in tropical areas all over the world. The first lines of the yellow silk webs of the genus are up to 3 m (10 ft) long and can even stretch across small rivers.

BIGGEST SCORPION
Steve Kutcher, seen left with his pet tropical emperor scorpion and Chilean rose tarantula, is famous for providing various trained creatures for big movies in the USA. He began by supplying the locusts for *The Exorcist 2* (1977) and went on to provide the spiders for *Arachnophobia* (1990) and a huge mosquito for *Jurassic Park* (1993). In order to get his creatures to behave exactly as he wants them to on set, Kutcher takes along tweezers, a fishing line and plastic cases full of waxes and glue. He sometimes also blasts his creatures with gusts of hot air and carbon dioxide to make them act in a certain way. Steve, who lives in Arcadia, California, USA, studied biology and entomology at university after becoming fascinated by bugs and starting a firefly collection one summer in New York. He now devotes an entire room in his house to insects, which live in glass and wooden boxes piled from floor to ceiling. The tropical emperor scorpion is one of the world's largest species of scorpion, reaching a length of up to 18 cm (7 in), but is totally harmless and makes a good housepet.

OLDEST SPIDERS

The tropical bird-eaters (family Theraphosidae) can live for up to 25 years.

STRONGEST SPIDERS' WEBS

Achaearenea tepidariorum weaves a web strong enough to trap a small mouse, completely lifting it off the ground.

The webs of the genus *Nephila* can trap small birds and even hamper the movements of humans.

Nephila senegalenis from tropical Africa has a special 'litter line' in its webs where the sucked-out remains of small birds may often be found.

LARGEST CONTINUOUS WEBS

The largest continuous areas of web in the world are built by spiders of the Indian genus *Stegodyphus*, which create three-dimensional, interwoven and overlapping webs. A single continuous silken mass can cover considerable vegetation, and extend unbroken over whole hedgerows.

SIMPLEST WEBS

Spider species of the genus *Miagrammopes* weave a single-stranded web that stretches for up to 1 m (3 ft) between two small branches.

The American bolas spider of the genus *Mastophora* uses a small single strand to attach itself to

a branch and a second, much longer, strand as a 'fishing-line' to catch passing moths.

The South African bolas spider *Cladomelea akermani* uses a similar technique but rotates the 'fishing line' continuously for about 15 minutes. If no prey is

ensnared, the spider consumes the sticky globe on the end of the line and replaces it with a new one.

LARGEST SCORPION

Heterometrus swannerdami from southern India frequently attains a length of more than 18 cm (7 in) from the tips of the pincers to the end of the sting. The longest specimen was found during WWII and had an overall length of 29.2 cm (11½ in).

STRONGEST SPIDER

When an intruder is trying to open its 'trap-door' (a silken structure covering the entrance to its underground burrow), the Californian trap-door spider *Bothriocyrtum californicum* is capable of resisting a force up to 38 times its own weight.

BIGGEST EYES

The net-casting spider (*Dinopis subrufa*) of the genus *Dinopis* has huge eyes that shine like headlights when staring at a bright light. The *Dinopis* genus has the biggest eyes of any spider, especially ogre-faced or gladiator spiders, which have the largest simple eyes of any arthropod. About 1.5 cm (½ in) in width, they do not produce very clear images but have excellent light-gathering power for night work.

The tropical emperor or imperial scorpion (*Pandinus imperator*) of West Africa can also be up to 18 cm (7 in) long. The largest on record is a 22.9-cm (9-in) male from Sierra Leone.

The tropical African species *Pandinus giganticus* may grow to almost 20 cm (8 in) in length.

SMALLEST SCORPION

Microbothus pusillus, a species which is found on the Red Sea coast, is the smallest scorpion in the world, with an approximate total length of 1.3 cm (½ in).

HEAVIEST SCORPION

The West African tropical emperor or imperial scorpion (*Pandinus imperator*) can weigh up to 60 g (2 oz).

DEEPEST-LIVING SCORPION

The *Alacran tartarus* species, which lives in South America, has been found in caves more than 800 m (2,625 ft) deep.

MOST SOCIABLE SCORPION

West African tropical emperor or imperial scorpion (*Pandinus imperator*) offspring may remain with the family group when they are adults, and families co-operate to capture prey.

insects and creepy crawlies

LONGEST INSECT

Measuring 54.6 cm (21½ in), the legs of *Pharnacia kirbyi*, a stick insect from the rainforests of Borneo, are so long that they can get trapped when it sheds its skin. The largest known specimen had a body length of 32.8 cm (12⁹/₁₀ in).

LIGHTEST INSECTS

The male bloodsucking banded louse (*Enderleinellus zonatus*) and the parasitic wasp (*Caraphractus cinctus*) may each weigh as little as 0.005 mg. This is equal to 1.6 billion creatures per gram (5,670,000 per ounce).

LARGEST FLEA

Hystrichopsylla schefferi females are up to 8 mm (¹/₃ in) long. The species was described from one specimen found in the nest of a mountain beaver in Washington, USA, in 1913.

LARGEST WINGED COCKROACH

A preserved *Megaloblatta longipennis* female in the collection of Akira Yokokura of Japan is 9.7 cm (3¹/₅ in) long and 4.5 cm (1¾ in) wide. The species originates in Columbia.

LARGEST TERMITE

Queens of the African termite species *Macrotermes bellicosus* are up to 14 cm (5½ in) long and 3.5 cm (1²/₅ in) wide. They can produce 30,000 eggs a day, barely move and spend their entire lives in a 'royal cell' in the centre of the colony.

GREATEST CONCENTRATION OF INSECTS

In July 1874 a swarm of Rocky Mountain locusts (*Melanoplus spretus*) covered an estimated 514,374-km² (198,600-mile²) area as they flew over the state of Nebraska, USA. The swarm

GREEDIEST ANIMAL

The larva of the polyphemus moth (*Antheraea polyphemus*) consumes 86,000 times its own birthweight in its first 56 days. This is equal to a 3.17-kg (7-lb) human baby taking in 273 tonnes of nourishment.

HEAVIEST INSECT

Goliath beetles (from the family Scarabaeidae) of equatorial Africa, especially *Goliathus regius*, *G. meleagris*, *G. goliathus* or *giganteus* and *G. druryi*, are the heaviest insects in the world. Males are up to 11 cm (4¹/₃ in) long from the tip of the frontal horns to the end of the abdomen and weigh up to 100 g (3½ oz).

MOST DESTRUCTIVE INSECT

The desert locust (*Schistocerca gregaria*) can eat its own weight in food every day. In a single day a 'small' swarm of about 50 million specimens can eat food that would sustain 500 people for a year.

contained 12.5 trillion (12.5 x 10¹²) insects and weighed 25 million tonnes.

MOST FERTILE ANIMAL

With unlimited food and no predators, one cabbage aphid (*Brevicoryne brassicae*) could theoretically create an 822 million-tonne mass of descendants every year – more than three times the weight of the world's human population.

FASTEST-FLYING INSECTS

The highest maintainable airspeed of any insect is 39 km/h (24 mph), by the deer bot-fly (*Cephenemyia pratti*), hawk moths (Sphingidae), horseflies (*Tabanus bovinus*) and some tropical butterflies (Hesperiidae).

The Australian dragonfly (*Austrophlebia costalis*) can reach a speed of 58 km/h (36 mph) for short bursts.

LONGEST JUMP BY A FLEA

The cat flea (*Ctenocephalides felis*) can make single jumps of up to 34 cm (13⅕ in), and the common flea (*Pulex irritans*) is capable of similar feats. In a 1910 US experiment, a common flea allowed to leap at will performed a long jump of 33 cm (13 in) and a high jump of 19.7 cm (7¾ in).

HIGHEST G FORCE ON AN INSECT

When 'jack-knifing' into the air to escape predators, the click beetle (*Athous haemorrhoidalis*)

averages 400 g (14 oz). One 12-mm-long (½-in), 40-mg (0.00014-oz) specimen jumped to a height of 30 cm (11¾ in), and was calculated to have endured a peak brain deceleration of 2,300 g.

LOUDEST INSECT

The tymbal organs of the male cicada (family Cicadidae) pulse 7,400 times a minute. The noise (which the US Department of Agriculture lists as 'Tsh-ee-EEEE-e-ou') is detectable more than 400 m (¼ mile) away.

SHORTEST-LIVED INSECTS

Mayflies (*Ephemeroptera*) can spend 2–3 years as nymphs at the bottom of lakes and streams and live for as little as an hour as winged adults.

MOST ACUTE SENSE OF SMELL

The male emperor moth (*Eudia pavonia*) can detect the sex attractant of the virgin female from a distance of 11 km (6⅘ miles). The chemoreceptors on the male moth's antennae can detect a single molecule of the attractant, of which the female carries less than 0.0001 mg.

BIGGEST COCKROACH

The *Macropanesthia rhinoceros* is the biggest cockroach species without wings. It is 8 cm (3 in) long, and 5 cm (2 in) wide, and weighs 35 grams (1¼ oz) about the same weight as two sparrows. The species is native to Queensland, Australia.

parasites

MOST BLOODTHIRSTY PARASITES
Blood-sucking hookworms inhabit about 700 million people worldwide and may be responsible for a daily blood loss of 7 million litres (12.3 million pints) — the total blood of more than 1 million people.

Each specimen of the digenean liver fluke *Fasciola hepatica*, a common mammalian parasite, consumes about 0.2 ml (0.007 fl.oz) of blood per day.

LONGEST PARASITIC FASTS
The common bedbug *Cimex lectularius* is famously able to survive without feeding for more than a year, but the soft tick *Ornithodoros turicata* can live through a period of starvation lasting up to five years.

MOST FERTILE PARASITES
One *Ascaris lumbricoides* female can produce up to 200,000 eggs every day of her adult life, and has a total productive capacity of 26 million eggs.

Echinococcus granulosus, a canine tapeworm, can also infect the liver, lungs and brain of humans, in which it produces cyst-like structures called hydatids. These can measure as much as 25.4 cm (10 in) across and can seriously damage the organs containing them. A fertile hydatid contains an average of 2 million larvae, which can yield innumerable adult tapeworms.

FASTEST PARASITIC WORM
Specimens of the subcutaneous eyeworm *Loa loa*, which is up to 7.6 cm (3 in) long, have been removed from all parts of patients' bodies. As adults their maximum migration rate through the human body equals 13 mm ($\frac{1}{2}$ in) per minute. The eyeworm is an endoparasite or internal parasite. The most common endoparasites are microparasites such as viruses.

MOST COMMON HUMAN PARASITE
Ascaris lumbricoides, a roundworm that inhabits the small intestine and is up to 45.7 cm (18 in) long, infects about 25% of the world's human population. Each host is usually infected with 10–20 specimens, but higher numbers have been recorded. The simultaneous migration of large numbers through the lungs can cause severe haemorrhagic pneumonia.

The body of the beef tapeworm *Taeniarhynchus saginatus* can consist of more than 1,000 segments, each of which contains about 80,000 eggs. A person infected with one specimen (which can live for up to 25 years) probably excretes about nine of its constantly-renewed segments, and therefore approximately 0.75 million eggs, each day.

LARGEST PARASITES
The broad or fish tapeworm *Diphyllobothrium latum*, which inhabits the small intestine of fish and sometimes humans, is usually 9.1–12.2 m (30–40 ft) long but can grow to 18.3 m (60 ft). If a specimen survived for 10 years, it could possess a chain of segments almost 8 km (5 miles) long containing about 2,000 million eggs.

Taeniarhynchus saginatus, the beef tapeworm, can usually grow to 15.2 m (50 ft), but one specimen measured more than 22.9 m (75 ft) — three times the length of the human intestine.

LARGEST PARASITIC FLUKE
A didymozoid digenean species found in the oceanic sunfish *Mola mola* can reportedly grow to 6.1–9.1m (20–30 ft) in length.

MOST BENEFICIAL PARASITE TO HUMANS
The medicinal leech *Hirudo medicinalis*, which was used by doctors for blood-letting up to the 19th century, has made a surprising comeback since physicians began to employ it for significant new purposes. Since 1990 the creatures have been used by a team of surgeons at Harper Hospital, Denver, USA, to improve blood circulation in gunshot wounds and in severed limbs or fingers that are being sewn back on. While in 1991 a team of Canadian surgeons used leeches to drain blood and prevent it from clotting under a patient's scalp that was being sewn back on after a grizzly bear had ripped it off. Leeches, which are both predatory and parasitic, are common in aquatic habitats and in moist situations on land. They have a very well developed sense of smell, which enables them to locate their prey, and suckers on both ends of their bodies with which to grasp their hosts. The saliva of parasitic leeches contains an anaesthetic, which prevents the host from detecting the parasite's presence, and powerful anti-coagulation compounds, which ensure that the blood of the prey remains fluid in the gut and can be easily digested by the leech.

LARGEST ROUNDWORM IN HUMANS
The largest parasitic nematode (roundworm) of humans is probably the Guinea worm *Dracunculus medinensis*, a subcutaneous species with females up to 1.2 m (4 ft) long.

LARGEST PARASITIC INSECT
The exceptionally large flea *Hystrichopsylla schefferi*, dubbed 'super flea', can exceed 9 mm (⁹/₂₅ in) in length. Its only known host is *Aplodontia rufa*, a North American rodent.

LARGEST TICKS
Ticks are small arachnids that often live on the skin of warm-blooded animals. The largest belong to the sub-order Ixodida and can be 3.6 cm (²/₅ in) long.

LARGEST LEECH
Haementeria ghilianii, an Amazonian species, is 30 cm (1 ft) long. A freshwater species, it has protruding mouth parts and no true jaws.

GREATEST SIZE DIFFERENCE
The biggest difference in size between the sexes of an animal associated with parasitism is in *Bonellia viridis*, a species of echiuroid or spoon worm. The adult female is around 0.9 m (3 ft) long and is non-parasitic, while the adult male is no more than 1.3 mm (¹/₂₀ in) long and lives as an endoparasite inside the female's brood pouch, where it fertilizes her eggs.

Female nematodes are typically larger than males, but this difference is extreme in *Trichosomoides crassicauda*, which inhabit the urinary bladder of rats. Compared with the female, the male — which lives as an endoparasite inside her uterus — is minute.

LONGEST-LIVING PARASITE
A life-span of 27 years has been reliably recorded for a medicinal leech *Hirudo medicinalis*.

MOST DANGEROUS MIGRATION
The far-flung migrations of the roundworm *Ascaris lumbricoides* can have severe and sometimes fatal consequences for its human host. These sizeable worms can block the bile and pancreatic ducts or penetrate the intestinal wall and cause peritonitis. There are even cases where, due to their sensitivity to anaesthetics, *Ascaris* worms have emerged out of the nose or mouth of a patient recovering from a surgical operation.

MOST PARASITIZED HOST SPECIES
Stagnicola emarginata, a freshwater snail, is a host for the larvae of at least 35 species of parasitic fluke.

MOST WIDESPREAD PARASITE ACROSS SPECIES
The liver fluke *Fasciola hepatica* has been found as an adult in the liver, gallbladder and associated ducts of a range of mammalian species, including sheep, cattle, goats, pigs, horses, rabbits, squirrels, dogs and humans, and its larval stage has been discovered in a variety of different species of freshwater snail.

MOST CUNNING PARASITE
In Jan 1998 scientists at Vrije University, Amsterdam, Netherlands, found that specimens of the freshwater snail *Lymnaea stagnalis* parasitized by the digenean fluke *Trichobilharzia ocellata* develop an aversion to sex. Instead they grow more quickly, allowing their parasites to thrive. The parasite achieves this behavioural change in its host by directly affecting the latter's gene expression.

MOST DRASTIC PARASITIC EFFECTS
The larvae of parasitic flukes often inhibit the growth of their snail host's gonads, sometimes even causing castration. Consequently, parasitized snails often cannot reproduce.

Bees, homopteran bugs and other insects hosting infections of tiny endoparasitic insects known as stylopids or strepsipterans often experience noticeable alterations of their secondary sexual characteristics.

The scientific literature contains mystifying reports of weasels that have been observed performing strange circular 'dances'. Some scientists suggest that these are due to the action of parasitic flukes inhabiting the weasels' brains.

Brain-dwelling flukes have been held responsible by some researchers for mysterious occurrences in which whales appear to have stranded themselves deliberately on beaches, from where they have been unable to return to the sea and have hence died.

MOST DRASTIC TRANSFORMATION OF A PARASITE
The larvae of the copepod crustacean *Sacculina carcini* are free-swimming and closely resemble those of typical, non-parasitic copepods, but when adult they bear no resemblance to any type of crustacean. Losing their limbs, gut and segmentation, their bodies transform into shapeless sac-like structures that pierce the body of a crab and send root-like branches permeating

MOST GROTESQUE EFFECTS
Extraordinary cases of frogs with six or more limbs may be the direct result of parasitic fluke activity. The bases of these extra limbs are packed with masses of metacercariae, an encysted larval stage in the lifecycle of various digenean parasitic flukes. These cysts may be disrupting the limb development of tadpoles, splitting the limb buds into several sections, each of which duly grows a limb.

throughout the crab's body and limbs. The crab then often undergoes a degree of sex reversal due to the modification of its gonads and/or release of inhibiting compounds by the now strangely plant-like *Sacculina*.

MOST DANGEROUS PARASITES
The most dangerous multicellular parasite is the rat flea *Xenopsylla cheopis*. The carrier of the bubonic plague (Black Death), it is believed to be to the cause of most of the world's catastrophic pandemics.

Malarial parasites of the genus *Plasmodium*, carried by *Anopheles* mosquitoes, are the most dangerous protozoan parasites. They are probably responsible for 50% of all human deaths (excluding wars and accidents) since the Stone Age. In sub-Saharan Africa 1.4–2.8 million people a year die from malaria.

animal attack

MOST POISONOUS ANIMAL
Poison-arrow frogs (*Dendrobates* and *Phyllobates*) from South and Central America secrete some of the deadliest biological toxins in the world. The skin secretion of the golden poison-arrow frog (*Phyllobates terribilis*) of western Colombia is the most poisonous of all — scientists have to wear thick gloves when handling them.

MOST VENOMOUS SCORPION
The Tunisian fat-tailed scorpion (*Androctomus australis*) is responsible for 80% of stings and 90% of deaths from scorpion stings in North Africa.

MOST VENOMOUS SPIDER
The Brazilian huntsman (*Phoneutria fera*) has the most active neurotoxic venom of any spider. Large and highly aggressive, huntsmen often hide in clothing or shoes and bite furiously several times if disturbed. Hundreds of accidents involving the Brazilian huntsman and other Brazilian wandering spiders are reported annually but an antivenin is now available. Most deaths that occur are of children under the age of seven.

MOST VENOMOUS SNAKE
The king cobra (*Ophiophagus hannah*) or hamadryad of South-east Asia and India averages 3.65–4.5 m (12–15 ft) in length and is both the deadliest and the longest venomous snake.

LONGEST SNAKE FANGS
The longest fangs of any snake are those of the highly venomous Gaboon viper (*Bitis gabonica*) of tropical Africa. In a 1.83-m-long (6-ft) specimen they measured 5 cm (2 in).

MOST DANGEROUS LIZARDS
Unusually for lizards, the Gila monster (*Heloderma suspectum*) of Mexico and the south-western USA and the Mexican beaded lizard (*Heloderma horridum*) from western coastal Mexico both have a venomous bite.

MOST DANGEROUS BIG CATS
Tigers seem to attack humans more than any other cats, probably because humans fall within the natural size range of a tiger's prey and are fairly easy to catch, particularly for old or injured tigers.

MOST DANGEROUS PRIMATE
Irate silverback gorillas are potentially the most dangerous of all primates. When defending their families, they rush towards intruders and emit roars. These displays are now known to be bluffs in most cases, although some end with the gorilla thumping or biting the intruder.

MOST DANGEROUS BEAR
The only species of bear that actively preys on humans is the polar bear (*Ursus maritimus*). Most attacks occur during the night and are made by hungry adolescent males that are probably inexperienced hunters, and therefore more likely to be driven from their usual prey by larger bears.

MOST DANGEROUS SMALL MAMMALS
The most dangerous small mammal to humans is the rat. More than 20 pathogens are carried by them, including the bacterium that causes bubonic plague (the 'Black Death'). They also carry leptospirosis (Weil's disease), Lassa fever, rat-bite fever and murine typhus, all of which can be fatal.

The Cuban solenodon (*Solenodon cubanus*) and the Haitian solenodon (*Solenodon paradoxus*) from the Caribbean have saliva that is toxic to prey and potentially dangerous to human beings.

MOST POISONOUS FISH
The puffer fish (*Tetraodon*) of the Red Sea and Indo-Pacific region delivers a fatal toxin called tetrodoxin, one of the most powerful non-proteinous poisons. Less than 0.1 g (0.004 oz) of the poison — which is contained in the fish's ovaries, eggs, blood, liver, intestines and skin — is enough to kill an adult human in as little as 20 minutes.

MOST DANGEROUS BEE
The venom of the Africanized honey bee (*Apis mellifera scutellata*) is no more potent than that of other bees, but the number of stings that it inflicts can kill humans.

MOST DANGEROUS BIRDS
The only birds known to have attacked and killed humans in the wild are ostriches (*Struthio camelus camelus*), mute swans (*Cygnus olor*) and the three cassowary species (family Casuariidae).

STRONGEST BITE
The strongest animal bite ever measured is that of the dusky shark (*Carcharhinus obscurus*): a 2-m-long (6-ft 6¾-in) specimen can exert a force of 60 kg

STRANGEST DEFENCE MECHANISM
The Texas horned lizard (*Phrynosoma douglassi*) remains motionless if approached but if it is picked up will often attempt to disconcert its attacker by puffing up its body and spraying blood from its eyes, sometimes for a considerable distance. Of the 14 species of the Phrynosoma genus, which is mainly found in the desert areas of North America and Mexico, only two or three can squirt blood from the corners of their eyes. They achieve this by increasing the blood pressure in their heads. The specimen pictured here was caught at the Chaparral Wildlife Management area in Artesia Wells, Texas, USA, in 1997.

(132 lb) between its jaws. This is equivalent to a pressure of 3 tonnes/cm^2 (19.6 tons/in^2) at the tips of the teeth. The bites of larger sharks, such as the great white shark (*Carcharodon carcharias*), may be stronger, but have never been measured.

BEST SENSE OF SMELL
Sharks have a better sense of smell and more highly developed scent organs than any other fish. Well known for their ability to smell blood from enormous distances, sharks can detect one part of mammalian blood in 100 million parts of water and are even believed to be able to pick up the scent of other fishes' fear.

MOST VENOMOUS FISH
The stonefish *Synanceia horrida*, found in the tropical waters of the Indo-Pacific, has the largest venom glands of any known fish. Direct contact with the spines of its fins, which contain a strong neurotoxic poison, can be fatal for humans.

MOST DANGEROUS SEA URCHIN
Toxin from the spines and pedicellaria (the small pincer-like organs) of the flower sea urchin (*Toxopneustes pileolus*) causes severe pain, respiratory problems and even paralysis in human beings.

MOST DANGEROUS HYDROID
The Pacific Portuguese man-of-war (*Physalia utriculus*) and the Atlantic Portuguese man-of-war (*P. physalus*) both carry a virulent poison and are the only hydrozoans known to endanger human life. Even when they are dead, the creatures can sting almost as effectively as when they were alive.

MOST VENOMOUS JELLYFISH
The cardiotoxic venom of the beautiful but deadly Australian sea wasp or box jellyfish (*Chironex fleckeri*) has caused the deaths of at least 70 people off the coast of Australia alone in the past century. If medical aid is unavailable, some victims die within four minutes. One effective defence is women's hosiery: Queensland lifesavers once wore outsized versions during surfing tournaments.

MOST VENOMOUS GASTROPOD
Cone shells of the genus Conus can all deliver a fast-acting neurotoxic venom. Several of these species are poisonous enough to kill human beings, but the geographer cone (*Conus geographus*) of the Indo-Pacific is considered to be one of the most dangerous.

MOST VENOMOUS MOLLUSC
Hapalochlaena maculosa and *H. lunulata*, the two closely-related species of blue-ringed octopus found around the coast of Australia and in parts of South-east Asia, both carry a neurotoxic venom so potent that their relatively painless bite can kill human beings in a matter of minutes. It has been estimated that a single specimen carries enough venom to cause the paralysis or even death of 10 adult people. The molluscs, which have a radial spread of just 10–20 cm (4–8 in), are not aggressive and generally only bite when they are taken out of the water and provoked.

MOST DANGEROUS PINNIPED
The carnivorous leopard seal (*Hydrurga leptonyx*) is the only species that has a reputation for apparently unprovoked attacks on human beings: at least one diver has been attacked and several people have been chased across the ice for a distance of up to 100 m (328 ft). However, experts believe that most leopard seal attacks are caused by the animals mistaking humans for emperor penguins or are due to provocation.

MOST DANGEROUS CROCODILIAN
The saltwater crocodile (*Crocodylus porosus*) kills an estimated 2,000 people every year, although the majority of these deaths go unrecorded. The largest reputed death toll in a crocodile attack occurred during WWII, on the night of 19–20 Feb 1945. Allied troops invaded Ramree Island off the coast of Burma, trapping between 800 and 1,000 Japanese infantrymen in a coastal mangrove swamp. By the following morning only 20 men were still alive: the majority of the infantrymen are believed to have been eaten alive by crocodiles.

MOST FEROCIOUS FISH
Razor-toothed piranhas of the genera *Serrasalmus* and *Pygocentrus* will attack any creature that is injured or makes a commotion in the water, regardless of its size. In 1981 more than 300 people were said to have been eaten when an overloaded passenger-cargo boat capsized and sank while docking at Obidos, Brazil.

endangered
and new species

MOST INFLUENTIAL RARE ANIMAL
Since becoming the symbol for the World Wildlife Fund in 1961, the giant panda *Ailuropoda melanoleuca* has attracted huge international support for the preservation of endangered species. There are around 700 giant pandas left in the world.

BIGGEST ELEPHANT RELOCATION PROJECT
In 1993 Care for the Wild International transported more than 500 elephants in family groups from Gonerauzou National Park, Zimbabwe, to the Save Valley Conservancy 250 km (155 miles) away.

MOST SUCCESSFUL RETURN TO THE WILD OF CAPTIVE-BRED ANIMALS
The sand gazelle (genus *Gazella*) has been returned to the Empty Quarter on the borders of Saudi Arabia and Oman after an absence of 40 years. It was thought extinct in the late 1950s but a few survivors, together with specimens from private collections, were involved in a 10-year breeding programme run by London Zoo, UK, and the Saudi National Commission for Wildlife Conservation and Development. There are now almost 600 specimens in the Empty Quarter.

RAREST LARGE LAND MAMMAL
The Javan rhinoceros *Rhinoceros sondaicus* is known only from a maximum of 70 specimens on Java in Indonesia, and in Vietnam.

SNOW LEOPARDS
On 30 Aug 1997 two eight-day-old snow leopard cubs were presented to the press at Lille Zoo, France. Snow leopards (of the genus *Panthera*) are an endangered species: only 5,000 specimens are believed to survive in the wild, more than half in Mongolia, and the rest in neighbouring areas of Russia, China, Pakistan, India, Nepal and Afghanistan and Kazakhstan. There are a further 150 in zoos.

RAREST MARINE MAMMAL
The baiji or Yangtze River dolphin (*Lipotes vexillifer*) has an estimated population of 150 and the number is still falling.

RAREST WILD CAT
There are currently less than 100 specimens of the Iriomote cat *Felis iriomotensis*, which is confined to Iriomote in the Ryukyu island chain, Japan.

MOST ENDANGERED BIRDS
The Spix's macaw *Cyanopsitta spixii* is now known from one wild and c. 30 captive specimens.

The Hawaiian songbird Kauai o-o (*Moho braccatus*) is known from just two wild pairs.

RAREST BIRDS OF PREY
There are approximately 70 captive Californian condors (*Gymnogyps californianus*) and about five wild specimens.

A single specimen of the Madagascan red owl *Tyto soumagnei* was recorded in 1994, the first since 1934.

RAREST INSECT
Still sought by entomologists, the giant earwig of Saint Helena (*Labidura herculeana*) was last recorded in 1965.

MOST ENDANGERED FISH
The 200–500 existing Devil's hole pupfish (*Cyprindon diabolis*) are restricted to one section of a single pool in Nevada, USA.

RAREST AMPHIBIAN
The last known sighting of the Costa Rican golden toad *Bufo periglenes* was in 1990, when 11 specimens were found.

LONELIEST CREATURES
Darwin, a 70-year-old Seychelles giant tortoise, is pictured with four-year-old Darren Short at Blackpool Zoo, UK. The species was believed to be almost extinct until the identification of Darwin. The world's loneliest creature is Lonesome George, an aged male Abingdon Island giant tortoise (*Geochelone elephantopus abingdoni*) who is the last known specimen of his species. Although it is possible that other specimens exist, there is little hope of finding another, so the subspecies is effectively extinct.

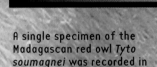

RAREST SNAKES
The burrowing boa *Bolyeria multicarinata* may already be extinct and the keel-scaled boa *Casarea dussumieri* is currently being maintained in Jersey Zoo, UK. Both come from the tiny Round Island, Mauritius.

GREATEST CONCENTRATION OF NEW ANIMALS
Twelve large new species of land mammal have been discovered or rediscovered in Vietnam, Laos and Cambodia in the 1990s, including the Vietnamese warty pig (*Sus bucculentis*).

MOST 'NEW' SPECIES FOUND IN ONE COUNTRY IN A YEAR
In 1997 biologists discovered more than 16,000 minute species in caves in Spain. These included numerous new species of crustacean belonging to a new class of animal.

'NEWEST' ECOSYSTEM
The Movile Cave mini-ecosystem of Romania, which is completely sealed off from sunlight, was discovered in the 1980s and houses more than 30 previously unknown invertebrate species.

NEWEST ANIMAL PHYLUM
A new species of tiny multicellular invertebrate called *Symbion pandora* (phylum Cyliophora), which lives on the lips of North Sea lobsters, was discovered in 1995.

FUR TRADE

The fur industry has declined dramatically over the last 10–15 years as people have come to realize the immense suffering endured by the animals. However, the $648-million-a-year (£405-million-a-year) trade continues to claim the lives of about 3.5 million animals annually, 2.5 million of which are raised on fur farms. In the past the fur trade has contributed to the extinction of animal species. Fur farms, which are estimated to number 500 in the USA alone, have stopped this, but the animals kept there are often treated brutally. Wild animals are often caught in traps, a practice that disrupts wildlife populations and encourages the spread of rabies. The majority of clothes designers today do not use fur in their collections, and many of the world's top models, including Kate Moss, Tyra Banks, Cindy Crawford, Christy Turlington, Elle MacPherson and Claudia Schiffer, have been designated 'models of compassion' by Peta, the world's largest animal rights movement. The latter has done much to convince the public that wearing fur is cruel through its powerful advertisement campaigns and publicity stunts. In London, UK, there remain just 14 of the 85 fur shops that existed in 1985.

MOST SENSATIONAL COMEBACK

The colonial marine invertebrate *Cephalodiscus graptolitoides*, formally described in 1993, is believed by some zoologists to be a living species of graptolite, hitherto known only from fossils and believed to have been extinct for 300 million years.

BIGGEST 'NEW' LAND MAMMAL

The Vu Quang ox (*Pseudoryx nghetinhensis*) of Vietnam is the largest species of land mammal discovered since 1936.

MOST ELUSIVE 'NEW' MAMMAL

The holy goat or kting voar (*Pseudonovibos spiralis*) of Vietnam, which was scientifically named in 1994, is only known from its distinctive horns.

LARGEST 'NEW' MARSUPIAL

The bondegezou or mbaiso tree kangaroo (*Dendrolagus mbaiso*), found in Irian Jaya, Indonesia, in 1994, is 1.2 m (4 ft) long.

'NEWEST' WHALE

Bahamonde's beaked whale (*Mesoplodan bahamondi*) was described in 1996 from a skull washed up on Robinson Crusoe Island, Chile.

MOST ELUSIVE 'NEW' BIRD

The Nechisar nightjar (*Caprimulgus solala*) was named a new species in 1995 but is only known from a wing found on a road in Nechisar Plain National Park, Ethiopia.

MOST RECENTLY DISCOVERED 'LIVING FOSSIL'

A Gulf snapping turtle that was discovered in Queensland, Australia, in 1996 resembles Australian freshwater tortoises that became extinct 5,000–20,000 years ago.

'NEWEST' LIZARD

Codling's lizard was discovered in the Kalahari Desert, Botswana, by Professor Charlemagne B'Nkobo of Durban University, South Africa, in 1996. Characterized by extremely blue eyes and a rippled brown skin, the species was named after Neil Codling, the keyboard player from British pop group Suede, of which Professor B'Nkobo is a fan.

'NEWEST' BIRD

The pink-legged graveteiro (*Acrobatornis fonsecai*), an ovenbird-related species from Brazil, is the most recently discovered bird. It was first sighted by a scientist in 1994.

BLUE-EYED LEMURS

Six-month-old blue-eyed lemur Dern and her mother Bacall are seen on their arrival at Los Angeles Zoo, USA, in Nov 1997. They were accompanied by Dern's father Cagney. The zoo is the fourth in the United States to display the Madagascan species (family Lemuridae), which is endangered.

MOST VOCALLY DISTINCTIVE 'NEW' SPECIES

The electric frog (*Litoria electrica*), which was discovered in Queensland, Australia, in 1990, has an extraordinary mating call that resembles the sound produced by a high-voltage, long-duration electric arc.

MOST GLAMOROUS PET WEDDING

In Sept 1996 two rare 'diamond-eyed' cats, Phet and Ploy, were married at a lavish ceremony at Phoebus House, Thailand's biggest discotheque. It cost their owner Wichan Jaratarcha $16,241 (£9,933), plus a dowry of $23,202 (£14,190). The groom, Phet arrived in a Rolls Royce. Ploy arrived by helicopter. Bride and groom wore matching pink satin outfits.

basket for less than £100 ($165) a day. At seven years old, Francky's vital statistics — he is 62 cm (24.4 in) tall and weighs 24 kg (3 st 11 lb) — have made him the favourite of photographers such as Patrick Demarchelier. He has starred in catwalk shows for Jean-Paul Gaultier alongside supermodel Karen Mulder and appeared in Robert Altman's film *Prêt-à-Porter* (USA, 1994).

HIGHEST-EARNING LITERARY DOG

In 1991 springer spaniel Mildred Kerr, Millie for short, brought in a salary more than four times bigger than that of her master, the then US president George Bush, when her 'autobiography' sold 400,000 copies. 'Dictated' to the First Lady Barbara Bush, *Millie's Book* was described as 'an under-the-table look at life in the Bush family'. It made a total of $900,000 (£510,000).

HIGHEST-EARNING ANIMAL ARTIST

Ruby the elephant has been painting for eight years, since her keepers at Phoenix Zoo, Arizona, USA, saw her making patterns in the dirt with a stick clutched in her trunk and provided her with paints, brushes and an easel. Ruby's canvasses now sell for up to $3,500 (£2,187). The 23-year-old has her own office, and assistants who change her brushes and hold her palette while she mixes colours.

MOST EXPENSIVE CATS

Bullseye and Cucamonga, who are Californian Spangled cats, were on sale in the Neiman-Marcus department store's 1986 Christmas catalogue for $1,400 (£853) each. In 1987 one of them sold for $24,000 (£15,925), to a film star who preferred to remain anonymous. Californian Spangled cats were bred by Hollywood scriptwriter Paul Casey, who crossed various types to develop a new breed of domestic cat that resembles spotted wildcats. There are currently less than 200 specimens in the world.

BEST-TRAVELLED CAT

Hamlet the cat escaped from his cage during a flight from Toronto, Canada, and travelled more than

MOST VALUABLE SHOWBIZ ANIMAL

The original *Lassie* star, Pal, was the first of nine male dogs to play the canine heroine. His great-great-great-great-great grandson 'Lassie IX', also known as Howard, is the most valuable animal in showbusiness history. He travels in his own aeroplane.

MOST SUCCESSFUL CONTEMPORARY TV DOG

Moose, the Jack Russell terrier who plays 'Eddie' in the US sitcom *Frasier*, was described by *Entertainment Weekly* as "the hottest pooch to be unleashed on the airways in years". He has had a starring role in Universal Studios' *Animal Actors Show*, appeared in several US print and TV commercials and featured on the covers of *Life* and *TV Guide*.

MOST FAMOUS ADVERTISING CAT

Morris was rescued from an animal shelter in Chicago, USA, by an animal trainer in 1968 and

was chosen to promote 'Nine Lives' cat food. He went on to appear in 40 advertisements over the next decade.

MOST 'PATSYS' WON BY AN ANIMAL

Francis the mule was the first animal to be awarded first place at the PATSY awards, which were held annually from 1951 to 1987 to honour the Picture/Performing Animal Top Stars of the Year and promote the health and safety of showbiz animals. Francis, the star of *Francis the Talking Mule* (USA, 1949), received his award from actor James Stewart. He went on to win a further six PATSYs. The original film was so successful that five sequels were made in as many years.

MOST SUCCESSFUL SHOWBIZ PIG

Luise from Hanover in Germany rose to fame when she became the world's first drug-sniffing pig at the age of three weeks in 1984. She turned to acting in

1987 and starred in her first movie, *Blutrausch* (*Blood Frenzy*), in which she played a porcine detective. Luise subsequently made almost 70 television appearances and was celebrity guest at the Hanover Opera, in a non-singing role.

MOST SUCCESSFUL CANINE SUPERMODELS

English bulldog Rosie Lee starred in shoe designer Patrick Cox's 1996 spring campaign, posed for fashion photographer Bruce Weber for a Pepe Jeans ad and appeared in an IBM commercial. Rosie is 46 cm (1ft 6 in) tall and weighs 22 kg (3 st 6 lb). She lives in New York, USA, with her owner Nikki Perry, who runs Tea and Sympathy, a restaurant popular with human supermodels such as Naomi Campbell and Kate Moss.

Magic Star Francky, known as Francky, is a top French fashion poodle who won't get out of his

ANIMAL AEROBICS

Catflexing, one of the latest crazes to hit the USA, was invented by Stephanie Jackson, who began to include her cat Bad (pictured left with Jackson) in workout sessions when the latter started demanding her attention while she was pumping iron. Jackson picked up the cat and continued exercising with Bad's additional 3.6-kg (8-lb) weight), incorporating her into bicep curls and behind-the-neck curls. She soon adapted other exercises to include Bad, such as the Catbell Press, where she lies down and lifts the cat above her chest, the Upright Cat Row, where she lifts the cat up to her chest, Cat Crunches, Cat Twists and the Dead Cat Lift, all of which are explained and illustrated in her book *Catflexing: A Catlovers Guide to Weight Training, Aerobics and Stretching*. Cats are not the only animals involved in regular workouts. In 1996 the Total Dog Inc. fitness centre opened on Santa Monica Boulevard in Los Angeles, USA. There, canine fitness freaks regularly work out on the treadmill, swim in the pool and complete the outdoor agility course. The centre also boasts therapists for massage and personal trainers to develop workout and weight-reduction programmes.

MOST PEOPLE AT A PET FUNERAL
In 1920 the funeral of Jimmy the canary from New Jersey, USA, was attended by 10,000 mourners. Jimmy's owner, cobbler Edidio Rusomanno, had his body placed in a white casket. The funeral cortege was followed by two coaches and a 15-piece band.

UGLIEST DOG
Chi Chi, a rare African sand dog, has won the World Championship Ugly Dog Contest at Petaluma, California, USA, a total of five times and took first place in the contest's 'Ring of Champions', which pits the winners from the previous 25 years against one another. Chi Chi was described by the *National Enquirer* as a 'space alien' and by his owner Doris Beezley as a 'bow-legged, pig-like dog'. He has made several television appearances and is the star of a comic strip called 'The Ugliest Dog'.

BIGGEST CHICKEN
The heaviest breed of chicken in the world is the White Sully, a hybrid of large Rhode Island Reds and other varieties. The largest on record, a rooster named Weirdo, reportedly weighed 10 kg (1 st 8 lb) in Jan 1973. Weirdo's prodigious size was the result of cross-breeding and was accompanied by a vicious streak: he once ripped through a wire fence to maul another giant rooster, and on another occasion maimed a dog and killed two cats.

965,600 km (600,000 miles) in just over seven weeks. He was caught in Feb 1984.

MOST JET-SETTING DOGS
Pumpkin Matthews, a tiny champagne-coloured toy poodle, used to commute by Concorde between her homes in New York, USA, and St Tropez, France, in the 1980s. By the time she was 10 years old she had visited Paris a total of 50 times. Her successor, Precious Pi, now travels as frequently as Pumpkin.

RICHEST DOG
The biggest legacy ever left to a dog was $15 million (£3 million), bequeathed by Ella Wendel of New York, USA, to her standard poodle Toby in 1931. Elsa was part of an eccentric family whose dogs were served prime lamb chops by personal butlers and slept in their own bedrooms in hand-carved miniature four-poster beds with silk sheets.

RICHEST CAT
Blackie, the last in a household of 15 cats, was left $15 million (£9.4 million) in the will of his millionaire owner, Ben Rea.

FATTEST CATS
Kato the cat from Sogndal in Norway, pictured above, is the fattest living cat in the world. In Feb 1998 he weighed in at 16.7 kg (36 lb) and had a neck measurement of 36 cm (14 in). The fattest-ever cat was Himmy, a tabby owned by Thomas Vyse of Cairns, Queensland, Australia. Himmy weighed 21.3 kg (46 lb 15 1/4 oz) and had an 84-cm (33-in) waist when he died at the age of 10 years 4 months on 12 March 1986. He was so huge that he had to be transported in a wheelbarrow.

MOST TRICKS PERFORMED BY A DOG
Chanda-Leah, a champagne-coloured toy poodle from Hamilton, Ontario, Canada, can perform a repertoire of more than 300 tricks. Chanda-Leah's owner Sharon Robinson has taught the four-year-old to play the piano, count and spell. The dog has appeared on numerous US television shows, including *Regis and Kathy Lee* and *The Maury Povich Show*, and now has her own publicist.

trees and plants

FASTEST-GROWING TREE
An *Albizzia falcata* planted in Sabah, Malaysia, in 1974 was found to have grown 10.74 m (35 ft 3 in) in 13 months — about 2.8 cm (1¹⁄₁₀ in) a day.

FASTEST-GROWING PLANT
Some species of bamboo grow at a rate of 91 cm (3 ft) per day, or 0.00003 km/h (0.00002 mph).

FASTEST-GROWING AQUATIC WEED
The mat-forming water weed *Salvinia auriculata* was detected when Lake Kariba on the Zimbabwe–Zambia border was filled in 1959. In 13 months it had choked a 518-km^2 (200-mile^2) area and by 1963 had overtaken a 1,002-km^2 (387-mile^2) area.

LONGEST SEAWEED
Macrocystis pyrifera, the Pacific giant kelp, does not exceed 60 m (196 ft) in length but can grow 45 cm (18 in) in a day.

DEEPEST-LIVING PLANT
In 1984 algae was found at a depth of 269 m (884 ft) off San Salvadore Island in the Bahamas, where 99.9995% of sunlight was filtered out.

TALLEST ORCHID
Galeola foliata, a saprophyte of the vanilla family, is known to have grown to a height of 15 m (49 ft) in the rainforests of Queensland, Australia.

BIRD OF PARADISE
The bird of paradise flower (*Strelitzia reginae*), belonging to the South African *Strelitzia* genus, has a type of inflorescence known as a cincinnus. The flower is grown for its exotic colourings.

LARGEST INFLORESCENCE
The erect panicle of *Puya raimondii*, a rare member of the Bromeliaceae family from Bolivia, has a diameter of 2.4 m (8 ft) and emerges to a height of 10.7 m (35 ft). Each can bear up to 8,000 white blooms.

LARGEST FUNGUS
A single living clonal growth of the underground fungus *Armillaria ostoyae* covers an area of about 600 ha (1,500 acres) in the forests of Washington state, USA. Its size suggests that it is between 500 and 1,000 years old.

HEAVIEST FUNGUS
One living mass of *Armillaria bulbosa* covering about 15 ha (37 acres) of forest in Michigan, USA, weighed more than 100 tonnes — approximately the same as a blue whale. It probably grew from a single fertilized spore at least 1,500 years ago.

LARGEST TREE FUNGUS
The bracket fungus *Rigidoporus ulmarius*, growing from dead elm wood in the grounds of the International Mycological Institute at Kew, Surrey, UK, measured 1.63 x 1.4 m (5 ft 4 in x 4 ft 7 in) in 1995 and had a circumference of 4.8 m (15 ft 9 in). In 1992 it was growing at an annual rate of 22.5 cm (9 in) a year but it has since slowed to about 3.5 cm (1⅓ in) a year.

LARGEST WEED
The giant hogweed (*Heracleum mantegazzianum*), originally from the Caucasus, can reach a height of 3.65 m (12 ft) and has 91-cm-long (3-ft) leaves.

LARGEST WEED COLONY
A colony of wild box huckleberry (*Gaylussacia brachycera*) covering about 40 ha (100 acres) was found in 1920, near the Juniata River, Pennsylvania, USA. It is estimated to be about 13,000 years old.

CLOVERS WITH THE MOST LEAVES
A 14-leaved white clover (*Trifolium repens*) was found by Randy Farland near Sioux Falls, South Dakota, USA, in 1975, and a 14-leaved red clover (*Trifolium pratense*) was reported by Paul Haizlip at Bellevue, Washington, USA, in 1987.

PLANT WITH THE GREATEST MASS
A network of quaking aspen trees (*Populus tremuloides*) growing from a single root system in the Wasatch Mountains, Utah, USA, covers 43 ha (106 acres) and weighs an estimated 6,000 tonnes. The clonal system is genetically uniform and acts as a single organism: all the trees change colour and shed leaves in unison.

BIGGEST TREES
'Lindsey Creek Tree', a coast redwood (*Sequoia sempervirens*) with a minimum trunk volume of 2,549 m^3 (90,000 ft^3) and a minimum total mass of 3,300 tonnes, had the greatest mass of any tree. It blew over in a storm in 1905.

The living tree with the greatest mass is 'General Sherman', a giant sequoia (*Sequoiadendron*

OLDEST PLANT
King's Holly (*Lomatia tasmanica*) was discovered at New Harbour in the south-western wilderness of Tasmania, Australia, by miner and amateur naturalist Denny King in 1934 and is the oldest known plant in the world. After being carbon dated from a fossil of an identical specimen found nearby, at Melaleuca Inlet, it was estimated to be at least 43,000 years old. King's Holly is extremely rare (it can only thrive naturally in a small area of the world), lacks genetic diversity (all individual specimens are genetically identical) and is a tripod — although it produces flowers, it has never produced fruit or seed and is therefore sterile, reproducing itself through vegetative means alone. The combination of these factors has resulted in its near extinction: there are currently only about 500 specimens in existence. In addition to these problems, the plant grows in areas that are extremely prone to disease and fire. It was therefore listed as endangered under the Threatened Species Protection Act 1995 and there have been many attempts to increase its chances of survival through fire and disease management planning.

giganteum) in
the Sequoia National Park,
California, USA. It is 83.82 m
(274 ft 11 in) tall with a 31.3-m
(102-ft 8-in) girth.

TALLEST TREES
The tallest tree standing today
is the 'Mendocino Tree', a coast
redwood (*Sequoia sempervirens*)
at Montgomery State Reserve,
California, USA. In 1996 it was
112.014 m (367 ft 6 in) in height
with a diameter of 3.139 m
(10 ft 4 in). It is estimated to
be about 1,000 years old.

A *Eucalyptus regnans* found at
Mt Baw Baw, Victoria, Australia,
is believed to have been 143 m
(470 ft) tall when it was
measured in 1885.

The tallest tree ever measured
was an Australian eucalyptus at
Watts River, Victoria, Australia.
Reported by forester William
Ferguson, in 1872, it was
132.6 m (435 ft) tall and had
almost certainly measured
more than 150 m (500 ft)
in height originally.

BIGGEST TREE CANOPY
The great banyan (*Ficus
benghalensis*) in the Indian
Botanical Garden, Calcutta,
has 1,775 prop or supporting
roots and a circumference of
412 m (1,350 ft). It covers an
area of approximately 1.2 ha
(3 acres) and is the biggest
known tree canopy.

LARGEST FLOWER
The blooms of the tropical
mottled orange-brown and white
parasite *Rafflesia arnoldi* are up
to 91 cm (3 ft) across with petals
1.9 cm (¾ in) thick. Each flower
weighs up to 11 kg (36 lb). The
plant is also known as the
'stinking corpse lily' because its
blossoms smell of rotten meat,
attracting flies that act as
pollinators. Local people have
often attributed medicinal
properties to the plant.

GREATEST TREE GIRTH
In the late 18th century a
European chestnut (*Castanea
sativa*) known as the 'Tree of
the Hundred Horses' on Mt Etna,
Sicily, Italy, was 57.9 m (190 ft)
in circumference. It has since
separated into three parts.

REMOTEST TREE
A Norwegian spruce on Campbell
Island, Antarctica, is believed
to be the most remote tree: its
nearest companion is more than
222 km (120 nautical miles)
away on the Auckland Islands.

OLDEST TREE
'Eternal God', a 12,000-year-old
redwood in Prairie Creek Redwoods
State Park, California, USA, is the
oldest living tree on record. It is
72.542 m (238 ft) tall and
5.974 m (19 ft 7 in) in diameter.

LARGEST LEAVES
The raffia plant (*Raffia
farinifera* or *R. ruffia*) of the
Mascarene Islands in the Indian
Ocean and the Amazonian
bamboo palm (*Raffia taedigera*)
of South America and Africa have
the largest leaves of any plant.
Their leaf blades may be up to
20 m (65 ft 6 in) in length with
4-m (13-ft) petioles.

LARGEST SEEDS
The giant fan palm *Lodoicea
maldivica* (also called
L. callipyge and *L. sechellarum*),
commonly known as the double
coconut or coco-de-mer, grows
wild exclusively in the
Seychelles. The palm produces
single-seeded fruit that weigh
up to 20 kg (44 lb) and can take
as long as 10 years to develop.

SMALLEST SEEDS
The epiphytic orchid has the
smallest seeds of any plant in
the world: it takes a total of
992.25 million seeds to make up
1 g (28,129.81 million/oz).

DEEPEST TREE ROOTS
The greatest depth to which
roots are known to have
penetrated is 120 m (400 ft),
by the roots of a wild fig
tree at Echo Caves, situated
near Ohrigstad, Transvaal,
South Africa.

LONGEST PLANT ROOTS
A single winter rye plant (*Secale
cereale*) can produce 622.8 km
(387 miles) of roots in 0.051 m³
(1⅘ ft³) of earth.

LARGEST CACTUS
The world's largest cactus is the
saguaro (*Cereus giganteus* or *Carnegiea
gigantea*), native to Mexico and to
California and Arizona, USA. The saguaro
grows just 2 cm (⁴/₅ in) during its first
10 years, and does not flower before
the age of 50, but it can live for up to
200 years and reach a height of 15 m
(49 ft). One specimen discovered in the
Maricopa Mountains, Arizona, USA, in
1988 has branches that rise to a height
of 17.67 m (57 ft 11¾ in).

dangerous and strange plantlife

MOST DAMAGING WEED
The weed that attacks the largest number of crops in the most countries is the purple nutgrass or nutsedge (*Cyperus rotundus*). The land weed is native to India but attacks 52 crops in 92 countries.

MOST THREATENING WATER WEED
The water hyacinth (*Eichhornia crassipes*), a native of South America, was introduced into Africa as an aquatic ornament and escaped into the River Nile in the 1950s. It spread rapidly in the absence of native predators and now seriously interferes with navigation in the Sudd region of Sudan and threatens to block the irrigation canals of the Gezira, the zone between the Blue Nile and the White Nile.

BIGGEST CARNIVOROUS PLANTS
Plants of the *Nepenthes* genus have vines that reach a length of up to 10 m (33 ft), making them the largest species of carnivorous plant. They capture some of the biggest prey of any plants, including creatures as large as frogs.

FASTEST-ACTING PLANT TRAP
The *Utricularia* genus of plants has the fastest-acting trap of any plant. The underwater plant acts by sucking its prey into bladders in $1/30$ of a second.

SMALLEST POISONOUS UNDERWATER PLANT
The toxins produced by the microscopic red tide algae are said to be among the most poisonous natural substances. The toxins have been known to poison humans, who digest them through the consumption of shellfish.

MOST EXPENSIVE CACTUS
An *Arocarpus kotschubeyanus* cactus sold in France in 1832 for $61 (£38) — more than it's own weight in gold, and in today's terms the equivalent of $2,353 (£1,471). Only three specimens were then known in cultivation.

ITCHIEST CACTUS
Opuntia, more commonly known as the prickly pear, has bristles barbed like bee stings. They are used to make the world's itchiest itching powder.

DEADLY FUNGI
The fly agaric (*Amanita muscaria*) is the best known of the *Amanita* genus of gill fungi. It is poisonous but rarely fatal, unlike its relatives the death cap (*Amanita phalloides*), destroying angel (*Amanita virosa*) and fool's mushroom (*Amanita verna*). The fly agaric earned its name in medieval times, when it was used as an insecticide. When crushed up with sugar — which acts as an attractant — it was used as a poison for flies.

OLDEST SURVIVING CACTUS REMAINS
Dried cactus samples that were taken from the burrows of pack rats in Arizona, USA, have been dated back to about 24,000 BC by scientists.

MOST SOUTHERLY PLANTS
The most southerly point at which plants grow is 86°48'S, 145°93'E, on top of Mt Roland in the La Gorce Mountains on Antarctica. *Carbonea vorticosa* and *Lecidea cancriformis*, both forms of lichen, can be found growing there.

MOST SOUTHERLY FLOWERING PLANTS
Atlantic hair grass (*Deschampsia Antarctica*) and Antarctic pearlwort (*Colobanthus quitensis*) both flower on the Terra Firma Islands in the South-West Antarctic Peninsula at 68°42'S, 67°32'W.

LOWEST TEMPERATURE AT WHICH PHOTOSYNTHESIS OCCURS
Although plants are capable of surviving for extensive periods without performing normal photosynthesis, they have to carry out this function in order to survive. The lowest temperature at which positive photosynthesis (carbon assimilation) has been recorded is −17°C (1°F), by the lichen *Umbilicaria aprina*.

LOWEST TEMPERATURE SURVIVED BY A PLANT
Experiments carried out by Otto Lange and Ludger Kappen as part of Antarctic Terrestrial Research put plants through prolonged periods of extreme temperatures. Several species of lichen managed to regain normal photosynthesis rates, surviving temperatures as low as −196°C (−320°F). This is the lowest temperature known to have been borne by plants.

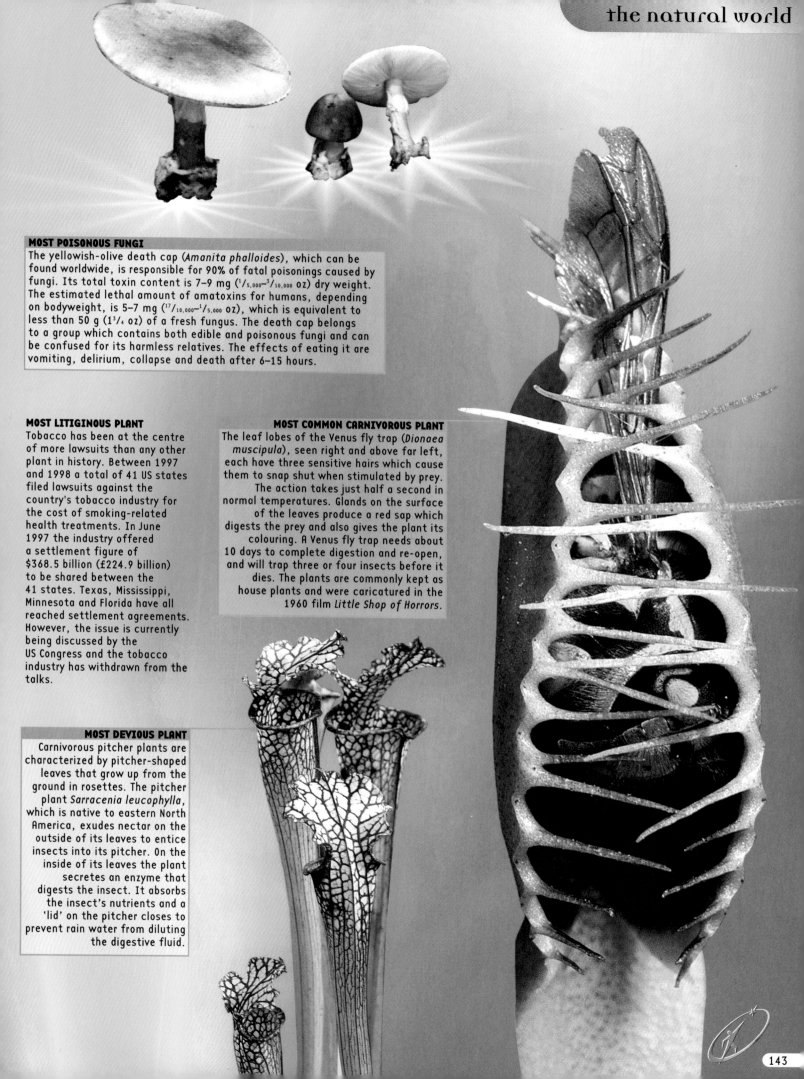

MOST POISONOUS FUNGI

The yellowish-olive death cap (*Amanita phalloides*), which can be found worldwide, is responsible for 90% of fatal poisonings caused by fungi. Its total toxin content is 7–9 mg ($^1/_{5,000}$–$^3/_{10,000}$ oz) dry weight. The estimated lethal amount of amatoxins for humans, depending on bodyweight, is 5–7 mg ($^{17}/_{10,000}$–$^1/_{5,000}$ oz), which is equivalent to less than 50 g (1$^3/_4$ oz) of a fresh fungus. The death cap belongs to a group which contains both edible and poisonous fungi and can be confused for its harmless relatives. The effects of eating it are vomiting, delirium, collapse and death after 6–15 hours.

MOST LITIGINOUS PLANT

Tobacco has been at the centre of more lawsuits than any other plant in history. Between 1997 and 1998 a total of 41 US states filed lawsuits against the country's tobacco industry for the cost of smoking-related health treatments. In June 1997 the industry offered a settlement figure of $368.5 billion (£224.9 billion) to be shared between the 41 states. Texas, Mississippi, Minnesota and Florida have all reached settlement agreements. However, the issue is currently being discussed by the US Congress and the tobacco industry has withdrawn from the talks.

MOST COMMON CARNIVOROUS PLANT

The leaf lobes of the Venus fly trap (*Dionaea muscipula*), seen right and above far left, each have three sensitive hairs which cause them to snap shut when stimulated by prey.
The action takes just half a second in normal temperatures. Glands on the surface of the leaves produce a red sap which digests the prey and also gives the plant its colouring. A Venus fly trap needs about 10 days to complete digestion and re-open, and will trap three or four insects before it dies. The plants are commonly kept as house plants and were caricatured in the 1960 film *Little Shop of Horrors*.

MOST DEVIOUS PLANT

Carnivorous pitcher plants are characterized by pitcher-shaped leaves that grow up from the ground in rosettes. The pitcher plant *Sarracenia leucophylla*, which is native to eastern North America, exudes nectar on the outside of its leaves to entice insects into its pitcher. On the inside of its leaves the plant secretes an enzyme that digests the insect. It absorbs the insect's nutrients and a 'lid' on the pitcher closes to prevent rain water from diluting the digestive fluid.

genetics

FIRST CLONED PRIMATES

In March 1997 geneticists at the Primate Research Center, Oregon, USA, announced that they had cloned two monkeys from embryos. They stripped the DNA from some monkey egg cells and replaced it with DNA taken from monkey embryos. In all, they created nine altered egg cells in this way. After they implanted them into female monkeys, three monkeys became pregnant and two went on to produce live offspring.

FIRST DNA FINGERPRINT

In 1985 Sir Alec Jeffreys and fellow researchers at the University of Leicester, UK, made the first DNA fingerprint. Looking a bit like a supermarket barcode, a DNA fingerprint is an image that shows the sequence of DNA unique to each person or living being. It can be used to identify people and to establish how they are related. DNA was first used to nail a crime suspect in 1987.

FASTEST DNA FINGERPRINT

The LightCycler was developed by Idaho Technology, USA, and can produce a DNA fingerprint in less than 10 minutes. It uses the polymerase chain reaction (PCR), a standard method of amplifying DNA, to produce a fingerprint from a sample of blood, or from other material with a volume of only 10 millionths of a litre (2 millionths of a gallon).

OLDEST DNA USED TO MAKE A FINGERPRINT

In 1993, R. J. Cano and fellow palaeontologists announced that they were able to extract and sequence DNA from a fossil that was about 125–130 million years old. According to Cano, their partial-DNA fingerprint was from a weevil trapped in amber. The claim remains controversial, however: other palaeontologists have been unable to replicate Cano's experiment. It has been suggested that the fossil may have recently been inadvertently contaminated, for instance with fungal material from the air.

MOST NOTORIOUS CRIMINAL IDENTIFIED USING DNA

In 1992 forensic scientists confirmed that the bones of a man who had drowned in Embú, Brazil, 13 years earlier belonged to the Nazi war criminal Josef Mengele. They were able to determine this by comparing DNA extracted from the bones with that of Mengele's surviving son Rolf. Dubbed the 'Angel of Death', Mengele was responsible for sending around 400,000 people to the gas chambers at the Nazi concentration camp in Auschwitz, Poland, during WWII.

BIGGEST PATENTED ANIMAL

The Oncomouse, a strain of mouse that has been genetically engineered to have a high predisposition to developing cancer, was produced in 1984 by geneticists at Harvard University, USA. Four years later, the US Patent Office granted the university a patent for this 'invention'. As early as 1972, a US Supreme Court hearing ruled that a patent should be granted to Ananada Chakrabarty for bacteria that he had genetically engineered to break down crude oil.

BIGGEST CROSS-SPECIES TRANSPLANT

In Aug 1996 scientists from Imutran, Cambridge, UK, reported that they had transplanted the hearts of seven pigs into monkeys. The pigs, some of whose DNA had been replaced with DNA taken from human cells, were the first of their kind. The genetic modification that they had undergone enabled them to make a human protein that would lower the risk of

HUMAN CLONING

In Feb 1998 Dr Richard Seed, a physicist from Chicago, USA, shocked the scientific community when he claimed that within 18 months he would develop the world's first human clone, using similar techniques to those used to produce Dolly the sheep. Dr Seed's views were greeted with consternation by some geneticists but he vowed to continue his work in Mexico if the US Congress obstructed it.

human beings, or any other primates, rejecting their hearts. The operations represented the first successful example of organ xenotransplantation (transplantation from one species to another) where the donor contained human genes.

MOST INSECT-RESISTANT POTATO

Introduced in 1995 by the US company Monsanto, the NewLeaf potato has been genetically engineered to protect itself against the Colorado potato beetle. Scientists genetically modified the NewLeaf potato to enable it to produce a protein that kills this beetle, which is the most damaging insect pest in potato crops.

COUNTRY WITH GREATEST NUMBER OF GENETICALLY-MODIFIED CROPS

More than 25% of cotton crops, 14% of soya and 10% of maize crops in the USA have been genetically modified. Genetic engineering by US agriculture companies such as Monsanto

and Calgene can provide these crops with resistance to herbicides and pests, or can endow them with new or enhanced commercially-useful properties, including extra strength and crispness.

MOST BENEFICIAL GENETICALLY-ENGINEERED DRUG

A synthetic version of insulin, the drug which is used to stabilize the disease diabetes, was first genetically-engineered by the US biotechnology firm Genetech in 1978. Genetech's synthetic insulin was engineered to be genetically close to the insulin that is produced by the human pancreas. Now called Humulin, it was first sold commercially by the US pharmaceutical giant Eli Lilly in 1982. Before then all insulin came from animal glands, so demand may eventually have outstripped supply — it is estimated that more than 100 million people around the world have diabetes.

MOST GENETICALLY SOPHISTICATED TOMATO

On 18 May 1994 the US Food and Drug Administration cleared the Flavr Savr tomato for sale to consumers, declaring it as safe as any traditionally-bred varieties. It was the firts such food to win approval. The Flavr Savr, which was developed by the agricultural company Calgene, takes far longer to soften than a convetional tomato, giving it a much longer shelf-life. The Flavr Savr in fact proved costly to produce, due to different regional growing conditions and the need for new picking equipment. By 1997 the advent of Israeli varieties grown in Mexico with a longer shelf life had lessened the need for a genetically engineered tomato.

BIGGEST GENETIC PROJECT

The Human Genome Project is a global effort to map the precise sequence of the 3 billion nucleotides that make up the human genome, the blueprint of human life. Scientists hope that the information will allow researchers to find the genetic causes and cures for many diseases. So far more than $10 billion (£6 billion) has been spent on the project, which began in 1990 and should end in 2005. It has been estimated that it would take one researcher 30,000 years to complete.

FIRST AUTOMATIC GENE SEQUENCER

Produced by Applied Biosystems in 1982, the world's first ever gene sequencer enabled a single researcher to sequence about 18,000 genes per day. Before the advent of this ground-breaking machine, researchers had to sequence genes by hand, and they could complete only a few hundred sequences at the most in a working day. Without the automatic gene sequencer it is unlikely that the Human Genome Project would have been viable.

FIRST MAMMAL CLONED FROM AN ADULT CELL

In Jan 1997 scientists from the Roslin Institute and PPL Therapeutics in Edinburgh, UK, announced the birth of Dolly, a Welsh mountain ewe cloned from a single udder cell of an adult ewe. Dolly's DNA was injected into another sheep's egg that had been stripped of its DNA. They had attempted the cloning of more than 220 sheep before they were able to produce one live, healthy lamb. Dolly is seen here with her daughter Bonnie, a Finn Dorset whose creation was completely natural. In Feb 1998, PPL Therapeutics revealed that they had cloned a calf. The 44.5-kg (98-lb) Holstein breed, named Mr Jefferson, was born in Virginia, USA, on 16 Feb. Unlike Dolly, who was produced from an adult cell line, Mr Jefferson was produced by nuclear transfer from a foetal cell. PPL has also genetically engineered sheep to produce alpha-1-antitrypsin (AAT), a human protein used to treat cystic fibrosis, in their milk.

amazing earth

LONGEST RIVERS
The two longest rivers are the Nile and the Amazon – which is the longer is more a matter of definition than measurement. The Amazon has several mouths, so the point where it ends is uncertain. If the Pará estuary (the most distant mouth) is counted, it is about 6,750 km (4,195 miles) long. The Nile was 6,670 km (4,145 miles) long before the loss of a few sections of meanders due to the formation of Lake Nasser behind the Aswan High Dam.

GREATEST RIVER FLOW
The greatest flow of any river is that of the Amazon, which discharges an average of 200,000 m³/sec (7.1 million cusec) into the Atlantic Ocean. This increases to more than 340,000 m³/sec (12 million cusec) in full flood.

HIGHEST WATERFALL
The Salto Angel in Venezuela has a total drop of 979 m (3,212 ft) and a longest single drop of 807 m (2,648 ft).

LARGEST SWAMP
The Pantanal in Mato Grosso and Mato Grosso do Sul states in Brazil covers about 109,000 km² (42,000 miles²).

LARGEST OCEAN
The Pacific makes up 45.9% of the world's oceans and covers an area of 166,241,700 km² (64,186,300 miles²).

SMALLEST OCEAN
The total surface area of the Arctic Ocean is 13,223,700 km² (5,105,700 miles²), making it the world's smallest.

DEEPEST OCEAN
In 1995 the Japanese probe *Kaiko* recorded a depth of 10,911 m (35,797 ft) when it reached the bottom of the Mariana Trench, Pacific Ocean.

THICKEST ICE
In 1975 4.7-km-thick (2⁹⁄₁₀-mile) ice was measured 440 km (270 miles) from the coast of Wilkes Land, Antarctica.

HIGHEST TSUNAMI
On 9 July 1958 a 160-km/h (100-mph) wave washed a record 524 m (1,720 ft) high along Lituya Bay in Alaska, USA. It was caused by a landslip.

FREAK WEATHER
The Pacific Ocean current El Niño is as old as the ocean itself. El Niño is cyclical and flows every few years, but the recent phenomenon is set to have the most devastating economic and environmental effects ever recorded. The see-saw in atmospheric pressure over the Pacific began in July 1997 and by early 1998 was estimated to have cost $33 billion (£20 billion) and caused the death of 5,000 people from floods, drought and the spread of disease, as well as malnutrition caused by crop damage. In Indonesia and Malaysia the land became so dry that man-made fires spread rapidly, resulting in more than 1,000 blazes, and causing widespread smog across South-east Asia. At the same time, El Niño fanned even more extensive fires in the Amazon rainforest.

LONGEST REEF

The Great Barrier Reef off the coast of Australia consists of thousands of separate reefs and is 2,027 km (1,260 miles) long.

TALLEST GEYSER

In 1903 the Waimangu geyser in New Zealand erupted every 30–36 hours to a height in excess of 460 m (1,500 ft). It has been inactive since 1904.

The tallest active geyser in the world is Steamboat Geyser in Yellowstone National Park, Wyoming, USA. It erupts to a height of 115 m (380 ft).

LARGEST 'BOILING RIVER'

The alkaline hot springs at Deildartunguhver, north of Reykjavik, Iceland, send out 245 litres (65 gallons) of boiling water a second.

HOTTEST PLACES

Between 1960 and 1966 the annual mean temperature at Dallol, Ethiopia, was recorded at 34°C (94°F).

Temperatures of over 49°C (120°F) were recorded in Death Valley, California, USA, on 43 consecutive days between 6 July and 17 Aug 1917.

Temperatures of 37.8°C (100°F) or more were recorded at Marble Bar, Western Australia, for 160 consecutive days between 31 Oct 1923 and 7 April 1924. The maximum was 120.5°F (49.2°C).

The temperature reached 32.2°C (90°F) or more at Wyndham, in Western Australia, on 333 days during 1946.

COLDEST PLACES

A record low of –89.2°C (–128.6°F) was registered at Vostok, Antarctica, at an altitude of 3,420 m (11,220 ft) on 21 July 1983.

The coldest permanently inhabited place is the village of Oymyakon (63°16'N, 143°15'E) at an altitude of 700 m (2,300 ft) in Siberia, Russia. The temperature there descended to –68°C (–90°F) in 1933 and to an unofficial –72°C (–98°F) more recently.

Polyus Nedostupnosti in Antarctica (78°S, 96°E) has an extrapolated annual mean of –58°C (–72°F).

The coldest measured mean is –57°C (–70°F), at Plateau Station, Antarctica.

MOST SUNSHINE

The annual average at Yuma, Arizona, USA, is 91% of the possible hours of sunshine (4,055 hours out of 4,456).

St. Petersburg, Florida, USA, had 768 consecutive sunny days from Feb 1967 to March 1969.

MOST RAINY DAYS

Mt Wai-'ale-'ale, Kauai, Hawaii, has up to 350 rainy days a year.

LONGEST DROUGHT

The Atacama Desert, northern Chile, has almost no rain. Squalls strike small areas several times a century.

MOST TORNADOES IN 24 HOURS

A total of 148 tornadoes swept through the southern and mid-western states of the USA from 3 to 4 April 1974.

FASTEST TORNADO

A tornado blew at 450 km/h (280 mph) at Wichita Falls, Texas, USA, on 2 April 1958.

HEAVIEST HAILSTONES

Hailstones weighing up to 1 kg (2 lb 3 oz) are reported to have killed 92 people in Gopalganj, Bangladesh, on 14 April 1986.

GREATEST VOLCANIC ERUPTIONS

The Taupo eruption in New Zealand c. AD 130 is estimated to have ejected 30,000 million tonnes of pumice at 700 km/h (400 mph). It flattened a 16,000-km² (6,200-mile²) area.

The total volume of matter that was discharged in the eruption of Tambora on Sumbawa, Indonesia, from 5 to 10 April 1815 was 150–180 km³ (36–43 miles³).

LARGEST ACTIVE VOLCANO

Mauna Loa on Hawaii is 120 km (75 miles) long and 50 km (31 miles) wide. Of its total volume, 84.2% is below sea level. Lava flows from Mauna Loa cover over 5,125 km² (1,980 miles²) of Hawaii.

LONGEST GLACIER

Icebergs are ice masses that have broken away from glaciers. The longest ever glacier, Lambert Glacier in the Antarctic, is at least 700 km (440 miles) long.

the universe

4.41. It was discovered in 1995 by a British team.

LARGEST STAR
The M-class supergiant Betelgeuse (*alpha Orionis*), which is 430 light years away from the Earth, has a diameter of 980 million km (610 million miles) – 700 times greater than that of the Sun.

BIGGEST STRUCTURE
A cocoon-shaped shell of galaxies about 650 million light years across is the largest structure found in the Universe to date. Its discovery by a team of French astronomers was announced in June 1994.

BIGGEST PLANET
With an equatorial diameter of 142,984 km (88,846 miles) and a polar diameter of 133,708 km (83,082 miles), Jupiter is the largest of the nine major planets. It also has the shortest period of rotation of any planet, resulting in a 9-hr 55-min 29.69-sec day.

LARGEST GALAXY
The central galaxy of the Abell 2029 galaxy cluster, which is 1,070 million light years away in Virgo, has a major diameter of 5.6 million light years – 80 times the diameter of the Milky Way. Its light output is equal to two trillion (2×10^{12}) Suns.

REMOTEST GALAXIES
In 1996 Esther M. Hu (USA) and Richard G. McMahon (UK) detected two star-forming galaxies with red shifts of 4.55 (a distance of 13,100 million light years).

The most remote radio galaxy, 6C0140 + 326, has a red shift of

SMALLEST STARS
Neutron stars, which may have a mass up to three times that of the Sun, are 10–30 km (6–19 miles) in diameter.

SMALLEST AND COLDEST PLANET
Pluto has a diameter of 2,320 km (1,442 miles) and a mass 0.0022 times that of the Earth. Its surface temperature is believed to be similar to that of Neptune's moon Triton, which is –233°C (–387°F) – the lowest surface temperature observed on a natural body in our solar system.

HOTTEST PLANET
Measurements by the *Venera* (USSR) and *Pioneer* (USA) probes indicate Venus' surface temperature to be 464°C (867°F).

FASTEST PLANET
Mercury orbits the Sun at a mean distance of 57,909,083 km (35,983,036 miles) and has an orbital period of 87.9684 days. This gives it the highest average speed in orbit of 172,341 km/h (107,088 mph).

LONGEST ECLIPSE
The longest possible lunar eclipse is 1 hr 47 min. This will occur on 16 July 2000.

LONGEST SOLAR ECLIPSE
The longest possible eclipse of the Sun is 7 min 31 sec. The longest of recent date lasted 7 min 8 sec, west of the Philippines in 1955. A 7-min 29-sec eclipse should occur in the mid-Atlantic Ocean in 2186.

LONGEST 'EXTENDED' ECLIPSE
A total eclipse of the Sun was extended to 1 hr 14 min for passengers aboard a Concorde flight that took off from Toulouse, France, and stayed in the Moon's shadow over the Atlantic from 10:51 to 12:05 GMT on 30 June 1973.

MOST ECLIPSES IN ONE YEAR
Seven eclipses are possible in one year. This occurred in 1935 (five solar and two lunar eclipses) and 1982 (four solar and three lunar eclipses).

FEWEST ECLIPSES IN ONE YEAR
It is possible for only two eclipses to occur in a year, both solar. This was seen in 1944, 1969 and 1984.

MOST ECLIPSES AT A SINGLE LOCATION
The most recent case of three total solar eclipses at a single location was east of the Aral Sea, Kazakhstan (44°N, 67°E), in 1941, 1945 and 1952.

MOST VOLCANIC BODY
The most volcanically active body in our solar system is Io, Jupiter's third largest moon. Its orange colour is caused by the hundreds of vents on its surface, which erupt sulphur.

LARGEST ASTEROID
The first asteroid discovered, 1 Ceres, has an average diameter of 941 km (585 miles).

SMALLEST ASTEROID
Discovered in 1993, 1993KA² is about 5 m (16 ft) in diameter.

CLOSEST ASTEROID APPROACH
The asteroid 1994XM₁ was discovered by James Scotti (USA) on 9 Dec 1994, 14 hours before it came within 100,000 km (62,000 miles) of the Earth. It is 10 m (33 ft) in diameter.

LARGEST COMET
Centaur 2060 Chiron has a diameter of 182 km (113 miles).

BIGGEST KUIPER BELT OBJECT
The object 1996T066, discovered in Oct 1996, has an estimated diameter of 800 km (500 miles).

LARGEST METEORITE
A 2.7-m (9-ft) x 2.4-m (8-ft) block was found near Grootfontein, Namibia, in 1920.

LARGEST STONY METEORITE
The largest piece of stony meteorite ever recovered weighs 1,770 kg (3,902 lb). It was part of a 4-tonne shower over Jilin, China, in 1976.

GREATEST METEORITE EXPLOSION
In 1908, an explosion over the Podkamennaya Tunguska River basin, Russia, devastated 3,900 km² (1,500 miles²) of land. It was equal to 10–15 megatons of high explosive.

GREATEST METEOR SHOWER
The Leonid meteors were calculated to have passed over Arizona, USA, at a rate of 2,300 per min for 20 minutes on 17 Nov 1966.

LARGEST METEOR CRATER
The largest crater definitely formed by a meteorite is Coon Butte or Barringer Crater, Arizona, USA. It is 1,265 m (4,150 ft) in diameter and about 175 m (575 ft) deep.

BRIGHTEST FIREBALL
The brightest known fireball passed over Sumava, Czechoslovakia (now the Czech Republic) in Dec 1974. For a few moments it was 10,000 times brighter than a full Moon.

LEAST DENSE PLANET
Made up of 70% water, Saturn has the lowest density of any planet. The image above was taken by *Voyager I*, one of the probes that showed that Saturn's 'rings' actually consist of thousands of closely spaced ringlets.

BIGGEST SUNSPOT
An infra-red image highlights sunspots. In 1947 a sunspot covering a record 18 billion km² (7 billion miles²) was seen.

BIGGEST CANYONS
The largest canyon system is the Valles Marineris on Mars. It is at least 4,500 km (2,800 miles) long and 600 km (370 miles) wide, with a maximum depth of about 7 km (4 miles).

weird science

STRANGEST SUBSTANCE
Scientifically speaking, water is the world's strangest substance. Where most substances shrink when they are cooled, water expands, and unlike most substances, water is less dense as a solid than as a liquid (ice floats). It needs 10 times as much energy to heat as solid iron and dissolves almost anything.

SALTIEST WATER
The lower layer of the Dead Sea has a salinity of 332 parts per 1,000, making it the world's saltiest water. The dry heat of the Middle East has caused much of the sea to evaporate over the centuries, and as it has shrunk, its saline content has increased.

MOST VITAL SUBSTANCE
Oxygen exists as molecules in the Earth's atmosphere, and all living things would die without it. Invisible, odourless, tasteless, it makes up 21% of the atmosphere.

MOST ABSORBENT SUBSTANCE
'H-span' or Super Slurper (which is 50% starch derivative and 25% each of acrylamide and acrylic acid) can, when treated with iron, retain water at 1,300 times its own weight.

SMALLEST TEST TUBES
The smallest ever test tubes for containing a chemical reaction were made at the Ecole Polytechnique Fédérale de Lausanne in Switzerland in 1996. Each is 1 micron (1 millionth of a metre) long and has an internal diameter of less than 10 nanometres (10 billionths of a metre). The carbon nanotubes contained silver nitrate, which was heated until it formed chains of tiny silver beads.

MOST HEAT-RESISTANT SUBSTANCE
NFAAR, or Ultra Hightech Starlite, is able to temporarily resist plasma temperatures (10,000°C or 18,032°F).

SMELLIEST SUBSTANCES
Ethyl mercaptan (C_2H_5SH) and butyl seleno-mercaptan (C_4H_9SeH) are among the most evil of the 17,000 smells classified to date. Each smells like a combination of rotting cabbage, garlic, onions, burnt toast and sewer gas.

BITTEREST SUBSTANCES
The world's bitterest substances are based on the denatonium cation and have been produced commercially as benzoate and saccharide. Taste detection levels are as low as one part in 500 million, and a dilution of one part in 100 million will leave a lingering taste in the mouth.

SWEETEST SUBSTANCE
Talin obtained from arils (appendages found on certain seeds) of the katemfe plant (*Thaumatococcus daniellii*), which was discovered in West Africa, is 6,150 times as sweet as a 1% sucrose solution.

DEADLIEST ARTIFICIAL CHEMICAL
The compound 2, 3, 7, 8-tetrachlorodibenzo-p-dioxin, or TCDD, is 150,000 times more deadly than cyanide.

MOST CARCINOGENIC CHEMICAL
The most carcinogenic substance ever tested is the compound 3-nitrobenzathrone, found in the exhaust fumes of diesel machines. In Oct 1997 it produced the highest score ever in an Ames test, a standard measure of the cancer-causing potential of toxic chemicals, carried out at Kyoto University, Tokyo, Japan.

MOST CHEMICALLY-COMPLEX FOOD
Chocolate, which was invented by the Maya 2,000 years ago, contains approximately 300 chemicals, including caffeine, phenylethylamine and N-acylethanolamines, which mimic the effects of some drugs.

MOST APHRODISIAC CHEMICAL
Inhabitants of the central African state of Cameroon discovered long ago that the bark of the yohimbine tree is a powerful aphrodisiac — just 10 mg ($^3/_{20}$ grains) is enough to have an effect. Chemists have since proved that this is due to its chemical content.

MOST HARMFUL RADIATION
Gamma rays, the most harmful form of radiation, can only be stopped by thick lead or concrete. They travel at the speed of light.

LEAST HARMFUL RADIATION
Alpha radiation, a stream of positively charged particles consisting of two protons and two neutrons, is the least harmful form of radiation. Its particles cannot pass through a piece of paper, and alpha rays can only travel at 10% of the speed of light.

STRONGEST SUPERACID
A 50% solution of antimony pentafluoride in hydrofluoric acid (fluoro-antimonic acid $HF:SbF_5$) is a record 10^{18} times stronger than concentrated sulphuric acid.

STRONGEST NATURAL FIBRE
Silk, the only major fibre obtained from an insect, is the strongest natural fibre. About 10,000 silk worms are needed to make a garment. To prevent the larva emerging as moths and breaking the cocoon filament, they are steamed alive.

NATURAL CHEMICALS
Unlike most amphibians, which are relatively defenceless, the cane toad (*Bufo marinus*), along with a number of other toads, salamanders and the great crested newt (order Urodela), secrete potent poisons called bufotoxins from their head and skin. These hallucinogenic toxins, which affect the blood pressure, nerves and muscles of the animal's predator, are used by Amazonian Indians to tip their arrows. Several other animals are believed to have chemical/medicinal properties: in Africa rhinos are killed for their horns, which are used in medicines in South-east Asia, tigers are slaughtered for their bones for use in Chinese medicines and bears are killed in the USA and Asia for their gallbladders, which are used in medicines and food in Taiwan. The shooting, poisoning, trapping and snaring of these animals has endangered a great number of species, despite being illegal in many of the countries where they takes place.

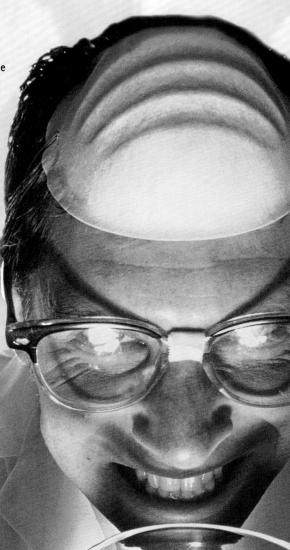

STRONGEST PLASTIC

Kevlar, which was discovered in 1965, is the strongest plastic substance in the world. Fire resistant, flexible and light, it is extremely strong (five times stronger than steel) and becomes even stronger when it is spun into fibre and heat-treated. Kevlar is used in the manufacture of bullet-proof vests, body armour, spacesuits and Formula 1 racing cars.

MOST DUCTILE ELEMENT

One gram of gold (Au) can be drawn to a distance of 2.4 km (1 oz to 43 miles).

MOST REACTIVE ELEMENT

Fluorine, which is used in the production of Teflon (the indestructible material used in space vehicles, protective clothing and non-stick cooking utensils) is the most reactive of all the elements — steel wool bursts into flames in fluorine.

SHORTEST-LIVED ELEMENT

Only a few atoms of seaborgium, element 106, have ever been produced, and none of them lasted more than half a minute. They were produced by bombarding californium with oxygen in a cyclotron.

HIGHEST ARTIFICIAL TEMPERATURE

The highest ever artificial temperature was 510 million°C (920 million°F) — 30 times hotter than the centre of the Sun. It was created using a deuterium-tritium plasma mix at the Tokamak Fusion Test Reactor at the Princeton Plasma Physics Laboratory, New Jersey, USA, on 27 May 1994.

LOWEST TEMPERATURE

Absolute zero (0K on the Kelvin scale) corresponds to −273.15°C (−459.67°F), a point when all atomic and molecular thermal motion ceases. The lowest temperature ever reached is 280 picoKelvin (280 trillionths of a degree), in a nuclear demagnetization device at the Low Temperature Laboratory of the Helsinki University of Technology, Finland. It was announced in 1993.

HOTTEST FLAME

At one atmosphere pressure, carbon subnitride (C_4N_2) can generate a flame calculated to reach 4,988°C (9,010°F).

MOST DENSE MATERIAL

A pinhead-sized piece of a neutron star weighs 1 million tonnes. The Geninga star, at 20–30 km (12–19 miles) across, weighs more than the Sun.

Crocus flowers are the most accurate natural thermometers in the world. The spring blooms can react to temperature differences of as little as 0.5°C (32.9°F) by opening and closing as the temperature rises and falls. The seed-producing element of spring crocuses is under the ground to protect it from the cold. Crocuses have been cultivated since the 16th century, and the flowers were used by the Romans to scent theatres and public places.

the
material
world

buildings and structures

TALLEST HOTEL
The 73-storey Westin Stamford in Raffles City, Singapore, is 226.1 m (742 ft) in height from the street level of its main entrance. It cost $235 million (£181 million) to build in 1985 and had a $54-million (£30-million) facelift in 1990/91.

The Ryujyong Hotel in Pyongyang, North Korea, is reportedly 105 storeys high. It has been under construction for 20 years.

LARGEST HOTEL
The MGM Grand Hotel and Casino which is situated in Las Vegas, Nevada, USA, has four 30-storey towers and covers 45.3 ha (112 acres). It has 5,005 rooms, a 15,200-seat arena and a 13.3-ha (33-acre) theme park.

LARGEST IGLOO
With a floor area of 3,000 m² (3,888 yd²) and the capacity to sleep up to 100 guests per night, the Ice Hotel in Jukkasjavi, Sweden, is the world's largest igloo. Rebuilt every December for the past five years, the igloo gets bigger every year. It currently features ice sculptures, a cinema, saunas, an ice bar and the world's only ice chapel.

TALLEST APARTMENT BLOCK
The John Hancock Center in Chicago, Illinois, USA, is 343.5 m (1,127 ft) tall and has 100 storeys, of which floors 44–92 are residential.

LARGEST PALACE
The Imperial Palace in Beijing, China, has a total area of 72 ha (178 acres).

LARGEST RESIDENTIAL PALACE
Istana Nurul Iman in Bandar Seri Begawan, Brunei, belongs to the Sultan of Brunei and is the world's largest residence. Completed in 1984 at a reported cost of $400 million (£300 million), it has 1,788 rooms, 257 toilets, and an underground garage housing 153 cars.

LARGEST AIR-SUPPORTED BUILDING
The 235-m-long (770-ft), 183-m-wide (600-ft) Pontiac Silverdome Stadium in Detroit, Michigan, USA, has a 4-ha (10-acre) 'Fiberglas' roof which reaches up to a height of 62 m (202 ft). The structure is supported by air pressure of 34.4 kPa (5 lb/ft²).

MOST EXPENSIVE STADIUM
The $466-million (£280-million) Stade de France in the Parisian suburb of Saint-Denis, France, was built for the 1998 World Cup. The stadium is able to seat 80,000 spectators and has a massive roof that has little visible means of support though

TALLEST MONUMENT
The stainless steel Gateway to the West arch in St Louis, Missouri, USA, spans 192 m (630 ft) and rises to the same height. Commemorating westward expansion after the Louisiana Purchase of 1803, it was completed in 1965 and cost $29 million (£10 million).

TALLEST BUILDING
The $63-million (£39.4-million) CN Tower in Toronto, Canada, was built from 1973 to 1975 and is 553.34 m (1,815 ft 5 in) tall.

it contains steelwork weighing as much as the Eiffel Tower.

LONGEST FRESHWATER SWIMMING POOL

The Hyatt Regency Cerromar Beach Resort in Puerto Rico has a 541-m-long (1,755-ft) swimming pool that covers 1.8 ha (4½ acres) and consists of five connected pools with water slides, a subterranean jacuzzi, tropical landscaping and 14 waterfalls. It takes 15 minutes to float from one end of the pool to the other.

TALLEST CEMETERY

The permanently illuminated Memorial Necrópole Ecumênica in Santos, Brazil, is 10 storeys high and covers 1.8 ha (4⅖ acres). Construction began in March 1983 and the first burial took place in July 1984.

LARGEST CEMETERY

Ohlsdorf Cemetery in Hamburg, Germany, covers 400 ha (990 acres). In use since 1877, it had hosted 984,006 burials and 418,323 cremations by the end of 1997.

LARGEST CREMATORIUM

The Nikolo-Arkhangelskiy Crematorium in Moscow, Russia, has seven British-designed twin cremators, the construction of which ended in 1972. It covers 210 ha (519 acres) and has six Halls of Farewell for atheists.

LARGEST CATHEDRAL

St. John the Divine, the cathedral of the Diocese of New York, USA, has a volume of 476,350 m³ (16,822,000 ft³) and a floor area of 11,240 m² (121,000 ft²). The building's cornerstone was laid in Dec 1892, but work on the building was stopped in 1941 and only restarted in earnest in July 1979.

LARGEST MOSQUE

The Shah Faisal Mosque near Islamabad, Pakistan, has a total area of 18.97 ha (46⁹/₁₀ acres). The prayer hall covers 0.48 ha (1⅕ acres) and together with the courtyard can accommodate 100,000 worshippers, while the adjacent grounds can accommodate a further 200,000 people.

LARGEST SYNAGOGUE

Temple Emanu-El in New York, USA, was completed in Sept 1929 and has a frontage of 45.7 m (150 ft) on Fifth Avenue and 77.1 m (253 ft) on 65th Street. The main sanctuary can take 2,500 people and the adjoining Beth-El Chapel seats 350. When the temple's other three sanctuaries are in use, a total of 5,500 worshippers can be accommodated.

LARGEST TEMPLE

Angkor Wat ('City Temple') in Cambodia is the largest religious structure ever built, covering 162.6 ha (402 acres). The entire temple complex has a total area of 24 x 8 km (15 x 5 miles) and consists of 72 major monuments, the construction of which began c. AD 900.

LARGEST BUDDHIST TEMPLE

The 8th-century Borobudur temple near Jogjakarta, Indonesia, covers an area of 123 m² (403 ft²) and is 31.4 m (103 ft) in height.

LONGEST BRIDGE

The Second Lake Pontchartrain Causeway, which joins Mandeville and Metairie, Louisiana, USA, is the longest bridge in the world. Completed in 1969, it is 38,422 m (23 miles 1,538 yd) long.

WIDEST BRIDGE

The widest long-span bridge in the world is the 503-m-long (1,650-ft) Sydney Harbour Bridge in Sydney, NSW, Australia. Officially opened on 19 March 1932, the bridge is 48.8 m (160 ft) wide and carries two electric overhead railway tracks, a total of eight lanes of roadway as well as a cycle track and footway.

LONGEST UNDERSEA TUNNEL

The £10-billion ($17-billion) Channel Tunnel beneath the English Channel running between Folkestone, Kent, UK, and Calais, France, was constructed between Dec 1987 and Dec 1990 and was officially opened by Queen Elizabeth II and President François Mitterrand of France on 6 May 1994. Each of the twin rail tunnels is 49.94 km (31 miles 53 yd) long and has a diameter of 7.6 m (24 ft 11 in).

LONGEST ROAD TUNNEL

The two-lane St Gotthard tunnel which runs between Göschenen and Airolo in Switzerland is the longest road tunnel in the world with a total length of 16.32 km (10 miles 246 yd). It was opened to traffic on 5 Sept 1980. Building began in 1969 and cost the then equivalent of $418 million (£175 million). The lives of 19 workers were lost during the construction of the tunnel.

TALLEST OFFICES

In 1996 the Petronas Towers in Malaysia became the tallest office building when 73.5-m-tall (241-ft) pinnacles were placed on top of the 88-storey towers, bringing their height to 451.9 m (1,482 ft 8 in).

future buildings

BIGGEST PURPOSE-BUILT GALLERY
At 130 m (450 ft) in length and 30 m (80 ft) in width, the biggest gallery in the Guggenheim Museum Bilbao, Spain, has been designed to hold some of the world's most spectacular 20th-century works of art. It presently houses *Snake*: three 30-m-long (100-ft), 3-m-high (13-ft) plates of steel sculpted by Richard Serra. The $100-million (£60-million) museum was designed by the Californian architect Frank Gehry.

MOST 'INTELLIGENT' TOWN
With living space for 20,000 people, Celebration, Florida, USA, is a futuristic city designed by Disney. All of the 8,000 homes in this $350-million (£211-million) city have a high-speed ISDN link with cable TV, multimedia resources, video on demand and an internet connection. Celebration, under construction since 1996, had 1,000 residents by summer 1997.

MOST 'INTELLIGENT' HOUSE
Bill Gates' house, which cost about $55 million (£33 million)

SELF-SUFFICIENT HOMES
Perfected by architect Michael Reynolds over the past 25 years, Earthships are self-sustaining structures that produce their own energy, catch their own water, recycle used water and gather their own heat. There are an estimated 1,000 such structures to date, all built from old tyres and aluminium tins, which are compressed and filled with earth. They have been built all around the world in a wide variety of climates (the Earthship pictured here is in the desert in New Mexico, USA). The most expensive one to date is a multi-million-dollar luxury Earthship belonging to the actor Dennis Weaver in Ridgeway, Colorado, USA.

to build over seven years, uses state-of-the-art information technology to tailor itself to the preferences of every guest. Everyone who enters is given an electronic pin that sensors in each room can detect, enabling the house to set the services and entertainments to their requirements. These sensors also control the lights and appliances, turning them off automatically when

someone leaves a room. Gates' hi-tech home is situated on the eastern shore of Lake Washington, USA.

MOST 'INTELLIGENT' STRUCTURE
Thousands of optical fibres are embedded between the segments of concrete that make up the recently built Winooski One Hydroelectric Dam in Vermont, USA. Sensors constantly monitor the light that these fibres receive for signs of the concrete structure shifting. Intelligent structures like this can help engineers spot the early signs that a dam, skyscraper, bridge or other high-performance structure is about to fail.

MOST ENERGY-EFFICIENT HOUSE
The Autonomous House in Southwell, Notts, UK, produces more energy than it consumes. Photovoltane panels provide electricity, and the 1,450 kWh produced by the house annually is sold back to the UK National Grid.

MOST EARTHQUAKE-PROOF AIRPORT
Built 5 km (3 miles) offshore on an artificial island in Osaka Bay, Japan, Kansai International Airport was virtually unscathed by the earthquake that hit the nearby city of Kobe in Jan 1995. The sea acted as a natural defence for the airport, damping out some of the vibrations and enabling the airport to move freely with minimal damage.

BIGGEST BUILDING CONSTRUCTED ON BASE ISOLATORS
The six-storey West Japan Building of the Ministry of Posts and Telecommunications, another survivor of the Kobe quake, sits on 120 vibration isolators, which act like shock absorbers. In an earthquake they compress, absorbing some of the energy of the quake and ensuring that as little as possible is transmitted to the building.

MOST EXPENSIVE COMPLETED GALLERY PROJECT
The Getty Center in Los Angeles, California, USA, cost $1 billion (£600 million) to build. The 90,000-m² (1 million-ft²)

BIGGEST BUILDING PROJECT
The Chinese authorities are trying to build a 21st-century financial and business centre from scratch on the east bank of Shanghai, and architects and engineers are fast at work on everything from sewers to airports. Highlights include a metro system and the Shanghai World Financial Centre (see below left). Pictured below is the Oriental Pearl TV tower.

complex was designed by Richard Meier and Partners. Along with countless other materials, 15,000 m² (165,000 ft²) of exterior glass, 225,000 m³ (8.1 million ft³) of concrete, 125,000 m² (4.4 million ft²) of steel stud and 295,000 pieces of Italian travertine were used.

BIGGEST SELF-SHAPING CONCRETE CONSTRUCTION

The Mega-City-Pyramid TRY-2004, which is still being developed, is a 2.004-km (1-mile 440-yd) ultra-high-rise pyramid intended to relieve overcrowding in Tokyo, Japan. It will accommodate

BIGGEST FUTURE BUILDING

Construction work officially began on the Shanghai World Financial Centre, China, on 27 Aug 1997. Due for completion in 2001, this skyscraper will be 460 m (1,509 ft) tall — higher than both the Sears and Petronas Towers. It will include a glazed viewing area on the 94th floor and a high, open-air walkway known as the 'bridge of world co-operation and friendship'.

1 million people but only take up 2,800 m² (30,000 ft²). It will use the Sun and wind as energy sources, and residents will move around it in circulatory cabins, some of which will be propelled by linear-induction motors.

BIGGEST PLANNED FLOATING BUILDING

First designed in the 1980s for an artificial island off the coast of Japan, X-Seed 4000 is a proposed dwelling for 1 million people, based on an open steel construction. The designers of X-Seed 4000, the Taisei Corporation, intend it to be used for research and mountain sports such as skiing, as well as accommodation. They have suggested magnetic lifts, which would carry 2,000 people to the top storey in 30 minutes.

BIGGEST T-UP BUILDING

The new headquarters of the Fuji Television Network in Tokyo Bay, Japan, was designed and constructed by the Taisei Corporation, the designers of X-Seed 4000 and inventors of the T-Up construction process. The latter was developed as a quick and safe way to erect high-rise buildings automatically. After each floor of a T-Up building is built, it is raised so that the next floor can be built below it.

MOST ADVANCED CONCERT HALL

Symphony Hall, Birmingham, UK, was opened in April 1991 and is famed for its acoustics, which can be modified in minutes by opening and closing large doors around its perimeter. The doors cover large chambers that increase the reverberation of the hall when they are revealed.

BIGGEST PUBLIC VENUE INSIDE A MOUNTAIN

Built for the 1994 Olympic Winter Games, Olympic Cavern Hall in Gjøvik, Norway, is now used as an exhibition centre, concert and sports venue and tourist attraction. Visitors have to venture 120 m (390 ft) inside Mt Hovdetoppen to reach the 61-m-wide (200-ft), 91-m-long (300-ft) venue.

FIRST UNDERWATER HOTEL

Situated 9 m (30 ft) underwater in a mangrove lagoon in Key Largo, Florida, USA, Jules' Undersea Lodge was opened as a hotel in 1986. It was formerly an aquatic research laboratory. Diving tuition and underwater natural history courses are the main attractions for guests.

BIGGEST UNDERGROUND HOUSE OF MODERN TIMES

Underhill in Holme, W Yorks, UK, has an internal area of 325 m² (3,500 ft²). The home of architect Arthur Quarmby since 1976, it cannot be seen from the surrounding moorland.

MOST ECO-FRIENDLY SKYSCRAPER

The new Commerzbank HQ in Frankfurt, Germany, is a 259-m-high (849-ft) skyscraper designed by Sir Norman Foster and Partners. An atrium towers 160 m (524 ft) through the core of the building, providing it with plenty of natural ventilation. Its spiralling sky gardens are places for occupants to meet and relax. The skyscraper has been designed to receive as much natural daylight as possible and has been positioned to minimize the amount of shadow it casts on nearby buildings.

cars

HIGHEST SPEEDS

The record for the highest speed attained in a rocket-engined car is 1,016.086 km/h (631.367 mph) over the first kilometre (1,056 yd) by *The Blue Flame*, a four-wheeled vehicle driven by Gary Gabelich on the Bonneville Salt Flats, Utah, USA, on 23 Oct 1970. He momentarily exceeded 1,046 km/h (650 mph). The car was powered by a liquid natural gas/hydrogen peroxide rocket engine that could develop thrust up to 9,979 kg (22,000 lb).

The highest land speed by a woman is 843.323 km/h (524.016 mph), by Kitty Hambleton in the rocket-powered three-wheeled *SM1 Motivator* over the Alvard Desert, Oregon, USA, on 6 Dec 1976. Her official two-way record was 825.126 km/h (512.710 mph) and she probably touched 965 km/h (600 mph) momentarily.

The highest speed reached in a wheel-driven car is 696.331 km/h (432.692 mph), by Al Teague (USA) in *Speed-O-Motive/Spirit of 76* over the final 40 m (132 ft) of a one-mile (1.6-km) run at Bonneville Salt Flats, Utah, USA, on 21 Aug 1991. His speed over the mile was 425.230 mph (684.322 km/h).

FASTEST SPEED ON LAND

The official one-mile (1.6-km) land speed record is 1,227.985 km/h (763.035 mph), by Andy Green (GB) in *Thrust SSC* over the Black Rock Desert, Nevada, USA, in Oct 1997. *Thrust SSC* is powered by two Rolls-Royce Spey 205 jet engines, which generate a total of 50,000 lb of thrust. It is the first car to have exceeded the speed of sound.

The highest ever speed reached by a diesel-engined car is 327.3 km/h (203.3 mph), by the prototype 3-litre Mercedes C 111/3 in tests on the Nardo Circuit, Italy, from 5 to 15 Oct 1978. In April 1978 the car averaged a speed of 314.5 km/h (195.4 mph) for 12 hours over a record distance of 3,773.5 km (2,344 miles 1,232 yd).

The record for the highest speed achieved by an electric vehicle is 295.832 km/h (183.822 mph) over a two-way flying kilometre (1,056 yd), by

General Motors' *Impact* driven by Clive Roberts (GB) at Fort Stockton Test Center, Texas, USA, on 11 March 1994.

Robert E. Barber broke the 79-year-old steam car world record when *Steamin' Demon*, built by the Barber-Nichols Engineering Company, attained a speed of 234.33 km/h (145.607 mph) at the Bonneville Salt Flats, Utah, USA, on 19 Aug 1985.

The record for the highest speed attained using solar/battery power was 135 km/h (83.88 mph), by Star Micronics' solar car *Solar Star* on 5 Jan 1991 at Richmond RAAF Base, NSW, Australia. The vehicle was driven by Manfred Hermann.

The record for the highest ever speed attained by a solely solar-powered land vehicle is 78.39 km/h (48.71 mph), by Molly Brennan in the General Motors' *Sunraycer* at Mesa, Arizona, USA, on 24 June 1988.

FASTEST ROAD CARS

The highest speed to have been reached by a standard production car is 349.21 km/h (217.1 mph), by a Jaguar XJ220 driven by British Formula 1 race driver Martin Brundle at the Nardo test track, Italy, on 21 June 1992.

The highest road-tested acceleration on record is 0–96 km/h (0–60 mph) in 3.07 sec, by a Ford RS200 Evolution driven by Graham Hathaway at Millbrook Proving Ground, Beds, UK, in May 1994.

LOWEST PETROL CONSUMPTION

In 1989 motoring writer Stuart Bladon drove a Citroën AX 14DTR 180.26 km (112 miles 18 yd) on one gallon of fuel on the M11 motorway, UK, in a test run arranged by Lucas Diesel Systems.

A vehicle designed by Team 1200 from Honda in Suzuka City, Japan, achieved 3,336 km/litre (9,426 mpg) in the Pisaralla Pisimmälle mileage marathon at Nokia, Finland, on 1 Sept 1996.

BIGGEST PRODUCTION RUN

More than 21.3 million Volkswagen 'Beetles' have been produced since 1937. The model was first developed in Germany in 1936, three years after Adolf Hitler asked Ferdinand Porsche for a blueprint for a 'Volkswagen' or 'people's car'. The result, which was nicknamed the 'Beetle' because it resembles the insect, went on to be produced in Nigeria, Belgium, Mexico and Brazil in addition to its native Germany. In 1994 a prototype for a new 'Beetle' (seen left) was unveiled at the Detroit Auto Show, USA, and was rapturously received, causing the value of the company on the stock market to increase. The new car, which was launched in North America in 1998, is significantly larger than the original and is built out of completely different components. Volkswagen do not see the vehicle as an update of the first 'Beetle' but as a completely new, futuristic car that should appeal both to people who loved the original and to young people who have little knowledge of it. Volkswagen expect that in the first year between 100,000 and 200,000 will be produced.

LONGEST FUEL RANGE

The greatest distance travelled by a vehicle on the contents of a standard fuel tank is 2,153.4 km (1,338 miles 18 yd) by an Audi 100 TDI diesel car (capacity 80.1 litres). Stuart Bladon, with RAC observer Robert Proctor, drove from John O'Groats to Land's End and returned to Scotland between 26 and 28 July 1992.

HIGHEST CAR MILEAGE

'Old Faithful', a 1963 Volkswagen 'Beetle' owned by Albert Klein of Pasadena, California, USA, clocked up 2.6 million km (1.6 million miles) before it was written off on 29 March 1997.

LARGEST ENGINE

The greatest ever engine capacity of a production car was 13.5 litres, by the US Pierce-Arrow 6–66 Raceabout (1912–18), the US Peerless 6–60 (1912–14) and the Fageol (1918).

LARGEST CAR

The largest car to have been produced for private use was the Bugatti 'Royale' type 41, which was assembled at Molsheim, France, by the Italian designer Ettore Bugatti. First built in 1927, it has an eight-cylinder engine with a capacity of 12.7 litres and is more than 6.7 m (22 ft long). The bonnet alone is 2.13 m (7 ft) long.

LONGEST CAR

A 30.5-m-long (100-ft), 26-wheeled limo designed by Jay Ohrberg of Burbank, California, USA, includes a swimming pool with a diving board and a king-sized waterbed among its many features. It can be driven as a rigid vehicle or altered to bend in the middle.

WIDEST CARS

The Koenig Competition:2417, built in 1989, and the Koenig Competition Evolution:2418, built in 1990, are both 2.195 m (86^2/$_5$ in) in width.

HEAVIEST CAR

The Soviet-built Zil–41047 limousine is probably the heaviest car in recent production. It has a 3.88-m (12-ft 9-in) wheel-base and weighs a total of 3,335 kg (7,352 lb). A 'stretched' Zil was used by the former Soviet president Mikhail Gorbachev until Dec 1991. It weighed 6 tonnes and had 7.5-cm-thick (3-in) armour-plated steel for protection in key areas. The eight-cylinder, seven-litre engine guzzled fuel at the rate of 2.1 km/litre (6 mpg).

SMALLEST CAR

The Peel P50, which was constructed by the Peel Engineering Company at Peel, Isle of Man, UK, in 1962, was 1.34 m (53 in) in length, 99 cm (39 in) in width and 1.34 m (53 in) in height. It weighed 59 kg (132 lb).

LIGHTEST CAR

The world's lightest ever car was built and driven by Louis Borsi of London, UK, and weighs 9.5 kg (21 lb). It has a 2.5-cc engine and can reach a maximum speed of 25 km/h (15 mph).

CHEAPEST CAR

The 1922 Red Bug Buckboard, built by the Briggs & Stratton Company, Milwaukee, Wisconsin, USA, sold for $125–$150 (£28–£34), the equivalent of $1,130–$1,870 (£680–£826) in

MOST POWERFUL CAR

The most powerful current production car in the world is the McLaren F1 6.1, which develops in excess of 627 bhp. The F1 is also the most expensive list-price British standard car, costing £634,500 (over $1 million) including tax. It can accelerate to 95.6 km/h (60 mph) in 3.2 seconds, and is capable of a top speed in excess of 370 km/h (230 mph).

1998 terms. It had a 1.57-m (62-in) wheel-base and weighed 111 kg (245 lb).

Early models of the King Midget cars that were made in the USA were sold in kit form for self-assembly for as little as $100 (£25) in 1948, the equivalent of $842 (£507) in 1998 terms.

LONGEST PRODUCTION RUN

The Morgan 4/4, built by the Morgan Motor Car Company of Malvern, Worcestershire, UK, celebrated its 63th birthday in Dec 1998. There is currently a waiting list of between six and eight years for the car.

MOST CARS PRODUCED IN A YEAR

In 1994 a record 49.97 million vehicles were constructed worldwide. Of this total, more than 36 million were cars, making 1994 a record-breaking year for car production.

LARGEST MANUFACTURER

The largest manufacturer of motor vehicles and parts in the world, and the largest manufacturing company, is the General Motors Corporation of Detroit, Michigan, USA. The company has about 610,000 employees worldwide. In 1997 General Motors sold a total of 8.776 million units to its retailers worldwide.

LOWEST PETROL CONSUMPTION

The lowest petrol consumption ever by a road legal vehicle in the Shell Mileage Marathon is 201.1 km/litre (568 mpg), by the diesel-powered Combidrive 'Mouse', at Silverstone race track, Northants, UK, in 1996.

concept cars

MOST ECO-FRIENDLY HYBRID SOLD

On 14 Oct 1997 Toyota launched the Prius, a hybrid-powertrain vehicle combining a 1.5-litre gasoline engine with a generator that halves emissions, cuts smog chemicals by up to 90% and goes twice as far as a standard car on 1 litre ($^{13}/_{50}$ gallon) of fuel. During one Japanese test cycle, the Prius achieved a fuel consumption of 123 km/litre (77 mpg). The car presently costs approximately $17,000 (£10,215) in Japan and is the most eco-friendly commercially available hybrid. Toyota had intended to produce 1,000 units a month but the car was so popular, with a total of 3,500 orders placed in the month after its launch, that they planned to double its production from June 1998. The Prius is set to be launched outside Japan in 1999.

MOST ECO-FRIENDLY CAR

A team of scientists working at Washington University, USA, have succeeded in developing the world's most eco-friendly car. The vehicle has a revolutionary zero-emission engine and is powered by energy produced by pressure build-up caused when liquid nitrogen is beaten by ambient air. Nitrogen gas then turns an air motor, propelling the car forwards, before being pumped out as clean air. The prototype is said to be a great deal cleaner than any other zero-emission vehicle but is unlikely to ever be seen on the market, as its fuel consumption works out at 3.2 km/litre (0.2 mpg), with an estimated maximum of 4.83 km/litre (3 mpg).

MOST ECO-FRIENDLY PETROL-POWERED CAR

The ZLEV (Zero Low Emission Vehicle), which was developed by the Japanese company Honda, has the lowest emission levels of any gasoline car. When tested on smoggy streets, the ZLEV's exhaust was cleaner in terms of hydrocarbon levels than the surrounding air. The car is not yet on the market.

MOST ECO-FRIENDLY CAR POWERED BY NATURAL GAS

The most eco-friendly natural gas vehicle in the world is the Civic GX, which was developed by Honda. Emissions of CO, HC and NOx from the car have been reduced to almost zero, while CO_2 emissions have been reduced by about 20%. The car is currently available in Japan and Honda plan to launch it worldwide in the near future.

MOST ECO-FRIENDLY CAR HIRE COMPANY

Kobe Ecocar, an auto rental business offering only clean-running cars, opened in Kobe, Japan, on 4 April 1998. The company, which is supplied by Pasona, Orix, Toyota, Nissan and Kansai Electric Power, initially offered customers a choice of 10 electric cars but plans to build up a fleet of 60 cars, including electric and gas vehicles, by April 1999. It announced that it will purchase 40 RAV4L-V-EV electric vehicles from Toyota, with Nissan providing natural gas cars. Toyota's Prius model will function as a backup.

LONGEST DISTANCES COVERED ON A SINGLE CHARGE

Solectria Corporation's Geo Metro conversion set a single-charge distance record for a 'production' motor vehicle of 249 m (817 ft) in May 1997. The production category requires that at least five vehicles must have been sold. The record was set using Ovonic nickel-metal hybrid batteries at the Tour de Sol in Portland, Maine, USA.

The greatest distance that a prototype electric vehicle has travelled on a single-charge is 343 m (1,125 ft), by Solectria Corporation's 'prototype' Sunrise at the 1996 Tour de Sol.

MOST 'INTELLIGENT' CARS

The Concept 2096 car of the future was unveiled at the 1996 British Motor Show. Designed at the University of Coventry, UK, the car is painted with 'smart' colours that change according to the environment, and the glass has the ability to change from transparent to opaque. The car has no steering wheel or engine and is controlled by a computer navigation system into which the user can enter a destination and desired route.

The Hypercar, an ultralight hybrid-electric car three times more efficient and 10 times cleaner than a conventional car, was under development at the Rocky Mountain Institute, USA, in 1998. The car uses space age materials, is rust-free, dent- and scratch-resistant and can absorb five times as much crash energy as steel. Its 'smart' windows reflect solar rays, and special paints, a vented roof and solar-powered vent fans monitor heat absorption to the interior.

The HSR (Highly Sophisticated Research) V1, which is computer driven but also has an optional

RENAULT ZO

In March 1998 Renault launched the ZO concept three-seater roadster at the Geneva Auto Show, Switzerland, to celebrate its 100th anniversary. The car is an all-terrain vehicle inspired by motorcycle scramblers. Special 43-cm (17-in) Michelin tyres have been designed to use the inner side for road driving and the outside for off-road and terrain surfaces. Its three seats are in a row, with the driver's in the centre and slightly further forward than the others. The ZO has no windshield or roof, but instead has an aperture directing the air over the passengers' heads. Powered by a new 2.0-litre engine with direct fuel injection, it has a four-speed automatic 'intelligent' gearbox and a chassis with hydraulic pumps to enable the clearance height to change within a range of 15–28 cm (6–11 in). Although the ZO is unlikely to hit the mass market in its present state, the engine may well appear in future Renaults.

WORLD SOLAR CHALLENGE WINNER

Honda's *Dream Solar* car is the current holder of the World Solar Challenge Race record. In 1996 it completed the 3,010-km (1,870-mile 669-yd) race from Darwin to Adelaide, Australia, in a record time of 33.32 hours. The car reached a maximum speed of 140 km/h (87 mph) and completed the race with an average speed of 85 km/h (53 mph). It can travel an estimated 90 km (56 miles) on pure solar power, and a further 100 km (62 miles) on energy collected from the solar cells into a silver oxide zinc battery.

RINSPEED E-GO ROCKET

The Swiss car manufacturer Rinspeed unveiled its E-Go Rocket at the 1998 Geneva Auto Show in Switzerland. Powered by a V8 aluminium 410-hp engine, it has a top speed of 260 km/h (162 mph) and claims 0–96.5 km/h (0–60 mph) acceleration in 4.8 seconds. The E-Go Rocket is a single-seater, with a stone-washed denim seat cover. The angle of the windshield adjusts to the vehicle's speed.

steering wheel concealed in the dashboard, was launched by Mitsubishi at the Tokyo Car Show in Japan in 1997. The car's ignition is turned on using a personal identity medallion in place of a key.

MOST ADVANCED IN-CAR COMPUTER SYSTEM

In 1998 Microsoft launched the AutoPC system, a specially programmed version of *Windows CE2* that runs on a single DIN hardware unit in place of a conventional car stereo and is the most advanced in-car computer system. The computer is fitted into the dashboard and is capable of operating a CD player and radio, sending and receiving e-mails and operating navigation and security systems. The Clarion unit, the first to adopt the system, can either be used directly or via remote control. The computer can also be voice-activated and responds to 200 commands.

FASTEST PRODUCTION OF A CAR

In 1997 Ford designed and developed their Puma in 135 days, setting a world record in the automotive industry. The company used computer processing power unrivalled by any institution bar the US government to design the Puma to approval stage in less than half the time it usually takes to turn a concept into reality. The Puma, a small coupé, is due on the market in Aug 1998.

MOST EXPENSIVE THREE-WHEELED CAR

The F300 Life-Jet, a vehicle that combines the safety of a car with the thrill of riding a motorcycle, was unveiled by Mercedes-Benz in 1998. The Life-Jet tips into bends rather than away from them — a sensation that is unavailable in a car because of Newton's law. If it makes it to production, it will be the most expensive three-wheeled car in the world.

MOST RECYCLABLE CAR

In 1998 Chrysler unveiled the CCV (Composite Compact Vehicle) ESX2, the most recyclable car in the world. The CCV is made out of plastic similar to that used for fizzy drinks bottles and can be made in six and a half hours. At the end of its life it can be melted down and recycled. With injection-moulded plastic, the car could be built using only 1,100 parts instead of the standard 4,000 components.

planes and helicopters

FASTEST FLYING BOAT
The Martin XP6M-1 SeaMaster, the four-jet-engined US Navy minelayer flown from 1955 to 1959, had a top speed of 1,040 km/h (646 mph).

FASTEST TRANSATLANTIC FLIGHTS
Major James Sullivan and Major Noel Widdifield flew a Lockheed SR-71A 'Blackbird' eastwards in 1 hr 54 min 56.4 sec in 1974. The average speed for the 5,570.80-km (3,461.53-mile) New York–London stage was 2,908.02 km/h (1,806.96 mph). It was reduced by refuelling from a Boeing KC-135 tanker aircraft.

The solo record is 8 hr 47 min 32 sec at an average speed of 426.7 km/h (265.1 mph), by Capt. John Smith in a Rockwell Commander 685 twin-turboprop in 1978. He flew from Gander, Newfoundland, Canada, to Gatwick, UK.

LONGEST CONTINUOUS FLIGHT
Robert Timm and John Cook flew for a total of 64 days 22 hr 19 min 5 sec in a Cessna 172 'Hacienda' from Dec 1958 to Feb 1959. The distance was the equivalent of flying six times round the world.

BIGGEST AIRCRAFT
The jet airliner with the highest capacity is the Boeing 747-400, which entered service with Northwest Airlines in 1989. It has a wing-span of 64.9 m (213 ft) and a range of 13,340 km (8,290 miles) and can carry up to 566 passengers.

The aircraft with the highest standard maximum take-off weight is the 600-tonne Antonov An-225 Mriya (Dream). One plane lifted a payload of 156,300 kg (344,582 lb) to a height of 12,410 m (40,715 ft) in March 1989. It covered 2,100 km (1,305 miles) in 3 hours 47 min.

The airliner with the greatest volume is the Airbus Super Transporter A300-600ST Beluga, which has a 1,400-m³ (49,441-ft³) main cargo compartment, a maximum

The fastest experimental propeller-driven aircraft is the turboprop-powered Republic XF-84H US fighter, which flew in July 1955 and had a top design speed of 1,078 km/h (670 mph).

The fastest propeller-driven aircraft was the former Soviet Tu-95/142, which has four 11,033-kW (14,795-hp) engines driving eight-blade contra-rotating propellers and a maximum level speed of Mach 0.82 or 925 km/h (575 mph).

The top speed by a piston-engined aircraft is 850.24 km/h (528.33 mph) over a 3-km (10-mile) course, by the *Rare Bear*, a modified Grumman F8F Bearcat piloted by Lyle Shelton, in Las Vegas, USA, in Aug 1989.

The fastest biplane was the one-off Italian Fiat CR42B, which had a 753-kW (1,010-hp) Daimler-Benz DB601A engine. It travelled at 520 km/h (323 mph) in 1941.

FASTEST HELICOPTER
Under FAI rules, the record for the highest helicopter speed in the world was set by John Trevor Eggington and his co-pilot Derek Clews in a Westland Lynx demonstrator. The pair averaged a speed of 400.87 km/h (249.09 mph) over Glastonbury, Somerset, UK, on 11 Aug 1986. It had taken a total of 10 years to design and develop the helicopter in order to achieve this speed.

FASTEST AIRCRAFT
The USAF Lockheed SR-71, a reconnaissance aircraft, was the world's fastest ever jet. First flown in its definitive form in 1964, the Lockheed was reportedly capable of attaining an altitude of about 30,000 m (100,000 ft). It was 32.73 m (107 ft 5 in) long, had a wing-span of 16.94 m (55 ft 7 in) and weighed 77.1 tonnes at take-off. Its reported range at Mach 3 was 4,800 km (3,000 miles) at 24,000 m (79,000 ft).

HIGHEST AIRSPEED
Capt. Eldon W. Joersz and Major George T. Morgan Jr attained a record speed of 3,529.56 km/h (2,193.17 mph) in a Lockheed SR-71A 'Blackbird' near Beale Air Force Base, California, USA, over a 25-km (15-mile 940-yard) course on 28 July 1976. The Lockheed SR-71A achieved an unofficial average speed of 3,608 km/h (2,242 mph) during a flight from St. Louis to Cincinatti, USA, in 1990.

take-off weight of 150 tonnes, a 44.84-m (147-ft 1-in) wing-span and an overall length of 56.16 m (184 ft 3 in). The usable length of its cargo compartment is 37.7 m (123 ft 8 in).

The production airliner with the greatest volume is the Ukrainian Antonov An-124 Ruslan, the cargo hold of which has a usable volume of 1,014 m³ (35,800 ft³) and a maximum take-off weight of 405 tonnes. The heavy-lift version of the An-124, the An-225 Mriya (Dream), has a stretched fuselage providing as much as 1,190 m³ (42,000 ft³) of usable volume. Its cargo compartment includes an unobstructed 43-m (141-ft) hold length and has a maximum width and height of 6.4 m (21 ft) and 4.4 m (14 ft 5 in) respectively.

LARGEST WING-SPANS
The $40-million (£24-million) Hughes H4 Hercules flying-boat, also known as the *Spruce Goose*, had the largest ever wing-span of any aircraft, at 97.51 m (319 ft 11 in). The 193-tonne, 66.65-m (218-ft 8-in), eight-engined aircraft was raised 21.3 m (70 ft) into the air in a 914-m (1,000-yd) test run piloted

by US tycoon Howard Hughes off Long Beach Harbor, California, USA, in 1947 but never flew again.

The record for the largest wing-span of a current aircraft is 73.3 m (240 ft 5¾ in), for the Ukrainian Antonov An-124.

SMALLEST AIRCRAFT
The smallest monoplane ever flown is the *Baby Bird*, which was designed and built by Donald Stits. First flown in 1984, the plane is 3.35 m (11 ft) in length and has a wing-span of 1.91 m (6 ft 3 in). It weighs just 114.3 kg (252 lb) when empty and has a maximum speed of 177 km/h (110 mph).

The smallest biplane ever flown was *Bumble Bee Two*, which was designed and constructed by Robert Starr of Tempe, Arizona, USA. Capable of carrying just one person, *Bumble Bee Two* was 2.69 m (8 ft 10 in) in overall length and had a wing-span of 1.68 m (5 ft 6 in). It weighed 179.6 kg (396 lb) when empty. The highest speed that it ever attained was 306 km/h (190 mph).

FASTEST AIRLINERS
The Tupolev Tu-144 (above left), first flown in 1968, was reported to have achieved Mach 2.4 (2,587 km/h or 1,600 mph) but had a normal cruising speed of Mach 2.2. In May 1970 it became the first commercial transport to exceed Mach 2. The BAC/Aérospatiale Concorde (above) was first flown in 1969. It cruises at up to Mach 2.2 (2,333 km/h or 1,450 mph) and is the fastest supersonic airliner.

In 1988 it crashed and was totally destroyed after having attained an altitude of 120 m (400 ft).

The world's smallest ever twin-engined aircraft is believed to have been the Colombian MGI5 Cricri, which was first flown in 1973. The Cricri has a wing-span of 4.9 m (16 ft) and an overall length of 3.91 m (12 ft 10 in). It is powered by two 11.25-kW (15-hp) JPX PUL engines.

LARGEST HELICOPTER
The largest helicopter in production is the Russian Mil Mi-26, which is 40.025 m (131 ft) in length and has a maximum take-off weight of 56,000 kg (55.1 tons). The eight-bladed main rotor is 32 m (105 ft) in diameter and powered by two 11,240 static HP turbo shaft engines.

LARGEST ROTORCRAFT
The 104.5-m-long (343-ft), 33.8-m-high (111-ft), 45.4-m-wide (149-ft) Piasecki Heli-Stat used four Sikorsky S-58 airframes attached to a surplus Goodyear ZPG-2 airship and was powered by four 1,525 hp piston engines. It first flew in Oct 1985 but was destroyed in a crash in July 1986.

SMALLEST HELICOPTER
The single-seat Seremet WS-8 ultra-light helicopter was built in Denmark in 1976 and had a 35-hp engine and an empty weight of 53 kg (117 lb). The rotor diameter was 4.5 m (14 ft 9 in).

FUTURE AIRCRAFT
The A3XX jumbo airbus, now in its prototype stage, will be the largest airliner in the world. Its manufacturer, Airbus Industrie, intends it to be in service by 2003, and is being assisted in its efforts by representatives from 19 airlines. The four-engined double-decker aircraft will be able to carry a record 1,000 passengers and will be the first airliner with four aisles (two on the main deck and two on the top deck). It will help to cope with the increase in air travel, which is estimated to triple over the next 20 years. The cost of developing the airbus is expected to reach $8 billion (£5 billion).

trains
and
boats

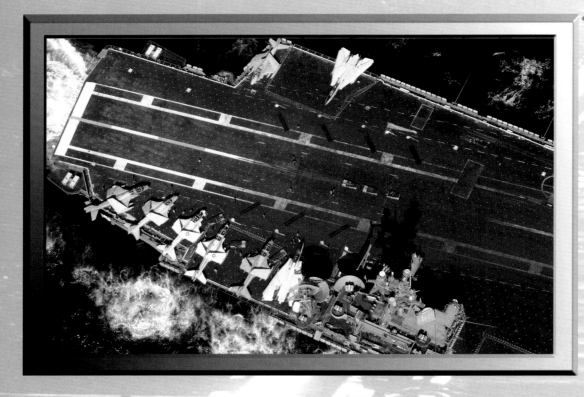

BIGGEST AIRCRAFT CARRIERS

The Nimitz class US Navy aircraft carriers *USS Nimitz, Dwight D. Eisenhower, Carl Vinson, Theodore Roosevelt, Abraham Lincoln, George Washington* and *John C. Stennis* (the last three of which displace 103,637 tonnes) have the biggest full-load displacement of any warships. They are 332.9 m (1,092 ft) long with 1.82 ha (4½ acres) of flight deck. Driven by four nuclear-powered 260,000-shp geared steam turbines, they can reach speeds of more than 56 km/h (30 knots). Two more ships of this class, *Harry S. Truman* and *Ronald Reagan*, are under construction. The Nimitz has four C-13 Mod 1 catapults that propel aircraft off the flight deck. The 'cats' can accelerate even the heaviest carrier-based aircraft to speeds of 273 km/h (170 mph) from a standing start.

FASTEST RAIL SYSTEM

The highest speed recorded on any national rail system is 515.3 km/h (320.2 mph), by the SNCF TGV Atlantique between Courtalain and Tours, France, on 18 May 1990. TGV Atlantique and Nord services now run at up to 300 km/h (186 mph), as does the Eurostar between Paris and Calais, France, though the train has to slow down when it reaches the UK. Cruising 30 km/h (18 mph) faster than the old TGV, Atlantique has eight rather than 12 motors, but can haul 10 trailer cars instead of eight, and can climb a 5% gradient at 12,000 hp without losing speed.

FASTEST TRAINS

The fastest point-to-point schedule in the world is between Hiroshima and Kokura in Japan on the Nozomi 500 and 503. The 192 km (119 miles) are covered in 44 minutes – an average of 261.8 km/h (162.7 mph).

The fastest train in Europe is the French TGV which runs between Lille and Roissy, France. It covers the 203.4 km (126 miles 704 yd) in 48 minutes, travelling at an average of 254.3 km/h (158 mph).

LONGEST FREIGHT TRAINS

From 26 to 27 Aug 1989 a record 660-wagon, 7.3-km-long (4½-mile) train with a tank car and a caboose made a 861-km (535-mile) run on the 1.065-m (3-ft 6-in) gauge Sishen–Saldanha railway, South Africa, in a time of 22 hr 40 min. The freight train was moved by a total of nine 50-kV electric and seven diesel-electric locomotives distributed along its length.

FASTEST DIESEL TRAIN

The record for the fastest ever speed by a diesel train is 238 km/h (148 mph), by an Intercity 125 train on a test run between Darlington and York, UK, on 1 Nov 1987. The train was one of a number of Intercity 125s used by British Rail for their HST (High Speed Train) daily service, which was inaugurated between London, Bristol and south Wales on 4 Aug 1976.

LONGEST PASSENGER TRAIN

On 27 April 1991 a 1,732.9-m (1-mile 135-yd), 2,786-tonne passenger train took 1 hr 11 min 5 sec to complete the 62.5-km (38-mile) journey from Ghent to Ostend, Belgium. Run by the National Belgian Railway Company, the train had a total of 70 coaches pulled by a single electric locomotive.

BIGGEST SAILING SHIP

The largest vessel built in the era of sail was the 5,899-gross-tonne *France II*, which was launched at Bordeaux, France, in 1911. The steel-hulled, five-masted barque had a 127.4-m (418-ft) hull, and although principally designed as a sailing vessel with a stump top gallant rig, was also fitted with two auxiliary engines. The latter were removed in 1919, and the ship became a pure sailing vessel. It was wrecked off New Caledonia in the South Pacific on 12 July 1922.

BIGGEST SAILING SHIP IN SERVICE

The biggest sailing ship in service is the 109-m (357-ft) *Sedov*, built in 1921 at Kiel, Germany, and now used by the Russian Navy. It is 14.6 m (48 ft) wide, has a displacement of 6,300 tonnes and a sail area of 4,192 m² (45,123 ft²). It can reach up to 17 knots, and has a crew of 65 cadets and 120 officer trainees.

LONGEST SAILING SHIP

The 187-m (613-ft) French-built *Club Med 1*, which has five aluminium masts and 2,800 m² (30,100 ft²) of computer-controlled polyester sails, operates as a Caribbean cruise vessel for 425 passengers for Club Med holiday company. With a small sail area and powerful engines it is really a motor-sailer.

BIGGEST CARGO VESSEL

The oil tanker *Jahre Viking* (formerly known as the *Happy Giant* and the *Seawise Giant*), weighs 564,763 dwt. The tanker, which is 458.45 m (1,504 ft) long overall, has a beam of 68.8 m (226 ft) and a draught of 24.61 m (80 ft 9 in). It was declared a total loss after being disabled during the Iran–Iraq war but underwent a $60-million (£33.9-million) renovation in Singapore and the United Arab Emirates and was relaunched under its new name in Nov 1991.

BIGGEST CONTAINER SHIP

The largest container vessel now in service is *Regina Maersk*, which was built at Odense, Denmark. Completed in Jan 1996, it has a gross tonnage of 81,488 and a capacity of 6,000 TEU (Twenty-foot Equivalent Units; the standard container is 6.096 m or 20 ft long).

BIGGEST HYDROFOIL

The 64.6-m-long (212-ft) *Plainview* naval hydrofoil, which weighs 314 tonnes with a full load, was launched by the Lockheed Shipbuilding and Construction Co. at Seattle, Washington, USA, on 28 June 1965, and has a service speed of 92 km/h (57.2 mph).

BIGGEST PASSENGER HYDROFOIL

Three 165-tonne *Supramar PTS 150 Mk III* hydrofoils, which carry up to 250 passengers at a speed of 40 knots across the Ore Sound between Copenhagen, Denmark, and Malmö, Sweden, were built by Westermoen Hydrofoil Ltd of Mandal, Norway.

BIGGEST HOVERCRAFT

The 56.38-m-long (185-ft) SRN4 Mk III, a British-built civil hovercraft, weighs 310 tonnes and is large enough to accommodate a total of 418 passengers and 60 cars. Powered by four Bristol Siddeley Marine Proteus engines, the hovercraft has a maximum speed in excess of 65 knots, which is the scheduled permitted cross-Channel operating speed.

BIGGEST YACHT

The Saudi Arabian royal yacht *Abdul Aziz*, which was built in Denmark and completed at Vospers Yard, Southampton, Hants, UK, on 22 June 1984, is 147 m (482 ft) long.

BIGGEST PRIVATE YACHT

The largest private (non-royal) yacht in the world is the 124-m (407-ft) *Savarona*, which was built for Turkish president Mustafa Ataturk in 1931 and privatized in 1992.

BIGGEST JUNK

The sea-going *Zheng He* had a displacement of 3,150 tonnes and an estimated length of up to 164 m (538 ft). The flagship of Admiral Zheng He's 62 treasure ships c. 1420, it is believed to have had nine masts.

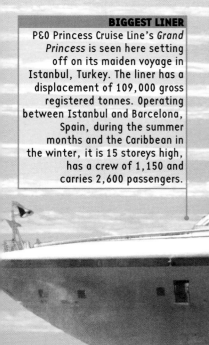

BIGGEST LINER

P&O Princess Cruise Line's *Grand Princess* is seen here setting off on its maiden voyage in Istanbul, Turkey. The liner has a displacement of 109,000 gross registered tonnes. Operating between Istanbul and Barcelona, Spain, during the summer months and the Caribbean in the winter, it is 15 storeys high, has a crew of 1,150 and carries 2,600 passengers.

bikes *and motorbikes*

MINIATURE MOTORCYCLE RACING
The first Spanish Miniature Motorcycling Championships were held on 1 Feb 1998 at the racing circuit at Albacete, Spain. The sport is acquiring a global following, and international championships are planned for 1999. They will be held in the USA.

HIGHEST BICYCLE SPEEDS
The record for the highest speed ever achieved on a bicycle is 268.83 km/h (166.94 mph), by Fred Rompelberg from the Netherlands behind a wind-shield at Bonneville Salt Flats, Utah, USA, on 3 Oct 1995. The slipstreaming effect of the lead vehicle provided considerable assistance in the record attempt.

The 24-hour behind pace record is 1,958.196 km (1,216 miles 1,310 yd), by Michael Secrest at Phoenix International Raceway, Arizona, USA, in April 1990.

FASTEST UNICYCLE SPRINT
Peter Rosendahl set a 100-m sprint record of 12.11 seconds (29.72 km/h or 18.47 mph) from a standing start at Las Vegas, Nevada, USA, on 25 March 1994.

FASTEST LAND SPEEDS BY HUMAN-POWERED VEHICLES
The world speed record by a single rider on a human-powered vehicle (HPV) over a 200-m flying start is 105.38 km/h (65.48 mph), by Fred Markham at Mono Lake, California, USA, on 11 May 1986.

The one-hour standing start record by a single rider was set by Pat Kinch, who averaged a speed of 75.57 km/h (46.96 mph) riding *Kingcycle Bean* at Millbrook Proving Ground, Bedford, UK, on 8 Sept 1990.

HIGHEST MOTORCYCLE SPEEDS
On 14 July 1990 US rider Dave Campos set AMA and FIM records on the 7-m-long (23-ft)

streamliner *Easyriders*, powered by two 1,491 cm³ (91 in³) Ruxton Harley-Davidson engines, at Bonneville Salt Flats, Utah, USA. Campos' overall average speed was 518.45 km/h (322.15 mph) and he completed the faster run at an average speed of 519.61 km/h (322.87 mph).

The fastest time for a single run over 440 yards (402 m) is 6.19 seconds, by Tony Lang (USA) riding a supercharged Suzuki at Gainesville, Florida, USA, in 1994.

The record for the highest terminal velocity at the end of a 440-yard (402-m) run is 343.17 km/h (213.24 mph), by Elmer Trett (USA) at Virginia Motorsports Park, Petersburg, USA, in 1994.

BIGGEST BICYCLE
The world's biggest bicycle by wheel diameter is *Frankencycle*, which is 3.40 m (11 ft 2 in) in height and has a wheel diameter of 3.05 m (10 ft). Built by Dave Moore of Rosemead, California, USA, it was first ridden by Steve Gordon of Moorpark, California, on 4 June 1989.

BIGGEST TRICYCLE
The Dillon *Colossal*, designed by Arthur Dillon and constructed by Dave Moore in 1994, has a back wheel diameter of 3.35 m (11 ft)

BIGGEST MOTORBIKE GATHERING
In March 1998 an estimated 500,000 bikers and motorbike enthusiasts from all over the world attended Bike Week at Daytona Beach, Florida, USA. The 10-day event has been held every winter for the last 57 years and has spawned a host of imitators across the USA, where a motorcycle event is held somewhere almost every weekend of the year. In conjunction with the gathering, the Daytona 200 — the most prestigious motorbike race in the USA — and the Daytona Supercross are held at the Daytona International Speedway. When bike gangs first began to show up in Daytona in the 1940s, the scene was much wilder than it is today. This continued until the 1980s, when a new set of followers began to appear: locals say that the event has been transformed from a gathering of outlaws to a well organized Mardi Gras with parades, displays and the chance to test drive the latest models.

and a front wheel diameter of 1.77 m (5 ft 10 in).

LONGEST BICYCLE

The longest bicycle built without a third stabilizing wheel is 22.24 m (72 ft 11½ in) in length and weighs 340 kg (750 lb). Designed and built by Terry Thessman of Pahiatua, New Zealand, it was ridden 246 m (807 ft) by four riders on 27 Feb 1988.

SMALLEST BICYCLE

The wheels of the smallest wheeled rideable bicycle in the world are 1.9 cm (19/25 in) in diameter. On 25 March 1988 the bike was ridden for 4.1 m (13 ft 5½ in) by its constructor Neville Patten of Gladstone, Queensland, Australia.

SMALLEST UNICYCLE

Peter Rosendahl (Sweden) rode a 20-cm-tall (8-in) unicycle with a wheel diameter of 18 mm (71/100 in) a distance of 4 m (13 ft 1½ in) at the University of Physical Education, Budapest, Hungary, on 28 July 1996. No attachments or extensions were fitted to the cycle.

LONGEST MOTORCYCLE

In 1996 Douglas and Roger Bell from Perth, Western Australia, designed and built a motorbike with a record length of 7.6 m

(24 ft 11 in). It weighed almost 2,000 kg (4,400 lb).

SMALLEST MOTORCYCLE

In 1990 Simon Timperley and Clive Williams of Progressive Engineering Ltd, Manchester, UK, designed and constructed a motorcycle with a wheel-base of 10.8 cm (4¼ in), a seat height of 9.5 cm (3¼ in), a front wheel diameter of 1.9 cm (¾ in) and a back wheel diameter of 2.4 cm (19/20 in). The motorbike was ridden a distance of 1 m (3 ft 2 in).

MOST EXPENSIVE MOTORCYCLE

The world's most expensive production motorbike is the Morbidelli 850 V8, which retailed for $98,400 (£61,500) in 1998.

MOST EXPENSIVE MOUNTAIN BIKE ON SALE

The most expensive retail mountain bike in the world costs £7,244 ($12,025) — about the same as many small cars. Made by the British company Stif, it weighs just 9.07 kg (20 lb) and is designed for off-road racing circuits. It has some of the world's most expensive components: the brakes, gears and pedals are made in Japan, the frame is from the USA, the forks and handlebar are British and the saddle is Italian.

SCOOTERS

The 125cc Vespa ET4 scooter was unveiled in Rome, Italy, in Sept 1996, together with the 50cc ET2, in a ceremony marking the 50th anniversary of the manufacturer Piaggio. The then chairman of Piaggio, Giovanni Agnelli, is pictured here sitting on the ET4 during the launch. Agnelli, who died in Dec 1997, was a member of the family that is the closest thing republican Italy has to a royal family. Piaggio's first Vespa scooter was launched more than 50 years ago, in the years following WWII, and has earned a reputation as an emblem of stylish two-wheeled transport in Europe and sold more than 15 million units. Despite 96 redesigns, the scooter — which was originally made from aircraft parts and is still the only scooter to be constructed from steel rather than plastic — has never moved away from its original image. Vespas have been used in worldwide advertising campaigns by IBM, Pepsi Cola, Absolut Vodka and American Express. In a recent ad for the launch of the Fiat Seicento, a Vespa acted as a referee in a football match between yellow and blue Seicentos.

HARLEY DAVIDSON MOTORCYCLES

In 1903 William Harley and Arthur Davidson hand-crafted three motorcycles in a backyard shed in Milwaukee, Wisconsin, USA. In 1909 they introduced the V-Twin engine, which is the company standard to this day. The Harley Davidson Owners Group (HOG) is the world's largest company-sponsored motorcycle enthusiasts group, with over 400,000 members in more than 1,000 branches worldwide.

hi-tech

computer games

PlayStation, and broke records set by some of the industry's biggest video games, including *Final Fantasy VII* and *Super Mario 64*. It was supported by a $5-million (£3-million) advertising campaign.

FASTEST-SELLING GAMES
Final Fantasy VII from Squaresoft was released in Nov 1997 and has sold about 3 million units on Sony PlayStation.

Riven, the sequel to *Myst*, was developed by Cyan and released by Broderbrund in Dec 1997. By May 1998 it had sold 1,003,414 units and taken $43.7 million (£26.3 million). *Riven* contains five CD-ROMs with twice the images and three times the amount of animation of *Myst*.

MOST SUCCESSFUL GAMES IN TERMS OF MERCHANDISING
Mario, the character who first appeared in *Donkey Kong* in 1982 and subsequently starred in the *Mario Bros.* games, was more frequently recognized than Mickey Mouse in a poll of children carried out in 1991. Together with his brother Luigi, he has featured in three cartoon series, one major movie and a number of toys ranging from board games to water guns. Together the video games have spawned more merchandising than any other.

Resident Evil by Capcom Entertainment, Sunnyvale, California, USA, had generated more than $200 million (£120.4 million) worldwide by Dec 1997 and sold about 4 million units. The success made it a popular licencing property and deals have been set for a feature film, a line of action figures and a series of comic

books. Released in March 1996, *Resident Evil* established a new genre in the gaming industry and became one of Sony PlayStation's highest-selling third-party franchises ever.

BEST-SELLING GAMES CONSOLE
The Sony PlayStation had sold approximately 30 million units (10 million in North America) worldwide up to Feb 1998, making it the biggest-selling computer games console in the world. Sony Computer Entertainment Inc. has spent more than $300 million (£180.7 million) developing the PlayStation, which runs hit games such as *Tomb Raider* and *Final Fantasy VII*. Japan, North America and Europe have produced about 135 million units of PlayStation software so far.

BIGGEST CHAIN OF VIDEO GAME ARCADES
In 1996 DreamWorks announced a partnership with Sega and MCA to develop Sega GameWorks, a

MOST ANTICIPATED GAME
Nintendo's *Diddy Kong races* had projected sales of 1.5 million copies between its launch on 24 Nov and Christmas 1997 — one copy for every 2 seconds. In 14 days it sold 800,000 units.

MOST ADVANCED 3-D ANIMATION
MediEvil, developed by Sony Computer Entertainment Europe-Cambridge Studios, uses N-World, a modelling and painting package from Nichimen Graphics Inc., which has also been used to produce *Super Mario 64* and *Final Fantasy VII*.

BEST-SELLING COMPUTER GAMES
After its release in 1993, *Myst* sold 500,000 copies in its first year and has now topped sales of 4 million and made more than $100 million (£60 million). It was the first CD-ROM entertainment to sell in excess of 2 million copies. *Myst* and its sequel *Riven* ranked first and second in computer games software in 1997. *Myst*, an interactive

fantasy game that takes place on Myst Island, incorporates 3-D animation and advanced sound and music technology. It was developed by Cyan and launched through Broderbrund.

Microsoft's *MS Flight Simulator* was released in April 1992 and had sold a total of 196,227 units by May 1998, taking in $99.2 million (£59.7 million).

Resident Evil 2 from Capcom Entertainment, California, USA, sold more than 380,000 units in its debut weekend — more than 60% of its initial production. It made more than $19 million (£11.4 million), surpassing the revenue of all but one Hollywood motion picture for the same weekend. The game was released on 21 Jan 1998 for the Sony

3-D SUPERHERO
Duke Nukem 3-D, the third chapter in the *Duke Nukem* series and the first to use 3-D perspective, was developed by Ritual Entertainment. Duke returns to 21st-century Earth to exterminate a race of aliens.

number of 322,800–538,000-m^2 (30,000–50,000-ft^2) video entertainment super-centres featuring Sega titles and games designed by movie director Steven Spielberg. The first centre opened in Seattle, USA, in 1997 and the company is planning a further 100 sites worldwide by 2002. Centres are already open in Pennsylvania, Ontario and Texas in the USA, and will soon be followed by Arizona, USA, and Rio de Janeiro, Brazil.

MOST PLAYERS AT ONE TIME IN A GAME ON THE INTERNET
The multi-player gaming engine *Ultima Online*, which was developed from *Ultima* — the best-selling role-playing series in the world ever — allows thousands of people to exist simultaneously in the same fantasy game world over the internet. When *Ultima Online* was released in 1997 it sold far more copies than had been predicted. Servers failed to cope as people flocked to play, and the game's manufacturer, Origin Systems Inc., had to add more servers and take on more employees in order

to cope with the overwhelming number of players logging on.

MOST SUCCESSFUL STRATEGY WAR GAMES
The *Command & Conquer* line of strategy war games, which was developed by Westwood Studios, USA, sold more than 5 million units between its release in 1995 and June 1997. The line includes the original *Command & Conquer* for MS-DOS, Windows '95, Macintosh, Sony PlayStation and Sega Saturn; *The Covert Operations*; and *Command & Conquer Red Alert* — the prequel to *Command & Conquer* and once the fastest-selling computer game in history.

BIGGEST COMPUTER GAME CULT
Quake took the games community by storm when it was released by Activision in 1996, and thousands of players are still blasting each other over the internet. Denis Fong (USA), known as 'Thresh', is the Internet's top *Quake* player. He has a sponsorship deal with Microsoft, and in 1997 became Intergraph's E3 *Quake* champion,

BEST-SELLING VIDEO GAME EVER
Super Mario Bros. from Nintendo was created by Shigeru Miyamoto, the Japanese game developer and creator of the *Donkey Kong* arcade games. Mario first appeared in *Donkey Kong* in 1982 and again in *Mario Bros.* in 1984. He has since starred in other games for the Super Nintendo, Game Boy and Virtual Boy. *Super Mario Bros. 3* has sold 15 million copies worldwide and is the best-selling video game ever.

winning $5,000 (£3,052), a computer system and a Ferrari.

MOST REALISTIC GRAPHICS
Video Reality, which was developed by the Australian company SouthPeak Interactive, uses video footage rather than computer-generated graphics, so that the background detail of games increases when seen close-up rather than losing sharpness. SouthPeak has used its Video Reality technology in its game *Temujin*, in which players navigate their way through a museum, deciphering puzzles and solving

mysteries. The backgrounds were filmed in an on-site video production facility before being transferred to computer.

MOST INTELLECTUALLY CHALLENGING GAME
Jane's Combat Simulations' game *688(I) Hunter/Killer* is reportedly the most realistic submarine simulation developed for PCs. The game was developed by defence contractors who design submarine simulators for the US Navy, and a knowledge of flight dynamics is an advantage for players, who have to master sonar and weapons systems, develop real target solutions and outfit a boat with the latest weaponry.

BIGGEST COMPUTER GAME MANUFACTURER
During the third quarter of 1997 Electronic Arts, of California, USA, reported sales of more than $391 million (£235 million) and profits of $58 million (£34.9 million). The company develops, publishes and distributes software for PCs and entertainment systems such as Sony PlayStation and Nintendo 64.

BIGGEST CYBERSTAR
Tomb Raider, starring the fearless Lara Croft, was launched by Eidos Interactive, Europe's biggest publisher and entertainment software developer, in Nov 1996. The game, which was designed by Core Design, has become one of the best-selling video game titles of all time and Lara was named one of the 50 most influential people in the computer industry by US magazine *Time Digital*. In Nov 1997 Lara was given a make-over and some new moves for *Tomb Raider II*, which sold more than 2 million copies within two months of its launch. By March 1998 the two games had sold 6 million copies worldwide. On 16 March 1998 Eidos announced that it had entered into an agreement to licence the worldwide film rights to *Tomb Raider* with Paramount Pictures. Lara Croft herself has appeared on more than 80 magazine and newspaper covers around the world, including *Time Digital*'s Dec 1997 issue, for which she was dressed in a Santa Claus outfit.

gadgets 1

THINNEST SPEAKERS
New Transducers Ltd have produced the thinnest full range speakers. They dispense with the magnets and voice coils of conventional dynamic speakers: instead an electromagnetic exciter creates dense waves across an acoustically inert slab, making sound waves from the mixing of pressure across the slab.

SMALLEST CELLULAR PHONE
The PHS (Personal Handyphone System), made by the Nippon Telegraph and Telephone Corp., is a wristwatch-style phone that dispenses with the conventional keypad. Numbers are selected by voice recognition circuitry within the phone. The unit weighs 70 g ($2^2/_5$ oz) and measures 5.5 x 4 x 1.6 cm (2 x $1^1/_2$ x $3/_5$ in).

SMALLEST MOBILE PHONE
The smallest GSM cellular phone is the Motorola StarTac Lite, which weighs 93.5 g (3 oz) but is capable of a standby time of more than 95 hours with an optional lithium ion battery. Users can 'hot-swap' batteries, allowing them to continue talking without interruption.

BIGGEST PLASMA TV SCREEN
NEC's Hi-Vision PlasmaX PX-50V2 features a 1.27-m (50-in) diagonal screen incorporating plasma display technology. The set, which is designed to work with Japan's analogue HDTV system, is also the world's slimmest high definition television to date: at a depth of just 9.7 cm ($3^4/_5$ in), the system is still capable of displaying more than 1 million pixels.

SMALLEST SOLID STATE STORAGE DEVICE
The SanDisk Multimedia Card, which was developed by SanDisk and Siemens for use in portable equipment such as mobile phones and digital voice recorders, is 3.2 x 2.4 x 0.14 cm ($1^1/_4$ x $9/_10$ x $1/_20$ in) thick and can store up to 10 megabytes in non-volatile memory.

SMALLEST WEARABLE PC
Seiko's RuPuter, which is slightly larger than a wristwatch, has 128 kilobytes of system memory and can exchange data with other computers by an Infra Red data link interface.

SMALLEST CAMERAS
In 1998 Nintendo's Game Boy, which was launched in 1989 and has sold more than 60 million units worldwide, was reinvented as a camera and printer. The digital still camera cartridge sits on top of the Game Boy (as seen left) and can take and store up to 30 low-resolution black and white photos. The camera comes with three games that allow players to create characters using photos. The printer can then produce passport-size prints or stickers. In 1997 the company reduced the size of the Game Boy and introduced the Game Boy Pocket, and a colour version of the Game Boy is due to be launched at the end of 1998. The world's smallest pinhole video camera is the PC-21XP, sold by Supercircuits Inc., USA. The CCD element occupies only 1.6 cm² ($1/_4$ in²) but has a 295,000-pixel array that outputs 380 video lines. It can see in low-level lighting of 0.5 lux. The overall unit is 7.4 cm² x 1.27 cm² ($1^{15}/_{100}$ in² x $1/_2$ in² deep) and can run for up to five hours on one PP3 battery.

THINNEST LAPTOP
Mitsubishi's Pedion portable PC, which has a fully featured MMX compatible Pentium 233 processor and 3.2-gigabyte hard drive, is 1.7 cm ($7/_{10}$ in) thick when folded.

SMALLEST VIDEO TRANSMITTER
The VID1 from AE Inc. allows the wireless transmission of a picture to a base station 609 m (2,000 ft) away, to compliment a remote camera in a covert monitoring situation. Measuring 1.5 x 2.28 x 0.76 mm ($3/_5$ x $9/_10$ x $3/_10$ in), it transmits either PAL or

In March 1998 the Polaroid Pocket Xiao, which was developed by toymaker Tomy Company Ltd. and U.S. Polaroid Corporation of Cambridge, Massachusetts, USA, was unveiled at the Tokyo Toy Show in Japan. It measures 4.4 x 13 x 4 cm ($1^7/_{10}$ x $5^1/_{10}$ x $1^1/_2$ in) and weighs 167 g ($5^4/_5$ oz) including batteries.

THINNEST PLASTIC WATCH
On 1 Oct 1997 the Swiss watchmakers Swatch launched the Swatch Skin, which has a paper-thin plastic strap and a 3.9-mm-high ($^{15}/_{100}$-in) case. It can be worn by divers down to a depth of 30 m (98 ft).

THINNEST MINIDISC RECORDER
Sony's MZ-R50 is 1.97 cm ($^7/_{10}$ in) thick and weighs 190 g (6 oz). It can play for up to 22 hours with its lithium ion battery and alkaline AA cells.

SMALLEST PRINTER
Citizen's PN60 printer measures 25.4 x 5.1 x 7.6 cm ($9^9/_{10}$ x 2 x $2^9/_{10}$ in) and weighs 498 kg (1 lb $1^1/_2$ oz). It has a thermal fusion print head and produces images of up to 140 x 140 dots/cm (360 x 360 dots/in) at a rate of two pages a minute.

SMALLEST DIGITAL PRINTER
JVC's V-HT1 is the smallest digital printer able to make hard copies of digital still camera images. It produces A7 size pictures from any camera with an IRTran-P infra-red data interface.

SMALLEST SHEET-FEED SCANNER
The CanoScan 300S, which uses Canon's LED InDirect Exposure (LIDE) technology, weighs just 1.5 kg (3 lb 4 oz).

SMALLEST DOCUMENT SHREDDER
Piranha's PR026 measures 17 x 6 x 4 cm ($6^1/_2$ x $2^1/_3$ x $1^1/_2$ in) and deals with any kind of document by nibbling off slices and shredding them into slivers.

SMALLEST FAX MACHINE
Phillips' smart phone add-on connects to the Phillips PCS 1900 Digital Phone to send faxes and e-mails, access the internet and provide other communication services. It makes the PCS 1900, at 17 cm ($6^7/_{10}$ in) in length and 159 g ($5^3/_5$ oz) in weight, the smallest and lightest mobile fax.

SMALLEST BINOCULARS
The U-C 8x18 series binoculars, with 8x magnification and optics that allow focusing down to 2 m

(6 ft 7 in), weighs 145 g (5 oz) and measures 8.5 x 7 x 1.8 cm (3 x $2^7/_{10}$ x $^7/_{10}$ in).

SMALLEST NIGHT VISION SCOPE
The smallest scope with a built-in illuminator is the Mini Night Vision from ASL Corp. At 13 x 6 cm ($5^1/_4$ x $2^1/_2$ in), it can amplify light by 15,000 times.

THINNEST PRIMARY CELL
Yuasa Exide's Power Film is a 1-mm-thick ($^3/_{100}$-in) primary cell of lithium manganese internal construction used in Smart Cards and other transportable media.

SMALLEST DIGITAL CAMERA
The world's smallest digital camera with a viewfinder is the Panasonic NV-DCF2B Card Shot, which measures 9 x 6 x 3.15 cm ($3^1/_2$ x 2 x $1^1/_5$ in), has a 350,000- pixel CCD element allowing images up to 640 x 480 to be captured in fine mode, or 320 x 240 in standard mode. The two-megabyte memory can store up to 24 images in fine or 85 in standard mode in JPEG picture file format.

NTSC encoded video at 900 MHz, reducing the need for powerful output and allowing use for up to 11 hours.

SMALLEST VIDEO RECORDER
Sony's EVO 220 Micro 8 mm weighs 680 g ($1^1/_2$ lb) and measures 6 x 21.7 x 14.6 cm ($2^3/_{10}$ x $8^1/_2$ x $5^7/_{10}$ in). It records up to five hours of video onto 8-mm ($^3/_{10}$-in) tape.

SMALLEST PORTABLE DVD PLAYER
Panasonic's DVD-L10 weighs less than 1 kg ($2^1/_5$ lb) and has its own 14.5-cm ($5^7/_{10}$-in) LCD screen and stereo speakers. Equipped with on-board and remote controls, it can also be used as a MPEG-2 video and Dolby Digital audio source for any home cinema set-up. It crams all of this into a box 16 x 16 x 4.3 cm ($6^1/_5$ x $6^1/_5$ x $1^3/_5$ in) deep.

SMALLEST VIDEO-CD PLAYER
The smallest video-CD player with its own screen is Panasonic's SL-DP70, which measures 13 x 3.6 x 14.4 cm (5 x $1^2/_5$ x $5^3/_5$ in). It can function for up to two hours with six AA batteries and costs about $528 (£330).

gadgets II

MOST POWERFUL GAMES CONSOLE
Nintendo's N64 is the fastest and the most powerful games console in the world to date. The console has true 64-bit processing architecture and was developed in a collaboration between Nintendo of Japan and Silicon Graphics Interactive Ltd of California, USA. Costing $158 (£99), it has graphic manipulation capabilities that would have only been present in multi-million-dollar systems 10 years ago.

MOST POWERFUL LAPTOP
In 1998 Apple launched the PowerPC 750 RISC chip, Powerbook G3 — the most powerful laptop in the world today. The Powerbook G3 looks and feels like Apple's 3400 model, but is twice as fast and has a 32-megabyte EDO DRAM memory that is upgradeable to 160 megabytes. Its power gives it a weight of 3.5 kg (7 lb 11 oz), making it difficult to carry in one hand.

MOST POWERFUL WEARABLE COMPUTER
The world's most powerful wearable computer is the Mentis system, which is manufactured by Teltronics Incorporated of Sarasota, Florida. The processing unit measures 19 x 13.9 x 2.5 cm (7½ x 5½ x 1 in) and contains a fully featured Pentium-equipped multimedia system on a single board. The wearer can access the system by voice command and view the display output either via a head-mounted LCD monocle or with the assistance of an external flat LCD panel.

CHEAPEST GPS RECEIVER
The cheapest portable Global Positioning by Satellite receiver in the world today is the GPS Pioneer, which is manufactured by Magellan Systems Corporation in the USA. The Pioneer is the first GPS receiver to cost less than $100 (£62) and allows users to find their location on the planet through its ability to decode information from the NavStar network of 24 orbiting geostationary satellites.

MOST SHOCK-PROOF CD PLAYER
The PCD-7900, which is manufactured by Sanyo-Fisher, is the first personal CD player in the world to incorporate a 40-second anti-shock memory, which compensates for errors in the disc tracking caused by external shock. The CD player has such an extensive shock-guard capability that listeners can continue to listen to the music from the original disk while they are changing discs.

INTERACTIVE CANDY
In Feb 1998 Hasbro Inc. introduced Sound Bites, a lollipop holder that plays tunes and noises inside the user's head. The toy is operated by the insertion of a lollipop into the Sound Bites holder. When someone bites into the lollipop, a computer chip inside the holder transmits vibrations through the person's teeth directly to their inner ear, providing sounds and melodies. The music is virtually inaudible to anyone standing nearby. Sound Bites, which was co-invented by Andrew Filo, a Silicon Valley engineer, and David Capper, a toy industry entrepreneur, has four buttons that can be pressed to mix and match the sound selection. The holder takes most standard makes of lollipop. There are six versions of the toy, including three musical themes and three special effects, with cartoon noises, funny voices and space noises. At Christmas Hasbro plans to introduce a new model that plays carols.

MOST EFFICIENT AUDIO AMPLIFIER
The Tact Millennium has a configuration known as Class D, or Pulse Width Modulation, which means that the amplifier converts almost 100% of the input power to audio power output, making it the most efficient audio amplifier in the world. It is the first Class D amplifier to be able to claim a fully digital signal path, and offers greater compatibility with new digital-only equalization equipment and effects.

MOST EXPENSIVE POWER AMPLIFIER
The AudioNote Ongaku costs $93,200 (£56,000), making it the world's most expensive power amplifier. The Ongaku has a valve amplifier with a Class A output configuration, giving purity of sound at the expense of electrical efficiency. The main reason for its high cost is the windings for the output transformers, which are made out of solid silver wire (silver is the most conductive metal at room temperature).

MOST EXPENSIVE HI-FI SPEAKERS
Dutch company OLS launched the Grand Enigma Reference System, a set of hi-fi speakers costing $1 million (£625,000), in 1998. The 10-kg (22-lb) speakers are charged with 100,000 watts.

MOST EXPENSIVE PRODUCTION 35-MM SLR CAMERA
The Canon Eos 1N-RS costs $3,840 (£2,400), making it the most expensive production 35-mm SLR camera in the world to date. The 1N-RS has a shutter speed of $\frac{1}{8000}$th of a second up to 30 seconds, accepts film speeds from 25 to 5,000 ASA and can shoot up to three frames every second. Its Penatprism viewfinder offers 100% of the view that is relayed to the film and the main body can accept any Canon EF mount lenses.

MOST EXPENSIVE MOBILE PHONE

In 1996 jewellers David Morris International of London, UK, designed and sold a one-off mobile telephone that was made entirely of 18-carat gold encrusted with pink and white diamonds. The price tag was a record-breaking £66,629 ($104,050). Other designs by the jewellers include a Game Boy made of gold and diamonds and a jelly-bean machine. The luxury gadgets are often purchased by royalty and other wealthy people. In 1971 David Morris International supplied all the jewellery worn in the James Bond movie *Diamonds Are Forever* (GB, 1971).

360° TV

The 360° television set was invented by Frank Gibshaw of E.S.P Electronics Inc. (pictured above with his invention) and unveiled at the International Consumer Electronics Show in Las Vegas, USA, in Jan 1998. The set displays the same images that are shown on normal televisions, but allows the viewer to watch from all sides of the unit. Aside from TV viewing, the potential applications of the set include video games, computer and video displays, educational presentations and movies.

FASTEST LINE MATRIX PRINTER

The world's fastest line matrix printer is the Tally T6180, which can print at speeds of up to 1,800 lines per minute. This is approximately 27% faster than its nearest rival.

MOST 'INTELLIGENT' PEN

Dutch computer company LCI have developed a 'smartpen' that is capable of verifying people's signatures. The smartpen's minuscule pressure pads, electronic spirit level and computer processor combine to record the pressure that is applied to it and the angle of tilt at which it is being used. The chip within the smartpen then encrypts the information and transmits it to a remote computer to be checked against a central database.

MOST EXPENSIVE CD PLAYER

A CD player with an 18-carat yellow gold case encrusted with pink pavé diamonds sold for £82,000 ($128,000) at David Morris International in London, UK, in 1996, making it the world's most expensive ever CD player. David Morris opened his shop in Conduit Street, Mayfair — an exclusive area of the British capital popular with wealthy socialites and movie stars — in 1969.

internet

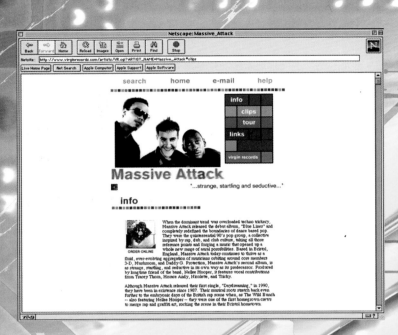

Netscape: Massive_Attack

http://www.virginrecords.com/artists/VR.cgi?ARTIST_NAME=Massive_Attack*clips

search   home   e-mail   help

info
clips
tour
links

virgin records

Massive Attack

"...strange, startling and seductive..."

info

ORDER ONLINE

When the dominant trend was overloaded techno trickery, Massive Attack released the debut album, "Blue Lines" and completely redefined the boundaries of dance based pop. They were the quintessential 90's pop group, a collective inspired by rap, dub, and club culture, taking all those reference points and forging a music that opened up a whole new range of aural possibilities. Based in Bristol, England, Massive Attack today continues to thrive as a fluid, ever-evolving aggregation of musicians orbiting around core members 3-D, Mushroom, and Daddy G. Protection, Massive Attack's second album, is as strange, startling, and seductive in its own way as its predecessor. Produced by long time friend of the band, Nellee Hooper, it features vocal contributions from Tracey Thorn, Horace Andy, Nicolette, and Tricky.

Although Massive Attack released their first single, "Daydreaming," in 1990, they have been in existence since 1987. Their musical roots stretch back even further to the embryonic days of the British rap scene when, as The Wild Bunch — also featuring Nellee Hooper — they were one of the first homegrown crews to merge rap and graffiti art, rocking the scene in their Bristol hometown.

BIGGEST ALBUM RELEASE

The British band Massive Attack launched the whole of their third album *Mezzanine* (1998) on-line, together with a preview of the video for the first single from the album, three weeks before it was available in the shops. The site received 1,313,644 hits, and the songs were downloaded a total of 101,673 times before the album went on sale on 20 April. A further 1,602,658 hits were recorded a month after the shop release. Despite its availability on the internet, *Mezzanine* went straight to No. 1 on the British album chart.

MOST ON-LINE SALES

The US firm Dell Computers generates a record-breaking $3 million (£1.8 million) a day from its websites.

MOST SPENT ON INTERNET ADVERTISING IN A YEAR

Microsoft spent more than $13 million (£8.58 million) on advertising on the internet in 1996, and between June 1997 and June 1998 it spent more than £600,000 ($960,000) in the United Kingdom alone.

MOST POPULAR WEBSITE

Yahoo, a directory in which websites have been compiled into categories, has the biggest audience of any on-line service or site on the internet in the world. Approximately 95 million page views per day were recorded in March 1998.

MOST MENTIONED MAN ON THE INTERNET

The internet search engine AltaVista links US president Bill Clinton's name to 1,842,790 sites, making him the most mentioned man on the internet. The word 'Clinton' has a monthly average of 45,080 hits on the directory Yahoo. 'Bill Clinton' receives a further 44,080 hits.

MOST QUESTIONS RECEIVED ON AN INTERNET SITE IN 30 MINUTES

On 17 May 1997 former Beatle Sir Paul McCartney received more than 3 million questions from fans in 30 minutes during a web event to promote his album *Flaming Pie*. On 19 Nov 1997 McCartney also set a record for the first ever debut performance

of a classical work live on the internet, when he performed his new work, the 75-minute symphonic poem *Standing Stones*, live from Carnegie Hall, New York, USA. The presentation involved radio, television, an interactive on-line interview and internet audio and video broadcast across the World Wide Web. McCartney had been composing *Standing Stones* for four years.

BIGGEST SHOPPING MALL ON THE INTERNET

Internet Mall, which is situated at mecklerweb.com/imall, has a record 800 on-screen virtual shops and more than 1 million subscribers in the United Kingdom alone. It uses a total of

65,000 shops around the globe to create the service, which is available in more than 150 countries. The products, which range from popcorn to car insurance, are delivered within 48 hours. Internet malls date back to 1993, when Jon Zeeff launched the Branch Mall. It had two virtual shops, Grant's Flowers and Calling Cards, and registered 400 hits in its first month. It now has 3 million visitors a month and is found at http://www.branchmall.com/.

MOST COMMERCE CONDUCTED ON THE INTERNET

In 1997 the USA saw $2 billion (£1.22 billion) worth of commerce over the internet — more than any other country.

MOST POPULAR SEARCH ENGINE

AltaVista has more than 1 billion page views and in excess of 21 million users every month worldwide. The engine works by trawling 140 million pages and 16,000 usenet newsgroups.

MOST POPULAR SEARCH WORDS

The most frequently-used search word recorded on Yahoo is 'sex', which receives an average of 1.55 million searches a month. In second place is 'chat', with 414,320 searches. Other top contenders are Netscape software, games and weather.

FIRST INTERNET VERDICT

In Nov 1997 Judge Hiller Zobel announced that he would post his 16-page ruling on the case of 19-year-old British au pair Louise Woodward on the internet before issuing hard copies, in order to avoid a media circus at the courthouse in Cambridge Massachusetts, USA. Woodward had been given a 15-year sentence after being found guilty of murdering Matthew Eappen, a baby who had been in her care. On 10 Nov 1997 this verdict was overturned by Judge Zobel, who reduced the sentence to 279 days and the conviction to one of involuntary manslaughter. His verdict was to be the first in legal history to be broadcast on the internet and via e-mail before being disseminated via other channels. However, demand for the site by millions of people around the globe caused the internet server delivering the verdict to crash, delaying the live announcement of the judgement on the Lawyer's Weekly Home Page on the World Wide Web. Pictured here, supporters of Woodward watch the announcement of the initial guilty verdict at her home village of Elton, Cheshire, UK.

MOST POPULAR NEWS SERVICE

CNN's seven sites have a combined average of 55 million page views per week. The sites also receive more than 3,000 user comments per day via the CNN message boards. The sites currently contain more than 210,000 pages but grow by 90–150 pages daily.

MOST POPULAR DOMAIN NAME

Of the 2.69 million domain names that were in existence worldwide by 16 Feb 1998, the most popular is '.com', at 1.65 million. According to NetNames Ltd, the number of domains registered grows by 7,983 a day.

BIGGEST DOMAIN OWNERSHIP

According to NetNames Ltd, the USA has a total of 1,353,550 domains, which represents 50.9% of the overall domain ownership in the world. The United Kingdom is the second largest, with 160,004, or 6%.

GREATEST NUMBER OF ACTIVE ON-LINE NET ACCOUNTS

Charles Schwab & Co., the US stockbrokers, have more than 900,000 on-line accounts holding in excess of $66.6 billion (£40.02 billion) in assets and accounting for more than one-third of their 99,000 daily trading operations.

BIGGEST SAVING OF PAPER THROUGH USING THE INTERNET

The delivery firm Federal Express has announced that it saves approximately 2 billion sheets of paper a year in the USA by tracking packages on-line.

MOST SUCCESSFUL INTERNET CRACKER

An internet cracker (similar to a hacker) is an electronic burglar who systematically breaks into computer systems and files. One cracker is reported to have managed the biggest invasion of supposedly secure computers since the creation of the internet. Uncharged because of the complexities of the case, he is said to have broken through

every known computer system, including NASA and Intel, as well as a number of nuclear weapons laboratories, government organizations and military sites. The technology used by hackers and crackers advances daily, and it is thought that internet crime is severely under-policed and out of control. It is estimated that $300 billion (£187.5 billion) a year is lost due to internet money laundering alone.

BIGGEST INTERNET CRASH

At approximately 11.30 EST on 25 April 1997, the global computer network ran into major problems, and much of the system became unusable. Human error and equipment failure had led a network in Florida to claim 'ownership' of 30,000 of the internet's 45,000 routes. Data packets were routed incorrectly and connections across the internet failed. Some service providers took action within 15 minutes, but the problem persisted until 19.00 EST.

MOST WIRED COUNTRY

It is estimated that more than 24 million adults in the USA will be connected to the internet by the end of 1998.

BIGGEST COMPUTER NETWORK

The number of computers using the internet has doubled every year since 1987. In Jan 1997 the figure was 16.2 million, although there may be a great number of computers that are connected but hidden behind corporate 'firewalls' designed to exclude electronic visitors, including hackers.

MOST MENTIONED WOMAN

Pamela Anderson is the most mentioned woman on the net. The search engine AltaVista links the star of US TV series *Baywatch* and the film *Barb Wire* (USA, 1996) to 1,542,282 sites. She inspires an average of 172,760 hits a month on the Yahoo internet browser.

HACKING

In 1995 an advertisement on the World Wide Web for the US movie *Hackers* was itself the victim of hackers. The controversial site had a hyperlink to sites that provided potentially dangerous and criminal information, including stolen credit-card numbers and instructions for creating home-made bombs and printing counterfeit banknotes with a laser printer. The site was submitted to the FBI's National Computer Crime Squad for potential investigation but in June 1998 it could still be accessed via the internet.

MOST WIRED COMMUNITY

Blacksburg, Montgomery County, Virginia, USA, claims to be the community with the most e-mail and internet users relative to its size. According to a survey carried out in 1995, there were about 30,000 regular users of wired data communications in a population of 70,000. Of these, 20,000 users had links through the local university, Virginia Tech.

computers

BEST CHESS COMPUTER

IBM's *Deep Blue* was the first supercomputer to beat a human chess grandmaster in a regulation game when it played Gary Kasparov in Philadelphia, USA, in 1995. On 11 May 1997 it beat a grandmaster (Kasparov again) in a series for the first time. It won the six-match series by 3½ points to 2½.

'MOST HUMAN' COMPUTER SYSTEM

In Jan 1997 a computer running the programme *Albert One version 1.0* was awarded the Loebner Prize for the 'most human' computer system. *Albert One* is a programme that a user can communicate with using human speech. The judges of the annual Loebner Prize put systems through a restricted version of the Turing Test, the classic test of machine intelligence.

WORST POTENTIAL BUG

The millennium bug, which will become active on 1 Jan 2000, could cause millions of computer systems to go haywire, including those in hospitals, banks, air traffic control centres, buildings, cars, planes and government databases. It occurs in all systems that record the year using only two figures (ie. '99' for '1999'). Unless they are fixed, these systems will be unable to interpret the year 2000 as a year that is one later than 1999. Pessimistic forecasters have said it will cost the world $4 trillion (£2.5 trillion) to fix systems containing the bug, deal with instances of it that are missed, and compensate any people that it affects.

MOST WIDESPREAD VIRUS

First detected in early 1997, the CAP computer virus infects Microsoft Word documents. It is a linked set of 'macros' (mini programmes that automate routines in Word) which change the way files are opened, closed and saved. CAP spreads by attaching itself to Word's 'global template', a file that is opened whenever a document is accessed. CAP has been reported more than any other virus in history, although this may be partly because it is very difficult for non-experts to deal with.

MOST MONEY LOST DUE TO COMPUTERS

On 19 Oct 1987 computers contributed to the loss of $1 trillion (£62,500,000 billion) in a rapid global stock-market crash. On the day of this catastrophe, which is now known as 'Black Monday', share prices began to tumble. This caused newly-installed computer trading programmes to jump into action, trading rapidly and selling shares automatically at ever-lower prices. 'Black Monday' wiped 22.6% off the US Dow Jones Index — the biggest drop ever recorded in stock-market history.

MOST NOTORIOUS HACKER CASE

US hacker Kevin Mitnick is alleged to have broken into several major organizations' computer systems, including those of Motorola, Sun Microsystems and the Pentagon. Mitnick was arrested on 16 Sept 1996 after an FBI computer expert tracked him down. He has since been charged with software theft, wire fraud, the interception of wire communications and computer vandalism. Mitnick, the first hacker ever to have appeared on an FBI Wanted poster, faces up to 12 years in prison if he is found guilty.

FASTEST COMPUTERS

The fastest general-purpose vector-parallel computer is the Cray Y-MP C90 supercomputer, which has two gigabytes of central memory and 16 CPUs (central processing units), giving a combined peak performance of 16 gigaflops.

Intel installed an even faster supercomputer at Sandia, Texas, USA, in 1996. Using 9,072 Intel Pentium Pro processors, each running at about 200 MHz, and 608 gigabytes of memory, it has a peak performance of about 1.8 teraflops.

'Massively parallel' computers, with enough processors, have a theoretical aggregate performance exceeding that of a C-90. The performance on real-life applications can often be less, because it may be harder to effectively harness the power of many small processors than a few large ones.

In Sept 1997 the US Defense Projects Research Agency (DARPA) commissioned computer researcher John McDonald to build the world's first PetOps supercomputer — a machine that can perform 1,000 trillion operations per second. DARPA gave $1 million (£625,000) to finance this three-year project, which will result in the fastest computer ever commissioned. They want to use the system to simulate battles and natural disasters for training purposes.

The World Supercomputing Speed Record was set in Dec 1994 by a team of scientists from Sandia National Laboratories and Intel Corporation, who linked together two of the largest Intel Paragon parallel-processing machines. The system achieved a performance of 281 gigaflops on the Linpack benchmark. The massively parallel supercomputer also achieved 328 gigaflops running a programme used for radar signature calculations. The two-Paragon system used 6,768 processors working in parallel.

FASTEST CHIP

The Deschutes Intel P6 microarchitecture processor is the fastest PC microchip on the high street. A 400Mhz version of this processor with a bus speed of 66 Mhz is already on the market and the company plan to bring out a 450Mhz chip, which will have a bus speed of 100 Mhz. In Sept 1997 IBM's Research and Microelectronics divisions unveiled the world's first copper-based microchip. Copper had long been recognized as a superior electrical conductor, but because it proved difficult to adapt it to semiconductor manufacturing, aluminium was used instead. The development enabled the company to shrink electronic circuitry and fit more 'intelligence' (computer logic) onto each microchip. The technology is called CMOS 7S (complementary metal oxide semiconductor) and will be used to build higher performing microprocessors for computer systems. It will also enable manufacturers to make products that need less power and less cooling and integrate more complex functions than those available on the market today, as well as being smaller and lighter. A month later IBM announced the first design tools and services to help electronics providers build products using the new microchip.

BIGGEST NUMBER CRUNCHED

In April 1997 it was announced that computer scientists at Purdue University, Indiana, USA, had co-ordinated researchers around the world to find the two largest numbers that, multiplied together, equal a known 167-digit number, $(3^{349}-1)\div2$. The breakthrough came after 100,000 hours of computing time. The two factors had 80 digits and 87 digits. The previous factorization record was 162 digits long.

LONGEST COMPUTER COMPUTATION FOR A YES/NO ANSWER

The 20th Fermat number, $2^{2^{20}}+1$, was tested on a CRAY–2 supercomputer in 1986 to see if it was a prime number. After 10 days of calculation the answer was no.

LARGEST PRIME NUMBER FOUND USING A COMPUTER

On 27 Jan 1998 19-year-old student Roland Clarkson discovered the prime number $2^{3,021,377}-1$. This number, which is 909,526 digits long when written out in full, was traced using software written by George Woltman and Scott Kurowski. It is the 37th known 'Mersenne prime'. Clarkson, one of several thousand volunteers contributing to the Great Internet Mersenne Prime Search (GIMPS), found the number on his ordinary 200 MHz Pentium desktop computer.

MOST POWERFUL COMPUTER IN SPACE

The lander of the Mars *Pathfinder* is controlled by an IBM RAD6000, a radiation-hardened single-board computer that is related to the PowerPC. It has a 32-bit architecture and can carry out 22 million instructions per second. It is used to store flight software, engineering and silence data and images, and data from the rover vehicle, in 128 million bytes of memory. *Pathfinder* landed on Mars in July 1997.

MOST REMOTE COMPUTER

Carrying microprocessors to control its operations and communications, the *Voyager 1* space probe was estimated to be approximately 11 billion km (6.7 billion miles) away from the Sun at the end of 1998 — 72.5 times the distance from Earth to the Sun and far too distant for scientists to communicate with it. *Voyager 1* was launched on 5 Sept 1977 and was used to collect data about Jupiter and Saturn. After it passed these planets, it was left to drift out of our solar system and into Outer Space.

MOST PROFITABLE COMPUTER COMPANY

The Microsoft Corporation was valued at $224 billion (£140 billion) in April 1998 and has an annual revenue in excess of $17.6 billion (£11 billion). The corporation produces, manufactures, sells and licenses software and online services to computer users around the world. Its chairman Bill Gates, who currently owns about 30% of Microsoft, founded the company with Paul Allen in 1975, and it has made him the richest man in the world.

BEST-SELLING SOFTWARE

Since its release on 24 Aug 1995, approximately 120 million copies of the Microsoft operating system *Windows '95* have been sold. *Windows '95* is bundled with 90% of the desktop

SMALLEST CALCULATOR

Scientists at IBM Research Division's Zürich Research Laboratory in Switzerland have designed a calculating device with a diameter of less than one millionth of a millimetre ($^{39}/_{10^8}$ in). The smallest handheld computer is the Psion Series 5 handheld computer, which weighs 345 g (12 oz) including batteries. It has a touch-type keyboard and touch-sensitive screen.

computers that are sold around the world. Only sales of MS DOS, the basic operating system that is pre-installed on almost all desktop PCs, have outstripped sales of this software.

BIGGEST LAWSUIT INVOLVING A COMPUTER COMPANY

On 20 Oct 1997 the US Justice Department filed a motion alleging that Microsoft had been trading unfairly. They objected to the fact that the company bundled its own browser, *Internet Explorer*, with *Windows '95* software. Microsoft claimed that they had acted within the law as *Internet Explorer* is just a new feature of *Windows '95* itself. Microsoft and the Department of Justice are currently fighting over this matter in court.

BIGGEST COMPUTERIZED BROKERAGE

The Institutional Network of Instinet Corp, which began operating in 1969, was purchased by Reuters in 1987 and became the world's largest computerized brokerage, with a 1996 volume of 100 million shares per day trading via its 54,000 terminals.

FASTEST COMPUTER IN USE

A 1,328-processor CRAY T3E-900TM built by Cray Research, USA, was found to be the fastest computer in use by weather researchers at the University of Oklahoma, USA, who used it to run storm prediction software. It is one of a small number of installed systems that can perform more than 1 trillion operations a second. Seen here is a Scarmjet computation made by a Cray supercomputer.

robots

MOST ANIMATED ROBOTS

In 1993 Steven Spielberg's company Amblin Entertainment in California, USA, created the most animated robots ever, for the director's movie *Jurassic Park*. The nine dinosaur species — which included a tyrannosaurus rex, dilophosaurs, velociraptors and a hatchling — were made of latex, foam rubber and urethane and had dilating pupils, twitching skin and saliva-moist mouths. To turn the complex machines into actors, a miniature version of each dinosaur was manipulated to capture the performance and relay it by computer to the dinosaur robots.

A team of Belgian and British scientists led by Dr Vassilios of Belgium is experimenting with robot technology to create dinosaurs that lie dormant and spring into life when humans appear. Ultra sensors built into the dinosaurs' eye sockets will allow them to watch and stalk people. The team is currently perfecting the first dinosaur, a 2.5-m (8-ft 2½-in) iguanodon.

BIGGEST FILM ROBOT

In 1993 Amblin Entertainment created a 5.5-m-tall (18-ft), 14-m-long (40-ft), 4,082-kg (9,000-lb) robotic tyrannosaurus rex for the film *Jurassic Park*. The biggest robot ever made for a motion picture, it was the same size as the original dinosaur.

SMALLEST ROBOT

The light-sensitive 'Monsieur' microbot, developed by the Seiko Epson Corporation, Japan, in 1992, measures less than 1 cm³ (³/₅₀ in³) and weighs 1.5 g (¹/₂₀ oz). Made from 97 separate watch parts (equivalent to two ordinary watches), it can move at 1.13 cm/sec (²/₅ in/sec) for about five minutes when charged. It won a design award at the International Contest for Hill-Climbing Micromechanisms.

MOST POPULAR ROBOT

Puma (Programmable Universal Machine for Assembly), designed by Vic Schienman in the 1970s and manufactured by Swiss company Staubli Unimation, is the most commonly used robot in university laboratories and assembly lines.

FASTEST INDUSTRIAL ROBOT

In July 1997 Japanese company Fanuc developed the LR Mate 100I high-speed conveyance robot, the axis speed of which is estimated to be 79% faster than previous models. The robot can carry objects for up to 3 km (1 mile 1,513 yd), and can move up and down 2.5 cm (1 in) and back and forth 30 cm (12 in) in a time of 0.58 seconds — 60% faster than previous models and an industry record.

MOST ADVANCED ROBOT TOY

In Jan 1998 Lego unveiled MindStorms: 'intelligent' plastic building blocks that can be made into 'thinking' robots and brought to life through a home computer. Developed over more than 10 years by Lego, together with Professor Papert of Massachusetts Institute of Technology, USA, the bricks contain a microchip and sensors.

CHEAPEST ROBOT

Walkman, a 12.7-cm (5-in) robot, was built from the wreckage of a Sony Walkman for $1.75 (£1.06) at the Los Alamos National Laboratory, USA, in 1996. In tests it struggled to get free when its legs were held, without being programmed to do so and without making the same movement twice.

MOST BIOLOGICAL ROBOTS

In March 1998 scientists at Tsukuba and Tokyo universities, Japan, created insect robots by fusing the antennae of silkmoths with wheeled robots containing electronic 'brains'. When the robots were lured by female moths, which secrete a sexual chemical, microchips with neural networks similar to those of male moths directed the wheels of the robots towards the scent of the females. It is hoped that these prototype 'cybugs', as they are known, will be of assistance in the destruction of locusts and similar pests in the future, as well as in the inspection of otherwise inaccessible areas. Japan is a major centre for bio-robotics: a brown cockroach attached to a hi-tech 'backpack' containing a microprocessor and electrode set is pictured here undergoing bio-robot trials in a research laboratory at Tokyo University in Jan 1997.

MOST AUTOMATED FACILITY

In March 1997 the Fanuc assembly plant in Yamanashi, Japan, became the most automated facility in the world when a number of two-armed intelligent robots began to assemble mini-robots, resulting in a completely automated manufacturing system.

COUNTRY WITH GREATEST NUMBER OF INDUSTRIAL ROBOTS

Since 1991 approximately 325,000 robots have been installed in Japan — more than half of the 580,000 installed worldwide. For every 10,000 people employed in the Japanese manufacturing industry, there are now 265 robots in use.

BIGGEST PRODUCER OF COMMERCIAL ROBOTS

Formed in 1982, Japanese robot manufacturer Fanuc is the largest producer of commercial robots. Fanuc Robotics in the USA has more than 1,100 employees and 21,000 robots in service.

MOST DISTANT REMOTE CONTROL ON EARTH

The record for the greatest distance over which a robot has been controlled by remote control on Earth was set on 31 July 1997, when the *Nomad* robot completed a 215-km (133-mile 1,057-yd) journey over the Atacama Desert, Chile, driving 20 km (12 miles 753 yd) autonomously. It was operated from NASA's Ames Research Center in Moffett Field, California, USA, and Carnegie Mellon's Robotics Institute in Pittsburgh, USA. The trek was part of a $1.6-million (£1-million) project preparing for missions to Antarctica, the Moon and Mars.

In Nov 1996 Professor Kevin Warwick used the Internet together with a 15.24-cm (6-in), 600-g (1-lb 5-oz) robot at the cybernetics department of

Reading University, UK, to programme an identical robot at the State University of New York, USA, to move around its environment. Once they were switched on the two robots required no remote control or human input.

MOST ADVANCED ROBOTIC ARM

In 1997, the US company Barret Technology developed a $250,000 (£152,000) robotic arm with cables that act like tendons and can hold weights of 5 kg (11 lb) in any position. The arm has a total of seven gearless arm and wrist joints, which are driven by brushless motors. It can throw a ball, and could also be developed for cleaning, assisting people in and out of the bath, opening doors and preparing meals.

MOST ADVANCED DOMESTIC ROBOT

On 1 Dec 1997 Electrolux unveiled a domestic robot that can clean efficiently without supervision. The miniature robot is equipped with an electronic brain and a navigational radar system that prevents it from bumping into obstacles. It is capable of cleaning up to 95% of an accessible area — this compares with an average of 75% for human beings. Although the Electrolux cannot climb stairs, it can clean an entire storey of a house if the doors are left open.

MOST SOPHISTICATED SURGICAL APPLICATION BY A ROBOT

In Feb 1998 Computer Motion of California, USA, unveiled *Zeus*, a robot that allows surgeons to perform heart bypasses through three incisions the width of pencils, using thin instruments that fit inside tubes in the patient's body. *Zeus* is designed to remove any shaking from the surgeon's hands. The company plans to produce a version that allows surgeons to operate over a high-speed telephone line.

MOST HUMANOID ROBOT

In 1997 Honda launched the 1.6-m-tall (5-ft 3-in) P3, seen here shaking the hand of former Chinese premier Li Peng. P3 can turn its head, step over obstacles, change direction and correct its balance if pushed, and has three-dimensional sight. Developed by 150 engineers over 11 years, at a total cost of $80 million (£36 million), it could be used in nursing and for tasks that are too dangerous or strenuous for humans.

MOST DISTANT REMOTE CONTROL

In July 1997 NASA Jet Propulsion Laboratory's 1.19-kg (2-lb 1-oz), six-wheeled *Sojourner Rover* landed on Mars. Remote-controlled from Earth, 384,399 km (238,854 miles) away, it transmitted more than 500 images back to scientists. A new model is being developed for 2001: it will be bigger, travel farther, last a year on Mars, and store Martian-surface materials for future pick-up.

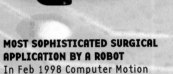

light, lasers and special effects

MOST POWERFUL TOUR LASERS

The British rock group Pink Floyd took a pair of 50-watt copper vapour lasers on their Division Bell tour, which ended in 1997. The green and red lasers, which cost (£250,000) $400,000 for the pair, were supplied by Oxford Lasers and are the most powerful and expensive lasers ever taken on a touring show.

MOST POWERFUL LASER BEAM

The world's most powerful laser beam is based at the top secret White Sands missile base, New Mexico, USA. The million-watt laser is driven by a rocket motor which is fuelled by a mixture of ethylene and nitrogen trifluoride. The laser beam itself is formed from microwaves at a wavelength of between 3.6 and 4.2 microns.

SMALLEST LASER

AT&T Bell Laboratories of Pasadena, California, USA, are the producers of the world's smallest laser. The laser is only 0.005 mm ($^1/_{5,000}$ in) in diameter and its reflecting disc is just 400 atoms thick. It is constructed from molecule-thick layers of indium gallium arsenide and phosphorus, over which is placed a thin protective coating.

BRIGHTEST FLASH OF LIGHT ON EARTH

The brightest flash of light ever produced on Earth was created by research staff at the Rutherford Appleton Laboratory, Oxfordshire, UK, in 1996. It was produced using an ultraviolet laser called *Titania*, which has a beam that is 42 cm ($16^1/_2$ in) in diameter and has a light intensity of 1,000 trillion watts, equivalent to 10 million trillion ordinary household light bulbs.

LONGEST BEAM OF ARTIFICIAL LIGHT

The longest beam of artificial light was fired by NASA scientists at a reflector placed on the Moon during the Apollo missions of the late 1960s and early 1970s. Astronauts positioned the reflector so that scientists on Earth could bounce a laser beam off it and get an accurate measurement of the distance from the Earth to the Moon (384,500 km or 238,920 miles). It sometimes took up to 1,000 attempts for the scientists to hit the target.

MOST POWERFUL SURFACE-TO-SPACE LASER WEAPON

The first test of a surface-to-space laser weapon occurred in Oct 1997. The weapon, a million-watt laser, was fired from the White Sands missile base in New Mexico, USA, and directed at a satellite which had been launched in May 1996. The satellite, which was orbiting 415 km (260 miles) above the surface of the Earth, was struck twice by the laser.

FASTEST LASER-POWERED SPACECRAFT

The world's fastest laser-powered spacecraft, which works by using laser beams to heat a jet of gases to extreme temperatures, was tested at White Sands missile base in New Mexico, USA, in Nov 1997. When the craft's lasers are used in conjunction with liquid hydrogen, it will be capable of speeds in excess of Mach 25 (27,000 km/h or 17,000 mph).

MOST LASERS USED IN COMBAT

The greatest use of laser-guided weapons in a war zone occurred during the Gulf War on 17 Jan 1991. Millions of people around the world watched live television coverage of lasers being used to guide missiles to their targets with pinpoint accuracy.

MOST MOTORISTS CAUGHT USING LASER SPEED DETECTION SYSTEM

Police in Hampshire, UK, set up a laser speed trap on a section of road works on the M27 motorway near Portsmouth over a six-month period from Dec 1996

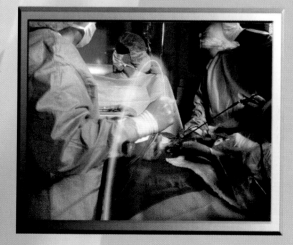

MOST SOPHISTICATED BONE-CUTTING LASER

The first practical bone-cutting laser was unveiled in 1995. Developed by surgeons at Hope Hospital, Manchester, UK, and physicists from the University of Manchester, it cuts through bone with precision without damaging surrounding tissue. This makes it especially useful for brain surgeons, who need to remove the top of the skull without damaging the brain. In 1990 American Dental Technologies introduced the first dental laser, and in 1998 it unveiled an advanced laser instrument for treating ulcers and gum disease. Ophthalmologists first used high-tech laser surgery in the early 1990s. Called photorefractive keratectomy (PRK), it involves altering the eye's focusing mechanism by shaving the cornea with a laser beam. The operation stemmed from radial keratotomy (RK), corrective microsurgery first attempted in Japan in the 1950s. Slava Fyodorov, a professor of ophthalmology in Moscow, Russia, later perfected the technique. The first experiments in PRK were made at St Thomas's Hospital, London, UK, and the University Eye Clinic, Berlin, Germany, between 1984 and 1986.

to May 1997. More than 1,900 motorists who exceeded the temporary 80-km/h (50-mph) speed limit were caught by the laser trap, and speeding tickets with a total value of £66,000 ($105,000) were issued.

BIGGEST LASER PROJECTION SCREEN
The largest laser projection screen in the world is the ITV (Inflatable Tower Vision), which was built by Advanced Entertainment Technologies of California, USA. The highly reflective inflatable nylon screen is more than 21 m (70 ft) high and is supported by two inflatable cones, each 7.5 m

(25 ft) in diameter. The screen is capable of withstanding continuous wind speeds of up to 48 km/h (30 mph) and has been seen by audiences at concerts all over the world.

MOST POWERFUL LIGHTING RIG
The most powerful lighting rig ever assembled, in terms of the amount of raw power that is needed to drive it, is generally agreed to be that used by the French rock star Johnny Halliday at the Zenith, Paris, France, in Dec 1984. The rig drew so much power from the Paris grid that a new electricity sub-station had to be installed in order for the show to go ahead.

MOST POWERFUL LASER PULSE
The 'Petawatt' laser at the Lawrence Livermore National Laboratory (LLNL), California, USA, produces laser pulses of more than 1.3 quadrillion watts (1.3 petawatts) at peak power. This is more than 1,300 times the entire electrical capacity of the USA. The record was previously held by the 'Nova' laser, pictured right, which is capable of generating 100×10^{12} watts and is also at the LLNL.

BIGGEST PRODUCER OF SPECIAL EFFECTS
The world's largest producer of digital special effects is Industrial Light And Magic, a division of Lucas Digital. The latter is owned by George Lucas, the director of *Star Wars* (USA, 1977). The film used spectacular computer-generated effects such as the animation of the Imperial Cruiser and the Millennium Falcon (above). The company has three times the computing power of its nearest rival and has created special effects for eight of the top 15 box office hits of all time, winning 14 Oscars and six Technical Achievement Awards along the way. The first computer-generated animation – the root of all computer-generated special effects – was created in the computer research department of the University of Utah, USA, in 1972. The animation sequence involved the recreation of a series of simple movements of a single human hand and took almost one year to produce. It laid the foundations for all subsequent computer generated special effects.

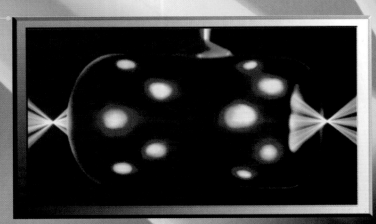

theme parks and rides

STRATOSPHERIC RIDES

The 135-storey, 350-m-tall (1,149-ft) Stratosphere Tower opened in Las Vegas, USA, in April 1996 and features a host of white-knuckle attractions, including the *Let It Ride High Roller*. In May the ride was visited by 79 beauty queens, including Andrea Deak of Hungary (below left) and Miriam Ruppert of Germany (below right), who were enjoying the city's sights prior to the Miss Universe contest.

MOST EXPENSIVE THEME PARK TO DEVELOP

Disney are reported to have spent approximately $1 billion (£625 million) on the design, development and realization of their Animal Kingdom in Florida, USA. The kingdom features fantastic creatures, a safari complete with real animals and a number of rides and landscaped areas. The centrepiece of the attraction, which opened on 22 April 1998, is a Tree of Life visible from any part of the park's 160 ha (500 acres).

BIGGEST THEME PARK

Disney World near Orlando, Florida, USA, covers 12,140 ha (30,000 acres), making it the largest theme park in the world today. Opened on 1 Oct 1971, it cost approximately $400 million (£163.5 million) to develop.

MOST-VISITED THEME PARK

In 1997 Tokyo Disneyland in Japan attracted a total of 17.83 million visitors. Opened on 15 April 1983, the 46.25-ha (114.2-acre) theme park, which includes areas dedicated to the Wild West, tropical exploration, fairy tales, space travel and the future, can accommodate up to 85,000 visitors at once.

MOST FUTURISTIC PLANNED THEME PARK

The Japanese construction company Obayashi plans to build a theme park in a crater on the Moon by the year 2050. Lunar City will accommodate approximately 10,000 tourists from Earth. It is still on the drawing board, but Obayashi has already specified some of the attractions that might be on offer. These include hang gliders and communal leisure centre activities that will make the most of the Moon's low gravitational field.

THEME PARK WITH GREATEST NUMBER OF RIDES

Cedar Point in Ohio, USA, has a total of 56 different rides — the most of any theme park in the world today. They include classic wooden roller coasters such as *Blue Streak*, which was built in 1964, hair-raising state-of-the-art rides such as *Mantis*, built in 1996, and children's rides such as *Jr. Gemini*, built in 1978.

THEME PARK WITH GREATEST NUMBER OF ROLLER COASTERS

A record-breaking 12 roller coasters dominate the skyline at Cedar Point, Ohio, USA, which has been nicknamed 'America's Roller Coast' as a result. At its opening in 1892, the theme park had just one roller coaster, which shuttled riders around at a sedate 16 km/h (10 mph). Today, it has some of the tallest, fastest and most technically advanced coasters in the world. In summer 1997 approximately 16.8 million people rode roller coasters at Cedar Point.

FASTEST ROLLER COASTER

On 4 Jan 1996 *Superman The Escape*, a steel coaster installed in Six Flags Magic Mountain, California, USA, became the world's first ever roller coaster to reach the psychologically significant speed of 160 km/h (100 mph). Riders sit in one of 15 aerodynamically-shaped cars and are accelerated to the maximum speed in a hair-raising seven seconds.

FASTEST STAND-UP ROLLER COASTER

The *Riddler's Revenge*, a steel stand-up coaster that went into service at Six Flags Magic Mountain, California, USA, on 4 April 1998, is 37.5 m (156 ft) tall and has a top speed of 105 km/h (65 mph) — the highest of any roller coaster in which the

BIGGEST THEME PARK WEDDINGS

On Valentine's Day 1997, 24 couples (including Matt Leddon and Melissa Williams, pictured far left) were married while hanging upside down aboard the *Montu* roller coaster at Busch Gardens in Tampa Bay, Florida, USA, reciting their vows to Reverend Chris Null via headsets. The biggest ever theme park wedding took place on 2 May 1997, at the opening of *Giant Drop*, a 69-m-high (227-ft) freefall tower at the Six Flags Great America theme park located mid-way between Chicago, Illinois, and Milwaukee, Wisconsin, USA, when 144 couples were pronounced man and wife seconds before a three-second plummet towards the Earth at a speed of 100 km/h (62 mph). Most of the wedding ceremony took place in the park's 3,200-seat stunt show arena. The couples then ascended to the 22-storey *Giant Drop*, where the Reverend Herring completed the ceremony. The brides and grooms, who came from all over the USA, including Indianapolis, Grand Rapids, Milwaukee and Chicago, had been selected by radio stations to participate in the mass wedding.

riders stand up. It boasts six inversions (sections that turn the rider upside down), including a 360° vertical loop with a record height of 37.8 m (124 ft).

HIGHEST ROLLER COASTER
With a difference of 126 m (415 ft) between its peak and its base, *Superman The Escape* has the biggest drop of any roller coaster. Opened in the 25th anniversary year of Six Flags Magic Mountain, California, USA, the ride has been built on a mountainside within the park.

Fujiyama in Fujikyu Highland Park, Japan, has a smaller drop than *Superman The Escape* but its tracks are raised by thousands of steel girders. With a maximum height of 72.8 m (239 ft), it is currently the world's tallest coaster.

TALLEST FREEFALL RIDE
The Power Tower, one of the newest rides at Cedar Point, Ohio, USA, blasts riders 73.2 m (240 ft) through the air at a speed of 80 km/h (50 mph). It takes three seconds for riders to complete their ascent or free fall on this attraction, which opened on 10 May 1998 and is constructed around four 914-m-high (300-ft) steel towers. Riders sit with their backs to these towers and with their legs dangling freely in the air.

COASTER GIVING MOST 'AIRTIME'
In total, *Superman The Escape* propels riders out of their seats for a record 6.5 seconds. It

begins by blasting them out of the Fortress of Solitude, a crystalline cavern. The riders experience weightlessness when they rocket to the peak of the ride then descend backwards to its base.

LONGEST ROLLER COASTER
The Ultimate roller coaster in Lightwater Valley, North Yorkshire, UK, is 2.298 km (7,542 ft) long and the ride lasts for 5 min 50 sec. The lift hill at the beginning of the ride is 2.29 km (1 mile 740 yd) long and takes riders 32.6 m (107 ft) above the ground. Built in 1991, *The Ultimate* has steel tracks fixed to a wooden structure that winds its way through the countryside theme park.

ROLLER COASTERS WITH MOST INVERSIONS
The twisting steel coaster *Dragon Khan* takes riders upside down eight times. The sit-down ride is the main attraction at Port Aventura, Salou, Spain. Built in 1995, the year the park opened, it has a top speed of 110 km/h (68 mph) and a maximum height of 49.1 m (161 ft).

The *Monte Makaya* at Terra Encantada, Rio de Janeiro, Brazil, also turns riders upside-down eight times during each complete circuit of its 851.36-m (2,793-ft 4-in) steel track. Track elements include one Vertical Loop, two Cobra Rolls, a Double Corkscrew and three Zero-G-Heart Rolls.

BIGGEST DARK RIDE
Opened in Aug 1969, *The Haunted Mansion* in Disney World, Florida, USA, transports passengers on a journey through a dark house inhabited by 999 scary beings. Horror icon Vincent Price recites a suitably spooky poem and visitors are treated to an array of classic special effects as the action unfolds around them.

LARGEST PORTABLE THRILL RIDE
Taz's Texas Tornado has been in service at Six Flags Astroworld, Texas, USA, since 14 March 1998, but was originally assembled in Germany in 1986. The twisting steel coaster is 34.1 m (112 ft) in total height and has a maximum speed of 97 km/h (60 mph). Its steepest turn is at an angle of 80°.

FIRST VERTICAL DROP RIDE
Oblivion, the world's first vertical drop ride at 87.5°, opened at Alton Towers in Staffordshire, UK, on 14 March 1998. The 360-m (1,222-ft) ride lasts about two minutes and features a 110-km/h (68-mph), 55-m (180-ft) drop into a pitch-black tunnel 30.5 m (100 ft) underground. Passengers endure 4.5 Gs and on exiting the tunnel are propelled through a sharp 90° turn. Around 5,500 bolts were used to build the ride.

space technology and rockets

HIGHEST SPEED
A speed of approximately 252,800 km/h (158,000 mph) is recorded by the NASA–German *Helios A* and *Helios B* solar probes each time they reach the perihelion (the point at which they are closest to the Sun) of their solar orbits.

FASTEST EVER ESCAPE VELOCITY FROM EARTH
The ESA *Ulysses* spacecraft, powered by an IUS-PAM upper stage, achieved an escape velocity of 54,614 km/h (34,134 mph) from the Earth after deployment from the space shuttle *Discovery* on 7 Oct 1990. The craft was en route to an orbit around the poles of the Sun via a fly-by of Jupiter.

SMALLEST ROCKET
The smallest satellite launch vehicle in the world was *Pegasus*, a 15-m-long (49-ft 3-in) three-stage booster. The original *Pegasus*, which has since been succeeded by an operational *Pegasus XL* version, was air-launched from an aircraft in 1990.

BIGGEST ROCKET
The US craft *Saturn 5* was the biggest ever rocket, at 110.6 m (363 ft) in height with the *Apollo* spacecraft on top. It weighed 2,903 tonnes on the launch pad.

LARGEST SPACE TELESCOPE
The NASA Edwin P. Hubble Space Telescope weighs 11 tonnes and is 13.1 m (43 ft) long, with a 2.4-m (7-ft 10$^1/_2$-in) reflector. It was placed in orbit aboard a US space shuttle on 24 April 1990. The telescope, which has made it possible to take photographs of Space of an unprecedented quality, cost a total of $2.1 billion (£1.4 billion) to construct.

MOST EXPENSIVE ROCKETS
The *Saturn 5* rocket was constructed for the *Apollo* moon landing programme, which had cost approximately $25 billion (£10.46 billion) by the time of the first flight to the Moon in July 1969.

Commercial customers have been charged more than $120 million (£72.7 million) in total for launches to orbit communications satellites aboard the US commercial rocket *Titan*, which is no longer in the market.

MOST POWERFUL ROCKET ENGINE
Built in the former USSR by the Scientific Industrial Corporation of Power Engineering in 1980, the RD-170 has a thrust of 806 tonnes in open Space and 740 tonnes at the Earth's surface. It also has a turbopump rated at 190MW, and burns liquid oxygen and kerosene. It powered the four strap-on boosters of the *Energiya* booster, launched in 1987, but is now grounded due to cuts in Russia's space budget.

MOST POWERFUL ROCKET
The NI booster, built by the former USSR, was launched from the Baikonur Cosmodrome at Tyuratam, Kazakhstan, on 21 Feb 1969, and exploded 70 seconds after take-off. Known as the G-1 in the West, it was the most powerful rocket of all time, with a thrust of 4,620 tonnes.

MOST INTELLIGENT ROCKETS
The launch and flight of the space shuttles are computer-controlled and guided from nine minutes before lift-off to the crafts' arrival in orbit eight minutes after launch.

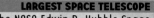

CHEAPEST SATELLITE LAUNCHER
The least expensive US satellite launcher is *Pegasus*, which was developed with a $45-million (£27.3-million) budget and costs approximately $10 million (£6.25 million) per launch. The rocket's inventor, Antonio Elias, is seen (top left) posing next to the craft in Spain in 1997. *Pegasus* was about to make history by playing a key role in the world's first ever space funeral. It took off from a Lockheed Tristar L-1011 at an altitude of 11,300 m (37,000 ft) over the Canary Islands (bottom left) with the ashes of Timothy Leary, *Star Trek* creator Gene Roddenberry and 23 other people on board, each of whom had paid $4,800 (£2,930) for the space funeral. *Pegasus* represents one of the most important breakthroughs in space technology for many years because it has finally made it possible to get small satellites into orbit cheaply. A number of companies had already tried to develop small rockets that could get into Space inexpensively, without success.

MOST RELIABLE OPERATIONAL LAUNCH SYSTEMS

The US space shuttle completed a total of 89 launches with one failure between April 1981 and Jan 1998 — a 98% success rate.

The Russian *Soyuz U* series has flown a total of 781 times with 766 successes since 1973, twice recording 100 consecutive successful launches.

LEAST RELIABLE OPERATIONAL LAUNCH SYSTEM

The Russian–Ukrainian *Zenit* launcher has had 21 successful and seven failed missions since 1985: a success rate of 72%.

LARGEST ORBITING OBJECT

The largest ever object in the Earth's orbit was the Russian *Mir* space station, which was docked to the US space shuttle. Comprising the core, *Kvant 1* and 2, *Kristall*, *Spektr* and *Priroda* modules, with docked *Soyuz* and *Progress* craft, it weighed more than 250 tonnes.

LARGEST OBJECT IN SPACE

The Italian Tethered Satellite was deployed for a distance of 19.7 km (12 miles) from the space shuttle *STS 75 Columbia* on 26 Feb 1996 before the tether snapped. The satellite and the tether continued to orbit until 19 March 1996.

MOST EXPENSIVE SATELLITE

The US military communications satellite project *Milstar* has cost more than $40 billion (£24 billion). Two satellites have been launched, in 1994 and 1995.

SOYUZ ROCKETS

A Russian *Soyuz TM-22* rocket is pictured blasting away from the Baikonur Cosmodrome, Kazakhstan, in 1995. The *Soyuz* rockets were first launched in manned flight in 1967, and since then have been major players in the Russian space programme.

CHEAPEST SATELLITES

Several satellites as small as hat boxes have been built by universities and launched as 'piggyback' payloads on commercial launches. They cost just $5 million (£3 million) to build and launch.

SATELLITES WITH LONGEST LIFE

The NASA Applications Technology Satellite *ATS 5*, which was launched on 12 Aug 1969, is still being used periodically for educational communications.

The US–European *International Ultraviolet Explorer*, which was launched in 1978 with an estimated operational lifetime of just three years, was shut down in 1996.

SMALLEST SATELLITE

The US satellite *Vanguard 1*, which was launched in March 1958, weighs 1.4 kg (3 lb 1 oz). In 1998 it was the oldest satellite still orbiting, although it is no longer operational.

BIGGEST SPACE LABORATORY

The biggest single research lab ever to have been launched is the US *Skylab*, which is 25 m (82 ft) long and weighs approximately 26,800 kg (59,000 lb). Launched in 1973, *Skylab* also became the largest piece of space debris after it was abandoned in 1974. The laboratory re-entered the Earth's atmosphere in 1979.

CLOSEST APPROACH TO THE SUN BY A ROCKET

The research spacecraft *Helios B* came within a record 43.5 million km (27 million miles) of the Sun on 16 April 1976. It was carrying instrumentation belonging to both the USA and West Germany.

REMOTEST MAN-MADE OBJECT

Voyager 1, which was launched from Cape Canaveral, Florida, USA, on 5 Sept 1977, was 10.4 billion km (6.5 billion miles) away from the Earth on 15 Feb 1998, making it the remotest man-made object ever known. The spacecraft's forerunner *Pioneer 10* became the first ever craft to leave our solar system on 17 Oct 1986, when it crossed the orbit of Pluto at a distance of 5.87 billion km (3.67 billion miles). *Pioneer 10* carries a plaque with messages from the Earth to any distant civilization that may find it. *Pioneer 11* and *Voyager 2* will follow these craft into interstellar Space.

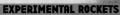

EXPERIMENTAL ROCKETS

The *Delta Blipper*, an experimental rocket, is seen here lifting off at White Sands Missile Range, New Mexico, USA, in 1993. The rocket is a precursor to the *X-33*, which is being developed as a potential predecessor to a Reusable Launch Vehicle. It is hoped by New Mexico Spaceport planners that the latter will replace the space shuttle at some point in the future.

space exploration

MOST TELEVISED EVENT IN SPACE
The first moonwalk by the *Apollo 11* astronauts in July 1969 was watched on TV by an estimated 600 million people (around one-fifth of the world's population at that time).

BIGGEST SPACE BUDGET
The US manned space program is estimated to have cost more than $100 billion (£62 billion) to the end of 1997.

FURTHEST FINAL RESTING PLACE
In Jan 1998 28.35 g (1 oz) of Dr Eugene Shoemaker's ashes were launched aboard NASA's *Lunar Prospector* as it set out on a one-year mapping mission above the Moon's surface. When its power fails after about 18 months, the craft will crash to the Moon's surface with Shoemaker's remains. The geologist had said that not going to the Moon was his greatest disappointment.

MOST PEOPLE ABOARD *MIR*
The Russian *Mir* space station, launched in 1986, is shown as photographed above Africa by a shuttle crew. In June 1995 a record 10 people were aboard the station (four Russians and six Americans).

BEST-KNOWN PAYLOAD SPECIALIST
The most famous payload specialist was US teacher Christa McAuliffe, who never reached Space. She was killed in the *Challenger* accident in 1986. Shuttles have flown dozens of non-NASA astronaut payload specialists, including politicians and an Arab prince.

LARGEST SPACE FUNERAL
The ashes of 24 space pioneers and enthusiasts, including the creator of *Star Trek* Gene Roddenberry, were sent into orbit in April 1997 on board Spain's *Pegasus* rocket, at a cost of $5,000 (£3,000) each. Held in lipstick-sized capsules inscribed with a name and message, they will stay in orbit for 18 months–10 years.

MOST SPACE DEBRIS
On 31 Jan 1998 there were a record 2,516 payloads in orbit, along with 6,172 pieces of trackable debris.

MOST DEBRIS CREATED BY A SINGLE LAUNCH
A *Pegasus* rocket that was launched in 1994 exploded in June 1996. About 700 pieces of its upper stage have been tracked to date.

LARGEST PIECES OF DEBRIS
Spent rocket stages form the largest pieces of space debris. A *Delta 2* third stage, for example, is 2.04 m (6 ft 8 in) long and 1.24 m (4 ft 1 in) in diameter.

LONGEST SPACEFLIGHTS
Russian doctor Valeriy Poliyakov was launched to the Russian *Mir 1* space station aboard *Soyuz TM15* on 8 Jan 1994 and landed aboard *Soyuz TM20* on 22 March 1995, after a 437-day 17-hr 58-min 16-sec spaceflight.

The longest spaceflight by a woman was 188 days 5 hr, by Shannon Lucid (USA). She was launched to the *Mir 1* space station aboard the US space shuttle *STS 76/Atlantis* on 22 March 1996 and landed aboard *STS 79/Atlantis* on 26 Sept.

SHORTEST SPACEFLIGHT
The shortest ever manned spaceflight was made by Cdr. Alan Bartlett Shepard (USA) aboard *Mercury-Redstone 3* on 5 May 1961. The sub-orbital mission lasted 15 min 28 sec.

LONGEST LUNAR MISSION
The crew of *Apollo 17* (Capt. Eugene Cernan and Dr Harrison Hagen Schmitt) were on the lunar surface for a record

LARGEST SHUTTLE CREW
Shuttles are reusable US manned spacecraft. The largest shuttle crew was eight (six Americans, two Russians), aboard *STS 71 Atlantis* in July 1995.

74 hr 59 min during a lunar mission lasting 12 days 13 hr 51 min (7–19 Dec 1972).

LONGEST SHUTTLE FLIGHT
Columbia's 21st mission, *STS 80*, began on 19 Nov 1996 and lasted for a total of 17 days 15 hr 53 min 26 sec (to main gear shutdown).

MOST EXPERIENCED TRAVELLER
Valeriy Poliyakov clocked up 678 days 16 hr 33 min 16 sec during two space missions.

MOST SPACE JOURNEYS
Storey Musgrave (USA) made a record six space shuttle missions between 1983 and 1996, giving him a total of 53 days' flight experience.

Capt. John Watts Young (USA) also made a total of six space flights, between 1965 and 1983. In doing so he acquired 34 days' flight experience.

MOST PEOPLE IN SPACE AT ONCE
On 14 March 1995 a record 13 people were in Space at the same time: seven Americans aboard the space shuttle *STS 67 Endeavour*, three CIS cosmonauts aboard the *Mir* space station and two cosmonauts and a US astronaut aboard *Soyuz TM21*.

MOST NATIONALITIES IN SPACE
Five countries had astronauts or cosmonauts in Space on 31 July 1992: four Russian cosmonauts and one Frenchman were aboard *Mir*, and one Swiss, one Italian and five US astronauts were on *STS 46 Atlantis*.

On 22 Feb 1996 there were one Swiss, four US and two Italian astronauts on *STS 75 Columbia* and one German and four Russian cosmonauts on board the *Mir* space station.

MOST ISOLATED HUMAN BEING
The greatest distance that a person has ever been from a fellow human being is 3,596.4 km (2,234 miles, 1330 yd). This was experienced by command module pilot Alfred Worden during the US *Apollo 15* lunar mission, which lasted from 30 July to 1 Aug 1971. David Scott and James Irwin were at Hadley Base exploring the Moon's surface.

GREATEST ALTITUDES ATTAINED
The crew of *Apollo 13* (which was made up of Capt. James Arthur Lovell Jr, Fred Wallace Haise Jr and John Swigert) were a record 254 km (158 miles) away from the Moon's surface and 400,171 km (248,655 miles) above the Earth's surface on 15 April 1970.

Kathryn Thornton (USA) attained an altitude of 600 km (375 miles) — a record for a woman — after an orbital engine burn on 10 Dec 1993 during the *STS 61 Endeavour* mission.

FASTEST SPEEDS ATTAINED
The record for the greatest speed at which a human being has ever travelled is 39,897 km/h (24,791 mph), achieved by the command module of *Apollo 10* (which comprised Col. Thomas Patten Stafford, Cdr. Eugene Andrew Cernan and Cdr. John Watts Young) at the 121.9-km (75$^{7}/_{10}$-mile) altitude interface on its trans-Earth return flight in May 1969.

HIGHEST SPEED
The highest speed by a woman is 28,582 km/h (17,864 mph), by Kathryn Sullivan (USA) at the start of re-entry during the *STS 31 Discovery* shuttle mission on 29 April 1990. Kathryn Thornton may have exceeded this at the end of the *STS 61 Endeavour* mission on 13 Dec 1993.

war

& disaster

war

MOST EXPENSIVE WAR
The material cost of WWII has been estimated at $1.5 trillion (£940 billion) — far in excess of all other wars put together.

MOST TELEVISED WAR
In terms of transmission hours, the Vietnam War is likely to remain the most televised war in history for many decades to come. In 1965 the NBC network screened *Actions of a Vietnamese Marine Battalion*, showing shocking action sequences, and as its ratings rocketed, CBS, ABC and foreign broadcasters rushed to put camera teams into Vietnam. It is estimated that in the USA the three major networks and their subsidiaries devoted about 10,000 hours of prime viewing time to coverage of the war between 1965 and 1975.

BLOODIEST SIEGE
About 1.3–1.5 million defenders and citizens are estimated to have died in the 880-day siege of Leningrad, USSR (now St Petersburg, Russia) by the German Army from 1941 to 1944. More than 150,000 shells and 100,000 bombs were dropped on the city. Pictured left is a WWII Russian army recruitment poster.

The collapse of Yugoslavia and associated conflicts between 1991 and 1996 eclipse Vietnam in density of TV coverage because by then it was easy for freelance journalists to travel with their own equipment and satellite dishes. During the five years of conflict they shot and recorded millions of hours of footage, of which only a tiny percentage has been broadcast.

BIGGEST ASSAULT ON THE ENVIRONMENT DURING WAR
In Jan 1991 the Iraqi dictator Saddam Hussein gave the order for crude Gulf oil to be pumped from Kuwait's Sea Island terminal and from seven large oil tankers. Provisional estimates put the loss at 816,000 tonnes. During the same campaign, Iraqi forces set fire to 600 oil wells, creating clouds of black smoke up to 2,133.6 m (7,000 ft) high, enveloping warships 80 km (50 miles) offshore and depositing soot as far away as the Himalayas. The last blazing well was extinguished on 6 Nov 1991.

MOST DEATHS CAUSED BY CHEMICAL WEAPONS IN ONE WAR
Exact figures for those wounded and killed by chemical weapons between Jan 1915 and Nov 1918, during WWI, are unreliable, but at least 100,000 died and 900,000 were injured. The Russian army, equipped with very inadequate respirators, sustained some 56,000 fatalities and 475,000 casualties.

BIGGEST MASSACRE
The largest ever massacre on record took place in Nanking, China, between 13 Dec 1937 and the end of Jan 1938, when Japanese troops overran the city, which was the capital of the Nationalist Chinese. Estimates vary as to the exact death toll, from 20,000 by the Japanese government to 300,000 by some US and Chinese experts.

BLOODIEST MODERN BATTLES
The 142-day Battle of the Somme, which took place in northern France in 1916, is estimated to have resulted in more than 1.22 million deaths and casualties.

The losses of the German Army Group Centre on the Eastern Front between 22 June and 8 July 1944 totalled 350,000 men.

The highest death toll in a battle was an estimated 1.11 million, in the Battle of Stalingrad, USSR, which ended when German forces surrendered on 31 Jan 1943. Only 1,515 civilians from a pre-war population of more than 500,000 were found alive afterwards.

The final drive on Berlin, Germany, by the Soviet Army and the ensuing battle for the city from 16 April to 2 May 1945 involved 3.5 million men, 52,000 guns and mortars, 7,750 tanks and 11,000 aircraft on both sides.

BLOODIEST WARS
The costliest war in terms of human life was WWII, in which the total number of fatalities, including battle deaths and civilians of all countries, is an estimated 56.4 million. In Poland, 6,028,000 people were killed — 17.2% of the pre-war population.

In Paraguay's war against Brazil, Argentina and Uruguay from 1864 to 1870, Paraguay's population was reduced from 407,000 to 221,000, of whom fewer than 30,000 were adult males.

BIGGEST EVACUATION
Between 26 May and 4 June 1940 1,200 allied craft evacuated 338,226 British and French troops from the beachhead at Dunkerque, France.

BIGGEST CIVILIAN EVACUATION
Following the Iraqi invasion of Kuwait in 1990, Air India evacuated 111,711 Indians on 488 flights over two months from 13 Aug.

BIGGEST MASS SUICIDE IN WAR
About 7,000 Japanese troops committed suicide — many by

PRECISION BOMBING
High-tech bombs changed the face of warfare during the Gulf War against Iraq, and precision bombing, which was used extensively by the allied nations during their liberation of Kuwait, enabled aerial weapons to be delivered with an accuracy that exceeded all expectations. In a videotape shown to US president George Bush during Operation Desert Storm, bombs exploded with pinpoint accuracy through the front door of an Iraqi Scud missile warehouse in Kuwait and into the air shaft of a building used by Iraqi president Saddam Hussein. The bombs, with names like Rockeye II Mk cluster bomb, ISCB-1 Area Denial Cluster weapon and the Paveway laser-guided bomb, could be sent to the target at the press of a button, and some of the 'smart' bombs could be programmed to explode their 160 'bomblets' over 24 hours to keep Iraqis from venturing within 5 m² (54 ft²) of a target. Others had time fuses to delay the explosion. Precision-guided weapons were said to have virtually eliminated the traditional military stance, which required a 3-to-1 advantage in troop numbers before an attack could be launched.

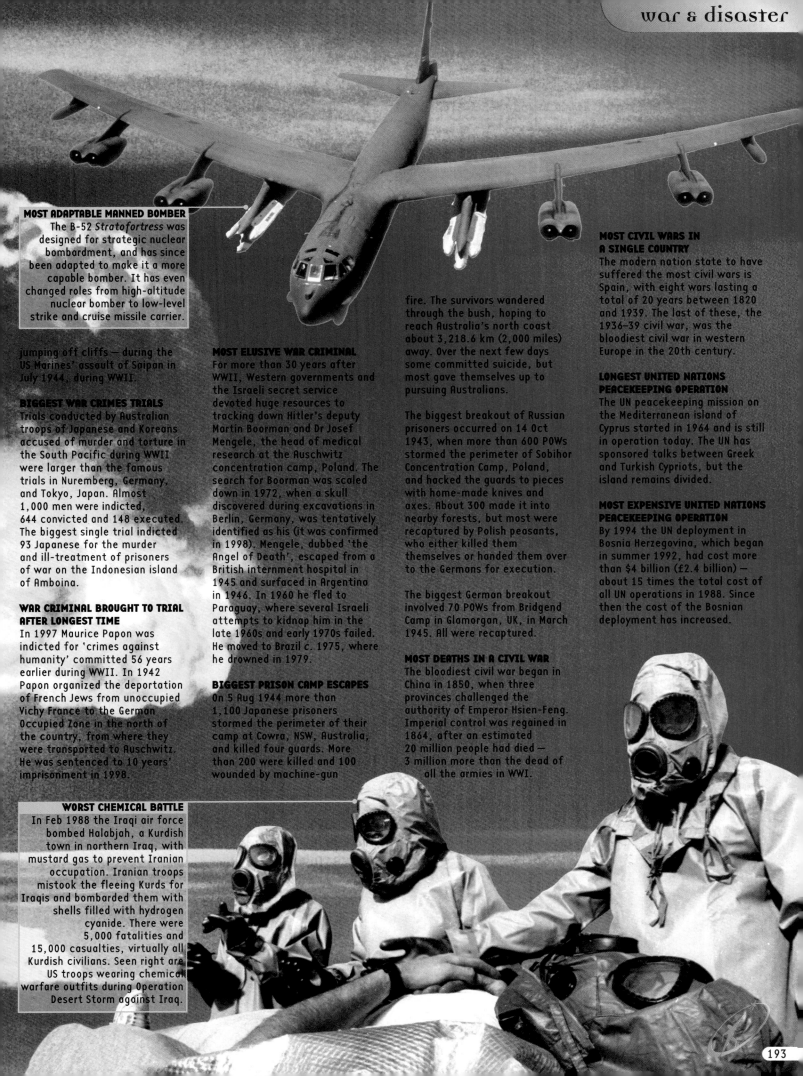

MOST ADAPTABLE MANNED BOMBER
The B-52 *Stratofortress* was designed for strategic nuclear bombardment, and has since been adapted to make it a more capable bomber. It has even changed roles from high-altitude nuclear bomber to low-level strike and cruise missile carrier.

jumping off cliffs — during the US Marines' assault of Saipan in July 1944, during WWII.

BIGGEST WAR CRIMES TRIALS
Trials conducted by Australian troops of Japanese and Koreans accused of murder and torture in the South Pacific during WWII were larger than the famous trials in Nuremberg, Germany, and Tokyo, Japan. Almost 1,000 men were indicted, 644 convicted and 148 executed. The biggest single trial indicted 93 Japanese for the murder and ill-treatment of prisoners of war on the Indonesian island of Amboina.

WAR CRIMINAL BROUGHT TO TRIAL AFTER LONGEST TIME
In 1997 Maurice Papon was indicted for 'crimes against humanity' committed 56 years earlier during WWII. In 1942 Papon organized the deportation of French Jews from unoccupied Vichy France to the German Occupied Zone in the north of the country, from where they were transported to Auschwitz. He was sentenced to 10 years' imprisonment in 1998.

WORST CHEMICAL BATTLE
In Feb 1988 the Iraqi air force bombed Halabjah, a Kurdish town in northern Iraq, with mustard gas to prevent Iranian occupation. Iranian troops mistook the fleeing Kurds for Iraqis and bombarded them with shells filled with hydrogen cyanide. There were 5,000 fatalities and 15,000 casualties, virtually all Kurdish civilians. Seen right are US troops wearing chemical warfare outfits during Operation Desert Storm against Iraq.

MOST ELUSIVE WAR CRIMINAL
For more than 30 years after WWII, Western governments and the Israeli secret service devoted huge resources to tracking down Hitler's deputy Martin Boorman and Dr Josef Mengele, the head of medical research at the Auschwitz concentration camp, Poland. The search for Boorman was scaled down in 1972, when a skull discovered during excavations in Berlin, Germany, was tentatively identified as his (it was confirmed in 1998). Mengele, dubbed 'the Angel of Death', escaped from a British internment hospital in 1945 and surfaced in Argentina in 1946. In 1960 he fled to Paraguay, where several Israeli attempts to kidnap him in the late 1960s and early 1970s failed. He moved to Brazil *c.* 1975, where he drowned in 1979.

BIGGEST PRISON CAMP ESCAPES
On 5 Aug 1944 more than 1,100 Japanese prisoners stormed the perimeter of their camp at Cowra, NSW, Australia, and killed four guards. More than 200 were killed and 100 wounded by machine-gun fire. The survivors wandered through the bush, hoping to reach Australia's north coast about 3,218.6 km (2,000 miles) away. Over the next few days some committed suicide, but most gave themselves up to pursuing Australians.

The biggest breakout of Russian prisoners occurred on 14 Oct 1943, when more than 600 POWs stormed the perimeter of Sobibor Concentration Camp, Poland, and hacked the guards to pieces with home-made knives and axes. About 300 made it into nearby forests, but most were recaptured by Polish peasants, who either killed them themselves or handed them over to the Germans for execution.

The biggest German breakout involved 70 POWs from Bridgend Camp in Glamorgan, UK, in March 1945. All were recaptured.

MOST DEATHS IN A CIVIL WAR
The bloodiest civil war began in China in 1850, when three provinces challenged the authority of Emperor Hsien-Feng. Imperial control was regained in 1864, after an estimated 20 million people had died — 3 million more than the dead of all the armies in WWI.

MOST CIVIL WARS IN A SINGLE COUNTRY
The modern nation state to have suffered the most civil wars is Spain, with eight wars lasting a total of 20 years between 1820 and 1939. The last of these, the 1936–39 civil war, was the bloodiest civil war in western Europe in the 20th century.

LONGEST UNITED NATIONS PEACEKEEPING OPERATION
The UN peacekeeping mission on the Mediterranean island of Cyprus started in 1964 and is still in operation today. The UN has sponsored talks between Greek and Turkish Cypriots, but the island remains divided.

MOST EXPENSIVE UNITED NATIONS PEACEKEEPING OPERATION
By 1994 the UN deployment in Bosnia Herzegovina, which began in summer 1992, had cost more than $4 billion (£2.4 billion) — about 15 times the total cost of all UN operations in 1988. Since then the cost of the Bosnian deployment has increased.

killing machines

BIGGEST UNMANNED AIR VEHICLE

The biggest unmanned aerial vehicle under construction is the Global Hawk, which was unveiled at Teledyne Ryan Aeronautical in San Diego, USA, on 20 Feb 1997. The aircraft, which has a 35.4-m (116-ft) wing-span and a 22,526-km (14,000-mile) range, will be used for aerial reconnaissance.

BIGGEST NUCLEAR WEAPONS

The most powerful ICBM (intercontinental ballistic missile) is the former USSR's SS-18 (Model 5), which is thought to be armed with 10,750-kilotonne MIRVs (multiple independently targetable re-entry vehicles). SS-18 ICBMs are located in Russia and Kazakhstan, although the dismantlement of those in Kazakhstan has begun. START 2 (Strategic Arms Reduction Talks 2) requires the elimination of all SS-18s and other ICBMs with more than one warhead.

MOST POWERFUL THERMONUCLEAR DEVICE

A thermonuclear device with a power equivalent to that of c. 57 megatonnes of TNT was detonated by the former USSR in the Novaya Zemlya area in Oct 1961. The shockwave circled the world three times, with the first circuit taking 36 hr 27 min. Some estimates put the power of the device at 62–90 megatonnes.

MOST PEOPLE KILLED IN A SINGLE CHEMICAL WARFARE ATTACK

In March 1988 an estimated 4,000 people were killed when Saddam Hussein used chemical weapons against Iraq's Kurdish minority for its support of Iran in the Iran–Iraq War.

MOST PEOPLE KILLED BY A BOMB

The atomic bomb dropped on Hiroshima, Japan, by the USA on 6 Aug 1945, instantly killed more than 100,000 people. A further 55,000 people died from radiation within one year.

MOST ADVANCED HELICOPTER

The Russian *Ka-52 Alligator*, is one of the world's most advanced helicopters. It is a two-seat derivative of the *Ka-50 Black Shark*. The helicopter is intended primarily as a gunship and is equipped with a wide range of weapons as well as devices which allow it to fly missions in extreme weather conditions.

LONGEST-RANGE ATTACKS

In Jan 1991 seven B-52G bombers took off from Barksdale Air Force Base, Louisiana, USA, to deliver cruise missiles against Iraq just after the start of the Gulf War. Each flew 22,526 km (14,000 miles), refuelling four times in the 35-hour round-trip. In Sept 1996, B-52s flew non-stop from Guam in the central Pacific to launch cruise missiles around Baghdad, Iraq.

MISSILES WITH GREATEST RANGE

The US *Atlas* missile entered service in 1959 and had a range of 16,669 km (10,360 miles) – about 4,827 km (3,000 miles) more than was necessary to hit any point in Soviet territory from launch sites in the West. The longest-range Russian missile is the SS-18, codenamed 'Satan', which entered service in the early 1980s and has a range of 12,067 km (7,500 miles).

MOST ACCURATE MAN-PORTABLE ANTI-AIRCRAFT MISSILE

In the early 1980s the USA introduced the *Stinger*, a 1.52-m-long (5-ft), 10-kg (22-lb) missile with a range of about 4.83 km (3 miles) and a speed of about 2,092 km/h (1,300 mph). The *Stinger*'s cryogenically cooled infra-red seeker distinguishes between an aircraft's infra-red signature and counter-measures such as flares. It was first used by the British against Argentina in the Falklands War and by the *Mujahedeen* in Afghanistan.

MOST FUTURISTIC COMBAT SHIP

In Oct 1996 Vosper Thornycroft of Southampton, UK, unveiled its design for the *Sea Wraith* corvette, a combat ship designed for patrolling regional waters, with the ability to hide and deceive the enemy. The latest in stealth technology, it uses similar principles to the radar-beating technology developed by the US aircraft industry which was used in the 1991 Gulf War against Iraq. The main areas of the vessel are covered with materials designed to deflect signals, making the corvette difficult to track or target on radar. Its mast, radar dishes and aerials are located inside flat-sided towers to make it hard for radar to lock on. To conceal itself and its exhaust, the ship sprays a mist of water when countering new infra-red missiles. The ship has state-of-the-art weapons and communications systems and its own signals are adjustable down to 1 watt of radiated energy. The first *Sea Wraith*, which has accommodation for 105 crew, will be operational in the 2000s.

MOST ADVANCED FIGHTER PLANE

The US *F22 Raptor* was developed by Lockheed Martin Aeronautical Systems, Lockheed Martin Fort Worth and Boeing in the late 1990s. Even before it had gone into production it had starred in a computer game called *F-22* by Microprose (pictured below). It cost around $13.3 billion (£8 billion), twice as much as its European counterpart the *Eurofighter*. It has a length of 18.9 m (62 ft 1 in) and a wing-span of 13.4 m (44 ft 6 in).

In the early 1990s the US Army took delivery of the *Stinger* POST (Passive Optical Seeker Technology), which is flown to target by a programmable microprocessor. The missile can 'think', and once locked on, there is little the pilot of the target aircraft can do, other than outfly the missile, or eject.

MOST POWERFUL TORPEDO

The Russian Type 65, a 66-cm (26-in) torpedo, carries a warhead of nearly one tonne of conventional explosive or a 15-kilotonne nuclear warhead — slightly less explosive power than the bombs that destroyed Hiroshima and Nagasaki. It can home in acoustically on the turbulence left by the wake of a ship more than 80.5 km (50 miles) away and can close at more than 80.5 km/h (50 knots) — far in excess of the speed of the fastest surface ships.

FASTEST FIRING MACHINE GUN

Designed for use in helicopters and armoured vehicles in the late 1960s, the 7.62-mm ($^3/_{10}$-in) M 134 Minigun is the fastest ever firing machine-gun. Based on the multiple-barrelled Gatling design, it has six barrels revolved by an electric motor and fed by a 4,000-round link belt — a configuration that allows a rate of fire of 6,000 rounds per minute (about 10 times that of an ordinary machine gun).

MOST FUTURISTIC WEAPON

Developed for the 'Star Wars' programme, the electromagnetic railgun may revolutionize war on Earth. If power problems are overcome, the gun will combine the capabilities of the anti-tank and anti-aircraft gun with the machine gun. Aircraft and tanks will be sawn to pieces by a stream of small high-velocity projectiles. The bullet speed that the railgun may be capable of will require millions of kilowats of power, at present only possible if it were linked to a high-capacity power station.

MOST REVOLUTIONARY RIFLE

In the first months of WWII, German weapons analysts began developing the *Sturmgewehr* (assault rifle), a fully automatic rifle with a level of accuracy of up to about 274 m (300 yd), the distance at which most actions were fought. A light bullet in a short cartridge case meant a magazine could hold 30 rather than the more usual 10 rounds. Introduced in 1943, its influence was profound: by the 1970s virtually every army in the world was using a small arm derived from the German model.

MOST EMBARRASSING TECHNICAL FAILURE

First used in Operation Just Cause in Panama in 1989, the F117A Stealth Fighter played a key role in the penetration of Iraqi air defences in the 1991 Gulf War. Its success depends on its radar signature, which has been much reduced by an angled fuselage and wings and by black ferrite paint that absorbs radar radiation. However, in 1997 the Pentagon reported that the paint was unstable and washed off in rain showers, making it visible and vulnerable because of its low speed (1,287 km/h or 800 mph) and poor manoeuverability.

FASTEST EVER BOMBERS

The US variable-geometry or 'swing-wing' General Dynamics FB-111A has a maximum speed of Mach 2.5, and the Russian 'swing-wing' Tupolev Tu-22M, known to NATO as 'Backfire', has an estimated over-target speed of Mach 2.0 but could be as fast as Mach 2.5.

FASTEST COMBAT JET

The world's fastest ever combat jet is the former Soviet Mikoyan MiG-25 fighter, the NATO codename for which is 'Foxbat'. The single-seat 'Foxbat-A' has a wing-span of 13.95 m (45 ft 9 in), is 23.82 m (78 ft 2 in) long and has an estimated maximum take-off weight of 37.4 tonnes. The reconnaissance 'Foxbat-B' has been tracked by radar at about Mach 3.2 (3,395 km/h or 2,110 mph).

FASTEST WARSHIP

On 25 Jan 1980, the 23.7-m-long (78-ft), 100-tonne test vehicle SES-100B, a US Navy hovercraft, achieved a record speed of 91.9 knots (170 km/h).

FASTEST DESTROYER

The record for the highest speed ever attained by a destroyer is 45.25 knots (83.42 km/h), by the 3,251-tonne French ship *Le Terrible* in 1935. Built in Blainville, France, and powered by four Yarrow small tube boilers and two Rateau geared turbines, giving 100,000 shaft horsepower, the destroyer was decommissioned at the end of 1957.

SMART WEAPONS

The AGM-130 is one of a new generation of 'smart' weapons being developed to destroy the chemical and biological weapons that Iraqi dictator Saddam Hussein is suspected of hiding in reinforced bunkers. Here Frank Robbins, director of the US Air Force's Precision Strike System Program Office, stands behind an AGM-130 missile at Eglin Air Force Base, Florida, USA, in early 1998.

spying

BIGGEST SECRET STOLEN BY A SPY IN THE 20TH CENTURY

Soviet spies penetrated the US atomic programme (codenamed the 'Manhattan Project') during WWII and continued spying after the war. Their success allowed Soviet scientists to explode their own nuclear weapon in Aug 1949.

LOWEST PRICE PAID FOR TOP SECRET MESSAGES

The KGB paid spy John Walker Jr. an estimated $1 million (£523,204) in total from 1968 to his arrest on 20 May 1985 for cipher secrets that allowed them to decipher more than 1 million secret messages — roughly $1 (52p) per secret.

MOST EFFECTIVE 'TRUTH SERUM'

During the Cold War a cocktail containing sodium pentothal, scopolamine, thiamin, sodium luminal, atropine sulfate and caffeine sulfate was used to create an alcohol-like disinhibition of normal behavioural restraints such as lying or deceit.

MOST EFFECTIVE SPY-TRACKING SUBSTANCE

During the Cold War a synthesized scent of a German Shepherd bitch in heat was made by East Germany's Ministry for State Security (STASI) and applied to a target's shoes or bicycle tyres. Trained male German Shepherd dogs could then track the target for up to three days.

MOST OVERRATED SPY

Margaretha Zelle, better known under her stage name Mata Hari, was the world's most overrated spy. As an 'exotic' dancer in Europe before WWI, her brief efforts to steal secrets from her lovers were amateurish and unsuccessful. Following a clumsy seduction of the German military attaché in Madrid, Spain, Mata Hari was arrested and executed as a German spy in 1917.

SMALLEST SUICIDE WEAPON

When US spy-plane pilot Francis Powers was shot down over Russia on 1 May 1960, he was carrying a grooved 'needle' coated with saxitoxin (paralytic shellfish poison) hidden inside a 2.8-cm-long (1^1/₁₀-in) common straight pin. It could cause death from respiratory paralysis and cardiovascular collapse within minutes of injection.

MOST LETHAL POISON USED IN AN ASSASSINATION

In 1978 a weapon disguised as an umbrella was used to inject a tiny RICIN-filled pellet into the thigh of the Bulgarian dissident Georgi Markov in London, UK. An outspoken opponent of the Bulgarian government, Markov died mysteriously within a matter of hours. RICIN is a lethal cytotoxin derived from the castor bean. The lethal dosage by injection is 3 ug/kg (1.36 ug/lb) of bodyweight.

LONGEST SPY TUNNEL

In 1955 the CIA and MI6 dug the 449-m (1,476-ft) Berlin Tunnel into East Berlin to monitor Soviet and East German voice and telegraphic communications on tapped underground cables. Codenamed 'Operation Gold', it was the most successful ever eavesdropping operation: a total of 443,000 conversations were recorded and transcribed, and more than 50,000 reels of magnetic tape were used prior to its discovery on 22 April 1956, following information from a KGB mole inside MI6. In Nov 1989 the Berlin Wall (above) came down, signalling the end of the Cold War. The wall had divided East and West Berlin since 1961.

HIGHEST-PAID SPY

KGB spy Rick Ames, who was a 'mole' in the CIA for nine years, was the highest-paid spy ever. The KGB paid him $2.7 million (£1.72 million) in cash, and promised him a further $1.9 million (£1.21 million). Ames' lavish lifestyle and 'free spending' contributed to his discovery and arrest in 1994.

MOST EFFECTIVE SPY FAMILY

John Walker Jr. joined the KGB in 1968 and eventually recruited his brother, son and best friend. His network inflicted more strategic damage on the USA than any other spy ring. Walker was arrested in 1985 after his ex-wife tipped off the FBI.

MOST INFORMANTS REPORTING TO AN INTELLIGENCE SERVICE

From 1985 to 1989, 260,000 people out of an adult population of 12 million were estimated to be acting as informants (known as IMS – *Inoffizielle Mitarbeiters* – or 'unofficial collaborators') for East Germany's Ministry for State Security. The density of the informer network was seven times that of Hitler's Germany. During the Cold War the East German Intelligence Service (HVA), led by spymaster Markus Wolf, pictured here with his wife Andrea, perfected the large-scale use of 'spying for love'. Rigorous screening of male candidates (only 1 in 100 was accepted) produced 'Romeos' who courted secretaries in NATO and the Bonn government with spectacular success, stealing both 'hearts and secrets'. Wolf, who is now in his mid 70s, served with the Red Army in WWII before becoming a journalist for Communist publications in his occupied homeland. In 1951 he was drafted into the East German Intelligence Service, which he led for 33 years. Since German re-unification in 1990 Wolf has made a living as an author and a chat-show guest.

MOST SECRET SPY-PLANE

A long-range, hypersonic stealth aircraft codenamed 'Aurora' and made by Lockheed's 'Skunkworks' in Burbank, California, USA, is reputed to have a top speed of 6,115 km/h (3,800 mph), a cruise range of 9,253.5 km (5,750 miles) and an operational altitude of more than 30,480 m (100,000 ft). The highly classified 'Aurora' is the apparent successor to Lockheed's SR-71 strategic reconnaissance craft.

SMALLEST OPERATIONAL SPY SUBMARINE

The 3.85-m-long (12-ft 8-in) MSC (Motorized Submersible Canoe), codenamed 'Sleeping Beauty', was built by the British SOE (Special Operations Executive) in WWII to transport spies or saboteurs into enemy territory.

DEEPEST UNDERWATER SPY OPERATION

In 1974 the CIA's 'Project Jennifer' salvaged part of a Soviet submarine from a depth of 5,029 m (16,500 ft). It used the *Glomar Explorer*, a recovery vessel built by the reclusive US tycoon Howard Hughes.

DEEPEST UNDERWATER TELEPHONE TAP

A joint US Navy and National Security Agency (NSA) operation in the Sea of Okhotsk in Russia used divers from a submarine to tap into a Soviet military communications cable at a depth of 121.9 m (400 ft). It was betrayed to the KGB by a former NSA employee in 1981.

SMALLEST WWII MICRODOT

German Military Intelligence operational microdots, ($^1/_{400}$ photographic reductions of the original document) could be hidden in the edge of a postcard or in the spine of a book.

SMALLEST VIDEO SPY CAMERA

The Supercircuits Model PC-51XP camera can be disguised as a button or hidden in a lipstick tube. The images it takes can be beamed to a receiver more than 152.4 m (500 ft) away using the tiny Model TXB transmitter.

MINI WEAPONRY

The Bulgarian key-ring gun, with its mounted barrel attachment, is just 7.62 cm (3 in) long and 2.54 cm (1 in) wide but can fire two 36-caliber rounds and could be deadly from a distance of 18.29 m (20 yd).

MOST SENSITIVE SPY SATELLITE CAMERA

The CCD digital camera, which was first carried on the US KH-11 satellite, can photograph targets on Earth with a resolution of 5.8 cm (2 in) in the visible light spectrum, including night imaging using a photomultiplier. Digital images are transmitted in 'real time' to receivers on Earth, where they are relayed to the USA for analysis.

SMALLEST 'BUG'

The ISG audio transmitter, codenamed 'Rice Grain', is the world's smallest listening device. The 10-mm x 5-mm ($^8/_{10}$-in x $^2/_{10}$-in) cylindrical 'bug' is smaller than a pharmaceutical capsule and when attached to a telephone line transmits the conversation on a frequency of 390–410 MHz to a listening post. It uses the telephone line for power and as an antenna.

MOST FAMOUS FICTIONAL SPY

Author Ian Fleming's spy character James Bond, seen here played by Roger Moore, the suave British Secret Service agent, is one of the most successful and widely imitated 20th-century heroes. The subject of 19 films, Bond is reputedly based on Fleming's older brother Peter, who was an officer in Special Operations Executive (SOE), a wartime espionage group.

disasters:
air, land and sea

WORST ATTACK ON TOURISTS
A terrorist attack at the Hatshepsut Temple in Luxor, Egypt, left 60 tourists dead on 17 Nov 1997. They were shot by militants dressed as police. Two policemen and two Egyptian civilians also died, as well as the six attackers. More than 1,500 people have been killed in the insurgency, which has haunted Egypt's tourist industry.

MOST KILLED IN TERRORIST ATTACK
A total of 329 people were killed when a bomb exploded aboard an Air India Boeing 747 in June 1985, causing the aircraft to crash into the Atlantic Ocean.

MOST KILLED IN MASS PANIC
In 1991, 1,426 Muslim pilgrims were trampled to death in a stampede along a tunnel from Mecca to Mina, Saudi Arabia.

MOST KILLED IN FOOTBALL STADIUM DISASTERS
In May 1964 a total of 318 fans were killed and 500 were injured in a riot that broke out at an Olympic qualifying match between Argentina and Peru at a football stadium in Lima, Peru. The riot was sparked by a Peruvian goal that was disallowed in the last minute. It would have sent Peru to the Tokyo Olympics.

On 21 Oct 1982 at Luzhniki Stadium, Moscow, USSR, many supporters of Spartak Moscow were crushed to death in an icy corridor at the end of a UEFA Cup game against Dutch side Haarlem. *Glasnost* allowed estimates of up to 340 fatalities to be given.

MOST FATALITIES IN A ROLLER COASTER CRASH
In May 1972 four people were killed and seven were injured when the big dipper at the Battersea fun fair in London, UK, collapsed on a Bank Holiday afternoon. Of the four fatalities, three were children.

WORST SKI LIFT ACCIDENT
On 9 March 1976 a total of 42 people were killed in a ski lift disaster at the Cavalese resort, northern Italy.

WORST LIFT DISASTER
A lift operating at the gold mine Vaal Reefs, South Africa, fell 490 m (1,600 ft) on 11 May 1995, killing 105 workers.

WORST UNDERGROUND TRAIN DISASTER
On 28 Oct 1995 approximately 300 people were killed in a fire that broke out in an underground train at Baku, Azerbaijan.

WORST TRAIN DISASTER
On 6 June 1981 more than 800 passengers died when their train plunged off a bridge into the Bagmati River in Bihar, India.

WORST HELICOPTER DISASTER
A Russian military helicopter carrying 61 refugees was shot down near Lata, Georgia, on 14 Dec 1992.

WORST AIR ACCIDENTS
The world's worst ever air disaster took place on 27 March 1977, when two Boeing 747s (Pan-Am and KLM) collided on the runway at Tenerife, Canary Islands, killing 583 people.

The worst air accident involving a single aircraft occurred on 12 Aug 1985, when JAL's Boeing 747, flight 123, crashed near Tokyo, Japan, killing 520 passengers and crew.

WORST SPACE DISASTERS
The worst ever disaster during actual spaceflight took place on 29 June 1971, when astronauts Georgi Dobrovolsky, Viktor Patsayev and Vladislav Volkov (all USSR), who were not wearing spacesuits, died when their *Soyuz 11* spacecraft depressurized during re-entry.

MOST ACCIDENTAL DEATHS ON A SHIP IN PEACETIME
A total of 1,513 people died when the cruise liner *Titanic* sank after hitting an iceberg 1,126.5 km (700 miles) east of Halifax, Canada, on 15 April 1912. Of the bodies that were subsequently recovered, 128 have never been identified. The ship, which was owned by White Star Line and built by Harland & Wolff in Belfast, Northern Ireland, was believed to be unsinkable. It was described at the time as a 'floating palace' — the people who travelled in the first-class accommodation paid $4,000 (£839) each for the voyage, which would be equivalent to $50,000 (£30,045) today. In 1985 the wreck was located by a robot submarine in an ocean canyon. Research and recovery operations carried out in 1987, 1993, 1994 and 1996 by the US company RMS Titanic brought around 5,000 artefacts back to land, many of which can be viewed in an exhibition at the Florida International Museum, USA. The company was granted salvor-in-possession rights to the wreck in 1995. Today just eight of the survivors of the tragedy are still alive.

The record for the greatest number of people known to have perished in any of the 207 manned spaceflights is seven (five men and two women), who were aboard the *Challenger 51L* on 28 Jan 1986. The spacecraft broke apart under extreme aerodynamic overpressure when an explosion occurred 73 seconds after lift-off from the Kennedy Space Center, Florida, USA. It had reached an altitude of 14,020 m (46,000 ft).

The worst ever Space disaster on the ground took place when an R-16 rocket exploded during fuelling at the Baikonur Cosmodrome, Kazakhstan, on 24 Oct 1960, killing 91 people.

WORST ACCIDENTAL EXPLOSION
The worst ever accidental explosion occurred on 17 Dec 1917, when the French freighter *Mont Blanc*, which was packed with 5,080 tonnes of explosives and combustibles, collided with another ship in Halifax Harbour, Nova Scotia, Canada, creating a blast that was felt more than 95 km (60 miles) away. A total of 1,635 people were killed.

BIGGEST MARITIME COLLISION
The world's worst ever collision at sea occurred on 16 Dec 1977 when the tanker *Venoil* (330,954 dwt) struck her sister ship *Venpet* (330,869 dwt) 35 km (22 miles) off the coast of southern Africa.

BIGGEST SHIPWRECK
The 321,186-deadweight tonne VLCC (very large crude carrier) *Energy Determination* blew up and broke in two in the Strait of Hormuz, Persian Gulf, on 12 Dec 1979, causing the world's largest ever shipwreck. The ship was in ballast at the time but its hull value was $58 million (£27.3 million).

WORST MID-AIR COLLISION
On 12 Nov 1996 a total of 351 people died in a collision between a Saudi Boeing 747 scheduled flight and a Kazakh Ilushin 76 charter flight 80 km (50 miles) south-west of New Delhi, India. Only the tail section of the Saudi aircraft remained intact after it plunged to the ground, where it left a 6-m (20-ft) crater. Mid-air collisions are rare, but at the time of this accident New Delhi airport was using the same route for arrivals and departures of civilian aircraft.

WORST FERRY DISASTER
The world's worst ferry disaster took place in the early hours of 21 Dec 1987, when the *Dona Paz* collided with a tanker, the *Victor*, while sailing from Tacloban to Manila, Philippines. After being engulfed in flames, both vessels sank in minutes. The *Dona Paz* officially had 1,550 passengers but may actually have had 4,000.

WORST SUBMARINE DISASTER DURING PEACETIME
On 10 April 1963 the 3,759-tonne US nuclear submarine *Thresher* failed to surface while carrying out deep-diving tests in the Atlantic, 354 km (220 miles) east of Cape Cod, Massachusetts. It had 112 officers and 17 civilian technicians on board. In 1964, the US Navy announced that the bathyscaphe *Trieste II* had obtained pictures of large sections of the vessel's hull, which lies at a depth of 2,560 m (6,400 ft), but the cause of the tragedy has never been determined.

WORST ATTACK ON A BUILDING
The most people killed in a terrorist attack on a building is 168, when a bomb exploded at 9:02 am outside the Alfred P. Murrah Federal Building in Oklahoma City, USA, on 19 April 1995. The death toll included 19 children from the building's Child Day Care Center and eight federal agents. A further 850 people were injured in what is reputed to be the worst mass murder in US history. Ex-army friends Timothy McVeigh and Terry Nichols were convicted in connection with the attack.

environmental *disasters*

MOST DESTRUCTIVE FIRES
The worst year in recorded history for the destruction of the natural environment was 1997, mainly because of fires that were deliberately lit to clear forest but also because of fires resulting from the droughts caused by the El Niño effect in the Pacific. The largest and most numerous fires occurred in Brazil, where they ranged on a 1,600-km (1,000-mile) front.

WORST DEFORESTATION
It is estimated that tropical forests are being cut down at a rate equivalent to 200 football pitches every minute. The country that is losing most forest in terms of area is Brazil, where about 30,000 km² (11,600 miles²) are destroyed every year. Rainforests are being felled and burned both by subsistence farmers and big business to provide new land for pastures and cultivation.

WORST AIR POLLUTION
More than 6,300 people have died from the effects of a poisonous cloud of methyl isocyanate that escaped from Union Carbide's pesticide plant near Bhopal, India, on 3 Dec 1984. The company made a settlement of $470 million (£267 million) to compensate victims and their relatives.

MOST POLLUTED MAJOR CITY
Levels of sulphur dioxide, carbon monoxide and suspended atmospheric particle levels in Mexico City, the capital of Mexico, are more than double those deemed acceptable by the World Health Organisation (WHO).

MOST POLLUTED TOWN
The Russian town of Dzerzhinsk, which has a population of 287,000, is home to dozens of factories producing chlorine and pesticides. In the past chemical weapons were also made there. The Kaprolaktam plant in particular emits 600 tonnes of vinyl chlorine, a carcinogenic gas, every year. Smog used to be so thick in the town that neighbours could not see one another's houses. Russia's leading authority on dioxins (toxic by-products of industrial processes or combustion) states that Dzerzhinsk, which has a life expectancy of 42 for men and 47 for women, should be evacuated.

MOST SULPHUR DIOXIDE POLLUTION
The Maritsa power complex in Bulgaria releases a record 350,000 tonnes of the acidic gas sulphur dioxide into the Maritsa River every year. Sulphur dioxide is a pungent gas and an atmospheric pollutant with an irritating odour. It is a major cause of acid rain.

GREATEST OZONE DEPLETION
The largest 'hole' in the ozone layer is above the Antarctic region. Each austral spring, a 23-km-high (14-mile) area of ozone 1¼ times the size of the USA disappears. Above this height the ozone remains unaffected, so the gap is actually a thinning rather than a hole.

BIGGEST EMISSIONS OF 'GREENHOUSE GASES'
The USA is home to 4% of the world's population but produces 25% of the world's annual emissions of carbon dioxide and other greenhouse gases.

The biggest emitter of carbon dioxide in relative terms is Luxembourg, which produces 18% more per head than the USA.

MOST ACIDIC ACID RAIN
A pH reading of 2.83 was recorded over the Great Lakes in the USA and Canada in 1982 and a reading of 1.87 was recorded at Inverpolly Forest, Highland, Scotland, in 1983.

LARGEST TOXIC CLOUD
In Sept 1990 a fire at a factory handling beryllium in Ust Kamenogorsk, Kazakhstan, released a toxic cloud that extended at least as far as the Chinese border, more than 300 km (190 miles) away.

WORST NUCLEAR ACCIDENTS
The worst ever nuclear reactor disaster took place at Chernobyl No. 4 in the USSR (now Ukraine) in 1986. Contamination was experienced over 28,200 km² (10,900 miles²) and about 1.7 million people were exposed to varying amounts of radiation. The official Soviet total of immediate deaths was 31, but it is not known how many of the 200,000 people involved in the clean-up operation died in the following five years. A total of 850,000 people are still living in contaminated areas.

The worst nuclear waste accident occurred at Kyshtym, Russia (then USSR), in 1957, when an overheated waste container exploded, releasing

MOST ACID RAIN DAMAGE TO FORESTS
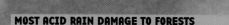
The most damage caused to the environment by acid rain is in the Czech Republic, where 71% of forests are affected. The main causes of acid rain are the burning of coal, which disperses sulphur dioxide into the atmosphere, and emissions from cars, which are responsible for most of the nitrogen dioxides in the air. Acid rain poses a threat to the balance of sensitive ecosystems, reduces crop yields and speeds up the decay of buildings. Lakes and water courses are also badly affected by acid rain, which disrupts the pH balance of the water and kills off wildlife. The trees that are most at risk are coniferous trees, which do not shed their needles at the end of the year if they have been exposed to a certain amount of acid rain. This interferes with the process of photosynthesis. In response to these problems Europe has cut its sulphur dioxide emissions by 25% in the last 10 years and in 1995 19 countries agreed to cut their emissions by 30%.

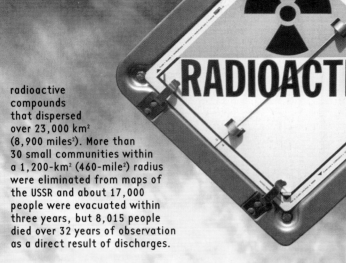

radioactive compounds that dispersed over 23,000 km² (8,900 miles²). More than 30 small communities within a 1,200-km² (460-mile²) radius were eliminated from maps of the USSR and about 17,000 people were evacuated within three years, but 8,015 people died over 32 years of observation as a direct result of discharges.

BIGGEST LAKE SHRINKAGE

The lake that has shrunk the most in recent times is the Aral Sea on the border between Uzbekistan and Kazakhstan. It decreased in area from 68,000 km² (26,300 miles²) to 66,000 km² (25,500 miles²) in 1960, 35,000 km² (13,500 miles²) by 1990 and 26,800 km² (11,000 miles²) by 1994 (by which time it had divided into two smaller bodies of water). The shrinkage is mainly due to the extraction of water (for irrigation) from the major rivers that feed it.

WORST RIVER POLLUTION

In Nov 1986 firemen who were fighting a blaze at the Sandoz chemical works in Basel, Switzerland, flushed 30 tonnes of agricultural chemicals into the River Rhine, killing around 500,000 million fish.

In Aug 1995 President Jagan of Guyana declared an 88-km (50-mile) stretch of the Esquibo River a disaster zone after the banks of a pond holding cyanide used in gold extraction leaked into the river.

WORST MARINE POLLUTION

A plastics factory on Minimata Bay, Kyushu, Japan, deposited mercury waste into the sea from 1953 to 1967. About 4,500 people were seriously harmed and different sources put the death toll at between 43 and 800.

MOST OVERFISHED WATERS

The United Nations has reported that 70% of the world's fisheries are either overfished or fished to the limit and the problem is worsening. Countries that have reduced their fleets include Canada, Japan, Australia, New Zealand and Taiwan.

MOST DAMAGE CAUSED TO AN ISLAND BY MINING

The entire centre of the 21-km² (8-mile²) Pacific island-state of Nauru has been mined, producing a 'lunar landscape'. Only a narrow strip of coast is under vegetation. Nauru's economy depends almost entirely on the extraction and export of phosphates.

MOST OIL SPILT IN A YEAR

The largest quantity of oil spilt into the sea in one year is 608,000 tonnes, in 1979. *The Atlantic Empress* produced the biggest offshore oil spill that year when it collided with the *Aegean Captain* off the coast of Tobago, the Caribbean. It was responsible for 287,000 tonnes of the spillage.

WORST COASTAL OIL DAMAGE

The *Exxon Valdez* oil tanker ran aground in Prince William Sound, Alaska, USA, in March 1989, spilling more than 30,000 tonnes of oil and polluting a 2,400-km-long (1,500-mile) stretch of coast. The company was fined $5 billion (£3.2 billion) and had to pay a clean-up bill of $3 billion (£1.9 billion).

WORST OIL SPILL

An oil spill beneath the Ixtoc 1 drilling rig in the Gulf of Campeche, Gulf of Mexico, in June 1979 caused a 640-km (400-mile) slick. The spill was halted in March 1980, after a loss of up to 500,000 tonnes.

WORST LAND POLLUTION

From Feb to Oct 1994 thousands of tonnes of crude oil flowed across the Arctic tundra of the Komi Republic, Russia. An estimated 100,000 tonnes of oil were lost in a slick up to 18 km (11 miles 35 yd) long.

BIGGEST SOUND POLLUTION

The loudest noise occurred when the island-volcano Krakatoa between Sumatra and Java, Indonesia, exploded in 1883. The explosion, which was heard a distance of 5,000 km (3,100 miles) away, is estimated to have had 26 times the power of the largest ever H-bomb test and is believed to have been heard over 8% of the Earth's suface.

MOST CONTAMINATED SPOT

Chelabinsk in Russia is the most radioactive point on the planet and has probably been so since 1940, when the Mayak weapons complex was built. Since then there have been three nuclear disasters in the area, affecting up to 500,000 people with levels of radiation similar to those in Chernobyl. Scientists designated it the most contaminated spot in 1992 and it was closed to foreign visitors.

MOST PUBLICIZED SMOG

Air pollution reached alarming levels in Kuching, Sarawak, Malaysia, in 1997, and many people wore protective masks. It was due to traffic fumes and to forest fires in neighbouring Indonesia. Although not the largest fires, these were the most publicized fires of 1997, covering large areas of South east Asia with smog and putting around 40,000 people in hospital with respiratory problems.

natural disasters

MOST PEOPLE KILLED IN EARTHQUAKES

In July 1201 approximately 1.1 million people are believed to have been killed by a quake in the eastern Mediterranean. Most of the casualties were in Egypt and Syria.

The earthquake that struck the Shaanxi, Shanxi and Henan provinces of China on 2 Feb 1556 is believed to have killed about 830,000 people.

The highest death toll in modern times was caused by the quake in Tangshan, eastern China, on 28 July 1976. According to the first official figure, 655,237 people were killed. This was subsequently adjusted to 750,000 and then to 242,000.

MOST MATERIAL DAMAGE CAUSED BY AN EARTHQUAKE

The earthquake on Japan's Kanto plain on 1 Sept 1923 destroyed 575,000 homes in Tokyo and Yokohama. The official total of people killed and missing in the quake and its resultant fires was 142,807.

MOST PEOPLE KILLED IN A VOLCANIC ERUPTION

When the Tambora volcano in Sumbawa, Indonesia (then Dutch East Indies), erupted from 5 to 10 April 1815, 92,000 people were killed, either directly or as a result of the subsequent famine.

MOST PEOPLE KILLED IN AVALANCHES

During WWI between 40,000 and 80,000 men are believed to have been killed by avalanches that were triggered by the sound of gunfire in the Tyrolean Alps, Austria.

BIGGEST MASS BURIAL IN AN AVALANCHE

On 11 Jan 1954 two avalanches roared into the village of Blons near the Arlberg Pass, Austria. The first avalanche occurred at 9.36 am and the second at 7.00 pm. Of the 376 residents of the village, 111 were killed, and 29 out of 90 homes were destroyed. In the Leduc mine 300 out of about 600 miners were buried alive.

MOST PEOPLE TRAPPED BY AVALANCHES

A total of 240 people died and more than 45,000 were trapped when a series of avalanches thundered through the Swiss, Austrian and Italian Alps on 20 Jan 1951. The avalanches were caused by a combination of hurricane force winds and wet snow overlaying powder snow.

MOST PEOPLE KILLED IN LANDSLIDES

On 16 Dec 1920 a series of landslides triggered by a single earthquake that hit Gansu province, China, killed about 180,000 people.

MOST MATERIAL DAMAGE CAUSED BY LANDSLIDES

From 18 to 26 Jan 1969 a series of mudslides brought about by nine days of torrential rain and a subtropical storm caused about $138 million (£57.7 million) worth of damage in southern California, USA.

MOST PEOPLE KILLED IN A FLOOD

In Oct 1887 the Huang He (Yellow River) in Huayan Kou, China, flooded its banks, killing about 900,000 people. Despite causing devastating seasonal floods, the Huang He suffers from water shortages and is the biggest river to dry up. In summer 1997 it ran totally dry along its lower section for more than 140 days, leaving farmland parched and threatening the harvest. The river's dry periods are getting longer, jeopardizing 7 million ha (17.3 million acres) of crops and the livelihoods of 52 million people.

MOST PEOPLE MADE HOMELESS BY FLOODS

In Sept 1978 monsoon rains caused extensive river flooding in West Bengal, India, drowning 1,300 people, making 15 million people out of a population of 44 million homeless, killing 26,687 cows and destroying 1.3 million homes. The economic loss was given as $11.3 million (£6.7 million), but unofficial estimates were up to three times that amount.

MOST PEOPLE KILLED BY A GEYSER

In Aug 1903 four people were killed when Waimangu geyser in New Zealand erupted. The victims were standing 27 m (90 ft) from it but their bodies were found up to 800 m (½ mile) away. One was jammed between rocks and another was suspended in a tree.

MOST DEVASTATING ICE STORM

In Jan 1998 an ice storm wreaked havoc across eastern Canada and parts of the north-eastern USA, shutting down

MOST PEOPLE KILLED IN A LANDSLIDE

On 31 May 1970 approximately 18,000 people were killed by a landslide on the slopes of Huascaran in the Yungay region of Peru, making it the most devastating single landslide in history. Huascaran, which is also called Nevada Huascaran, is a mountain peak of the Andes in west-central Peru. The snow-capped peak, which is 6,768 m (22,205 ft) high, is the highest point in Peru and is a favourite destination for mountain climbers and tourists. Its slopes have been the scene of two major disasters. In 1962 a sudden thaw caused a portion of the sheer northern summit to break off, resulting in an avalanche that destroyed several villages and killed 3,500 people. The 1970 disaster occurred when an earthquake caused a landslide that buried 10 villages and most of the town of Yungay. It was one of the worst natural disasters of the 20th century in terms of the number of fatalities. On 17 Jan 1998 a mudslide in San Mateo, about 80.5 km (50 miles) from Lima, Peru, blocked a major road to the capital city but no injuries were reported. Pictured here are the remains of a truck covered in debris from the slide.

MOST PEOPLE MADE HOMELESS BY AN EARTHQUAKE

More than 1 million Guatemalans in a 1,310-km^2 (3,400-mile^2) radius were made homeless at 3.02 am on 4 Feb 1976, when a giant earthquake ripped along the Montagua Fault (the boundary between the Caribbean and North American plates) and devastated their houses. The material damage was estimated at $1.4 billion (£780 million) and the quake is widely cited as the worst natural disaster in Central American history. In terms of material damage it was almost matched by the 1972 Nicaraguan earthquake, which devastated Managua and caused $1.3 billion (£720 million) worth of material damage.

airports and train stations, blocking roads and cutting off power to 3 million people. About 600 giant transmission towers collapsed and five days of freezing rain coated power lines with up to 10 cm (4 in) of ice — many times more weight than they could support. After a fortnight 1 million people were still without power, and some areas remained without power for three weeks. The total cost of the damage was estimated at $650 million (£406 million).

MOST DEVASTATING CYCLONE

Between 300,000 and 500,000 people are estimated to have died in the worst known

cyclone, which hit East Pakistan (now Bangladesh) on 12 Nov 1970. Winds that reached speeds of up to 240 km/h (150 mph) and a 15-m-high (50-ft) tidal wave lashed the coast, the Ganges Delta and the offshore islands of Bhola, Hatia, Kukri Mukri, Manpura and Rangabali.

MOST PEOPLE KILLED IN A TORNADO

On 26 April 1989 approximately 1,300 people lost their lives

and as many as 50,000 people were made homeless when a tornado hit the town of Shaturia in Bangladesh.

MOST MATERIAL DAMAGE CAUSED BY A TORNADO

A tornado cluster that hit the states of Iowa, Illinois, Wisconsin, Indiana, Michigan and Ohio, USA, in April 1985 killed a total of 271 people, injured thousands more and caused more than $400 million (£308.3 million) worth of damage.

MOST PEOPLE MADE HOMELESS BY A TYPHOON

Typhoon 'Ike' hit the Philippines with 220-km/h (137-mph) winds on 2 Sept 1985. It killed 1,363 people, injured 300 and made 1.12 million people homeless.

MOST PEOPLE KILLED IN A TYPHOON

Approximately 10,000 people died when a violent typhoon with winds reaching speeds of up to 161 km/h (100 mph) struck Hong Kong on 18 Sept 1906.

WORST MONSOONS

Monsoons raged through Thailand in 1983, killing around 10,000 people and causing more than $396 million (£264 million) worth of damage. Up to 100,000 people are estimated to have contracted waterborne diseases as a result of the monsoons and around 15,000 people had to be evacuated.

MOST PEOPLE KILLED IN A DAM BURST

The Banqiao and Shimantan Dams burst almost simultaneously onto Henan province, China, in Aug 1975, killing a total of 230,000 people.

MOST PEOPLE KILLED BY A DROUGHT

A drought in northern China between 1876 and 1879 led to the deaths of between 9 million and 13 million people.

MOST PEOPLE KILLED BY A LIGHTNING STRIKE

On 8 Dec 1963 a Boeing 707 jet airliner was struck by lightning near Elkton, Maryland, USA, and crashed, killing 81 passengers.

MOST KILLED IN A HAILSTORM

The hailstone pictured here fell near Huron, South Dakota, USA, during a severe thunderstorm in May 1998. The worst hailstorm on record occurred at Moradabad, Uttar Pradesh, India, on 20 April 1888. It claimed the lives of 246 people. Hailstones are usually between 5 mm and 10 mm ($^1/_5$ in and $^1/_4$ in) in diameter, but stones up to 15 cm (6 in) are not unknown in the mid-west USA.

danger zones

WORST AREA FOR PIRACY

In the last 10 years about 1,500 acts of piracy have been reported in South-east Asia. Most pirates operating in the region, such as these pictured in the South China Sea, are armed with sub-machine guns and use small speedboats to 'jump' targeted vessels. Financial losses from piracy in the Pacific area are estimated to exceed $100 million (£60 million) a year.

MOST LIKELY PLACE IN WHICH TO DIE YOUNG

Palm Island off Queensland, Australia, has been designated the most violent place on Earth outside a combat zone. The island's murder rate is currently 15 times higher than that of the entire state of Queensland and the life expectancy of the 3,500 inhabitants is 40 years. Palm Island also has the highest rate of youth suicide per capita in the world today: since 1994 there has been a total of 40 suicide fatalities on the island and the community is now burying an average of one youth each day.

MOST LIKELY PLACE IN WHICH TO BE SHOT DEAD OUTSIDE WAR

There are currently more than 200 million guns in the USA, where one in four adults own a firearm and where there are estimated to be about 40,000 fatalities from guns each year. In the last 10 years, gun-related homicides in the country have risen by 18%.

MOST LIKELY PLACE IN WHICH TO BE KIDNAPPED

Of the 8,000 kidnap cases reported in 1996, 6,500 were in Latin America and more than 4,000 were in Colombia, where 10 people are kidnapped every day. The crime is alleged to be worth $200 million a year (£120 million) in Colombia. Only 3% of its kidnappers are convicted, compared to 95% in the USA.

MOST LIKELY PLACE IN WHICH TO BE HIT BY SPACE DEBRIS

Since the 1970s approximately 10,000 meteorites have been discovered in Antarctica, making it the most likely place on Earth in which to be hit by space debris.

MOST LIKELY PLACES IN WHICH TO BE INVOLVED IN AN AIR CRASH

China currently accounts for 16% of all global flights and for 70% of all air accidents. Chinese pilots are reputed to average 280 flight hours a month — 180 hours more than Chinese regulations allow — because of a shortage of pilots.

WORST AREA FOR LANDMINES

Of the 120 million landmines buried in 64 countries, about 35 million are in Afghanistan. Landmines cause an injury or fatality every 15–20 minutes, 85% of which occur in Cambodia, Afghanistan and Angola. Pictured left are Kosal Song and Tun Channareth, victims of landmines in Cambodia. Channareth accepted the Nobel Peace Prize for the International Campaign to Ban Landmines in 1997.

The chances of dying in a plane crash in Russia are about 10 times higher than in the USA, making it one of the most dangerous countries in the world in which to fly.

The chances of being involved in an air accident in Africa are one in 50,000. This is 20 times greater than in the USA and about the same odds as being killed in a car accident.

In 1996 more than 550 people died in plane crashes in Latin America. The danger is most acute in Colombia, which is reputed to have the worst air-safety record in the Americas.

LARGEST CITY TO BE THREATENED BY AN EARTHQUAKE

Every year thousands of small tremors occur in the Tokai area south-west of Tokyo, Japan. Since a quake struck with a magnitude of 8.4 in the Tokai fault in Dec 1854, the Tokyo region has become an urban sprawl housing almost 30 million people, with skyscrapers, overhead expressways and millions of tonnes of fuel oil and poisonous chemicals stored in tanks around Tokyo Bay. At some point in the future, an earthquake will occur on the Tokai fault. It is predicted that it will be much larger than the quake that wrecked the Japanese city of Kobe in 1995.

LARGEST CITY TO BE THREATENED BY A VOLCANIC ERUPTION

Vesuvius near Naples, Italy, is regarded as one of the most dangerous volcanoes: more than 700,000 people live on its slopes within a 10-km (6-miles 376-yd) radius of the summit crater, and the outskirts of Naples are within 15 km (9 miles 564 yd) of the vent. If enough warning can be given, the Italian government envisages an evacuation of at least 600,000 people in the event of an eruption. This would take a week, during which time Naples' outer suburbs could suffer the same fate as Pompeii.

HIGHEST RISK OF RADIATION-RELATED ILLNESS FROM FOOD

The former Soviet republic of Belarus suffered the greatest damage from the Chernobyl disaster in 1986 — 70% of the fallout from the nuclear reactor fell on the country. In addition to radiation-related illnesses, Belarus has large areas of contaminated ground, and private plots in these areas are still being used to grow food. Almost 99% of Belarus has been contaminated to degrees above internationally accepted levels, but produce from the greater part of that land continues to be consumed.

MOST LIKELY PLACE IN WHICH TO BE EATEN BY A TIGER

In the Sundarban mangrove forests of Bangladesh and India, fatal attacks on humans by Siberian tigers (*Panthera tigris*) average around 60 a year. Siberian tigers, which can grow to a length of 4 m (13 ft), are the largest of the big cats.

MOST LIKELY PLACE IN WHICH TO BE EATEN BY A SHARK

The most likely place in the world in which to be eaten by a great white shark (*Carcharodon Carcharias*) — the species responsible for one-third of shark attacks on humans — is in the Indian Ocean, off the coasts of Indonesia and Australia. The annual tally for fatal shark attacks globally is estimated at 40, with the chances of being attacked by a shark estimated to be 300 million to one.

MOST LIKELY PLACE IN WHICH TO BE KILLED BY A SNAKE

Human beings are most likely to die of a snakebite in Sri Lanka, where an average of 800 people a year are killed by snakes.

MOST LIKELY PLACE IN WHICH TO BE KILLED BY A SCORPION

Approximately 1,000 people a year die after being stung by scorpions in Mexico. The worst year to be there was 1946, when a total of 1,933 people were killed.

WORST AREA FOR JOURNALISTS

Since 1993 a total of 70 journalists have been murdered in Algeria, making it the most dangerous place in the world in which to be a journalist. On arriving in Algeria, journalists are met by a government protection team. Here firefighters are seen carrying a wounded bomb victim in Algiers, the nation's capital. The majority of the killing takes place just outside Algiers and in the Mitidja Plain. A total of 474 journalists were killed worldwide between 1987 and 1996, 128 in Europe and the republics of the former Soviet Union, 116 in the Americas, 94 in the Middle East and Africa, 85 in Asia and 51 in sub-Saharan Africa.

GREATEST DANGER ZONE

The part of Afghanistan that is controlled by the Islamic fundamentalist Taliban movement is a dangerous place in which to dance, play music, watch videos, play football, read magazines, drink alcohol, fly a kite or use a paper bag. All of these are banned by the Taliban. Women are also prohibited from seeking employment or education and talking to foreigners.

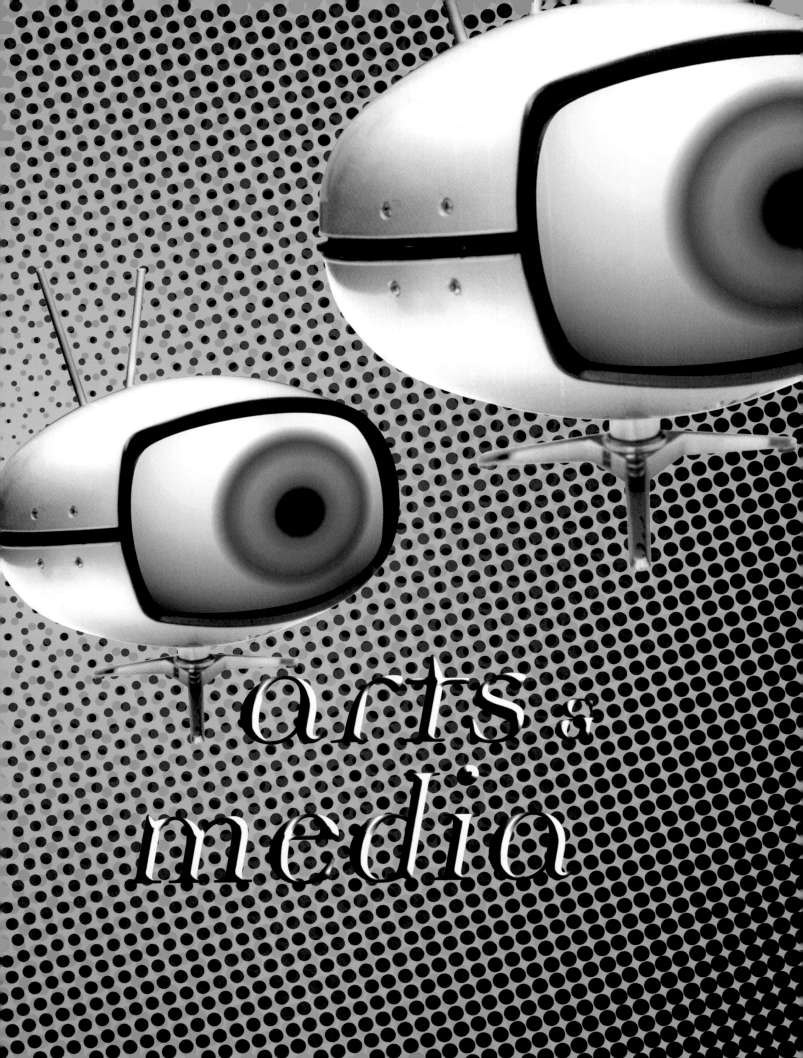

arts & media

movies I

MOST FILMED AUTHOR

A total of 309 straight or relatively straight version films have been made of plays by William Shakespeare, in addition to 41 modern versions, where the storyline is loosely based on a play (such as *West Side Story*). There have also been innumerable parodies. *Hamlet* is the most popular choice, with 75 versions, followed by *Romeo and Juliet* with 51. The most recent of these was *William Shakespeare's Romeo and Juliet* (1996), starring Leonardo DiCaprio and Claire Danes.

HIGHEST BOX OFFICE GROSS

The Oscar-winning *Titanic* (USA, 1997) was released on 19 Dec 1997 and had made a 10-week gross of $918.6 million (£552 million) worldwide by 2 March 1998.

MGM's *Gone With The Wind* (USA, 1939) took $193.6 million (£43.4 million) from 197.55 million admissions in North America — equivalent to $871.2 million (£523.5 million) today, taking into account inflation and the increased price of cinema tickets. In an inflation-adjusted list, *Gone With The Wind* has the highest ever box office gross and *Titanic* is 15th.

FASTEST BOX OFFICE GROSS

The Lost World: Jurassic Park (USA, 1997), made its $74-million (£46-million) budget back in just three days from 23 May 1997 and passed the $100-million (£60-million) mark in 5½ days — faster than any other movie.

TOP FIRST-DAY BOX OFFICE GROSS

The Lost World: Jurassic Park took $22 million (£13.75 million) from 3,281 cinemas on 23 May 1997, beating the biggest single-day gross of $20 million (£12.5 million) set by *Batman Forever* on 16 June 1995.

BIGGEST LOSS

MGM's *Cutthroat Island* (USA, 1995), starring Geena Davis and directed by her then husband Renny Harlin, cost more than $100 million (£60 million) to produce, promote and distribute. By May 1996 it had reportedly earned back just $11 million (£6.9 million).

MOST PROFITABLE FILM SERIES

The 19 James Bond movies, from *Dr No* (UK, 1962) to *Tomorrow Never Dies* (UK/USA, 1997), have grossed more than $1 billion (£625 million) worldwide — more than any other film series.

TOP BUDGET/BOX OFFICE RATIO

Mad Max (Australia, 1980), which starred Mel Gibson and was directed by George Miller, cost $350,000 (£125,000) to make and grossed $100 million (£60 million) in its first two years of international distribution — a budget/box office ratio of 1:285.

LONGEST FIRST RUN

The record for the longest first run in one cinema is 10 years 32 weeks, by *Emmanuelle* (France, 1974), starring Sylvia Kristel and directed by Just Jaeckin. It played at the Paramount City Cinema, Paris, France, from 1974 to 1985, during which time it was seen by a total of 3,268,874 people.

LARGEST PUBLICITY BUDGET

Universal and its licensed merchandisers spent $68 million (£45 million) promoting Steven Spielberg's *Jurassic Park* (USA, 1993) in the USA alone — $8 million (£5.3 million) more than the cost of the film.

MOST EXPENSIVE FILM RIGHTS

The highest price ever paid for film rights was $9.5 million (£6.3 million), for the Broadway musical *Annie*. The deal was announced in 1978 by Columbia and the film was released in 1982. It was directed by John Huston and starred Albert Finney.

A contract worth $4 million (£2.6 million) plus profit-sharing was signed by New Line on 20 July 1993 for the psycho-thriller *The Long Kiss Goodnight* (USA), by 32-year-old Shane Black.

HIGHEST PAY FOR AN ACTOR

Through a percentage of the film's receipts in lieu of salary, Jack Nicholson stood to receive up to $60 million (£40 million) for playing the Joker in the $50-million (£30-million) movie *Batman* (USA, 1989).

HIGHEST FEES FOR A SCRIPT

Carolco Pictures paid a record $3 million (£1.7 million) to Joe Eszterhas for his speculative script for *Basic Instinct* (USA, 1992). The controversial thriller, starring Michael Douglas and Sharon Stone and directed by Paul Verhoeven, was nominated for two Oscars in 1993. It made Stone — a former model who had spent the 1980s playing minor roles — into a major star. She won awards for both Best Female Performance and Most Desirable Female at the 1993 MTV Movie Awards. Since *Basic Instinct* her films have included *Intersection* (1993) with Richard Gere, *The Specialist* (1994) with Sylvester Stallone and *Casino* (1995) with Robert de Niro. She has become one of the most highly paid actresses in Hollywood and has her own production company, Chaos.

MOST EXPENSIVE FILMS

The film *Titanic* (USA, 1997), starring Leonardo DiCaprio and Kate Winslett and directed by James Cameron, was due to be released in July 1997 but was delayed until Dec 1997 due to post-production problems. This delay added at least $20 million (£12.5 million) to the budget, making *Titanic* the most expensive movie ever made, at almost $250 million (£152 million). The film went on to win a total of 11 Oscars, equalling the record that was set by *Ben-Hur* in 1959.

The most expensive film ever made in terms of real costs adjusted for inflation was *Cleopatra* (USA, 1963), which starred Elizabeth Taylor and Richard Burton. The $44-million (£15.7-million) budget would equal more than $260 million (£158 million) in 1998.

MOST SUCCESSFUL DIRECTOR

Seven of US director Steven Spielberg's movies are in the all-time top 10, and collectively his films have grossed more than $2.17 billion (£1.35 billion). He won an Oscar for Best Director with *Schindler's List* (1993).

LARGEST FILM OUTPUT

India produces more feature-length films than any other country, with a peak output of 948 films in 1990. It has three major centres of production, Bombay, Calcutta and Madras, making films in 16 languages.

LARGEST FILM STUDIO COMPLEX

Universal City in Los Angeles, California, USA, covers 170 ha (420 acres) and has 561 buildings and 34 sound stages.

LONGEST FILM

The 85-hour *Cure for Insomnia* (USA, 1987), which was directed by John Henry Timmis IV, premiered in its entirety at the School of Art Institute of Chicago, USA, from 31 Jan to 3 Feb 1987. Much of the film consists of L. D. Groban reading his own 4,080-page poem, interspersed with scenes of a rock band and some X-rated footage.

MOST DEATHS DURING THE PRODUCTION OF A FILM

In 1989 a fire killed more than 40 people on the set of the Indian TV movie *The Sword of Tipu Sultan*.

MOST COSTUMES IN ONE FILM

A record 32,000 costumes were worn in *Quo Vadis* (USA, 1951).

MOST COSTUME CHANGES IN ONE FILM

Madonna changed costume a record 85 times in *Evita* (USA, 1996) and wore a total of 39 hats, 45 pairs of shoes and 56 pairs of earrings. The costumes were based on Eva Perón's own clothes, many of which are kept in an Argentinian bank vault. Madonna chose each pattern herself.

CHARACTERS PORTRAYED IN THE MOST FILMS

The French emperor Napoleon Bonaparte was the subject of a total of 177 films between 1897 and 1986 – a record for any historical character.

The fictional character most frequently portrayed on the big screen is Sherlock Holmes, who was created by Sir Arthur Conan Doyle. He has been portrayed by 75 actors in more than 211 films since 1900.

MOST FILMED STORY

There have been a record 95 productions of the classic fairy tale *Cinderella*, including cartoon, modern ballet, operatic, all-male, parody and pornographic versions. The first ever version was *Fairy Godmother* (UK, 1898) and the most recent version was *The Magic Riddle* (Australia, 1991).

MOST MERCHANDISING LICENCES

Warner Bros. issued 160 merchandising licences at the time of the premier of *Batman* (USA, 1989). It was the most successful merchandising operation in terms of licence fees, adding an estimated $50 million (£30 million) to the $250-million (£147-million) box office gross. The 'caped crusader' is seen here portrayed by George Clooney in *Batman and Robin* (1997).

movies II

HIGHEST EARNINGS FROM A SINGLE FILM

As the producer of *Star Wars* (USA, 1977), George Lucas was entitled to 40% of net profits, worth almost $50 million (£28.6 million). In addition Lucas held all the merchandising rights, which Fox allowed him under the contract because they could see little value in them. His cut of the estimated $4-billion (£2.4-billion) revenue from retail sales of *Star Wars*-related products is undisclosed.

HIGHEST EARNINGS FROM A HORROR FILM

William Peter Blatty, the author and producer of *The Exorcist* (USA, 1973), earned 40% of the film's gross. The exact amount of money is not known, but the film grossed approximately $89 million (£36 million).

HIGHEST-GROSSING HORROR MOVIES

Miramax's *Scream* (USA, 1996), directed by Wes Craven and starring Drew Barrymore and Neve Campbell, cost about $15 million (£9.3 million) to make and had grossed $103 million (£64 million) by July 1997. *Scream II* (USA, 1997), grossed $33 million (£20.65 million) on its opening weekend and took $96 million (£60 million) from Dec 1997 to March 1998. A second sequel is due for release in 1999.

MOST TAKES FOR A DIALOGUE SCENE

Stanley Kubrick is reputed to have required a record 127 takes for a scene with Shelley Duvall in *The Shining* (GB, 1980). Kubrick, a notoriously demanding director, also required 85 takes for a scene with Duvall, Scatman Crothers and five-year-old Danny Lloyd, and 50–60 takes for a long tracking shot where Jack Nicholson pursues Duvall up the staircase as she brandishes a baseball bat at his face.

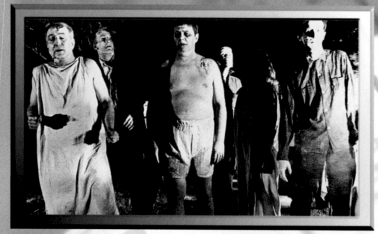

LOWEST BUDGET HORROR MOVIES

Night of the Living Dead (USA, 1968) was made on a tiny budget of about $114,000 (£47,000) and went on to become one of the most successful independent films of all time. It was shot in and around the director George Romero's home in Pittsburgh, Pennsylvania, USA, over three weekends. Romero raised finances by selling $300 (£125) shares in the film. The cast of unknowns was made up of local talent and the film was shot by people who had previously made ads and industrial films. Two of the investors had to play minor roles due to a shortage of talent, while another — a butcher — provided blood and guts. The end result, said to be the first truly modern horror movie, was rejected by Columbia because it was not in colour. It spawned two sequels and a series of Italian zombie and cannibal films in the 1970s.

In an inflation-adjusted list, *The Exorcist* (USA, 1973), directed by William Friedkin, had the highest-ever box office gross of any horror movie. If the rate of inflation and the rise in the price of cinema tickets since 1973 are taken into account, the film grossed the equivalent of more than $381 million (£238 million) in today's terms.

HIGHEST-GROSSING SCI-FI MOVIES

Including its recent re-release, *Star Wars* (USA, 1977) has grossed about $910 million (£568 million). Taking into account the rate of inflation and the rise in the price of cinema tickets, it has the highest box office gross of any science-fiction film.

Fox's *Independence Day* (USA, 1996), which starred Bill Pullman, Will Smith and Jeff Goldblum, grossed $811 million (£506 million) worldwide — the highest box office gross of a sci-fi film on its original release.

MOST EXPENSIVE SCI-FI FILM

Waterworld (USA, 1995), starring Kevin Costner, suffered a series of setbacks when the set broke free from its moorings in the Pacific Ocean on several occasions. This problem and additional technical failures made it the most expensive sci-fi movie ever, at an estimated $160 million (£103 million).

MOST PROLIFIC HORROR DIRECTOR

Roger Corman directed 27 horror movies over 35 years, from *Swamp Women* (USA, 1955) to *Frankenstein Unbound* (USA, 1990). He also produced more than 100 other horror films.

MOST PROLIFIC HORROR ACTORS

US actor John Carradine starred in a record 67 horror films during his acting career, from

The Black Cat (USA, 1934) to The Alien Within (USA, 1991).

Christopher Lee, the British actor who rose to fame with his portrayal of Dracula, has starred in 59 movies since 1959. He was first cast by Hammer Films in The Curse of Frankenstein (GB, 1956) and most recently appeared in Talos the Mummy (GB, 1998).

MOST PORTRAYED HORROR CHARACTER
Count Dracula, who was created by the Irish writer Bram Stoker in 1897, has been portrayed in more horror films than any other character. Representations of the Count or his immediate descendants outnumber those of his closest rival, Frankenstein's

monster (created by Mary Shelley in 1818), by 161 to 117.

MOST HORROR NOVELS FILMED
More than 20 of horror writer Stephen King's novels and short stories have been made into movies, including Carrie (USA, 1976), directed by Brian de Palma and starring Sissy Spacek, The Shining (GB, 1980), Children of the Corn (USA, 1984) and Misery (USA, 1990).

MOST HORROR SEQUELS
House (USA, 1986), directed by Steve Miner, was followed by House II: The Second Story (1987) and a further eight sequels. Many of the sequels by-passed cinema release and went straight to video.

MOST SCI-FI SEQUELS
The most sequels to a US sci-fi movie is seven, for Star Trek — The Motion Picture (USA, 1979), directed by Robert Wise. An eighth sequel is due for release in Dec 1998.

MOST SECRETIVE FILM SCRIPTS
George Lucas's new Star Wars trilogy is the most secretive project in film history. For the first prequel it was reputed that Lucasfilm Ltd gave characters bogus names, filmed scenes that were never to be used and employed different versions of the script. People who have seen the script have had to sign a confidentiality document. The first film is due to be released in May 1999.

BIGGEST HORROR FILM LINK-UP
Friday the 13th (USA, 1980), which was directed by Sean S. Cunningham, had eight sequels by May 1998, and a ninth sequel, Jason Versus Freddy, is planned. The NewLine film will pit Jason Vorhees from Friday the 13th against Freddy Krueger from A Nightmare on Elm Street (USA, 1984), pictured below.

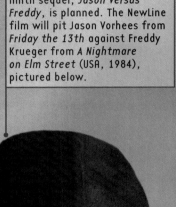

MOST SCI-FI SEQUELS
There have been 24 sequels to the original Japanese version of Godzilla, King of the Monsters (1954). In 1998 a big-budget US version of the story was released after one and a half years of publicity and marketing.

movie stunts

MOST EXPENSIVE AERIAL STUNT

Simon Crane performed one of the most dangerous ever aerial stunts when he moved from one jet plane to another while flying at 4.752 km (2 miles 1,480 yds) for *Cliffhanger* (USA, 1993). The stunt was performed only once because it was so dangerous, and cost a record $1 million (£568,000). Sylvester Stallone (left), the film's star, is said to have offered to reduce his fee by the same amount to ensure that the stunt was made.

MOST STUNTS BY A LIVING ACTOR

Jackie Chan, the Hong Kong actor, director, producer, stunt co-ordinator and writer, has appeared in more than 65 films since his debut in *Big and Little Wong Tin Bar* (Hong Kong, 1962) at the age of eight. No insurance company will underwrite Chan's productions, in which he performs all his own stunts. After a number of stuntmen were injured during the making of *Police Story* (Hong Kong, 1985), the star formed the Jackie Chan Stuntmen Association, trained the stuntmen personally and paid their medical bills out of his own pocket.

MOST STUNTS BY A HOLLYWOOD ACTOR

Buster Keaton starred in more than 100 films from *The Butcher Boy* (USA, 1917) to *A Funny Thing Happened on the Way to the Forum* (USA, 1966) and has been described as 'the Jackie Chan of silent film'. He is believed to have been the only star of his time to have performed all his own death-defying stunts, despite studio claims that actors such as Harold Lloyd and Douglas Fairbanks did all their own stunts.

MOST STUNTS BY AN ACTRESS

Michele Yeoh, a former Miss Malaysia, was the first actress that Jackie Chan allowed to do all her own stunts. In *Ah Lahm: The Story of a Stuntwoman* (Hong Kong, 1996) a mistimed jump off a 20-m (65-ft) bridge put Yeoh in hospital for three months, but she went on to complete the film. Her most dangerous stunt was riding a speeding motorbike on a moving train without safety nets or catch wires for *Police Story 3: Supercop* (Hong Kong, 1992). She has starred in 18 movies since 1979, achieving international fame as a Bond girl with Pierce Brosnan in *Tomorrow Never Dies* (GB/USA, 1997).

MOST PROLIFIC STUNTMEN

Vic Armstrong has doubled for every actor playing James Bond, and in a career spanning three decades has performed stunts in more than 200 films, including *Raiders of the Lost Ark* (USA, 1981). He has co-ordinated stunts for movies such as *Tomorrow Never Dies* (GB/USA, 1997) and is married to stuntwoman Wendy Leech, who he met when they doubled for the stars of *Superman* (USA, 1978).

Yakima Canutt performed stunts in more than 150 films in his 15-year career. He was also a stunt double for John Wayne and Clark Gable. In 1941 he broke his ankles and began creating stunts and handling the action scenes in Hollywood movies, including the chariot race in *Ben Hur* (USA, 1959). In 1966 he was awarded an Oscar for his stunt work.

HIGHEST FREEFALL

The greatest height from which a stuntman has ever leapt in a freefall is 335 m (1,100 ft), by Dar Robinson from a ledge at the summit of the CN Tower in Toronto, Canada, for *Highpoint* (Canada, 1979). Robinson's parachute opened just 91 m (300 ft) from the ground after a freefall lasting six seconds.

HIGHEST JUMP

The highest ever jump made by a movie stuntman without a parachute is 70.71 m (232 ft), by A. J. Bakunus while he was doubling for Burt Reynolds in the film *Hooper* (USA, 1978). He fell onto an air mattress.

BRAVEST LIVING HOLLYWOOD LEAD

Mel Gibson, who was born in New York, USA, but moved to Australia at the age of 12, starred in the action film *Lethal Weapon* (USA, 1987) and its three sequels. He performs his own stunts and is said to be the bravest actor in Hollywood. He is the only actor to have been credited as both leading man and a stuntman in a movie, in *Mad Max Beyond Thunderdome* (Australia, 1985), pictured left, in which he starred alongside Tina Turner. He made his first big screen appearance in 1977 and since then has starred in more than 30 films.

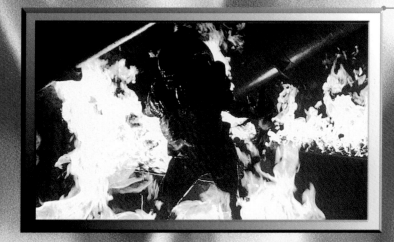

LONGEST FIRE BURN

Nick Gillard withstood a full fire burn without air for two minutes for *Alien 3* (USA, 1992), starring Sigourney Weaver. Stuntpeople performing a full fire burn have to refrain from breathing while on fire to prevent the oxygen in their lungs from igniting. During his 20-year career Gillard has been on fire at least 100 times and has performed and co-ordinated stunts in more than 15 major films including the boat and tank sequences in *Indiana Jones and the Last Crusade* (USA, 1989) and sword-work in *Robin Hood: Prince of Thieves* (USA, 1991) and *The Three Musketeers* (USA, 1993). His most recent work is as stunt co-ordinator on the set of George Lucas's *Star Wars: Episode I*, due to be released in 1999. Gillard has responsibility for training actors Liam Neeson and Ewan McGregor, the two Jedi Knights, in swordplay. At 12 years of age Gillard ran away from military school to join the circus, becoming a world class horse-trick rider in the Moscow State Circus by the age of 16. His career in stunts began when he was offered work on *The Thief of Baghdad* (USA, 1978).

LONGEST LEAP IN A CAR

The world's longest ever leap made in a car that was being propelled by its own engine was performed by the stunt driver Gary Davis for the movie *Smokey and the Bandit II* (USA, 1981), starring Burt Reynolds. Davis raced a stripped-down Plymouth at a speed of 128 km/h (80 mph) up a ramp that was butted up against the back of a double-tiered car-carrier. He flew 49.6 m (163 ft) through the air before landing safely on the desert floor.

BIGGEST CO-ORDINATOR OF AERIAL STUNTS

Flying Pictures of Surrey, UK, has planned and co-ordinated air stunts for more than 200 feature films, including *Cliffhanger* (USA, 1993), *GoldenEye* (GB/USA, 1995) and *Mission Impossible* (USA 1996), and co-ordinated the aerial stunts for hundreds of TV shows and ads.

HIGHEST PAY FOR A SINGLE STUNT

Dar Robinson was paid $150,000 (£70,671) for his freefall from Toronto's CN Tower for *Highpoint* (Canada, 1979).

BIGGEST STUNT BUDGET

More than $3 million (£1.87 million) of the $200-million (£125-million) budget for *Titanic* (USA, 1997) went towards the movie's stunts. In the most complex scene, 100 stuntpeople leap, fall and slide 229 m (70 ft) as the ship breaks in half and rises out of the water to a 90° angle. The ship was docked in a tank filled with 77 million litres (17 million gallons) of water.

MOST STUNT DAYS WORKED

The record for the greatest number of stunt days worked on any film is 6,000, by the 100 stuntpeople who worked on the set of *Titanic*. The team was led by British stunt co-ordinator Simon Crane.

HIGHEST STUNTMAN:ACTOR RATIO

The Rookie (USA, 1990), directed by Clint Eastwood, who also starred in the film along with Charlie Sheen and Raul Julia, featured a total of 87 stuntmen and just 37 actors.

OLDEST STUNTMAN TO STAND IN FOR CHILDREN

The only adult stuntman who stands in for children is Bobby Porter, who is 1.43 m (4 ft 9 in) tall. One of Porter's most famous films is *Annie* (USA, 1982), in which he dangled from a 20-storey-high drawbridge as the stand-in for the nine-year-old lead Aileen Quinn.

LONGEST BOAT JUMP

Stuntman Nick Gillard performed a record 67-m (220-ft) powerboat jump over two bridges for Dick Maas's *Amsterdamned* (Netherlands, 1988), a murder mystery involving a psychopathic diver in the Dutch capital. Gillard, who has appeared on numerous *World's Greatest Stunts* videos, believes that fear is good because it keeps him on his toes.

tv and video

MOST EXPENSIVE PROGRAMME

In Jan 1998 the NBC network in the USA agreed to pay $13 million (£8.2 million) for each hourly episode of the top-rated medical drama *ER*, which stars George Clooney (right) and Julianna Margulies. It had previously paid $1.6 million (£1 million) per episode. The hospital drama is the No. 1 US primetime show, with a weekly audience of 32 million. The three-year deal with *ER* creators Warner Bros. will work out at $873.68 million (£536 million) for 22 episodes.

BIGGEST AUDIENCES

Baywatch, whose stars have included David Hasselhoff and Pamela Anderson, is the world's most widely viewed TV series, with an estimated weekly audience of more than 1.1 billion people in 142 countries.

'Goodbye, Farewell and Amen', the final episode of *M*A*S*H*, was transmitted to 77% of all US viewers on 28 Feb 1983. It was estimated that about 125 million people tuned in.

MOST VIEWED TRIAL

From Jan to Oct 1995 a daily average of 5.5 million US viewers watched the trial of O. J. Simpson, the American footballer and actor charged with the murder of his ex-wife Nicole and her friend Ronald Goodman.

LARGEST SOAP OPERA PRODUCTION

Brazil, Mexico and Puerto Rico dominate the trade in *telenovelas*, which run on average for more than 100 episodes. They supply them for stations throughout Latin America, Spain, Italy and Portugal.

The Brazilian network Globo is the largest and most profitable producer of *telenovelas* in Latin America. It shows soaps from 6 pm onwards each night.

MOST SUCCESSFUL *TELENOVELA*

In the 1960s *Simply Mary* was sold to every Spanish-speaking country and once attracted more viewers than the World Cup.

MOST SUCCESSFUL SOAP OPERA

Dallas, starring Larry Hagman and Victoria Principal, began in 1978 and by 1980 had an estimated 83 million US viewers (a then record 76% share of the TV audience) and had been seen in more than 90 countries.

LONGEST RUNNING SHOW

NBC's *Meet the Press* was first transmitted on 6 Nov 1947 and was shown weekly from 12 Sept 1948. By 28 June 1998, 2,557 shows had been aired.

LARGEST TV CONTRACT

In March 1994 US talk show queen Oprah Winfrey reportedly signed a contract with the King World Corporation guaranteeing her company Harpo $300 million (£193 million) by 31 Dec 2000, or $46.15 million (£29.7 million) a year for 6½ years.

MOST EXPENSIVE TV DEAL

In Jan 1998, the National Football League (NFL) signed contracts with CBS, ABC and Fox, and with the cable sportscaster ESPN totalling $17.6 billion (£10.6 billion). The contracts give each network rights to NFL games for eight years starting with the 1998–99 season. ESPN will pay the NFL $600 million (£360.5 million) per year, ABC and Fox will each pay $550 million (£330.5 million) per year, and CBS will pay $500 million (£300.4 million) per year.

BIGGEST GLOBAL TV NETWORK

CNN International news is the only global TV network. Distributed via 15 satellites, CNN and CNNI are seen by 184 million households in more than 210 countries.

MOST PROLIFIC TV PRODUCERS

Aaron Spelling has produced more than 3,784 TV episodes since 1956. Projected 24 hours a day they would take just over four months to screen. His output has included *Starsky and Hutch*, *Dynasty* and *Beverly Hills 90210*.

TALK SHOW WARS

Jerry Springer, who once worked on Senator Robert F. Kennedy's political campaigns and became one of the youngest ever US mayors at the age of 33 in 1971, rose to international fame after being asked to launch *The Jerry Springer Show*, a one-hour talk show, in 1991. Today his controversial programme is a success throughout the USA and is seen in more than 30 other countries around the world. In May 1996 Springer signed a contract to continue making the show for another six years, and by 1997 the show was so popular that it began to be aired twice a week on US television. Much of its appeal lies in the fact that half of all episodes end up in fights and brawls, which are encouraged by the live studio audience. It is for this reason that the show employs several security guards for each episode. Guests who appear on the programme have to sign a form stipulating that if they lie they must pay production costs of up to $80,000 (£50,000). In 1998 *The Jerry Springer Show* was ranked second only to *Oprah* in the talk show ratings. The latter's host, Oprah Winfrey, is the most successful woman on TV to date.

MOST VISITED WEBSITES

The most visited TV series websites, in descending order, are those of US sitcoms *Seinfeld*, *Friends* and *Caroline in the City*. *Friends*, which first aired in the United States in 1994, stars Lisa Kudrow, Matthew Perry, Jennifer Aniston, David Schwimmer, Courteney Cox and Matt LeBlanc (left to right). Now in its fourth series, it is watched by about 16.5 million US viewers.

The most prolific game show producer is Mark Goodson. He has produced more than 39,000 episodes of game shows, totalling 21,240 hours of airtime.

MOST EXTREME GAME SHOW

First shown in 1984, the Japanese game show *Gaman* tests the endurance of contestants who willingly put themselves in perilous situations, and face challenges ranging from starvation to self-dousing with petrol or experiments with live maggots.

MOST QUIZ SHOW CONTESTANTS

A record 5,000 contestants took part in Japan's *Ultra Quiz*, which was produced by Nippon Television. Competitors who correctly answered a general knowledge question had to board a plane but were obliged to disembark if they failed to answer a second question correctly. Those who remained aboard had to sit an 800-question, two-hour exam. The two finalists faced a play-off on top of the Pan Am skyscraper in New York, USA. Prizes included a racehorse, a helicopter and a plot of land in Nevada, USA.

The All-Japan High-School Quiz Championship, which was televised by NTV on 31 Dec 1983, had a record 80,799 participants.

MOST EXPENSIVE TV RIGHTS FOR A FILM

The Fox network paid $82 million (£50 million) for the TV rights to Steven Spielberg's *Jurassic Park: The Lost World* in June 1997, before its international release.

MOST EXPENSIVE TV RIGHTS FOR A MINI SERIES

In 1991 a group of US and European investors, led by CBS, paid $8 million (£4.5 million) for the TV rights to Alexandra Ripley's *Scarlett*, the sequel to Margaret Mitchell's *Gone With the Wind* (USA, 1939).

MOST EXPENSIVE TV MINI SERIES

The 14-episode mini-series *War and Remembrance* cost $110 million (£61 million) to make over three years, and will be aired in Nov 1998.

HIGHEST EXPENDITURE ON TV AND VIDEO PRODUCTS

The leading consumer market for video and TV products is Japan, with an average expenditure of $43.66 (£26.23) per person a year.

COUNTRY WITH THE MOST TV SETS

There are 227.5 million households with TV sets in China (one in six people) — almost twice as many as in the USA.

COUNTRY WITH MOST VCRS

A record 81% of US households (78,125,000) own at least one video recorder.

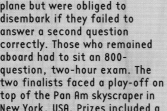

MOST SPIN-OFFS FROM A SERIES

Star Trek has spawned a record seven feature films and five syndicated programmes: *Star Trek* (1966–69), the *Star Trek* cartoon (1973–75), *Star Trek: The Next Generation* (1987–94), *Star Trek: Deep Space Nine* (1993–present) and *Star Trek: Voyager* (1995–present). The first feature film adaptation was *Star Trek: the Motion Picture* (1980), starring William Shatner and Leonard Nimoy.

MOST RENTED VIDEO

Fox's reissue of George Lucas' *Star Wars* trilogy, featuring digitally remastered versions of *Star Wars*, *The Empire Strikes Back* and *Return of the Jedi*, has made a record $270.9 million (£166.2 million) through video rentals. Steven Spielberg's *E.T.: the Extra Terrestrial* (USA, 1982) had previously held the record for 14 years, making a total of $228.16 million (£114.6 million).

BEST-SELLING VIDEO

Walt Disney's *The Lion King* (1994) had sold more than 55 million copies worldwide by Aug 1997. The 32nd Disney animated feature, it was the first without human characters and the first based on an original story. It featured the voices of Whoopi Goldberg, Jeremy Irons and Rowan Atkinson.

FASTEST-SELLING FILM ON VIDEO

The Full Monty (UK/USA, 1997) sold 1.8 million copies in its first week of release — almost 700,000 more than *Star Wars*, the previous record-holder in the UK. It also nearly doubled the previous record of 351,000 for UK first-day sales, held by *Independence Day*.

FASTEST VIDEO PRODUCTION

Videos of Prince Andrew and Sarah Ferguson's wedding in London, UK, in 1986 were made in 5 hr 41 min by Thames Video Collection. Live filming ended when the couple left for their honeymoon at 4:42 pm and the first tapes were available from the Virgin Megastore, Oxford Street, London, UK, at 10:23 pm.

MOST VIDEO LIBRARIES

Bombay (Mumbai), India, has 15,000 video libraries and 500 video parlours.

books, newspapers and magazines

TOP NEWSPAPER CIRCULATIONS

Japanese newspapers have some of the highest circulation figures in the world. The newspaper with the world's highest circulation is Tokyo's *Yomiuri Shimbun*, which has a combined morning and evening circulation of 14.5 million copies daily. The most popular periodical in Japan is the countryside magazine *Le-no-Hikari*, which has an average readership of 1.11 million people every month.

MOST TRANSLATED NOVELIST

The world's most translated novelist is Sidney Sheldon, pictured here with his wife Alexandra. Sheldon's novels, which include *Rage of Angels*, 1987, have been translated into 51 languages and distributed in more than 180 countries to date. He sold his first piece of writing — a poem — when he was 10 years old and by the age of 18 was working in Hollywood as a screenwriter, going on to create such series as *Hart to Hart*.

BEST-SELLING BOOKS

The world's best-selling and most widely distributed book is the Bible, with an estimated 3.88 billion copies sold between 1815 and 1998.

Excluding non-copyright works such as the Bible and the Koran, the all-time best-selling book is the *Guinness Book of Records*, which was first published by Guinness Superlatives in Oct 1955. Global sales in about 37 languages had surpassed 81 million by June 1998.

BEST-SELLING WORKS OF FICTION

Three novels have been credited with sales of about 30 million: *Valley of the Dolls* (1966, now out of print) by Jacqueline Susann, which sold 6.8 million copies in its first six months; *To Kill a Mockingbird* (1960) by Harper Lee; and *Gone With the Wind* (1936) by Margaret Mitchell.

Alistair MacLean wrote 30 novels, 28 of which sold more than 1 million copies each in the United Kingdom alone. It has been estimated that one of his novels is purchased somewhere in the world every 18 seconds.

LONGEST ON A BEST-SELLER LIST

The Road Less Traveled by M. Scott Peck had spent 694 weeks on the *New York Times* paperback best-seller list by the time it exited on 6th April 1997. More than 5 million copies of the book are in print.

TOP-SELLING AUTHORS

The top-selling fiction writer is Agatha Christie, whose 78 crime novels have sold an estimated 2 billion copies in 44 languages.

The top-selling living author is British novelist Dame Barbara Cartland, with global sales of more than 650 million for her 635 titles.

RICHEST AUTHOR

US horror novelist Stephen King is the richest author in the world today, with an estimated worth of $84 million (£52.5 million). His top-selling works include *Carrie* (1974), *The Shining* (1978), *Pet Sematary* (1983) and *Misery* (1987), all of which have been made into successful films.

HIGHEST SUM PAID FOR THE SERIALIZATION OF A NOVEL

US author Tom Wolfe, who wrote the best-selling *The Bonfire of the Vanities* (1988), received a record $600,000 (£360,000) for the serialization of his new novel, which will be titled either *Red Dogs* or *The Stoic's Game* and has taken him 12 years to complete. *Rolling Stone* magazine outbid *Vanity Fair*, *Esquire* and the *New Yorker* in the secret auction for the rights.

MOST PROLIFIC NOVELIST

The Brazilian novelist José Carlos Ryoki de Alpoim Inoue had a total of 1,046 sci-fi novels, westerns and thrillers published between June 1986 and Aug 1996 — more than any other writer.

OLDEST AUTHORS

US sisters Sarah and Elizabeth Delany wrote their autobiography in 1993, when they were 103 and 102 years old respectively. In 1997 Sarah wrote its sequel *On my Own at 107*.

MOST RECLUSIVE NOVELIST

J. D. Salinger has guarded his privacy and resisted publicity to such an extent that a book about efforts to find him has been published. *In Search of J. D. Salinger* was written by Ian Hamilton after his original biography was blocked from publication by Salinger.

TOP NEWSPAPER CIRCULATIONS

The United Kingdom has the highest newspaper circulation of any European Union country. *The Sun* has the highest circulation of any British daily newspaper, at 4.064 million, while *The News of the World* has a record Sunday circulation of 4.307 million. The most popular British periodical is *Reader's Digest*, with a circulation of 1.67 million.

MOST NEWSPAPERS

In 1995 India had more than 4,235 newspapers, most of them regional and published in different languages for a rural readership. Those with higher circulations include the daily *Malayala Manorama*, with a circulation of 800,000, and *Punjab Kesari*, a Sunday paper with a circulation of 892,000. India's most popular magazine is *India Today*, which is printed in five languages and has a circulation of 970,000 every fortnight.

BIGGEST SHORTAGE OF PRINT MATERIALS

Russia's shortage of materials, increasing taxes and high costs make it hard for daily papers to keep in constant print, and some low circulation papers appear intermittently. The highest circulation is 3.6 million, by the weekly *Argumenty y Fakty*. Russia's top-selling magazine is *Rabotmitsa*, a magazine for working women with a monthly circulation of 20.5 million.

TOP-SELLING FRENCH NEWSPAPERS AND MAGAZINES

France's top-selling newspaper is *Ouest-France* from Rennes, with a circulation of 797,091.

France's top-selling magazine is the TV listings magazine *Télé 7 Jours*, with a weekly circulation of 2.8 million.

Modes et Travaux is France's top monthly fashion magazine, with a circulation of 1.5 million.

Paris Match is France's most popular news periodical, with a circulation of 690,000.

TOP-SELLING GERMAN NEWSPAPERS AND MAGAZINES

Germany has no national papers but the regional *Zeitung* papers printed in 15 cities are Germany's most popular, with a combined circulation of 2.4 million.

The top-selling German magazine is *Hörzu*, a TV listings magazine with a circulation of 3.86 million. The top-selling non-TV listings magazine is fashion and cookery magazine *Burda Moden*, with a monthly circulation of 2.3 million.

TOP-SELLING ITALIAN NEWSPAPERS AND MAGAZINES

Italy's top circulating paper is *Corriere della Sera*, a regional paper based in Milan but with a national circulation of 720,239.

The top-selling periodical is the monthly motoring magazine *L'Automobile*, with a circulation of 1.08 million.

TOP-SELLING SPANISH NEWSPAPERS AND MAGAZINES

El Pais is Spain's top-selling newspaper, with a circulation of 1.12 million.

TV listings magazine *TP Teleprogramma* has a circulation of 1 million.

TOP-SELLING CHINESE NEWSPAPERS AND MAGAZINES

In 1996 China had 2,235 newspapers, all state run. *Sichuan Ribao*, which services the Chengdu region, is China's top-selling newspaper, with a circulation of 8 million readers.

Ban Yue Tan is the top-selling Chinese magazine, with a circulation of 6 million.

BIGGEST ADVANCES

Tom Clancy was allegedly paid a $33.4-million (£25-million) advance for *The Hunt for Red October* (1984) and *Patriot Games* (1987). In 1997 he is said to have beaten this with a $75-million (£46.8-million), two-book deal with Penguin. In 1992 he had received the biggest known advance for one book, with a reported $14 million (£7.3 million) for the North American rights to *Without Remorse*.

TOP-SELLING US NEWSPAPERS AND MAGAZINES

The *Wall Street Journal* has a circulation of 1.84 million.

The most popular periodical in the USA is the *Reader's Digest*, with a circulation of 16.26 million.

TOP-SELLING BRAZILIAN NEWSPAPERS AND MAGAZINES

Fôlha de Sao Paulo has a daily circulation of 558,000 and a Sunday circulation of 1.4 million.

Veja, a weekly magazine, has a circulation of 800,000.

TOP-SELLING AUSTRALIAN NEWSPAPERS AND MAGAZINES

Sydney's *Sunday Telegraph* has a circulation of 705,000. The most popular daily is the *Herald Sun*, with a circulation of 675,193.

Motoring magazine *The Open Road* has a circulation of 1.5 million.

BIGGEST-SELLING GAY MAGAZINE

Los Angeles-based *Advocate* magazine sells more than 2 million copies a year in the USA.

TOP-SELLING SOCIETY MAGAZINE

Spain's *¡Hola!* sells 622,292 copies a week — 47,434 more copies than its British equivalent *Hello!*.

TOP-SELLING NEWS MAGAZINE

Time, which was launched in 1923, has a worldwide weekly circulation of 4.15 million.

TOP-SELLING STREET MAGAZINE

The *Big Issue* sells 800,000 copies a month worldwide, making it the biggest-selling street magazine. The magazine is sold by the homeless and helps 8,000–10,000 vendors a year in Los Angeles, USA, Melbourne, Sydney and Brisbane, Australia, Cape Town, South Africa (pictured below), and the United Kingdom.

animation and comic strips

Animated Film. This is a record for any Oscar category. Three of the nominations, *The Lyp Synch* series featuring *Creature Comforts*, *The Wrong Trousers* and *A Close Shave*, which were all directed by Nick Park, went on to win Oscars.

MOST CELEBRITIES FEATURED IN AN ANIMATION SERIES
The Simpsons became a regular series on 14 Jan 1990 and has featured a total of 120 celebrities. Guest stars have included Gillian Anderson, Magic Johnson and Elizabeth Taylor.

MOST VIDEO GAMES INSPIRED BY AN ANIMATED SERIES
Gundam, a Japanese TV series about enemies who become robots to fight one another, has inspired Robotec (which in turn inspired the toys Transformers), as well as countless Sony PlayStation spin-offs.

after the broadcast with epilepsy-type symptoms. An explosion scene followed by five seconds of red lights flashing from the eyes of a rat-like creature called Pikachu was said by experts to be to blame for causing the fits.

MOST EXPENSIVE CELLS
One of the 150,000 colour cells from Walt Disney's animated

TOP FIRST-RUN GROSS
Walt Disney's *The Lion King* (USA, 1994) grossed a record $766.15 million (£499.80 million) worldwide and was screened in more than 60 countries. A 600-strong animation crew spent three years making the film, which featured the voices of Jeremy Irons, James Earl Jones, Rowan Atkinson and Whoopi Goldberg. In 1995, Elton John and Tim Rice's *Can You Feel the Love Tonight*, the hit theme tune from *The Lion King*, won an Oscar for Best Original Song.

MOST EXPENSIVE ANIMATED FILM
Walt Disney's *Beauty and the Beast* (USA, 1992) cost $35 million (£20 million). The remake of *Fantasia*, which is not expected to be completed for another two years, is expected to be more expensive.

TOP-GROSSING ANIMATED FILM
The Jungle Book (USA, 1967) is the highest-grossing animated film ever. In an inflation-adjusted list of the top-grossing movies of all time it would come eighth. *The Lion King* would be 23rd.

MOST CONSECUTIVE OSCAR NOMINATIONS
From 1991 to 1997 Aardman Animation of Bristol, UK, received six consecutive Oscar nominations for Best Short

MOST FITS CAUSED BY A TV SHOW
In Dec 1997 more than 700 children in Japan were rushed to hospital when an episode of an animated series based on the Nintendo game Pocket Monsters triggered convulsions. A total of 208 people from the age of three upwards were detained in hospital

fairy tale *Snow White* (USA, 1937) was sold in 1991 for a record £115,000 ($203,000).

A black-and-white drawing from Walt Disney's *Orphan's Benefit* (1934) raised £171,250 ($280,000) when it was sold at Christie's, London, UK, in 1989.

BEST-KNOWN MANGA TITLE
The Japanese animation known as manga became a hit after its first title *Akira* was made into a film and released on video in 1991. Japan produces an estimated 2.3 billion manga titles a year, which accounts for 38% of all books and magazines sold in Japan. The manga business is worth $7–9 billion (£4–5 billion) in Japan alone.

MOST SUCCESSFUL ANIMATED FILM CHARACTER

Steamboat Willie (USA, 1928) premiered at the Colony Theater, New York, USA, on 18 Nov 1928 and marked the debut of Mickey Mouse, who went on to become the most successful cartoon character of all time.

LONGEST ANIMATED SERIES

Harry 'Bud' Fisher's *Mutt and Jeff* began as a comic supplement to *Pathe's Weekly* on 10 Feb 1913 and continued as separate weekly reels from 1 April 1916 until 1 Dec 1926, although no titles have been traced for 1923–24. There were at least 323 films produced.

OLDEST ANIMATED FILMS IN REGULAR DISTRIBUTION

Several of the *Mutt and Jeff* films have been colourized and synchronized for video release.

LONGEST SERIES OF 'TALKIES'

Max Fleisher's *Popeye The Sailor Man*, which was produced for the cinema between 1933 and 1957, consisted of 233 one-reelers and a single two-reeler. A further 220 Popeye cartoons were produced for television by King Features during the 1970s.

LONGEST AMATEUR ANIMATION

The British Film Institute has accepted a film which has been produced by a British man over a period of 28 years for inclusion in their film archives. It involves 100,000 hand-painted cells and runs for 2 hr 33 min.

MOST VALUABLE COMIC BOOK

The rarest comic book is an issue of *Detective* (No.27) in which Batman first appears. It was sold at auction for a record $85,000 (£52,000).

MOST FILMED COMIC STRIP CHARACTER

Zorro has been portrayed in 69 films to date. Originated by Johnston McCulley, he was also the first comic strip character to be the subject of a major feature film, *The Mark of Zorro* (USA, 1920) starring Douglas Fairbanks. The movie appeared just one year after the comic strip was printed, making Zorro the fastest comic strip character to make it from strip to the silver screen.

LONGEST-RUNNING NEWSPAPER STRIP

The 'Katzenjammer Kids', created by Rudolph Dirks, was first published in the *New York Journal* in Dec 1897, making it the longest-running newspaper strip in the world. It is now drawn by cartoonist Hy Eisman and is syndicated to 50 newspapers by King Features Syndicate.

MOST SYNDICATED COMIC STRIP

'Peanuts' by Charles Schulz was first published in Oct 1950 in the USA. The comic strip, featuring characters including Charlie Brown and Snoopy, now appears in 2,620 newspapers in 75 countries and 26 languages.

MOST COMIC BOOKS BY A WRITER

Paul S. Newman has written more than 4,000 published stories for 360 different comic book titles, including *Superman*, *Mighty Mouse*, *Prince Valiant*, *Fat Albert*, *Tweety and Sylvester* and *The Lone Ranger*.

LONGEST SERIES

On 26 April 1998 the 200th episode of *The Simpsons* was aired on the Fox network, making it the longest-running prime-time animation series. Now in its ninth prime-time series on Fox, *The Simpsons* has been screened in 70 countries.

art and installations

BIGGEST OUTDOOR INSTALLATION

Desert Breath covers 10 ha (25 acres) and is made up of 178 cones, 89 sand cones and 89 conical depressions cut into the floor of the desert near the town of Hurghada in Egypt. It took a team of three Greek artists nine months to create, and will erode within a few years.

BIGGEST ARCHITECTURAL INSTALLATION

Tight Roaring Circle, a 12-m-tall (39-ft), 19-m-wide (62-ft) bouncy castle made of 2,725 m² (29,333 ft²) of white PVC-coated polyester was designed by Dana Caspersen and William Forsythe and constructed in three weeks inside the Roundhouse, a circular railway turntable shed in London, UK, by Southern Inflatables in 1997. Visitors were invited to interact with the structure, spurred on by low lighting, an ambient soundtrack by Joel Ryan and text by the late Japanese writer Yukio Mishima printed on the courtyard walls.

BIGGEST INSTALLATION ON THE NEW YORK SUBWAY

In Dec 1996 Alexander Brodsky placed four gondolas on an unused track of a downtown subway in New York, USA. The project, *Arts for Transit*, was funded by the US Public Arts Fund.

MOST EXPENSIVE LANDSCAPE ARTWORK

Christo's $23-million (£13.37-million) work *The Umbrellas* (1991) involved 1,340 huge yellow umbrellas on farmland in California, USA, and a further 1,760 blue umbrellas in Japan. They were simultaneously opened by 810 workers.

BIGGEST FLOWER SCULPTURE

In 1992 US artist Jeff Koons erected *Puppy*, a 12.3-m x 5.5-m x 6-m (40-ft 5-in x 18-ft x 19-ft 6-in) flower sculpture at the Documenta exhibition in Kassel, Germany.

LONGEST SKETCH PROJECT

Alan Whitworth has been sketching Hadrian's Wall on the border of Scotland and England for more than 12 years. His sketch will be 117 km (73 miles) long when it is finished in 2007.

MOST VALUABLE PAINTING

The *Mona Lisa* (*La Gioconda*) by Leonardo da Vinci was assessed at $100 million (£35 million) for insurance purposes for its move to Washington DC and New York, USA, for exhibition from 1962 to 1963. Insurance was not concluded, as the cost of the closest security precautions was less than that of the premiums.

MOST EXPENSIVE PAINTING

Portrait of Dr Gachet by Vincent van Gogh sold at Christie's, New York, USA, for $82.5 million (£49.1 million) in May 1990. It depicts Van Gogh's doctor and was completed weeks before the artist's suicide in 1890.

MOST EXPENSIVE PAINTING BY A FEMALE ARTIST

In the Box by the US artist Mary Cassatt, who died in 1926, sold at Christie's, New York, USA, for $3.67 million (£2.45 million) on 23 May 1996. Seven of the 10 highest prices paid for female artists have been for works by Mary Cassatt.

MOST SUCCESSFUL GRAFFITI ARTIST

Keith Haring, who died in 1990, began his graffiti career by chalkdrawing on black paper pasted over expired adverts on the subway in New York, USA. He went on to paint murals all over the world and had 85 solo and more than 50 group exhibitions. There are permanent Haring collections in more than 15 countries. Seen here is *Untitled (Breakers)*.

MOST SUCCESSFUL POP ARTIST

Andy Warhol has had more than 80 exhibitions worldwide since 1952 and boasts eight permanent collections in the USA, as well as one at the Moderna Museet in Stockholm, Sweden, and another at the Tate Gallery in London, UK. Warhol, who began as a window dresser in Pittsburgh, USA, and designed adverts for sanitary towels after moving to New York in the 1950s, went on to become the most iconic figure in the Pop Art movement. From the age of six he was fascinated by glamour and collected film memorabilia, including magazines, movie posters and photographs. He filmed and taped much of his own life, and by his death in 1987 had captured about 6,000 hours of his life on film. Among the subjects that he painted were Campbell soup cans, Coca-Cola bottles and Marilyn Monroe. His most expensive work, *Marilyn X100*, sold for $17.3 million (£10.6 million) – more than four times the previous price for a Warhol – at Sotheby's, New York, USA, in May 1998.

BIGGEST LAND PORTRAIT

Crop artist Stan Herd uses his tractor to carve pictures into the landscape. His largest work to date is his 65-ha (160-acre) portrait of cowboy Will Rogers on the planes of south-west Kansas, USA. His other well-known works include a sunflower still life and a portrait of Native American Saginaw Grant (pictured here) in a 12-ha (30-acre) wheat field.

MOST EXPENSIVE 20TH-CENTURY PAINTING

Les Noces de Pierette by Pablo Picasso sold for $80.44 million (£51.89 million) in Paris, France, in 1986.

MOST EXPENSIVE PAINTING BY AN ANONYMOUS ARTIST

Departure of the Argonauts (1487) sold at Sotheby's, London, UK, for £4.2 million ($6.7 million) on 9 Dec 1989.

HIGHEST PRICE PAID AT AUCTION FOR A PHOTOGRAPH

Hand With Thimble (1920), Alfred Stieglitz's photograph of one of artist Georgia O'Keeffe's hands, raised $398,500 (£260,458) at auction at Christie's, New York, USA, on 8 Oct 1993.

MOST EXPENSIVE POSTER

A poster by Charles Rennie Mackintosh advertising an 1895 art show at the Glasgow Institute of Fine Arts, UK, sold for £68,200 ($105,028) at Christie's, London, UK, in Feb 1993.

MOST AUCTION SALES BY AN ARTIST

By May 1997 works by Picasso had been sold at auction 3,579 times. The total value of these sales is $1.07 billion (£668.8 million).

MOST RAISED BY A PRIVATE ART COLLECTION AT AUCTION

Victor and Sally Ganz's collection, which included works by Picasso and Johns, raised $207.04 million (£129.4 million) at Christie's, New York, USA, in Nov 1997. A two-week exhibition prior to the auction had 25,000 visitors.

MOST STOLEN WORKS OF ART

The artist believed to have had the most works stolen is Picasso, with around 350 pieces missing worldwide. Also missing are nearly 270 Mirós and 250 Chagalls.

BIGGEST GALLERY ENDOWMENT

The J. Paul Getty Museum, Malibu, California, USA, was set up in Jan 1974 for $1.64 billion (£700 million) and has an annual budget of $100 million-plus (£60 million) to stock its 38 galleries with art.

MOST VISITORS TO AN ART GALLERY IN A YEAR

In 1995 the Centre Pompidou in Paris, France, had a record 6,311,526 visitors.

MOST VISITED OUTDOOR EXHIBIT

In 1995 Christo attracted 5 million people to Berlin, Germany, when he wrapped the former parliament building, the Reichstag, in 109 km (68 miles) of silver polypropylene fabric. The cost of the installation was $7 million (£4.5 million).

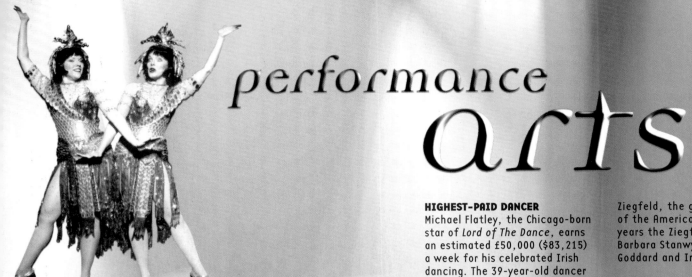

performance arts

HIGHEST-PAID DANCER

Michael Flatley, the Chicago-born star of *Lord of The Dance*, earns an estimated £50,000 ($83,215) a week for his celebrated Irish dancing. The 39-year-old dancer first found fame through dancing at the 1994 Eurovision Song Contest in Dublin, Republic of Ireland, and in the phenomenally successful *Riverdance* show.

MOST CURTAIN CALLS FOR A BALLET

The record for the greatest number of curtain calls known to have been received at any ballet is 89, by Dame Margot Fonteyn and Rudolf Nureyev after a performance of *Swan Lake* at the Vienna Staatsoper, Austria, in Oct 1964.

LONGEST CHORUS LINES

The longest chorus lines in performing history contained up to 120 dancers, in some of the early Ziegfeld's Follies, which were created by Florenz Ziegfeld, the greatest exponent of the American revue. Over the years the Ziegfeld girls included Barbara Stanwyck, Paulette Goddard and Irene Dunn.

HIGHEST-INSURED SHOW

The producers of *Barnum*, which opened at the London Palladium, UK, on 11 June 1981, insured the musical for the sum of £5 million ($10 million). The individual insurance for its star Michael Crawford, who had to walk a high-wire and slide down a rope from the topmost box to the stage, accounted for £3 million ($6 million) of the total.

LONGEST-RUNNING ANNUAL REVUE

The Ziegfeld Follies went through a total of 25 editions between 1907 and 1957, making them the world's longest-running annual revue. The elaborate costumes accounted for half of the cost of the productions.

BIGGEST THEATRICAL LOSSES

Side Show, a musical about real-life Siamese twins who became performers, is the third-biggest flop in Broadway history, closing after just three months in 1998. The biggest-ever theatrical loss was $7 million (£4.2 million), by the US producers of the Royal Shakespeare Company's musical *Carrie*, which closed in May 1988 after five performances on Broadway. The musical was based on the successful Stephen King novel of 1974 and the 1976 film starring Sissy Spacek and John Travolta.

LONGEST-RUNNING MUSICAL ON BROADWAY AND IN THE WEST END

On 19 June 1997 the musical *Cats*, which was composed by Andrew Lloyd Webber, became the longest-running musical on Broadway when it was performed at the Winter Garden Theater, New York, USA, for the 6,138th time since 7 Oct 1982. The record was previously held by *A Chorus Line*, which was last staged in April 1990. By the time *Cats* took the record, more than 8.25 million people had seen the show and it had grossed $329 million (£200 million) on Broadway alone. In its first 15 years on Broadway the show used 1 tonne of yak hair for wigs, more than 48,000 condoms to protect body microphones from perspiration, as well as 327 litres (72 gallons) of shampoo and 684,000 kg (1,508,000 lb) of dry ice. The show opened at the New London Theatre on Drury Lane, London, UK, on 11 May 1981 and became London's longest-running musical in Jan 1996. On 2 June 1998 it was performed in London's West End for the 7,315th time and by that date had grossed more than $2 billion (£1.25 billion) worldwide. *Cats* has been seen by an estimated 50 million people in approximately 250 cities.

LONGEST CONTINUOUS THEATRICAL RUN

The Mousetrap, written by Agatha Christie, opened at the Ambassadors Theatre, London, UK, on 25 Nov 1952. On 25 March 1974, after a total of 8,862 performances, it moved to St Martin's Theatre next door. On 1 June 1998 the 18,944th performance took place. The box office has grossed £20 million ($33.3 million) from more than 9 million theatre-goers.

SHORTEST THEATRICAL RUN

Scene changes during *The Intimate Revue* at the Duchess Theatre, London, UK, on 11 March 1930 took up to 20 minutes each and in order to reach the finale before midnight the management had to scrap seven scenes, leaving what was described as 'half a performance'.

MOST STRUTTERS

When *A Chorus Line* broke the record as the then longest-running Broadway show ever on 29 Sept 1983, the show's finale featured a total of 332 top-hatted 'strutters'.

MOST FREQUENTLY-ADAPTED PLAY

A Day Well Spent, a one-act farce written by John Oxenford in 1835, has been adapted as *Einen Jux will er sich machen* (1842) by Johann Nestroy, *The Merchant of Yonkers* (1938) by Thornton Wilder, *The Matchmaker* (1954) by Thornton Wilder, *Hello Dolly* (1963) by Jerry Herman and Michael Stewart and *On The Razzle* (1981) by Tom Stoppard.

BIGGEST ARTS FESTIVAL

The annual Edinburgh Fringe Festival, UK, began in 1947 and saw its busiest year in 1993, when 582 theatre groups gave a total of 14,108 performances of 1,643 shows between 15 Aug and 4 Sept.

LONGEST PLAY

The longest known play is *The Non-Stop Connolly Show* by John Arden, which took 26½ hours to perform in Dublin, Republic of Ireland, in 1975.

SHORTEST PLAY

The world's shortest ever play is the 30-second *Breath*, which was written by the Irish playwright and novelist Samuel Beckett in 1969.

MOST LEAD PERFORMANCES

Kanmi Fujiyama played the lead role in 10,288 performances by the Japanese comedy company Sochiku Shikigeki from Nov 1966 to June 1983.

MOST THEATRICAL ROLES

Kanzaburo Nakamura performed in 806 Kabuki titles from 1926 to 1987. As each title in this classical Japanese theatrical form lasts for 25 days, he had given 20,150 performances.

MOST DURABLE UNDERSTUDY

In March 1994 79-year-old Nancy Seabrooke retired from *The Mousetrap* after understudying the part of Mrs Boyle for 15 years

and 6,240 performances. She had performed the part 72 times.

MOST FAMILY MEMBERS ON STAGE AT ONCE

A record 22 members of the Terry family (including Sir John Gielgud's mother, Kate) appeared in a Masked Dance from Shakespeare's *Much Ado About Nothing* at Ellen Terry's Jubilee Matinée, Drury Lane, London, UK, on 12 June 1906.

MOST TIME SPENT IN BED TOGETHER BY A STAGE COUPLE

Jessica Tandy and Hume Cronyn were married in 1942 and spent more time in bed together than any other stage couple. They opened at the Ethel Barrymore Theater, New York, USA, in Jan de Hartog's *The Fourposter* in Oct 1951 and played the bed-bound characters on Broadway and on tour for the next two years.

circus stunts and feats

HIGHEST CROSSING OF THE THAMES

On 14 Sept 1997 Didier Pasquette of France (pictured left in front of St Pauls Cathedral) and Jade Kindar-Martin from the USA became the first tightrope walkers to cross the River Thames, London, UK, simultaneously in opposite directions. The 300-m-long (1,000-ft), 2.5-cm-thick (1-in) wire was 45.7 m (150 ft) above the river. At the point where they met, in the centre of the high wire, Pasquette squatted down and Kindar-Martin stepped over him. They had planned to celebrate their meeting in the middle with a glass of champagne, but instead shook hands and threw white roses into the river in memory of Diana, Princess of Wales. The pair, who belong to French acrobatic team Les Tréteaux du Cœur Volant, then performed a series of stunts while sitting, kneeling and lying on the wire. The death-defying feat, which was accomplished without safety nets, was only the third successful crossing of the river, as well as being the highest and longest ever. Had the pair fallen, they would have plunged into 2.44 m (8 ft) of water at about 96.56 km/h (60 mph). The first completed tightrope walk across the River Thames was by another Frenchman, Charles Elleano, in 1951. A German, Franz Burbach, followed him in 1972.

HIGHEST AERIAL ACT

On 10 Aug 1995 Mike Howard performed a trapeze act at a record altitude of 6,000–6,200 m (19,600–20,300 ft). The trapeze was suspended from a hot-air balloon between Glastonbury and Street, Somerset, UK.

BIGGEST HUMAN MOBILE

In 1996 a record 16 performers from the Circus of Horrors, which is based at Addlestone Moor, Surrey, UK, were suspended from a crane to form a human mobile in Munich, Germany.

HIGHEST HIGH-WIRE

The world's highest ever ground-supported high-wire feat took place at an altitude of 411 m (1,350 ft). It was performed by Philippe Petit of France between the towers of the World Trade Center, New York, USA, on 7 Aug 1974.

GREATEST TIGHTROPE DROP

On 4 Aug 1989 Michel Menin from Lons-le-Saunier, France, walked a record-breaking 3,150 m (10,335 ft) on a tightrope above the French countryside.

LONGEST TIGHTROPE WALK

The world tightrope endurance record of 205 days was set by Jorge Ojeda-Guzman from Orlando, Florida, USA, between 1 Jan and 25 July 1993. The 11-m-long (36-ft) wire was 10.7 m (35 ft) above the ground. Ojeda-Guzman entertained the crowds of spectators by walking, balancing on a chair and dancing. He had a 91 x 91-cm (3 x 3-ft) wooden cabin at one end of the tightrope.

MOST PEOPLE JUMPED OVER ON A HIGH-WIRE

On 26 Dec 1996, during a performance for Ringling Brothers and Barnum & Bailey Circus, Tampa, Florida, USA, Walter Guerrero from Colombia jumped over a total of four people who were sitting on the high-wire.

GREATEST DISTANCE COVERED BY A HUMAN ARROW

The Bulgarian artiste Vesta Gueschkova, whose stage name was 'Airiana', was fired a record distance of 22.9 m (75 ft) from a crossbow at Ringling Brothers and Barnum & Bailey Circus, Tampa, Florida, USA, on 27 Dec 1995.

MOST SWORDS SWALLOWED

Edward Benjamin of Binghamton, New York, USA, known by his stage name of 'Count Desmond', swallowed 13 blades 58.4 cm (23 in) in length to below his xiphisternum. The circus performer injured himself in the process of breaking the record.

MOST PEOPLE ON ONE BICYCLE

In 1996 a record 17 people from the Shan Dong Acrobatic Troupe with Phillip Gandey's Chinese State Circus rode one bicycle.

TALLEST STILTS

Eddy Wolf ('Steady Eddy') from Loyal, Wisconsin, USA, mastered aluminium stilts which measured 12.36 m (40 ft 9½ in) from the ground to his ankle. He walked 25 steps without touching his safety handrail wires on 3 Aug 1988.

TALLEST UNICYCLE

The tallest unicycle was 31 m (101 ft 9 in) in height. Steve McPeak rode the unicycle, with a safety wire suspended from an overhead crane, for a distance of 114.6 m (376 ft) in Las Vegas, USA, in Oct 1980.

BIGGEST OUTDOOR ILLUSION

In 1993 magician David Copperfield made the Statue of Liberty in New York, USA, 'disappear': a helicopter overhead shone lights on what appeared to be an empty space.

MOST DANGEROUS PERFORMANCE GROUPS

French group Archaos' shows have featured chainsaw jugglers, stock cars and pyrotechnics. More recently, the group DNTT have shocked audiences with electric chairs and fire-based phenomena. Their show in Berlin, Germany, boasted green fire, exploding bodies, slimy people descending from hanging pods and a finale in which the whole set is destroyed.

LONGEST HUMAN CANNONBALL

Dave Smith Sr. and his son Dave Smith Jr. are seen here in the US TV show *Guinness World Records™: Primetime* attempting a new world record for the greatest distance travelled by a human cannonball. Dave Sr. equalled his own world record of 54.86 m (180 ft), but Dave Jr. went further than his dad, setting a new distance of 59.43 m (185 ft).

HIGHEST-EARNING CIRCUS GROUP
Global theatre group Cirque du Soleil has an annual turnover of more than $88 million (£53 million). It has grown from a company started by two French performers to a multinational corporation employing 1,250 people in Las Vegas, USA.

BIGGEST GATHERING OF STREET/CIRCUS PERFORMERS
Glastonbury Festival, UK, which attracts acts from all over the world every year, is the largest gathering of street/circus performers to date. In 1994 a total of 700 people juggled at one time.

MOST METAL BENT
Uri Geller reputedly bent 5,000 pieces of cutlery by the power of his mind, and stuck them onto his custom-built 1976 Cadillac. The car featured in *Mindbender*, the film inspired by Geller's life and directed by Ken Russell in 1995.

SCORPION HANDLING
Rohayo Ramli plays with hundreds of deadly scorpions in a cage at an exhibition in Seremban, in Negeri Sembilan, Malaysia, on 21 March 1998. Ramli, who used to be a dancer, began scorpion handling two years ago, having discovered that she enjoyed the feel of arachnids on her skin. People have long been fascinated by the behaviour of arachnids and insects and their reactions to human contact. In June 1924 Frank Bornhofer was photographed wearing a helmet and chin strap covered in bees in Cincinnati, Ohio, USA. The purpose of the exercise was to prove that bees rarely sting. As Bornhofer had predicted, he did not receive a single sting.

SNAKE CHARMING
The annual International Snake Charmers Competition was first held in Perlis state, Malaysia, in Sept 1997. It attracted more than 40 snake tamers from around the world, who competed for a first prize of $2,000 (£1,210). Snake charmer Osman Ayub from Langkawi Island, Perlis, Malaysia, is pictured holding a poisonous cat snake (family Colubridae) in his mouth during the first competition.

WORLD TRADE CENTER FEATS
Former professional stuntman Daniel Goodwin climbed the sheer face of the North Tower of the World Trade Center, New York, USA, in May 1983. Almost a decade previously, in Aug 1974, the 419-m-high (1,375-ft) towers had also been the location for the world's highest ever ground-supported high-wire feat, which was performed by the French trapeze artist Philippe Petit.

225

music &
fashion

pop

BIGGEST-SELLING ALBUM

Michael Jackson's *Thriller* (1982) has sold more than 45 million copies globally. Of these, 25 million were sold in the USA, making it the biggest-selling album in the country.

Sgt Pepper's Lonely Hearts Club Band by the Beatles has sold more than 4.3 million copies in the UK. Since it was first released in June 1967 it has re-charted on several occasions and last reached the Top 40 in April 1998.

BIGGEST-SELLING ALBUM BY A MALE SOLOIST IN THE UK

Michael Jackson's *Bad* (1987) has sold 3.9 million copies in the UK. His *Thriller* (1982) is the second most successful album, with sales of more than 3.3 million.

BIGGEST-SELLING ALBUM IN THE UK BY A FEMALE SOLOIST

The Immaculate Collection by Madonna (1990) has had UK sales of more than 2.7 million.

BIGGEST UK ADVANCE ORDERS

Spiceworld (1997) by the Spice Girls had record UK advance orders of 1.4 million. The global advance order was 6 million.

YOUNGEST SINGER TO TOP US SINGLES CHART

Michael Jackson was 11 years five months old when he sang lead on *I Want You Back* by the Jackson Five, which reached No. 1 on the US chart in 1970.

YOUNGEST SINGER TO TOP UK SINGLES CHART

Jimmy Osmond was nine years eight months old when he reached No. 1 in 1972, with *Long Haired Lover From Liverpool*.

LONGEST PERIOD AT NO. 1 ON US SINGLES CHART

Mariah Carey was at No. 1 on the US chart for 26 out of 33 weeks between Sept 1995 and May 1996, with the singles *Fantasy* (eight weeks), *One Sweet Day* – recorded with Boyz II Men – (16 weeks) and *Always Be My Baby* (two weeks). She broke the record of 25 weeks set by Elvis Presley in 1956.

MOST WEEKS ON SINGLES CHART IN THE USA

You Were Meant For Me/Foolish Games by Jewel spent a record 65 weeks on the US chart from 30 Nov 1996 to 21 Feb 1998.

MOST CONSECUTIVE WEEKS AT NO. 1 IN THE USA

One Sweet Day by Mariah Carey & Boyz II Men spent 16 consecutive weeks at the top of the US singles chart in 1995/96. Boyz II Men feature in three of the six records to have topped the US charts for the longest time.

MOST CONSECUTIVE TOP 5 SINGLES IN THE USA

Madonna had a record-breaking 16 successive US Top 5 singles between 1984 and 1989 and 27 consecutive Top 20 entries between 1983 and 1992.

MOST BRIT AWARDS (NON-UK)

The most successful ever non-UK/US solo artist at the annual Brit Awards is the Icelandic singer/songwriter Björk, with a total of three. Björk began her recording career at the age of 11 with an eponymously-titled album of covers and went on to front the Sugarcubes in Iceland. In 1993 her album *Debut* secured her international fame.

MOST SUCCESSFUL FEMALE ARTIST

No female artist has sold more records around the world than Madonna, who has had total sales of more than 100 million. She is the most successful female artist on both the US chart, with a total of 35 Top 20 singles and 10 Top 10 albums since 1983, and the UK chart, with 45 Top 20 entries and 13 Top 10 albums (including six No. 1s — a UK chart record for any female artist).

MOST SUCCESSFUL SIBLINGS

Michael and Janet Jackson are the only siblings to have separately topped the US singles and album charts. Michael has amassed 13 No. 1 singles and four chart-topping albums and Janet has had eight No. 1 singles and three No. 1 albums.

MOST SUCCESSFUL DUOS

The most successful duo in the USA is Daryl Hall & John Oates, with 22 Top 20 singles.

The most successful duo in the UK is the Pet Shop Boys, who have had 28 Top 20 singles.

MOST SUCCESSFUL SONGWRITER

Lionel Richie wrote at least one No. 1 hit in the USA every year between 1978 and 1987.

MOST SUCCESSFUL CONCERT SERIES

Michael Jackson sold out for seven nights at Wembley Stadium, UK, in Aug 1988.

YOUNGEST GROUP TO EARN A PLATINUM SINGLE IN THE UK

Mmmbop by the American trio Hanson went to No. 1 in a total of 20 countries and passed the 600,000 sales mark in the UK in 1997, when the Hanson brothers' average age was 14. When the single was at No. 1 in the USA, the group's youngest member, drummer Zachary, was 11 years six months old — just one month older than Michael Jackson had been when the Jackson Five went to the top of the US charts with *I Want You Back* in 1970. Hanson's album *Middle of Nowhere* has sold about 6 million copies worldwide and been widely acclaimed as a classic pop album. Zachary and his brothers Taylor, the band's 14-year-old vocalist and keyboard player, and Isaac, the 17-year-old guitarist, all studied classical piano for at least five years and write a proportion of their songs. Now managed by their father, they were spotted at the South By Southwest music conference at Austin, Texas, by an entertainment lawyer and Grateful Dead fanatic, Christopher Sabec, in 1994. They join a long line of youthful pop stars, including the Osmonds, the Jackson Five, Five Star, Musical Youth, Aaron Carter and Cleopatra.

MUSIC RECORDS

Because of the localized nature of the music industry, the records on the music pages are a mixture of US, British and World records.

MOST SUCCESSFUL SINGLES DEBUT IN THE USA

Mariah Carey's first 11 singles all reached the US Top 5. She had 13 No. 1 singles in the 1990s and has topped the chart for 58 weeks — a record only bettered by Elvis Presley and the Beatles. Carey also holds the records for the most successive US No. 1 singles by a newcomer (her first five singles reached No. 1) and for the most singles to enter at No. 1, with three by April 1998.

MOST SUCCESSIVE UK NO. 1 SINGLES BY A NEWCOMER

The Spice Girls reached No. 1 with their first six singles in the UK.

MOST CONSECUTIVE TOP 10 HITS IN THE UK

From 1984 to 1994 Madonna amassed a record 32 successive Top 10 entries in the UK.

BIGGEST-SELLING DEBUT ALBUM

Spice (1996), the debut album by the Spice Girls, is both the biggest- and fastest-selling debut album by a British act. The five-piece band, now four after the departure of Geri Halliwell ('Ginger Spice'), topped the charts in 14 countries and had worldwide sales of more than 20 million. It is also the biggest-selling debut album by any recording artist in the UK, with certified sales of 3 million.

MOST SUCCESSFUL SINGLE BY A GERMAN ACT IN THE UK

Nena's *99 Red Balloons* topped the UK chart for three weeks in 1984. The original German version reached No. 2 in the USA.

MOST SUCCESSFUL SINGLE BY A SWEDISH ACT IN THE USA

The Sign by Swedish group Ace of Base remained at No. 1 in the USA for four weeks in 1994.

MOST NO. 1S BY A SINGLE

Chubby Checker's *The Twist* topped the US chart in Sept 1960 and Jan 1962, and *Bohemian Rhapsody* by Queen was No. 1 in the UK in Nov 1975 and Dec 1991.

MOST SUCCESSFUL BOY BANDS

The biggest-earning boy band in the world were New Kids on the Block, who were reported to have had gross revenues of $861 million (£512.5 million) at the peak of their career from 1989 to 1991. No US band has beaten the nine consecutive US Top 10 entries by the band between 1988 and 1990. New Kids on the Block also hold the record for the greatest number of UK Top 10 hits in a calendar year, with eight in 1990.

The greatest number of No. 1 singles on the UK chart by a British boy band is eight, by Take That, between 1993 and 1996.

MOST BRIT AWARDS

The most Brit Awards won by a British performer is seven, by Annie Lennox.

The most successful US artist at the Brit Awards is The Artist (formerly known as Prince), who has won seven awards, one of which was for the music from the film *Batman* (1989).

MOST SUCCESSFULL NON UK DEBUT

Former Australian soap star Kylie Minogue's first 11 singles all reached the UK Top 5. Kylie was also the youngest female artist to top the UK album chart with *Kylie* in 1988, when she was 20 years 8 months old. It sold nearly 2 million copies in the UK. Kylie's record for the most succesful foreign debut was equalled by Boyzone in 1998.

MOST AUSTRALIAN AWARDS

The record for the greatest ever number of Aria (Australian Record Industry Association) awards won by an act in one year is 10, by Savage Garden in 1997. In all they were nominated in a record 13 out of 26 categories.

LONGEST-RUNNING POP SHOW

The BBC show *Top of the Pops* was first presented by Jimmy Saville on 1 Jan 1964 and featured, among other acts, the Rolling Stones and the Beatles. The programme's 1,782th episode was aired on 1 May 1998.

pop classics

MOST SUCCESSFUL GROUP
The Beatles have sold around 1 billion records and cassettes and had a record 18 US No. 1 albums, and 14 UK No. 1 albums.

MOST SUCCESSFUL FAMILY GROUP IN THE USA AND UK
Between 1968 and 1998 the Bee Gees accumulated 24 Top 20 singles in the USA and UK. They have also had 13 Top 20 albums in the USA and 11 in the UK.

MOST SUCCESSFUL SONGWRITERS
The most US No. 1s in a calendar year is seven, by John Lennon and Paul McCartney with *I Want To Hold Your Hand*, *She Loves You*, *Can't Buy Me Love*, *Love Me Do*, *A World Without Love*, *A Hard Day's Night* and *I Feel Fine* in 1964. Their songs held the top spot for 19 weeks of the year.

Barry Gibb wrote or co-wrote seven No. 1s in the 12-month period from 30 July 1976: *I Just Want To Be Your Everything*, *How Deep Is Your Love*, *Stayin' Alive*, *Love Is Thicker Than Water*, *Night Fever*, *If I Can't Have You* and *Shadow Dancing*. Together they held the top spot for 26 weeks.

MOST US NO. 1 ALBUMS IN A YEAR
The Monkees had a record four No. 1 albums on the US chart in one year: *The Monkees*, *More Of The Monkees*, *Headquarters* and *Pisces, Aquarius, Capricorn and Jones* in 1967.

LONGEST CAREER ON US TOP 20
Barbra Streisand first entered the US singles chart with *People* in May 1964. Her most recent hit, *I Finally Found Someone* (a duet with Bryan Adams), exited 32 years seven months later in Jan 1997. In 1987 she founded the Barbra Streisand Foundation for liberal causes and later founded a Streisand Chair in Cardiology and a Streisand Chair in Contemporary Gender Studies at two US universities.

MOST SUCCESSFUL SOLO ARTISTS
Elvis Presley was the world's most successful solo artist of the rock era, with 18 No. 1 singles and nine No. 1 albums in the USA and 17 No. 1 singles and six No. 1 albums in the UK. The first artist to reportedly sell 1 billion records, he had a record 94 chart entries in the USA and 98 in the UK.

In the pre rock era, Bing Crosby had 299 Top 20 entries in the USA, including 38 No. 1s.

ALBUM WITH MOST WEEKS AT NO. 1 IN THE USA (ROCK ERA)
The soundtrack to *West Side Story* charted in May 1962 and held the top spot on the stereo album chart for 54 weeks.

ALBUM WITH MOST WEEKS AT NO. 1 IN THE UK
The soundtrack to *South Pacific* (USA, 1958) headed the first ever UK album chart and remained at No. 1 for 115 weeks, of which 70 were consecutive.

MOST WEEKS ON SINGLES CHART IN THE UK
My Way by Frank Sinatra entered the UK chart on 10 separate occasions and spent a total of 124 weeks there between 1969 and 1994. In the USA Sinatra had a record career span of 39 years 7 months on the Top 20 album chart, from 1955 to 1994.

MOST ENTRIES ON THE UK TOP 5
Frankie Laine had three entries in the UK Top 5 on 7 Nov 1953, with *Answer Me* at No. 2, *Hey Joe* at No. 3 and *I Believe* at No. 5.

BIGGEST CD SET BY A SOLO ARTIST
France's most consistently successful recording artist is Johnny Hallyday, who released a 40-CD, 730-track set to mark his 50th birthday in 1993. The singer, who was still scoring big hits in 1998, is reported to have sold 80 million records worldwide – a record for a French artist.

TOP FRENCH LANGUAGE ALBUM
Celine Dion's *D'eux* (1995) has sold more than 8 million globally.

MOST SUCCESSFUL SINGLE BY FRENCH ACT IN THE UK
She by Charles Aznavour headed the chart for four weeks in 1974.

MOST FRENCH ACTS ON UK CHART
On 1 Oct 1977 the UK Top 10 included *Magic Fly* by Space, *Oxygene Part IV* by Jean Michel Jarre and *Black Is Black* by La Belle Epoque.

MOST SUCCESSFUL SINGLE BY A GERMAN ACT IN THE USA
Wunderland Bei Nacht by Bert Kaempfert & His Orchestra was No. 1 for three weeks in 1961.

MOST SUCCESSFUL SINGLE BY AUSTRALIAN ACT IN THE UK
Two Little Boys by Rolf Harris was at No. 1 for six weeks in 1969.

MOST AUSTRALIAN ACTS ON THE US CHART
On 14 November 1981 *The Night Owls* by the Little River Band, *Here I Am* by Air Supply and *I've Done Everything For You* by Rick Springfield were in the US Top 10 alongside *Physical* by Australian-raised Olivia Newton-John.

MOST SUCCESSFUL SINGLE BY AN ITALIAN ACT IN THE USA
Nel Blu Dipinto Di Blu (Volare) by Domenico Modugno spent five weeks at No. 1 in 1958.

MOST SUCCESSFUL EUROVISION SONG CONTEST WINNERS
The 1974 Eurovision Song Contest winner *Waterloo* launched the international career of Abba, who went on to become the most commercially successful group of the 70s and one of the biggest-selling acts of all time. They also became the most successful ever Swedish act in the UK, with a total of 19 Top 20 singles (nine of which went to No. 1) and eight No. 1 albums between 1974 and 1982. Abba split up in 1982 but experienced a revival in the early 1990s, when they topped the charts worldwide. In 1992 band members Bjorn Ulvaeus and Benny Anderson joined U2 on stage when the latter performed the Abba classic *Dancing Queen* during their *Zoo* tour. Nelson Mandela's favourite pop group, Abba's other hits included *Thank You For the Music*, *Super Trouper*, *Fernando*, *The Winner Takes It All*, *Chiquitita*, *I Do, I Do, I Do, I Do, I Do* and *Knowing Me Knowing You*. Six other Eurovision Song Contest winners have topped the British chart: three British (Sandie Shaw, Brotherhood Of Man and Bucks Fizz), two Irish (Dana and Johnny Logan) and one German (Nicole).

MOST SUCCESSFUL SINGLE BY JAPANESE ACT IN THE USA AND UK

Sukiyaki (Ue O Muite Aruko) by Kyu Sakamoto topped the US chart for three weeks in 1963 and reached the UK Top 10.

BIGGEST-SELLING SOUNDTRACK ALBUM IN THE UK & USA

The Bodyguard, starring Whitney Houston and Kevin Costner, has sold a record 2.1 million copies in the UK and more than 16 million in the USA since its release in 1992. It is also the top-selling international album in Japan, with sales of more than 2.5 million.

BIGGEST-SELLING FILM SCORE

The score of *Titanic* (1997) is the biggest- and fastest-selling film score ever. In the USA it sold 9 million copies in 15 weeks. A No. 1 album in more than 20 countries, it was the first record containing incidental film score music to top the UK charts. As of June 1998, it had sold close to 24 million copies worldwide.

MOST SUCCESSFUL INSTRUMENTAL ACT ON US ALBUM CHART

Herb Alpert & The Tijuana Brass had a record nine successive US Top 10 albums between 1963 and 1968. On 2 April 1966 they had four albums in the US Top 10.

MOST SUCCESSFUL INSTRUMENTAL SINGLE IN THE USA (ROCK ERA)

Cherry Pink And Apple Blossom White by Perez Prado & His Orchestra topped the chart for 10 weeks in 1955.

BIGGEST-SELLING RELIGIOUS ALBUM (IN THE ROCK ERA)

Chant (aka *Canto Gregoriano/ Major Works of Canto Gregori*) by the Benedictine Monks Of Santo Domingo De Silos (aka Monks Chorus Silos) from Spain sold more than 6 million copies worldwide in 1994 and reached the Top 10 in many countries, including the UK and USA.

MOST WINS IN THE EUROVISION SONG CONTEST

The most Eurovision Song Contest wins by one country is seven, by Ireland (1970, 1980, 1987, 1992, 1993, 1994, 1996).

Ireland's Johnny Logan won twice, in 1980 and 1987.

BIGGEST EUROVISION HIT IN USA

Abba's Eurovision Song Contest winner *Waterloo* reached No. 6 on the US singles chart in 1974.

The most successful finalist is *L'Amour est Bleu*, which came fourth in the 1967 contest sung by Vicky (Luxembourg). As *Love Is Blue* by Paul Mauriat & His Orchestra, the song topped the chart in 1968. It is the most successful ever single by a French act in the USA.

HIGHEST POINTS IN EUROVISION SONG CONTEST

The 1997 winner, the UK entry *Love Shine A Light* by Katrina & The Waves, scored 227 points.

MOST SUCCESSFUL JAMES BOND THEME IN THE USA AND UK

Duran Duran's *A View To A Kill* reached No. 1 in the USA and No. 2 in the UK in 1985.

MOST SUCCESSFUL COVER OF A JAMES BOND THEME

The highest chart position by a James Bond cover in the UK is No. 5, by *Live And Let Die* by Guns 'N' Roses in Dec 1991.

LONGEST TIME TAKEN BY A JAMES BOND THEME TO BECOME A HIT

Louis Armstrong's *We Have All The Time In The World*, the theme song to *On Her Majesty's Secret Service* (1969), reached No. 3 in the UK in Dec 1994, more than 25 years after it was originally released and 23 years 5 months after Armstrong's death.

MOST JAMES BOND THEMES

Of the 11 James Bond themes sung by women, three have been by Shirley Bassey: *Goldfinger*, *Diamonds Are Forever* and *Moonraker*. Bassey also holds the record for the longest career on the UK Top 20 singles chart by a female artist, at 40 years nine months. Born in Tiger Bay, Cardiff, UK, she now lives in Monte Carlo.

MOST SUCCESSFUL UK SOLO ARTIST

Elton John, pictured at his 50th birthday party with his partner David Furnish, is the most successful British solo singer of all time in both the USA and the UK. In his 30-year career, he has sold more than 150 million albums worldwide and in the USA his 56 Top 40 hits put him second only to Elvis Presley.

rock

BIGGEST-SELLING ALBUM BY A GROUP
The Eagles' *Greatest Hits 1971-75* is estimated to have sold more than 25 million copies worldwide. It is also the biggest-selling rock album in the USA, with certified sales of 24 million.

MOST WEEKS ON US ALBUM CHART
Dark Side Of The Moon by Pink Floyd entered the US chart on 17 March 1973 and is still there. It spent 741 weeks in the Top 200 and 353 weeks on the Pop Catalogue chart up to April 1998, topping the latter on its 1,075th chart week.

BIGGEST-SELLING HEAVY ROCK ALBUMS IN THE USA
Led Zeppelin IV (Four Symbols) by British band Led Zeppelin has sold 17 million copies since 1971.

Bruce Springsteen's *Born In The USA* (1984) is the top-selling album by a US rock act in the USA, with sales of 15 million.

BIGGEST-SELLING HEAVY ROCK ALBUM IN THE UK
Bat Out Of Hell by Meatloaf has sold more than 2.1 million copies in the UK since 1978. It had also spent a record 472 weeks on the UK album chart by April 1998.

BIGGEST-SELLING NON UK/US ROCK ALBUM IN THE USA
Australian group AC/DC's *Back In Black* (1980) has sold more than 12 million copies in the USA.

BIGGEST-SELLING NON UK/US ROCK ALBUM IN THE UK
Irish group U2's *Joshua Tree* (1987) has sold 1.8 million copies in the UK.

BEST-SELLING ALBUM IN JAPAN
Japan's top-selling album of all time is *Review*, by Japanese rock band Glay. The album has sold more than 4.7 million copies in Japan alone.

MOST SUCCESSFUL POSTHUMOUS ALBUMS IN THE USA
Kurt Cobain and his group Nirvana topped the US chart with *MTV Unplugged In New York* in Nov 1994 and with *From The Muddy Banks Of The Wishkah* in Oct 1996. Cobain died in April 1994.

BIGGEST-SELLING DEBUT ALBUM
Jagged Little Pill (1995) by Canada's Alanis Morissette has sold almost 30 million copies worldwide. It is also the biggest-selling album in the USA by a female artist.

MOST SUCCESSFUL ROCK SINGLE
Bryan Adams' *(Everything I Do) I Do It For You* spent a record 16 consecutive weeks at No. 1 in the UK and seven weeks at No. 1 in the USA in 1991.

MOST WEEKS AT NO. 1 ON US AIRPLAY CHART
Don't Speak by No Doubt spent 16 weeks at No. 1 on the US airplay chart in 1997 but was never available as a single so did not enter the US Top 100 sales chart.

MOST SUCCESSFUL SINGLE BY AN AUSTRALIAN ACT IN THE USA
Down Under by Men At Work was No. 1 for four weeks in 1983.

MOST SIMULTANEOUS 'INDIE' HITS IN THE UK
The Smiths held the top three places on the UK indie chart on 28 Jan 1984.

On 1 July 1995 Oasis had six singles in the top seven of the UK indie chart.

BIGGEST ROCK CONCERT
On 21 July 1990 an estimated 200,000 people watched Roger Water's production of Pink Floyd's *The Wall* at Potsdamer Platz on the border between East and West Berlin, Germany. It involved 600 performers.

BIGGEST CONCERT ATTENDANCES
The biggest audience at a paying concert was an estimated 195,000 people, who saw Norway's A-Ha play at the Rock in Rio festival, Brazil, in 1990.

The largest paying audience for a solo performer was an estimated 180,000-184,000, for Paul McCartney at the Macaranã Stadium, Rio de Janeiro, Brazil, on 21 April 1990. About 180,000 people are also believed to have watched Tina Turner's concert at the Macaranã Stadium in 1988.

The largest audience for a free concert by a solo artist was 3.5 million, to see Rod Stewart at Copacabana Beach, Rio de Janeiro, Brazil, on 31 Dec 1994.

BIGGEST SCREEN AT A CONCERT
The largest LED (light-emitting diodes) screen measures 16.7 x 51.8 m (55 x 170 ft) and was part of the set at U2's 1997 *PopMart* tour. It showed animation and art, including material by pop artists Andy Warhol and Roy Lichtenstein.

FASTEST-SELLING ALBUM (UK)
Be Here Now (1997) by Oasis sold a record 345,000 copies in the UK on its first day of release. By the third day it had sold 700,000 copies and within 17 days it had passed the 1 million mark. Like Oasis' first two albums, it entered the chart at No. 1, breaking the record for the most consecutive releases to enter in pole position. It also headed the charts in nine other countries in its first week of release.

MOST HIGHLY-PAID ROCK STARS
The Rolling Stones had an estimated gross income of $68 million (£40.4 million) in the year 1996-97, putting them 12th in the *Forbes* list of the world's highest-paid entertainers. The British band narrowly beat Celine Dion, who earned $65 million (£38.7 million), and David Bowie, who earned $63 million (£37.5 million). Formed in 1962, the Stones are the world's most enduring rock band: they had their first UK hit in 1963 with a version of Chuck Berry's *Come On* and made their debut on the US chart in 1964 with *(Tell Me) You're Coming Back*. The band were still charting on both sides of the Atlantic as recently as 1998. In 1994 and 1995 the band proved that they could still pull in the crowds when their *Voodoo Lounge* tour became the most successful tour of all time, taking an estimated $400 million (£238 million) in receipts. During the tour the band, most of whom are now in their 50s, put on 62 concerts instead of the scheduled 28. Their 1997 *Bridges to Babylon* tour surpassed this record, taking approximately $500 million (£297.6 million). The band currently consists of Keith Richards, Ron Wood, Charlie Watts, Darryl Jones and frontman Mick Jagger.

MOST DEATHS AT A ROCK CONCERT
Eleven Who fans were trampled to death at the band's gig in Cincinnati, USA, in 1979.

MOST CONTINENTS IN A DAY
Def Leppard staged shows on three continents on 24 Oct 1995, when they appeared in Tangiers, Morocco, London, UK, and Vancouver, Canada.

BIGGEST ROCK COLLECTION
The Hard Rock Cafe, Philadelphia, USA, has 45,000 pieces of rock memorabilia on display, including Madonna's black bustier and Sid Vicious' vinyl trousers.

MOST EXPENSIVE ROCK ITEM
John Lennon's 1965 psychedelic Rolls-Royce *Phantom V* touring limousine was sold at Sotheby's, New York, USA, on 29 June 1995, for $2.8 million (£1.8 million).

BIGGEST ROCK MUSEUM
Paul Allen, the co-founder of Microsoft and eighth richest man in the world, is donating his tens of thousands of pieces of Jimi Hendrix memorabilia to the new 12,077-m^2 (130,000-ft^2) Experience Music Project museum in Seattle, USA, which will be the world's largest rock museum. A legendary guitarist, songwriter and singer, Hendrix died in 1970 at the age of just 28. On 14 Sept 1997, more than a quarter of a century after his death, he became the first ever rock artist to have a prestigious English Heritage Blue Plaque placed on a building associated with him (his former house at 23 Brook Street, London, UK).

MOST EXPENSIVE ROCK INSTRUMENT
The most expensive rock instrument sold at auction is an acoustic guitar owned at various times by David Bowie, George Michael and Paul McCartney, which sold for £220,000 ($369,600) at Christie's, London, UK, on 18 May 1994.

MOST VALUABLE US ROCK RECORDING
There are only two copies of Bob Dylan's *The Freewheelin' Bob Dylan* (Columbia CS-8796, in stereo), because the album was later re-pressed without four of the songs. Near-mint condition copies would be worth $20,000–30,000 (£12,000–18,000).

MOST IMPRESSIVE CHART ENTRY
On 5 Oct 1991 *Use Your Illusion II* by Guns 'N' Roses entered the US album chart at No. 1 and *Use Your Illusion I* entered at No. 2 — the most impressive entry in US chart history. In total, 4.2 million copies of these albums were shipped in the first week. The group also hold the record for the biggest-selling album by a US rock group: their *Appetite For Destruction* (1987) has sold 14 million copies.

MOST SUCCESSFUL ROCK WIDOW
Courtney Love, who married Kurt Cobain of Nirvana in 1992, is the most successful rock widow of the 1990s. After an early acting appearance in Alex Cox's *Sid and Nancy* (1986), Love achieved rock fame with her band Hole, whose second album *Live Through This* coincided with Cobain's suicide in 1994. In 1996 she was nominated for a Golden Globe for her role in *The People vs. Larry Flynt*.

MOST ARRESTS OF A ROCK STAR
Jim Morrison of the Doors was arrested five times from 1967 to 1970, for harassment; public drunkenness (twice); indecent exposure and profanity; drunk and disorderly conduct; and interfering with personnel aboard an aircraft. Morrison died in 1971.

dance music

BEST-SELLING FILM SOUNDTRACK

Saturday Night Fever (1978) is the biggest-selling film soundtrack worldwide, with sales of more than 30 million. Of these, 11 million copies were sold in the USA. The disco album featured the hits *Jive Talkin'*, *Stayin' Alive*, *You Should Be Dancing* and *How Deep Is Your Love* by the Bee Gees, *If I Can't Have You* by Yvonne Elliman, *More Than a Woman* by Tavares and *Disco Inferno* by the Trammps. The film starred John Travolta, who was nominated for an Oscar for Best Actor.

BIGGEST-SELLING DANCE ALBUM IN THE UK

Bizarre Fruit (1994) by the British group M People has sold more than 1.5 million copies in the United Kingdom — more than any other dance album. It features the hits *Sight for Sore Eyes*, *Open Your Heart* and *Search for the Hero*.

MOST SUCCESSFUL DANCE SINGLE IN THE USA

That's The Way Love Goes by Janet Jackson topped the singles chart in the USA for a record eight weeks in 1993.

MOST SUCCESSFUL DANCE SINGLE IN THE UK

Ride On Time (1989) by the Italian act Black Box shares the record for the most successful ever dance single in the United Kingdom with *Rhythm is a Dancer* (1992) by Snap. Both European-produced singles topped the chart for six weeks. *Ride on Time* is also the most successful ever single by an Italian act in the United Kingdom.

MOST SUCCESSFUL DANCE MUSIC CAREER IN THE UK

Prodigy have had the best ever run of dance hit singles in the United Kingdom, with a record 12 successive releases reaching the top 15 of the chart. The British group, which is made up of Keith Flint, Leroy Thornhill, Liam Howlett and Maxim Reality (Keith Palmer) debuted with *Charly* in Aug 1991 and its 12th entry, the controversially titled *Smack My Bitch Up*, entered the chart in Nov 1997.

MOST DANCE CLUB PLAY NO. 1 SINGLES IN THE USA

Madonna has had a total of 19 No. 1 singles on the Billboard Dance Club Play chart.

The group with the most ever No. 1s on the Billboard Dance Club Play chart is the C&C Music Factory, with eight.

The record for the most No. 1s by a male soloist on the chart is seven, by ♀ (The Artist formerly known as Prince).

TOP-SELLING DANCE ALBUM, USA

The soundtrack to *Purple Rain* by Prince topped the US chart for a record 24 weeks and has sold more than 13 million copies there since its release in 1985. The movie, which starred Prince, was an apparently autobiographical story set in the club scene of Minneapolis, USA. The album yielded the hits *When Doves Cry* and *Let's Go Crazy*. In Sept 1993 the singer announced that he had changed his name to   .

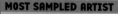

MOST SAMPLED ARTIST

James Brown, who had his first hit in 1956, has been the most influential artist in the dance field: he has been an inspiration for dance music for five decades and is the most sampled artist of all time. The stage acts of many of today's top performers, including Michael Jackson, Mick Jagger and ♀ (The Artist formerly known as Prince), owe a great deal to Brown's showstopping dance routines, in which he thrusts his hips, twists his feet and ends his act by doing the splits. Brown was born in the southern USA in 1933 and began his career as a performer by dancing for money in the street. At the age of 16 he was convicted of armed robbery and sent to a juvenile detention centre, where he began to sing gospel music with fellow inmate Bobby Byrd. The duo formed a rock 'n' roll group called the Flames and had a million-selling debut single *Please Please Please* in 1956, but their subsequent compositions had more of an R&B flavour. Brown's first solo album was *Live at the Apollo*, which was recorded in 1965 and sold 1 million copies. Throughout the 1970s he used his position as one of the most popular figures in the music world to promote social issues and write songs with a strong social message.

BRITISH ACT WITH MOST US DANCE CLUB PLAY NO. 1 SINGLES

The British artist with the most ever No. 1s on the Billboard Dance Club Play chart is Lisa Stansfield, with a total of seven. They included *All Around the World*, which was her third UK hit, and *Change*.

MOST NO. 1 HITS ON US 12-INCH DANCE SINGLES CHART

Madonna has had a record 16 singles reach the top of the US 12-inch singles chart — more than double the total of the three joint runners-up, ♀ (The Artist formerly known as Prince), Janet Jackson and Michael Jackson, all of whom have had a total of seven No. 1 hits. Madonna's dance No. 1s include *Like A Prayer*, *Vogue*, *Into the Groove* and *Papa Don't Preach*.

MOST NO. 1 US 12-INCH DANCE SINGLES BY A NON-US ACT

British band Soul II Soul, fronted by Jazzie B and Nellee Hooper, is the most successful non-US act on the US 12-inch singles chart, with a record four No. 1s — *Keep on Movin'* (1989), *Back to Life* (1989), *Jazzie's Groove* (1990) and *A Dream's a Dream/Courtney Blows* (1990). Hooper is also a successful dance producer and has worked with acts such as Madonna and Björk.

DANCE ACT WITH GREATEST NUMBER OF SIMULTANEOUS HITS

On 20 April 1996 all of Prodigy's 10 hit singles were in the UK Top 100. Their previous nine singles (*Charly*, *Everybody in the Place*, *Fire/Jericho*, *Out of Space/Ruff in the Jungle Bizness*, *Wind it Up (Rewound)*, *One Love*, *No Good (Start The Dance)*, *Voodoo People* and *Poison*) had been re-issued after *Firestarter* gave them their first No. 1.

TOP-SELLING DANCE ALBUM

The biggest-selling dance album by a female artist in the USA is *Janet* (1993) by Janet Jackson, which topped the chart for six weeks and sold more than 6 million copies. Born in 1966, Janet had an eventful childhood, singing with her brothers' band, the Jackson Five, and appearing in the TV shows *Diff'rent Strokes* and *Fame*. She made her movie debut in *Poetic Justice* (1993), opposite rapper Tupac Shakur.

FASTEST-SELLING DANCE ALBUM

The fastest-selling dance album in the UK is *The Fat Of The Land* (1997) by Prodigy, which sold a record 317,000 copies in its first week. In the USA it sold more than 200,000 copies in its first week. The album entered the chart at No. 1 in a total of 20 countries, including the USA, the United Kingdom, Canada, Australia, Germany, Austria and Norway. Prodigy are distinctive not only for their 'hardcore' style of dance music, but also for their unique looks — Keith Flint (left) has dyed, shaved hair and a pierced septum, while Maxim wears cat's-eye contact lenses.

hip hop rap reggae and R&B

TOP-SELLING REGGAE ALBUM

Legend (1984), by the late Bob Marley, is the biggest-selling reggae album of all time. In the UK, where it topped the chart, it has had certified sales of 1.8 million, and although it did not reach the Top 40 in the USA it sold more than 9 million copies there. Marley was awarded the Jamaican Order of Merit after his death in 1981 and is officially known as The Honourable Bob Marley.

TOP-SELLING GROUP R&B ALBUM

The biggest-selling R&B album by a group in the USA is *II* (1994) by Boyz II Men, with sales of more than 12 million. The group made their chart debut in 1991 and in 1992 their *End of the Road* (from the Eddie Murphy movie *Boomerang*) beat Elvis Presley's record for the most weeks at No. 1 on the US chart, with 13. They have since broken the record twice, with *I'll Make Love to You*, which was No. 1 for 14 weeks in 1994 and *One Sweet Day* (with Mariah Carey), which topped the chart for 16 weeks in 1995.

BIGGEST-SELLING HIP HOP/RAP ALBUM IN THE USA

Please Hammer Don't Hurt 'Em (1990) by M. C. Hammer and *Crazysexycool* (1994) by female trio TLC share the record for the biggest-selling hip hop/rap album in the USA, with certified sales of 10 million.

MOST SUCCESSFUL HIP HOP/RAP SINGLE IN THE UK & USA

I'll Be Missing You by Puff Daddy & Faith Evans headed the US pop chart for 11 weeks and the UK pop chart for six weeks in 1997, and is the most successful hip hop/rap single to date.

MOST US NO. 1 RAP SINGLES

The artist who has had the greatest number of No. 1 singles on the Billboard Rap Chart is L. L. Cool J, with a total of eight. These included *I'm That Type of Guy*, *Around the Way Girl*, *Loungin'* and *Father*.

The female rapper with the most No. 1 singles on the Billboard Rap Chart is MC Lyte, with four (*Cha Cha Cha*, *Poor Georgie*, *Ruffneck* and *Cold Rock a Party*).

LABEL WITH THE MOST US NO. 1 RAP SINGLES

The label with the greatest number of No. 1 singles on the Billboard Rap Chart is Def Jam, with 15 by April 1998. Def Jam acts include Public Enemy, MC Serch, Boss and L. L. Cool J.

MOST SUCCESSFUL NON-ENGLISH LANGUAGE RAP RECORDS

In 1993 *Dur Dur D'Etre Bébé* (*It's Tough To Be A Baby*) by the five-year-old French rapper Jordy (Lemoine) sold more than 1 million copies in France and was also a minor hit in the USA.

Da Ya Ne by Japanese rap act East End X Yuri sold 1 million copies in Japan in 1995.

MOST SUCCESSFUL RAP PRODUCER

Sean (Puff Daddy) Coombs produced four singles that consecutively headed the US Rap chart for 36 weeks in 1997. They included *Hypnotize* and *Mo Money, Mo Problems* by The Notorious B.I.G.

MOST SUCCESSFUL TRIBUTE RECORD IN THE UK & USA

I'll Be Missing You, which was recorded in 1997 by Puff Daddy & Faith Evans, and featured 112, topped the singles chart in the UK for six weeks and led the US list for 11 weeks. The record was made as a tribute to rapper The Notorious B.I.G.

MOST SUCCESSFUL REGGAE SINGLE IN THE USA

Informer by Canadian performer Snow and *Can't Help Falling In Love* by British group UB40 share the title of most successful reggae single in the USA. Both recordings topped the pop chart for seven weeks in 1993.

MOST SUCCESSFUL GANGSTA RAP ACT

The world's most successful gangsta rap act to date was 2 Pac (Tupac Shakur), who died at the age of 25 in Sept 1996. Four of his albums reached the US pop Top 3 and three of them (*Me Against The World*, *All Eyez on Me* and *The Don Killuminati – The 7 Day Theory*) reached No. 1 in the USA. Shakur died a week after being gunned down as he was driven to a party for the boxer Mike Tyson in Las Vegas, USA. A man in a white Cadillac drew up beside his vehicle and opened fire, injuring both Shakur and his boss Suge Knight, the head of Death Row Records. Shakur's death focused the media's attention on the sometimes brutal nature of the gangsta rap genre, in which singers boast of their violent crimes and sexual conquests, and police suspected that the murder was gang-related: the public rivalry between West Coast rappers such as Shakur, Dr Dre and Snoop Doggy Dog and East Coast stars such as The Notorious B.I.G. certainly resembled gang warfare at times. Shakur himself had been arrested for assault and battery, and in 1995 he had spent 10 months in jail for sexual assault. Shakur's anti-authoritarian stance, as well as his 'hardcore' musical style, earned the rapper both respect and record sales.

BEST WEEK FOR REGGAE ON THE UK CHART

On 27 March 1993, for the only time in history, the top three singles on the British chart were reggae recordings. Shaggy was at No. 1 with *Oh Carolina*, Snow was at No. 2 with *Informer* and Shabba Ranks was at No. 3 with *Mr Loverman*.

LONGEST TIME AT UK NO. 1 BY POSTHUMOUS ALBUM

The record for the longest ever stay at the top of the UK album chart by a posthumously released album is 12 weeks, by Bob Marley's best-selling *Legend*. The album was released in 1984, three years after the artist's death in 1981 at the age of 36. Of the 11 artists who have posthumously topped the UK album chart, Otis Redding was the first, with his *Dock Of The Bay* in 1968.

MOST US NO. 1 R&B ALBUMS

The Temptations have had 15 No. 1 R&B albums in the USA, including *With a Lot O'Soul* (1967) and *Masterpiece* (1973).

The most No. 1 R&B albums in the USA by a female artist is 10, by Aretha Franklin. The list includes *I Never Loved a Man* (1967) and *Lady Soul* (1968).

The most No. 1 R&B albums in the USA by a male soloist is 10, by Stevie Wonder. Among these were the albums *Fulfillingness First Finale* (1974) and *Songs in the Key Of Life* (1976).

BIGGEST-SELLING R&B ALBUM IN THE USA BY A FEMALE ARTIST

Whitney Houston's self-titled 1985 debut album, which has had certified sales of 12 million, is the biggest-selling R&B album in the USA by a female artist. It featured *Saving All My Love for You* and *Greatest Love of All*.

BIGGEST-SELLING R&B ALBUM IN THE UK

Bad (1987) by Michael Jackson is the biggest-selling R&B album in the UK, with certified sales of 3.9 million.

MOST SINGLES ON THE R&B CHART IN THE USA

The artist with the most ever singles on the US Billboard R&B chart is James Brown, with a total of 118 entries between 1956 and 1993. He has also had more Top 10 entries than any other artist, with 58. Brown's most famous hits include *Papa's Got a Brand New Bag* (1965), *I Got You (I Feel Good)* (1965), *It's a Man's Man's Man's World* (1966) and *Living in America* (1986).

The greatest number of singles on the US R&B chart by a female artist is 96, by Aretha Franklin. She also holds the record for the most Top 10 entries, with a total of 52. The greatest hits of her career include *Respect* (1967), *I Say a Little Prayer* (1968) and *Who's Zoomin' Who* (1985).

MOST NO. 1 R&B HITS IN THE USA

Stevie Wonder and Aretha Franklin have both had a record 20 No. 1 R&B hits in the USA.

MOST SUCCESSFUL R&B SINGLE IN THE UK

The most successful single by an R&B artist in the UK is *I Will Always Love You* by Whitney Houston, which topped the pop chart for 10 weeks in 1992.

LONGEST CAREER ON THE R&B CHART IN THE USA

Balladeer Nat 'King' Cole, who died in 1965, made his debut on the US R&B chart on 21 Nov 1942, with *That Ain't Right*. His last chart entry came 48 years seven months later on 29 June 1991, with *Unforgettable* (a posthumously created duet with his daughter Natalie Cole).

Aretha Franklin holds the record for the longest chart career in the USA by a female artist, at 37 years five months by April 1998. Her first chart hit was *Today I Sing the Blues* in 1960 and her most recent was *A Rose is Still a Rose* in 1998.

YOUNGEST ARTIST TO TOP THE US ALBUM CHART

The youngest artist to have ever got to No. 1 on the US album pop chart was Stevie Wonder, with *The 12 Year Old Genius* in 1963, when the singer was 13 years three months old. Wonder's most famous hits include *You Are the Sunshine of my Life* (1972) and *I Just Called to Say I Love You* (1984).

TALLEST US NO. 1 SINGLES ARTIST

At 2.64 m (6 ft 8 in) in height, Montell Jordan is the tallest artist to have ever reached the top of the US chart. His recording of *This Is How We Do It* reached No. 1 in April 1995.

FASTEST RAPPER

Rebel X.D. of Chicago, Illinois, USA, rapped 67 syllables in 54.9 seconds at the Hair Bear Recording Studio, Alsip, Illinois, on 27 Aug 1992. This works out at 12.2 syllables per second.

TOP GANGSTA RAP ALBUM

Life After Death by The Notorious B.I.G. (Christopher Wallace) charted one month after his death in March 1997 and is the most successful gangsta rap album to date. It was No. 1 for four weeks and sold more than 7 million copies in the USA alone. Its leap from No. 176 to No. 1 was the biggest US album chart jump of all time. Wallace was gunned down as he left a party in Los Angeles, USA.

country music

MOST SUCCESSFUL COUNTRY ARTISTS IN THE USA
Garth Brooks is the most successful country recording artist of all time, with sales of more than 80 million albums between 1989 and 1998. His greatest hits include *If Tomorrow Never Dies* (1989), *The Dance* (1992) and *Red Strokes* (1993).

Reba McEntire is the biggest-selling female country vocalist in the USA, with 12 platinum and six gold albums to her credit by April 1998, including *Sweet Sixteen* (1989), *Read My Mind* (1994) and *If You See Him* (1998).

HIGHEST-PAID COUNTRY SINGER
In 1997 Garth Brooks earned $26 million (£16.25 million) — more than any other country music star.

BIGGEST-SELLING COUNTRY SINGLE IN THE USA
The only country single with certified sales of 3 million in the USA is *How Do I Live* by Leann Rimes, which reached No. 2 on the pop chart in 1998.

MOST NO. 1 COUNTRY SINGLES IN THE USA
The most No. 1 hits on the Billboard country chart is 40, by Conway Twitty.

MOST CONSECUTIVE NO. 1 US COUNTRY SINGLES
The group Alabama notched up a record-breaking 21 consecutive country No. 1 singles between 1980 and 1987.

MOST SINGLES SIMULTANEOUSLY ON US COUNTRY CHART
On 6 Dec 1997 Garth Brooks had a record 12 separate tracks on the Billboard Top 75 country chart, including *Long Neck Bottle*, *Two Pina Coladas* and *Cowboy Cadillac*.

BIGGEST ONE-WEEK SALE OF A COUNTRY ALBUM IN THE USA
The Hits by Garth Brooks sold a record 907,000 copies during Christmas week 1994.

BIGGEST-SELLING COUNTRY ALBUMS IN THE USA
Garth Brooks' 1990 album *No Fences* sold a record total of more than 14 million copies.

The top-selling country album by a female artist in the USA is *The Woman In Me* (1996) by Shania Twain, which has had certified sales of 10 million.

The best-selling country album by a group in the USA is *Greatest Hits* (1986) by Alabama, with sales of 5 million.

MOST WEEKS AT NO. 1 ON ANY US ALBUM CHART
No record has topped any US album chart for longer than the 8-million-selling *12 Greatest Hits* (1967) by Patsy Cline, which headed the country catalogue chart in Billboard for 251 weeks (almost five years).

MOST SIMULTANEOUS ALBUM HITS IN THE USA
On 10 Oct 1992 four of the Top 5 albums on the US country chart were by Garth Brooks. The albums — *The Chase*, *Beyond The Season*, *No Fences* and *Ropin' The Wind* — were all in the US Top 20 pop album chart too, and reportedly accounted for 37% of all Top 20 album sales.

MOST HIT SINGLES IN THE USA
The most successful group on the Billboard country chart is Alabama, with 24 chart-topping singles, including *Tennessee River* (1980), *Feels So Right* (1981) and *If You're Gonna Play In Texas* (1984).

MOST NO. 1 COUNTRY ALBUMS IN THE USA
Willie Nelson and Merle Haggard have both had a record 15 No. 1 country albums.

The best-selling female country artist in terms of No. 1 albums in the USA is Loretta Lynn, with 10, including *You Ain't Woman Enough* (1966).

The most No. 1 country albums by a group is 10, by Alabama.

TOP SELLING COMEDY ALBUM IN THE USA
You Might Be A Redneck If (1994), by country comedian Jeff Foxworthy, is the only comedy album to have been certified triple platinum in the USA.

MOST NO. 1 SINGLES
The record for the most No. 1 hits on the Billboard country chart by a woman is 24, by Dolly Parton, from *Joshua* (1970) to *Rockin' Years* (1991) with Ricky Van Shelton. Dolly has also had 56 Top 10 singles and 41 weeks in total at No. 1. In 1986 her company, Parton Enterprises, opened Dollywood, a 35-ha (87-acre) theme park near her birthplace in Sevier County, Tennessee, USA.

FIRST FEMALE COUNTRY SINGER TO SELL 1 MILLION RECORDS
Tammy Wynette, who recorded more than 50 albums and sold more than 30 million records in her 25-year career, was the first female country singer to sell 1 million records. The winner of the Country Music Association's female vocalist of the year award in 1968, 1969 and 1970, she was widely known as 'The First Lady of Country Music'. Her signature song *Stand By Your Man* (1968), which she wrote with her producer Billy Sherrill, was a US country chart-topper, won a Grammy Award in 1969 and went on to become the UK No. 1 on its sixth reissue in 1975. Born Wynette Pugh in Itawamba County, Mississippi, USA, Tammy changed her name in 1969, after auditioning for Billy Sherrill at Epic Records. She released her first single, *Apartment No. 9*, in 1966 and went on to record 32 No. 1 country hits. Her 1969 album *Tammy's Greatest Hits* sold more copies worldwide than any other album by a female country recording artist and crossed over to the Top 40 pop lists. Tammy died in her sleep at the age of 55 on 6 April 1998.

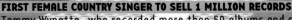

MOST SIMULTANEOUS ALBUM HITS IN THE UK

On 24 Sept 1964 the late Jim Reeves had a record-breaking eight entries on the UK Top 20 pop album chart — or in other words, an unprecedented 40% of the chart.

On the UK country album chart, Irish singer Daniel O'Donnell occupied a record six of the top seven places on 16 Nov 1991.

BIGGEST GAP BETWEEN POP AND COUNTRY CHART ENTRIES IN USA

The biggest gap between a first pop chart entry and a first country chart entry is 34 years 6 months, by the Beach Boys, whose newly-recorded version of *Little Deuce Coupe* (featuring James House) entered the country chart in Aug 1996.

ONLY COUNTRY/RAP/POP HIT IN THE USA

The only act to have had hits on the US country, rap and pop charts is Sting. In Dec 1997, the pop chart veteran and former leader singer of the Police climbed the country chart with *I'm So Happy I Can't Stop Crying* (a duet with Toby Keith) and the rap chart with *Roxanne '97*, the Puff Daddy remix of the 1979 Police hit.

MOST WEEKS AT NO. 1 ON ANY US SINGLES CHART

On 14 March 1998 *How Do I Live*, by the 15-year-old country singer Leann Rimes, spent the last of 32 weeks at the top of the country singles sales chart — the most ever weeks that a single has been at No. 1 on any US singles chart. Rimes, the first country singer to win a Grammy for Best New Artist (1997), was also the youngest performer to top either the country album or singles chart. She headed the album chart when she was 13 years 11 months old with *Blue* (1996), and the singles chart when she was 14 years 4 months old with *One Way Ticket* (1996). She is also the youngest female of all time to reach No. 1 on the US pop album chart, which she did with *Blue* when she was 13 years 11 months old. In addition to this, Rimes is the only teenage artist to have put four albums in the US pop Top 3 and the youngest US female singer to reach the UK Top 10 singles chart.

latino music

BEST-SELLING LATIN ARTISTS

Spanish vocalist Julio Iglesias is the most successful Latin music artist in the world, with reported global sales of more than 200 million albums. His album *Julio* (1983) was the first foreign language album to sell more than 2 million copies in the USA and the only foreign language record to go double platinum there.

Cuban-born singer Gloria Estefan is the most successful female Latin artist in the world. In the USA she has amassed eight gold albums, four of which have passed the 3-million sales mark: *Primitive Love* (1985), *Let It Loose* (1987), *Cuts Both Ways* (1989) and *Greatest Hits* (1992). In the United Kingdom her *Anything For You* (aka *Let It Loose*) and *Cuts Both Ways* both sold more than 1 million copies. In 1990 Estefan was presented with a Golden Globe award for album sales of more than 5 million outside the USA. Her current total world sales are more than 35 million.

TOP GROSSING LATIN PERFORMER

Mexican superstar Luis Miguel grossed a record $6.77 million (£4.13 million) for a series of 17 concerts at the Auditória Nacionál in Mexico City during Oct and Nov 1997, which put him into the Top 20 all-time grossing performers. The shows came soon after Miguel's debut in the US Top 20 with *Romances* — the best-selling Spanish language album of 1997.

BIGGEST-SELLING LATIN ALBUM IN THE USA

Julio Iglesias' *1100 Bel Air Place* (1984) is the only Latin album to date to be certified as quadruple platinum in the USA.

GREATEST DOMINATION OF THE US LATIN ALBUM CHART

In the months following her murder on 31 March 1995, the albums of 23-year-old Texas-born Selena (Quintanilla Perez) took over the US Latin chart: on 6 May 1995 they held the top five

TOP-SELLING MALE LATIN ARTIST

Julio Iglesias is the most successful male Latin artist on the UK album chart, with a total of six Top 20 albums: *Begin the Beguine* (1981), *Amor* (1982), *Julio* (1983), *1100 Bel Air Place* (1984), *Crazy* (1994) and *La Carretera* (1995). Iglesias learnt to compose, sing and play the guitar after a near-fatal car crash ended his hopes of becoming a professional footballer. He was signed by Discos Columbia after winning the Spanish Song Festival in 1968 and soon became a huge star throughout Europe and Latin America. He has recorded songs in French, Italian, German, Portuguese and English, as well as Spanish.

BIGGEST UK CHART JUMP

Macarena, which broke the record for the biggest ever jump on the UK singles chart when it leapt from No. 74 to No. 11, was inspired by Diana Patricia Cubillan, seen above. Released in Spain in April 1993, the song became a huge success around the world, especially in Mexico and the USA. It was written and recorded by Los Del Rio, aka Antonio Romero and Rafael Ruiz (left), a prolific duo who had already composed 300 songs. It inspired the equally popular *Macarena* dance, a giant version of which was held in Key Biscayne, Florida, USA, involving 10,000 people.
How to *Macarena*: Right hand forward, left hand forward, right hand on left arm, left hand on right arm, right hand on head, left hand on head, right hand on behind, left hand on behind, sway three times, jump to the left and start again.

places and were all in the US pop album chart too. In a 21-month chart-span a record five albums by Selena reached No. 1 on the Latin chart. Selena is also the only non UK/US act to have entered the US album chart at No. 1, with her first posthumous album *Dreaming Of You* on 5 Aug 1995.

MOST SUCCESSFUL LATIN SINGLE IN THE USA

Macarena by the Spanish duo Los Del Rio is the most successful non UK/US Latin hit of the rock era. It topped the US chart for a total of 14 weeks in 1996 and spent 60 weeks on the Top 100 — both are records for non-US acts. It also has the distinction of having been the slowest record to get to No. 1 in the USA, reaching the top spot in its 33rd chart week. More than 4 million copies of the single were sold in the USA alone, and more than 10 million were sold around the globe.

MOST SUCCESSFUL SPANISH-LANGUAGE SINGLE IN THE UK

The only Spanish-language record to have topped the UK chart is *Begin the Beguine (Volver a Empezar)*, by Latin superstar Julio Iglesias in 1981. Iglesias was not the first Spanish act to reach the top of the UK chart: female duo Baccara got to No. 1 in 1977 with *Yes Sir I Can Boogie*.

MOST SUCCESSFUL INSTRUMENTAL SINGLE IN THE USA

Cherry Pink and Apple Blossom White by Cuban-born Perez Prado and his orchestra, which topped the US chart for 10 weeks in 1955, was the most successful instrumental single in the USA in the rock era. It was also the first Latin track to top the UK chart. Prado, known as 'The King of the Mambo', also holds the record for the longest gap between hits on the UK Top 20: his *Patricia* left the Top 20 on 24 Oct 1958 and his *Guaglione*, first released in 1958 as the follow-up to *Patricia*, returned to the chart 36 years 6 months later on 6 May 1995.

BEST-SELLING LATIN ARTIST, UK

Gloria Estefan has had more successful albums in the United Kingdom than any other Latin artist, with seven Top 20 entries, four of which reached the Top 3. Estefan, the daughter of a Cuban revolutionary, became a global star with *Dr Beat* in 1984. Throughout the 1990s she has concentrated on exploring her diverse musical heritage. In 1993 she revisited classic Cuban music with *Mi Tierra*, while in 1994 her album *Hold Me, Thrill Me, Kiss Me* brought together some of her favourite rock and pop classics. In 1995 she released *Abriendo Puertas*, a Spanish-language pop/dance album drawing on different strands of Latin music.

TOP-SELLING ENGLISH-LANGUAGE RECORD ON US LATIN CHART

The only English-language record to have ever topped the Latin chart in the USA is *My Heart Will Go On*, by Celine Dion in Feb 1998. The song is the theme from the Oscar-winning 1997 film *Titanic*.

BIGGEST LATIN HIT

Puerto Rico-born performer Ricky Martin's recording of *(Un, Dos, Tres) Maria*, was a hit in many countries around the world in 1997 and sold over 5 million copies. The singer, who was a member of the top Latin teen group Menudo for five years, is best known in the USA for his role as Miguel Morez in the ABC network's popular daytime soap opera *General Hospital*. Martin also sang *La Copa de la Vida*, which was the official song of the 1998 soccer World Cup, France '98.

classical music
opera and jazz

BEST-SELLING CLASSICAL ALBUM
The Three Tenors In Concert, recorded by José Carreras, Placido Domingo and Luciano Pavarotti for the 1990 football World Cup Finals, has sold an estimated 13 million copies.

MOST GRAMMYS TO ONE ARTIST
Hungarian-born conductor Sir Georg Solti was awarded 31 Grammys (one posthumously).

BIGGEST CLASSICAL AUDIENCE
An estimated 800,000 people attended a free open-air concert by the New York Philharmonic on the Great Lawn of Central Park, New York, USA, on 5 July 1986.

QUIETEST PIECE
In John Cage's *4'33"* the performer or performers sit silently on the concert platform and the 'music' is any noise that comes from the audience and from outside the concert hall.

LARGEST MUSICAL PERFORMER
And God Created Great Whales (1970) by Alan Hovhaness (USA) is scored for orchestra and a solo by a humpback whale (recorded).

BEST-SELLING OPERA SINGER
Luciano Pavarotti made his professional debut in 1961 and has sold about 60 million albums worldwide. His entire stage repertory has reached disc and every recording is a best-seller.

LONGEST EVER OPERA
The seven-act *Life and Times of Joseph Stalin* by Robert Wilson lasted almost 13 hr 25 min from 14 to 15 Dec 1973 at the Brooklyn Academy of Music, New York, USA.

SHORTEST OPERA
The shortest published opera is *The Sands of Time* by Simon Rees and Peter Reynolds, which lasted 4 min 9 sec when first performed by Rhian Owen and Dominic Burns at The Hayes, Cardiff, UK, in March 1993. A 3-min 34-sec version was performed under the direction of Peter Reynolds in London, UK, in Sept 1993.

LONGEST OPERATIC APPLAUSE
Placido Domingo was applauded for a record 1 hr 20 min through a total of 101 curtain calls after a performance of *Otello* at the Vienna Staatsoper, Austria, on 30 July 1991.

MOST CURTAIN CALLS IN AN OPERA
On 24 Feb 1988 Luciano Pavarotti received 165 curtain calls and was applauded for 1 hr 7 min after singing the part of Nemorino in Donizetti's *L'Elisir d'Amore* at the Deutsche Oper, Berlin, Germany.

MOST TUNELESS OPERA
Lulu (1937) by German composer Alban Berg is a modern 12-tone opera with no tunes. The composer constrained his writing by a set of mathematical rules.

LARGEST OPERA HOUSE
The Metropolitan Opera House at the Lincoln Center, New York, USA, which was completed in Sept 1966 at a cost of $45.7 million (£16.3 million), can seat and stand 4,065 people.

LOWEST NOTES
The lowest note by a human voice was sung in 1997 by Dan Britton, who produced a

MOST POPULAR JAZZ ARTIST
Miles Davis' *Milestones* (1958) has been acclaimed as the best album in the history of jazz by more jazz writers than any other. Its only rival is *Kind of Blue*, another Miles Davis album. The trumpeter and composer was consistently voted most popular artist in all major US jazz polls from 1954 to the mid-60s, but by the 1970s he had alienated jazz purists through his adoption of rock styles.

WORST RECEPTION FOR A NEW WORK
Russian composer Igor Stravinsky's controversial ballet *The Rite of Spring* sparked violent reactions among the audience at the Théatre des Champs-Elysées, Paris, France, at its premiere in 1913. The first few bars evoked laughter that soon escalated into full-scale riots as the audience protested against the complexity of the music, which challenged the accepted musical norms of the time. The noise made by the protestors was so loud that the dancers were unable to hear the orchestra, but Stravinsky remained unfazed by the reaction and continued with the performance. *The Rite of Spring* was eventually recognized as a masterpiece and the composer became regarded as one of the most important musical figures of the 20th century.

recognizable note that measured electronically at 16.45 Hz and is below the musical note C-0.

The lowest vocal note in the classical repertoire is in Osmin's aria in Mozart's *Die Entführung aus dem Serail*. It calls for a low D (73.4 Hz).

HIGHEST NOTE

The highest vocal note to be found in the classical repertoire is giii, which occurs in Mozart's *Popolo di Tessaglia*.

MOST SHOCKING MODERN OPERA

Salome, seen here in a 1920s production played by Maud Allan, was the granddaughter of Herod the Great and gained notoriety when she demanded the head of John the Baptist. Her story has been retold in many works of art, including Richard Strauss' *Salome* (1905), which was banned from the New York Metropolitan Opera for 27 years after audiences were shocked by its subject matter.

GREATEST VOCAL RANGE

Ivan Rebroff, the Russian bass, has a voice that easily extends over four octaves, from low F to high F, 1¼ octaves above C.

LOUDEST MUSICAL INSTRUMENT

The loudest and largest musical instrument ever made is the now partially functional Auditorium Organ in Atlantic City, New Jersey, USA. Completed in 1930, it had 1,477 stop controls and 33,112 pipes, and its volume equalled that of 25 brass bands.

GRANDEST GRAND PIANO

A 3.55-m-long (11-ft 8-in) grand piano was made by Chas H. Challen & Son Ltd of London, UK,

in 1935. Its longest bass string was 3.02 m (9 ft 11 in).

MOST EXPENSIVE PIANO

A Steinway grand piano made *c.* 1888 was sold for $390,000 (£177,272) at Sotheby's, New York, USA, on 26 March 1980.

MOST EXPENSIVE VIOLIN

The highest price paid for a violin at auction was £947,500 ($1,572,850), for a 1729 Stradivarius 'The Kreutzer' at Christie's, London, UK, in 1998.

MOST EXPENSIVE JAZZ INSTRUMENT

A saxophone owned by Charlie Parker sold for £93,500 ($146,328) at Christie's, London, UK, in Sept 1994.

BEST-SELLING JAZZ ARTIST

US saxophonist Kenny G has sold an estimated 50 million albums.

BEST-SELLING JAZZ RECORD

Kenny G's *Breathless* has sold an estimated 13 million copies.

LONGEST JAZZ CAREER

Saxophonist and pianist Benny Waters from Maryland, USA, has been performing since his mid teens and is still recording at the age of 96.

OLDEST JAZZ CLUB

The Village Vanguard cellar jazz club opened in New York, USA, in the 1930s and has hosted mainstream jazz ever since.

BIGGEST JAZZ FESTIVAL

An 11-day multimedia extravaganza, the Festival International de Jazz de Montreal in Québec, Canada, is the world's largest jazz festival.

LONGEST PERFORMED OPERA

German composer Richard Wagner revolutionized opera in the late 19th century in works such as *Der Ring des Nibelungen*, which includes *Die Walküre* (1856), seen below. The longest frequently performed opera in the world is Wagner's *Die Meistersinger von Nürnberg* (1868). An uncut version performed by the Sadler's Wells company in London, UK, in 1968 lasted a total of 5 hr 15 min.

clubs, parties and _festivals_

BIGGEST STREET FESTIVALS

Rio de Janeiro Carnival is the world's largest street festival, attracting around 2 million people each day of the festival, 300,000 of whom are tourists. In 1998 the four-day event generated more than $165 million (£100 million). A seat in the Sambadrome for one of the parades costs between $300 and $600 (£180 and £360). In 1998 14 Samba schools contributed to the parade, each with six to eight floats and up to 5,000 elaborately dressed dancers. The Notting Hill Carnival, London, UK, is the biggest street festival in Europe and the world's second largest carnival, with 1 million visitors annually.

MOST POPULAR CLUBBING DESTINATION

Ibiza has a total of 740 clubs, restaurants and bars and attracts 1.5 million visitors each year.

MOST SUCCESSFUL CLUB DJ

British DJ Paul Oakenfold has sold 1 million records and owns the Perfecto music label. He is reported to earn £250,000 ($400,000) a year. The remixer and producer has worked with U2 and the Rolling Stones, making him the most influential DJ to have moved from club culture into the mainstream. He has worked in Australia, the USA, Hong Kong, Brazil, Argentina and all over Europe and played at private parties for Madonna, Naomi Campbell and Grace Jones.

BIGGEST TECHNO PARTY

On 12 July 1997 an estimated 1 million people congregated in the centre of Berlin, Germany, for the city's ninth annual, and biggest ever, Love Parade. The ravers danced behind 38 decorated floats equipped with turbo-powered sound systems down a 6-km (4-mile) boulevard starting at the Brandenburg Gate, the landmark that has become a symbol of Berlin's reunification. Parties took place in more than 130 dance clubs, as well as in parks and on Potsdamer Platz, Europe's biggest construction site. Revenue from the parade, which attracted people from around the world, was estimated at $84 million (£51 million). A rival 'hate parade' organized by disc jockeys who objected to the main event's 'commercialism' attracted about 500 people and broke up after a few hours.

MOST SUCCESSFUL CLUB ENTERPRISE

The Ministry of Sound in London, UK, is reported to be worth £20 million ($32 million). Since opening in 1991, the club has spawned a record company, a clothing brand and a magazine. Its record company sells 1 million records a year, mainly dance music compilations.

BIGGEST NIGHTCLUB

Gilley's Club (formerly Shelly's) on Spencer Highway, Houston, Texas, USA, was built in 1955 and was extended to seat 6,000 people in 1971, making it the biggest club.

BIGGEST NEW YEAR'S PARTY

In 1996 more than 400,000 revellers descended on the city of Edinburgh, UK, Europe's most popular New Year destination. Despite raising an estimated £23 million ($38 million) in spin-off revenue, the city has now restricted the number of people attending to 180,000.

BIGGEST MILLENNIUM PARTIES

The Times Square Business Improvement District plans a 24-hour televised entertainment production in Times Square, New York, USA. The millennium party will cost millions of dollars and will feature the world's biggest hologram strobe-lit spinning ball.

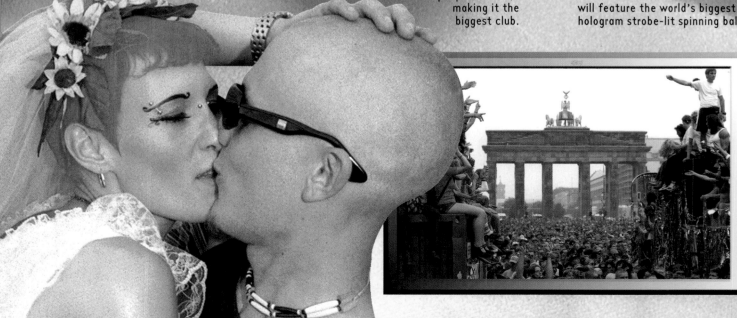

On 31 Dec 1999 Sydney, NSW, Australia – which is hosting the 2000 Olympic Games – will hold the world's biggest firework display. The event is expected to be 10 times larger than the city's bicentennial celebrations.

King Taufa'ahau Tupou of Tonga is inviting tourists to celebrate the millennium at what he claims will be the world's biggest party. He asserts that Tonga will see the dawn of the new millennium before anywhere else, and threatens to sue any islands who challenge his claim. The Chatham Islands state that they will be the first to see the dawn, and a British consortium plans to fly 100 party-goers there at $53,000 (£32,000) a head in the world's biggest airship, which will be called *Nelson* and will be twice as big as a jumbo jet.

BIGGEST MULTICULTURAL FESTIVAL

The annual Folklorama festival in Winnipeg, Manitoba, Canada, draws more than 500,000 people from all over the world. First held in 1970 to celebrate the province's 100th birthday and show the diverse cultural heritage of its people, it has grown into a two-week festival put on by 20,000 volunteers.

BIGGEST MUSIC FESTIVAL ON THE INTERNET

The 1998 Intel New York Music Festival featured more than 300 bands performing in 20 clubs in Manhattan, New York, USA. The festival website broadcast video and audio from the clubs.

MOST PEOPLE AT A ROCK FESTIVAL

An estimated 670,000 people attended Steve Wozniak's 1983 US Festival at Devore, California. Artists included The Clash, Van Halen and David Bowie.

WOODSTOCK

Woodstock Music and Art Fair, one of the most famous music events ever, was held at Bethel, New York, USA, from 15 to 17 Aug 1969 and attracted 300,000–500,000 people.

OLDEST ROCK FESTIVAL

Pinkpop has been staged in Geleen, Netherlands, every year since May 1970 and now attracts 40,000–60,000 people.

BIGGEST FESTIVAL OF PERFORMANCE ART

The annual Cleveland Performance Art Festival, Ohio, USA, is held every May and is seen as a showcase for both emerging and established performance artists. It attracts some of the most outrageous international artists.

BIGGEST WINTER CARNIVAL

The Annual Winter Carnival in Québec City, Canada, began in 1955 but has its origins in the city's first carnival in 1894. The most popular event is the snow-sculpting demonstration. Other highlights include the canoe race, the dog-sled race, a car race on ice, and snow-rolling in swimsuits. It attracts more than 500,000 people a year from all over the world and is the third biggest carnival after Rio and Notting Hill.

BIGGEST GAY FESTIVALS

The Gay and Lesbian Mardi Gras (pictured above) in Sydney, NSW, Australia, began in 1978 and is now the world's biggest gay festival. In 1998 it was attended by 700,000 people, and a post-parade dance party attracted over 17,000 people and live performers including Kylie and Dannii Minogue. The biggest of the Gay Pride events takes place in San Francisco, USA. One of the largest gay events in the world, it attracted 500,000 people in 1997, its 27th parade.

street fashion

Calvin Klein
underwear

BIGGEST-SELLING BRAND OF UNDERWEAR

The world's most popular underwear brand is made by the US designer Calvin Klein. In the 1980s Klein capitalized on the trend among women of buying his men's underwear for themselves by launching boxer shorts for women. He even kept the flies, telling *Time* magazine that they looked sexy on women. In 1984 a record 400,000 pairs of 'Calvins' (seen left on supermodel Christy Turlington) were bought and the company made $50 million (£37.4 million). Klein is largely responsible for popularizing designer clothing by attaching his name to the back pocket of his jeans, setting a precedent for other designers, and the brand name has become one of the most recognized symbols of US fashion since it was founded by Klein and Barry Schwartz in 1968.

FASTEST-GROWING BRAND OF CLOTHING

Dockers, a brand of casual wear by Levi Strauss and Co, was launched in the USA in 1986 and by the early 1990s had become the fastest-growing apparel brand in US history, with the highest level of brand awareness of any casual trousers. The brand was initially conceived as a comfortable alternative to jeans for the 'baby boomer' generation, but the promotion, which had cost a total of $10 million (£6.25 million) within two years, propelled them to the top of the casual wear market, with sales of $6.9 billion (£4.31 billion) in 1997.

BIGGEST UNDERWEAR MANUFACTURER

According to *Fortune 500 1998*, the biggest underwear manufacturer in the world is Fruit of the Loom, which is based in Chicago, Illinois, USA. In 1997 the company had a revenue of $488 million (£305 million), making it the 596th largest company in the world.

BEST-SELLING BRA

The Wonderbra, made by Sara Lee, is the most popular bra in the world. It currently sells at a rate of more than 30,000 units a week in the United Kingdom alone and is available in the USA, South Africa, Australia and across Europe. Clients include Gwyneth Paltrow, Caprice and Kate Moss.

BIGGEST TIGHTS MANUFACTURER

One in every five pairs of tights in the world are made by Sara Lee, making it the largest tights manufacturer. The company's 31 brands also include Playtex and Wonderbra, each of which has sales of more than $100 million (£62.5 million).

FIRST SHOE BRAND IN AN ENGLISH DICTIONARY

Dr. Martens boots, which have been manufactured since 1960, are now so famous that they warrant an entry in the *Oxford English Dictionary*. It reads as follows: "Dr. Martens (n. phr.) Propriety name for a type of heavy (esp. laced) boot or shoe with a cushioned sole". The company is said to make two pairs of boots every second of the working week.

BIGGEST SELLING OWN BRAND UNDERWEAR

Marks & Spencer sell 52 million pairs (counting multi-packs as a pair) of its own brand St Michael women's knickers globally each year — the equivalent of 1 million pairs every week.

BIGGEST SURFWEAR MANUFACTURER

Quiksilver has an annual revenue of approximately $230 million (£143.75 million) in the USA and Europe, making it the largest manufacturer of surfwear in the world to date. The company sells to more than 130 countries and sponsors hundreds of athletes, including surf champions Robbie Naish, Kelly Slater and Lisa Andersen.

FASTEST-SELLING WATCH IN HISTORY

The Swatch watch, which was invented by the Swiss watchmaker Dr. Ernest Thomke and Nicholas Hayelk in 1981, had sold more than 100 million units within a period of 10 years, making it the fastest-selling brand of watch in history. In 1986 the graffiti artist Keith Haring, who was famous for his work in the New York subway, was commissioned to design a series of four Swatch watches, some of which have sold at auction for more than $5,000 (£3,125) in the 1990s. In 1989 the company asked Mimmo Paladino, the well-known Italian artist, to design a watch, which was produced in limited editions of 120. Two years later a Paladino Swatch sold at an auction in Europe for $24,000 (£13,946).

BEST-SELLING SUNGLASSES

Ray-Ban is one of the most widely recognized brands in the sunglass market: surveys carried out in the early 1990s found that 80% of sunglass wearers in Europe, Asia and the USA could identify with the name. The brand was developed by Bausch & Lomb Inc. of Rochester, New York, USA, in response to a request from US Army Corps, who needed an optical quality glass lens that could resist the harsh glare endured by their fighter pilots. Scientists worked through the late 1920s and early 1930s to develop the green tinted lens. The Aviator model was introduced to the public in 1936 and has become a fashion icon, along with the Wayfarer style. This was achieved through high-profile product placement in cult films such as *The Blues Brothers* (USA, 1980). The Wayfarer is the best-selling sunglass style in history, and remains one of the world's most popular styles 40 years after its launch in the early 1950s. In 1989 alone, Ray-Bans were featured in more than 110 movies and in 1997 the Predator 2 style was prominent in *Men in Black* (USA), starring Will Smith.

BEST-SELLING FACIAL MOISTURIZER

Oil of Ulay, which is now made by Procter and Gamble, has 28% of the world market in facial moisturizers. It was formulated by Graham Wulff of South Africa to prevent the dehydration of British pilots' burn wounds during WWII. After the war Wulff refined the product and teamed up with Shaun Adams to sell it door to door.

BIGGEST CHARITY SHOP CHAIN

Oxfam opened its first charity shop in 1948 and now has 862 shops in the United Kingdom and Ireland, making it the biggest charity shop chain in the world. In 1997 the company — which fights hunger, disease, exploitation and poverty worldwide regardless of race or religion — had an income of £17.1 million ($27.36 million) from its shops. This is almost one third of its annual income from voluntary work.

BIGGEST SECONDHAND CLOTHES SHOP

Domsey's Warehouse and Annex in Brooklyn, New York, USA, is the largest secondhand clothes shop, with an area of 23,225 m² (250,000 ft²), of which 3,251 m² (35,000 ft²) is the sales floor. The family business has been handed down through three generations and has been based in Brooklyn for 17 years. It stocks about 350,000 garments at any one time.

BIGGEST SPORTSWEAR FIRM

The sportswear giant Nike, based in Oregon, USA, had revenue of $9.19 billion (£5.74 billion) and profits of $796 million (£497.5 million) in 1997, making it the world's 198th largest company. One of its most successful lines, Nike Air training and running shoes, was inspired by Frank Rudy, a NASA engineer. Here a model wears clothes designed by basketball player Michael Jordan and produced by Nike.

BIGGEST CLOTHING INDUSTRIES

The largest clothing industry in the world in terms of the value of the goods produced is that of the USA, which manufactured approximately $39.5 billion (£24.7 billion) worth of clothing, excluding footwear, in 1996. It had about 800,000 employees in 1997.

The biggest clothing industry in terms of the number of employees is China, which had about 1.75 million people on the payroll in 1997. They made clothing (excluding footwear) worth $17.9 billion (£11.2 billion) in 1996.

high fashion

MOST SPENT ON A DESIGNER CLOTHING STORE

Gianni Versace's shop in Bond Street, London, UK, is said to have cost more than any other designer store, at £12 million ($21.2 million). The shop opened in 1992 and features Carrera marble, gilt and frescoes. His store in Paris, France, may have cost more but the figure is undisclosed. Versace was born in Italy in 1946 and began his career working with his mother in a workshop and clothing store. He moved to Milan in 1972 and in 1978 he established his own fashion house with his brother Santo and sister Donatella. Versace is now one of the most commercially successful houses in the world, grossing $50.8 million (£26.5 million) in 1978 and $742.2 million (£463.9 million) in 1993. In July 1997 Versace was shot dead on the steps of his home in Miami, Florida, USA. His funeral was attended by a host of top fashion luminaries and supermodels, as well as Diana, Princess of Wales, and singer Elton John.

RICHEST DESIGNER

Ralph Lauren has an estimated personal fortune of $1 billion (£625 million) — the highest of any designer. Born Ralph Lipschitz in New York, USA, in 1939, Lauren began his career as a sales assistant and had his first success when he designed a collection of ties. He opened his first independent Polo shop in Beverly Hills, USA, in 1971, and in 1993 launched his Polo Sport range. By 1988 his fashion house had sales of $925 million (£630 million) a year, compared with $7 million (£3 million) a year in 1974. It has supplied clothes for the Woody Allen movies *Annie Hall* (USA, 1977) and *Manhattan* (USA, 1979), and also *The Great Gatsby* (USA, 1974), starring Robert Redford, Mia Farrow and Patsy Kensit.

BEST-SELLING DESIGNER

The biggest-selling designer clothing brand in the world is Giorgio Armani. The Italian designer began his fashion career in 1954, doing the displays at La Rinascente department stores, before working for the design house Cerruti. In 1975 Armani sold his car and started up his own fashion label. The label was hugely successful throughout the late seventies and early eighties, when his clothing began to epitomise both style and wealth. Although he does not advertise as much as his main competitors (Versace, Calvin Klein and Valentino) Armani has been a favourite of a number of celebrities, including Michelle Pfeiffer, Cindy Crawford and Richard Gere. Annual global sales of Armani clothing now exceed $320 million (£200 million).

YOUNGEST INTERNATIONALLY ESTABLISHED DESIGNER

The British designer Julian MacDonald got his lucky break at the age of 24 at his graduation from the Royal College Of Art in London, UK, where he was spotted by Karl Lagerfeld and asked to design a knitwear range for the Chanel ready-to-wear collection. After great success in Paris, France, MacDonald presented his own collection, 'Mermaids', in 1997.

FASTEST RISE TO DESIGN STARDOM

Stella McCartney, the daughter of Paul McCartney, was appointed as the new designer at Parisian fashion house Chloé, in April 1997, just 18 months after graduating from Central Saint Martins College of Art and Design, London, UK. McCartney, who replaced Karl Lagerfeld, had designed three successful lines under her own label. Supermodels Naomi Campbell and Kate Moss modelled at her graduation show. Now 26, McCartney commands a six-figure salary.

OLDEST DESIGNER

The oldest international couturier in the world is the 71-year-old US designer Geoffrey Beene, who moved on to fashion after originally studying medicine.

MOST EXPENSIVE JACKET

In 1998 Naomi Campbell modelled the world's most expensive jacket for Gai Mattioli's 1998 collection. Worth $1 million (£625,000), the jacket has 100-carat Burmese rubies — the biggest on the market — and 250-year-old, 36-carat emeralds as buttons.

MOST EXPENSIVE CANCELLED CATWALK SHOW

Giorgio Armani's Emporio show during Paris fashion week in March 1998 was cancelled by French police concerned about safety at the venue. By that time Armani had spent $300,000 (£187,500) on the show and a

BIGGEST CATWALK WEDDING DRESS

Japanese designer Yohji Yamamoto astounded audiences at his March 1998 show in Paris, France, when he unveiled a beige crinoline wedding dress with a 4-m-wide (13-ft) skirt and outsize hat. The designer wanted to add humour to his collection, and the stage was set up so that the audience could see under the dress, which is not for sale. Born in Tokyo, Japan, in 1943, Yamamoto studied law before helping in his mother's dress shop and studying fashion at the famous Bunkafukuso Gaukin School. He started his own company in 1972 and in 1976 unveiled his first collection in Tokyo. Yamamoto's clothes are usually functional and understated. According to model agency chiefs, he likes to use 'real' looking women to model his collections. He also makes clothes for men, and his designs for both sexes conceal rather than emphasise the body. Yamamoto made his Paris debut in 1981, and is the only Japanese designer to have been awarded the French Chevalier de l'Ordre des Arts et des Lettres. In 1987 he opened a new headquarters in London, UK, for his company which now has an estimated annual turnover of $100 million (£60 million).

further $1 million (£625,000) on the after-show party, making it the most expensive fashion show never to have happened.

FASTEST DESIGN HOUSE REVAMP

Over a period of just three years Gucci's creative director Tom Ford has transformed the Italian fashion house into one of the most desired labels in the world. Gucci's annual turnover has increased from $250 million (£156.25 million) to approximately $1.2 billion (£750 million) in that time. One of Ford's innovations has been to abandon the crossed Gs that were attached to many Gucci products for a long time. Ford himself, who started his fashion career with an internship at Chloé, has appeared in commercials for a number of companies, including McDonalds, Old Spice and Bell Shampoo.

STORE THAT STOCKS THE MOST DESIGNER LABELS

The US department store Saks Fifth Avenue currently stocks a total of 1,252 designer labels — more than any other store in the world. Saks' flagship store on Fifth Avenue, New York, USA, was opened in 1924 by Horace Saks and Bernard Gimbel. There are now 41 full-line fashion speciality stores, eight fashion resort stores and seven main street stores in 23 states, and the company employs around 12,000 people.

BIGGEST-SELLING DESIGNER PERFUME

The most successful designer perfume in the world is Chanel No. 5, which sells more than 10 million bottles a year. Created in 1925, Chanel No. 5 has more than 80 ingredients. Its creator, Coco Chanel, was the first ever couturier to attach her name to a perfume. The market is now worth an estimated $7.5 billion (£4.7 million) a year, and some designers spend huge sums on advertising — Christian Lacroix, for instance, spent $40 million (£24 million) advertising his C'est La Vie.

MOST EXPENSIVE BRA

The Diamond Dream bra, the world's most expensive bra, was created by Harry Winston in 1997 and made by Victoria's Secret, one of the most popular US lingerie companies. The bra, which has a 42-carat, pear-shaped flawless diamond in the centre and 100 diamonds on each side, costs $3 million (£1.87 million). It is seen here modelled by Tyra Banks, the supermodel who rose to fame in the TV show *The Fresh Prince of Bel-Air* alongside Will Smith.

MOST VALUABLE COUTURE HOUSE

In 1998 Valentino and his business partner Giancarlo Giammetti sold the design house Valentino for a record $300 million (£187.5 million), after running the company for 38 years. Valentino, which makes $17.3 million (£10.8 million) a year, was bought by Holding di Part. Industriali. German supermodel Claudia Schiffer is pictured here wearing a Valentino dress.

sporting
heroes

soccer

MOST APPEARANCES

The record for the greatest number of matches played for a national team is 147, by Majed Abdullah Mohammed of Saudi Arabia from 1978 to 1994.

British goalkeeper Peter Shilton made a record 1,390 senior appearances, including a record 1,005 national league matches (286 for Leicester City, 1966–74, 110 for Stoke City, 1974–77, 202 for Nottingham Forest, 1977–82, 188 for Southampton, 1982–87, 175 for Derby County, 1987–92, 34 for Plymouth Argyle, 1992–94, one for Bolton Wanderers in 1995, nine for Leyton Orient, 1996–97, one League play-off, 86 FA Cup matches, 102 League Cup matches, 125 internationals, 13 Under-23 matches, four Football League XI matches and 53 European and other club competitions).

MOST GOALS IN A MATCH

The most goals scored by one player in a first-class match is 16, by Stephan Stanis for Racing Club de Lens v. Aubry-Asturies in a wartime French Cup game in Lens, France, on 13 Dec 1942.

The most goals by a player in an international match is 10, by Sofus Nielsen for Denmark v. France (17–1) in the 1908 Olympics and by Gottfried Fuchs for Germany v. Russia (16–0) in the 1912 Olympic tournament (consolation event) in Sweden.

MOST CAREER GOALS

Artur Friedenreich of Brazil scored an undocumented 1,329 goals in a 26-year first-class career from 1909 to 1935.

Franz 'Bimbo' Binder scored 1,006 goals in 756 games in Austria and Germany between 1930 and 1950.

MOST SUCCESSFUL GOALKEEPERS

The longest period that a goalkeeper has prevented goals being scored past him in top-class competition is 1,275 minutes, by Abel Resino of Athlético Madrid, Spain, to 17 March 1991.

The longest period that a goalkeeper has prevented goals in international matches is 1,142 min, by Dino Zoff (Italy) from Sept 1972 to June 1974.

HIGHEST SCORES

The highest winning margin in an international is 17, by England in their 17–0 victory over Australia at Sydney, Australia, on 30 June 1951 (not listed by England as a full international) and by Iran in their 17–0 win over the Maldives at Damascus, Syria, in June 1997.

The highest score recorded in a first-class match was 36, in the Scottish Cup match between Arbroath and Bon Accord on 5 Sept 1885. Arbroath won 36–0 at their home ground.

FASTEST GOALS

In first-class football the record for the fastest goal is six seconds, by Albert Mundy for

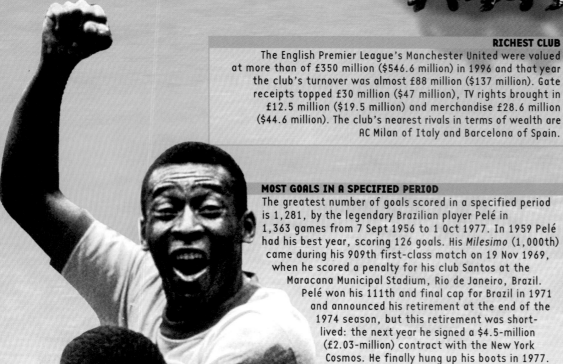

RICHEST CLUB

The English Premier League's Manchester United were valued at more than of £350 million ($546.6 million) in 1996 and that year the club's turnover was almost £88 million ($137 million). Gate receipts topped £30 million ($47 million), TV rights brought in £12.5 million ($19.5 million) and merchandise £28.6 million ($44.6 million). The club's nearest rivals in terms of wealth are AC Milan of Italy and Barcelona of Spain.

MOST GOALS IN A SPECIFIED PERIOD

The greatest number of goals scored in a specified period is 1,281, by the legendary Brazilian player Pelé in 1,363 games from 7 Sept 1956 to 1 Oct 1977. In 1959 Pelé had his best year, scoring 126 goals. His *Milesimo* (1,000th) came during his 909th first-class match on 19 Nov 1969, when he scored a penalty for his club Santos at the Maracana Municipal Stadium, Rio de Janeiro, Brazil. Pelé won his 111th and final cap for Brazil in 1971 and announced his retirement at the end of the 1974 season, but this retirement was short-lived: the next year he signed a $4.5-million (£2.03-million) contract with the New York Cosmos. He finally hung up his boots in 1977.

Aldershot v. Hartlepool United in a Fourth Division match at Victoria Ground, Hartlepool, Co. Durham, UK, in Oct 1958; by Barrie Jones for Notts County v. Torquay United in a British Third Division match in March 1962, and by Keith Smith for Crystal Palace v. Derby County in a Second Division match at the Baseball Ground, Derby, UK, on 12 Dec 1964.

The international record is three goals in 3½ minutes, by George Hall of Tottenham Hotspur for England against Ireland at Old Trafford, Greater Manchester, UK, on 16 Nov 1938.

Maglioni is said to have scored a hat-trick in a record time of 1 min 50 sec whilst playing for Independiente against Gimnasia y Escrima de la Plata in Argentina on 18 March 1973.

MOST EXPENSIVE DEFENDER

In May 1998 Dutch defender Jaap Stam struck a deal to go to Manchester United for a record £10.75 million ($18 million). The 26-year-old PSV Eindhoven star accepted a seven-year deal that is worth £11 million ($18.3 million) with bonuses. He began his professional career at 19 and made his international debut in 1996 for Holland.

BIGGEST VICTORY MARGINS IN NATIONAL SOCCER CUP FINALS

In 1935 Lausanne-Sports beat Nordstern Basel 10-0 in the Swiss Cup Final, but were defeated by the same scoreline by Grasshopper Club (Zürich) in the 1937 Swiss Cup Final.

MOST SUCCESSIVE NATIONAL LEAGUE CHAMPIONSHIPS

Dinamo Berlin of Germany had 10 successive championships from 1979 to 1988.

CSKA Sofia of Bulgaria hold a European post-war record of 26 league titles, including two under the name CFKA Sredets (renamed CSKA).

LONGEST-HELD NATIONAL SOCCER LEAGUE TITLE

The Cairo club Al Ahly maintained the national soccer title from the 1948/49 season until the 1959/60 season. However, the 1952 championship was abandoned because of the Egyptian revolution and the 1955 league programme also went uncompleted.

FURTHEST DISTANCE TRAVELLED FOR A LEAGUE GAME

The furthest distance travelled between two clubs in the top division of a national soccer league is 4,766 km (2,979 miles), from the grounds of LA Galaxy, California, and New England Revolution, Massachusetts, in the US Major League.

BIGGEST CROWDS

The record attendance for any European Cup match is 136,505, at the semi-final between Glasgow Celtic and Leeds United at Hampden Park, Glasgow, UK, on 15 April 1970.

The highest recorded attendance at an amateur match was 120,000, to see North Korea v. Indonesia at the pre-Olympic Group II final in Senayan Stadium, Jakarta, Indonesia, on 26 Feb 1976.

BIGGEST FOOTBALL STADIUM

The Maracana Municipal Stadium in Rio de Janeiro, Brazil, has a normal capacity of 205,000 with seats for 155,000. It was built for the 1950 World Cup, when a crowd of nearly 200,000 packed the arena for the final, which Brazil lost to Uruguay. It was also the stage for Brazilian victories in 1958, 1962 and 1970.

MOST UNDISCIPLINED MATCH

On 1 June 1993 it was reported that referee William Weiler sent off 20 players in a league match between Sportivo Ameliano and General Caballero in Paraguay. Trouble flared after two Sportivo players were sent off. A 10-minute fight ensued, and Weiler dismissed a further 18 players, including the rest of the Sportivo team. The match was then abandoned.

HIGHEST TRANSFER FEE

On 28 Aug 1997 Real Betis (Spain) paid a world record $36 million (£22.6 million) for midfielder Denilson de Oliveira, who was 20 at the time, before immediately loaning him back to Sao Paolo. Denilson signed a 10-year contract said to be worth $127 million (£77.5 million). He was first capped for Brazil aged 19 in Nov 1996 and now has his left foot insured for more than $1.6 million (£1 million).

soccer: world cup

BIGGEST CROWDS
The largest ever crowd at a football match consisted of 199,854 people, for the 1950 World Cup match between Brazil and Uruguay at the Maracana Municipal Stadium, Rio de Janeiro, Brazil.

The record for the greatest number of spectators at a tournament is 3,587,538, for the 52 matches in the 1994 World Cup in the USA.

BUSIEST WORLD CUP HOTLINE
British Telecom estimate that 20 million callers in the United Kingdom tried to get through to the French hotline when tickets went on sale on 22 April 1998.

MOST TEAMS IN A TOURNAMENT
In 1998, 32 countries played — more than double the number that took part in the first World Cup in 1930, when a total of 18 matches were played by 13 countries. In 1998 64 games were played.

MOST TEAM WINS
Brazil have won the World Cup a record four times (1958, 1962, 1970 and 1994).

Overall, Brazil have won a record 53 matches from 80 matches in the finals stage.

MOST TEAM APPEARANCES
Brazil have taken part in all 16 finals tournaments.

France and the USA are the only other nations to have entered every World Cup competition (the USA withdrew without playing a match in 1938).

MOST INDIVIDUAL WINS
Pelé (Brazil) is the only player to have been with a record three winning teams, in 1958, 1962 and 1970.

MOST GOALS SCORED OVERALL
Brazil have scored a record-breaking 173 goals in a total of 80 matches.

Gerd Müller (Germany) scored 10 goals in 1970 and four in 1974 for a record total of 14.

MOST GOALS IN A TOURNAMENT
A record 171 goals were scored in France in 1998.

The record for the greatest number of goals scored in one finals tournament is 27 (in five games), by Hungary in 1954.

Just Fontaine (France) scored a total of 13 goals in six matches in the final stages of the 1958 competition in Sweden.

The only players to have scored in every match in a final series are Fontaine (France),

WORLD CUP TROPHIES
Brazil are pictured above with the World Cup after victory in 1994. The first trophy for the World Cup — a gold statuette weighing about 1.5 kg (3 lb) — was commissioned from French sculptor Abel Lafleur by FIFA and named after the FIFA president Jules Rimet, a Frenchman who had initiated the first tournament. In 1966 the 'Jules Rimet Cup' was stolen for the first time, in London, UK. The thief, Edward Bletchley, demanded a ransom of £15,000 ($40,500) but was arrested when he went to collect it. He did not reveal where the cup was but it was eventually found by a dog called Pickles under a bush in his owner's back garden. The trophy was presented to Brazil — the first country to have won three World Cups — in 1970, but was stolen again and never retrieved. Since then, a copy of the original has been given to the winning team. Following the first theft a secret version of the trophy was made by London silversmiths Alexander Clarke and exhibited until 1970 around England, under heavy guard to maintain the illusion that it was the original. This trophy was auctioned by Sotheby's for £254,500 ($407,200) in 1997. The present trophy is the work of Italian sculptor Silvio Gazamiga, and is made of solid gold.

Jaïrzinho (Brazil) and Alcide Ghiggia (Uruguay). Jaïrzinho scored seven goals in six games in 1970 and Ghiggia scored four goals in four games in 1950.

MOST GOALS IN A GAME
Iran beat the Maldives 17-0 in a qualifying match on 2 June 1997.

The highest score in the final stages was achieved by Hungary in a 10-1 win over El Salvador at Elche, Spain, on 15 June 1982.

The highest match aggregate in the finals tournament was 12, when Austria beat Switzerland 7-5 in Switzerland in June 1954.

Oleg Salenko scored five goals in Russia's 6-1 win over Cameroon in the USA on 28 June 1994.

MOST APPEARANCES
Antonio Carbajal kept goal for Mexico in five World Cup finals tournaments, in 1950, 1954, 1958, 1962 and 1966, playing 11 games in all. This record was equalled by Lothar Matthäus (Germany), who played a record 25 games from 1982 to 1998. Matthäus, below right, is pictured during a challenge from Croatia's Davor Suker during Germany's quarter-final match against Croatia in Lyon, France, in July 1998. Croatia won 3–0, knocking Germany out of the tournament.

Of the nine players to have scored four goals in a match, three — Sándor Kocsis (Hungary), Just Fontaine (France) and Gerd Müller (West Germany) — have achieved one of the 35 hat-tricks scored in finals matches.

MOST GOALS IN A FINAL
Geoff Hurst scored three goals for England against West Germany on 30 July 1966.

MOST WORLD CUP FINAL MATCHES SCORED IN
Vava (Brazil) scored in 1958 and 1962, Pelé (Brazil) in 1958 and 1970, and Paul Breitner (West Germany) in 1974 and 1982.

MOST GOALS CONCEDED
The record for the greatest number of goals to have been conceded is 103 in 78 matches, by Germany.

YOUNGEST AND OLDEST PLAYERS
The youngest person to play in a finals match is Norman Whiteside, who played for Northern Ireland v. Yugoslavia at the age of 17 years 41 days in June 1982.

The youngest scorer in a finals match is Pelé, who was 17 years 239 days old when he scored for Brazil against Wales, at Gothenburg, Sweden, in 1958.

YOUNGEST SCORER, 1998
The youngest scorer in the 1998 finals was England's Michael Owen (right), who was 18 years 191 days old when he scored against Romania at Toulouse, France, on 22 June 1998. The oldest scorer during the 1998 finals was Saudi Arabia's Youssef Al Tunian, who was 34 years 220 days old when he scored a penalty against South Africa at Bordeaux, France, on 24 June 1998.

The youngest player in the 1998 finals was Samuel Eto'o (Cameroon), who was 17 years 99 days old when he came on as a substitute v. Italy on 17 June.

The oldest person to play in a finals match was Roger Milla for Cameroon v. Russia at the age of 42 years 39 days on 28 June 1994.

The oldest player in the 1998 finals was Jim Leighton, Scotland's goalkeeper, who was 39 years 334 days old in his team's final group match against Morocco at St Etienne, France, on 23 June 1998.

FASTEST GOAL
The quickest official goal in a World Cup finals match was 27 seconds by Bryan Robson for England v. France at Bilbao, Spain, on 16 June 1982.

Based on timing from film, Vaclav Masek of Czechoslovakia scored against Mexico in 15 seconds at Viña del Mar, Chile, in 1962.

FASTEST GOAL BY A SUBSTITUTE PLAYER
Denmark's Ebbe Sand was sent on in the 59th minute of the match against Nigeria on 28 June 1998 and was on the pitch 16 (ball in play) seconds before he scored the fourth goal.

MOST SENDINGS OFF IN ONE GAME
The record for the greatest number of sendings off to have occurred in a single game is three, by Brazil (2) against Czechoslovakia (1) at Bordeaux, France, on 12 June 1938; Brazil (2) against Hungary (1) at Berne, Switzerland, on 27 June 1958, and Denmark (2) against South Africa (1) at Toulouse, France, on 18 June 1998.

MOST UNDISCIPLINED TOURNAMENT
The worst ever World Cup tournament in terms of bookings and sendings off was France '98, with a total of 22 sendings off and 257 bookings from 64 games.

track and field

STEEPLECHASE CHAMPION

Moses Kiptanui (Kenya) was the first athlete to complete the 3,000-m steeplechase in less than 8 minutes. His first ambition was to play football, but he was directed towards athletics and began training seriously in 1989. His first breakthrough came in 1990, when he won the World junior and the African senior 1,500-m titles. He has set up a coaching centre in the mountains of his native Kenya.

FASTEST RUNNING SPEEDS

Ben Johnson (Canada) and Carl Lewis (USA) both reached a peak speed of 0.83 sec over 10 m (43.37 km/h or 26.95 mph) during the 1988 Olympic Games 100-m final in Seoul, South Korea, on 24 Sept 1988. Johnson won but his world record was disallowed after a positive drugs test.

In the women's final, Florence Griffith-Joyner (USA) was timed at 0.91 sec for each 10 m from 60 m to 90 m (a speed of 39.56 km/h or 24.58 mph).

MOST OLYMPIC TITLES

The most gold medals won is 10 (an absolute Olympic record), by Raymond Ewry (USA): standing high, long and triple jumps in 1900, 1904, 1906 and 1908.

The most gold medals won by a woman is four, by Fanny Blankers-Koen (Netherlands) in the 100 m, 200 m, 80-m hurdles and 4 x 100-m relay, 1948; Betty Cuthbert (Australia) in the 100 m, 200 m and 4 x 100-m relay, 1956, and the 400 m, 1964; Bärbel Wöckel (GDR) in the 200 m and 4 x 100-m relay, 1976 and 1980; and Evelyn Ashford (USA) in the 100 m, 1984, and 4 x 100-m relay, 1984, 1988 and 1992.

MOST OLYMPIC MEDALS

The most medals is 12 (nine gold, three silver), by long-distance runner Paavo Nurmi (Finland) in 1920, 1924 and 1928.

The most medals by a female athlete is seven, by Shirley de la Hunty (Australia), with three gold, one silver and three bronze in 1948, 1952 and 1956. A re-read of the photo-finish indicated that she was third, not fourth, in the 1948 200-m event, thus unofficially making her medal count eight. Irena Szewinska (Poland), the only female athlete to win a medal in four successive Games, also won seven medals (three gold, two silver and two bronze in 1964, 1968, 1972 and 1976), as did Merlene Ottey (Jamaica), with two silver and five bronze in 1980, 1984, 1992 and 1996.

MOST WINS AT ONE GAMES

The most gold medals at one Games is five, by Paavo Nurmi (Finland) in 1924 (1,500 m, 5,000 m, 10,000-m cross-country, 3,000-m team and cross-country team).

The most medals at individual events is four, by Alvin Kraenzlein (USA) in 1900 (60 m, 110-m hurdles, 200-m hurdles and long jump).

OLDEST AND YOUNGEST OLYMPIC CHAMPIONS

The oldest athlete was Patrick 'Babe' McDonald (USA), who was 42 years 26 days old when he won the 25.4-kg (56-lb) weight throw in Belgium in Aug 1920.

The oldest female champion was Lia Manoliu (Romania), who was 36 years 176 days old when she won the discus in Mexico in 1968.

The youngest gold medallist was Barbara Jones (USA), who was a member of the winning 4 x 100-m relay team at Helsinki, Finland, at the age of 15 years 123 days in July 1952.

The youngest male champion was Robert Mathias (USA), who won the decathlon aged 17 years 263 days in London, UK, in 1948.

OLDEST AND YOUNGEST RECORD-BREAKERS

Marina Styepanova (USSR) set a 400-m hurdle record (52.94 sec) at Tashkent, USSR, in 1986, at the age of 36 years 139 days.

RECORD-BREAKING SPRINTER

Donovan Bailey was born in Manchester, Jamaica. He began his track career running for Canada at the 1991 Pan-Am Games in Cuba and went on to win an Olympic gold at the 1996 Summer Games in Atlanta, USA, setting a new 100-m world record of 9.84 sec, and reaching a top speed of more than 43.45 km/h (27 mph). He set a new indoor 50-m world record of 5.56 sec in 1996.

Wang Yan (China) set an individual women's 5,000-m walk record of 21 min 33.8 sec aged 14 years 334 days in China on 9 March 1986.

The youngest man to break an individual record was Thomas Ray (GB), who pole-vaulted 3.42 m (11 ft 2¼ in) aged 17 years 198 days on 19 Sept 1879.

WORLD CHAMPIONSHIPS

The most medals won is 10, by Carl Lewis (USA): a record eight gold (100 m, long jump and 4 x 100-m relay, 1983; 100 m, long jump and 4 x 100-m relay, 1987; and 100 m and 4 x 100-m relay, 1991), a silver at long jump in 1991 and a bronze at 200 m in 1993.

The most medals won by a woman is 14, by Merlene Ottey (Jamaica), with three gold, four silver and seven bronze from 1983 to 1997.

The most gold medals won by a woman is four, by Jackie Joyner-Kersee (USA) in the long jump in 1987 and 1991 and the heptathlon in 1987 and 1993.

Sergey Bubka (Ukraine) won the same event at a record six consecutive championships in the pole vault from 1983 to 1997

WORLD INDOOR CHAMPIONSHIPS

The most individual titles is four, by Stefka Kostadinova (Bulgaria) in the high jump in 1985, 1987, 1989 and 1993, Mikhail Shchennikov (Russia) in the 5,000-m walk in 1987, 1989, 1991 and 1993 and Sergey Bubka (Ukraine) in the pole vault in 1985, 1987, 1991 and 1995.

MOST RECORDS SET IN A DAY

Jesse Owens (USA) set six world records in 45 minutes at Ann Arbor, Michigan, USA, on 25 May 1935. He ran 100 yd in 9.4 sec at 3:15 pm, made an 8.13-m (26-ft 8¼-in) long jump at 3:25 pm, ran 220 yd (and 200 m) in 20.3 sec at 3:45 pm and covered the 220-yd (and 200-m) low hurdles in 22.6 sec at 4 pm.

LONGEST WINNING SEQUENCES

The record winning sequence at a track event is 122, by Edwin Corley Moses (USA) at the 400-m hurdles between Aug 1977 and June 1987.

Iolanda Balas (Romania) won a record 150 consecutive high jump competitions between 1956 and 1967.

HIGHEST JUMP ABOVE OWN HEAD

The greatest height cleared by an athlete above their own head was 59 cm (1 ft 11¼ in), by 1.73-m-tall (5-ft 8-in) Franklin Jacobs (USA), who jumped 2.32 m (7 ft 7¼ in) at New York, USA, on 27 Jan 1978.

The greatest height cleared by a female athlete above her own head was 32 cm (1 ft ¾ in), by 1.68-m-tall (5-ft 6-in) Yolanda Henry (USA), who jumped 2.00 m (6 ft 6¾ in) at Seville, Spain, on 30 May 1990.

BEST STANDING JUMPS

The best high jump from a standing position was 1.90 m (6 ft 2¾ in), by Rune Almen (Sweden) at Karlstad, Sweden, on 3 May 1980.

The women's best is 1.52 m (4 ft 11¾ in), by Grete Bjørdalsbakka (Norway) in 1984.

The best ever long jump was 3.71 m (12 ft 2 in), by Arne Tvervaag (Norway) in 1968.

The best long jump by a woman was 2.92 m (9 ft 7 in), by Annelin Mannes (Norway) in March 1981.

FASTEST MASS RELAYS

The fastest 100 x 100-m was 19 min 14.19 sec, by a team from Antwerp in Belgium on 23 Sept 1989.

The fastest time over 160.9 km (100 miles) by 100 runners was 7 hr 53 min 52.1 sec, by Baltimore Road Runners Club, Maryland, USA, on 17 May 1981.

The greatest distance ever covered by a team of 10 runners in 24 hours is 487.343 km (302 miles 494 yd), by Puma Tyneside RC at Monkton Stadium in Jarrow, UK, in Sept 1994.

DOUBLE RECORD-BREAKER

Svetlana Masterkova (Russia) holds the 1,000-m record, after finishing in 2 min 28.98 sec on 23 Aug 1996 in Brussels, Belgium. Nine days earlier she set a new one-mile record of 4 min 12.56 sec in Zürich, Switzerland. She is the first woman to hold world records at both 1,000 m and one mile since 1936.

POLE VAULTING CHAMPION

On 21 March 1998 Emma George (Australia) set a world outdoor pole vault record of 4.58 m (15 ft ¼ in), an improvement of 1 cm (²/₅ in) on the existing record which she had set herself just the week before. Five days later, on 26 March, George cleared 4.55 m (14 ft 11 in), breaking the world indoor pole vault record by 7 cm (2¾ in). George, who is 23 years old, is a former circus performer.

golf

The best score in four rounds is 267 (66, 68, 69, 64), by Greg Norman at Royal St George's, UK, from 15 to 18 July 1993.

Nick Faldo completed the first 36 holes at Muirfield, UK, in a record 130 strokes (66, 64) from 16 to 17 July 1992.

US OPEN

The best score in a round is 63, by Johnny Miller on the 6,328-m (6,921-yd), par-71 Oakmont Country Club course, Pennsylvania, in June 1973 and by Jack Nicklaus and Tom Weiskopf (USA) at Baltusrol Country Club (6,414-m or 7,015-yd), Springfield, New Jersey, both on 12 June 1980.

The best score over two rounds is 134, by Jack Nicklaus (63, 71) at Baltusrol in 1980, Chen Tze-Chung of Taiwan (65, 69) at Oakland Hills, Michigan, in 1985, and Lee Janzen of the USA (67, 67) at Baltusrol in June 1993.

The best score over four rounds is 272, by Jack Nicklaus (63, 71, 70, 68) at Baltusrol in June 1980 and Lee Janzen (67, 67, 69, 69) at Baltusrol in June 1993.

US MASTERS

The top score in a round is 63, by Nicholas Price (Zimbabwe) in 1986 and Greg Norman in 1996.

The best score over two rounds is 131 (65, 66), by Raymond Floyd (USA) in 1976.

OLDEST US OPEN CHAMPION

US golfer Hale Irwin won the US Open at the age of 45 years 15 days on 18 June 1990. Irwin won in 1974 and 1979, but he had not been a contender for several years, and was only eligible via a special exemption given him by the USGA. Although he has never been the top player in the world, he has been in the US top 10 money winners a total of eight times, from 1973 to 1978, in 1981 and in 1990.

THE OPEN

The best score in a round is 63, by Mark Hayes (USA) at Turnberry, UK, in 1977, Isao Aoki (Japan) at Muirfield, UK, in 1980, Greg Norman (Australia) at Turnberry, UK, in 1986, Paul Broadhurst (GB) at St Andrews, UK, in 1990, Jodie Mudd (USA) at Royal Birkdale, UK, in 1991, Nick Faldo (GB) at Royal St George's, UK, in 1993, and William Stewart (USA) in 1993, also at St George's.

US PGA

The best score in any round is 63, by Bruce Crampton (Australia) at Firestone, Akron, Ohio, in 1975; Raymond Floyd (USA) at Southern Hills, Tulsa, Oklahoma, in 1982; Gary Player (South Africa) at Shoal Creek, Birmingham, Alabama, in 1984; Vijay Singh (Fiji) at Inverness Club, Toledo, Ohio, in 1993; and Michael Bradley (USA) and Brad Faxon (USA) at Riviera Pacific Palisades, California, in 1995.

The record aggregate is 26.7 by Steve Elkington (Australia), with 68, 67, 68, 64, and Colin Montgomerie (GB), with 68, 67, 67, 65, at Riviera GC, Pacific Palisades, in 1995.

WORLD CUP

The USA has won the World Cup 21 times between 1955 and 1995.

The lowest aggregate score for 144 holes is 536, by the USA (Fredrick Couples and Davis Milton Love III) at Dorado, Puerto Rico, from 10 to 13 Nov 1994.

The lowest ever individual score was 265, by Fredrick Couples on the same occasion.

WORLD CUP

Arnold Palmer and Jack Nicklaus have been on a record six winning teams, Palmer in 1960, 1962–64, and 1966–67, and Nicklaus in 1963–64, 1966–67, 1971 and 1973.

Jack Nicklaus has taken the individual title a record three times (1963–64, 1971).

WALKER CUP

The USA has won the Walker Cup a record 31 times.

Jay Sigel (USA) won a record 18 matches from 1977 to 1993.

Joseph Carr (GB and Ireland) played in 10 contests, 1947–67.

MOST TOURNAMENT WINS

John Nelson (USA) won a record 18 tournaments and an unofficial tournament in a year, including a record 11 consecutive wins, from 8 March to 4 Aug 1945.

After turning professional in 1934, Sam Snead had won 84 official US PGA tour events by 1965.

The ladies' PGA record is 88, by Kathy Whitworth (USA), 1959–91.

The most career victories in European Order of Merit tournaments is 55, by Severiano Ballesteros (Spain), 1974–95.

BIGGEST WINNING MARGIN

The greatest margin of victory in a major tournament is 21 strokes, by Jerry Pate (USA), who won the 1981 Colombian Open with 262.

Charlotte Pitcairn Leitch won the Canadian Ladies' Open in 1921 by the biggest margin for a major title: 17 up and 15 to play.

EUROPEAN VICTORY IN THE RYDER CUP

The Ryder Cup, golf's most prized team trophy, began in 1927 at the instigation of wealthy British seed merchant Samuel Ryder. The idea was the result of a match between professionals from Great Britain and the USA at Wentworth, Surrey, UK, the previous year. The biennial event was originally contested between the USA and Great Britain (Great Britain and Ireland 1973–77). In 1979 the British team was opened up to include European players, a reflection of the rapidly growing European Tour, although it was not until 1985 that a European side gained victory in the event. Prior to this, Britain had won only three times (1929, 1933 and 1957), while the USA had won 21 times. Since 1985, however, Europe has won a further four times and interest has grown in the event. In 1997 it was held outside the British Isles and the USA for the first time, at Valderrama, Spain. Europe (seen left), captained by Spaniard Severiano Ballesteros, secured victory by 14.5 to 13.5 points.

YOUNGEST AND OLDEST NATIONAL CHAMPIONS

Thuashni Selvaratnam won the Sri Lankan Ladies' Amateur Open Golf Championship aged 12 in 1989.

Isa Goldschmid won the Italian Women's Championship at the age of 50 in 1976.

MOST HOLES

Eric Freeman (USA) played 467 holes, using a cart, at Glen Head Country Club, New York, USA, in 12 hours in 1997. The nine-hole course is 2,992 m long (3,272 yd).

Ian Colston played 401 holes in 24 hours at Bendigo GC, Victoria, Australia (par-73, 5,542 m or 6,061 yd), in 1971.

Steve Hylton played 1,128 holes in a week at Mason Rudolph GC (5,541 m or 6,060 yd), Clarksville, Tennessee, USA, in Aug 1980.

LONGEST CARRY

The greatest recorded carry of a ball is 418.8 m (458 yd), by Jack Hamm (USA) at Highlands Ranch, Colorado, USA, on 20 July 1993.

The record for the longest carry below an altitude of 1,000 m (3,281 ft) is 333.6 m (365 yd), by Karl Woodward (GB) at the Boca Raton Country Club, Florida, USA, in 1996.

LONGEST PUTT

The longest known holed putt in a major tournament is 100.6 m (110 ft), by Jack Nicklaus in the 1964 Tournament of Champions, and Nick Price in the 1992 United States PGA.

MOST BALLS HIT IN ONE HOUR

The most balls driven in one hour, over 91.5 m (100 yd) and into a target area, is 2,146, by Sean Murphy of Canada at Swifts Practice Range, Carlisle, Cumbria, UK, on 30 June 1995.

LONGEST STRAIGHT HOLE ACHIEVED IN ONE SHOT

The longest straight hole ever holed in one shot was the 10th (408 m or 447 yd) at Miracle Hills GC, Omaha, Nebraska, USA, by Robert Mitera on 7 Oct 1965. Mitera stood 1.68 m (5 ft 6 in) tall and weighed 75 kg (11 st 11 lb). He was a two-handicap player who normally drove 224 m (245 yd). An 80 km/h (50 mph) gust carried his shot over a 265-m (290-yd) drop-off.

LONGEST 'DOG LEG' HOLE

The record for the longest 'dog-leg' hole achieved in one stroke is the 453 m (496 yd) 17th, by Shaun Lynch at Teign Valley GC, Christow, Devon, UK, on 24 July 1995.

VARE TROPHY WINNER

Annika Sörenstam (Sweden) began playing golf at the age of 12, winning the World Amateur Championship in 1991. She began her professional career at 23 on the WPG European Tour (1993), and became the first foreign-born player to win the Vare Trophy for low scoring average. Sörenstam was the first player in seven years to win six events in one season and is the eighth woman to have been player of the year more than once.

BEST FOUR ROUNDS IN US MASTERS

Tiger Woods holds the record for the best score in four rounds in the US Masters, with 270 (70, 66, 65, 69) in 1997, the year in which he became the youngest player to win the Masters. Born in 1975, Woods apparently swung his first golf club at the age of 11 months. He turned professional on 26 Aug 1996, and became the first player to record five consecutive top-10 finishes on a US tour.

tennis

MOST GRAND SLAM WINS

The most singles championships in grand slam tournaments is 24, by Margaret Court (Australia): 11 Australian, five US, five French and three Wimbledon, 1960–73.

The record for the most men's singles championships in grand slam tournaments is 12, by Roy Emerson (Australia): six Australian and two each French, US and Wimbledon, 1961–67.

The most grand slam tournament wins by a doubles partnership is 20, by Althea Brough (USA) and Margaret Du Pont (USA): 12 US, five Wimbledon and three French 1942–57; and Martina Navrátilová and Pam Shriver (both USA): seven Australian, five Wimbledon, four French and four US, 1981–89.

Pam Shriver and Martina Navrátilová (both USA) won a record eight successive grand slam tournament women's doubles titles and 109 successive matches in all events from April 1983 to July 1985.

Six successive grand slam tournaments were won by Maureen Connolly (USA) in 1953, Margaret Court (Australia) in 1970 and Martina Navrátilová (USA) from 1983 to 1984.

MOST WIMBLEDON WINS

Billie-Jean King (USA) won a record 20 women's titles between 1961 and 1979: six singles, 10 women's doubles and four mixed doubles.

Martina Navrátilová (USA) has won a record nine women's singles titles in 1978–79, 1982–87 and 1990.

Elizabeth Montague Ryan (USA) won a record 19 women's doubles titles (12 women's, seven mixed), 1914–34.

The most titles by a man is 13, by Hugh Doherty (GB) with five singles titles (1902–06) and a record eight men's doubles (1897–1901 and 1903–05), partnered by his brother Reginald.

The most men's singles wins since the Challenge Round was abolished in 1922 is five, by Björn Borg (Sweden), 1976–80.

The most men's mixed doubles titles is four, by Elias Seixas (USA) from 1953 to 1956; Kenneth Fletcher (Australia) in 1963, 1965, 1966 and 1968; and Owen Davidson (Australia) in 1967, 1971, 1973 and 1974.

OLDEST AND YOUNGEST WIMBLEDON CHAMPIONS

Margaret Du Pont (USA) was 44 years 125 days old when she won the mixed doubles in 1962.

Arthur Gore (GB) won the men's singles at the age of 41 years 182 days in 1909.

Lottie Dod (GB) was 15 years 285 days old when she won the women's singles in 1887.

The youngest seed was Jennifer Capriati (USA), who was 14 years 89 days old at her first match in 1990. She won, making her the youngest ever Wimbledon winner.

MOST US CHAMPIONSHIP WINS

Margaret Du Pont (USA) won 25 titles from 1941 to 1960: a record 13 women's doubles (12 with Althea Brough, USA), nine mixed doubles and three singles.

The most women's singles titles is seven, by Molla Mallory (USA), 1915–16, 1918, 1920–22, 1926, and Helen Newington Moody (USA), 1923–25, 1927–29, 1931.

The most men's titles is 16, by William Tilden (USA), including seven singles (1920–25, 1929). Seven singles titles were also won by Richard Sears (USA), 1881–87, and William Larned (USA), 1901–02, 1907–11.

YOUNGEST AND OLDEST US CHAMPIONSHIP WINNERS

Vincent Richards (USA) was 15 years 139 days old when he won the men's doubles in 1918.

The youngest singles champion was Tracy Austin (USA), who was 16 years 271 days old when she won the 1979 women's title.

The youngest men's singles champion was Pete Sampras (USA), who was 19 years 28 days old when he won the title in 1990.

The oldest ever champion was Margaret Du Pont (USA), who won the mixed doubles title at the age of 42 years 166 days in 1960.

The oldest ever singles champion was William Larned (USA), who won at the age of 38 years 242 days in 1911.

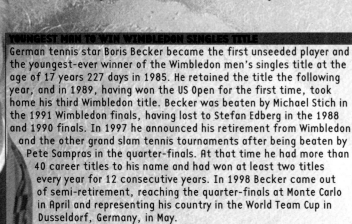

MOST WINS IN THE AUSTRALIAN CHAMPIONSHIP

Margaret Court (Australia) won 21 titles: 11 women's singles (1960–66, 1969–71 and 1973), eight women's doubles, and two mixed doubles.

Roy Emerson (Australia) won six men's singles (1961, 1963–67).

Thelma Long (Australia) won a record 12 women's doubles and four mixed doubles for a record total of 16 doubles titles.

Adrian Quist (Australia) won 10 consecutive men's doubles (1936 to 1950) and three men's singles.

YOUNGEST AND OLDEST WINNERS AT AUSTRALIAN CHAMPIONSHIP

Rodney Heath (Australia) was 17 when he won the men's singles in 1905.

The oldest champion was Norman Brookes (Australia), who was 46 years 2 months old when he won the 1924 men's doubles.

Kenneth Rosewal (Australia) won the men's singles at the age of 37 years 62 days in 1972.

MOST FRENCH OPEN WINS

Margaret Court (Australia) won a record 13 titles from 1962–73: five singles, four women's doubles and four mixed doubles.

The men's record is nine, by Henri Cochet (France), with four singles, three men's doubles and two mixed doubles, 1926–30.

The singles record is seven by Chris Evert (USA): 1974–75, 1979–80, 1983 and 1985–86.

Björn Borg (Sweden) won six men's singles from 1974 to 1975, and 1978 to 1981.

OLDEST AND YOUNGEST FRENCH OPEN CHAMPIONSHIPS

Elizabeth Ryan (USA) won the 1934 women's doubles at the age of 42 years 88 days.

The oldest singles champion was Andrés Gimeno (Spain), at the age of 34 years 301 days in 1972.

The youngest doubles champions were the 1981 mixed doubles winners Andrea Jaeger and Jimmy Arias (both USA). Jaegar was 15 years 339 days old and Arias 16 years 296 days old.

The youngest women's singles winner is Monica Seles (Yugoslavia), who won at the age of 16 years 169 days in 1990.

MOST WINS IN THE ATP TOUR CHAMPIONSHIP

Ivan Lendl (Czechoslovakia/USA) won five titles: 1982, 1983, 1986 (two) and 1987.

Seven doubles titles were won by John McEnroe and Peter Fleming (both USA) from 1978 to 1984.

MOST DAVIS CUP WINS

The USA has won the Davis Cup 31 times from 1900 to 1997.

LONGEST GRAND SLAM MATCH

The 1992 semi-final of the US Championships between Stefan Edberg (Sweden) and Michael Chang (USA) lasted a total of 5 hr 26 min. Edberg won 6–7, 7–5, 7–6, 5–7, 6–4.

FASTEST SERVE

The fastest service timed with modern equipment was 239.8 km/h (149 mph), by Greg Rusedski (GB) during the ATP Champions' Cup at Indian Wells, California, USA, on 14 March 1998. The record for the fastest timed women's service was set by Brenda Schultz-McCarthy (Netherlands) during the Australian Championships on 22 Jan 1996, and stands at 196 km/h (121.8 mph).

YOUNGEST WIMBLEDON CHAMP

The youngest ever Wimbledon champion is Martina Hingis (Switzerland), who was 15 years 282 days old when she won the women's doubles in 1996. In 1997 Hingis also became the youngest ever winner of the women's singles title at the Australian Championship, at the age of 16 years 117 days.

national football league (NFL)

LARGEST TV AUDIENCE
Around 138.5 million viewers in the USA and a further 800 million worldwide tuned in to watch Super Bowl XXX between the Dallas Cowboys and the Pittsburgh Steelers on 28 Jan 1996.

LARGEST CROWD
On 20 Jan 1980 Super Bowl XIV between the Pittsburgh Steelers and the LA Rams at the Rose Bowl, Pasadena, California, was watched by 103,985 spectators.

MOST SUPER BOWL WINS
The greatest number of team wins is five, by the San Francisco 49ers (1982, 1985, 1989–90 and 1995) and by the Dallas Cowboys (1972, 1978, 1993–94 and 1996).

The most wins by an individual player is five, by Charles Hayley for the San Francisco 49ers (1989–90) and the Dallas Cowboys (1993–94 and 1996).

Chuck Noll holds the record for the most wins by a coach. He led the Pittsburgh Steelers to four Super Bowl titles: IX, X, XIII and XIV.

MOST SUPER BOWL APPEARANCES BY A COACH
Don Shula has been the head coach of six Super Bowl teams: the Baltimore Colts (III) and the Miami Dolphins (VI, VII, VIII, XVII and XIX). He won two games and lost four.

HIGHEST SUPER BOWL SCORES
The highest team score was set by the San Francisco 49ers when they beat the Denver Broncos 55–10 at New Orleans, Louisiana, on 28 Jan 1990. This was also the highest victory margin.

In 1995, the San Francisco 49ers set the record for the highest aggregate score, beating the San Diego Chargers 49–26.

HIGHEST NFL ATTENDANCE
The greatest number of spectators at a regular season game is 102,368, on 10 Nov 1957. The game was between the LA Rams and the San Francisco 49ers, and was played at the Los Angeles Coliseum, California.

MOST NFL TITLES
The Green Bay Packers have won a record 12 NFL/NFC titles: 1929–31, 1936, 1939, 1944, 1961–62, 1965–67 and 1997. The last three wins were also Super Bowl championships.

The record for the most AFL/AFC titles is held by the Buffalo Bills, who won six titles from 1964 to 1965 and from 1990 to 1993.

MOST CONSECUTIVE NFL WINS
The Chicago Bears had the most consecutive NFL victories, winning 17 games in succession from 1933 to 1934.

LONGEST UNBEATEN NFL RUN
The most consecutive games without defeat is 25, by Canton, with 22 wins and 3 ties from 1921 to 1923.

MOST NFL WINS IN A SEASON
The most wins in a season is 15, by the San Francisco 49ers in 1984 and the Chicago Bears in 1985.

The Miami Dolphins won all their games in the 1972 season (14 regular season matches and three playoff games, including the Super Bowl).

HIGHEST NFL SCORES
The highest individual team score in a regular season game is 72, by the Washington Redskins against the New York Giants (who scored 41) on 27 Nov 1966. This was also the highest aggregate score for a match.

The Chicago Bears beat the Washington Redskins by 73 to 0 in the NFL Championship game on 8 Dec 1940.

MOST NFL GAMES PLAYED
George Blanda played in 340 games in a record 26 seasons in the NFL (Chicago Bears 1949–58, Baltimore Colts 1950, Houston Oilers 1960–66 and Oakland Raiders 1967–75).

MOST EXPENSIVE TV ADVERTISING SLOT
A 30-second advertising slot for Super Bowl XXXII between the Denver Broncos and the Green Bay Packers on 25 Jan 1998 cost a record $1.3 million (£780,000) — four times the cost of a normal advertising slot at a similar time. It is estimated that 45% of US homes tune in to the annual Super Bowl and a single 30-second slot is estimated to reach about 100 million viewers. There were more than 30 advertisers for the 1998 Super Bowl, including Pizza Hut (top picture), Pepsi (bottom picture), Budweiser, Doritos, Intel and Coca-Cola, and all 58 spots are reported to have been sold two months before the game. TV networks claim to have paid a total of $18 billion (£10.8 billion) for Super Bowl, and one network estimates that it lost more than $1 billion (£601 million) in profits by not renewing a franchise.

LONGEST RUN FROM SCRIMMAGE
Tony Dorsett scored on a touchdown run of 99 yd for the Dallas Cowboys against the Minnesota Vikings on 3 Jan 1983. Dorsett, the winner of the 1976 Heisman Trophy, is the leading rusher in the Dallas Cowboys' history and is third on the all-time rushers list, with 12,739 yd.

MOST SUCCESSFUL NFL COACH
The record for the greatest number of games won as coach is 347, by Don Shula for the Baltimore Colts (1963–69) and the Miami Dolphins (1970–95).

MOST NFL GAMES LOST
The Tampa Bay Buccaneers lost a record 26 consecutive games from 1976 to 1977.

LONGEST NFL PASS COMPLETION
A pass completion of 99 yd has been achieved on eight occasions and has always resulted in a touchdown. The most recent 99-yd pass was from Brett Favre to Robert Brooks of the Green Bay Packers against the Chicago Bears on 11 Sept 1995.

LONGEST NFL FIELD GOAL
The longest field goal kicked is 63 yd, by Tom Dempsey of the New Orleans Saints against the Detroit Lions on 8 Nov 1970.

LONGEST NFL PUNT
Steve O'Neal kicked a punt of 98 yd for the New York Jets against the Denver Broncos on 21 Sept 1969.

LONGEST NFL PUNT RETURN
The longest return is 103 yd, by Robert Bailey for the Los Angeles Rams against the New Orleans Saints on 23 Oct 1994.

LONGEST INTERCEPTION RETURNS IN AN NFL GAME
The longest recorded return for a touchdown is 104 yd. It was achieved by James Willis and Troy Vincent for the Philadelphia Eagles in a game against the Dallas Cowboys on 3 Nov 1996. Willis returned the ball 14 yd and lateralled it to Vincent, who returned it for the remaining 90 yd.

The longest interception return for a touchdown by an individual player is 103 yd. The record was set by Venice Glenn for the San Diego Chargers in a game against the Denver Broncos, on 29 Nov 1987. It was equalled by Louis Oliver for the Miami Dolphins against the Buffalo Bills, on 4 Oct 1992.

LONGEST NFL KICKOFF RETURN
The record for the longest ever NFL kickoff return for a touchdown is 106 yd, by three players: Al Carmichael for the Green Bay Packers against the Chicago Bears on 7 Oct 1956; Noland Smith for the Kansas City Chiefs against the Denver Broncos on 17 Dec 1967; and Roy Green for the St. Louis Cardinals against the Dallas Cowboys on 21 Oct 1979.

BIGGEST CONTRACT
The biggest player contract is believed to average $6–6.5 million (£3.6–3.9 million) a year for seven years and include a signing bonus of $12 million (£7.2 million), but the terms were not officially disclosed. It was signed by Brett Favre in July 1997, when he re-joined the Green Bay Packers. Favre was also the most recent player to equal the longest pass completion record.

olympics

SUMMER OLYMPICS

The next Summer Games will take place in Sydney, Australia, in 2000. More than 30 disciplines will be competed, including, for the first time, trampolining, triathlon and taekwondo. At the first modern Games in 1896 nine sports were contested: athletics, cycling, fencing, gymnastics, shooting, swimming, tennis, weightlifting and wrestling.

LONGEST LIVE BROADCAST

The French-language, state-owned Swiss TV station Suisse 4 broadcast the 1996 Olympic Games in Atlanta, USA, non-stop for 16 days 22 hr 45 min from 19 July to 5 Aug 1996.

MOST GAMES COMPETED

Five countries have competed at all 24 Summer Games: Australia, France, Greece, Great Britain and Switzerland (the latter only competed in the Equestrian events in Stockholm, Sweden, in 1956 and did not attend the Games in Melbourne, Australia). France, Great Britain and Switzerland have also competed at every Winter Games.

MOST PARTICIPANTS

The most competitors at a Summer Games is 10,744 (7,060 men, 3,684 women), at Atlanta, USA, in 1996.

The most competitors at a single Winter Games is 1,801 (1,412 men and 489 women) at Albertville, France, in 1992.

A record 72 countries competed at the 1998 Winter Games at Nagano, Japan.

MOST GOLD MEDALS

The record for the most individual gold medals by a male competitor in the modern Games is 10, by Raymond Ewry (USA) in athletics from 1900 to 1908.

The record for the greatest number of individual gold medals ever won by a female competitor is seven, by Vera Caslavska-Odlozil (Czechoslovakia) in gymnastics: three in 1964 and four (one shared) in 1968.

Swimmer Mark Spitz (USA) won a record seven golds (including three for relay) at a single celebration, at Munich, Germany, in 1972.

The record for the greatest number of gold medals won in individual events at one celebration is five, by speed skater Eric Heiden (USA) at Lake Placid, New York, USA, in 1980.

The greatest number of consecutive individual titles won in the same event is four, by Alfred Oerter (USA) in the discus (1956–68) and Carl Lewis (USA) in the long jump (1984–96).

Raymond Ewry (USA) won both the standing long jump and the standing high jump at four games in succession (1900, 1904, 1906 and 1908). This includes the official Intercalated Games of 1906.

Paul Elvstrøm (Denmark) won four successive gold medals at monotype yachting events from 1948 to 1960, but there was a class change (1948 Firefly class, 1952–60 Finn class).

MOST MEDALS

Gymnast Larisa Semyonovna Latynina (USSR) won a record 18 medals from 1956 to 1964.

The men's record is 15, by gymnast Nikolay Andrianov (USSR) from 1972 to 1980.

The most medals won at one celebration is eight, by gymnast Aleksandr Dityatin (USSR) in 1980.

MOST GAMES ENTERED

Yachtsman Hubert Raudaschl (Austria) competed in nine Games from 1964 to 1996.

WOMEN'S ICE HOCKEY

The 1998 Winter Olympics at Nagano, Japan, was the first Games to feature women's ice hockey, with four countries competing for medals – Canada, USA, Finland and China. Although detractors argued that there were not enough teams participating, the Olympics represented a great breakthrough for women's ice hockey, and it is hoped that the event will help the sport to attract the kind of serious financial backing that is enjoyed by men's ice hockey. However, the current lack of support is regarded as a major hindrance to the women's game. In Canada, for example, female players currently have to rely on monthly stipends provided by Sport Canada, ranging from $800 (£500) for A-card athletes to $400 (£250) for less experienced players. Despite this, women's ice hockey is increasingly popular – the number of women and girls registered with USA Hockey has quadrupled since the 1990 Women's World Championship, while the total number participating in the sport in the USA is an estimated 23,000 or more. The most prominent US player is Cammi Granato, who had an endorsement deal with Nike for the Olympics. She scored the first ever women's Olympic ice hockey goal against China.

LUGEING
Stefan Krausse and Jan Behrendt from Germany are pictured in action on their way to winning a second Olympic gold and completing a German clean sweep at the 1998 Winter Games at Nagano, Japan. German lugers have dominated the sport at the Olympics, winning 21 out of a possible 30 gold medals since the introduction of lugeing to the Games in 1964.

Fencer Kerstin Palm (Sweden) holds the women's record, with seven Games (1964–88).

LONGEST OLYMPIC CAREERS
The record for the longest Olympic career is 40 years, by Dr Ivan Osiier (Denmark) in fencing (1908–32 and 1948), Magnus Konow (Norway) in yachting, (1908–20, 1928 and 1936–48), Paul Elvstrøm (Denmark) in yachting (1948–60, 1968–72 and 1984–88), and Durward Knowles (Great Britain 1948, then Bahamas) in yachting (1948–72 and 1988).

The longest Olympic career by a woman is 28 years, by Anne Ransehousen (USA), in dressage (1960, 1964, 1988) and Christilot Hanson-Boylen (Canada) in dressage (1964–76, 1984, 1992).

MOST MEDALS *
SUMMER GAMES (1896–1996)
USA 2,015:
833 gold, 634 silver, 548 bronze
Soviet Union[1] 1,234:
485 gold, 395 silver, 354 bronze
Great Britain 635:
177 gold, 233 silver, 225 bronze
France 562:
176 gold, 181 silver, 205 bronze
Germany[2] 516:
151 gold, 181 silver, 184 bronze
Sweden 459:
134 gold, 152 silver, 173 bronze

Italy 444:
166 gold, 136 silver, 142 bronze
Hungary 425:
142 gold, 128 silver, 155 bronze
GDR (East Germany)[3] 410:
153 gold, 130 silver, 127 bronze
Australia 294:
87 gold, 85 silver, 122 bronze
Finland 292:
99 gold, 80 silver, 113 bronze
Japan 280:
93 gold, 89 silver, 98 bronze
Romania 239:
63 gold, 77 silver, 99 bronze
Poland 227:
50 gold, 67 silver, 110 bronze
Canada 217:
49 gold, 77 silver, 91 bronze
FRG (West Germany)[4] 200:
56 gold, 64 silver, 80 bronze
Netherlands 187:
49 gold, 57 silver, 81 bronze
Bulgaria 182:
43 gold, 76 silver, 63 bronze
Switzerland 174:
46 gold, 68 silver, 60 bronze
China 164:
52 gold, 63 silver, 49 bronze

This excludes medals that were won in Official Art competitions from 1912 to 1948.

WINTER GAMES (1924–98)
Norway 239:
83 gold, 87 silver, 69 bronze
Soviet Union[1] 217:
87 gold, 63 silver, 67 bronze
USA 159: *59 gold, 59 silver, 41 bronze*
Austria 145:
39 gold, 53 silver, 53 bronze
Finland 135:
38 gold, 49 silver, 48 bronze
GDR[3] 110:
39 gold, 36 silver, 35 bronze
Germany[2] 106:
46 gold, 38 silver, 32 bronze
Sweden 102:
39 gold, 28 silver, 35 bronze
Switzerland 92:
29 gold, 31 silver, 32 bronze
Canada 79:
25 gold, 25 silver, 29 bronze
Italy 77:
27 gold, 27 silver, 23 bronze

Netherlands 61:
19 gold, 23 silver, 19 bronze
France 61:
18 gold, 17 silver, 26 bronze
Russia[6] 42:
21 gold, 14 silver, 7 bronze
FRG (West Germany)[4] 39:
11 gold, 15 silver, 13 bronze
Japan 29:
8 gold, 9 silver, 12 bronze
Czechoslovakia[6] 26:
2 gold, 8 silver, 16 bronze
Great Britain 24:
7 gold, 4 silver, 13 bronze
Korea 16:
9 gold, 3 silver, 4 bronze
China 15:
0 gold, 10 silver, 5 bronze

* Totals are for all the leading nations for all Summer and Winter Olympic disiplines and include events which have now been discontinued.

[1] Includes CIS (Unified team) 1992
[2] Germany 1896–1964 and 1992–94
[3] GDR (East Germany) 1968–88
[4] FRG (West Germany) 1968–88
[5] Includes Bohemia
[6] Includes Czarist Russia

SPEED SKATING
Gianni Romme (Netherlands) won both the 5,000-m and the 10,000-m gold medals in world record times at the 1998 Winter Games. Speed skating is one of the sports that was contested at the first Winter Olympics, held at Chamonix, Switzerland, in 1924. Technical innovations such as aerodynamically-designed suits and 'clap' skates have lowered times considerably since the first Games.

paralympics

FASTEST 100-M BREASTSTROKE
Kaspar Engel of Germany celebrates after setting a world record in the men's 100-m breaststroke at the Atlanta Paralympics on 24 Aug 1996. His time was 1:31.50.

FASTEST 100-M ICE SLEDGE
Norway's Anne Mette Samdal set a world record in the women's 100-m ice sledge speed race at the Winter Paralympic Games in Nagano, Japan, on 7 March 1998. Her time was 15.69 sec. The 26-year-old bank clerk also won gold in the 500-m race in a Paralympic record time of 1:17.26 on the same day. The 1998 Winter Paralympics were the largest ever, with around 1,200 athletes and officials from more than 32 countries.

BIGGEST PARALYMPICS
A record 4,912 athletes from a record 104 countries competed in the Xth Summer Paralympics at Atlanta, Georgia, USA, in 1996.

MOST WORLD RECORDS BY A MALE TRACK ATHLETE
Spain's Javier Conde, an amputee, set eight records in track events at the Barcelona Paralympics, Spain, in 1992, and the marathon record at Atlanta.

MOST WORLD RECORDS BY A FEMALE TRACK ATHLETE
Rima Batalova (USSR/Russia), a blind athlete, holds six records in track events. The last was set in an 800-m class at Atlanta.

MOST WORLD RECORDS BY A MALE FIELD ATHLETE
Wheelchair athlete Stephanus Lombaard of South Africa set three records in shot put and javelin between 1994 and 1996.

MOST WORLD RECORDS BY A FEMALE FIELD ATHLETE
Maria Buggenhagen (Germany) set four wheelchair records in shot put and discus from 1992 to 1996, when she set a shot put record at Atlanta.

MOST WORLD RECORDS BY MALE SWIMMERS
Duane Kale (New Zealand) and Alwin De Groot (Netherlands) set four world records at Atlanta.

MOST WORLD RECORDS BY A FEMALE SWIMMER
Beatrice Hess of France set six records at Atlanta. All still stand.

MEN'S TEAM ARCHERY: STANDING
The record for the 3 x 72 archery event was set by Poland, with 1.73 points at Atlanta.

The 27 + 27 event record was set by South Korea, with 457 points at Atlanta.

The record for the 27 event is 232 points, which was set by South Korea at Atlanta.

WOMEN'S TEAM ARCHERY, OPEN
The record for the 3 x 72 archery event was set by Italy, with 1.58 points at Atlanta.

The 27 + 27 record is 438 points, by Italy at Atlanta.

The record for the 27 archery event was set by Italy, with 220 points at Atlanta.

MEN'S 100 M
The fastest 100 m by a blind man is 10.96 sec, by A. Managaro (Italy) at Valencia, Spain, in 1995.

The record for the fastest 100 m by a male athlete with cerebral palsy is 11.79 sec, by Hoon Son (South Korea) at Seoul, South Korea, on 17 Oct 1988.

The fastest 100 m by a male amputee is 10.72 sec, by Ajibola Adeoye (Nigeria) at Barcelona, Spain, on 5 Sept 1992.

The best 100 m by a male athlete in a wheelchair is 14.45 sec, by David Holding (GB) at Atlanta.

WOMEN'S 100 M
The best 100 m by a blind woman is 12.43 sec, by R. Takbulatova (USSR) in Bulgaria in 1983.

The fastest 100 m by a female athlete with cerebral palsy is 14.56 sec, by Alison Quinn (Australia) at Berlin, Germany, in July 1994.

The record for the 100 m by a female amputee is 12.51 sec, by Petra Buddelmeyer (Germany) in Belgium, in May 1957.

MEN'S 1,500 M
The fastest 1,500 m by a blind man is 3:55.00, by Noel Thatcher (GB) at Leeds, UK, in 1991.

The record for the 1,500 m by a male athlete with cerebral palsy is 4:19.90, by Ross Davis (USA) in a wheelchair at Hartford, Connecticut, USA, in Aug 1996.

The fastest 1,500 m by a male amputee is 3:58.53, by Javier Conde (Spain) at Barcelona.

WOMEN'S 1,500 M
The fastest 1,500 m by a blind female athlete is 4:37.02, by Rima Batalova (Russia) at Berlin, Germany, in July 1994.

The record for the 1,500 m by a female athlete with cerebral palsy is 5:20.50, by Linda Mastandrea (USA) in a wheelchair at Hartford, USA, on 5 Aug 1995.

The fastest 1,500 m by a female amputee is 6:09.43, by Britta Brockskothon (Germany) at Hasselt, Belgium, in May 1987.

The fastest 1,500 m by a female athlete in a wheelchair is 3:30.45, by Louise Sauvage (Australia) at Atlanta.

MOST SUCCESSFUL WHEELCHAIR TENNIS PLAYER
Ricky Molier of the Netherlands has been ranked No. 1 on the International Wheelchair Tennis Federation Tour for the past two seasons (1996 and 1997) and was the Paralympic champion in Atlanta, USA, in 1996. The 1997 season reinforced his dominance: he won almost 50% of Tour events, including the British, Austrian, Swiss, Czech, Polish, French and Finnish opens, and the Sportement and USTA nationals. The major difference between standard tennis and the wheelchair version is that the ball is allowed to bounce twice before it has to be returned in the latter, although it is often returned after just one bounce in top-level wheelchair tennis. Due to the nature of the game a full-blown backhand can be difficult and is usually sliced. Spin plays a more prominent part in wheelchair tennis than standard tennis, but that is not to say that it lacks speed and power — Ricky Molier's serve has been clocked at speeds in excess of 160 km/h (100 mph).

MEN'S HIGH JUMP
The best high jump by a blind man is 2.02 m (6 ft 7¹/₂ in), by Olaf Mehlmann (Germany) in 1994.

The best high jump by a male amputee is 1.96 m (6 ft 5 in), by Arnold Boldt (Canada) at Arnhem, Netherlands, on 17 June 1980.

WOMEN'S HIGH JUMP
The best high jump by a blind woman is 1.80 m (5 ft 11 in), by Maria Runyan (USA) in 1995.

FASTEST 1,500 M, WHEELCHAIR
The record for the 1,500 m by a male athlete in a wheelchair is 3:02.00, by Swiss sportsman Franz Nietlispach (seen below left) at Zürich, Switzerland, on 14 Aug 1996. Nietlispach is seen here in the men's 1,500-m wheelchair final at Barcelona, Spain, in 1992, where he came second to Claude Issorat of France (right of picture).

The best high jump by a female amputee is 1.66 m (5 ft 5 in), by Petra Buddelmeyer (Germany) at New York, USA, on 24 June 1986.

MEN'S LONG JUMP
The best long jump by a blind man is 7.23 m (23 ft 8¹/₂ in), by Enrique Cepeda (Cuba) in Argentina, 1995.

The longest jump by a male athlete with cerebral palsy is 5.92 m (19 ft 5 in), by Darren Thrupp (Australia) in China, 1994.

The best long jump by a male amputee is 6.75 m (22 ft 2 in), by Ruben Alvarez (Spain) at Atlanta.

WOMEN'S LONG JUMP
The best jump by a blind woman is 6.11 m (20 ft), by Purification Ortiz (Spain) in Spain in 1995.

The best long jump by a woman with cerebral palsy is 4.49 m (14 ft 8³/₄ in), by A. Grigalluniene (Lithuania) at Atlanta.

The record for the long jump by a female amputee is 5.70 m (18 ft 8¹/₄ in), by Irina Leontiouk (Belarus) at Atlanta.

MEN'S SWIMMING
The fastest 100-m butterfly by a male swimmer is 1:02.44, by Jody Cundy (GB) at Atlanta.

The fastest 100-m freestyle by a man is 56.40 sec, by Alwin Houtsma (Netherlands) at Atlanta.

The fastest 100-m freestyle by a severely disabled male swimmer is 1:31.35, by Ricardo Oribe (Spain) at Atlanta.

The fastest 100-m freestyle by a very severely disabled male swimmer is 2:41.94, by James Anderson (GB) at Atlanta.

The fastest 100-m backstroke by a male swimmer is 1:04.10, by Alwin DeGroot (Netherlands) at Atlanta.

The record for the fastest 100-m backstroke by a blind male swimmer is 1:04.80, by Walter Wu (Canada) at Atlanta.

WOMEN'S SWIMMING
The fastest 100-m butterfly by a woman is 1:08.88, by Gemma Dashwood (Australia) at Atlanta.

The fastest 100-m freestyle by a woman is 1:08.16, by Joyce Luncher (USA) at Atlanta.

The fastest 100-m freestyle by a severely disabled female swimmer is 1:36.23, by Mayumi Narita (Japan) at Atlanta.

The fastest 100-m freestyle by a very severely disabled female swimmer is 3:09.00, by Betiana Basualdo (Argentina) at Atlanta.

The record for the 100-m backstroke by a female swimmer is 1:26.41, by Kristin Hakonard (Iceland) at Atlanta.

basketball

SPORTS ICON

Michael Jordan, who holds many NBA records, including highest career average for players exceeding 10,000 and highest career scoring average for play-offs, is the most famous basketball player in the world. His rise to superstardom began in 1984 when he was drafted by the Chicago Bulls, and in 1991 he was named the NBA Finals Most Valuable Player, a feat he repeated in 1992 and 1993. He has signed lucrative endorsement deals with a host of well known companies, including Nike, Coke, Gatorade and McDonalds. The biggest of these contracts is with Nike, who have produced an Air Jordan range of sneakers, some of which fetch up to $2,000 (£1,200) second-hand. Jordan is reputed to receive $12 million (£7.5 million) a year for the deal. He is also the co-chairman of P.L.A.Y, a $10-million (£6-million) Nike-sponsored initiative to provide recreational facilities for children. In addition, he owns a restaurant, has hosted *Saturday Night Live* and has appeared in the movie *Space Jam*, in which he plays basketball with cartoons. He has been described by one commentator as "the ultimate sports icon of the generation".

MOST OLYMPIC TITLES

The USA has won 11 men's Olympic titles. From 1936 to 1972 they won 63 consecutive matches until they lost 50–51 to the USSR in the disputed final in Munich, Germany. Since then they have won a further 37 matches and had another loss to the USSR (in 1988).

The women's title has been won a record three times by the USSR in 1976, 1980 and 1992 (by the Unified team from the republics of the ex-USSR) and the USA in 1984, 1988 and 1996.

MOST WORLD TITLES

The record for most men's World Championships (instituted 1950) titles is three by the USSR (1967, 1974 and 1982) and Yugoslavia (1970, 1978 and 1990).

The USSR has won six women's World Championships (instituted 1953) titles (1959, 1964, 1967, 1971, 1975 and 1983).

HIGHEST INTERNATIONAL SCORE

In a senior international match Iraq scored 251 against Yemen, who scored 33, at New Delhi, India, in Nov 1982 at the Asian Games.

MOST TITLES: NBA

The Boston Celtics have won 16 NBA titles: in 1957, from 1959 to 1966, and in 1968, 1969, 1974, 1976, 1981, 1984 and 1986.

HIGHEST SCORES: NBA

The highest aggregate score in a match was 370, when the Detroit Pistons beat the Denver Nuggets 186–184 at Denver, Colorado, USA, on 13 Dec 1983. Overtime was played after a 145–145 tie in regulation time.

The highest ever aggregate score in regulation time was 320, when the Golden State Warriors beat the Denver Nuggets 162–158 at Denver, Colorado, on 2 Nov 1990.

The highest-scoring individual was Wilt Chamberlain, who scored a record 100 points for Philadelphia against New York at Hershey, Pennsylvania, on 2 March 1962. This included a record 36 field goals and 28 free throws from 32 attempts, as well as a record 59 points in one half.

Chamberlain's free throws record was equalled by Adrian Dantley for Utah against Houston at Las Vegas, Nevada, in Jan 1984.

MOST SEASON WINS: NBA

The Chicago Bulls had 72 NBA wins in the 1995–96 season, a record number of NBA wins within a single season.

MOST GAMES: NBA

Robert Parish played 1,611 regular season

TALLEST NBA PLAYER

Gheorghe Muresan of the Washington Wizards is 2.31 m (7 ft 7 in) tall. He made his pro debut in 1994. Born in Transylvania, Romania, in 1971, his height is due to a pituitary gland condition. His nickname is 'Ghitza', which translated into English means 'Little Gheorghe'.

games over 21 seasons for the Golden State Warriors (1976–80), the Boston Celtics (1980–94), the Charlotte Hornets (1994–96) and the Chicago Bulls (1996–97).

The record for the greatest number of complete games played in a single season is 79, by Wilt Chamberlain for Philadelphia in 1962. During this period he was on court for a record total of 3,882 minutes. Chamberlain is also unique in having never fouled out during his entire 1,045-game career.

MOST POINTS: NBA
Kareem Abdul-Jabbar scored a record total of 38,387 points during his career, which works out at an average of 24.6 points per game. This included a total of 15,837 field goals and 5,762 points in regular season games and 2,356 field goals in play-off games.

The highest career average for players exceeding 10,000 points is 31.7, by Michael Jordan, who scored a total of 26,290 points in 748 games for the Chicago Bulls from 1984 to 1997.

The highest career average for play-offs is 33.6, by Michael Jordan, who scored 5,307 points in 158 games from 1984 to 1997. Jordan has earnt more from endorsement deals than any other basketball player.

GREATEST WINNING MARGIN: NBA
A record winning margin of 68 points was achieved when the Cleveland Cavaliers beat the Miami Heat 148–80 on 17 Dec 1991.

BEST WINNING STREAK: NBA
The Los Angeles Lakers won a record 33 games in succession from 5 Nov 1971 to 7 Jan 1972 during the 1971/72 season.

YOUNGEST PLAYER: NBA
Jermaine O'Neal was 18 years 53 days old when he made his debut for the Portland Trail Blazers against the Denver Nuggets on 5 Dec 1996.

OLDEST REGULAR PLAYER: NBA
Robert Parish of the Chicago Bulls was still playing at the age of 43 years 231 days on 19 April 1997, making him the oldest regular player in the NBA.

TALLEST EVER PLAYER
The tallest ever player is thought to be Suleiman Ali Nashnush, who was reputed to be 2.45 m (8 ft ¼ in) in height when he played for the Libyan team in 1962.

HIGHEST MATCH ATTENDANCE
The biggest ever crowd was 80,000, for the final of the European Cup Winners' Cup between AEK Athens and Slavia Prague at the Olympic stadium, Athens, Greece, on 4 April 1968.

HIGHEST VERTICAL DUNK
Sean Williams and Michael Wilson, both of the Harlem Globetrotters, dunked a basketball at a rim height of 3.58 m (11 ft 8 in) at Disney-MGM Studios, Orlando, Florida, USA, on 16 Sept 1996.

LONGEST GOAL
Christopher Eddy scored a 27.49-m (90-ft 2¼-in) field goal for Fairview High School against Iroquois High School at Erie, Pennsylvania, USA, on 25 Feb 1989. The shot was made as time expired in overtime and won the game 51–50 for Fairview.

TOP SHOOTING SPEEDS
Jeff Liles scored 231 goals out of 240 attempts in 10 min using one ball and one rebounder at Southern Nazarene University, Bethany, Oklahoma, USA, on 11 June 1992. He scored 231 goals out of 241 attempts on 16 June.

In 24 hours (29–30 Sept 1990) Fred Newman scored 20,371 free throws from a total of 22,049 taken (a success rate of 92.39%) at Caltech, Pasadena, California, USA. Ted St. Martin scored a record 5,221 consecutive free throws at Jacksonville, Florida, USA, on 28 April 1996.

In one minute Jeff Liles scored goals in 25 of 29 attempts (50 points) from seven scoring positions at Bethany, Oklahoma, USA, on 18 Sept 1994.

LONGEST DRIBBLE
Ashrita Furman dribbled a basketball 155.41 km (96 miles 1,003 yd) in 24 hours without 'travelling' at Victory Field Track, Forest Park, Queens, New York, USA, from 17 to 18 May 1997.

MOST BALLS SPUN
Bruce Crevier span 18 basketballs at the ABC-TV studios in New York, USA, on 18 July 1994.

MOST BALLS DRIBBLED
A record four basketballs have been dribbled simultaneously by four Americans: Bob Nickerson from Gallitzin, Pennsylvania; Dave Davlin from Garland, Texas; Jeremy Kable from Highspire, Pennsylvania; and Joseph Odhiambo from Mesa, Arizona.

baseball

OUTSTANDING PITCHER

Roger Clemens of the Toronto Blue Jays has won the Cy Young award for outstanding pitcher in the major leagues a record four times, together with Stephen Carlton and Greg Maddux. Clemens won the award in 1986, 1987 and 1991 for Boston and in 1997 for Toronto (both American League). Cy Young was a record-breaking pitcher of the late 19th and early 20th century.

BASEBALL
BIGGEST CONTRACTS

The top baseball contracts (based on the average annual salary for the duration of the contract) are for $11.5 million (£6.9 million). They were signed by pitchers Greg Maddux of the Atlanta Braves in Aug 1997 and Pedro Martinez of the Boston Red Sox in Dec 1997. Maddux's contract is worth $57.5 million (£34.5 million) over five years and Martinez's is worth $69 million (£41.5 million) over six years. Martinez has the option for a seventh year, however, which could bring the total value of the contract to $90 million (£54 million)— an average of $12.85 million (£7.72 million) per year.

MOST SPECTATORS

An estimated 114,000 spectators watched a demonstration game between Australia and an American Services team during the Olympic Games in Melbourne, Australia, on 1 Dec 1956.

MOST TITLES

The New York Yankees won a record 23 World Series between 1923 and 1996. They also won a record 34 American League pennants between 1921 and 1996.

The most National League titles is 19, by the Dodgers (Brooklyn 1890–1957, Los Angeles 1958–88).

MOST VALUABLE PLAYER

The most awards for Most Valuable Player is two, by Sandy Koufax (Los Angeles NL 1963 and 1965), Bob Gibson (St. Louis NL, 1964 and 1967) and Reggie Jackson (Oakland AL 1973, New York AL 1977).

MOST HOME RUNS

Hank Aaron scored a record 755 career home runs: 733 for the Milwaukee Braves (1954–65) and the Atlanta Braves (1966–74) in the National League, and 22 for the Milwaukee Brewers (AL) from 1975 to 1976. By 8 April 1974 he had bettered the previous record of 714 by Babe Ruth.

The most home runs in a US major league season is 61, by Roger Eugene Maris in 162 games for the New York Yankees in 1961.

Babe Ruth hit 60 home runs in 154 games for the New York Yankees in 1927.

The record for the most home runs in a major league game is four. This was first achieved by Bobby Lowe for Boston against Cincinnati on 30 May 1894 and has been repeated 10 times since.

LONGEST HOME RUN

The record for the longest measured home run in a major league game is 193 m (634 ft), by Mickey Mantle for the New York Yankees against the Detroit Tigers at Briggs Stadium, Detroit, USA, in Sept 1960.

MOST CONSECUTIVE HITS

Pinky Higgins had 12 consecutive hits for Boston (AL) from 19 to 21 June 1938. This was equalled by Moose Droppo for Detroit (AL) from 14 to 15 July 1952.

Joe DiMaggio hit in a record 56 consecutive games for New York in 1941. He was 223 times at bat, had 91 hits and scored a total of 16 doubles, four triples and 15 home runs.

MOST GAMES PLAYED

Pete Rose played in a total of 3,562 games and was at bat a record 14,053 times for Cincinnati NL (1963–78, 1984–86), Philadelphia NL (1979–83) and Montreal NL (1984).

BIGGEST REPLICA BAT

The world's biggest ever replica baseball bat is 36.6 m (120 ft) in height and weighs 30,845 kg (68,000 lb). Here it is seen being placed in front of bat manufacturer Hillerich & Bradsby's new headquarters in Louisville, Kentucky, in Oct 1995. The bat is modelled on the 'R43' bat made for Babe Ruth, who is credited with inventing the modern baseball bat. In early spring 1927, he strode into the Hillerich & Bradsby plant and asked them to make him some bats. He hit his then record of 60 home runs with the resulting bats that year. The largest actual baseball bat, made from a solid cypress log, is 3.7 m (12 ft 2 in) long, has a diameter of 28.5 cm (11¼ in) at the handle and 35 cm (14 in) at the barrel, and weighs 127 kg (280 lb). The bat, completed in 1996, was made by Thomas Timm, his father Russ, and his son Joshua of Custom Woodcrafter in Summerville, South Carolina, USA.

MOST GAMES WON BY A PITCHER

The greatest number of games won by a pitcher is 511, by Cy Young, who also played a record 749 complete games from a total of 906 games and 815 starts in his career for Cleveland NL (1890 to 1898), St. Louis NL (1899 to 1900), Boston AL (1901 to 1908), Cleveland AL (1909 to 1911) and Boston NL (1911). Young also pitched a record total of 7,357 innings.

MOST GAMES PITCHED

The record for the most games pitched in a single career is 1,070, by James Hoyt Wilhelm for a total of nine teams between 1952 and 1972. He also set the career record of 143 wins by a relief pitcher.

MOST CONSECUTIVE SCORELESS INNINGS

Orel Hershiser IV pitched a record 59 consecutive scoreless innings from 30 Aug to 28 Sept 1988.

MOST CY YOUNG AWARDS

Four Cy Young awards have been won by Stephen Carlton (Philadelphia NL 1972, 1977, 1980, 1982); Greg Maddux (Chicago NL 1992, Atlanta NL 1993–95); and Roger Clemens (Boston AL in 1986, 1987, 1991 and Toronto AL in 1997).

FASTEST PITCHER

Lynn Nolan Ryan (then of the California Angels) pitched at 162.3 km/h (100.9 mph) at Anaheim Stadium, California, USA, on 20 Aug 1974.

LONGEST THROW

Glen Edward Gorbous threw a distance of 135.88 m (445 ft 10 in) on 1 Aug 1957.

FASTEST BASE RUNNER

The record for the fastest time for circling bases is 13.3 sec and was set by Ernest Evar Swanson at Columbus, Ohio, USA, in 1932. His average speed was 29.7 km/h (18.45 mph).

SOFTBALL
MOST WORLD TITLES

The men's fast-pitch World Championship has been won a record four times by the USA, in 1966, 1968, 1976 (shared) and 1980, and by Canada, in 1972, 1976 (shared), 1988 and 1992.

The women's fast-pitch World Championship has been won a record four times by the USA, in 1974, 1978, 1986 and 1990.

Dot Richardson (USA) won a record eight individual world titles. Her most recent international title was a gold medal at the Olympic Games in Atlanta, in 1996, and her first was in 1979 at the Pan American Games in Puerto Rico.

MOST RUNS

The most runs scored by an individual in a World Championship tournament is 19, by Marty Kernaghan (Canada) in 1988.

The most runs scored by a woman in a World Championship tournament is 13, by Kathy Elliott (USA) in 1974.

MOST STRIKEOUTS

The most strikeouts by a pitcher in a World Championship tournament is 99, by Kevin Herlihy (New Zealand) in 1972.

The record for the most strikeouts by a woman in a World Championship tournament is 76, by Joan Joyce (USA) in 1974.

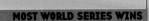

MOST WORLD SERIES WINS

The New York Yankees hold the record for the most wins in the World Series, with 23 victories. One of the team's newest recruits is Orlando Hernandez, a former Cuban star pitcher who signed a $6.6-million (£4-million), four-year contract in 1998. Before signing with the NYY, Hernandez made about $8 (£4.80) per month in Cuba.

BIGGEST CONTRACT

In Aug 1997 pitcher Greg Maddux signed a record-breaking contract worth $11.5 million (£6.9 million) a year when he re-signed with the Atlanta Braves. His record was equalled later that year by Pedro Martinez, who was acquired by the Boston Red Sox. Maddux is also one of three players to have won four Cy Young awards (1992, 1993, 1994 and 1995).

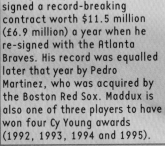

auto sports

MOST WINS AT LE MANS

Porsche cars have won Le Mans, France, a record 15 times (1970–71, 1976–77, 1979, 1981–87, 1993 and 1996–97). These wins represent just a fraction of their successes in the International Sports Car World Championships: with well over 100 wins, the German company is the world's most successful sports car manufacturer. Porsche have won the Manufacturers' World title 13 times between 1969 and 1985.

GRAND PRIX
MOST SUCCESSFUL DRIVERS

The World Drivers' Championship has been won five times by Juan-Manuel Fangio (Argentina), in 1951 and from 1954 to 1957. When Fangio retired in 1958 he had won 24 Grand Prix races (two shared) from 51 starts.

Alain Prost (France) had 51 wins from a total of 199 races between 1980 and 1993. During his career he gained a record 798.5 Grand Prix points.

The most pole positions is 65, by the late Ayrton Senna (Brazil) from 161 races (41 wins) between 1985 and 1994.

The most Grand Prix starts is 256, by Ricardo Patrese (Italy) from 1977 to 1993.

The most Grand Prix wins in a year is nine, by Nigel Mansell (GB) in 1992 and by Michael Schumacher (Germany) in 1995.

MOST SUCCESSFUL MANUFACTURERS

Williams have won a record nine World Championships (1980–81, 1986–87, 1992–94 and 1996–97).

McLaren won 15 of the 16 Grand Prix in the 1988 season: Ayrton Senna had eight wins and three seconds and Alain Prost had seven wins and seven seconds.

Excluding the Indianapolis 500 race (then included in the World Drivers' Championship), Ferrari won all seven races in 1952 and the first eight (of nine) in 1953.

FASTEST RACE

Peter Gethin (GB) averaged a speed of 242.623 km/h (150.759 mph), in a BRM in the 1971 Italian Grand Prix at Monza.

FASTEST QUALIFYING LAP

Keke Rosberg (Finland) set a record of 1 min 5.59 sec in a Williams-Honda in the 1985 British Grand Prix at Silverstone. His average speed was 258.802 km/h (160.817 mph).

CLOSEST FINISHES

Peter Gethin (GB) beat Ronnie Peterson (Sweden) by 0.01 sec in the 1971 Italian Grand Prix.

Ayrton Senna (Brazil) beat Nigel Mansell (GB) by 0.014 sec in the 1986 Spanish Grand Prix at Jerez de la Frontera.

INDIANAPOLIS 500
MOST SUCCESSFUL DRIVERS

Three drivers have had four wins: A. J. Foyt Jr (USA) in 1961, 1964, 1967 and 1977; Al Unser Sr (USA) in 1970, 1971, 1978 and 1987; and Rick Ravon Mears (USA) in 1979, 1984, 1988 and 1991.

Rick Mears has started from pole position a record six times (1979, 1982, 1986, 1988–89 and 1991).

A. J. Foyt Jr started in a record 35 races from 1958 to 1992.

FASTEST RACE

Arie Luyendyk (Netherlands) won in 2 hr 41 min 18.404 sec, driving a Lola-Chevrolet on 27 May 1990. His average speed was 299.307 km/h (185.981 mph).

FASTEST QUALIFYING LAPS

The highest average speed for the four qualifying laps is 381.392 km/h (236.986 mph), by Arie Luyendyk (Netherlands) in a Reynard-Ford-Cosworth on 12 May 1996. This included a one-lap record of 382.216 km/h (237.498 mph). On 9 May 1996 Luyendyk also set the unofficial track record of 385.051 km/h (239.260 mph).

BIGGEST PRIZES

The record for the largest ever prize fund is $8.11 million (£5.4 million), in 1996.

The biggest individual prize was $1.37 million (£915,875), won by Al Unser Jr (USA) in 1994.

LE MANS
GREATEST DISTANCE COVERED

Dr Helmut Marko (Austria) and Gijs van Lennep (Netherlands) covered 5,335.302 km (3,315 miles 363 yd) in a 4,907 cc flat-12 Porsche 917K Group 5 sports car from 12 to 13 June 1971.

The greatest distance covered on the current circuit is 5,331.998 km (3,313 miles 264 yd), by Jan Lammers (Netherlands), Johnny Dumfries and Andy Wallace (both GB) in a Jaguar XJR-9 from 11 to 12 June 1988. Their average speed was 222.166 km/h (138.047 mph).

FASTEST LAPS

The fastest ever race lap is 3 min 21.27 sec, by Alain Ferté (France) in a Jaguar XJR-9 on 10 June 1989. His average speed over the 13.536-km (8-mile 728-yd) lap was 242.093 km/h (150.429 mph).

Hans Stück (West Germany) set the record for the fastest ever practice lap speed on 14 June 1985, reaching a speed of 251.664 km/h (156.377 mph).

MOST GRAND PRIX WINS

In 1995 German driver Michael Schumacher, pictured left celebrating his victory in the Monaco Grand Prix in 1997, equalled Nigel Mansell's record nine Grand Prix wins in a year, which was set in 1992. Now 28 years of age, Schumacher is one of the world's best racing drivers: he won two World Championships when he was driving for Benetton (1994 and 1995) and clinched a $56-million (£35-million), two-year deal with Ferrari in 1996, although he has yet to win a championship with the manufacturer. The same year he earned approximately $60 million (£37.5 million), making him one of the wealthiest sportsmen in the world. Michael's younger brother Ralph began Formula 1 racing in 1997, after a career in Formula 3000. He signed a three-year contract with Jordan–Peugeot and earns an estimated $8 million (£4.8 million) a year, but he has yet to win a race.

MOST WINS

The most wins by one driver is six, by Jacky Ickx (Belgium): 1969, 1975–77 and 1981–82.

RALLYING
LONGEST RALLIES

The Singapore Airlines London–Sydney Rally covered 31,107 km (19,329 miles) from Covent Garden, London, UK, to Sydney Opera House, Australia. It was won by Andrew Cowan, Colin Malkin and Michael Broad in a Mercedes 280E in 1977.

The longest annual rally is the Safari Rally, first run through Kenya, Tanzania and Uganda but now restricted to Kenya. The 17th Safari in 1971 covered 6,234 km (3,874 miles). The race has been won a record five times by Shekhar Mehta (Kenya), in 1973 and from 1979 to 1982.

MOST MONTE CARLO WINS

The Monte Carlo Rally has been won four times by Sandro Munari (Italy), in 1972, 1975, 1976 and 1977, and Walter Röhrl (West Germany), with co-driver Christian Geistdorfer, in 1980 and from 1982 to 1984.

SMALLEST CAR TO WIN
MONTE CARLO RALLY

An 851-cc Saab driven by Erik Carlsson and Gunnar Häggbom and by Carlsson and Gunnar Palm (all Sweden) won the Monte Carlo Rally in 1962 and 1963.

MOST RAC RALLY WINS

Hannu Mikkola (Finland), with co-driver Arne Hertz (Sweden), has had four wins, in a Ford Escort in 1978 and 1979 and an Audi Quattro in 1981 and 1982.

MOST WORLD CHAMPIONSHIP WINS

The World Drivers' Championships has been won four times by Juha Kankkunen (Finland), in 1986, 1987, 1991 and 1993.

The record for the most wins in World Championship races is 21, by Juha Kankkunen (Finland) and Carlos Sainz (Spain).

The most wins in a season is six, by Didier Auriol (France) in 1992.

Lancia won a record-breaking total of 11 manufacturers' World Championships between 1972 and 1992.

FASTEST RACE

The Busch Clash race over a distance of 80.5 km (50 miles) on a 4-km-long (2½-mile), 31° banked track at Daytona, Florida, USA, is the world's fastest race. In 1987 Bill Elliott averaged a speed of 318.331 km/h (197.802 mph) in a Ford Thunderbird. Elliott won a record 11 races in 1985, and has been voted the Most Popular Driver in the NASCAR Winston Cup series 12 times.

BEST RACE TIMES
FASTEST CIRCUIT

The record for the highest ever average lap speed on any closed circuit in the world is 403.878 km/h (250.958 mph). It was achieved by Dr Hans Liebold (Germany) when he lapped the 12.64-km (7-mile 1,496-yd) high-speed track at Nardo, Italy, in a Mercedes-Benz C111-IV experimental coupé in a time of 1 min 52.67 sec on 5 May 1979. The car was powered by a V8 engine with two KKK turbochargers, with an output of 500 hp at 6,200 rpm.

FASTEST 805-KM RACE

Al Unser Jr (USA) set the world record for any 805-km (500-mile) race on 9 Aug 1990, when he won the Michigan 500A in the USA at an average speed of 305.2 km/h (189.7 mph).

MOST GRAND PRIX WINS

The greatest number of Grand Prix race victories by a manufacturer is 114, by Ferrari following the 1998 San Marino Grand Prix. Pictured here is the new Ferrari F300, which first raced in 1998. Ferrari have won the Manufacturers' World title eight times, although their last success was in 1983. They had their first Grand Prix success in July 1951 at Silverstone, UK, and dominated the next two seasons. The first Manufacturers' championship was contested in 1958, and Ferrari's first success came in 1961. That year they won five of the eight races, but their final success was marked by the tragic death of German driver Wolfgang von Trips, who was killed along with 14 spectators when his Ferrari crashed at the Italian Grand Prix.

swimming and diving

SWIMMING

MOST OLYMPIC MEDALS

The most individual gold medals is five, by Krisztina Egerszegi (Hungary) with the 100-m backstroke in 1992, the 200-m backstroke in 1988, 1992 and 1996 and the 400-m medley in 1992.

The most individual gold medals by a man is four by: Charles Daniels (USA) in the 100-m freestyle in 1906 and 1908, the 220-yd freestyle in 1904 and the 440-yd freestyle in 1904; Roland Matthes (GDR) in the 100-m and 200-m backstroke in 1968 and 1972; Tamás Daryni (Hungary) in the 200-m and 400-m medley in 1988 and 1992, Aleksandr Popov (Russia) in the 50-m and 100-m freestyle in 1992 and 1996; and Mark Spitz (see below).

The most gold medals by a woman is six, by Kristin Otto (GDR) at Seoul, South Korea, in 1988: the 100-m freestyle, backstroke and butterfly, the 50-m freestyle, the 4 x 100-m freestyle and the 4 x 100-m medley.

The most Olympic golds won by a swimmer is nine, by Mark Spitz (USA) in the 100-m and 200-m freestyle in 1972, the 100-m and 200-m butterfly in 1972, the 4 x 100-m freestyle in 1968 and 1972, the 4 x 200-m freestyle in 1968 and 1972 and the 4 x 100-m medley in 1972. In all but one (the 1968 4 x 200-m freestyle) he set a world record.

FASTEST MALE SWIMMER

Tom Jager (USA) had an average speed of 8.64 km/h (5.37 mph) over 50 yards in a 25-yd pool at Nashville, Tennessee, USA, on 23 March 1990. His time was 19.05 seconds. If Jager, winner of two Olympic golds, a silver and a bronze, was able to maintain this pace indefinitely, he would be able to halve the record time for crossing the English Channel (7 hr 17 min).

Mark Spitz won a record total of 11 medals: a silver (100-m butterfly) and a bronze (100-m freestyle) in 1968 as well as his nine golds. This record was equalled by Matt Biondi (USA), with a gold in 1984, five gold, one silver and one bronze in 1988, and two golds and a silver in 1992.

Spitz's record of seven medals at a single Games (1972) was also equalled by Matt Biondi in 1988.

The most medals won by a woman is eight, by Dawn Fraser (Australia) with four gold and four silver from 1956 to 1964, Kornelia Ender (GDR) with four gold and four silver from 1972 to 1976 and Shirley Babashoff (USA) with two gold and six silver from 1972 to 1976.

MOST WINS IN ONE EVENT

Two swimmers have won the same event on three occasions: Dawn Fraser (Australia) in the 100-m freestyle (1956, 1960, 1964) and Krisztina Egerszegi (Hungary) in the 200-m backstroke (1988, 1992, 1996).

MOST MEDALS IN THE WORLD CHAMPIONSHIPS

Michael Gross (West Germany) won 13 World Championship medals (five gold, five silver and three bronze) from 1982 to 1990.

The most medals by a woman is 10, by Kornelia Ender (eight gold and two silver in 1973 and 1975).

The most gold medals by a man is six (two individual and four relay) by James Montgomery (USA) in 1973 and 1975.

The most medals at a single championship is seven, by Matt Biondi (USA) with three gold, one silver and three bronze in 1986.

MOST WORLD RECORDS

The most world records set by a man is 32, by Arne Borg (Sweden) between 1921 and 1929.

The most world records set by a woman is 42, by Ragnhild Hveger (Denmark) from 1936 to 1942.

The most world records set by a man in currently recognized events (metric distances in 50-m pools) is 26, by Mark Spitz (USA) from 1967 to 1972.

The greatest number of world records set by a woman in currently recognized events is 23, by Kornelia Ender (GDR) from 1973 to 1976.

FASTEST FEMALE SWIMMER

The fastest ever speed by a female swimmer was 7.34 km/h (4.56 mph), by Le Jingyi (China) when she set her 50-m world record in Rome, Italy, on 11 Sept 1994. Jingyi, who was born in 1975 stands 1.78 m (5 ft 8 in) in height and weighs 68 kg (150 lb). She is one of the best swimmers ever to come out of China.

The most world records set in one pool is 86, in the North Sydney pool, NSW, Australia, between 1955 and 1978. This includes 48 imperial distance records.

LONGEST SWIMS
Fred Newton swam 2,938 km (1,826 miles) down the Mississippi River, USA, between Ford Dam (near Minneapolis, Minnesota) and Carrollton Ave, New Orleans, Louisiana, from 6 July to 29 Dec 1930. He was in the water for 742 hours.

The greatest distance swum in 24 hours is 101.9 km (63 miles 559 yd), by Anders Forvass (Sweden) at the 25-m Linköping public swimming pool, Sweden, from 28 to 29 Oct 1989.

The greatest distance swum by a woman in 24 hours is 95.657 km (59 miles 771 yd), by Kelly Driffield at the 50-m Mingara Leisure Centre pool, Tumbi Umbi, NSW, Australia, in June 1997.

The greatest distance swum underwater is 78.92 km (49 miles 68 yd) in 24 hours, by Paul Cryne (GB) and Samir Sawan al Awami (Qatar) from Doha to Umm Said, Qatar, and back again in 1985.

The greatest distance swum underwater by a relay team is 151.987 km (94 miles 774 yd), by six people in a pool in Czechoslovakia (now Czech Republic) from 17 to 18 Oct 1987.

LONGEST RELAYS
The 20-strong New Zealand national relay team swam a record 182.807 km (113 miles 1,040 yd) in Lower Hutt, New Zealand, in a time of 24 hours from 9 to 10 Dec 1983.

The 24-hour club record by a team of five is 162.52 km (100 miles 1,045 yd), by the Portsmouth Northsea SC at the Victoria Swimming Centre, Portsmouth, Hants, UK, from 4 to 5 March 1993.

DIVING
MOST OLYMPIC MEDALS
The greatest number of Olympic medals ever won by a diver is five, by Klaus Dibiasi (Italy) with three gold and two silver from 1964 to 1976, and by Greg Louganis (USA) with four gold and one silver in 1976, 1984 and 1988. Dibiasi is also the only diver to have ever won the same event (highboard) at three successive Olympic Games (1968, 1972 and 1976).

The record for the greatest number of highboard and springboard doubles wins is two, by Patricia McCormick (USA) in 1952 and 1956 and by Greg Louganis (USA) in 1984 and 1988.

MOST WORLD TITLES
Greg Louganis has won a record five world titles (highboard in 1978 and both highboard and springboard in 1982 and 1986, as well as four Olympic gold medals in 1984 and 1988).

HIGHEST DIVING SCORES
The US diver Greg Louganis achieved record scores at the 1984 Olympic Games in Los Angeles, California, USA, with 754.41 points for the 11-dive springboard event and 710.91 for the highboard. Louganis, who has won an unprecedented 47 national titles during his career, revealed his HIV-positive status after the 1988 Summer Olympics in Seoul, where he injured his head while diving.

The record for the greatest number of gold medals ever to have been won in a single event since the inaugural World Championship in 1973 is three, by Philip Boggs (USA) in the springboard in 1973, 1975 and 1978. Boggs also won the 1976 Olympic springboard title.

skiing

HIGHEST SCORING JUMP

The Chinese skier Xu Nannan performs her jump during the women's aerials qualification round at the 1998 Winter Olympics in Nagano, Japan. A former gymnast, Nannan was in a highly advantageous position after the qualifying round, which she led. She remained on form and executed the highest scoring jump of the competition but went on to win silver rather than gold.

MOST WORLD ALPINE CHAMPIONSHIP TITLES

The most titles won by a man in the World Alpine Championship is seven, by Toni Sailer (Austria), who won all four (giant slalom, slalom, downhill and the non-Olympic Alpine combination) in 1956 and the downhill, giant slalom and combined in 1958.

The record for the most titles by a woman is 12, by Christl Cranz (Germany), who won seven individual (four slalom, 1934 and 1937–39, and three downhill, 1935, 1937 and 1939) and five combined (1934–35 and 1937–39). Cranz also won the gold medal for the combined in the 1936 Olympics.

MOST WORLD NORDIC CHAMPIONSHIP TITLES

The most titles won by a woman is 17, by Yelena Välbe (Russia), with 10 individual titles and seven relay titles from 1989 to 1998.

The most titles by a jumper is five, by Birger Ruud (Norway) in 1931 and 1932 and from 1935 to 1937. Ruud is the only person to have won Olympic events in the Alpine and Nordic disciplines: the ski-jumping and the Alpine downhill in 1936.

MOST WORLD NORDIC CHAMPIONSHIP MEDALS

The most medals won is 23, by Raisa Petrovna Smetanina (USSR, later CIS), including seven golds (1974–92).

FASTEST OLYMPIC DOWNHILL SPEED

The record for the highest ever average speed achieved in the Olympic downhill race is 107.24 km/h (66.64 mph), by the French skier Jean-Luc Cretier at the 1998 Nagano Winter Olympics. A jubilant Cretier is pictured here seconds after receiving his medal for men's downhill alpine skiing on 15 Feb. He had been competing at the highest level for a total of 11 years but had so far failed to win a single race or medal. He announced his retirement at the end of the season.

MOST WORLD CUP WINS

The record for the greatest number of individual event wins is 86 (46 giant slalom and 40 slalom) from a total of 287 races, by Ingemar Stenmark (Sweden) from 1974 to 1989. This included a men's record of 13 wins in one season (1978/79). Of these, 10 were part of a record 14 successive giant slalom wins from 18 March 1978 to 21 Jan 1980.

Franz Klammer (Austria) won 25 downhill races, 1974–84.

Annemarie Moser (Austria) won a women's record 62 individual events from 1970 to 1979. She also had a record 11 consecutive downhill wins from 1972 to 1974.

Vreni Schneider (Switzerland) won a record total of 13 events (and one combined event), including all seven slalom events, in 1988/89.

MOST WORLD NORDIC TITLES

The most titles won by any skier (including Olympics) is 18, by Bjørn Dæhlie (Norway), who won 12 individual and six relay from 1991 to 1998. At the 1998 Nagano Olympics, Daehlie become the most successful individual in the history of the Winter Games when he won an eighth gold medal. He plans to add to his Olympic victories at the 2002 Games at Salt Lake City, Utah, USA.

MOST FREESTYLE TITLES

Edgar Grospiron (France) has won a record three titles (moguls in 1989 and 1991 and aerials in 1995). He also won an Olympic title in 1992.

The record for the most men's overall titles in the World Cup is five, by Eric Laboureix (France) from 1986 to 1988 and in 1990 and 1991.

The most women's overall titles in the World Cup is 10, by Connie Kissling (Switzerland) from 1983 to 1992.

LONGEST SKI-JUMPS

The longest ski-jump recorded in a World Cup event is 204 m (669 ft), by Andreas Goldberger (Austria) at Harrachov, Czech Republic, on 9 March 1996.

The longest ski-jump by a woman is 112 m (367 ft), by Eva Ganster (Austria) at Bischofshofen, Austria, on 7 Jan 1994.

The longest ever dry ski-jump was 92 m (302 ft), by Hubert Schwarz (West Germany) at Berchtesgarten, Germany, on 30 June 1981.

HIGHEST SPEEDS

The official world speed record is 241.448 km/h (150.028 mph), by Jeffrey Hamilton (USA) at Vars, France, on 14 April 1995.

The official women's record is 226.700 km/h (140.864 mph), by Karine Dubouchet (France) at Les Arcs, France, on 20 April 1996.

The highest speed reached in a World Cup downhill is 112.4 km/h (69.8 mph), by Armin Assinger (Austria) at Sierra Nevada, Spain, on 15 March 1993.

The record time for 50-km (31-mile) race in a major championship is 1 hr 54 min 46 sec, by Aleksey Prokurorov (Russia) at Thunder Bay, Canada,

in 1994. His average speed was 26.14 km/h (16.24 mph).

The record for the fastest speed ever attained by a person skiing on one leg is 185.567 km/h (115.306 mph), by Patrick Knaff (France) in 1988.

LONGEST RACES

The longest Nordic ski race is the 89-km (55-mile 528-yd) annual Vasaloppet in Sweden. There were 10,934 starters in 1977.

The longest downhill race is the 15.8-km (9-mile 1,408-yd) Inferno from the top of the Schilthorn to Lauterbrunnen, Switzerland. The record time is 13 min 53.4 sec, by Urs von Allmen (Switzerland) in 1991.

LARGEST RACE

The Finlandia Ski Race is 75 km (46 miles 1,056 yd) long from Hämeenlinna to Lahti, Finland. In Feb 1984 it had a record 13,226 starters and 12,909 finishers.

LONGEST ALL-DOWNHILL SKI RUN

The Weissfluhjoch-Küblis Parsenn skiing course near Davos, Switzerland, is a record 12.23 km (7 miles 1,056 yd) long.

GREATEST DISTANCE COVERED

Seppo-Juhani Savolainen (Finland) covered 415.5 km (258 miles 352 yd) in 24 hours at Saariselkä, Finland, from 8 to 9 April 1988.

The women's 24-hour record is 330 km (205 miles), by Sisko Kainulaisen (Finland) at Jyväskylä, Finland, from 23 to 24 March 1985.

MEN'S DOWNHILL

Brian Stemmle of Canada trains for the men's downhill at the Nagano Winter Olympics. The men's downhill is the Blue Riband event of the Winter Olympics and is always eventful: 1998 was no exception. The race was delayed on numerous occasions due to heavy snow and eventually took place on 13 Feb, which was a Friday. It proved unlucky for some — 13 skiers failed to finish.

ice hockey

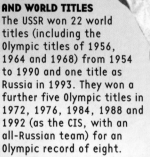

Canada have won the first four world championships for women (1990, 1992, 1994 and 1997) without losing a single game.

MOST STANLEY CUP WINS

The Montreal Canadiens had a record 24 wins (1916, 1924, 1930–31, 1944, 1946, 1953, 1956–60, 1965–66, 1968–69, 1971, 1973, 1976–79, 1986 and 1993) from a record 32 finals.

Joseph Henri Richard played on a record 11 winning teams for the Canadiens from 1956 to 1973.

MOST STANLEY CUP POINTS

The most points scored in a game is eight, by Patrik Sundström (Sweden), with three goals and five assists for New Jersey against Washington in April 1988, and by Mario Lemieux, with five goals and three assists for Pittsburgh against Philadelphia in April 1989.

MOST STANLEY CUP GOALS

The most goals in a season is 19, by Reggie Leach for Philadelphia in 1976 and by Jari Kurri (Finland) for Edmonton in 1985.

The most goals in a game is five, by Maurice Richard in Montreal's 5–1 win over Toronto on 23 March 1944, Darryl Sittler in Toronto's 8–5 win over Philadelphia on 22 April 1976, Reggie Leach in Philadelphia's 6–3 win over Boston on 6 May 1976, and Mario Lemieux in Pittsburgh's 10–7 win over Philadelphia in April 1989.

MOST STANLEY CUP ASSISTS

The most assists in a game is six, by Mikko Leinonen in New York Rangers' 7–3 victory over Philadelphia on 8 April 1982 and by Wayne Gretzky in Edmonton's 13–3 victory over Los Angeles on 9 April 1987.

MOST GAMES PLAYED

Gordie Howe (Canada) played in a record 1,767 regular season games (and 157 play-off games) over a record 26 seasons, from

MOST OLYMPIC AND WORLD TITLES

The USSR won 22 world titles (including the Olympic titles of 1956, 1964 and 1968) from 1954 to 1990 and one title as Russia in 1993. They won a further five Olympic titles in 1972, 1976, 1984, 1988 and 1992 (as the CIS, with an all-Russian team) for an Olympic record of eight.

The most gold medals is three, by Soviet players Vitaliy Davydov, Anatoliy Firsov, Viktor Kuzkin and Aleksandr Ragulin (1964, 1968, 1972), Vladislav Tretyak (1972, 1976, 1984) and Andrey Khomutov (1984, 1988, 1992).

ICE HOCKEY COMPETITIONS

World ice hockey championships were first held for amateur players in 1920 in conjunction with the Olympic Games, which were also considered as world championships up to 1968. Since 1976 world championships have also been open to professional players. Women's ice hockey was first introduced to the Olympic Games in 1998. The winner was the USA, who beat Canada in the final.

MOST HIGHLY-PAID PLAYER

Sergey Federov (Russia) of the Detroit Red Wings is reported to have earned the record sum of $20 million (£12 million) for the 1997/98 season, making him the highest-paid ice hockey player ever. His basic salary was $2 million (£1.2 million); the rest was made up of bonuses. Federov had been instrumental in the Red Wings' Stanley Cup success the previous season.

ICE HOCKEY SUPERSTAR

Wayne Gretzky, who has played for the Edmonton Oilers, the Los Angeles Kings, the St. Louis Blues and the New York Rangers, is the most successful ice hockey player today, earning an estimated $6.5 million (£3.9 million) a year. He holds numerous Stanley Cup records: most points (382), most goals (122) and most assists (260), as well as most points in a season, with 47 (16 goals and a record 31 assists) in 1985. He also holds the NHL scoring records for the regular season and play-off games, with 837 goals and 1,771 assists for a record 2,608 points from 1,253 games. In 1981/82 he scored a record 92 goals in a season for the Edmonton Oilers and in all his 1981/82 games (including Stanley Cup play-offs and matches for Canada in the world championship) he scored 238 points (103 goals and 135 assists). In 1985/86 he scored an NHL record of 215 points, including a record 163 assists. Born in Canada in 1961, Gretzky began his professional career in 1978. Nicknamed 'the Great One', he is now regarded by many as the greatest ice hockey player of all time. He is pictured here on the pages of the 1998 *Sports Illustrated* swimsuit edition with his wife, actress Janet Jones.

1946 to 1971 (Detroit Red Wings) and in the 1979/80 season (Hartford Whalers). He also played 419 games (and 78 play-off games) for the Houston Aeros and for the New England Whalers in the World Hockey Association (WHA) from 1973 to 1979, and a grand total of 2,421 major league games.

MOST GOALS, POINTS AND ASSISTS

The most points scored in a North American major league game is 10, by Jim Harrison (three goals, seven assists) for Alberta, later Edmonton Oilers, in a WHA match at Edmonton on 30 Jan 1973, and by Darryl Sittler (six goals, four assists) for Toronto Maple Leafs against Boston Bruins in an NHL match at Toronto on 7 Feb 1976.

The most goals in a game is seven, by Joe Malone in Québec's 10–6 win over Toronto St. Patricks at Québec City in 1920.

The most assists is seven, by Billy Taylor for Detroit against Chicago in March 1947 and by Wayne Gretzky for Edmonton against Washington in Feb 1980, against Chicago in Dec 1985 and against Québec in Feb 1986.

The most goals by a team in a world championship match was 58, by Australia against New Zealand (0) at Perth, Australia, on 15 March 1987.

The most team goals scored in a season is 446, by the Edmonton Oilers in the 1983/84 season, when they also achieved a record 1,182 scoring points.

The Montreal Canadiens scored a record 132 team points (60 wins, 12 ties) from 80 games played in 1976/77. Their tally of eight losses was also the lowest ever in a season of 70 or more games.

MOST TEAM WINS

The Detroit Red Wings won a record 62 games in 1995/96.

The highest percentage of wins in a season was .875% by the Boston Bruins, with 30 wins in 44 games in the 1929/30 season.

LONGEST UNDEFEATED RUN

The longest unbeaten run in a season is 35 games (25 wins, 10 ties), by the Philadelphia Flyers from 14 Oct 1979 to 6 Jan 1980.

MOST SUCCESSFUL GOALTENDERS

Terry Sawchuk played a record 971 games as goaltender for Detroit, Boston, Toronto, Los Angeles and New York Rangers from 1950 to 1970. He had a record 435 wins (to 337 losses and 188 ties) and a record 103 career shutouts.

Jacques Plante had 15 wins in his one season in the WHA and 434 NHL wins, making a senior league total of 449 from 868 games.

Bernie Parent had 47 wins in one season, with 13 losses and 12 ties for Philadelphia, 1973/74.

Gerry Cheevers (Boston Bruins) played in 32 successive games without a defeat, 1971–72.

FASTEST GOAL

The fastest goal from the opening whistle is five seconds, by Doug Smail for the Winnipeg Jets on 20 Dec 1981 and by Bryan Trottier for the New York Islanders on 22 March 1984.

STANLEY CUP

The Stanley Cup was first presented in 1893 by Lord Stanley of Preston, then the governor-general of Canada. From 1894 onwards the contest was played out by amateur teams for the Canadian Championship. This lasted until 1910, when it became the award for the winners of the professional league play-offs.

powerboats and jetskiing

POWERBOATS

FASTEST WATER SPEEDS, OFFICIAL

The official world water speed record is 511.11 km/h (317.6 mph), by Kenneth Warby in an unlimited hydroplane on Blowering Dam Lake, NSW, Australia, on 8 Oct 1978.

The official world water speed record by a woman is 317 km/h (197 mph), by Mary Rife at Flint, Texas, USA, in 1977.

FASTEST WATER SPEEDS, UNOFFICIAL

Kenneth Warby achieved an unofficial record speed of 556 km/h (345.48 mph) in his unlimited hydroplane *Spirit of Australia* on Blowering Dam Lake, NSW, Australia, on 20 Nov 1977.

Mary Rife set a women's unofficial record speed of 332.67 km/h (206.72 mph) in her blown fuel hydro *Proud Mary* in Tulsa, Oklahoma, USA, on 23 July 1977.

FASTEST SPEED IN AN ELECTRIC POWERBOAT

David Mischke set the APBA electric powerboat speed record of 133.57 km/h (70.6 mph) in a 4.27-m (14-ft) outboard hydroplane with a 48-volt motor at the Kilometer Speed Trials in Oregon, USA, on 14 Oct 1995.

FASTEST CIRCUIT RACING

In 1997 Guido Cappellini of Italy achieved a Formula 1 speed of 214 km/h (132.97 mph) in a DAC/Mercury. Formula 1 boats must be at least 4.8 m (15 ft 8 in) long, weigh no more than 390 kg (860 lb) and have a maximum engine capacity of 2 litres.

In 1996 L. Norman of Sweden set the record Formula 2 speed of 174 km/h (108.08 mph) in a Molgard/Mercury. Formula 2 boats must be no longer than 4.8 m (15 ft 8 in), weigh at least 390 kg (860 lb) and have a maximum engine capacity of 2 litres.

In 1995 P. Sandown of Hungary set the Formula 3 speed record of 170.3 km/h (105.82 mph) in a Hungasv/Johnson. Formula 3 boats must be no longer than 3.9 m (12 ft 9 in), weigh at least 250 kg (551 lb) and have an engine capacity of no more than 850cc.

Andy Chesman (GB) attained a Formula 500 record speed of 163.3 km/h (101.5 mph) in 1996. The boat used was a Fort/Konig. Formula 500 boats must be at least 3.85 m (12 ft 8 in) long, weigh at least 130 kg (286 lb 9 oz) and have an engine capacity of no more than 500cc.

FASTEST SPEEDS IN OFFSHORE RACING

In 1994 Tom Gentry (USA) set the offshore Class 1 speed record of 253.35 km/h (157.43 mph) in a 12.2-m (40-ft) Skater with twin Mercury V8 engines. Class 1 boats are 12–14.63 m (39–48 ft) long, weigh no less than 4,500 kg (9,920 lb) and have a top engine capacity of 16 litres.

Charles Burnett III (GB) set the offshore Class 2 speed record of 220 km/h (137.32 mph) in a 8.5-m (28-ft) Skater with triple Mercury 2.5 EFI outboards in 1996. Class 2 boats are 9.75–12 m (32–39 ft) long, with a minimum

POWERBOATING

Powerboating began in 1863, when Frenchman Jean Lenoir installed a petrol engine on a boat. Competitive racing started around 1900 and the first major race was between Calais, France, and Dover, UK, in 1903. The American Power Boat Association (APBA) was formed in that same year and held its first Gold Cup on the Hudson River, New York, USA, in 1904. The Cowes to Torquay race was instituted in 1961. It was originally run from Cowes to Torquay, UK, but from 1968 also included the return journey.

FASTEST TRANSATLANTIC CROSSINGS

In 1989 Tom Gentry (second from left, with Virgin boss Richard Branson far left) set the transatlantic speed record in *Gentry Eagle*, then the world's fastest motoryacht, crossing the ocean in 2 days 14 hr 7 min 47 sec. In 1992 the Italian-owned *Destriero* broke his record, crossing in 58 hr 34 min. The voyage marked the 500th anniversary of Columbus' arrival in America and its promoters included the Aga Khan and Giovanni Agnelli, the late chairman of Fiat. When the record fell, Gentry set out to win it back, but in 1994 he fell into a coma after a boating accident and died in 1998.

weight of 2,750 kg (6,063 lb) and an engine capacity of no more than 8 litres.

In 1995 Bo Warelius of Finland attained a record Class 3 speed of 181 km/h (113.11 mph) in an 8.5-m (28-ft) Skater with twin Mercury 2.5 EFI outboards. Class 3 boats are 7.6–10 m long (25–33 ft), weigh no less than 1,600 kg (3,528 lb) and have a maximum engine capacity of 6 litres.

HIGHEST APBA GOLD CUP AVERAGE SPEED
The highest ever average speed in the APBA Gold Cup race is 240.05 km/h (149.160 mph), by Chip Hanauer (USA) piloting *Miss Budweiser* in 1995.

MOST APBA GOLD CUP WINS
The most wins by a driver is 10, by Chip Hanauer (USA): 1982–88, 1992, 1993 and 1995.

Bornie Little, the owner of *Miss Budweiser* (registered at Hydroplane Inc.), holds the record for the most wins by an owner, at 10: in 1969 (driven by Bill Sterett Sr.), in 1970, 1973, 1980 and 1981 (driven by Dean

Chenoweth), in 1989 and 1990 (driven by Tom D'eath), in 1992, 1993 and 1995 (driven by Chip Hanauer) and in 1997 (driven by Dave Villwock).

Chip Hanauer (USA) has had a record seven successive victories, winning the APBA Gold Cup from 1982 to 1988.

MOST COWES TO TORQUAY WINS
The most wins in the 320.4-km (199-mile) race from Cowes to Torquay, UK, is four by Renato della Valle (Italy), 1982–85.

FASTEST COWES TO TORQUAY SPEED
The highest ever average speed in the race was 138.24 km/h (85.89 mph), by Fabio Fuzzi (Italy) piloting *Cesa* in 1988.

LONGEST RACES
The longest ever offshore race was the Port Richborough London to Monte Carlo Marathon Offshore international event, which covered 4,742 km (2,947 miles) in 14 stages from 10 to 25 June 1972. It was won by *H.T.S.* (GB), piloted by Mike Bellamy, Eddie Chater

and Jim Brooker in 71 hr 35 min 56 sec — an average speed of 66.24 km/h (41.15 mph).

The longest circuit race is the 24-hour race on the River Seine at Rouen, France, which has been held annually since 1962.

JETSKIING
LONGEST JETSKI JOURNEY
In 1993 Gary Frick (USA) travelled a record 8,109 km (5,040 miles) along the US coastline on a stand-up Kawasaki 650sx Jet Ski. He left Lubec, Maine, on 8 May and arrived in Seattle, Washington, on 16 Sept.

FASTEST SPEED ON A SOLO BIKE
In 1994 D. Condemine of France attained a record speed of 69 km/h (43.09 mph) on a Solo Yamaha bike. A solo bike is the original type of jetski with a pivoting handbole.

POWERBOATING CHAMPION
La Gran Argentina, piloted by Daniel Scioili (Argentina) and throttleman Jorge Bordas, won the 1997 UIM Class Three (6 litre) World Offshore Championships, securing success in home waters off the coast of Buenos Aires. It was a fourth consecutive world title for Scioili, who was partnered by Fabio Buzzi of Italy when they won the Superboat Vee class world championship at the Key West World offshore powerboat race in 1996.

FASTEST SPEED ON A SPORT BIKE
In 1997 Ray Purkiss (GB) set the record speed for a sport bike when he attained a speed of 91 km/h (56.68 mph) on a Sport Yamaha bike. A sport bike is a two seater jetski.

FASTEST SPEED ON A RUNABOUT
In 1997 Steve Longbottom (GB) attained a record-breaking speed of 98.76 km/h (61.38 mph) on a Runabout Bombardier bike. A Runabout is a three-seater jetski.

JETSKIING
Jetskiing was developed by Clayton Jacobsen of the USA in the early 1960s. He loved the excitement of moto-cross and waterskiing and dreamed of combining the two. He spent the 1960s refining his craft and in 1971 presented his idea to Kawasaki, the Japanese motorcycle manufacturer. In 1973 the first commercially available jetskis were produced. Since then jetskiing has evolved into a highly competitive sport with a global following.

wrestling boxing
and martial arts

SUMO
MOST SUCCESSFUL WRESTLERS
Yokozuna (grand champion) Sadji Akiyoshi, alias Futabayama, holds the all-time record of 69 consecutive wins (1937–39).

Yokozuna Koki Naya, alias Taiho (meaning 'Great Bird'), won the Emperor's Cup a record 32 times to his retirement in 1971.

The *ozeki* Tameemon Torokichi, alias Raiden, won 254 bouts and lost only 10 in 21 years, giving him the highest ever winning percentage of 96.2.

MOST WINS
Yokozuna Mitsugu Akimoto, alias Chiyonofuji, won the Kyushu Basho (one of the six annual tournaments) for eight successive years (1981–88). He also holds the record for the most career wins (1,045) and the most *Makunouchi* (top division) wins (807).

In 1978 Toshimitsu Ogata, alias Kitanoumi, won 82 of the 90 bouts that the top *rikishi* fight each year. In 1974, at the age of 21 years 2 months, he became the youngest ever man to become a *yokozuna*.

MOST TOP-DIVISION BOUTS
Jesse Kuhaulua (Takamiyama) (USA) fought 1,231 consecutive bouts (1981). He was the first non-Japanese to win an official top-division tournament, in 1972.

The most consecutive bouts in all six divisions is 1,631, by Yukio Shoji, alias Aobajo (1964–86).

The most career bouts is 1,891, by Kenji Hatano (Oshio) from 1962 to 1988.

WRESTLING
MOST OLYMPIC TITLES
Three titles were won by: Carl Westergren (Sweden) in 1920, 1924 and 1932; Ivar Johansson (Sweden) in 1932 (two) and 1936; Aleksandr Medved (USSR) in 1964, 1968 and 1972; and Aleksandr Karelin (Russia) in 1988, 1992 and 1996.

MOST OLYMPIC MEDALS
Four Olympic medals were won by: Eino Leino (Finland) at

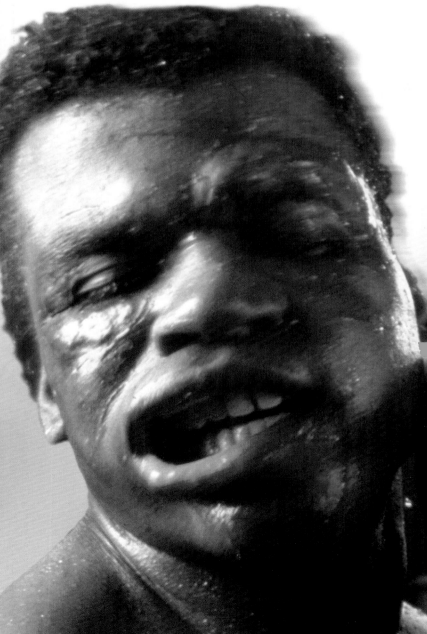

BIGGEST *YOKOZUNA*
The Hawaiian-born sumo wrestler Chad Rowan, alias Akebono, is pictured lifting his opponent Tochinowaka during a bout. The tallest and heaviest *yokozuna* in sumo history, Akebono is 2.04 m (6 ft 8 in) tall and weighs 227 kg (35 st 11 lb). In Jan 1993 he became the first foreign *rikishi* ever to be promoted to the rank of *yokozuna* and in 1996 he became a Japanese citizen.

BIGGEST PAY-PER-VIEW TV AUDIENCE
In July 1997 boxing superstar Mike Tyson was fined $3 million (£1.8 million) by the court of Nevada and had his boxing licence revoked for a year after biting a chunk out of the ear of his opponent Evander Holyfield during the World Boxing Association heavyweight championship fight on 28 June. After the incident, the chunk of ear was found on the canvas by Mitch Libonati, an employee of the MGM Grand Hotel, who is said to have wrapped it up in a latex glove and taken it to Holyfield's dressing room. Holyfield was then rushed to hospital, where the piece was reattached. The fight was watched by the biggest pay-per-view audience in boxing history, while celebrities such as Whitney Houston and Robert de Niro were among 16,000 spectators who paid up to $1,440 (£900) to watch the fight live in the MGM Grand Arena, Las Vegas, USA.

freestyle from 1920 to 1932; Imre Polyák (Hungary) at Greco-Roman from 1952 to 1964; and Bruce Baumgartner (USA) at freestyle from 1984 to 1996.

MOST WORLD TITLES
Freestyler Aleksandr Medved (USSR) won a record 10 titles at three weight categories (1962–64 and 1966–72).

LONGEST BOUT
The longest recorded bout lasted 11 hr 40 min, when Martin Klein (Estonia representing Russia) beat Alfred Asikáinen (Finland) for the Greco-Roman 75-kg 'A' event silver medal in the 1912 Olympics.

BOXING
SHORTEST FIGHT
The shortest world title fight lasted 20 seconds, when Gerald McClellan (USA) beat Jay Bell in an WBC middleweight bout in Puerto Rico on 7 Aug 1993.

MOST KNOCK-OUTS
The most finishes classed as 'knock-outs' in a career is 145 (129 in professional bouts), by Archie Moore (USA), 1936–63.

LONGEST REIGNS
Joe Louis (USA) was champion for 11 years 252 days, from 1937 to his retirement in 1949. This heavyweight duration record stands for all divisions.

Rocky Marciano (USA) is the only world champion at any weight to have won every fight of his entire professional career (49 fights), from 1947 to 1955.

LONGEST FIGHT
The longest world title fight under Queensberry Rules was between lightweights Joe Gans and Oscar Nelson (both USA) at Goldfield, Nevada, USA, on 3 Sept 1906. It was terminated in the 42nd round when Gans was declared the winner on a foul.

JUDO
MOST TITLES
Yasuhiro Yamashita (Japan) won four world and one Olympic title: the Over 95 kg in 1979, 1981 and 1983, the Open in 1981 and the Olympic Open in 1984. He retired undefeated after 203 successive wins (1977–85).

Four world titles were also won by Shozo Fujii (Japan) in the Under 80 kg in 1971, 1973 and 1975 and the Under 78 kg in 1979 and by Naoya Ogawa (Japan) in the Open in 1987, 1989 and 1991 and the Over 95 kg in 1989.

MOST WOMEN'S TITLES
Ingrid Berghmans (Belgium) has won a record six women's world titles: the Open in 1980, 1982, 1984 and 1986 and the Under 72 kg in 1984 and 1989. She has also won four silver medals and a bronze. She won the Olympic 72-kg title in 1988, when women's judo was introduced as a demonstration sport.

KARATE
MOST WORLD TITLES
Great Britain has won a record six world titles at the Kumite team event (1975, 1982, 1984, 1986, 1988 and 1990).

The record for the most men's individual kumite titles is two, by: Pat McKay (GB) at the Under 80 kg in 1982 and 1984; Emmanuel Pinda (France) at the Open in 1984 and the Over 80 kg in 1988; Thierry Masci (France) at the Under 70 kg in 1986 and 1988; and José Manuel Egea (Spain) at the Under 80 kg in 1990 and 1992.

A record four women's kumite titles have been won by Guus van Mourik (Netherlands) at the Over 60 kg in 1982, 1984, 1986 and 1988.

The most men's individual kata titles is three, by Tsuguo Sakumoto (Japan) in 1984, 1986 and 1988.

The record for the greatest number of individual kata titles in women's competition is three, by Mie Nakayama (Japan) in 1982, 1984 and 1986 and by Yuki Mimura (Japan) in 1988, 1990 and 1992.

BOXING RULES
In 1867 the sport of boxing came under the Queensberry Rules, which were formulated for John Sholto Douglas, the eighth Marquess of Queensberry. The rules stipulated the wearing of gloves (earlier contests had been fought by bareknuckled boxers). The first champion under the Queensberry Rules was the heavyweight James Corbett, in 1892.

gymnastics and weightlifting

GYMNASTICS

MOST MEN'S WORLD TITLES

The most individual men's titles is 13, by Vitaliy Scherbo (Belarus) between 1992 and 1995. He also won a team gold medal in 1992.

Boris Anfiyanovich Shakhlin (USSR) won a record 10 individual titles and three team titles between 1954 and 1964.

The USSR won the team title a record 13 times (eight World Championships and five Olympics) between 1952 and 1992.

MOST WOMEN'S WORLD TITLES

The record for the most titles won in the World Championships (including Olympic Games) is 18 (12 individual, six team), by Larisa Semyonovna Latynina (USSR) between 1954 and 1964.

The USSR won the team title on a record 21 occasions (11 World Championships and 10 Olympics).

YOUNGEST WORLD TITLE WINNERS

Aurelia Dobre (Romania) won the women's overall world title at the age of 14 years 352 days at Rotterdam, Netherlands, on 23 Oct 1987.

In 1990 Daniela Silivas (Romania) revealed that she was born a year later than she had previously claimed and was in fact 14 years 185 days old when she won the gold medal for balance beam in 1985.

The youngest male world champion was Dmitriy Bilozerchev (USSR), who was 16 years 315 days old when he competed at Budapest, Hungary, on 28 Oct 1983.

MOST MEN'S OLYMPIC TITLES

The men's team title has been won five times by Japan (1960, 1964, 1968, 1972 and 1976) and the USSR (1952, 1956, 1980, 1988 and 1992).

The greatest number of men's individual gold medals is six, by Boris Shakhlin (USSR) — one in 1956, four (two shared) in 1960 and one in 1964 — and by Nikolay Andrianov (USSR) — one in 1972, four in 1976 and one in 1980.

MOST MEN'S OLYMPIC MEDALS

Male gymnast Nikolay Andrianov (USSR) won a record 15 Olympic medals (seven gold, five silver and three bronze), from 1972 to 1980.

Aleksandr Dityatin (USSR) won a record eight medals at one Games, in Moscow, Russia (then USSR), in 1980. He won a medal in all eight categories (three gold, four silver and one bronze).

MOST WOMEN'S OLYMPIC TITLES

The USSR won the Olympic women's title a record 10 times (from 1952 to 1980 and in 1988 and 1992). The last title was won by the Unified team from the republics of the former USSR.

Vera Caslavska-Odlozil (Czechoslovakia) holds the record for the most individual gold medals: three in 1964 and four (one shared) in 1968.

MOST WOMEN'S OLYMPIC MEDALS

Larisa Latynina (USSR) won six individual gold medals and three team golds from 1956 to 1964. She also won five silver and four bronze medals, making an Olympic record total of 18.

YOUNGEST INTERNATIONAL

Pasakevi 'Voula' Kouna (Greece) was just 9 years 299 days old at the start of the Balkan Games at Serres, Greece, in 1981.

MOST WORLD CUP TITLES

Male gymnasts Li Ning (China), Nikolay Andrianov (USSR) and Aleksandr Dityatin (USSR) and female gymnast Maria Yevgenyevna Filatova (USSR) have each won two World Cup overall titles.

FASTEST SOMERSAULTS

On 30 April 1986 Ashrita Furman performed 8,341 forward rolls in 10 hr 30 min over 19.67 km (12 miles 390 yd) from Lexington to Charleston, Massachusetts, USA.

On 21 July 1996, Ashrita Furman somersaulted 1.6 km (1 mile) in 19 min 38 sec, at Edgewater Park, Cleveland, Ohio, USA.

Vitaliy Scherbo (Belarus) backwards somersaulted 50 m (54 yd) in just 10.22 sec at Makuhar Messe Event Hall, Chiba, Japan, on 31 Aug 1995.

MOST TITLES

Alexei Nemov is seen performing on the parallel bars for the USSR. The former Soviet Union was the most successful nation in men's gymnastics, winning 13 world titles. Russia continued the success, taking the Olympic title in 1996.

RHYTHMIC SPORTIVE GYMNASTICS
MOST WORLD TITLES
The most overall individual world titles in rhythmic gymnastics is three, by Maria Gigova (Bulgaria) in 1969, 1971 and 1973 (shared) and by Maria Petrova (Bulgaria) in 1993, 1994 and 1995 (shared).

Bianka Panova (Bulgaria) won all four apparatus gold medals (all with maximum scores) and a team gold in 1987.

Bulgaria has won a record nine team titles in rhythmic gymnastics: 1969, 1971, 1981, 1983, 1985, 1987, 1989 (shared), 1993 and 1995.

PERFECT SCORES IN GREATEST NUMBER OF DISCIPLINES
At the 1988 Olympics in Seoul, South Korea, Marina Lobach (USSR) won the rhythmic gymnastic title with perfect scores in all six disciplines.

TRAMPOLINING
MOST TITLES
The most men's trampolining titles is five, by Aleksandr Moskalenko (Russia): three individual from 1990 to 1994 and two pairs from 1992 to 1994.

Brett Austine (Australia) also won three individual men's trampolining titles (double mini from 1982 to 1986).

Judy Wills (USA) has won a record nine women's titles: five individual from 1964 to 1968 (a record), two pairs in 1966 and 1967 and two tumbling in 1965 and 1966.

WEIGHTLIFTING
MOST MEN'S TITLES
Naim Suleymanoğlu (Turkey) won 10 world titles (including Olympic Games) in 1985, 1986, 1988, 1989 and from 1991 to 1996.

Naim Suleymanoğlu has won three Olympic golds: the 60 kg in 1988 and 1992 and the 64 kg in 1996.

MOST MEN'S MEDALS
Norbert Schemansky (USA) won a record four Olympic medals: gold for middle-heavyweight in 1952, silver for heavyweight in 1948 and bronze for heavyweight in 1960 and 1964.

MOST WOMEN'S GOLD MEDALS
Li Hongyun (China) won 13 medals in the 60/64-kg class from 1992 to 1996.

YOUNGEST AND OLDEST WORLD RECORD HOLDERS
Naim Suleimanov (Bulgaria) set world records for clean and jerk (160 kg or 352$\frac{1}{2}$ lb) and total (285 kg or 628$\frac{1}{2}$ lb) in the 56-kg class at the age of 16 years 62 days at Allentown, New Jersey, USA, on 26 March 1983. Suleimanov changed his name to Suleymanoğlu and now competes for Turkey.

Norbert Schemansky (USA) was 37 years 333 days old when he snatched 164.2 kg (362 lb) in the then unlimited heavyweight class at Detroit, USA, in 1962.

RHYTHMIC SPORTIVE GYMNASTICS
An Olympic sport since 1984, rhythmic sportive gymnastics (seen left and far left) is popular throughout the world.

POWERLIFTING
MOST WORLD TITLES
The most men's world titles is 17, by Hideaki Inaba (Japan) at 52 kg from 1974 to 1983 and 1985 to 1991.

The most women's powerlifting titles is six, by Beverley Francis (Australia) at 75 kg in 1980 and 1982 and 82.5 kg in 1981 and from 1983 to 1985, and Sisi Dolman (Netherlands) at 52 kg in 1985 and 1986 and from 1988 to 1991.

BEST TIMED LIFTS
A world deadlifting record of 3.14 million kg (6.92 million lb) was set by a team of 10 people at the Pontefract Sports and Leisure Centre, W Yorks, UK, from 3 to 4 May 1997.

The individual deadlift record is held by Chris Lawton, who lifted 450,095 kg (992,288 lb) at Barnsdale Country Club, Rutland, UK, from 5 to 6 April 1997.

A bench press record of 4.5 million kg (9.95 million lb) was set by a team of nine men at the Pulse 8 Fitness Studio in Reading, Berks, UK, from 31 May to 1 June 1997.

An individual bench press record of 815,434 kg (1.8 million lb) was set by Glen Tenove (USA) in 12 hours at Irvine, California, USA, on 17 Dec 1994.

A squat record of 2.17 million kg (4.78 million lb) was set by a team of 10 men at St Albans Weightlifting Club and Ware Boys Club, Herts, UK, from 20 to 21 July 1986.

WOMEN'S WEIGHTLIFTING
China's Chen Yanqing sets a new world record lift of 131.5 kg (290 lb) during the women's 54-kg class at the World Weightlifting Championships in Chang Mai, Thailand. Women's weightlifting will become an Olympic sport for the first time at the Sydney Olympics in 2000. Although there have been World Championships for women since 1987, the Olympics are seen as the highlight of athletes' careers. There will be 74 women lifters competing at the Sydney Games compared with 176 men, and there will be seven body weight classes for female lifters, ranging from 48 kg to 75 kg plus.

bike sports

CYCLING

MOST OLYMPIC TITLES

The most gold medals won is three, by Paul Masson (France) in 1896, Francisco Verri (Italy) in 1906, Robert Charpentier (France) in 1936 and Daniel Morelon (France) in 1968 (two) and 1972. Morelon also won a silver medal in 1976 and a bronze medal in 1964.

Marcus Hurley (USA) won four events in the 'unofficial' 1904 cycling programme.

MOST WORLD CHAMPIONSHIP TITLES

The most wins at one event is 10, by Koichi Nakano (Japan) in the professional sprint from 1977 to 1986.

The most wins at a men's amateur event is seven, by Daniel Morelon (France) in the sprint (1966, 1967, 1969–71, 1973 and 1975) and Leon Meredith (GB) in the 100-km motor paced (1904–05, 1907–09, 1911 and 1913).

beat Laurent Fignon (France) by just eight seconds, after 3,267 km (2,030 miles) over 23 days. LeMond's time was 87 hr 38 min 35 sec.

MOST CYCLO-CROSS TITLES

The most World Championship titles is eight, by Eric De Vlaeminck of Belgium, who won the Amateur and Open in 1966 and six professional titles from 1968 to 1973.

LONGEST ONE-DAY CYCLING RACE

The longest single-day 'massed start' road race in the world is the 551–620-km (342–385-mile) event from Bordeaux to Paris, France. Paced over all or part of the route, the highest average speed was 47.186 km/h (29.32 mph), by Herman van Springel (Belgium) in 1981. He covered 584.5 km (363 miles 176 yd) in 13 hr 35 min 18 sec.

HIGHEST CYCLING ALTITUDE

Canadians Bruce Bell, Philip Whelan and Suzanne MacFadyen cycled at a record altitude of 6,960 m (22,834 ft) on the peak of Mt Aconcagua, Argentina, on 25 Jan 1991. This achievement was equalled by Mozart Hastenreiter Catão (Brazil) on 11 March 1993 and by Tim Sumner and Jonathon Green (GB) on 6 Jan 1994.

MOTORBIKES

FASTEST MOTORBIKE CIRCUITS

The highest ever average lap speed attained on any closed circuit on a motorcycle is 257.958 km/h (160.288 mph), by Yvon du Hamel (Canada) on a modified 903cc four-cylinder Kawasaki Z1 at the 31° banked 4.02-km (2-mile 880-yd) Daytona International Speedway, Florida, USA, in March 1973. His lap time was 56.149 sec.

MOST MOTO-CROSS WINS

Moto-cross first began as an organized sport during the 1920s in the United Kingdom. It gained international status after WWII with the inauguration of a team event, the Moto-Cross des Nations. Joël Robert (Belgium) won a record six 250cc Moto-Cross World Championships, in 1964 and from 1968 to 1972. Between 25 April 1964 and 18 June 1972 he also won a record 50 250cc Grand Prix.

The fastest ever road circuit was Francorchamps near Spa, Belgium. At 14.12 km (8 miles 1,250 yd) in length, it was lapped in 3 min 50.3 sec — an average speed of 220.721 km/h (137.150 mph) — by Barry Sheene (GB) on a 495cc four-cylinder Suzuki during the Belgian Grand Prix on 3 July 1977. Sheene set a record time of 38 min 58.5 sec for the 10-lap race, giving him an average speed of 217.370 km/h (135.068 mph) over the course.

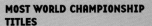

MOST WOMEN'S WORLD TITLES

The most women's titles is 10, by Jeannie Longo (France) in pursuit (1986 and 1988–89), road (1985–87, 1989 and 1995), points (1989) and the time-trial (1995 and 1996). In addition to her world titles, Longo has set numerous world records, including the current 1-hour mark, and in 1996 won an Olympic gold. She is widely considered to be the greatest ever female cyclist.

MOST TOUR DE FRANCE WINS

The greatest ever number of wins in the annual Tour de France race is five, by Jacques Anquetil (France) in 1957 and from 1961 to 1964; Eddy Merckx (Belgium) from 1969 to 1972 and in 1974; Bernard Hinault (France) from 1978 to 1979, 1981 to 1982 and in 1985; and Miguel Induráin (Spain) from 1991 to 1995.

CLOSEST TOUR DE FRANCE RACE

The closest race took place in 1989, when Greg LeMond (USA)

LONGEST MOTORBIKE CIRCUIT

The 60.72-km (37-mile 1,284-yd) 'Mountain' circuit on the Isle of Man has hosted the principal TT races since 1911 (with minor amendments in 1920). It has 264 curves and corners and is the longest circuit used for any motorcycle race.

MOST SUCCESSFUL MOTORCYCLISTS

The most World Championship titles won is 15, by Giacomo Agostini (Italy): seven at 350cc from 1968 to 1974 and eight at 500cc from 1966 to 1972 and in 1975. Agostini is also the only man to have won two World Championships in five consecutive years (350cc and 500cc titles from 1968 to 1972).

Giacomo Agostini won 122 races (68 at 500cc and 54 at

FASTEST TOUR DE FRANCE SPEED

The fastest average speed in the Tour de France was 39.504 km/h (24.547 mph), by Miguel Induráin (Spain) in 1992. Induráin is the winner of five consecutive Tour de France races, and has also won both the Giro d'Italia and the Tour de France in 1992 and again in 1993. He retired at the end of 1996, having never won the Vuelta a España, the major tour of his native country.

350cc) in the World Championship series between 24 April 1965 and 25 Sept 1977, including a record-breaking 19 in 1970. This season's total was equalled by Mike Hailwood (GB) in 1966.

Angel Roldan Nieto (Spain) won a record seven 125cc titles (1971–72, 1979 and 1981–84) and a record six titles at 50cc (1969–70, 1972 and 1975–77).

Phil Read (GB) won a record four 250cc titles, in 1964, 1965, 1968 and 1971.

Switzerland's Rolf Biland won a record seven world side-car titles from 1978 to 1979, in 1981 and 1983 and from 1992 to 1994.

The greatest number of career wins in any one class is 79, by Rolf Biland at the side-car.

MOST TOURIST TROPHY WINS

The record for the greatest number of victories in the Isle of Man TT races is 23, by Joey Dunlop (Ireland) between 1977 and 1998.

The most events won in the Isle of Man TT races in one year is four (Formula 1, Junior, Senior and Production), by Phillip McCallen (Ireland) in 1996.

HIGHEST TOURIST TROPHY SPEEDS

The Isle of Man TT circuit record is 198.92 km/h (123.61 mph), by Carl Fogarty on 12 June 1992.

On 12 June 1992 Steve Hislop set the race speed record of 1 hr 51 min 59.6 sec — an average speed of 195.17 km/h (121.28 mph) — when he won the Senior TT on a Norton.

The record for the fastest average women's speed around the 'Mountain' circuit is 181.29 km/h (112.65 mph), by Sandra Barnett (GB) in the Junior TT on 4 June 1997.

MOST TRIALS WINS

Jordi Tarrès (Spain) won six World Trials Championships, in 1987, from 1989 to 1991 and from 1993 to 1994.

horse sports

HORSE RACING
MOST SUCCESSFUL RACE CAREER
Chorisbar won 197 out of 324 races in Puerto Rico between 1937 and 1947.

Lenoxbar won a record 46 races from 56 starts in one year, in Puerto Rico in 1940.

HIGHEST RACE SPEEDS
The record for the highest known race speed is 69.62 km/h (43.26 mph) — 402 m (440 yd) in 20.8 seconds — by *Big Racket* at Mexico City, Mexico, on 5 Feb 1945 and by *Onion Roll* at Thistledown, Cleveland, Ohio, USA, on 27 Sept 1993.

The highest speed over a distance of 2,414 m (1 mile 880 yd) is 60.86 km/h (37.82 mph), by three-year-old *Hawkster* at Santa Anita Park, Arcadia, California, USA, on 14 Oct 1989. Carrying 54.9 kg (121 lb), its time was 2 min 22.8 sec.

OLDEST WINNERS
The oldest horses to have ever won at flat racing were the 18-year-olds *Revenge* at Shrewsbury, UK, on 23 Sept 1790, *Marksman* at Ashford, Kent, UK, on 4 Sept 1826 and *Jorrocks* at Bathurst, Australia, on 28 Feb 1851.

Wild Aster was 18 when it won three hurdle races in six days in March 1919 and *Sonny Somers* was 18 when it won two steeplechases in Feb 1980.

MOST SUCCESSFUL JOCKEYS
Bill Shoemaker (USA), whose racing weight was 44 kg (97 lb) at 1.5 m (4 ft 11 in), rode a record 8,833 winners from a total of 40,350 mounts between 1949 and 1990.

The most races won in a year is 598 from 2,312 rides, by Kent Desormeaux (USA) in 1989.

Christopher McCarron (USA) earned a career record of $204 million (£127.5 million) from 1974 to May 1997.

The most money won in a year is c. £19 million ($28.4 million), by Yutaka Take in Japan in 1993.

MOST WINS
Chris Antley (USA) rode nine winners in one day on 31 Oct 1987 – four in the afternoon at Aqueduct, New York, USA, and five in the evening at The Meadowlands, New Jersey, USA.

The most winners ridden on one card is eight by six riders, most recently (and from the fewest rides) by Patrick Day (USA) from nine rides at Arlington International, Illinois, USA, on 13 Sept 1989.

The longest winning streak is 12, by Sir Gordon Richards (GB) (one race at Nottingham, UK, on 3 Oct, six races out of six at Chepstow, UK, on 4 Oct and the first five races on 5 Oct at Chepstow, UK, in 1933) and by

Pieter Stroebel (Rhodesia) at Bulawayo, Southern Rhodesia (now Zimbabwe), from 7 June to 7 July 1958.

MOST SUCCESSFUL OWNERS
The most lifetime wins by an owner is 4,775, by Marion Van Berg (USA) in North America over 35 years from 1936 to 1971.

The most wins in a year is 494, by Dan Lasater (USA) in 1974.

MOST SUCCESSFUL TRAINERS
The most career wins is 7,200, by Dale Baird (USA), 1962–97.

Jack Van Berg (USA) had a record 496 wins in a year, in 1976.

MOST RUNNERS
The record for the greatest number of horses in a race is 66 in the Grand National, Aintree, UK, on 22 March 1929.

The record for the Flat is 58, in the Lincolnshire Handicap at Lincoln, UK, on 13 March 1948.

LONGEST FLAT RACE
The Queen Alexandra Stakes, run at Ascot, Berks, UK, in June each year, is competed over a record 4.425 km (2³⁄₄ miles).

SHOW JUMPING
MOST OLYMPIC WINS
The most team wins in the Prix des Nations is seven, by Germany (as West Germany from 1968 to 1990) in 1936, 1956, 1960, 1964, 1972, 1988 and 1996.

The record for the most individual gold medals is two, by Pierre Jonquères d'Oriola (France) in 1952 and 1964.

The greatest number of Olympic gold medals is five, by Hans Winkler (West Germany): four team in 1956, 1960, 1964 and 1972 and the individual Grand Prix in 1956. He also won team silver in 1976 and team bronze in 1968, making a record seven medals overall.

LOWEST SCORE AT OLYMPICS
The record for the lowest score obtained by a winner is no faults, by: Frantisek Ventura (Czechoslovakia) on *Eliot* in 1928; Alwin Schockemöhle (West Germany) on *Warwick Rex* in 1976; and Ludger Beerbaum (Germany) on *Classic Touch* in 1992.

MOST WORLD CHAMPIONSHIP WINS
The record for the greatest number of team wins is three, by France in 1982, 1986 and 1990.

The most men's titles is two, by Hans Winkler (West Germany) in 1954 and 1955 and Raimondo d'Inzeo (Italy) in 1956 and 1960.

The record for the greatest number of women's titles is two, by Jane Tissot (France) on *Rocket* in 1970 and 1974.

MOST WORLD CUP WINS
Hugo Simon (Austria) won three times, in 1979, 1996 and 1997.

OLDEST CONTESTED RACE
The most famous claimant to the title of oldest contested horse race is the *Palio*, which is contested by 10 of the 17 *contrade* (parishes) of the city of Siena, Italy, to confirm who is the strongest. Traditionally believed to have begun in the 13th century, it has been run twice yearly (on 2 July and 16 August) since 1701, except during wartime. During the three days preceding the *Palio* the horses are kept under guard and each jockey is held incommunicado. On the day itself, the contestants march into town under their banners. The course winds through the town's maze of streets, making the event highly dangerous, and many horses have been killed during the race. The jockeys are very well paid, currently earning more than £250,000 ($416,100) to ride with the *Palio* (a banner depicting the Virgin Mary) for the *contrade*. The most successful *contrade* is Oca (Goose) with 59 victories. An edict passed by Mussolini in 1935 gave the Siennese exclusive control of the word 'Palio', preventing towns in any other part of Italy from holding similar *festivals*. The *Palio* which now attracts spectators from across the world.

HIGHEST JUMP

The official Fédération Equestre Internationale high-jump record is 2.47 m (8 ft 1¼ in), by *Huasó* ridden by Capt. Alberto Morales (Chile) at Viña del Mar, Santiago, Chile, on 5 Feb 1949.

LONGEST JUMP

The record for a long jump over water is 8.4 m (27 ft 6¾ in) by *Something*, ridden by André Ferreira (South Africa) at Johannesburg, South Africa, on 25 April 1975.

THREE DAY EVENTING
MOST OLYMPIC WINS

Charles Pahud de Mortanges (Netherlands) won a record four Olympic gold medals: team in 1924 and 1928 and individual (riding *Marcroix*) in 1928 and 1932, when he also won a team silver medal.

MOST WORLD CHAMPIONSHIP WINS

Bruce Oram Davidson (USA) has won two titles, on *Irish Cap* in 1974 and *Might Tango* in 1978.

DRESSAGE
MOST OLYMPIC WINS

Germany (as West Germany from 1968 to 1990) have won a record nine team gold medals: 1928, 1936, 1964, 1968, 1976, 1984, 1988, 1992 and 1996.

A record two individual gold Olympic medals were won by Henri St Cyr (Sweden) in 1952 and 1956 and by Nicole Uphoff (Germany) in 1988 and 1992.

Dr Reiner Klimke (West Germany) won a record six Olympic golds (team from 1964 to 1988 and individual in 1984). He also won individual bronze in 1976.

MOST WORLD CHAMPIONSHIP WINS

Germany (as West Germany from 1968 to 1990) have had a record seven team wins (1966, 1974, 1978, 1982, 1986, 1990, 1994).

A record two world titles were won by Dr Reiner Klimke (West Germany), on *Mehmed* in 1974 and *Ahlerich* in 1982.

MOST WORLD CUP WINS

The record for the most wins is two, by Christine Stückelberger (Switzerland) on *Gauguin de Lully* in 1987 and 1988, Monica Theodorescu (Greece) on *Ganimedes Tecrent* in 1993 and 1994, and Anky van Grunsven (Netherlands) on *Camelion Bonfire* in 1995 and 1996.

CARRIAGE DRIVING
MOST WORLD CHAMPIONSHIP WINS

The most team titles is three, by Great Britain (1972, 1974 and 1980), Hungary (1976, 1978 and 1984), Netherlands (1982, 1986 and 1988) and Germany (1992, 1994 and 1996).

A record two individual titles have been won by György Bárdos (Hungary) in 1978 and 1980, Tjeerd Velstra (Netherlands) in 1982 and 1986 and Ijsbrand Chardon (Netherlands) in 1988 and 1992.

POLO
HIGHEST HANDICAP

The highest handicap based on six 7½-min 'chukkas' is 10 goals (introduced in the USA in 1891 and in the United Kingdom and Argentina in 1910). A total of 56 players have received 10-goal handicaps: for the 1998 season there are eight 10-goal handicap players in the United Kingdom.

HIGHEST SCORE

The most goals in an international match was 30, when Argentina beat the USA 21–9 at Long Island, New York, USA, in 1936.

ROYAL ASCOT

Gold Cup day at Royal Ascot, the most important meeting on the British racing calendar and the most famous in the world, sees thousands of women donning hats of all shapes and sizes. In the Royal Enclosure morning dress must be worn by the gentlemen and hats worn by the ladies. In June 1997, Gold Cup day, the third day of the four-day meeting, was attended by a record 77,543 people.

HORSE RACING

Jockeys urge their horse on to the winning post at a horse race in Hong Kong. Horsemanship was an important part of the Hitite culture of Turkey, dating from 1400 BC. In 648 BC, the 33rd ancient Olympic Games in Greece featured horse racing. Since then, it has spread across the globe and has become both a multi-million-dollar industry and a popular sport.

cricket

HIGHEST TEAM INNINGS
Victoria scored 1,107 runs in
10 hr 30 min v. New South Wales
in an Australian Sheffield Shield
match at Melbourne in Dec 1926.

The Test record is 952 for six,
by Sri Lanka v. India at Colombo,
Sri Lanka, from 4 to 6 Aug 1997.

LOWEST TEAM INNINGS
The traditional first-class record
is 12, by Oxford University (a
man short) v. Marylebone Cricket
Club at Cowley Marsh, Oxford, UK,
in 1877, and Northamptonshire
v. Gloucestershire at Gloucester,
UK, in June 1907.

'The Bs' scored six in their
second innings against England
at Lord's, London, UK, in 1810.

The Test match record is 26,
by New Zealand v. England at
Auckland, New Zealand, in 1955.

HIGHEST INDIVIDUAL INNINGS
Brian Lara scored 501 not out in
7 hr 54 min for Warwickshire
against Durham at Edgbaston,
UK, in June 1994. His innings
included the most runs in a day
(390) and the most runs from
strokes worth four or more
(308: 62 fours and 10 sixes).

MOST CAREER MATCHES PLAYED
Mohammad Azharuddin of India
has played 282 games, including
90 test matches, from the start
of his career in 1985 to 1998. He
has also made the most career
catches by a fielder, at 134, and
scored 100 in his first three test
matches. In 1996 Azharuddin was
relieved of his captaincy of the
Indian team and in 1997 he was
dropped altogether, but he was
reinstated as captain in 1998.

The Test record is also held by
Brian Lara, with 375 in 12 hr
48 min for the West Indies against
England at Recreation Ground, St
John's, Antigua, in April 1994.

MOST SIXES IN AN INNINGS
Andrew Symonds hit 16 in an
innings of 254 not out for
Gloucestershire v. Glamorgan in
a County Championship match at
Abergavenny, UK, in Aug 1995.
He added four in his second
innings of 76, for a record
match total of 20.

Chris Cairns hit a record 14 sixes
in a limited-overs international,
in his 157 (from 89 deliveries) for
New Zealand against Kenya at
Nairobi, Kenya, on 7 Sept 1997.

MOST WICKETS IN A MATCH
Jim Laker took 19 wickets for
90 runs (9–37 and 10–53) for
England v. Australia at Old
Trafford, UK, in July 1956.

MOST WICKETS IN AN INNINGS
Alfred Freeman of Kent, UK,
took all 10 wickets in an innings
on a record three occasions,
against Lancashire in 1929 and
1931 and against Essex in 1930.

The fewest runs scored off a
bowler taking all 10 wickets is
10, off Hedley Verity for
Yorkshire v. Nottinghamshire
at Leeds, UK, in 1932 (the full
analyses for early performances
of the feat are unknown).

John Wisden bowled out all
10 for North against South at
Lord's, London, UK, in 1850.

FASTEST BOWLER
The highest electronically
measured speed for a bowled
ball is 160.45 km/h (99.7 mph),
bowled by Jeffrey Thomson of
Australia against the West Indies
in Dec 1975.

MOST CATCHES
The greatest number of catches
in an innings is seven, by
Michael Stewart for Surrey
against Northamptonshire at
Northampton, UK, on 7 June
1957, and by Anthony Brown for
Gloucestershire against
Nottinghamshire at Trent Bridge,
Nottingham, UK, on 26 July 1966.

MOST CATCHES IN A MATCH
Walter Hammond held 10 catches
for Gloucestershire against
Surrey at Cheltenham, UK, from
16 to 17 Aug 1928.

MOST CATCHES IN A TEST MATCH
Seven catches were made by
Greg Chappell for Australia
v. England at Perth, Australia, in
1974, Yajurvindra Singh for India
v. England at Bangalore, India,
in 1977, and Hashan Prasantha
Tillekeratne for Sri Lanka v. New
Zealand at Colombo, Sri Lanka,
from 7 to 9 Dec 1992.

MOST DISMISSALS
The most ever dismissals in an
innings is nine, by Tahir Rashid
(eight catches and a stumping)
for Habib Bank against Pakistan
Automobile Corporation at
Gujranwala, Pakistan, in Nov
1992 and by Wayne James (seven
catches and two stumpings) for
Matabeleland against Mashonaland
Country Districts at Bulawayo,
Zimbabwe, on 19 April 1996.

The most stumpings in an innings
is six, by Hugo Yarnold for
Worcestershire against Scotland
at Broughty Ferry, Dundee, UK,
on 2 July 1951.

The most dismissals in a match is
13, by Wayne James (11 catches,
two stumpings) for Matabeleland
v. Mashonaland Country Districts
at Bulawayo, Zimbabwe, from
19 to 21 April 1996. The record
of 11 catches has been equalled
on six other occasions.

The most stumpings in a match
is nine, by Frederick Huish for
Kent v. Surrey at The Oval,
London, UK, in 1911.

SHORTEST TEST MATCH IN TERMS OF BALLS BOWLED
The shortest ever Test, in terms of the number of balls bowled, was
the First Test of the West Indies–England series in 1998. Only
10.1 overs were possible during England's first innings at Sabina Park
in Kingston, Jamaica, on 29 Jan. For the first time in Test history,
play was abandoned not because of the weather but because the
pitch was deemed too dangerous. Faced by the quick bowling of the
West Indies opening pair, Curtly Ambrose and Courtney Walsh, England
struggled to 17–3. Such was the spiteful nature of the wicket that
England's physiotherapist, Wayne Morton, was called on to treat the
batsmen six times for blows to hands and body. No player sustained
broken bones, but the team captains and match umpires decided to
halt play following Morton's sixth visit. The details of the match have
been noted in the record books, so the West Indies fast bowler Nixon
McLean, who was making his Test debut, 'played' but never bowled a
ball. Bookmakers William Hill paid out to every customer who had
backed Alec Stewart to be the highest-scoring batsmen. Stewart
scored possibly the lowest highest total ever, with nine.

MOST SIXES IN A TEST INNINGS
Wasim Akram hit a record 12 sixes in his 257 not out for Pakistan against Zimbabwe at Sheikhupura, Pakistan, from 18 to 20 Oct 1996. Akram also holds the record for the greatest number of wickets taken in a career, with a total of 356 in 247 matches — an average of 22.79 — between 1985 and 1998.

MOST DISMISSALS IN TESTS
The record in an innings is seven (all caught), by Wasim Bari for Pakistan v. New Zealand at Auckland, New Zealand, in Feb 1979, Bob Taylor for England v. India at Bombay, India, in Feb 1980, and Ian Smith for New Zealand v. Sri Lanka at Hamilton, New Zealand, in Feb 1991.

The record in a match is 11, all caught, by Jack Russell for England v. South Africa at Johannesburg, South Africa, from 30 Nov to 3 Dec 1995.

MOST TEST APPEARANCES
Allan Border of Australia played a record 156 Test matches between 1979 and 1994.

SHORTEST MATCH
The shortest playing time was during the first Test between England and Australia at Trent Bridge, Nottingham, UK, in June 1926. There were 50 minutes of play, in which 17.2 overs were bowled and England scored 32–0.

MOST CAREER RUNS SCORED
Desmond Haynes of the West Indies scored a total of 8,648 runs in 238 matches (an average of 41.37 a match) from 1977 to 1994. This total includes a record 17 centuries.

MOST CAREER DISMISSALS
Ian Healy of Australia made 234 (195 caught, 39 stumped) in 168 matches from 1988 to 1997.

The highest innings score between Test-playing nations in a one day international is 371–9, by Pakistan against Sri Lanka at Nairobi, Kenya, on 4 Oct 1996.

The lowest completed innings total in a one day international is 43, by Pakistan against the West Indies at Newlands, Cape Town, South Africa, on 25 Feb 1993.

LONGEST MATCH
The 1939 England v. South Africa test in South Africa was stopped after 10 days, as the ship taking the England team home was due to leave. The total playing time was 43 hr 16 min and a record Test match aggregate of 1,981 runs was scored.

HIGHEST AND LOWEST INNINGS IN A MATCH
The record for the highest innings score in a one day international is 398–5. It was set by Sri Lanka against Kenya in a World Cup match played at Kandy, Sri Lanka, on 6 March 1996.

MOST FEARED BOWLER
Shane Warne is Australia's most effective spinner, and one of cricket's most talented bowlers ever. Born in 1969, Warne made his international debut against New Zealand at Wellington in March 1993. He is master of the 'googley' and has invented his own lethal variations of many deliveries. In 1993 he bowled the 'ball of the century' in the Ashes against Mike Gatting at Old Trafford, UK.

street and beach sports

HIGHEST JUMP ON IN-LINE SKATES

The first in-line skates date back to the 1100s, when Arctic dwellers made skates by attaching animal bones to their boots in order to improve ice travel. The first modern-day skates were made in 1960 by Chicago Skate Company. The highest ever jump on in-line skates was 2.7 m (8 ft 11 in), by Randolph Sandoz (Switzerland) at Amsterdam, Netherlands, on 15 Dec 1996.

STREET LUGE
TOP SPEED

On 29 May 1998 Tom Mason from Van Nuys, California, USA, set an official world record for street luge when he achieved a speed of 130.8 km/h (81.28 mph) at Mount Whitney, California, USA. Mason, who took up street luge in 1995, set the record on a 10-kg (23-lb) board and was timed by Bob Pererya from the street luge sanctioning body RAIL (Road Racing Association for International Luge).

SKATEBOARDING
TOP SPEEDS

The highest speed recorded on a skateboard is 126.12 km/h (78.37 mph) by Roger Hickey (USA) on a course near Los Angeles, California, USA, on 15 March 1990. He was in a prone position.

The stand-up speed record is 89.20 km/h (55.43 mph), by Roger Hickey at San Demas, California, USA, on 3 July 1990.

Eleftherios Argiropoulos covered 436.6 km (271 miles 510 yd) in 36 hr 33 min 17 sec at Ekali, Greece, from 4 to 5 Nov 1993.

IN-LINE SKATING AND ROLLER HOCKEY
BIGGEST CASH PRIZE

The Ultimate In-line Challenge offers a record cash purse of $60,000 (£36,054). The event is presented by Rollerblade and includes 20-km and 1,500-m sprints.

FASTEST ROAD TIMES

Eddy Matzger (USA) skated 34.82 km (21 miles 1,126 yd) in an hour at Long Beach, California, USA, in Feb 1991.

Jonathan Seutter (USA) holds the 12-hr road record, covering a distance of 285.86 km (177 miles 1,109 yd) at Long Beach, California, USA, on 2 Feb 1991.

Kimberly Ames (USA) set the 24-hour road record when she skated 455.5 km (283 miles 123 yd) in Portland, Oregon, USA, on 2 Oct 1994.

LONGEST DISTANCE SKATED

In March 1996 Fabrice Gropaiz of France began a 30,500-km (19,000-mile) round-the-world trek on skates, setting out from San Francisco, USA. In Aug he skated into Mexico after crossing the USA and by early 1997 he was skating across Europe. In Oct 1997 he skated from Paris, France, to St Petersburg, Russia, where he stopped due to freezing road conditions and to raise more funds. In April 1998 Gropaiz crossed Australia before returning to Russia, where the roads were now skateable.

HIGHEST MOUNTAIN SKATED

In Jan 1998 Eddy Matzger (USA) and Dave Cooper (USA) skated up and down the Murango Route of Mt Kilimanjaro, the highest peak in Africa. It took them six days to complete the 5.895 km (3 miles 1,162 yd) climb. Conditions allowed them to roll about 30% of the time.

MOST ROLLER HOCKEY WORLD CHAMPIONSHIP VICTORIES

Portugal won 14 titles between 1947 and 1993.

MOST STREET LUGE TITLES

Michael Sherlock (USA), known as 'Biker', began competing in 1995. He won the EDI series race in 1996 and in 1997, and has won three gold medals at the ESPN Summer X Games – for Mass Luge in 1996 and for Mass Luge and Dual Luge in 1997. In 1997 he also took the silver medal for Super Mass Luge at the ESPN Summer X Games.

FASTEST 'ROCKET' STREET LUGER

On 15 May 1998 Billy Copeland, a machine press operator from Ashland City, Tennessee, USA, set a world speed record for 'Rocket' street luge when he held a jet-assisted speed of 113 km/h (70 mph) over 45.7 m (150 ft) of level ground on Granite Road in Kern County, California, USA. He began the 3.6 km (2¼ mile) course on an incline, and when he reached a speed of about 105 km/h (65 mph) ignited the rockets that were attached with steel to the back of the 2.1 m long (7 ft) street luge to achieve the record speed on level ground. Copeland's speed was clocked using a radar speed gun and was filmed for the hit US TV show *Guinness World Records™: Primetime*. Copeland has been street lugeing as a hobby since 1992 and claims to have unofficially reached speeds of more than 129 km/h (80 mph) since he began attaching the rockets to his board. The eight Aerotech G64 White Lightning rocket motors can be fired in pairs or all at once. He was inspired to try out the rockets by a Mountain Dew ad that featured street lugers in California, USA, having realized that the hills around his home town were not steep enough to enable him to reach speeds of more than 97 km/h (60 mph).

HIGHEST SKATEBOARD JUMPS

World skateboarding championships have been staged intermittently since 1966 and the sport is popular around the world. The skateboarding high-jump record is 1.67 m (5 ft 5¾ in), by Trevor Baxter of Burgess Hill, E Sussex, UK, at Grenoble, France, on 14 Sept 1982. The high air-jump record from a half pipe is 3.6 m (11 ft 10 in), by Sergie Ventura (USA).

VOLLEYBALL
MOST WORLD TITLES

The USSR has won a record six titles (1949, 1952, 1960, 1962, 1978 and 1982).

The greatest number of women's titles is five, by the USSR (1952, 1956, 1960, 1970 and 1990).

MOST OLYMPIC TITLES

The USSR has won a record three men's titles (1964, 1968, 1980).

The most women's titles is four, by the USSR (1968, 1972, 1980 and 1988).

MOST OLYMPIC MEDALS

The record for the greatest number of Olympic medals won by a volleyball player is four, by Inna Valeryevna Ryskal (USSR), who won women's silver medals in 1964 and 1976 and gold medals in 1968 and 1972.

The greatest number of Olympic medals won by male volleyballers is three, by Yuriy Mikhailovich Poyarkov (USSR), who won gold medals in 1964 and 1968 and a bronze in 1972, and by Katsutoshi Nekoda (Japan), who won gold in 1972, silver in 1968 and bronze in 1964.

BEACH VOLLEYBALL
HIGHEST-EARNING PLAYERS

Karch Kiraly of San Clemente, California, USA, left the indoor volleyball circuit after leading the US indoor team to victory in the 1984 and 1988 Olympic Games. He became a five-time MVP (Most Valuable Player) on the US professional circuit and the first beach volleyball player to amass winnings of more than $2 million (£1.25 million). Kiraly is the highest-earning beach volleyballer of all time, having earned $2.58 million (£1.61 million) by March 1997.

Karolyn Kirby from San Diego, California, USA, is the highest-earning woman in beach volleyball today, with total winnings of more than $650,000 (£405,000). She has earned a record $110,000 (£68,000) in 30 grand slam events, including a record 25 appearances in the final four. Kirby has finished in first place on the WPVA (Women's Professional Volleyball Association) tour 61 times.

SAND YACHTING
HIGHEST SPEEDS

The official world record for a sand yacht is 107 km/h (66.48 mph), by Christian-Yves Nau (France) in *Mobil* at Le Touquet, France, on 22 March 1981. The wind speed reached 120 km/h (75 mph).

A speed of 142.26 km/h (88.4 mph) was attained by Nord Embroden (USA) in *Midnight at the Oasis* at Superior Dry Lake, California, USA, on 15 April 1976.

LONGEST SAND RACE

The Transat des Sables, which was held in the desert in Mauritania from 8 to 18 March 1997, was the longest and toughest sand race ever. It was organized by the French Federation of Sand & Land Yachting and the French Ministry of Sport, and was competed by sand yachts, kite yachts and speed-sails. Yachters had to cover 100–200 km (60–120 miles) daily, which required 6–8 hours of sailing every day.

MOST BEACH VOLLEYBALL WINS

Beach volleyball is particularly popular in the USA, and made its Olympic debut at the 1996 Summer Games in Atlanta, USA. The world's most successful beach volleyballer is Sinjin Smith (USA), who won his first career open in 1977 and has gone on to win a record 139 times. He has been a beach volleyball pro for 21 years and was the second player to earn $1 million (£625,000), in 1992.

snow and ice sports

SNOWBOARDING
MOST WORLD CUP TITLES
The record for the most World Cup titles won is 11, by Karine Ruby (France): the overall from 1996 to 1998, the slalom from 1996 to 1998, the giant slalom from 1995 to 1998 and the snowboard cross in 1997.

The most men's World Cup titles won is three, by Mike Jacoby (USA): the overall in 1996 and the giant slalom in 1995 and 1996.

MOST WORLD CHAMPIONSHIP TITLES WON
The most World Championship titles (including Olympics) is three, by Karine Ruby (France): the giant slalom in 1996 and 1998 (Olympic) and the snowboard cross in 1997. No man has won more than one title.

SKI-BOB
HIGHEST SPEED
The record for the highest speed ever attained in a ski-bob is 166 km/h (103.1 mph), by Erich Brenter (Austria) at Cervinia, Italy, in 1964.

MOST WORLD TITLES
The most World Championship titles by a man is three, by Walter Kronseil (Austria) from 1988 to 1990.

The record for the most individual World Championship combined titles is four, by Petra Tschach-Wlezcek (Austria) from 1988 to 1991.

CRESTA RUN
MOST CRESTA RUN WINS
The most wins in the Grand National is eight, by the 1948 Olympic champion Nino Bibbia (Italy) from 1960 to 1964 and in 1966, 1968 and 1973, and by Franco Gansser (Switzerland) in 1981, from 1983 to 1986, from 1988 to 1989, and in 1991.

The most wins in the Curzon Cup is eight, by Nino Bibbia (1950, 1957–58, 1960, 1962–64, 1969).

FASTEST CRESTA RUN TIMES
The record for the fastest ever time on the 1,212-m-long (3,977-ft) Cresta Run course, which has a drop of 157 m (514 ft), is 50.41 seconds, by Christian Bertschinger (Switzerland) on 23 Feb 1992. Bertschinger's average speed was 86.56 km/h (53.79 mph).

On 15 Jan 1995 Johannes Badrutt (Switzerland) set a record of 41.27 seconds from Junction, at an altitude of 890 m (2,920ft).

BOBSLEIGH
MOST TITLES AND MEDALS
The world four-man bobsleigh title has been won a record 20 times by Switzerland (1924, 1936, 1939, 1947, 1954–57, 1971–73, 1975, 1982–83, 1986–90 and 1993). This total includes a record five Olympic victories (1924, 1936, 1956, 1972 and 1988).

Switzerland have won the two-man title a record 17 times (1935, 1947–50, 1953, 1955, 1977–80, 1982–83, 1987, 1990, 1992 and 1994). This total includes a record four Olympic successes (in 1948, 1980, 1992 and 1994).

Eugenio Monti was a member of 11 world championship crews from 1957 to 1968 (eight two-man and three four-man).

The record for the greatest number of Olympic gold medals won by an individual is three, by Meinhard Nehmer and Bernhard Germeshausen (both of the GDR) in the 1976 two-man and the 1976 and 1980 four-man events.

The greatest number of medals won is seven (one gold, five silver, one bronze), by Bogdan Musiol (GDR, later Germany) from 1980 to 1992.

LUGEING

MOST TITLES

The record for the most World Championship lugeing titles won (including Olympics) is six, by Georg Hackl (GDR/Germany): single-seater in 1989, 1990, 1992, 1994, 1997 and 1998.

Stefan Krausee and Jan Behrendt (both GDR/Germany) have won a record six two-seater titles (1989, 1991–93, 1995 and 1998).

Margit Schumann (GDR) has won a record five women's titles, from 1973 to 1975 and in 1976 (Olympic) and 1977.

Steffi Walter (GDR) has won a record two Olympic single-seater luge titles, at the women's event in 1984 and 1988.

FASTEST SPEED

The record for the highest photo-timed speed is 137.4 km/h (85.38 mph), by Asle Strand (Norway) at Tandådalens Linbana, Sälen, Sweden, on 1 May 1982.

ICE-YACHTING

HIGHEST SPEED

The highest officially recorded speed by an ice-yacht is 230 km/h (143 mph), by John Buckstaff in a Class A stern-steerer on Lake Winnebago, Wisconsin, USA, in 1938. Such a speed is possible in a wind of 115 km/h (72 mph).

LARGEST ICE-YACHT

Icicle, an ice-yacht built for Comm. John Roosevelt for racing on the Hudson River, New York, USA, in 1869, was 21 m (68 ft 11 in) long and carried 99 m² (1,070 ft²) of canvas.

WINTER X GAMES

The Winter X Games, the world's largest extreme sports extravaganza, was launched by ESPN in 1997. It features ice climbing, where competitors scale a 20-m-high (66-ft) man-made frozen waterfall, snow mountain bike racing, free skiing, skiboarding, snowboarding and snowcross. Competitors from the USA, Russia, Australia, South Korea, Germany and Sweden competed in the 1998 Winter X Games at Crested Butte in Colorado, USA.

MOST ICE CLIMBING MEDALS

The most ice climbing medals won is three, by Will Gadd (USA): the bronze difficulty medal in 1997 and the gold speed and gold difficulty medals in 1998.

MOST MEDALS FOR SNOW MOUNTAIN BIKING

The most snow mountain biking medals is three, by Cheri Elliott (USA): the 1997 gold speed medal and the 1998 silver speed and silver difficulty medals.

FASTEST SPEED ON A SNOW MOUNTAIN BIKE

The fastest speed recorded on a snow mountain bike at the Winter X Games is 117.48 km/h (73 mph), by Jan Karpie (USA).

SNOWBOARDING COMPETITIONS

Klas Vangen (Norway) is seen training for the snowboard halfpipe in preparation for the 1998 Winter Olympics. Snowboarding is now part of the Fédération Internationale de Ski. A World Cup series began in 1995 and World Championships were inaugurated the following year. Competitions are held at halfpipe, slalom, parallel slalom, giant slalom and snowboard cross.

water sports

SURFING
BIGGEST SURFING COMPETITION
The G-Shock US Open of Surfing, which takes place at Huntington Beach, California, USA, is generally regarded as the biggest surfing competition in the world today. The competition, which forms part of the world qualifying series, has attracted approximately 200,000 spectators every year since it started in 1994, and has about 700 competitors. The total prize money is $155,000 (£97,000). Of this, $100,000 (£62,500) goes to the winner of the men's surfing contest and $15,000 (£9,375) goes to the winner of the women's contest.

HIGHEST EARNINGS IN A SEASON
Kelly Slater (USA) earned a record $208,200 (£130,125) in the 1997 season. Slater turned professional at the age of 19, after winning about 200 amateur competitions, and became the youngest ever world champion at the age of 20 in 1992. *Black and White*, a video released in 1990, showed him redefining surfing's traditional manoeuvres. He has won three more world titles, in 1994, 1995 and 1996.

The women's record is $55,510 (£34,695), by US surfer Lisa Andersen in 1996.

HIGHEST CAREER EARNINGS
Kelly Slater (USA) had earned a record $654,495 (£409,060) by the end of the 1997 season. In 1991 the surfer was the subject of a fierce sponsorship bidding war between the major surfwear companies. It was eventually won by Quiksilver, the world's biggest surfwear manufacturer.

The women's career record is $270,275 (£168,922), by Pam Burridge (Australia) to the end of the 1997 season.

MOST WORLD PROFESSIONAL SERIES TITLES
The men's title has been won five times, by Mark Richards (Australia) in 1975 and from 1979 to 1982.

The women's professional title has been won four times by: Frieda Zamba (USA), 1984–86 and 1988, and by Wendy Botha (Australia, formerly South Africa), 1987, 1989, 1991 and 1992.

MOST WORLD AMATEUR CHAMPIONSHIP TITLES
The most titles is three, by Michael Novakov (Australia) in the Kneeboard event in 1982, 1984 and 1986.

The most titles by a woman is two, by Joyce Hoffman (USA) in 1965 and 1966 and Sharon Weber (USA) in 1970 and 1972.

WATERSKIING
MOST WATERSKIING TITLES
The USA won the team championship on 17 successive occasions from 1957 to 1989.

The World Overall Championships have been won five times by Patrice Martin (France), in 1989, 1991, 1993, 1995 and 1997.

The record for the most women's titles in the World Overall Championships is three, by Willa McGuire (USA) in 1949, 1950 and 1955, and Liz Allan-Shetter (USA) in 1965, 1969 and 1975.

HIGHEST WAVES
Waimea Bay, Hawaii, USA, is reputed to provide the most consistently high waves, which often reach the rideable limit of 9–11 m (30–35 ft). In 1998 K2, the ski and snowboard manufacturer, announced that it was launching a new K2 Surf line of clothing and with it the inaugural K2 'Big Wave Challenge', which offered a $50,000 (£30,000) prize for the rider of the biggest wave of the winter. The challenge, which attracted surfers from around the world, was won by 26-year-old Taylor Knox of Carlsbad, California, USA. His winning ride (pictured left) took place at Todos Santos, an isolated surf spot off the Mexican coast, on a wave just under 15.24 m (50 ft) in height. Knox, who was rated No. 9 in the world at the end of 1997, has been competing on the surfing pro tour since 1992 and now travels on the world pro tour for elite surfers. The coasts of Mexico offer some of the world's top surfing spots: the longest sea wave rides experienced cover approximately 1.7 km (1 mile 298 ft) and are possible four to six times a year when rideable surfing waves break in Matanchen Bay near San Blas, Nayarit, Mexico.

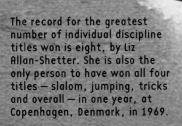

The record for the greatest number of individual discipline titles won is eight, by Liz Allan-Shetter. She is also the only person to have won all four titles — slalom, jumping, tricks and overall — in one year, at Copenhagen, Denmark, in 1969.

The most World Barefoot Championship Overall titles is four, by Kim Lampard (Australia) in 1980, 1982, 1985 and 1986.

The greatest number of men's World Barefoot Championship Overall titles is three, by Brett Wing (Australia) in 1978, 1980 and 1982.

The World Barefoot Championship team title has been won by Australia five times, in 1978, 1980, 1982, 1985 and 1986.

HIGHEST SPEED

The highest speed known to have been attained by any waterskier is 230.26 km/h (143.08 mph), by Christopher Massey (Australia) on the Hawkesbury River, Windsor, NSW, Australia, on 6 March 1983. His drag boat driver was Stanley Sainty.

Donna Patterson Brice (USA) set a women's record of 178.8 km/h (111.11 mph) at Long Beach, California, USA, on 21 Aug 1977.

The official barefoot speed record is 218.44 km/h (135.74 mph), by Scott Pellaton (USA) over a 402-m (440-yd) course at Chandler, Arizona, USA, in Nov 1989.

MOST WATERSKIERS TOWED BY ONE BOAT

On 18 Oct 1986 a record-breaking 100 skiers were towed on double skis over a nautical mile (1.8 km) by the cruiser *Reef Cat* at Cairns, Queensland, Australia. This feat, which was organized by the Cairns and District Powerboating and Ski Club, was then replicated by 100 skiers on single skis.

CANOEING
MOST OLYMPIC MEDALS

Gert Fredriksson (Sweden) won a record six Olympic gold medals from 1948 to 1960. He also won a silver and a bronze, for a record total of eight medals.

The most gold medals won by a woman is five, by Birgit Schmidt (GDR/Germany) from 1980 to 1996. Schmidt has also won three silvers, to equal Fredriksson's total of eight medals.

MOST WORLD AND OLYMPIC TITLES

A record 25 world titles (including Olympic titles) were won by Birgit Schmidt from 1979 to 1996.

The men's record is 13, by Gert Fredriksson from 1948 to 1960, Rüdiger Helm (GDR) from 1976 to 1983, and Ivan Patzaichin (Romania) from 1968 to 1984.

HIGHEST SPEEDS

At the 1995 World Championships, the Hungarian four won the 200-m title in 31.227 seconds, at an average speed of 23.05 km/h (14.32 mph).

On 4 Aug 1992 the German four-man kayak Olympic champions at Barcelona, Spain, covered 1,000 m in 2 min 52.17 sec — an average speed of 20.90 km/h (12.98 mph).

BIGGEST CANOE RAFT

On 17 Aug 1996 a raft made up of 649 kayaks and canoes free-floated for 30 seconds, held together by participants' hands only, on the Rock River, Byron, Illinois, USA. The feat was organized by the United States Canoe Association.

WHITE WATER RAFTING AND KAYAKING
MOST SUCCESSFUL NATION IN WHITE WATER RAFTING

Slovenia has been the overall world champion at every World Rafting Challenge Championship (1995, 1996 and 1997). In each championship it gained first place in all three elements (raft sprint, raft slalom and raft down river) except for the raft down river in 1996, which was won by South Africa.

MOST SUCCESSFUL NATIONS IN WHITE WATER KAYAKING

The most successful nations to date are Croatia (who won the World Championship in 1996) and Zimbabwe (who won the title in 1997). White water kayaking has been part of the World Rafting Challenge Championship since 1996.

BOARDSAILING

Boardsailing was introduced to the Olympic Games in 1984. The first gold was won by Stephan van den Berg (Netherlands), who also won a record five world titles from 1979 to 1983. The fastest overall speed by a boardsailer is 45.34 knots (84.02 km/h or 52.21 mph), by Thierry Bielak (France) at Camargue, France, in 1993. The women's record is 40.36 knots (74.74 km/h or 46.44 mph), by Elisabeth Coquelle of France at Tarifa, Spain, on 7 July 1995.

TOUGHEST WHITE WATER RIVER

The Kali Gandaki River in central Nepal — a popular course for white water rafting — winds through remote canyons and deep gorges filled with intense rapids and is classified as 6+, making it the most difficult white water river regularly rafted. Rivers are graded 1 to 6 in terms of difficulty. The World Rafting Challenge Championship has been held three times, in Zimbabwe.

high sports

LONGEST BUNGEE JUMP

A record 249.9-m-long (820-ft) bungee was used by Gregory Riffi during a jump from a helicopter above the Loire Valley, France, in Feb 1992. Riffi's cord stretched to a length of 610 m (2,000 ft) during the jump.

MOST JUMPS BY A SKYSURFER

Eric Fradet from Le Tignet, France, has logged more than 14,700 jumps during his skysurfing career.

LONGEST PARACHUTE FALL

William Rankin fell for 40 minutes, due to thermals, at North Carolina, USA, on 26 July 1956.

LONGEST DELAYED DROPS BY PARACHUTE

Joseph Kittinger fell 25.82 km (16 miles) from a balloon at 31.33 km (19 miles 872 yd) at Tularosa, New Mexico, USA, on 16 Aug 1960.

Elvira Fomitcheva (USSR) made the longest ever delayed parachute drop by a woman, falling 14.8 km (9 miles 352 yd) over Odessa, USSR (now Ukraine), on 26 Oct 1977.

HIGHEST BASE JUMP BY PARACHUTISTS

Dr Glenn Singleman and Nicholas Feteris jumped from a 5.88-km (3-mile 1,102-yd) ledge on the Great Trango Tower, Kashmir, on 26 Aug 1992.

LOWEST MID-AIR RESCUE BY A PARACHUTIST

On 16 Oct 1988 Eddie Turner saved Frank Farnan, who was unconscious after being injured in a collision while jumping out of an aircraft at 3.95 km (2 miles 792 yd). Turner pulled Farnan's ripcord at 550 m (1,800 ft) over Clewiston, Florida, USA.

HIGHEST PARACHUTE ESCAPE

Flight Lieutenant J. de Salis and Flying Officer P. Lowe (both GB) escaped at 17.1 km (10 miles 1,108 yd) over Derby, UK, in 1958.

LOWEST PARACHUTE ESCAPE

Terence Spencer (GB) made the lowest ever escape, at 9–12 m (30–40 ft) over Wismar Bay in the Baltic Sea in 1945.

BIGGEST CANOPY STACK BY PARACHUTISTS

The world's largest ever canopy stack involved a total of 46 people from a number of different countries at Davis, California, USA, on 12 Oct 1994. They held the stack for 37.54 seconds.

BIGGEST PARACHUTE FREEFALL FORMATIONS

The biggest official freefall formation involved a total of 200 people from 10 countries over Myrtle Beach, South Carolina, USA, on 23 Oct 1992. It was held for 6.47 seconds from 5.03 km (3 miles 229 yd).

The unofficial freefall record is 297 people from a total of 26 countries, who held a formation from 6.5 km (4 miles 70 yd) over Anapa, Russia, on 27 Sept 1996.

LONGEST UPSIDE-DOWN FLIGHT

The longest inverted flight was 4 hr 38 min 10 sec, by Joann Osterud from Vancouver to Vanderhoof, Canada, in July 1991.

MOST LOOPS DURING FLIGHT

On 9 Aug 1986 David Childs performed 2,368 inside loops in a Bellanca Decathlon over the North Pole, Alaska, USA.

Joann Osterud made 208 outside loops in a 'Supernova' Hyperbipe over North Bend, Oregon, USA, on 13 July 1989.

In Sept 1987 British daredevil Ian Ashpole set a world altitude record for toy balloon flight when he reached a height of 3.05 km (1 mile 1,575 yd) over Ross-on-Wye, Herefordshire, UK. Ashpole was lifted to the target altitude by the hot-air balloon *Mercier*. When he reached the desired height he cut himself free from the hot-air balloon, then one by one from the 400 helium-filled toy balloons that suspended him in mid-air. Once freed from all the balloons, each of which was 61 cm (2 ft) in diameter, he began freefalling at approximately 144 km/h (90 mph) before parachuting to the ground.

SKYSURFING

The skysurfing World Championships were first staged in 1997 in Turkey. The men's title was won by Oliver Furrer and the women's by Vivian Wegrath (both Switzerland).

LONGEST DISTANCE COVERED IN A MICROLIGHT

The greatest ever distance covered in a straight line was 1,627.78 km (1,011 miles 845 yd), by Wilhelm Lischak (Austria) from Volsau, Austria, to Brest, France, on 8 June 1988.

GREATEST ALTITUDE ACHIEVED IN A MICROLIGHT

The record for the greatest altitude ever reached in a microlight is 9.72 km (6 miles 70 yd), by Serge Zin (France) over Saint Auban, France, in 1994.

LONGEST HANG GLIDES

The record for the greatest straight line and declared goal distance is 495 km (307 miles 1,056 yd), by Larry Tudor (USA) from Rock Springs, Wyoming, USA, on 1 July 1994.

The greatest distance by a woman is 335.8 km (208 miles 1,165 yd), by Kari Castle (USA) over Owens Valley, California, USA, on 22 July 1991.

GREATEST HEIGHT GAINS BY HANG GLIDERS

Larry Tudor gained 4.343 km (2 miles 1,232 yd) over Owens Valley, California, USA, in 1985.

The greatest height gain by a woman was 3.97 km (2 miles 822 yd), by British hang glider Judy Leden over Kuruman, South Africa, on 1 Dec 1992.

LONGEST PARAGLIDING FLIGHTS

The men's record is 283.9 km (176 miles 722 yd), by Alex François Louw (South Africa) from Kuruman, South Africa, on 31 Dec 1992.

The greatest distance flown by a woman is 285 km (177 miles 169 yd), by British paraglider Kat Thurston from Kuruman, South Africa, on 25 Dec 1995.

The greatest distance flown on a tandem paraglider is 200 km (124 miles 493 yd), by Britons Richard and Guy Westgate from Kuruman, South Africa, on 23 Dec 1995 and 1 Jan 1996 respectively.

GREATEST HEIGHT GAINS BY PARAGLIDERS

The height gain record is 4.53 km (2 miles 1,426 yd), by the British paraglider Robby Whittal at Brandvlei, South Africa, on 6 Jan 1993.

The women's height gain record is 4.32 m (2 miles 1,209 yd), by Kat Thurston (GB) at Kuruman, South Africa, on 23 Dec 1993.

The height gain record on a tandem paraglider is 4.38 km (2 miles 1,271 yd), by Richard and Guy Westgate (GB) at Kuruman, South Africa, on 23 Dec 1995 and 1 Jan 1996 respectively.

HIGHEST DIVES

The highest ever dive into a lake was made by Harry Froboess of Switzerland, who jumped 120 m (394 ft) into Lake Constance from the airship *Hindenburg* on 22 June 1936.

The highest dive from a diving

board was 53.9 m (176 ft 10 in), by Olivier Favre of Switzerland at Villers-le-Lac, France, on 30 Aug 1987.

The highest dive from a diving board by a woman was 36.8 m (120 ft 9 in), by US diver Lucy Wardle at Ocean Park, Hong Kong, on 6 April 1985.

The highest regularly performed head-first dives are made by professional divers from a height of 26.7 m (87 ft 6 in) from La Quebrada ('the break in the rocks') at Acapulco, Mexico. The base rocks, which are 6.4 m (21 ft) out from the take-off, necessitate an outwards leap of 8.22 m (27 ft). The water there is 3.65 m (12 ft) deep.

BUNGEE JUMPING

Bungee jumping originated on Pentecost Island in the South Pacific, where for thousands of years locals have climbed towers 15–24 m (50–80 ft) tall, attached vines to their ankles, and dived head-first to the ground. In 1970 photographer and author Kal Muller visited the island and became the first foreigner to attempt the plunge. The first commercial operation opened in 1988 in Ohakune, New Zealand.

mountain sports

LARGEST VERTICAL FACES
The Trango Towers, which are situated next to the Baltoro Glacier on the approach to K2, the Gasherbrums and Broad Peak in Kashmir, are home to the largest vertical faces in the world. The Great Trango Tower's three summits are all over 6,000 m (19,700 ft) in altitude, with the main summit at 6,286 m (20,625 ft). The latter was climbed for the first time in 1977, two years after the area was opened for climbing after being closed for many years.

MOST SUCCESSFUL MOUNTAINEER
Reinhold Messner (Italy) has scaled all 14 of the world's mountains that are more than 8,000 m (26,250 ft) in altitude, without oxygen. In 1982 he also became the first person to have climbed the three highest mountains when he ascended Kanchenjunga, having previously climbed Mt Everest and K2.

FIRST ASCENT OF SEVEN SUMMITS
The first person to climb the highest mountain on all seven continents, including Kosciusko in Australia, was Richards Bass (USA), who scaled the last of the peaks with his conquest of Mt Everest in 1985.

Ngga Pulu (formerly Carstensz Pyramid) on Irian Jaya, Indonesia, is the highest mountain in Australasia (New Zealand, New Guinea, Tasmania, the Pacific Islands and Australia). The first person to scale the highest peak on every continent including Australasia was Patrick Morrow (Canada), who completed his conquest on 7 May 1986.

FASTEST SEVEN-SUMMIT ASCENT
In 1990, New Zealanders Gary Ball, Peter Hillary (son of Sir Edmund Hillary) and Andy Hall completed an ascent of the seven summits in a record time of seven months.

MOST EUROPEAN SUMMITS
British climber Eamon Fullen has climbed the highest summits in 44 European countries — more than any other person. He began with Elbrus in Russia, Europe's highest point, in Aug 1992 and is set to complete the ascent of the final three peaks by Aug 1998.

FIRST ASCENT OF MT EVEREST
The summit of Mt Everest (8,848 m or 29,029 ft in altitude) was first reached in May 1953 by Edmund Hillary (New Zealand) and Tenzing Norgay (Nepal), in an expedition led by Henry Hunt (GB).

FIRST SOLO ASCENT OF MT EVEREST
The first person to make the entire climb solo was Reinhold Messner (Italy), in Aug 1980.

FIRST SOLO ASCENT OF MT EVEREST BY A WOMAN
In May 1994 33-year-old Alison Hargreaves (GB) became the first woman to reach the summit of Mt Everest alone and without oxygen tanks. In Aug 1995, having reached the summit of K2, Hargreaves was one of seven climbers who were swept to their death during the descent.

MOST ASCENTS OF MT EVEREST
Sherpa Ang Rita has scaled Mt Everest a record 10 times (in 1983, 1984, 1985, 1987, 1988, 1990, 1992, 1993, 1995 and 1996), each time without the use of bottled oxygen.

MOST PEOPLE ON MT EVEREST PEAK
The Mount Everest International Peace Climb, a team of US, Soviet and Chinese climbers led by James Whittaker (USA), succeeded in putting a record 10 people on the summit of Mt Everest from 7 to 10 May 1990.

MOST PEOPLE TO REACH MT EVEREST SUMMIT IN ONE DAY
On 10 May 1993 40 climbers (32 men and eight women) from nine expeditions and 10 different countries (USA, Canada, Australia, United Kingdom, Russia, New Zealand, Finland, Lithuania, India and Nepal) reached the summit of Mt Everest.

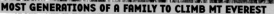

MOST GENERATIONS OF A FAMILY TO CLIMB MT EVEREST
Tashi Wangchuk Tenzing, a travel agent from Sydney, NSW, Australia, climbed the world's highest mountain in May 1997, reaching the summit almost 44 years to the day that his grandfather Tenzing Norgay made the first ever ascent of Mt Everest with Edmund Hillary in 1953. At the peak Tashi, who is a devout Buddhist, left a 15-cm-tall (6-in) statue of the Buddha. A record three generations of the Tenzing family have now climbed the mountain, and Tashi is the first grandson of an Everest conqueror to reach the peak (Sir Edmund Hillary's son Peter was the first son of an Everest mountaineer to reach the summit). Tashi, who made the ascent in just under nine hours, first tried to climb Mt Everest in 1993 to mark the 40th anniversary of his grandfather's climb, but the attempt came to a tragic end when his uncle Lobsang, who was climbing with him, died. Now that he has achieved his goal, Tashi has no plans to scale the mountain again, although 90% of the 700-plus people from 43 different countries who have climbed Mt Everest have attempted to repeat the experience.

FASTEST TIME FROM EVEREST BASE CAMP TO KATHMANDU

Hélène Diamantides and Alison Wright (both GB) travelled from Everest base camp to Kathmandu, Nepal, in a time of 3 days 10 hr 8 min from 8 to 10 Oct 1987. They covered 288 km (180 miles), climbed 9,800 m (32,000 ft) and descended 14,000 m (46,000 ft).

HIGHEST BIVOUAC

Mark Whetu (New Zealand) and Michael Rheinberger (Australia) reached the summit of Mt Everest on 26 May 1994 and bivouacked just 20 m (66 ft) below the summit that night. Rheinberger died the next day during the descent.

MOST SUCCESSFUL SKI DOWN MT EVEREST

In Sept 1992, Pierre Tardivel (France) skied 3,200 m (10,500 ft) from the South Summit of Mt Everest to base camp in three hours of jump turns. Tarduvel has notched up more than 60 first descents, mostly in the Alps.

WORST YEAR ON MT EVEREST

In 1996, 15 of the 98 people who reached the summit of Mt Everest died during the descent.

BIGGEST CLIMBING WALL

The 5,000-m (16,404-ft) Rupal Face on the southern side of the Nanga Pardat, Pakistan, is the biggest climbing wall in the world. The equivalent of two-and-a-half Eigers guard the 8,108-m (26,600-ft) summit of Nanga Pardat, also known as the 'Naked Mountain'.

MOST DIFFICULT FREE CLIMB

The world's most difficult free climb is reputed to be Action Direkt in the Frankenjua, Germany, which has a 9A rating. The climb has earned its reputation because of its overhang and small holds. Action Direkt was first climbed by Wolfgang Gullich in 1994.

FASTEST RACES: MT CAMEROON

Reginald Esuke (Cameroon) descended from the summit of Mt Cameroon (4,095 m or 13,435 ft) to Buea Stadium (915 m or 3,002 ft) in a time of 1 hr 2 min 15 sec on 24 Jan 1988. This gives a vertical rate of 51 m (167.5 ft) a minute.

Timothy Leku Lekunze (Cameroon) set a record time of 3 hr 46 min 34 sec for the race to the summit of Mt Cameroon and back in 1987. The temperature varied between 35°C (95°F) at the foot and 0°C (32°F) at the summit.

The fastest ever ascent of Mt Cameroon was 2 hr 25 min 20 sec, by Jack Maitland (GB) in 1988.

The fastest ascent of Mt Cameroon in a women's race was 4 hr 42 min 31 sec, by Fabiola Rueda (Colombia) in 1989.

FASTEST RACES: BEN NEVIS (SCOTLAND)

The record time for the race from Fort William Town park to the summit of Ben Nevis (1,347 m or 4,418 ft) and return is 1 hr 25 min 34 sec, by Kenneth Stuart (GB) on 1 Sept 1984.

The women's record is 1 hr 43 min 25 sec, by Pauline Haworth (GB) on 1 Sept 1984.

FASTEST RACES: SNOWDON (WALES)

The record for the fastest time from Llanberis to the summit of Snowdon (1,085 m or 3,560 ft) is 1 hr 2 min 29 sec, by Kenneth Stuart in 1985.

The best women's time is 1 hr 12 min 48 sec, by Carol Greenwood (GB) in 1993.

ABSEILING

Abseiling, the descent of a steep slope or vertical drop by a rope secured from above, gets its name from the German verb *abseilen*, which means to descend by a rope. Abseiling is not only a recreational activity, it is also practised in army training and rescue operations. The record for the greatest overall distance covered by abseilers is 1,105.5 m (3,627 ft). It was achieved by a team of four Royal Marines, each of whom abseiled down the Boulby Potash Mine, Cleveland, UK, from 7.6 m (25 ft) below ground level to the shaft bottom on 2 Nov 1993.

MOUNTAIN CLIMBING

Mountaineering began as a sport in the 18th century, when Swiss scientist Horace-Bénédict de Saussure offered a prize for the first person to scale Mont Blanc. The prize was not claimed until 20 years later in 1786. The 19th century saw an emphasis on the climbing of alpine and other European mountains, but climbers were expected to not only scale the peaks but to reach them by ever-more demanding routes.
The worldwide spread of mountaineering continued from the end of the 19th century, when attention turned towards the Himalayas, particularly Mt Everest, which was eventually scaled in 1953.

marathons and endurance

MOST MARATHONS RUN
Horst Preisler (Germany) ran a total of 631 races of 42.195 km (26 miles 385 yd) or longer from 1974 to 29 May 1996.

Henri Girault (France) ran a total of 330 100-km races — an IAAF recognized distance — from 1979 to June 1996 and has completed a run on every continent except Antarctica.

FASTEST HALF MARATHON
The world best time on a properly measured course is 59 min 17 sec, by Paul Tergat (Kenya) at Milan, Italy, on 4 April 1998.

OLDEST MARATHON FINISHERS
Dimitrion Yordanidis (Greece) was 98 when he raced in Athens, Greece, in Oct 1976. His time was 7 hr 33 min.

The oldest woman to complete a marathon was Thelma Pitt-Turner (New Zealand), who was 82 when she raced in New Zealand in Aug 1985. Her time was 7 hr 58 min.

LONGEST RUNNING RACE
The world's longest ever race covered a distance of 5,898 km (3,665 miles) from New York City to Los Angeles, USA, in 1929. Finnish-born Johnny Salo won in 79 days and an elapsed time of 525 hr 57 min 20 sec, averaging 11.21 km/h (6.97 mph).

FASTEST MALE MARATHON
The fastest ever marathon (42.195 km or 26 miles 385 yd) by a man was 2 hr 6 min 50 sec, by Belayneh Dinsamo (Ethiopia) at Rotterdam, Netherlands, on 17 April 1988. Dinsamo bettered the previous world record, which had been set at Rotterdam three years earlier by Carlos Lopes of Portugal, by 22 sec.

PENTATHLON: MOST WORLD TITLES
András Balczó (Hungary) won six individual titles: 1963, 1965–67, 1969 and 1972 (Olympic) and seven team titles (five world and two Olympic, 1960–70).

The USSR won 14 world and four Olympic team titles.

Hungary has also won a record four Olympic team titles.

The most women's titles is three, by Eva Fjellerup (Denmark), with individual titles in 1990, 1991 and 1993.

Poland has won a record seven women's world team titles (1985, 1988–92, 1995).

MOST OLYMPIC TITLES
The record for the greatest number of Olympic gold medals won is three, by András Balczó of Hungary (team in 1960 and 1968 and individual in 1972).

The record for the most individual championships won is two, by Lars Hall (Sweden) in 1952 and 1956.

MOST OLYMPIC MEDALS
Pavel Serafimovich Lednyev (USSR) won a record seven medals (two team gold, one team silver, one individual silver and three individual bronze) from 1968 to 1980.

FASTEST FEMALE IRONMAN
The record for the fastest Hawaii Ironman time by a woman is 8 hr 55 min 28 sec, by Paula Newby-Fraser (Zimbabwe) in 1992. Newby-Fraser also holds the records for the fastest time by a woman over the Ironman distances, at 8 hr 55 min, at Roth, Germany, on 12 July 1992, and for the greatest number of race wins by a woman, with eight (1986, 1988, 1989, 1991 to 1994 and 1996). Surprisingly, Newby-Fraser has never won the official World Championships.

RECORD-BREAKING RUNNER
Haile Gebreselassie has broken 14 world records since 1994, making him one of the greatest distance runners of all time. The 1.62-m-tall (5-ft 4-in) athlete is soon to be immortalized in a Disney biographical movie tracing his life from his humble beginnings as one of 10 children from a poor district in Ethiopia to victory at the Olympics in 1996. The 24-year-old has won two Mercedes in competitions, but they remain unused, as he has not yet learnt to drive. His sponsorship deal with sports manufacturer Adidas stands to net him $1 million (£625,000) over five years.

BIATHLON: MOST TITLES

Frank Ullrich (GDR) won a record six individual world titles: four at 10 km from 1978 to 1981, including the 1980 Olympics, and two at 20 km in 1982 and 1983.

Aleksandr Tikhonov was in a record 10 winning Soviet relay teams (1968–80) and won four individual titles.

The most individual World Championship titles is three, by Anne-Elinor Elvebakk (Norway): 10 km in 1988 and 7.5 km from 1989 to 1990.

Kaya Parve (USSR) won six titles: two individual and four relay from 1984 to 1986 and in 1988.

The most men's Olympic individual titles is two, by Magnar Solberg (Norway) in 1968 and 1972 and Frank-Peter Rötsch (GDR) at both 10 km and 20 km in 1988.

Aleksandr Tikhonov (USSR) won four relay golds (1968–80) and a silver in the 20 km in 1968.

The most women's titles is two, by Anfissa Restzova of Russia: 7.5 km in 1992 and 4 x 7.5-km in 1994, and by Myriam Bédard of Canada: 7.5 km and 15 km in 1994.

The Biathlon World Cup was won four times by Frank Ullrich (GDR) (1978, 1980–82) and Franz Rötsch (GDR) (1984, 1985, 1987, 1988).

TRIATHLON: BEST IRONMAN TIMES

The fastest time for the Hawaii Ironman, which consists of a 3.8-km (2-mile 440-yd) swim, a 180-km (112-mile) cycle ride and a full marathon of 42.195 km (26 miles 385 yd), is 8 hr 4 min 8 sec, by Luc van Lierde (Belgium) in 1996.

The fastest ever time over the Ironman distances is 7 hr 50 min 27 sec, by Luc van Lierde (Belgium) at Roth, Germany, on 13 July 1997.

The most wins in the men's race is six, by Dave Scott (USA): 1980, 1982–84 and 1986–87; and by Mark Allen: 1989–93 and 1995.

TRIATHLON: MOST WORLD CHAMPIONSHIP WINS

The World Championship consists of a 40-km (24-mile 1,496-yd) cycle, a 10-km (6-mile 370-yd) run, and a 1,500-m (4,921-ft 3-in) swim. Simon Lessing (UK) has won three (1992, 1995 and 1996).

The most wins in the women's event is two, by Michelle Jones (Australia) in 1992 and 1993 and Karen Smyers (USA) in 1990 and 1995.

Prior to 1989 a race held annually in Nice, France, was regarded as the unofficial World Championship. Mark Allen (USA) won 10 titles from 1982 to 1986 and from 1989 to 1993.

Paula Newby-Fraser (Zimbabwe) had four women's wins, 1989–92.

TRIATHLON: BEST WORLD CHAMPIONSHIP TIMES

The best men's time is 5 hr 46 min 10 sec, by Mark Allen (USA) in 1986.

The best women's time is 6 hr 27 min 6 sec, by Erin Baker (New Zealand) in 1988.

STAMINA: MOST PRESS-UPS

The most press-ups in 24 hours is 46,001, by Charles Servizio, in Fontana, California, USA, in 1993.

The most one-arm press-ups in five hours is 8,794, by Paddy Doyle in Birmingham, UK, in 1996.

The most fingertip press-ups in five hours is 8,200, by Terry Cole in Walthamstow, London, UK, in 1996.

STAMINA: MOST SQUAT THRUSTS

Paul Wai Man Chung did 3,552 in an hour in Hong Kong in 1992.

STAMINA: MOST BURPEES

The most burpees in an hour is 1,840, by Paddy Doyle in Birmingham, UK, in Feb 1994.

FASTEST FEMALE MARATHON

The fastest women's half marathon is 66 min 40 sec, by Ingrid Kristiansen (Norway) at Sandnes, Norway, on 5 April 1987, although the measurement of the course has not been confirmed. Kristiansen had held the full marathon world record for nearly 14 years until it was bettered by Tegla Loraipe (Kenya) at Rotterdam, Netherlands, on 19 April 1998 with a time of 2 hr 20 min 7 sec.

sports reference

In the following pages are more than 800 sports records. Entries are arranged alphabetically for easy reference.

american football

World American Football Records
NFL Records
MOST POINTS
Career: 2,002
George Blanda, Chicago Bears, Baltimore Colts, Houston Oilers,

Game: 336
Willie Anderson, Los Angeles Rams v. New Orleans Saints, 26 Nov 1989
MOST COMBINED NET YARDS GAINED
Career: 21,803
Walter Payton, Chicago Bears, 1975–87
Season: 2,535
Lionel James, San Diego Chargers, 1985
Game: 404
Glyn Milburn, Denver Broncos v. Seattle Seahawks, 10 Dec 1995
MOST YARDS GAINED PASSING
Career: 55,416
Dan Marino, Miami Dolphins, 1983–97
Season: 5,084
Dan Marino, Miami Dolphins, 1984
Game: 554
Norm Van Brocklin, Los Angeles

Joe Kapp, Minnesota Vikings v. Baltimore Colts, 28 Sept 1969
FIELD GOALS
Career: 385
Gary Anderson, Pittsburgh Steelers, Philadelphia Eagles, San Francisco 49ers, 1982–97
Season: 37
John Kasay, Carolina Panthers, 1996
Game: 7
Jim Bakken, St. Louis Cardinals, v. Pittsburgh Steelers, 24 Sept 1967
Rich Karlis, Minnesota Vikings v. Los Angeles Rams, 5 Nov 1989
Chris Boniol, Dallas Cowboys v. Green Bay Packers, 18 Nov 1996

Jerry Rice, 1989
Career: 512
Jerry Rice, 1989–90, 1995
YARDS GAINED RUSHING
Game: 204
Timmy Smith (Washington Redskins), 1988
Career: 354
Franco Harris (Pittsburgh Steelers), 1975–76, 1979–80
PASSES COMPLETED
Game: 31
Jim Kelly (Buffalo Bills), 1994
Career: 83
Joe Montana, 1982, 1985, 1989–90
PASS RECEPTIONS
Game: 11
Dan Ross (Cincinnati Bengals), 1982
Jerry Rice, 1989

TERRELL DAVIS OF THE DENVER BRONCOS WAS VOTED THE MOST VALUABLE PLAYER OF SUPER BOWL XXXII, HAVING SCORED A RECORD-EQUALLING THREE TOUCHDOWNS. DENVER WON THE SUPER BOWL FOR THE FIRST TIME IN FIVE ATTEMPTS, DEFEATING REIGNING CHAMPIONS GREEN BAY 31–24.

JACK TRAGIS PROUDLY DISPLAYS HIS RECORD-BREAKING PACIFIC HALIBUT, WHICH HE LANDED OFF THE COAST OF ALASKA, USA. THE SIDE SHOWN IS THE CHARACTERISTICALLY WHITE 'BLIND' SIDE OF THE FLATFISH. THE EYES ARE FOUND ON THE OTHER SIDE, WHICH IS NORMALLY BROWN, DARK GREEN OR BLACK.

Oakland Raiders, 1949–75
Season: 176
Paul Hornung, Green Bay Packers, 1960
Game: 40
Ernie Nevers, Chicago Cardinals v. Chicago Bears, 28 Nov 1929
MOST TOUCHDOWNS
Career: 166
Jerry Rice, San Francisco 49ers, 1985–97
Season: 25
Emmitt Smith, Dallas Cowboys, 1995
Game: 6
Ernie Nevers, Chicago Cardinals v. Chicago Bears, 28 Nov 1929
William Jones, Cleveland Browns v. Chicago Bears, 25 Nov 1951
Gale Sayers, Chicago Bears v. San Francisco 49ers, 12 Dec 1965
MOST YARDS GAINED RUSHING
Career: 16,726
Walter Payton, Chicago Bears, 1975–87
Season: 2,105
Eric Dickerson, Los Angeles Rams, 1984
Game: 275
Walter Payton, Chicago Bears v. Minnesota Vikings, 20 Nov 1977
MOST YARDS GAINED RECEIVING
Career: 16,455
Jerry Rice, San Francisco 49ers, 1985–97
Season: 1,848
Jerry Rice, San Francisco 49ers, 1995

Rams v. New York Yanks, 28 Sept 1951
MOST PASSES COMPLETED
Career: 4,453
Dan Marino, Miami Dolphins, 1983–97
Season: 404
Warren Moon, Houston Oilers, 1991
Game: 45
Drew Bledsoe, New England Patriots v. Minnesota Vikings, 13 Nov 1994
PASS RECEPTIONS
Career: 1,057
Jerry Rice, San Francisco 49ers, 1985–97
Season: 123
Herman Moore, Detroit Lions, 1995
Game: 18
Tom Fears, Los Angeles Rams v. Green Bay Packers, 3 Dec 1950
MOST TOUCHDOWN PASSES
Career: 385
Dan Marino, Miami Dolphins, 1983–97
Season: 48
Dan Marino, Miami Dolphins, 1984
Game: 7
Sid Luckman, Chicago Bears v. New York Giants, 14 Nov 1943
Adrian Burk, Philadelphia Eagles v. Washington Redskins, 17 Oct 1954
George Blanda, Houston Oilers v. New York Titans, 19 Nov 1961
Y. A. Tittle, New York Giants v. Washington Redskins, 28 Oct 1962

Super Bowl Game & Career Records
POINTS
Game: 18
Roger Craig (San Francisco 49ers), 1985
Jerry Rice (San Francisco 49ers), 1990 and 1995
Ricky Watters (San Francisco 49ers), 1995
Terrell Davis (Denver Broncos), 1998
Career: 42
Jerry Rice, 1989–90, 1995
TOUCHDOWNS
Game: 3
Roger Craig, 1985
Jerry Rice, 1990 and 1995
Ricky Watters, 1990
Terrell Davis, 1998
Career: 7
Jerry Rice, 1989–90, 1995
TOUCHDOWN PASSES
Game: 6
Steve Young (San Francisco 49ers), 1995
Career: 11
Joe Montana (San Francisco 49ers), 1982, 1985, 1989–90
YARDS GAINED PASSING
Game: 357
Joe Montana, 1989
Career: 1,142
Joe Montana, 1982, 1985, 1989–90
YARDS GAINED RECEIVING
Game: 215

Career: 28
Jerry Rice, 1989–90, 1995
FIELD GOALS
Game: 4
Don Chandler (Green Bay Packers), 1968
Ray Wersching (San Francisco 49ers), 1982
Career: 5
Ray Wersching, 1982, 1985
MOST VALUABLE PLAYER
Joe Montana, 1982, 1985, 1990

angling

World Angling Records
FRESHWATER AND SALTWATER
A selection of All-Tackle records ratified by the International Game Fish Association as at Jan 1998.
Barracuda, Great: 38.55 kg (85 lb)
John W. Helfrich
Christmas Island, Kiribati, 11 April 1992
Bass, Striped: 35.60 kg (78 lb 8 oz)
Albert R. McReynolds
Atlantic City, New Jersey, USA, 21 Sept 1982

Catfish, Flathead: 41.3 kg (91 lb 6 oz)
Mike Rogers
Lake Lewisville, Texas, USA, 28 March 1982

Cod, Atlantic: 44.79 kg (98 lb 2 oz)
Alphonse J. Bielevich
Isle of Shoals, New Hampshire, USA,
8 June 1969

Conger: 60.44 kg (133 lb 6 oz)
Vic Evans
Berry Head, Devon, UK, 5 June 1995

Halibut, Pacific: 459.0 kg (208 lb 3 oz)
Jack Tragis
Dutch Harbor, Alaska, USA, 11 June 1996

Mackerel, King: 40.82 kg (90 lb)
Norton I. Thomton
Key West, Florida, USA, 16 Feb 1976

Marlin, Black: 707.61 kg (1,560 lb)
Alfred C. Glassell Jr
Cabo Blanco, Peru, 4 Aug 1953

Pike, Northern: 25.00 kg (55 lb 1 oz)
Lothar Louis
Lake of Grefeern, Germany, 16 Oct 1986

Sailfish (Pacific): 100.24 kg (221 lb)
C. W. Stewart
Santa Cruz Island, Ecuador, 12 Feb 1947

Salmon, Atlantic: 35.89 kg (79 lb 3 oz)
Henrik Henriksen
Tana River, Norway, 1928

Shark, Hammerhead: 449.50 kg (991 lb)
Allen Ogle Sarasota
Florida, USA, 30 May 1982

Aulds Cove, Nova Scotia, Canada,
26 Oct 1979

Tuna, Yellowfin: 176.35 kg (388 lb 2 oz)
Curt Wiesenhutter
San Benedicto Island, Mexico,
1 April 1977

Wahoo: 158.8 kg (71 lb 14 oz)
Keith Winter
Loreto, Baja California, Mexico,
10 June 1996

archery

World Archery Records
Men (Single FITA rounds)
FITA: Oh Kyo-moon (South Korea) scored
1,368 points from a possible 1,440
in 1995

90 m: Vladimir Yesheyev (USSR) scored
330 points from a possible 360 in 1990

70 m: Jackson Fear (Australia) scored
345 points from a possible 360 in 1997

50 m: Kim Kyung-ho (South Korea) scored
351 points from a possible 360 in 1997

30 m: Han Seuong-hoon (South Korea)
scored 360 points from a possible 360
in 1994

Women
Petra Ericsson (Sweden) scored 592
points from a possible 600 in 1991

athletics

World Athletics Records
Men
World outdoor records for the men's
events scheduled by the International
Amateur Athletic Federation. Fully
automatic electric timing is mandatory
for events up to 400 metres.
Running
100 m: 9.84*
Donovan Bailey (Canada)
Atlanta, USA, 27 July 1996
200 m: 19.32
Michael Johnson (USA)
Atlanta, USA, 1 Aug 1996
400 m: 43.29
Harry Lee 'Butch' Reynolds Jr (USA)
Zürich, Switzerland, 17 Aug 1988
800 m: 1:41.11
Wilson Kipketer (Denmark)
Cologne, Germany, 24 Aug 1997

1 hour: 21,101 m
Arturo Barrios (Mexico, now USA)
La Flèche, France, 30 March 1991
110-m hurdles: 12.91
Colin Ray Jackson (GB)
Stuttgart, Germany, 20 Aug 1993
400-m hurdles: 46.78
Kevin Curtis Young (USA)
Barcelona, Spain, 6 Aug 1992
3,000-m steeplechase: 7:55.72
Bernard Barmasai (Kenya)
Cologne, Germany, 24 Aug 1997
4 x 100-m: 37.40
USA (Michael Marsh, Leroy Burrell,
Dennis A. Mitchell, Carl Lewis)
Barcelona, Spain, 8 Aug 1992
and: USA (John A. Drummond Jr, Andre
Cason, Dennis A. Mitchell, Leroy Burrell)
Stuttgart, Germany, 21 Aug 1993
4 x 200-m: 1:18.68
Santa Monica Track Club (USA)
(Michael Marsh, Leroy Burrell, Floyd
Wayne Heard, Carl Lewis)
Walnut, California, USA, 17 April 1994
4 x 400-m: 2:54.29
USA (Andrew Valmon, Quincy Watts,
Butch Reynolds, Michael Duane Johnson)
Stuttgart, Germany, 21 Aug 1993
4 x 800-m: 7:03.89
Great Britain (Peter Elliott, Garry Peter
Cook, Steve Cram, Sebastian Coe)

KIM KYUNG-WOOK OF SOUTH KOREA WINNING
THE 1996 OLYMPIC INDIVIDUAL WOMEN'S
GOLD. SOUTH KOREA ARE ONE OF THE DOMINANT
FORCES IN ARCHERY AND SINCE 1984 NO OTHER
NATION HAS WON AN OLYMPIC GOLD IN
WOMEN'S EVENTS.

MICHAEL JOHNSON WINNING THE 1996 200-M
OLYMPIC TITLE IN A RECORD TIME OF
19.32 SECONDS. HE BETTERED HIS OWN RECORD
OF 19.66 SECONDS. WITH THIS RECORD, HE
SURPASSED THE LONGEST STANDING ATHLETICS
RECORD OF THE TIME, PIETRO MENNEA'S
19.79 SECONDS ACHIEVED IN FEB 1979.

Shark, Porbeagle: 230.00 kg (507 lb)
Christopher Bennett
Pentland Firth, Caithness, UK, 9 March 1993

Shark, Thresher: 363.80 kg (802 lb)
Dianne North
Tutukaka, New Zealand, 8 Feb 1981

Shark, White: 1,208.38 kg (2,664 lb)
Alfred Dean
Ceduna, South Australia, 21 April 1959

Sturgeon, White: 212.28 kg (468 lb)
Joey Pallotta III
Benicia, California, USA, 9 July 1983

Swordfish: 536.15 kg (1,182 lb)
L. Marron, Iquique, Chile, 17 May 1953

Trout, Brook: 6.57 kg (14 lb 13 oz)
Dr W. J. Cook
Nipigon River, Ontario, Canada,
July 1916

Trout, Brown: 18.25 kg (40 lb 6 oz)
Howard L. Collins
Heber Springs, Arkansas, USA,
9 May 1992

Trout, Lake: 30.16 kg (66 lb 13 oz)
Rodney Harback
Great Bear Lake, NWT, Canada,
19 July 1991

Trout, Rainbow: 19.10 kg (42 lb 3 oz)
David Robert White
Bell Island, Alaska, USA, 22 June 1970

Tuna, Bluefin: 679.00 kg (1,496 lb)
Ken Fraser

Team: South Korea (Oh Kyo-moon, Lee
Kyung-chul, Kim Jae-pak) scored 4,053
points from a possible 4,320 in 1995
Women (Single FITA rounds)
FITA: Kim Jung-rye (South Korea) scored
1,377 points from a possible 1,440 in 1995
70 m: Chung Chang-sook (South Korea)
scored 341 points from a possible 360
in 1997
60 m: He Ying (China) scored 349 points
from a possible 360 in 1995
50 m: Kim Moon-sun (South Korea)
scored 345 points from a possible 360
in 1996
30 m: Joanne Edens (GB) scored 357
points from a possible 360 in 1990
Team: South Korea (Kim Soo-nyung,
Lee Eun-kyung, Cho Yuon-jeong) scored
4,094 points from a possible 4,320
in 1992
INDOOR (18 M)
Men
Magnus Pettersson (Sweden) scored 596
points from a possible 600 in 1995
Women
Lina Herasymenko (Ukraine) scored 591
points from a possible 600 in 1996
INDOOR (25 M)
Men
Magnus Pettersson (Sweden) scored 593
points from a possible 600 in 1993

1,000 m: 2:12.18
Sebastian Coe (GB)
Oslo, Norway, 11 July 1981
1,500 m: 3:27.37
Noureddine Morceli (Algeria)
Nice, France, 12 July 1995
1 mile: 3:44.39
Noureddine Morceli (Algeria)
Rieti, Italy, 5 Sept 1993
2,000 m: 4:47.88
Noureddine Morceli (Algeria)
Paris, France, 3 July 1995
3,000 m: 7:20.67
Daniel Komen (Kenya)
Rieti, Italy, 1 Sept 1996
5,000 m: 12:39.36
Haile Gebreselassie (Ethiopia)
Helsinki, Finland, 13 June 1998
10,000 m: 26:22.75
Haile Gebreselassie (Ethiopia)
Hengelo, Netherlands, 1 June 1998
20,000 m: 56:55.6
Arturo Barrios (Mexico, now USA)
La Flèche, France, 30 March 1991
25,000 m: 1:13:55.8
Toshihiko Seko (Japan)
Christchurch, New Zealand, 22 March 1981
30,000 m: 1:29:18.8
Toshihiko Seko (Japan)
Christchurch, New Zealand,
22 March 1981

Crystal Palace, London, 30 Aug 1982
4 x 1,500-m: 14:38.8
West Germany (Thomas Wessinghage,
Harald Hudak, Michael Lederer, Karl
Fleschen)
Cologne, Germany, 17 Aug 1977
* Ben Johnson (Canada) ran 100 m in
9.79 seconds at Seoul, South Korea, on
24 Sept 1988, but was subsequently
disqualified on a positive drugs test for
steroids. He later admitted to having
taken drugs over many years, and this
invalidated his ratified 9.83 seconds at
Rome, Italy, on 30 Aug 1987.
Field Events
High Jump: 2.45 m (8 ft 1/2 in)
Javier Sotomayor (Cuba)
Salamanca, Spain, 27 July 1993
Pole Vault (A): 6.14 m (20 ft 1 3/4 in)
Sergey Nazarovich Bubka (Ukraine)
Setriere, Italy, 1 July 1994
Long Jump: 8.95 m (29 ft 4 1/2 in)
Mike Powell (USA)
Tokyo, Japan, 30 Aug 1991
Triple Jump: 18.29 m (60 ft 1/4 in)
Jonathan Edwards (GB) Gothenburg,
Sweden, 7 Aug 1995
Shot: 23.12 m (75 ft 10 1/4 in)
Randy Barnes (USA)
Los Angeles, California, USA,
20 May 1990

Discus: 74.08 m (243 ft)
Jürgen Schult (GDR)
Neubrandenburg, Germany, 6 June 1986
Hammer: 86.74 m (284 ft 7 in)
Yuriy Georgiyevich Sedykh (USSR, now Russia), Stuttgart, Germany, 30 Aug 1986
Javelin: 98.48 m (323 ft 1 in)
Jan Zelezny (Czech Republic)
Jena, Germany, 25 May 1996
A record set at high altitude. The best mark at low altitude 6.13 m (20 ft 1¼ in) by Sergey Bubka at Tokyo, Japan, on 19 Sept 1992.
Decathlon: 8,891 points
Dan Dion O'Brien (USA)
Talence, France, 4–5 Sept 1992
Day 1: 100 m: 10.43 sec; long jump: 8.08 m (26 ft 6¼ in); shot: 16.69 m (54 ft 9¼ in); high jump: 2.07 m (6ft 9½ in); 400 m: 48.51 sec
Day 2: 110-m hurdles: 13.98 sec; discus: 48.56 m (159 ft 4 in); pole vault: 5.00 m (16 ft 4¼ in); javelin 62.58 m (205 ft 4 in); 1,500 m: 4:42.10 sec

WOMEN'S WORLD RECORDS

World outdoor records for the women's events scheduled by the International Amateur Athletic Federation. Fully automatic electric timing is mandatory for all events up to 400 metres.

10,000 m: 29:31.78
Wang Junxia (China)
Beijing, China, 8 Sept 1993
20,000 m: 1:06:48.8
Isumi Maki (Japan)
Amagasaki, Japan, 20 Sept 1993
25,000 m: 1:29:29.2
Karolina Szabo (Hungary)
Budapest, Hungary, 23 April 1988
30,000 m: 1:47:05.6
Karolina Szabo (Hungary)
Budapest, Hungary, 23 April 1988
1 hour : 18,084 m
Silvana Cruciata (Italy)
Rome, Italy, 4 May 1981
100-m hurdles: 12.21
Yordanka Donkova (Bulgaria)
Stara Zagora, Bulgaria, 20 Aug 1988
400-m hurdles: 52.61
Kim Batten (USA)
Gothenburg, Sweden, 11 Aug 1995
4 x 100-m: 41.37
GDR (Silke Gladisch, Sabine Rieger, Ingrid Auerswald, Marlies Göhr)
Canberra, Australia, 6 Oct 1985
4 x 200-m: 1:28.15
GDR (Marlies Göhr, Romy Müller, Bärbel Wöckel, Marita Koch)
Jena, Germany, 9 Aug 1980
4 x 400-m: 3:15.17
USSR (Tatyana Ledovskaya, Olga

Potsdam, Germany, 9 Sept 1988
Heptathlon: 7,291 points
Jacqueline Joyner-Kersee (USA)
Seoul, South Korea, 23–24 Sept 1988
100-m hurdles: 12.69 sec; high jump: 1.86 m (6 ft 1¼ in); shot: 15.80 m (51 ft 10 in); 200 m: 22.56 sec; long jump: 7.27 m (23 ft 10¼ in); javelin: 45.66 m (149 ft 10 in); 800 m: 2 min 8.51 sec

MEN'S INDOOR RUNNING RECORDS

Track performances around a turn must be made on a track of circumference no longer than 200 metres.
50 m: 5.56*
Donovan Bailey (Canada)
Reno, NV, USA, 9 Feb 1996
Set at high altitude. Best at low altitude: 5.61 sec, Manfred Kokot (GDR), Berlin, Germany, 4 Feb 1973 and James Sanford (USA), San Diego, California, USA, 20 Feb 1981.
60 m: 6.39
Maurice Greene (USA)
Madrid, Spain, 3 Feb 1998
200 m: 19.92
Frank Fredericks (Namibia)
Liévin, France, 18 Feb 1996
400 m: 44.63
Michael Johnson (USA)
Atlanta, Georgia, USA, 4 March 1995

Seville, Spain, 10 March 1991
5,000-m walk: 18:07.08
Mikhail Shchennikov (Russia)
Moscow, Russia, 14 Feb 1995
* Ben Johnson (Canada) ran 50 m in 5.55 sec at Ottawa, Canada, on 31 Jan 1987 but this was invalidated due to his admission of having taken drugs, following his disqualification at the 1988 Olympics.
Field Events
High Jump: 2.43 m (7 ft 11½ in)
Javier Sotomayor (Cuba)
Budapest, Hungary, 4 March 1989
Pole Vault: 6.15 m (20 ft 2¼ in)
Sergey Nazarovich Bubka (Ukraine)
Donetsk, Ukraine, 21 Feb 1993
Long Jump: 8.79 m (28 ft 10¼ in)
Carl Lewis (USA)
New York, USA, 27 Jan 1984
Triple Jump: 17.83 m (58 ft 6 in)
Alliacer Urrutia (Cuba)
Sindelfingen, Germany, 1 March 1997
Shot: 22.6674 m (4 ft ¼ in)
Randy Barnes (USA)
Los Angeles, California, USA, 20 Jan 1989
Heptathlon: 6,476 points
Dan Dion O'Brien (USA)
Toronto, Canada, 13–14 March 1993
60 m: 6.67 sec; long jump: 7.84 m (25 ft 8 in); shot: 16.02 m (52 ft 6 in);

SERGEY BUBKA OF UKRAINE HAS DOMINATED POLE VAULTING FOR OVER 15 YEARS, SETTING NUMEROUS WORLD RECORDS, BOTH INDOORS AND OUT, AND IS THE ONLY ATHLETE, MALE OR FEMALE, TO HAVE WON THE SAME EVENT AT ALL SIX ATHLETICS WORLD CHAMPIONSHIPS.

ASHIA HANSEN OF GREAT BRITAIN SETTING A NEW WOMEN'S INDOOR TRIPLE JUMP WORLD RECORD OF 15.16M DURING THE EUROPEAN INDOOR CHAMPIONSHIPS AT VALENCIA, SPAIN.

Running
100 m: 10.49
Delorez Florence Griffith Joyner (USA)
Indianapolis, Indiana, USA, 16 July 1988
200 m: 21.34
Delorez Florence Griffith Joyner (USA)
Seoul, South Korea, 29 Sept 1988
400 m: 47.60
Marita Koch (GDR)
Canberra, Australia, 6 Oct 1985
800 m: 1:53.28
Jarmila Kratochvílová (Czechoslovakia)
Munich, Germany, 26 July 1983
1,000 m: 2:28.98
Svetlana Masterkova (Russia)
Brussels, Belgium, 23 Aug 1996
1,500 m: 3:50.46
Qu Yunxia (China)
Beijing, China, 11 Sept 1993
1 mile: 4:12.56
Svetlana Masterkova (Russia)
Zürich, Switzerland, 14 Aug 1996
2,000 m: 5:25.36
Sonia O'Sullivan (Ireland)
Edinburgh, UK, 8 July 1994
3,000 m: 8:06.11
Wang Junxia (China)
Beijing, China, 13 Sept 1993
5,000 m: 14:28.09
Jiang Bo (China)
Beijing, China, 23 Oct 1997

Nazarova, Maria Pinigina, Olga Bryzgina)
Seoul, South Korea, 1 Oct 1988
4 x 800-m: 7:50.17
USSR (Nadezhda Olizarenko, Lyubov Gurina, Lyudmila Borisova, Irina Podyalovskaya)
Moscow, USSR, 5 Aug 1984
Field Events
High Jump: 2.09 m (6 ft 10¼ in)
Stefka Kostadinova (Bulgaria)
Rome, Italy, 30 Aug 1987
Pole Vault: 4.59 m (15 ft ¾ in)
Emma George (Australia)
Brisbane, Australia, 20 March 1998
Long Jump: 7.52 m (24 ft 8¼ in)
Galina Chistyakova (USSR)
Leningrad, USSR, 11 June 1988
Triple Jump: 15.50 m (50 ft 10¼ in)
Inessa Kravets (Ukraine)
Gothenburg, Sweden, 10 Aug 1995
Shot: 22.6374 m (74 ft 3 in)
Natalya Venedictovna Lisovskaya (USSR)
Moscow, USSR, 7 June 1987
Discus: 76.80 m (252 ft)
Gabriele Reinsch (GDR)
Neubrandenburg, Germany, 9 July 1988
Hammer: 69.58 m (228 ft 3 in)
Mihaela Melinte (Romania)
Bucharest, Romania, 11 March 1997
Javelin: 80.00 m (262 ft 5 in)
Petra Felke (GDR)

800 m: 1:42.67
Wilson Kipketer (Denmark)
Paris, France, 9 March 1997
1,000 m: 2:15.26
Noureddine Morceli (Algeria)
Birmingham, W Mids, UK, 22 Feb 1992
1,500 m: 3:31.18
Hicham El Gerrouj (Morocco)
Stuttgart, Germany, 2 Feb 1997
1 mile: 3:48.45
Hicham El Gerrouj (Morocco)
Ghent, Belgium, 12 Feb 1997
3,000 m: 7:24.90
Daniel Komen (Kenya)
Budapest, Hungary, 6 Feb 1998
5,000 m: 12:51.48
Daniel Komen (Kenya)
Stockholm, Sweden, 19 Feb 1998
50-m hurdles: 6.25
Mark McKoy (Canada)
Kobe, Japan, 5 March 1986
60-m hurdles: 7.30
Colin Jackson (GB)
Sindelfingen, Germany, 6 March 1994
4 x 200-m: 1:22.11
United Kingdom (Linford Christie, Darren Braithwaite, Ade Mafe, John Regis)
Glasgow, UK, 3 March 1991
4 x 400-m: 3:03.05
Germany (Rico Lieder, Jens Carlowitz, Karsten Just, Thomas Schönlebe)

high jump: 2.13 m (7 ft); 60-m hurdles: 7.85 sec; pole vault 5.20 m (17 ft); 1,000 m: 2:57.96
WOMEN'S INDOOR RUNNING RECORDS
50 m: 5.96
Irina Privalova (Russia)
Madrid, Spain, 9 Feb 1995
60 m: 6.92
Irina Privalova (Russia)
Madrid, Spain, 11 Feb 1993
200 m: 21.87
Merlene Ottey (Jamaica)
Liévin, France, 13 Feb 1993
400 m: 49.59
Jarmila Kratochvílová (Czechoslovakia)
Milan, Italy, 7 March 1982
800 m: 1:56.36
Maria Lurdes Mutola (Mozambique)
Liévin, France, 22 Feb 1998
1,000 m: 2:31.23
Maria Lurdes Mutola (Mozambique)
Stockholm, Sweden, 25 Feb 1996
1,500 m: 4:00.27
Doina Melinte (Romania)
East Rutherford, NJ, USA, 9 Feb 1990
1 mile: 4:17.14
Doina Melinte (Romania)
East Rutherford, NJ, USA, 9 Feb 1990
3,000 m: 8:33.82
Elly van Hulst (Netherlands)
Budapest, Hungary, 4 March 1989

5,000 m: 15:03.17
Elizabeth McColgan (GB)
Birmingham, W Mids, UK, 22 Feb 1992
50 m hurdles: 6.58
Cornelia Oschkenat (GDR)
Berlin, Germany, 20 Feb 1988
60 m hurdles: 7.69*
Lyudmila Narozhilenko (Russia)
Chelyabinsk, Russia, 4 Feb 1993
4 x 200 m: 1:32.55
S. C. Eintracht Hamm (West Germany)
(Helga Arendt, Silke-Beate Knoll,
Mechthild Kluth, Gisela Kinzel)
Dortmund, Germany, 19 Feb 1988
4 x 400 m: 3:26.84
Russia (Tatyana Chebykina, Olga
Goncharenko, Olga Kotlyarova, Tatyana
Alekseyeva)
Paris, France, 9 March 1997
3,000 m walk: 11:44.00
Alina Ivanova (Ukraine)
Moscow, Russia, 7 Feb 1992
FIELD EVENTS
High jump: 2.07 m (6 ft 9½ in)
Heike Henkel (Germany)
Karlsruhe, Germany, 9 Feb 1992
Pole vault: 4.55 m (14 ft 11 in)
Emma George (Australia)
Adelaide, Australia, 26 March 1998
Long jump: 7.37 m (24 ft 2¼ in)
Heike Drechsler (GDR)

1973, 1976, 1979, 1984, 1994 and
1996).
The most wins at the women's World
Team Badminton Championships for the
Uber Cup (instituted 1956) is five by:
Japan (1966, 1969, 1972, 1978 and
1981); and China (1984, 1986, 1988,
1990 and 1992).

baseball

World Baseball records
US MAJOR LEAGUE
BATTING RECORDS
Average
Career: .366
Ty Cobb (Detroit AL, Philadelphia AL),
1905–28.
Season: .440
Hugh Duffy (Boston NL), 1894.
Runs
Career: 2,245
Ty Cobb, 1905–28.
Season: 192
William Hamilton (Philadelphia NL), 1894.

Michael Franklin Pinky Higgins (Boston AL),
19–21 June 1938; Moose Dropo (Detroit
AL), 14–15 July 1952.
Consecutive games batted safely: 56
Jo DiMaggio (New York AL),
15 May–16 July 1941.
Stolen bases
Career: 1,231
Rickey Henderson (Oakland AL, New York
AL, Oakland AL, Toronto AL, Oakland AL,
San Diego NL, Anaheim AL), 1979–97.
Season: 130
Rickey Henderson, 1982.
Consecutive games played: 2,478
Calvin Ripken Jr (Baltimore AL),
30 May 1982–1997.
PITCHING
Games won
Career: 511
Cy Young (Cleveland NL, St Louis NL, Boston
AL, Cleveland AL, Boston NL), 1890–1911.
Season: 60
Charles Gardner Radbourn (Providence NL),
1884.
Consecutive games won: 24
Carl Owen Hubbell (New York NL), 1936–37.
Shutouts
Career: 113
Walter Perry Johnson (Washington AL),
1907–27.

Most series played by pitcher: 11
Edward Charles 'Whitey' Ford (New York,
AL), 1950–64
Most home runs in a game: 3
Babe Ruth (New York, AL), 6 Oct 1926
and 9 Oct 1928; and Reginald Martinez
Jackson (New York, AL), 18 Oct 1977
Runs batted in: 6
Robert C. Richardson (New York, AL),
8 Oct 1960
Strikeouts: 17
Robert Gibson (St Louis, NL), 2 Oct 1968
Perfect game: (9 innings)
Donald Larson (New York, AL) v.
Brooklyn, 8 Oct 1956
AL – American League/NL – National League

canoeing

World Canoeing Records
Most titles, World and Olympic
The record is 13 by Gert Fredriksson,
1948–60, Rüdiger Helm (GDR), 1976–83,
and Ivan Patzaichin (Romania), 1968–84.
Most titles, World and Olympic
Including Olympics, 25 world titles have
been won by Birgit Schmidt, 1979–95.

US SPRINTER MAURICE GREEN, WINNER OF THE
1997 100-M WORLD CHAMPIONSHIP TITLE,
CONTINUED HIS GOOD FORM INTO THE 1997/98
INDOOR SEASON, SETTING A NEW 60-M WORLD
RECORD AT SEVILLE IN FEBRUARY.

CAL RIPKEN HAS FAILED TO MISS A REGULAR
SEASON GAME FOR THE BALTIMORE ORIOLES FOR
NEARLY 16 YEARS, PLAYING A STAGGERING
TOTAL OF MORE THAN 2,500 GAMES.

Vienna, Austria, 13 Feb 1988
Triple jump: 15.16 m (49 ft 8¾ in)
Ashia Hansen (GB)
Valencia, Spain, 28 Feb 1998
Shot: 22.50 m (73 ft 10 in)
Helena Fibingerová (Czechoslovakia)
Jablonec, Czechoslovakia, 19 Feb 1977
Pentathlon: 4,991 points
Irina Belova (Russia)
Berlin, Germany, 14–15 Feb 1992
60-m hurdles: 8.22 sec; high jump:
1.93 m (6 ft 3¼ in); shot: 13.25 m
(50 ft 5½ in); long jump: 6.67 m
(21 ft 10 in); 800 m: 2:10.26
* Narozhilenko recorded a time of
7.63 at Seville, Spain, on 4 Nov 1993,
but was disqualified on a positive drugs
test. u=unratified

badminton

World Badminton Records
World Championships
The most wins at the men's World Team
Badminton Championships for the
Thomas Cup (instituted 1948) is 10, by
Indonesia (1958, 1961, 1964, 1970,

Home runs
Career: *1,755
Hank Aaron (Milwaukee NL, Atlanta NL,
Milwaukee AL), 1954–76.
Season: 61
Roger Eugene Maris (New York AL), 1961.
Runs batted in
Career: 2,297
Hank Aaron, 1954–76.
Season: 190
Hack Wilson (Chicago NL), 1930.
Game: 12
James LeRoy Bottomley (St Louis NL),
16 Sept 1924; Mark Whiten (St Louis NL),
7 Sept 1993.
Innings: 7
Edward Cartwright (St Louis AL), 23 Sept
1890.
Base hits
Career: 4,256
Peter Edward Rose (Cincinnati NL,
Philadelphia NL, Montreal NL,
Cincinnati NL), 1963–86.
Season: 257
George Harold Sisler (St Louis AL), 1920.
Total bases
Career: 6,856
Hank Aaron, 1954–76.
Season: 457
Babe Ruth (New York AL), 1921.
Consecutive hits: 12

Season: 16
George Washington Bradley (St Louis NL),
1876; Grover Cleveland Alexander
(Philadelphia NL), 1916.
Strikeouts
Career: 5,714
Lynn Ryan (New York NL, California AL,
Houston NL, Texas AL), 1966–93.
Season: 383
Lynn Ryan (California AL), 1973. (513
Matthew Aloysius Kilroy (Baltimore AA),
1886).
Game (9 innings): 20
Roger Clemens (Boston AL) v. Seattle, 29
April 1986 and v. Detroit, 18 Sept 1996.
No-hit games
Career: 7
Lynn Ryan, 1973–91.
Earned run average
Season: .90 Ferdinand Schupp (140 inns)
(New York NL), 1916; 0.96 Dutch Leonard
(222 inns) (Boston AL), 1914;
1.12 Robert Gibson (305 inns)
(St Louis NL), 1968.
* Japanese League records that are
superior to those in the US major
leagues: 1,868 Sadaharu Oh (Yomiuri),
1959–80.
WORLD SERIES RECORDS
Most series played: 14
Yogi Berra (New York, AL), 1947–63

Highest speed
The German four-man kayak Olympic
champions in 1992 at Barcelona, Spain,
covered 1000 m in 2 min 52.17 sec.
Canoe raft
A raft of 649 kayaks and canoes,
organized by the United States Canoe
Association, was held together by hands
only, while free floating for 30 seconds,
on the Rock River, Byron, Illinois, USA,
on 17 Aug 1996.

cricket

Individual Cricket Records
FIRST-CLASS (FC) AND TEST CAREER
BATTING
Most runs: FC 61,237
Sir Jack Hobbs (1882–1963) (av. 50.65)
Surrey/England, 1905–34
Test: 11,174 Allan Border (av. 50.56)
Australia (156 Tests), 1978–94
Most centuries: FC 197
Sir Jack Hobbs (in 1,315 innings),
Surrey/England, 1905–34
Test: 34 Sunil Gavaskar
(in 214 innings), India, 1971–87

Highest average: FC 95.14
Sir Donald Bradman, NSW/South
Australia/Australia, 1927–49
(28,067 runs in 338 innings, including
43 not outs)
Test: 99.94
Sir Donald Bradman (6,996 runs in 80
innings), Australia (52 Tests), 1928–48
Bowling
Most wickets: FC 4,187
Wilfred Rhodes (av. 16.71),
Yorkshire/England, 1898–1930
Test: 434
Kapil Dev Nikhanj (av. 29.62), India
(131 Tests), 1978–94
Lowest average: Test 10.75
George Lohmann
(112 wkts), England (18 Tests), 1886–96
(min 25 wkts)
Wicket-keeping
Most dismissals: FC 1,649
Robert Taylor, Derbyshire/England,
1960–88
Test: 355
Rodney Marsh, Australia (96 Tests),
1970–84
Most catches: FC 1,473
Robert Taylor, Derbyshire/England,
1960–88
Test: 343
Rodney Marsh, Australia, 1970–84

Wicket-keeping
Most dismissals: 28
Rodney Marsh (all caught), Australia v.
England (5), 1982/83
Most stumpings: 9
Percy Sherwell, South Africa v. Australia
(5), 1910/11
Fielding
Most catches: 15
Jack Gregory, Australia v. England (5),
1920/21
All-round
400 runs/30 wkts 475/34, George Giffen
(1859–1927), Australia v. England (5),
1894/95

World Cycling Records
These records are those recognized by
the Union Cycliste Internationale (UCI).
From 1 Jan 1993 their list no longer
distinguished between those set by
professionals and amateurs, indoor and
outdoor records, or records set at
altitude and sea level.

Mexico City, Mexico, 26 Oct 1996
Unpaced flying start
200 m: 10.831
Olga Slyusareva (Russia)
Moscow, Russia, 25 April 1993
500 m: 29.655
Erika Salumäe (USSR)
Moscow, USSR, 6 Aug 1987

Darts Scoring Records
24-Hour
Men
(8 players): 1,722,249
Broken Hill Darts Club at Broken Hill,
NSW, Australia, 28–29 Sept 1985.
Women
(8 players): 830,737
By a team from the Cornwall Inn, Killurin,
Co Wexford, Ireland, 1–2 Aug 1997.
Individual: 567,145
Kenny Fellowes at The Prince of Wales,
Cashes Green, Glos, UK, 28–29 Sept 1996.
Bulls and 25s: (8 players) 526,750 by a
team at the George Inn, Morden,
Surrey, UK, 1–2 July 1994.

International Football Competitions
Most Wins
NATIONAL LEVEL
Olympic Games (1896)
(unofficial until 1908): 3
Great Britain 1900, 1908, 1912
Hungary, 1952, 1964, 1968
S. American Championships (1910) (Copa
America since 1975): 15
Argentina, 1910, 1921, 1925, 1927,
1929, 1937, 1941, 1945–47, 1955,
1957, 1959, 1991, 1993
Asian Cup (1956): 3
Iran, 1968, 1972, 1976
Saudi Arabia 1984, 1988, 1996
African Cup of Nations (1957): 4
Ghana, 1963, 1965, 1978, 1982
Egypt, 1957, 1959, 1986, 1998
European Championships (1958): 3
West Germany/Germany, 1972, 1980, 1996
Club level
World Club Championship (1960): 3
Peñarol (Uruguay), 1961, 1966, 1982
Nacional (Uruguay), 1971, 1980, 1988
Milan (Italy), 1969, 1989, 1990

CHRIS BOARDMAN IN ACTION IN THE 1996
WORLD INDOOR CHAMPIONSHIPS, DURING
WHICH HE BETTERED THE WORLD RECORD TIME
FOR THE 4,000 M INDIVIDUAL PURSUIT BY
MORE THAN NINE SECONDS.

RONALDO COMPETING FOR BARCELONA DURING
THE 1997 EUROPEAN CUP WINNERS' CUP FINAL
AGAINST AJAX, BEFORE HIS RECORD-BREAKING
TRANSFER TO INTER MILAN. BARCELONA WON
1–0, WINNING FOR A RECORD FOURTH TIME.

Most stumpings: FC 418
Leslie Ames, Kent/England,
1926–51
Test: 52
William Oldfield, Australia (54 Tests),
1920–37
Fielding
Most catches: FC 1,018
Frank Woolley, Kent/England, 1906–38
Test: 156
Allan Border, Australia (156 Tests), 1978–94
TEST SERIES
Batting
Most runs: 974
Sir Donald Bradman (av. 139.14),
Australia v. England (5), 1930
Most centuries: 5
Sir Clyde Leopold Walcott, West Indies v.
Australia (5), 1954/55
Highest average: 563.00
Walter Hammond, England v.
New Zealand (2), 1932/33
(563 runs, 2 inns, 1 not out)
Bowling
Most wickets: 49
Sydney Barnes (av. 10.93), England v.
South Africa (4), 1913/14
Lowest average: 5.80
George Alfred Lohmann (35 wkts),
England v. South Africa (3), 1895/96
(min 20 wkts)

Men
Unpaced standing start
1 km: 1:00.613
Shane Kelly (Australia)
Bogotá, Colombia, 26 Sept 1995
4 km: 4:11.114
Chris Boardman (GB)
Manchester, UK, 29 Aug 1996
4 km team: 4:00.958
Italy
Manchester, UK, 31 Aug 1996
1 hour (kms): 56.3759
Chris Boardman (GB)
Manchester, UK, 6 Sept 1996
Unpaced flying start
200 m: 9.865
Curtis Harnett (Canada)
Bogotá, Colombia, 28 Sept 1995
500 m: 26.649
Aleksandr Kiritchenko (USSR)
Moscow, USSR, 29 Oct 1988
Women
Unpaced standing start
500 m: 34.017
Felicia Ballanger (France)
Bogotá, Colombia, 29 Sept 1995
3 km: 3:30.974
Marion Clignet (France)
Manchester, UK, 31 Aug 1996
1 hour (kms): 48.159
Jeanie Longo-Ciprelli (France)

10-Hour
Most trebles: 3,056 (from 7,992 darts)
Paul Taylor at the Woodhouse Tavern,
Leytonstone, London, UK, 19 Oct 1985.
Most doubles: 3,265 (from 8,451 darts)
Paul Taylor at the Lord Brooke,
Walthamstow, London, UK, 5 Sept 1987.
Highest score: 465,919
(retrieving own darts)
Jon Archer and Neil Rankin at the Royal
Oak, Cossington, Leics, UK, 17 Nov 1990.
Bulls (individual) 1,321: Jim Damore
(USA) at the Parkside Pub, Chicago,
Illinois, USA, 29 June 1996.
6-Hour
Men: 210,172
Russell Locke at the Hugglescote
Working Mens Club, Coalville, Leics, UK,
10 Sept 1989.
Women: 99,725
Karen Knightly at the Lord Clyde, Leyton,
London, UK, 17 March 1991.
Million and One Up
Men: (8 players) 36,583 darts
Team at Buzzy's Pub and Grub, Lynn,
Massachusetts, USA, 19–20 Oct 1991.
Women: (8 players) 70,019 darts
'Delinquents' team at the Top George,
Combe Martin, Devon, UK, 11–13 Sept
1987.

Europe
UEFA Cup (1955): 3
Barcelona (Spain), 1958, 1960, 1966
European Cup (1956): 6
Real Madrid, 1956–60, 1966
Cup Winners Cup (1960): 4
Barcelona, 1979, 1982, 1989, 1997
South America
Copa Libertadores (1960): 7
Independiente (Argentina), 1964–65,
1972–75, 1984
Africa
Cup of Champion Clubs (1964): 4
Zamalek (Eygpt), 1984, 1986, 1993,
1996
Cup Winners Cup (1975): 4
Al Alhy Cairo (Eygpt), 1984–86, 1993

World Gliding Single-Seater Records
Straight Distance: 1,460.8 km
(907 miles 1,232 yd)
Hans-Werner Grosse (West Germany)
Lübeck, Germany, to Biarritz, France,
25 April 1972

Declared Goal Distance: 1,383 km (859 miles 704 yd)
Gérard Herbaud (France), Vinon, France, to Fes, Morocco, 17 April 1992
Jean Nöel Herbaud (France)Vinon, France, to Fes, Morocco, 17 April 1992
Goal and Return: 1,646.68 km (1,023 miles 352 yd)
Thomas L. Knauff (USA)
Gliderport to Williamsport, Pennsylvania, USA, 25 April 1983
Absolute Altitude: 14,938 m (49,009 ft)
Robert R. Harris (USA)
California, USA, 17 Feb 1986
Height Gain: 12,894 m (42,303 ft)
Paul F. Bikle (USA)
Mojave, Lancaster, California, USA, 25 Feb 1961
SPEED OVER TRIANGULAR COURSE
100 km: 217.41 km/h (135.09 mph)
James Payne (USA)
California, USA, 4 March 1997
300 km: 176.99 km/h (109.97 mph)
Beat Bünzli (Switzerland)
Bitterwasser, Namibia, 14 Nov 1985
500 km: 171.7 km/h (106.7 mph)
Hans-Werner Grosse (West Germany)
Mount Newman, Australia, 31 Dec 1990
750 km: 161.33 km/h (100.24 mph)
Hans-Werner Grosse (West Germany)

US PGA: 5
Walter Hagan 1921, 24–27
Jack Nicklaus 1963, 71, 73, 75, 80
US Masters: 6
Jack William Nicklaus 1963, 65–66, 72, 75, 86
US Women's Open: 4
Betsy Earle-Rawls 1951, 53, 57, 60
Mickey Wright 1958–59, 61, 64
US Women's Amateur: 6
Glenna Collett Vare 1922, 25, 28–30, 35
British Women's: 4
Charlotte Pitcairn Leitch 1914, 20–21, 26
Joyce Wethered 1922, 24–25, 29
Note: Nicklaus is the only golfer to have won five different major titles (The Open, US Open, Masters, PGA and US Amateur titles) twice and a record 20 all told (1959–86). In 1930 Bobby Jones achieved a unique 'Grand Slam' of the US and British Open and Amateur titles.

hockey

World Hockey Records
World Cup
The most women's wins is five by the Netherlands, 1974, 1978, 1983, 1986 and 1990.The most men's wins is four by Pakistan, 1971, 1978, 1982 and 1994.
Most Olympic medals
India was Olympic champion from the re-introduction of Olympic hockey in 1928 until 1960. They had their eighth win in 1980. Of the six Indians who have won three Olympic team gold medals, two have also won a silver medal – Leslie Walter Claudius, in 1948, 1952, 1956 and 1960 (silver), and Udham Singh, in 1952, 1956, 1964 and 1960 (silver).
Most Olympic titles
A women's tournament was added in 1980, and Australia have won twice – in 1988 and 1996.
Champions' Trophy
The most wins is six, by Australia, 1983–85, 1989–90 and 1993. The first women's Champions' Trophy was held in 1987, Australia has won four times, 1991, 1993, 1995 and 1997.

Most wins (trainer): 7
John Scott 1842, 43, 49, 53, 56, 60, 62
Most wins (owner): 5
Duke of Grafton 1820, 21, 22, 26, 27
Earl of Jersey 831, 34, 35, 36, 37
1000 GUINEAS (1814)
Record time: 1 min 36.71 sec
Las Meninas 1994
Most wins (jockey): 7
George Fordham 1859, 61, 65, 68, 69, 81, 83
Most wins (trainer): 9
Robert Robson 1818, 19, 20, 21, 22, 23, 25, 26, 27
Most wins (owner): 8
Duke of Grafton 1819, 20, 21, 22, 23, 25, 26, 27
OAKS (1779)
Record time: 2 min 34.19 sec
Intrepidity 1993
Most wins (jockey): 9
Frank Buckle 1797, 98, 99, 1802, 03, 05, 17, 18, 23
Most wins (trainer): 12
Robert Robson 1802, 04, 05, 07, 08, 09, 13, 15, 18, 22, 23, 25
Most wins (owner): 6
Duke of Grafton 1813, 15, 22, 23, 28, 31

Alice Springs, Australia, 10 Jan 1988
1,250 km: 143.46 km/h (89.14 mph)
Hans-Werner Grosse (West Germany)
Alice Springs, Australia, 10 Jan 1987

golf

World Golf Records
Most Major Golf Titles
The Open: 6
Harry Vardon 1896, 1898–89, 1903, 11, 14
The Amateur: 8
John Ball 1888, 90, 92, 94, 99, 1907, 10, 12
US Open: 4
Willie Anderson 1901, 03–05
Robert Tyre 'Bobby' Jones Jr 1923, 26, 29–30
William Hogan 1948, 50–51, 53
Jack Nicklaus 1962, 67, 72, 80
US Amateur: 5
Robert Jones Jr:
1924–25, 27–28, 30

hang gliding

Hang Gliding World Records
The Fédération Aéronautique Internationale recognizes world records for rigidwing, flexwing and multiplace flexwing. These records are the greatest in each category.
Greatest distance in straight line:
495 km (307 miles 880 yd), Larry Tudor (USA), from Rock Springs, Wyoming, 1 July 1994.
Height gain: 4.343 km (14,250 ft), Larry Tudor (USA), Owens Valley, California, 4 Aug 1985.
Greatest distance (woman): 335.8 km (208 miles 1,056 yd), Kari Castle (USA), Owens Valley, 22 July 1991.
Height gain (woman): 3.97 km (13,025 ft), Judy Leden (GB) Kuruman, South Africa, 1 Dec 1992.
World Championships
The World Team Championships (officially instituted 1976) have been won most often by Great Britain (1981, 1985, 1989 and 1991).

horse racing

Major Race Records
Derby (1780)
Record time: 2 min 32.31 sec
Lammtarra 1995
Most wins (jockey): 9
Lester Piggott 1954, 57, 60, 68, 70, 72, 76, 77, 83
Most wins (trainer): 7
Robert Robson 1793, 1802, 09, 10, 15, 17, 23
John Porter 1868, 82, 83, 86, 90, 91, 99
Fred Darling 1922, 25, 26, 31, 38, 40, 41
Most wins (owner): 5
Earl of Egremont 1782, 34, 1804, 05, 07, 26
Aga Khan III 1930, 35, 36, 48, 52
2000 GUINEAS (1809)
Record time: 1 min 35.08 sec
Mister Baileys 1994
Most wins (jockey): 9
Jem Robinson 1825, 28, 31, 33, 34, 35, 36, 47, 48

ST LEGER
Record time: 3 min 01.6 sec
Coronach 1926 and *Windsor Lad* 1934
Most wins (jockey): 9
Bill Scott 1821, 25, 28, 29, 38, 39, 40, 41, 46
Most wins (trainer): 16
John Scott 1827, 28, 29, 32, 34, 38, 39, 40, 41, 45, 51, 53, 56, 57, 59, 62
Most wins (owner): 7
9th Duke of Hamilton 1786, 87, 88, 92, 1808, 09, 14
KING GEORGE VI AND QUEEN ELIZABETH DIAMOND STAKES
Record time: 2 min 26.98 sec
Grundy 1975
Most wins (jockey): 7
Lester Piggott 1965, 66, 69, 70, 74, 77, 84
Most wins (trainer): 5
Dick Hern 1972, 79, 80, 85, 89
Most wins (owner): 3
Sheikh Mohammed 1990, 93, 94
MAJOR INTERNATIONAL RACE RECORDS
Prix de l'Arc de Triomphe
Record time: 2 min 24.6 sec
Peintre Célèbre 1997
Most wins (jockey): 4
Jacques Doyasbère 1942, 44, 50, 51
Frédéric Head 1966, 72, 76, 79
Yves St-Martin 1970, 74, 82, 84
Pat Eddery 1980, 85, 86, 87

Most wins (trainer): 4
Charles Semblat 1942, 44, 46, 49
Alec Head 1952, 59, 76, 81
François Mathet 1950, 51, 70, 82
Most wins (owner): 6
Marcel Boussac 1936, 37, 42, 44, 46, 49
VRC MELBOURNE CUP
Record time: 3 min 16.3 sec
Kingston Rule 1990
Most wins (jockey): 4
Bobby Lewis 1902, 15, 19, 27
Harry White 1974, 75, 78, 79
Most wins (trainer): 10
Bart Cummings 1965, 66, 67, 74, 75, 77, 79, 90, 91, 96
Most wins (owner): 4
Etienne de Mestre 1861, 62, 67, 78
KENTUCKY DERBY
Record time: 1 min 59.4 sec
Secretariat 1973
Most wins (jockey): 5
Eddie Arcaro 1938, 41, 45, 48, 52
Bill Hartack 1957, 60, 62, 64, 69
Most wins (trainer): 6
Ben Jones 1938, 41, 44, 48, 49, 52
Most wins (owner): 8
Calumet Farm 1941, 44, 48, 49, 52, 57, 58, 68
IRISH DERBY
Record time: 2 min 25.60 sec
St Jovite 1992

hurling

World Hurling Records
Most titles
The greatest number of All-Ireland Championships won by one team is 27 by Cork between 1890 and 1990.
Most appearances
The most appearances in All-Ireland finals is 10, shared by Christy Ring (Cork and Munster), John Doyle (Tipperary) and Frank Cummings (Kilkenny). Ring and Doyle also share the record of All-Ireland medals won, with eight each. Ring's appearances on the winning side were in 1941–44, 46 and 52–54, while Doyle's were in 1949–51, 58, 61–62 and 64–65. Ring also played in a record 22 inter-provincial finals (1942–63) and was on the winning side 18 times.

World Championships/World Cup/Women
The first World Cup was held in 1982, replacing the World Championships which had been held three times since 1969. The USA have won four times, in 1974, 1982, 1989 and 1993.
Highest scores/Men
The highest score in a World Cup match is Scotland's 34–3 win over Germany at Greater Manchester on 25 July 1994. In the World Cup Premier Division, the record score is the USA's 33–2 win over Japan at Greater Manchester, UK, on 21 July 1994.
Highest score/Women
The highest score by an international team was by Great Britain and Ireland with their 40–0 defeat of Long Island during their 1967 tour of the USA.

powerlifting

World Powerlifting Records
(All weights in kilograms)
Men
52 kg
Squat: 277.5

Daniel Austin (USA), 1991
Total: 765
Aleksey Sivokon (Kazakhstan), 1994
75 kg
Squat: 328
Ausby Alexander (USA), 1989
Bench press: 217.5
James Rouse (USA), 1980
Deadlift: 337.5
Daniel Austin, 1994
Total: 850
Rick Gaugler (USA), 1982
82.5 kg
Squat: 379.5
Mike Bridges (USA), 1982
Bench press: 240
Mike Bridges, 1981
Deadlift: 357.5
Veli Kumpuniemi (Finland), 1980
Total: 952.5
Mike Bridges, 1982
90 kg
Squat: 375
Fred Hatfield (USA), 1980
Bench press:255
Mike MacDonald (USA), 1980
Deadlift: 372.5
Walter Thomas (USA), 1982
Total: 937.5
Mike Bridges, 1980

Most wins (jockey): 6
Morny Wing 1921, 23, 30, 38, 42, 46
Most wins (trainer): 6
Vincent O'Brien 1953, 57, 70, 77, 84, 85
Most wins (owner): 5
HH Aga Khan III 1925, 32, 40, 48, 49
JUMPING
GRAND NATIONAL
Record time: 8 min 47.8 sec
Mr Frisk 1990
Most wins (jockey): 5
George Stevens 1856, 63, 64, 69, 70
Most wins (trainer): 4
Fred Rimell 1956, 61, 70, 76
Most wins (owner): 3
James Machell 1873, 74, 76
Sir Charles Assheton-Smith 1893, 1912, 13
Noel Le Mare 1973, 74, 77
CHELTENHAM GOLD CUP
Record time: 6 min 23.4 sec
Silver Fame 1951
Most wins (jockey): 4
Pat Taaffe 1964, 65, 66, 68
Most wins (trainer): 5
Tom Dreaper 1946, 64, 65, 66, 68
Most wins (owner): 7
Dorothy Paget 1932, 33, 34, 35, 36, 40, 52
CHAMPION HURDLE
Record time: 3 min 48.4 sec
Make A Stand 1997

World Gaelic Football Records
All-Ireland Championships
The greatest number of All-Ireland Championships won by one team is 31 by Kerry between 1903 and 1997. The greatest number of successive wins is four by Wexford (1915–18) and Kerry twice (1929–32, 1978–81).
The highest team score in a final was when Dublin, 27 (5 goals, 12 points), beat Armagh, 15 (3 goals, 6 points), on 25 Sept 1977. The highest combined score was 45 points when Cork (26) beat Galway (19) in 1973. A goal equals three points.

lacrosse

World Lacrosse Records
Most World titles
The USA has won six of the seven World Championships, in 1967, 1974, 1982, 1986, 1990 and 1994. Canada won the other world title in 1978 beating the USA 17–16 after extra time – this was the first drawn international match.

Andrzej Stanaszek (Poland), 1997
Bench press: 177.5
Andrzej Stanaszek, 1994
Deadlift: 256
E S Bhaskaran (India), 1993
Total: 592.5
Andrzej Stanaszek, 1996
56 kg
Squat: 287.5
Magnus Carlsson (Sweden), 1996
Bench press:187.5
Magnus Carlsson, 1996
Deadlift: 289.5
Lamar Gant (USA), 1982
Total: 637.5
Hu Chun-hsing (Taipei), 1997
60 kg
Squat: 295.5
Magnus Carlsson, 1994
Bench press: 185
Magnus Carlsson, 1997
Deadlift: 310
Lamar Gant,1988
Total: 707.5
Joe Bradley, 1982
67.5 kg
Squat: 303
Wade Hooper (USA), 1997
Bench press: 200.5
Aleksey Sivokon (Kazakhstan), 1997
Deadlift: 316

100 kg
Squat: 423
Ed Coan (USA), 1994
Bench press: 261.5
Mike MacDonald, 1977
Deadlift: 390
Ed Coan, 1993
Total: 1035
Ed Coan, 1994
110 kg
Squat: 415
Kirk Karwoski (USA), 1994
Bench press: 270
Jeffrey Magruder (USA), 1982
Deadlift: 395
John Kuc (USA), 1980
Total: 1,000
John Kuc, 1980
125 kg
Squat: 455
Kirk Karwoski, 1995
Bench press: 278.5
Tom Hardman (USA), 1982
Deadlift: 387.5
Lars Norén (Sweden), 1987
Total: 1,045
Kirk Karwoski, 1995
125+ kg
Squat: 447.5
Shane Hamman (USA), 1994
Bench press: 322.5

James Henderson (USA), 1997
Deadlift: 406
Lars Norén, 1988
Total: 1,100
Bill Kazmaier (USA), 1981

Women

44 kg
Squat: 162.5
Raija Koskinen (Fin), 1997
Bench press: 85
Svetlana Tesleva (Russia), 1996
Deadlift: 165.5
Anna-Liisa Prinkkala (Finland), 1998
Total: 397.5
Raija Koskinen, 1997

48 kg
Squat: 171
Raija Koskinen (Finland), 1997
Bench press: 100
Marlina (Indonesia), 1997
Deadlift: 182.5
Majik Jones (USA), 1984
Total: 415
Yelena Yamkich (Russia), 1997

52 kg
Squat: 182.5
Oksana Belova (Russia), 1997
Bench press: 107.5
Anna Olsson (Sweden), 1997
Deadlift: 197.5
Diana Rowell (USA) 1984

75 kg
Squat: 245
Anne Sigrid Stiklestad (Norway), 1997
Bench press: 145.5
Marina Zhguleva (Russia), 1997
Deadlift: 252.5
Yelena Sukhoruk, 1995
Total: 605
Yelena Sukhoruk, 1995

82.5 kg
Squat: 242.5
Anne Sigrid Stiklestad (Norway), 1997
Bench press: 151
Natalia Rumyantseva (Russia), 1997
Deadlift: 257.5
Cathy Millen (New Zealand), 1993
Total: 637.5
Cathy Millen, 1993

90 kg
Squat: 260
Cathy Millen, 1994
Bench press: 162.5
Cathy Millen, 1994
Deadlift: 260
Cathy Millen, 1994
Total: 682.5
Cathy Millen, 1994

90+kg
Squat: 277.5
Juanita Trujillo (USA), 1994
Bench press: 175

The most wins at single sculls is five by: Peter-Michael Kolbe (West Germany), 1975, 1978, 1981, 1983 and 1986; Pertti Karppinen, 1979 and 1985 and three Olympic 1976, 1980 and 1984; Thomas Lange (GDR/Germany), 1987, 1989 and 1991 and two Olympics 1988 and 1992; and in the women's events by Christine Hahn (née Scheiblich) (GDR), 1974–75, 1977–78 (and the 1976 Olympic title).

Most Olympic golds
The most golds is four by Steven Redgrave (GB), coxed fours (1984), coxless pairs (1988, 1992 and 1996).

Most Olympic golds
The most by women is three, by Canadian pair Kathleen Heddle and Marnie McBean, coxless pairs 1992, eights 1992 and double sculls 1996.

Highest speed
The record time for 2,000 m (1 mile 427 yd) on non-tidal water is 5 min 23.90 sec (22.22 km/h or 13.80 mph) by the Dutch National team (eight) at Duisburg, Germany, on 19 May 1996.

Highest speed
The women's record time for 2,000 m (1 mile 427 yd) on non-tidal water is 5 min 58.50 sec (20.08 km/h or 12.48 mph) by Romania at Duisburg, Germany on 18 May 1996.

Individual international records
The most points scored in a game is 32 by: Andrew Johns (Australia) (2 tries, 12 goals) v. Fiji at Newcastle, NSW, Australia on 12 July 1996 and Bobby Goulding (GB) (3 tries, 10 goals) v. Fiji at Nadi, Fiji, on 5 Oct 1996.
Jim Sullivan (Wigan) played in most internationals (60 for Wales and Great Britain, 1921–39), kicked most goals (160) and scored most points (329).

Rugby Union Titles
On the three occasions the World Cup has been held, 1987, 1991 and 1995, the winners have been New Zealand, Australia and South Africa respectively.

Highest team score
New Zealand beat Japan 145–17 at Bloemfontein, South Africa, on 4 June 1995. During this match New Zealand scored a record 21 tries.

Most international appearances
Philippe Sella (France) has played in 111 internationals for France, 1982–95.

Internationals
The highest score in any full international is when Hong Kong beat Singapore 164–13 in a World Cup qualifying match at Kuala Lumpur, Malaysia, on 27 Oct 1994.
The highest aggregate score for any

STEVE REDGRAVE, WITH LONG-TIME ROWING PARTNER MATTHEW PINSENT, ON THE WAY TO WINNING THE COXLESS PAIRS GOLD AT THE 1996 OLYMPICS. IT WAS REDGRAVE'S FOURTH CONSECUTIVE OLYMPIC GOLD AND HE WENT ON TO WIN A RECORD 11TH WORLD TITLE IN 1997.

PERCY MONTGOMERY OF SOUTH AFRICA ON HIS WAY TO SCORING THE FIRST TRY IN HIS TEAM'S 68–10 DEMOLITION OF SCOTLAND, THE HEAVIEST DEFEAT IN AN INTERNATONAL BY AN OVERSEAS SIDE IN THE BRITISH ISLES.

Total: 475
Oksana Belova, 1997

56 kg
Squat: 191.5
Carrie Boudreau (USA), 1995
Bench press: 122.5
Valentina Nelubova (Russia), 1997
Deadlift: 222.5
Carrie Boudreau, 1995
Total: 522.5
Carrie Boudreau, 1995

60 kg
Squat: 210
Beate Amdahl (Norway), 1993
Bench press: 118
Helena Heiniluoma (Finland), 1996
Deadlift: 213.5
Ingeborg Marx (Belgium), 1997
Total: 525
Ingeborg Marx, 1997

67.5 kg
Squat: 230
Ruthi Shafer (USA), 1984
Bench press: 120
Vicki Steenrod (USA), 1990
Deadlift: 244
Ruthi Shafer, 1984
Total: 572.5
Lisa Sjöstrand (Sweden), 1997

Chao Chen-yeh (Taipei), 1997
Deadlift: 262.5
Katrina Robertson (Australia), 1997
Total: 657.5
Lee Chia-sui (Taipei), 1997

rowing

World Rowing Records
World Championships
World Rowing Championships distinct from the Olympic Games were first held in 1962, at first four yearly, but from 1974 annually, except in Olympic years. The most gold medals won at World Championships and Olympic Games is 11 by Steven Redgrave who, in addition to his four Olympic successes, won world titles at coxed pairs 1986, coxless pairs 1987, 1991, 1993–95, coxless fours, 1997. Francesco Esposito (Italy) has won nine titles at lightweight events, coxless pairs, 1980–84, 1988, 1994 and coxless fours, 1990, 1992. At women's events Yelena Tereshina has won a record seven golds, all eights for the USSR, 1978–79, 1981–83 and 1985–86.

Highest speed
The single sculls record is 6 min 37.03 sec (18.13 km/h or 11.26 mph) by Juri Jaanson (Estonia) at Lucerne, Switzerland on 9 July 1995.

Highest speed
The single sculls record is 7 min 17.09 sec (16.47 km/h or 10.23 mph). Silken Laumann (Canada) at Lucerne, Switzerland, on 17 July 1994.

rugby

World Rugby Records
Rugby League
World Cup
The World Cup competition was first held in 1954. Australia have most wins, with seven, (1957, 1968, 1970, 1977, 1988, 1992 and 1995) as well as a win in the International Championship of 1975.

International match
The highest score in an international match is Australia's 86–6 defeat of South Africa at Gateshead, Tyne & Wear, UK, on 10 Oct 1995.

international match between the Four Home Unions is 82, when England beat Wales by 82 points (7 goals, 1 drop goal and 6 tries) to nil at Blackheath, London, UK, on 19 Feb 1881. (Note: there was no point scoring in 1881.) The highest aggregate score under the modern points system between two of the eight major nations is 93, when New Zealand beat Scotland 62–31 at Dunedin, New Zealand, on 15 June 1996. The highest score by an overseas side in an international in the British Isles is 68 points by South Africa v. Scotland (10) at Murrayfield, Edinburgh, on 6 Dec 1997.

shooting

Shooting – Individual World Records
In 1986, the International Shooting Union (UIT) introduced new regulations for major championships and world records. Now the leading competitors undertake an additional round with a target sub-divided to tenths of a point for rifle and pistol shooting, and an extra 25, 40 or 50 (depending

on category) shots for trap and skeet. Harder targets have since been introduced and the table below shows the world records, as recognised by the UIT, for the 15 Olympic shooting disciplines, the score for the number of shots specified is in brackets plus the score in the additional round.

Men
Free Rifle 50 m 3 x 40 shots
1,287.9 (1,186+101.9)
Rajmond Debevec (Slovenia)
Munich, Germany, 29 Aug 1992
Free Rifle 50 m 60 Shots Prone
704.8 (600 + 104.8)
Christian Klees (Germany)
Atlanta, Georgia, USA, 25 July 1996
Air Rifle 10 m 60 shots
700.2 (596 + 104.2)
Leif Steinar Rolland (Norway)
Munich, Germany, 20 May 1997
Free Pistol 50 m 60 shots
675.3 (580 + 95.3)
Taniu Kiriakov (Bulgaria)
Hiroshima, Japan, 21 April 1995
Rapid-Fire Pistol 25 m 60 shots
699.7 (596 + 107.5)
Ralf Schumann (Germany)
Barcelona, Spain, 8 June 1994
Air Pistol 10 m 60 shots
695.1 (593 + 102.1)

Havana, Cuba
12 April 1996
Sport Pistol
25 m 60 shots
696.2 (594 + 102.2)
Diana Jorgova (Bulgaria)
Milan, Italy, 31 May 1994
Air Pistol 10 m 40 shots
492.7 (392 + 100.7)
Jasna Sekaric (Yugoslavia)
Nafels, Switzerland, 22 Sept 1996
Double Trap 120 targets
149 (113 + 36)
Deborah Gelisio (Italy)
Nicosia, Cyprus, 19 June 1995

skating

World Speed Skating Records
Men
500 m: 34.82
Hiroyasu Shimizu (Japan)
Calgary, Canada, 28 March 1998
1,000 m: 1:09.60
Sylvain Bouchard (Canada)
Calgary, Canada, 29 Dec 1998

WORLD RECORDS – SHORT TRACK
Men
500 m: 41.938
Nicola Franceschina (Italy)
Bormio, Italy, 29 March 1998
1,000 m: 1:28.23
Marc Gagnon (Canada)
Seoul, South Korea, 4 April 1997
1,500 m: 2:15.50
Kai Feng (China)
Habin, China, 11 Nov 1997
3,000 m: 4:53.23
Lee Seung-chan (South Korea)
Beijing, China, 23 Nov 1997
5,000 m relay: 7:00.042
South Korea
Nagano, Japan, 30 March 1997
Women
500 m: 44.867
Isabelle Charset (Canada)
Nagano, Japan, 29 March 1997
1,000 m: 1:31.991
Yang Yang (China)
Nagano, Japan, 21 Feb 1998
1,500 m: 2:25.17
Kim Yun-mi (South Korea)
Harbin, China, 2 Dec 1995
3,000 m: 5:02.19
Chun Lee-kyung (South Korea)
Gyovik, Norway, 19 March 1995

The record score achieved for the world overall title is 153.367 points by Ids Postma (Netherlands) at Heerenven, Netherlands, on 13-15 March 1998.
Most world titles/Women
The most titles won in the women's events (instituted 1936) is seven by Gunda Neimann-Stirnemann (Germany), 1991-93 and 1995-98.
The record low women's score is 163.02 points by Gunda Neimann-Stirnemann (Germany), at Heerenven, Netherlands, on 13-15 March 1998.

FIGURE SKATING
Most world titles – Individual
The greatest number of men's individual world figure skating titles (instituted 1896) is 10 by Ulrich Salchow (Sweden), 1901-05 and 1907-11. The women's record (instituted 1906) is also 10 individual titles by Sonja Henie between 1927 and 1936.
Most world titles – Pairs
Irina Rodnina won 10 pairs titles (instituted 1908), four with Aleksey Nikolayevich Ulanov, 1969–72, and six with her husband Aleksandr Gennadyevich Zaitsev, 1973–78. The most ice dance titles (instituted 1952)

CHRISTIAN KLEES ON HIS WAY TO WINNING OLYMPIC GOLD AT THE 1996 GAMES IN THE 50-M FREE RIFLE PRONE EVENT. HAVING SCORED A PERFECT 600 IN THE CLASSIFICATION ROUND, HE WENT ON TO SCORE 104.8 IN THE FINAL ROUND TO SET A WORLD RECORD.

CANADIAN SKATER CATRIONA LE MAY DOAN WINNING THE 500-M RACE DRING THE ICE SPEED WORLD CHAMPIONSHIPS IN BERLIN, GERMANY, WHERE SHE SET A NEW TRACK RECORD. LE MAY DOAN ALSO HOLDS THE WORLD RECORD FOR 500 M WITH A TIME OF 37.55 SECS.

Sergey Pyzhyanov (USSR)
Munich, Germany, 13 Oct 1989
Running Target 10 m 30/30 shots
687.9 (586 + 101.9)
Ling Yang (China)
Milan, Italy, 6 June 1996
Skeet 125 targets
150 (125 + 25)
Marcello Tittarelli (Italy)
Suhl, Germany, 11 June 1996
Ennio Falco (Italy)
Lonato, Italy, 13 May 1997
Trap 125 targets
150 (125 + 25)
Jan Henrik Heinrich (Germany)
Lonato, Italy, 5 June 1996
Andrea Benelli (Italy)
Suhl, Germany, 11 June 1996
Double trap 150 targets
191 (143 + 48)
Joshua Lakatos (USA)
Barcelona, Spain, 15 June 1993
Women
Standard Rifle
50 m 3 x 20 shots
689.7 (592 + 97.7)
Vessela Letcheva (Bulgaria)
Munich, Germany, 15 June 1995
Air Rifle 10 m 40 shots
501.5 (398 + 103.5)
Vessela Letcheva (Bulgaria)

1,500 m: 1:46.43
Ådne Søndrål (Norway)
Calgary, Canada, 28 March 1998
3,000: 3:48.91
Bart Veldkamp (Netherlands)
Calgary, Canada, 21 March 1998
5,000 m:
Gianni Romme (Netherlands)
Calgary, Canada, 27 March 1998
10,000 m: 13:08.71
Gianni Romme (Netherlands)
Calgary, Canada, 29 March 1998
Women
500: 37.55
Catriona Le May Doan (Canada)
Calgary, Canada, 29 Dec 1997
1,000 m: 1:14.96
Christine Witty (USA)
Calgary, Canada, 28 March 1998
1,500: 1:56.93
Anni Friesinger (Germany)
Calgary, Canada, 29 March 1998
3,000 m: 4:01.67
Gunda Niemann-Stirnemann (Germany)
Calgary, Canada, 27 March 1998
5,000: 6:58.63
Gunda Niemann-Stirnemann (Germany)
Calgary, Canada, 28 March 1998

3,000-m relay: 4:16.26
South Korea
Nagano, Japan, 17 Feb 1998
Most Olympic titles/Men
The most Olympic gold medals won by a man is five by: Clas Thunberg (Finland) (including one tied) in 1924 and 1928; and Eric Arthur Heiden (USA), uniquely at one Games at Lake Placid, New York, USA, in 1980. The most medals is seven by Clas Thunberg, who additionally won one silver and one tied bronze; and Ivar Ballangrud (Norway), four gold, two silver and a bronze, 1928–36.
Most Olympic titles/Women
The most Olympic gold medals won in speed skating is six by Lidiya Pavlovna Skoblikova (USSR), in 1960 (two) and 1964 (four). The most medals is eight by Karin Kania (GDR), three gold, four silver and a bronze, 1980–88.
Most world titles/Men
The greatest number of world overall titles (instituted 1893) won by any skater is five; by Oscar Mathisen (Norway) in 1908-09 and 1912-14; and by Clas Thunberg in 1923, 1925, 1928-29 and 1931. A record six men's sprint overall titles have been won by Igor Zhelezovskiy (USSR/Belarus), 1985-86, 1989 and 1991-93.

won is six by Lyudmila Alekseyevna Pakhomova and her husband Aleksandr Georgiyevich Gorshkov (USSR), 1970-74 and 1976. They also won the first ever Olympic ice dance title in 1976.
Triple Crown
Karl Schäfer (Austria) and Sonja Henie achieved double 'Grand Slams', both in the years 1932 and 1936. This feat was repeated by Katarina Witt (GDR) in 1984 and 1988. The only British skaters to win the 'Grand Slam' of World, Olympic and European titles in the same year are John Curry (1949-94) in 1976 and the ice dancers Jayne Torvill and Christopher Dean in 1984.

skiing

World Skiing Records
Most Olympic Skiing Titles
Men
ALPINE: 3
Toni Sailer (Austria)
Downhill, slalom, giant slalom, 1956
Jean-Claude Killy (France)

Downhill, slalom, giant slalom, 1968, Alberto Tomba (Italy)*
Slalom, giant slalom, 1988; giant slalom, 1992
NORDIC: 8
Bjørn Dæhlie (Norway)
15 km, 50 km, 4 x 10-km 1992; 10 km, 15 km 1994
10 km, 50 km, 4 x 10-km 1998
JUMPING: 4
Matti Nykänen (Finland) 70-m hill 1988; 90-m hill 1984, 1988; Team 1988
Women
ALPINE: 3
Vreni Schneider (Switzerland)*
Giant slalom, slalom 1988; slalom 1994
Katja Seizinger (Germany)*
Downhill 1994; combined, downhill 1998
Deborah Campagnoni (Italy)
Super giant slalom 1992; giant slalom 1994; giant slalom 1998
NORDIC: 6
Lyubov Yegorova (Russia)
10 km, 15 km, 4 x 5-km 1992; 5 km, 10 km, 4 x 5-km 1994
*Most medals
12 (men), Bjørn Dæhlie (Norway) also won four silver in Nordic events, 1992-98.
10 (women), Raisa Smetanina (USSR/CIS), four gold, five silver and one bronze in Nordic events, 1976-92.

1967; and Pirmin Zurbriggen (Switzerland) won four of the five possible disciplines (downhill, giant slalom, super giant slalom [added 1986] and overall) in 1987.
Women
Overall: 6
Annemarie Moser-Pröll (Austria), 1971-75, 1979
Downhill: 7
Annemarie Moser-Pröll, 1971-75, 1978-79
Slalom: 6
Vreni Schneider (Switzerland) 1989-90, 1992-5
Giant Slalom: 5
Vreni Schneider (Switzerland), 1986-7, 1989, 1991, 1995
Super Giant Slalom: 5
Katja Seizinger (Germany), 1993-96, 1998
NORDIC SKIING (instituted 1981)
Men
Jumping: 4
Matti Nykänen (Finland), 1983, 1985-86, 1988
Cross-country: 5
Gunde Svan (Sweden), 1984-86, 1988-89
Bjørn Dæhlie (Norway), 1992-93, 1995-97
Women
Cross Country: 4
Yelena Välbe (USSR/Russia), 1989, 1991-92, 1995

swimming

World Swimming Records
WORLD RECORDS
(set in 50-m pools)
Men
Freestyle
50 m: 21.81
Tom Jager (USA)
Nashville, Tennessee, USA, 24 March 1990
100 m: 48.21
Aleksandr Popov (Russia)
Monte Carlo, 18 June 1994
200 m: 1:46.69
Giorgio Lamberti (Italy)
Bonn, Germany, 15 Aug 1989
400 m: 3:43.80
Kieren John Perkins (Australia)
Rome, Italy, 9 Sept 1994
800 m: 7:46.00
Kieren John Perkins (Australia)
Victoria, Canada, 24 Aug 1994
1,500 m: 14:41.66
Kieren John Perkins (Australia)
Victoria, Canada, 24 Aug 1994
4 x 100 m: 3:15.11
USA (David Fox, Joe Hudepohl,

Medley
200 m: 1:58.16
Jani Nikanor Sievinen (Finland) Rome, Italy 11 Sept 1994
400 m: 4:12.30
Tom Dolan (USA) Rome, Italy, 6 Sept 1994
4 x 100-m: 3:34.84
USA (Gary Hall Jr, Mark Henderson, Jeremy Linn, Jeff Rouse)
Atlanta, Georgia, USA, 26 July 1996
Women
Freestyle
50 m: 24.51
Le Jingyi (China)
Rome, Italy, 11 Sept 1994
100 m: 54.01
Le Jingyi (China)
Rome, Italy, 5 Sept 1994
200 m: 1:56.78
Franziska van Almsick (Germany)
Rome, Italy, 6 Sept 1994
400 m: 4:03.8
Janet B Evans (USA)
Seoul, South Korea, 22 Sept 1988
800 m: 8:16.22
Janet Evans (USA)
Tokyo, Japan, 20 Aug 1989
1,500 m: 15:52.10
Janet Evans (USA)
Orlando, FL, USA, 26 March 1988

KATJA SEIZINGER HAD A SUCCESSFUL 1997/98 SEASON, WINNING THE SUPER GIANT SLALOM WORLD CUP TITLE FOR A RECORD FIFTH TIME AND TWO GOLDS AND A BRONZE AT THE 1998 WINTER OLYMPICS. HER OVERALL TOTAL OF THREE GOLDS AND FIVE MEDALS ARE BOTH RECORDS.

REMARKABLY, MARK WARNECKE OF GERMANY, HOLDER OF THE SHORT-COURSE WORLD RECORD FOR 50M BREASTSTROKE, HAS SET THE RECORD TIME OF 26.97 SECONDS FOR THE EVENT ON NO FEWER THAN THREE OCCASIONS.

In Alpine skiing, the record is five: Alberto Tomba won silver in the 1992 and 1994 slalom; Vreni Schneider won silver in the combined and bronze in the giant slalom in 1994; Katja Seizinger won bronze in the 1992 and 1998 super giant slalom; and Kjetil André Aamodt (Norway) won one gold (super giant slalom 1992), two silver (downhill, combined 1994) and two bronze (giant slalom 1992, super giant slalom 1994).
Most World Cup Titles
ALPINE SKIING (instituted 1967)
Men
Overall: 5
Marc Girardelli (Luxembourg), 1985-86, 1989, 1991, 1993
Downhill: 5
Franz Klammer (Austria), 1975-78, 1983
Slalom: 8
Ingemar Stenmark (Sweden), 1975-81, 1983
Giant Slalom: 7
Ingemar Stenmark (Sweden), 1975-76, 1978-81, 1984
Super Giant Slalom: 4
Pirmin Zurbriggen (Switzerland) 1987-90
Two men have won four titles in one year: Jean-Claude Killy (France) won all four possible disciplines (downhill, slalom, giant slalom and overall) in

squash

World Squash Records
World Championships
The most men's world team titles is six by: Australia 1967, 1969, 1971, 1973, 1989 and 1991; and Pakistan 1977, 1981, 1983, 1985, 1987 and 1993.
The women's title has been won four times by, England, 1985, 1987, 1989 and 1990 (Great Britain won in 1979) and Australia, 1981, 1983, 1992 and 1994.
Jansher Khan (Pakistan) has won eight World Open (instituted 1976) titles, 1987, 1989-90, 1992-96. Jahangir Khan (Pakistan) won six World Open titles, 1981-85 and 1988, and the International Squash Rackets Federation world individual title (formerly World Amateur, instituted 1967) in 1979, 1983 and 1985. Geoffrey B. Hunt (Australia) won four World Open titles, 1976-77 and 1979-80 and three World Amateur, 1967, 1969 and 1971.
The most women's World Open titles is four by Susan Devoy (New Zealand), 1985, 1987, 1990 and 1992.

Jon Olsen, Gary Hall)
Atlanta, GA, USA, 12 Aug 1995
4 x 200-m: 7:11.95
CIS (Dmitriy Lepikov, Vladimir Pyechenko, Venyamin Tayanovich, Yevgeniy Sadovyi)
Barcelona, Spain, 27 July 1992
Breaststroke
100 m: 1:00.60
Frédéric Deburghgraeve (Belgium)
Atlanta, GA, USA, 20, July 1996
200 m: 2:10.16
Michael Ray Barrowman (USA)
Barcelona, Spain, 29 July 1992
Butterfly
100 m: 52.15
Michael Klim (Australia)
Australia, 9 Oct 1997
200 m: 1:51.76
James Hickman (GB)
Paris, France, 28 March 1998
Backstroke
100 m: 53.86
Jeff Rouse (USA)
Barcelona, Spain, 31 July 1992
200 m: 1:56.57
Martin López-Zubero (Spain)
Tuscaloosa, Alabama, USA, 23 Nov 1991

4 x 100-m: 3:37.91
China (Le Jingyi, Shan Ying, Le Ying, Lu Bin)
Rome, Italy, 7 Sept 1994
4 x 200-m: 7:55.47
GDR (Manuela Stellmach, Astrid Strauss, Anke Möhring, Heike Friedrich)
Strasbourg, France, 18 Aug 1987
Breaststroke
100 m: 1:07.02
Penelope Heyns (South Africa) Atlanta, Georgia, USA, 21 July 1996
200 m: 2:24.76
Rebecca Brown (Australia)
Brisbane, Australia, 16 March 1994
Butterfly
100 m: 57.93
Mary Terstegge Meagher (USA)
Brown Deer, Wisconsin, USA, 16 Aug 1981
200 m: 2:05.96
Mary Terstegge Meagher (USA)
Brown Deer, Wisconsin, USA, 13 Aug 1981
Backstroke
100 m: 1:00.16
He Cihong (China)
Rome, Italy, 10 Sept 1994
200 m: 2:06.62
Krisztina Egerszegi (Hungary)
Athens, Greece, 25 Aug 1991

Medley
200 m: 2:09.72
Wu Yanyan (China)
Shanghai, China, 17 Oct 1997
400 m: 4:34.79
Chen Yan (China)
Shanghai, China, 17 Oct 1997
4 x 100-m: 4:01.67
China (He Cihong, Dai Guohong, Liu Limin, Le Jingyi)
Rome, Italy, 10 Sept 1994

Short-Course Swimming World Records
(set in 25-m pools)
Men
Freestyle
50 m: 21.50
Aleksandr Popov (Russia)
Desenzano, Italy, 13 March 1994
100 m: 46.74
Aleksandr Popov (Russia)
Gelsenkirchen, Germany, 19 March 1994
200 m: 1:43.64
Giorgio Lamberti (Italy)
Bonn, Germany, 11 Feb 1990
400 m: 3:40.46
Danyon Loader (New Zealand)
Sheffield, S Yorks, UK, 11 Feb 1995
800 m: 7:34.90
Kieren Perkins (Australia)
Sydney, NSW, Australia, 25 July 1993

200 m: 2:07.79
Andrey Korneev (Russia)
Paris, France, 28 March 1998
Butterfly
50 m: 23.35
Denis Pankratov (Russia)
Paris, France, 8 Feb 1997
100 m: 51.07
Michael Klim (Australia)
Sydney, NSW, Australia, 22 Jan 1998
200 m: 1:51.76
James Hickman (GB)
Paris, France, 28 March 1998
Medley
100 m: 53.10
Jani Nikanor Sievinen (Finland)
Malmö, Sweden, 30 Jan 1996
200 m: 1:54.65
Jani Sievinen (Finland)
Kuopio, Finland, 21 Jan 1994
400 m: 4:05.41
Marcel Wouda (Netherlands)
Paris, France, 8 Feb 1997
4 x 50-m: 1:36.69
Auburn Aquatics
Auburn, New York, USA, 9 April 1996
4 x 100-m: 3:30.66
Australia
Gothenburg, Sweden, 17 April 1997

Backstroke
50 m: 27.64
Bai Xiuyu (China)
Desenzano, Italy, 12 March 1994
100 m: 58.50
Angel Martino (USA)
Palma de Majorca, Spain, 3 Dec 1993
200 m: 2:06.09
He Cihong (China)
Palma de Majorca, Spain, 5 Dec 1993
Breaststroke
50 m: 30.77
Han Xue (China)
Gelsenkirchen, Germany, 2 Feb 1997
100 m: 1:05.70
Samantha Riley (Australia)
Rio de Janeiro, Brazil, 2 Dec 1995
200 m: 2:20.85
Samantha Riley (Australia)
Rio de Janeiro, Brazil, 1 Dec 1995
Butterfly
50 m: 26.48
Jenny Thompson (USA)
Toronto, Canada, 29 Nov 1997
100 m: 57.79
Jenny Thompson (USA)
Gothenburg, Sweden, 19 April 1997
200 m: 2:05.65
Mary Terstegge Meagher (USA)
Gainesville, Florida, USA, 2 Jan 1981

Women: 1 buoy on 10.25-m (34-ft) line
Kristi Overton Johnson (USA)
West Palm Beach, Florida, USA,
14 Sept 1996
TRICKS
Men: 11,680 points
Cory Pickos (USA)
Zachary, Louisiana, USA, 10 May 1997
Women: 8,580 points
Tawn Larsen (USA)
Groveland, Florida, USA, on 4 July 1992.
JUMPING
Men: 67.8 m (222 ft)
Bruce Neville (Australia)
Orangeville, Canada, 27 July 1997
John Swanson (USA)
Bow Hill, Washington, USA, 13 Sept 1997
Women: 50.5 m (165 ft)
Brenda Nichols Baldwin (USA)
Okahumpka, Florida, USA, 27 April 1997.

weightlifting

World Weightlifting Records
From 1 Jan 1993, the International Weightlifting Federation (IWF) introduced modified bodyweight

JAMES HICKMAN (GB), CENTRE IN THE YELLOW CAP, STARTS THE 100-M BUTTERFLY AT SHEFFIELD, UK, ONE OF THE WORLD CUP SHORT COURSE SERIES VENUES FOR THE 1997/98 SEASON. HICKMAN DOMINATED LONGER DISTANCE BUTTERFLY EVENTS IN THE SEASON AND SET A NEW 200-M WORLD RECORD IN THE FINAL WORLD CUP MEET IN PARIS, FRANCE.

OF THE THREE DISCIPLINES IN WATER SKIING, JUMPING IS CONSIDERED THE MOST EXCITING. IN 1997 THE FIRST JUMP IN EXCESS OF 50 METRES BY A WOMAN WAS ACHIEVED, BRENDA NICHOLS BALDWIN LEAPING TO 50.5 M IN APRIL. THE MEN'S FIRST 50 M-PLUS JUMP HAD BEEN MADE IN 1970 BY AMERICAN MIKE SUYDERHOUD.

1,500 m: 14:26.52
Kieren Perkins (Australia)
Auckland, New Zealand, 14 July 1993
4 x 50-m: 1:27.62
Sweden
Stavanger, Norway, 2 Dec 1994
4 x 100-m: 3:12.11
Brazil
Palma de Majorca, Spain, 5 Dec 1993
4 x 200-m: 7:02.74
Australia
Gothenburg, Sweden, 18 April 1997
Backstroke
50 m: 24.25
Chris Renaud (Canada)
St Catharine's, Canada, 28 Feb 1997
100 m: 51.43
Jeff Rouse (USA)
Sheffield, S Yorks, UK, 12 April 1993
200 m: 1:52.51
Martin Lopez-Zubero (Spain)
Gainesville, Florida, USA, 10 April 1991
Breaststroke
50 m: 26.97
Mark Warnecke (Germany)
Paris, France, 8 Feb 1997
Sydney, NSW, Australia, 22 Jan 1998
Paris, France, 28 March 1998
100 m: 59.02
Frédéric Deburghgraeve (Belgium)
Bastogne, Belgium, 17 Feb 1996

Women
Freestyle
50 m: 24.23
Le Jingyi (China)
Palma de Majorca, Spain, 3 Dec 1993
100 m: 53.01
Le Jingyi (China)
Palma de Majorca, Spain, 2 Dec 1993
200 m: 1:54.17
Claudia Poll (Costa Rica)
Gothenburg, Sweden, 18 April 1997
400 m: 4:00.03
Claudia Poll (Costa Rica)
Gothenburg, Sweden, 19 April 1997
800 m: 8:15.34
Astrid Strauss (GDR)
Bonn, Germany, 6 Feb 1987
1,500 m: 15:43.31
Petra Schneider (GDR)
Gainesville, Florida, USA, 10 Jan 1982
4 x 50-m: 1:40.63
Germany
Espoo, Finland, 22 Nov 1992
4 x 100-m: 3:34.55
China
Gothenburg, Sweden, 19 April 1997
4 x 200-m: 7:51.92
China
Gothenburg, Sweden, 17 April 1997

Medley
100 m: 1:01.03
Louise Karlsson (Sweden)
Espoo, Finland, 22 Nov 1992
200 m: 2:07.79
Allison Wagner (USA)
Palma de Majorca, Spain, 5 Dec 1993
400 m: 4:29.00
Dai Gouhong (China)
Palma de Majorca, Spain, 2 Dec 1993
4 x 50-m: 1:52.44
Germany
Espoo, Finland, 21 Nov 1992
4 x 100-m: 3:57.73
China
Palma de Majorca, Spain, 5 Dec 1993

water skiing

World Water Skiing Records
Slalom
Men: 1 buoy on 9.75-m (32-ft) line
Jeff Rogers (USA)
Charleston, South Carolina, USA, 31 Aug 1997.

categories, thereby making the then world records redundant. This is the current list for the new weight categories (as of 31 Dec 1997).
Bodyweight 54 kg (119 lb)
Snatch: 132.5 kg (292 lb)
Halil Mutlu (Turkey)
Atlanta, USA, 20 July 1996
Jerk: 160.5 kg (353³/₄ lb)
Lan Shizang (China)
Chiang Mai, Thailand, 6 Dec 1997
Total: 290 kg (639¹/₄ lb)
Halil Mutlu (Turkey)
Istanbul, Turkey, 18 Nov 1994
Bodyweight 59 kg (130 lb)
Snatch: 140 kg (308¹/₂ lb)
Hafiz Suleymanoğlü (Turkey)
Warsaw, Poland, 3 May 1995
Jerk: 170 kg (374³/₄ lb)
Nikolai Peshalov (Bulgaria)
Warsaw, Poland, 3 May 1995
Total: 307.5 kg (677³/₄ lb)
Tang Ningsheng (China)
Atlanta, USA, 21 July 1996

Bodyweight 64 kg (141 lb)
Snatch: 150 kg (330¹/₂ lb)
Wang Guohua (China)
Pusan, South Korea, 12 May 1997
Jerk: 187.5 kg (413¹/₄ lb)
Valerios Leonidis (Greece)
Atlanta, USA, 22 July 1996
Total: 335 kg (738¹/₂ lb)
Naim Suleymanoğlu (Turkey)*
Atlanta, USA, 22 July 1996
Bodyweight 70 kg (154¹/₄ lb)
Snatch: 163 kg (359¹/₄ lb)
Wan Jianhui (China)
Guangzhou, China, 9 July 1997
Jerk: 195.5 kg (429³/₄ lb)
Zhan Xugang (China)
Chiang Mai, Thailand,
9 Dec 1997
Total: 357.5 kg (788 lb)
Zhan Xugang (China)
Atlanta, USA, 23 July 1996
Bodyweight 76 kg (167¹/₂ lb)
Snatch: 170 kg (374³/₄ lb)
Ruslan Savchenko (Ukraine)
Melbourne, Australia, 16 Nov 1993
Jerk: 208 kg (458¹/₂ lb)
Pablo Lara (Cuba)
Szekszárd, Hungary, 20 April 1996
Total: 372.5 kg (821 lb)
Pablo Lara (Cuba)
Szekszárd, Hungary, 20 April 1996

Bodyweight 108 kg (238 lb)
Snatch: 200 kg (440³/₄ lb)
Timur Taimazov (Ukraine)
Istanbul, Turkey, 26 Nov 1994
Jerk: 236 kg (520¹/₂ lb)
Timur Taimazov (Ukraine)
Atlanta, USA, 29 July 1996
Total: 435 kg (959 lb)
Timur Taimazov (Ukraine)
Istanbul, Turkey, 26 Nov 1994
Bodyweight Over 108 kg
Snatch: 205 kg (451³/₄ lb)
Aleksandr Kurlovich (Belarus)
Istanbul, Turkey, 27 Nov 1994
Jerk: 262.5 kg (578¹/₂ lb)
Andrey Chemerkin (Russia)
Chiang Mai, Thailand,
14 Dec 1997
Total: 462.5 kg (1,019¹/₂ lb)
Andrey Chemerkin (Russia)
Chiang Mai, Thailand, 14 Dec 1997
* Formerly Naim Suleimanov or Neum
Shalamanov of Bulgaria

Bodyweight 59 kg (130 lb)
Snatch: 100 kg (220¹/₄ lb)
Zou Feie (China)
Pusan, South Korea, 13 May 1997
Jerk: 125 kg (275¹/₂ lb)
Suta Khassaraporn (Thailand)
Jakarta, Thailand, 13 Oct 1997
Total: 220 kg (485 lb)
Chen Xiaomin (China)
Hiroshima, Japan, 4 Oct 1994
Bodyweight 64 kg (141 lb)
Snatch: 107.5 kg (237 lb)
Chen Xiaomin (China)
Guangzhou, China, 10 July 1997
Jerk: 130.5 kg (287¹/₂ lb)
Shi Lihua (China)
Lahti, Finland, 9 Aug 1997
Total: 235 kg (518 lb)
Li Hongyun (China)
Istanbul, Turkey, 22 Nov 1994
Bodyweight 70 kg (154¹/₄ lb)
Snatch: 105.5 kg (232¹/₂ lb)
Xiang Fenglan (China)
Chiang Mai, Thailand, 11 Dec 1997
Jerk: 131 kg (288³/₄ lb)
Xiang Fenglan (China)
Chiang Mai, Thailand, 11 Dec 1997
Total: 235 kg (518 lb)
Xiang Fenglan (China)
Chiang Mai, Thailand, 11 Dec 1997

yachting

World Yachting Records
Olympic titles
The first sportsman ever to win
individual gold medals in four
successive Olympic Games was Paul
Elvstrøm (Denmark) in the Firefly
class in 1948 and the Finn class in
1952, 1956 and 1960.
Paul Elvstrøm also won eight other world
titles in a total of six classes.
AMERICA'S CUP
There have been 29 challenges since
8 Aug 1870, with the USA winning on
every occasion except 1983 (to
Australia) and 1995 (to New Zealand).
In individual races sailed, US boats have
won 81 races
Foreign challengers have won 13 races.
Most appearances in the America's Cup
Dennis Conner – six appearances
since 1974.

ZHAN XUGANG OF CHINA AT THE 1996
OLYMPICS IN ATLANTA, WHERE HE SET WORLD
RECORDS IN SNATCH, JERK AND TOTAL. HIS
TOTAL RECORD REMAINED THE BEST MARK WHEN
THE GOVERNING BODY RESTRUCTURED THE
CATEGORIES AND CONSIGNED THE RECORDS AS
OF 31 DEC 1997 TO THE ARCHIVES.

THE USA COMPETING DURING THE AMERICA'S
CUP. THE USA HAVE DOMINATED THE
COMPETITION THROUGHOUT ITS HISTORY,
LOSING ONLY TWO CHALLENGES SINCE THE FIRST
WAS MADE IN 1870.

Bodyweight 83 kg (183 lb)
Snatch: 180 kg (396³/₄ lb)
Pyrros Dimas (Greece)
Atlanta, USA, 26 July 1996
Jerk: 214 kg (471¹/₄ lb)
Zhung Yong (China)
Guangzhou, China, 12 July 1997
Total: 392.5 kg (865¹/₄ lb)
Pyrros Dimas (Greece),
Atlanta, USA, 26 July 1996
Bodyweight 91 kg (200¹/₂ lb)
Snatch: 187.5 kg (413¹/₄ lb)
Aleksey Petrov (Russia)
Atlanta, USA, 27 July 1996
Jerk: 228.5 kg (503³/₄ lb)
Akakide Kakhiasvilis (Greece)
Warsaw, Poland, 6 May 1995
Total: 412.5 kg (909¹/₄ lb)
Aleksey Petrov (Russia)
Sokolov, Czech Republic,
7 May 1994
Bodyweight 99 kg (218¹/₄ lb)
Snatch: 192.5 kg (424¹/₄ lb)
Sergey Syrtsov (Russia)
Istanbul, Turkey, 25 Nov 1994
Jerk: 235 kg (518 lb)
Akakide Kakhiasvilis (Greece)
Atlanta, USA, 28 July 1996
Total: 420 kg (925³/₄ lb)
Akakide Kakhiasvilis (Greece)
Atlanta, USA, 28 July 1996

WOMEN'S WEIGHTLIFTING RECORDS
Bodyweight 46 kg (101¹/₄ lb)
Snatch: 81.5 kg (179¹/₂ lb)
Jiang Yinsu (China)
Pusan, South Korea, 11 May 1997
Jerk: 105.5 kg (232¹/₂ lb)
Xing Fen (China)
Guangzhou, China, 8 July 1997
Total: 185 kg (407³/₄ lb)
Guang Hong (China)
Yachiyo, Japan, 4 April 1996
Bodyweight 50 kg (110¹/₄ lb)
Snatch: 88 kg (194 lb)
Jiang Baoyu (China)
Pusan, South Korea, 3 July 1995
Jerk: 110.5 kg (243¹/₂ lb)
Liu Xiuhua (China)
Hiroshima, Japan, 3 Oct 1994
Total: 197.5 kg (435¹/₄ lb)
Liu Xiuhua (China)
Hiroshima, Japan, 3 Oct 1994
Bodyweight 54 kg (119 lb)
Snatch: 93.5 kg (206 lb)
Yang Xia (China)
Guangzhou, China, 9 July 1997
Jerk: 117.5 kg (259 lb)
Mengh Xiajuan (China)
Chiang Mai, Thailand, 8 Dec 1997
Total: 207.5 kg (457¹/₄ lb)
Yang Xia (China)
Guangzhou, China, 9 July 1997

Bodyweight 76 kg (167¹/₂ lb)
Snatch: 107.5 kg (237 lb)
Hua Ju (China)
Chiang Mai, Thailand, 12 Dec 1997
Jerk: 140.5 kg (309³/₄ lb)
Hua Ju (China)
Chiang Mai, Thailand, 12 Dec 1997
Total: 247.5 kg (545¹/₄ lb)
Hua Ju (China)
Chiang Mai, Thailand, 12 Dec 1997
Bodyweight 83 kg (183 lb)
Snatch: 117.5 kg (259 lb)
Tang Weifang (China)
Chiang Mai, Thailand, 13 Dec 1997
Jerk: 143 kg (315¹/₄ lb)
Tang Weifang (China)
Chiang Mai, Thailand, 13 Dec 1997
Total: 260 kg (573 lb)
Tang Weifang (China)
Chiang Mai, Thailand, 13 Dec 1997
Bodyweight over 83 kg (183 lb)
Snatch: 112.5 kg (248 lb)
Wang Yanmei (China)
Guangzhou, China, 14 July 1997
Jerk: 155 kg (341¹/₄ lb)
Li Yajuan (China)
Melbourne, Australia, 20 Nov 1993
Total: 260 kg (573 lb)
Li Yajuan (China)
Melbourne, Australia, 20 Nov 1993

Admiral's Cup
The ocean racing team series to have
had the most participating nations
(three boats allowed to each nation) is
the Admiral's Cup, organized by the
Royal Ocean Racing Club.
A record 19 nations competed in 1975,
1977 and 1979.
Britain has had a record nine wins.
Highest speeds
Men
The highest speed reached under sail on
water by any craft over a 500-m timed
run is 46.52 knots (86.21 km/h or
53.57 mph) by trifoiler *Yellow Pages
Endeavour* piloted by Simon McKeon and
Tim Daddo, both of Australia, at Sandy
Point near Melbourne, Australia, on
26 Oct 1993.
Highest speeds
Women
The highest speed reached under sail on
water by any craft over a 500-m timed
run is by Elisabeth Coquelle (France),
with 40.38 knots (74.83 km/h or
46.5 mph) at Tarifa, Spain, on
7 July 1995.

index

A/S Svindlands 60
A View To Kill 231
A Rose is Still a Rose 237
A-Ha 232
A3XX airbus 163
Aardman Animation, UK 218
Aaron, Hank 270
Abba 230-31
Abdul Aziz al-Saud, Prince 23
Abdul Aziz royal yacht 165
Abdul-Jabbar, Kareem 269
Abell 2029 galaxy cluster 148
Abingdon Island giant tortoise 136
Aboriginal art 37
Abraham-Louis Breguet watches 35
Abreindo Puertas 241
abseiling 301
absorbency 150
AC Milan football club 252
AC/DC 232
Academy Awards 12-13
acceleration: cars 158
Ace of Base 229
Achaearanea tepidariorum 129
acid rain 200
Aconcagua, Mount 286
acoustics 157
Action Direkt 301
Activision 171
actors 234; horror films 210;
    youngest 70
Adamkus, Valdus 26
Adams, Bryan 232
Adelaide Herald 50
Adeoye, Ajibola 266
Adidas 42, 302
advances: publishers' 217
Adventures of Hercules 110
advertisement: shortest 44
advertising 42-43, 44-45, 262;
    internet 176; pets 138;
    spending 249
Advertising Standards Authority 45
Advocate magazine 217
Adwatch 45
AE Inc. 172
aerial stunts 212-13
aerials: photography 58
aeroplane sickbags: collection 57
aeroplanes 162-63; escapes 92
aerospace companies 49
Afghanistan: landmines 204;
    purdah 91
African bush elephant 116
African giant frog 122
African lion 116
African sand dog 139
Africanized honey bee 134
Aga Khan 280
Agassi, Andre 29
age, old 102
age: oldest fish 120;
    oldest plant 140; oldest tree 141
AGM-130 missile 195
Agnelli, Giovanni 167, 280
Agostini, Giacomo 287

*Ah Lahm: The Story of a
    Stuntwoman* 212
Ahlerich (horse) 289
aid donation 47
AIDS: charities 22, 28-29; virus 104
air accidents 198, 199, 204
air crashes: royal accident 23
Air Jordans (Nike) 43
air pollution: India 200;
    Mexico City 200
Airbus Industrie 163
Airbus Super Transporter 162
aircraft: carriers 164; fastest
    propeller 162; fighter planes 195;
    manufacturers 49;
    spy-planes 197; unmanned 194
'Airiana' 224
airliners 163
airlines 49
airspeed 162
Akimoto, Mitsugu (Chiyonofuji) 282
Akira 218
Akiyoshi, Sadji (Futabayama) 282
Akram, Wasim 291
Al Ahly football club 253
al Awami, Samir Sawan 275
Al Fayed, Dodi 22, 33
Al Safi dairy farm, Saudi Arabia 49
Al Tunian, Youssef 255
al-Ayoub, Mouna 41
Ala Moana Center 40
Alabama (group) 238
Alacran tartarus 129
Albert One 178
Albina, Leontino 102
Albizziata falcata 140
albums: charts 232-33; classical
    music 242; jazz 243;
    on internet 176; sales 24, 228-29
Alcatraz prison 86
Aldous, Jay 79
algae 140
Algeria: journalists 205
Alice's Day At Sea 37
Alien 3 213
Alien Within Us, The 211
Alkana, Dr Ronald 60
All Around the World 235
All-Japan High-School Quiz 215
Allan-Shetter, Liz 296
Allen, Mark 303
Allen, Paul 179, 233
Allen, Ron 108
Allen, Sandy 96
Allmen, Urs von 277
Almas caviar 62
Almen, Rune 257
Alpert, Herb 231
Alpoim Inoue, José Carlos Ryoki de
    216
AltaVista 176
Althorp, UK 22
altitude, from Moon 189
Alton Towers, UK 74, 185
aluminium cans: building 68
Alvard Desert, USA 158
Alvarez, Reuben 267
Alves de Lima e Silva, Luís 71
Always Be My Baby 228
Alzheimer's disease 105

Amanita fungi 142
Amanpour, Christiane 14
amatoxins 143
Amazon, River 146
Amazon rainforest 146
Amazonian bamboo palm 141
Ambassadors Theatre 223
ambassadors: royal reception 29
Amber Room 35
Amblin Entertainment 180
Amboina, Indonesia 193
Ambrose, Curtly 290
American Airlines 49
American bolas spider 129
American Express 16, 41
American football 262-63;
    reference 304
American Power Boat Association
    280
American Telephone and Telegraph
    Company (AT&T) 48-49
American woodcock 126
Ames Research Centre 181
Ames, Kimberly 292
Ames, Rick 196
'Amityville Horror' 89
amplifiers 174
AMR Corporation 49
Amsterdamned 213
An Unseen Enemy 10
anaesthetic, in leeches 132
And God Created Great Whales 242
Andean condor 126
Andersen, Lisa 296
Anderson, Gillian 218
Anderson, James 267
Anderson, Pamela 177, 214
Andersson, Uf 75
Andes: landslide 202; plane crash 93
Andrew, Prince, wedding 215
Andrianov, Nikolay 264, 284
Anelosimus eximus 128
'Anémone' fountain pen 35
Ang Rita, Sherpa 300
'Angel of Death' 144
Angkor Wat, Cambodia 155
anglerfish, dwarf 120
angling: reference 304-05
Anglo-Chinese School, Singapore 74
Angola: landmines 23
Angolan currency 47
Anhalt, Prince Frederick von 11
Anheuser-Busch Inc. 49
Animal Actors Show 138
Animal Kingdom 48, 184
animals: endangered 136-37;
    new species 136-37
animated films 218-19
animation, computer 183
animators: insured hands 98
Annenberg, Walter 33
Annie 208, 213
Annie Hall 248
annual general meetings 49
Anquetil, Jacques 286
Answer Me 230
Antarctic crossings 79
Antarctica 146-47; ozone hole 200;
    space debris 204
Anthony, Barbara Cox 50
anti-aircraft missile 194

Antiquorum 35
Antley, Chris 288
Antonov An-225 Mriya plane 162
Antonov An-124 163
Antwerp, Belgium: relay run 257
Aoki, Isao 258
apartment blocks, tallest 154
Apartment No. 9 238
aphids 131
aphrodisiacs 150
apnea 107
Apollo 11 moon landing 188
Apollo 13 spacecraft 189
Apollo spacecraft 186;
    space missions 182
appendectomy 106
Appetite For Destruction 233
applause, opera 242
Apple Computers 174
Apple Macintosh 44
apple strudel, biggest 61
Appleby, Phil 75
Applied Biosystems 145
Arabian camel 119
arachnids 225
Arachnophobia 128
Aral Sea 148; 201
Arapaima gigas 120
Archaos 224
archery: Paralympics 266;
    reference 305
Archie, snail 74
Arctic Ocean 146
Arctic: oil pollution 201
Arden, John 223
Arfeuille, Walter 64
Argentina: polo 289
Argiropoulos, Eleftherios 292
Argumenty y Fakty newspaper 216
Aria Awards 229
Arias, Jimmy 261
Ark of the Covenant 90
armadillo 119
Armani, Georgio 248
Armenia: GNP 47
arms: robots 181
Armstrong, Louis 72, 231
Armstrong, Vic 212
Army Corps of Brasília 76
Arnold Classic title 110
Arocarpus kotschubeyanus 142
arrests 87
arrow, human 224
Arsovic, Goran 75
art: collections 51;
    galleries 156; stolen treasures 35;
    supermarket 40; thefts 221;
artists: body 112-13; earnings 53;
    elephant 138
Arts for Transit 220
As Good as It Gets 12
Asahi, Japan 16
Ascaris lumbricoides 132
ascendants, living 102
Ascot 289
Ashes, 1993 (cricket) 291
Ashford, Evelyn 256
Ashpole, Ian 299
Asikáinen, Alfred 283
Aspel, Michael 15

aspen trees 140
assassination 84, 196, 236;
    Versace 248
assets, company 49
Assinger, Armin 277
asteroids 149
astronauts: oldest 72
astronomy 148-49
At Close Range 111
AT&T Bell Laboratories 182
AT&T Corporation 45
Atacama Desert 147, 181
Atahualpa, Inca emperor 85
Ataturk, Mustafa 165
Athletico Madrid 252
athletics 256-57; reference 305
Atkin, Anne 56
Atkinson, Rowan 215
Atkisson, Andee and Gil 34
Atlanta Braves 51, 270
Atlanta Hawks 51
Atlantic Empress 201
Atlantic hair grass 142
Atlantic ridley (turtle) 125
Atlas missile 194
atomic bomb 194
ATS 5 satellite 187
auctions 34-35, 36; art 220-21;
    clothes 22
Audi 100 TDI 159
audiences: boxing 282; classical
    concert 242; musicals 222;
    rock concerts 232; TV 44
audio transmitters 197
AudioNote Ongaku 174
Auditória Nacionál 240
Auditorium Organ 243
Auerman, Nadja 21
Aurangamirri 37
Auriol, Didier 273
'Aurora' spy-plane 197
Auschwitz 144, 193
Austin, Megan 102
Austin, Tracy 260
Austine, Brett 285
Australia, gambling 38
Australian dragonfly 131
Australian pelican 126
Australian sea wasp 135
auto flight 76
autobiographies: canine 138;
    youngest writer 71
automation 181
Autonomous House, UK 156
AutoPC car computer system 161
avalanches 93, 202
Ayub, Osman 225
Azagury, Jacques 23
Azharuddin, Mohammad 290
Aznavour, Charles 230
Aztecs 90

B'Nkobo, Professor Charlemagne 137
B-52 bombers 194

Babashoff, Shirley 274
babies 102, 103; weight 97
Baby Bird plane 163
Baby Leroy 70
Baby Woman 20
Babylon 26
Babylon Zoo 44
Baccara 241
Back In Black 232
Bacrot, Etienne 70
bacteria: genetically engineered 144
Bad (cat) 138
Bad 228, 237
'Bad Boy Drive', Hollywood 11
badminton: reference 306
Badrutt, Johannes 294
Bagmati River 198
Baha'i religion 91
Bahamonde's beaked whale 137
Bahrein: taxation 46
baiji (Yangtze River dolphin) 136
Baikonur Cosmodrome 186-87, 199
Bailey, Alison and Ian 81
Bailey, David 20
Bailey, Donovan 256
Bailey, Robert 263
Baird, Dale 288
Baker, Erin 303
Baku, Azerbaijan 198
Bakunus, A. J. 212
balance of payments: Japan 46;
    USA 46
balancing, one foot 67
Balas, Iolanda 257
Balczó, András 302
bald eagle 127
Baldwin, Brenda Nichols 314
Baldwin, William Ivy 72
Ball, Gary 300
Ballesteros, Severiano 258
ballet 222
balloons 72; hot-air balloons 78;
    toy balloon flights 299
Baltimore Colts 262
Baltimore Road Runners Club 257
Baluchistan pygmy jerboa 117
bamboos 140
Ban Yue Tan magazine 217
bananas: eating 60; Somalia 46
Banca Nazionale del Lavoro 85
Band Aid 28
Bandaranaike, Sirimavo 27
banded louse 130
Bangladesh: marriages 71
Banham, Carl 74
banks 49; bank robbery 85; fraud 85
Bank of Tokyo-Mitsubishi 49
bankers 52
banknotes: collection 57
bankruptcies 49; Maxwell 51
Banks, Tyra 249
Banqiao dam, China 203
banyan, great 141
Bapu, Mastram 67
Barbara Sinatra Children's Center 29
Barbaric, Juraj 64
barbeque 60
Barber, Robert E. 158
Barber-Nichols Engineering Company
    158
Barbie dolls 56; creator 11; fans 58
Barcelona football club 252, 254
Bárdos, György 289
Bari, Wasim 291
Barilla pasta advertisement 12
Barindelli, Fiorenzo 56
Barings Bank 85
bark painting 37
Barnes, Maggie 102
Barnett, Sandra 287
Barnum, P. T. 88

Barnum 222
Barnum and Bailey Circus 100, 224
Barr, Roseanne 15
Barret Technology, USA 181
Barrie, Patrick 75
Barrymore, Drew 71, 210
Barry (dog) 93
Bartlett, Brother Michael 78
Barty, Billy 13
Barzan Ibrahim 26
baseball 270-71;
    baseball bat (replica) 270;
    reference 306
Basic Instinct 10, 53, 208
Basinger, Kim 13
basketball 268; earnings 16
bass strings 243
bass voices 242-43
Bass, Richards 300
Basseto, Leandro Henrique 76
Bassey, Shirley 231
Bassogigas 120
Basualdo, Betiana 267
Bat Out Of Hell 232
bat rescue 93
Bata, Sonja 56
Batalova, Rima 266
Bates, Anna 97
Bates, Martin van Buren 96
bath tub racing 75
Bathori, Elizabeth 84
bathyscaphe 79; survey 199
Batman 208-09, 219, 229
Batman and Robin 14, 111
Batman Forever 208
bats 116, 119
Battersea funfair 198
battles: deaths 192
Baumann, Roberta 37
Baumgartner, Bruce 283
Baxter, Trevor 293
Bayfield School 67
Baywatch 177, 214
BCF Holland b.v. 74
Be Here Now 232
Bédard, Myriam 303
Beach Boys 239
beach volleyball 293
bead implants 112
Beale, Fiona 76
beards 100; beard hair 99
bears: polar 134; attack 70
Beatles, The 18, 228, 230;
    memorabilia 36
Beatty, Warren 11
Beaujolais Nouveau 62
Beauty and the Beast 218
beauty contests 109
beavers 119
Becker, Boris 260
Beckett, Samuel 223
bed making 67, 68
bed racing 75
bedbug, common 132
Bedtime for Bonzo 12
Bedtime Story 70
Bee Gees 230, 234
bee hummingbirds 126
Beeding, Eli 107
beef: Japanese 62; tapeworm 132
Beene, Geoffrey 248
beer 49; beer keg lifting 64;
    festivals 63; sampling 58
Beerbaum, Ludge 288
bees 133, 225; Africanized honey
    bee 134
Beethoven, Ludwig van 99
beetles 130-31
'Beetles' cars 158-59
Beezley, Doris 139
Begin the Beguine 241

Behram, a Thug 84
Behrendt, Jan 265, 295
Beilinson Hospital 106
Belarus 205; economy 46
Belaur, Eugene 67
Belgian Grand Prix 286
Belgian Railway Company 165
Bell, Douglas and Roger 167
Bell, Jay 283
Bellamy, Mike 281
Bellanca Decathalon 298
Ben Nevis, Scotland 301
Ben Hur 212
bench-pressing 111;
    bench press record 285
Benedictine Monks 231
Benetton 272; advertising 45
Benjamin, Edward 224
Benkel, Michelle 68
Benn, Nigel 98
Bentalls store delivery van: Dinky 37
benzoate 150
bequests: corporation 49
Berbick, Trevor 16
Berezovsky, Boris 52
Berg, Alban 242
Berg, Stephan van den 297
Bergen, Candice 110
Berghmans, Ingrid 283
Berkley-White, Sheila 23
Berlin: battle of 192: Berlin,
    Germany: Love Parade 244;
    Tunnel 196; Berlin Wall 196
Bernhardt, Sarah 19
Bertelsmann AG 49
Bertschinger, Christian 294
beryllium 200
Best Little Girl in the World 12
Best Actor Awards 12
Best Actress Awards 13
best-sellers 216-17
Bester, Madge 96
Betelgeuse 148
Bettencourt, Liliane 32
betting 38-39; odds 39
beverage companies 49
Beverly Hills 90210 11, 214
Beverly Hills High School 10
Beverly Hills Hotel 10
Beyond The Season 238
Bhutto, Benazir 26
Bianchini, Maria Esperanza Medrano
    90
biathlon 303
Bibbia, Nino 294
Bible: best-seller 216
biceps 110
bicycles 166-67; acrobatics 224;
    eating 63
Bielak, Thierry 297
Big and Little Wong Tin Bar 212
big dipper crash 198
Big Foot 88
Big Issue 217
Big Racket (racehorse) 288
Bike Week, Daytona Beach 166
Biland, Rolf 287
Billboard charts 234-35;
    country charts 238; Health and
    Fitness Chart 111; R&B chart 237;
    Rap Chart 236
billiard tables 34
billionaires 32-33, 50-51, 52-53
Bilozerchev, Dmitriy 284
biltong 126
Binder, Franz 'Bimbo' 252
bingo 39
Binion's Horseshoe, Las Vegas 38
binoculars 173
Biondi, Matt 274
biplanes 163

bird of paradise flower 140
bird-eating spider 128-29
bird-ringing 58
birds 126-27; birds of prey 126, 136;
    dangerous 134; endangered
    136-37; birdspotters 58
Birdwatch Kenya '86 58
birth certificate 36
birthday parties 28-29
births 103; post mortem 106
bite, strength in sharks 134-35
Bizarre Fruit 234
Bjørdalsbakka, Grete 257
Björk 228
Black, Cilla 15
Black, Shane 52
Black and White 296
Black Box 234
Black Cat, The 211
Black death 104, 133-34
black-legged falconet 126
'Black Monday' 178
Black Rock Desert 158
black-tailed prairie dogs 119
black timber rattlesnake 124
Blackie (cat) 139
blackjack 39
Blackout, The 20
Blackwell, Rory 64
Bladon, Stuart 158, 159
Blair, Tony 26
Blake, Margaret 103
Blake, Peter and Knox-Johnston,
    Robin 79
Blanco, Ramón 72
Blanda, George 262
Blankers-Koen, Fanny 256
Blatty, William 210
Blessitt, Arthur 80
Bletchley, Edward 254
Blind Date 15
blind sprinting 266
Blons, Austria 202
blood-letting 85
blood-suckers 130, 132
blood sugar 106
blood transfusion 106
bloodsucking insects 130
Bloomingdales 18
Blow, Isabella 20
Blue 239
blue-eyed lemur 137
Blue Flame 158
Blue Lagoon 14
blue-ringed octopus 135
Blue Streak roller coaster 184
blue whales 119
Blue Wolf Productions 53
bluefin tuna 62, 120
Blume, Martin 76
Blutrausch (Blood Frenzy) 138
Boardman, Chris 308
boardsailing 72, 297
boats 165
bobsleigh 294
body art 112-13
body temperature 106
Body World exhibition 98
bodybuilding 110-11
Bodyguard, The 18, 231
Boeing Company 49, 195;
    Boeing 747-400 162; bomb 198;
    collision 198, 199; lightning strike
    203; pulled by hand 64
bog snorkelling 74
Boggs, Philip 275
Bogotá, Colombia, murder rate 84
Bohemian Rhapsody 29, 229
Bois, Curt 12
Bokassa, Emperor 35
Bol, Manute 96

bird of paradise flower 140
Bolaffi, Alberto 36
Boldt, Arnold 267
Boldt, Beth 20
Bollig, Christopher 102
Bolsheviks 23
bomb explosions 198-99
Bombay, India 215; office rents 48
bombers 195
bombers, long-range 193
bombing, precision 192
Bon Marché 44
bondegezou 137
bone-cutting lasers 182
Bonfire (clothing) 294
Bonfire of the Vanities 216
Bonham's auctioneers 36
Bonneville Salt Flats, USA 158
bonuses 53
books 216-17; auctioned 22
bookmakers 39
Boomerang 12
boomerang throwing 67
Boorman, Martin 193
boots: Dr. Martens 246
Bootscooting Boogie 68
Border, Allen 291
Borg, Arne 274
Borg, Björn 260
Born, Jorge and Juan 85
Born In The USA 18, 232
Bornhofer, Frank 225
Borobudur temple, Indonesia 155
Borsi, Louis 159
Bosnia, crying statue 91
Bosnia Herzegovina 193
Boston Bruins 279
Boston Celtics 268
Boston Red Sox 270
Botha, Wendy 296
Boucher, Denis and Andre 80
Boulby Potash Mine, UK 301
bouncy castle installation 220
Bourgnon, Laurent 78
bovine spongiform encephalitis (BSE)
    105
Bowden, Jim 79
Bowen, Joe 81
Bower, Ron and Williams, John 78
Bowie, David 18, 232
box office takings 208, 210, 218
boxing 283; earnings 16;
    gloves 37, 283; memorabilia 37
Boxing Helena 13
boy bands 228-29
Boy Scouts of America 69
Boyz II Men 228, 236
Boyzone 229
brachiosaurids 125
bracket fungus 140
Bradford, Rosalie 97, 108
Bradley, Michael 258
Bragg, Professor Sir Lawrence 70
Brahminy blindsnake 124
brain-size: dinosaur 125
brains 99; surgery 182
Branch Dravidians 90
Branch Mall: internet 176
brand names 42-43
Brandenburg Gate 244
Brando, Marlon 11
Branson, Richard 52, 78, 280
bras 246
bratwurst, longest 60
bravery award 70
bravery: honey badger 119
Brazil: deforestation 200; fires 200;
    leprosy 105; soap operas 214;
    World Cup 254
'Brazil's girlfriend' 15
Brazilian football team 42, 254

Brazilian huntsman spider 134
breasts: implants 109; largest 109;
multiple 101
Breath 223
Breathless 243
breeding: mole rats 119
Breedlove, Norman 77
Breitner, Paul 255
Brenna, Mario 22
Brennan, Molly 158
Brenter, Erich 294
Brett, James Henry 106
Brett, Sylvia 72
breweries 49
Brice, Donna Patterson 297
Bricka, Rémy 81
bridge building 68
Bridgend Camp, UK 193
bridges 155; Europe's longest 63
Bridges to Babylon 232
Briers, Steve 65
Brigadoon 10
Briggs & Stratton 159
brisingid starfish 123
bristlemouth, fish 121
Brit Awards 228-29
British Airways 42, 45
British Bank of the Middle East 85
British Film Institute 51, 219
British Motor Show 160
British Rail 164
British Telecom 45, 254
Britton, Dan 242
Broad, Eli 41
Broad, Michael 273
broad tapeworm 132
broadcasting: Olympics 264
Broadhurst, Paul 258
Broadway, New York 222
Brockskothen, Britta 266
Broderbrund 170
Broderick, Matthew 110
Brodrick, Geraldine 103
Brodsky, Alexander 220
brokers 46
Bromeliaceae 140
Bronson, Charles and Ireland, Jill 12
Brooker, Tim 281
Brookes, Norman 261
Brooks, Garth 238
Brooks, Robert 263
Brooks and Dunn 68
Broomfield, Nick 24
Brosnan, Pierce 212
Brough, Althea and Du Pont,
Margaret 260
Brown, Anthony 290
Brown, Dick 67
Brown, James 234, 237
brown antechinus 118
brown rat 118
Brundle, Martin 158
Bryant, Kobe 269
Bryant, Rob 81
BSE: bovine spongiform encephalitis
105
bubble blowing 66
bubble cars 37
bubblegum: blowing 66;
collection 57
Bubka, Sergey 257, 306
bubonic plague 104, 133-34;
rats 118
bucket chain 69
Buckingham Palace 22; parties 29
Buckstaff, John 295
Buddelmeyer, Petra 266-67
Buddha 90
Buddhism 90
Buddhist temples 155
Buderim Tavern 61

Buffalo Bills 262
Buffet, Warren 50, 53
Bufo taitanus beiranus, smallest
toad 122
bufotoxins 150
Bug Bowl, Indiana 74
Bugatti, Ettore 159;
'Royale' 159
Buggenhagen, Maria 266
bugs: spying 197
building: beavers 119
buildings 154-55; expensive 48;
future 156-57
Bulgaria: CD piracy 43;
pollution 200; rhythmic
gymnastics 285
bullet-proof bra 56
Bumble Bee Two 163
bumblebee bat 116
Bunge, Augusta 102
bungee jumping 298
Bungkas 67
Bunker, Chang and Eng 100
Bunny, John 98
Burbach, Franz 224
Burda Moden magazine 216
Burge, Heather and Heidi 96
Burnett, Charles III 280
burning: film stunts 213
burpees 303
Burridge, Pam 296
burrowing boa 136
Burt, Tal 79
Burton, Richard 10, 13, 209
Busch Clash car race 273
Busch Gardens theme park 184
Bush, George 26, 138
bush babies 118
business 42-43
business tycoons 50-51
businessmen 52-53
Butcher Boy 212
Buthelezi, Chief Mangosuthu 27
Buttle, Elizabeth 103
butyl seleno-mercaptan 150

C&C Music Factory 234
C'est La Vie perfume 249
cabbage aphids 131
cacti 141-42; oldest 142
Caesar's Palace 77
Cage, John 242
Cage, Nicolas 10, 12
Cairns, Chris 290
Cairns and District Powerboating
and Ski Club 297
cake, tallest 61
calculation: computer 179
Caldera, Rafael 27
calf (cloned) 145
Calgene, USA 145
California Angels 271
Californian condors 126, 136
Californian Spangled cats 138
Californian trap-door spider 129
Calle Ocho 68
Calment, Jeanne 102
Calvin Klein 20, 246
Cambodia: King Norodom 23
Camelion Bonfire (horse) 289
cameo cast 18
cameras, Game Boy 172
cameras: digital 173;
expensive 174; Polaroid 173;
spying 197

Campbell, Naomi 20, 248
Campbell, Winifred 106
camping 67
Camping Cosmos 109
Campos, Dave 166
Can You Feel the Love Tonight 218
Can't Help Falling In Love 236
Canada: education budget 47;
lacrosse 310
Canadian Championship (ice hockey)
279
cancer 105; cure 98
Candle In The Wind 22
cane toad 122, 150
Canfield Fair, Ohio 68
cannibalism 93
cannonballs, human 224
Cano, R. J. 144
canoe raft 297
canoeing 297; reference 306
Canon Eos 1N-RS 174
Canon scanners 173
canopy stack, parachuting 298
Canton 262
Canutt, Yakima 212
canyons: Mars 149
CAP virus 178
Capablanca, José Raúl 75
Capcom Entertainment 170
Cape Canaveral 187
capital punishment 86-87
Cappellini, Guido 280
Capper, David 174
Capriati, Jennifer 260
Caprice 246
capybaras 116
caravans: horse-drawn 80; towing 76
Carbajal, Antonio 255
carbon subnitride 151
carbon monoxide 160, 200
carcinogens 150, 200-01
cardiac arrest 106
Cardiff Giant 88
Cardwell, Faith, Hope and Charity 102
Care for the Wild International 136
career earnings, sport 16-17
Carey, Mariah 228
cargo capacity: aeroplanes 162-63
Carlsson, Erik 273
Carlton, Stephen 270
Carmichael, Al 263
Carne, Simon 212
Carnegie, Andrew 51
Carnegie Peace Fund 51
carnivals 244-45
carnivorous plants 142-43
Caroline in the City sitcom 216
Carr, Joseph 258
Carradine, John 210
Carreras, José 242
carriage driving 289
Carrie 211, 222
cars 158-59; crashes 24;
diesel-powered 158;
driving 76-77; future 160-61;
largest 159; powerful 159;
production 159; racing 272-73;
smallest 159; solar 158;
stunts 213; washing 68
Carson, Brian 76
Cartell International 24-25
Cartier jewellers 34
Cartland, Dame Barbara 216
Casablanca, John 21
Casey, Paul 138
Casino Royale 10
casinos 38-39
Caslavska-Odlozil, Vera 264, 284
Casperson, Dana 220
Cassatt, Mary 220

Casserly, Peter 65
cassowaries 134
Castle, Carry 299
Castlemaine XXXX 45
Castro, Fidel 27
cat flea 131
cat snakes 225
catalogue, Diana's dresses 22
Catão, Mozart Hastenreiter 286
catfish 120
Catflexing 138
cathedrals 155
Cats musical 222
cats 116, 136; advertisements 138
Cavalese ski resort 198
Cavanagh, Walter 41
caviar 62, 121
CBS Television City 28
CCD digital camera 197
CD players 173, 174-75
CD piracy 43
César awards 12
Cedar Point 184
Celebration, Florida 156
celebrities 24-25; in advertising 44;
hair 56
cells: human 98
cellular phones 172
cemeteries 24, 155; Hollywood 10
Centaur 2060 Chiron 149
centenarians 102
centipede, human 68
Centre Pompidou 221
Centre Socio-Cultural d'Endoume 74
Cepeda, Enrique 267
Cephalodiscus graptolitoides 137
ceratopsids 125
Cernan, Capt. Eugene 188
Cesa 281
Cessna 172 'Hacienda' 162
chainsaw, surgical 35
chair balancing 64
Chakrabarty, Ananada 144
Chakraborty, Rajkumar 67
Challenge Dunlop gumboots 66
Challenger spacecraft 188, 199
chamber pots: collection 57
Chamberlain, Richard 10
Chamberlain, Wilt 268
Chambers, Anne Cox 50
champagne 62
Chan, Jackie 212
Chan, Paul 59
Chanda-Leah (poodle) 139
Chander, Jagdish 66
Chandlers Restaurant, Seattle 122
Chanel 248; dress 41;
No. 5 perfume 249
Chanel, Coco 249
Chang, Michael 260
Change 235
Change Your Smile 109
Channareth, Tun 204
Channel Tunnel 155
Chant 231
Chaplin, Charlie 24, 98
Chapman, Roger and Mallinson,
Roger 92
Chappell, Greg 290
Chardon, Ijsbrand 289
Charisse, Cyd 10
charities: Diana 22; donations 51;
fundraising 28, 68-69;
philanthropists 33; shops 247
Charles I, King of England 99
Charles Schwab & Co. 177
Charlie Brown 219

Charly 234
Charpentier, Robert 286
charts: Latin music 240-41; pop 230
Chas H. Challen & Son, UK 243
Chasen's, Hollywood 63
Château de Savigny-Les-Beaune 56
Château Lafite claret 62
Chater, Eddie 281
Chatham Islands: millennium 245
Chaumet jewellers 34
Checker, Chubby 229
cheetah 118
Cheevers, Gerry 279
chefs, TV 14
Chek Lap Kok airport 41
chelonians 124-25
Chelsea Hotel, New York 19, 25
chemical warfare 192-93, 194
Chen Tze-Tung 258
Chen Yanqing 285
Chenoweth, Dean 281
Chernobyl 200, 205
cherry pie 61
Cherry Pink and Apple Blossom White
231, 241
cherry stone spitting 66
Chesman, Andy 280
chess: computer 178; titles 75;
youngest Grand Master 70
chest measurements: gorilla 116;
strongmen 110
Chester Zoo 117
chestnut, European 141
Chevrolet Caprice Classic 76
Chi Chi (dog) 139
Chiburdanidze, Maya Grigoryevna 75
Chicago Bears 262
Chicago Bulls 16, 268
Chicago Skate Company 292
Chicken Dance 68
chicken eating 60
chickens 139
child performers 12
children 70-71
Childs, David 298
Chilean rose tarantula 128
Chillag, Yosef and Victoria 106
Chillal, Shridar 101
chilli: expensive 63
chimpanzees 119
China: air accidents 204; Buddha's
ashes 90; clothing industry 247;
crime 84; death penalty 86;
hepatitis B 105; prisoners 86;
TV sets 215
Chinachem Group 52
Chinese dumpling 61
'Chinese Elvis' 59
Chinese State Circus 67, 224
Chloé 248
chocolate 150
cholera 104
Chorisbar (racehorse) 288
Chorus Line 222
chorus lines 222
Choudhury, Mohammed Salahuddin
and Neena 77
Chow Tai Fook Jewellery Co. 34
Christian Lacroix 21
Christie, Agatha 216, 223
Christie's: London 19, 34-36, 62,
218, 243; New York 22, 36
Christmas cards 59
Christo 220-21
chromosomes 98
Chrysler 18, 49, 161
Chung Ju Yung 51
CIA 196-97
cicadas 131
Ciccone, 'Madonna' Louise 19
cichlid, mouth-brooding 121

cigars 35
cincinnus flower 140
Cinderella 209
circulation: newspapers 216
circumnavigation: balloon 78;
    car 77; flight 78; motorbike 79;
    sailing 79; skating 292; youngest
    person 70
circuses 224-225;
    Circus of Horrors 224;
    Cirque du Soleil 225; stars 112
Citicorp 52
Citizen printers 173
Citroën AX 14DTR 158
Civic GX vehicle 160
civil war: China 193
clam, marine giant 122
Clancy, Tom 217
claret, expensive 62
Clarion in-car computer unit 161
Clark, Mary Higgins 53
Clarkson, Roland 179
Classic Touch (horse) 288
classical music 242-43
claws: dinosaur 125
cleaning, by robot 181
Clemens, Roger 270
Cleopatra 10, 209
Cleveland Cavaliers 269
Cleveland Performance Art
    Festival 245
click beetle 131
Cliffhanger 212-13
Cline, Patsy 238
Clinton, Hillary Rodham 27
Clinton, Bill 109, 176
cloning: human 144; monkeys 144
Clooney, George 14, 209, 214
clothes 22, 248-49
clothing: brands 43; ex-pop star 18;
    secondhand 247
Clouse, John D. 80
clovers 140;
    four-leaved collection 57
Club Med I motor-sailer 165
clubs 244
CN Tower 154
CNN: international news 214;
    internet news 177
Co-operative movement anniversary
    61
coaches (football) 262
coal: carrying race 74; shovelling 68
coast redwood trees 141
Cobain, Kurt 24, 232
cobra, king 134
Coca-Cola 42; company 49;
    recycled cans 68; Museum 49
cocaine 84
Cochet, Henri 261
cockroaches 12, 130-31; robot 180
cocktail, biggest 61
coco-de-mer 141
Coconut Tree Climbing Competition
    65
Codling's lizard 137
coffee 63
'Cola Wars' 43
cold, common 105
cold survival 92
Cold War 196
Cole, Nat 'King' 237
Cole, Terry 74, 303
collections 56-57
collisions: at sea 199;
    mid-air 199
Colombia: kidnapping 204;
    murder rate 84
Colombian Open golf 258
Color Purple, The 14
Colorado potato beetle 145

Colston, Ian 259
Colt 600 hot-air balloon 78
Columbia spacecraft 189
comas 106
Combat Simulation game 171
Combidrive 'Mouse' 159
Come Fly With Me 24
comedians: earnings 53;
    insurance 98
comets 149
Comic Relief 28
comic strips 219
Command & Conquer 171
Comme un Ouragan 23
Comme des Garçons 21
commercials 44-45
Commerzbank HQ 157
common flea 131
common tern 126
companies 48-49; clothing 246-47;
    losses 46
Compaq Computer Corporation 49
Composite Compact Vehicle 161
Compsognathus (dinosaur) 125
computers 178-79; animation 183;
    cars 161; computer-controlled
    shuttles 186; games 170-71;
    graphics 171; laptop 172;
    manufacture 49; networks 177;
    in space 179; viruses 88, 178
Computer Motion 181
Concept 2096 car 160
concert halls 157
conch, trumpet 123
Concorde 139, 163; oldest
    passenger 72; painted blue 43
Conde, Javier 266
Condemine, D. 281
condolence messages 22
condors 126
Conesco company 52
Coney Island Circus Sideshow 112
confinements 103
Confucius (K'ung Ch'iu) 102
conga dancing 68
Congo, Democratic Republic:
    Church 91; Ebola fever 105
Connery, Sean 109
Connolly, Maureen 260
conscription, of babies 71
Constance, Lake 299
Constantin, Prince of Liechenstein
    72
consultants' fees 53
consumer price index: Seychelles 47
consumption: food 60;
    hummingbirds 126
container ships 165
contract: breach 13
contracts: baseball 270-71;
    ethical 13; supermodels 20;
    US football 263
Conus, gastropod genus 135
Cook, Captain 125
Cook, John 162
Cooke, Leslie 63
Cooke, Norman 92
cooks: TV 14
Coombs, Sean (Puff Daddy) 236
Coon Butte 149
Cooper, Dave 292
Copeland, Billy 292
copepods 133
copper microchips 178
Copperfield, David 53, 224
Coquelle, Elisabeth 297
coral 122
Corbett, James 283
Core Design 171
Corlett, Robert and King, Mary Ann 56
Corman, Roger 210

Cornish, Clarence 73
corporations 48-49
Corriere della Sera 217
corset (Madonna's) 19
Corta, Rosanna Dalla 102
Cosmetic Surgery Network 108
cosmetics: contracts 20;
    industry 32
cosmopolitan sailfish 120
Coss, Lawrence 53
cost: rockets 186
Costa Rican golden toad 136
Costner, Kevin 210
costumes: film 209
Cottingley fairies 89
cotton: genetically modified 145
counterfeit goods 42
country and western music 238-39
Couples, Frederick 258
Court, Margaret 260
court cases 18
Cover Girl 20-21
Cowan, Andrew 273
Cowan, Nicholas 39
Cowboy Cadillac 238
Cowes to Torquay race 280-81
Cowra, Australia 193
cows 119; cow pat throwing 66
Cox, James 50
Cox, Patrick 138
Cox Enterprises 50
coxwains: youngest 71
crabs 122; Crabfest 122;
    parasitized 133
crackers: internet 177
Crampton, Bruce 258
crane, paper 61
Crane, Simon 213
cranes (birds) 126
Cranz, Christl 276
crash: internet 177
crashes: racing car 107
Craven, Wes 210
Crawford, Cindy 21, 29, 110-11
Crawford, Michael 222
crawling 66
Cray Research 179
Cray Y-MP C90 computer 178
crayfish 122
credit cards: collection 41;
    transaction 41
cremation: mass 105
crematoria 155
Cresta Run 72, 294
Crested Butte 295
Cretier, Jean-Luc 276
Creutzfeld Jacob Disease (CJD) 105
Crevier, Bruce 269
Crichton, Michael 53
cricket 290-91; bats 37;
    reference 307-08
cricket-spitting 74
Cricri aircraft 163
crime: internet 177
criminal organizations 84
criminals: plastic surgery 108
Criswell, Matt 74
Croatia: kayaking 297
crocodiles 124; saltwater 135
crocus flowers 151
Croft, Lara 171
crop circles 88
crop pictures 221
Crosby, Bing 230
cross-species transplants 144
crowds 262; basketball 269;
    football 262; World Cup
    football 254
cruise missiles 194
crustaceans 122; new species 136
Cryne, Paul 275

CSKA, Sofia football club 253
Cuba: presidency 27; cigars 35;
    music 240-41
Cuban solenodon 134
Cubillan, Diana Patricia 240
cues: billiard 34
Culinary Voyage Through Germany 26
Culkin, Macaulay 12
Cundy, Jody 267
Cunningham, Sean S. 211
Cure for Insomnia 209
Curse of Frankenstein, The 211
curtain calls 222, 242
Curtis, Bill 58
Curzon Cup (ski-bob) 294
cut-throat razor shaving 65
Cuthbert, Betty 256
Cuts Both Ways 240
Cutthroat Island 208
Cy Young Awards 270-71
Cyan 170
cyanide poisoning 90
cyanide pollution 201
Cybervention: Barbie dolls 58
cybugs 180
cycling: circumnavigation 79;
    journeys 79; racing 286-87;
    reference 308
cyclo-cross 286
cyclones 203
Cyprinodontidae 121
Cyprus: peacekeeping 193
Cyrano de Bergerac 12
Czech Republic: acid rain 200;
    president 26

D'Arros, Seychelles 33
D'eath, Tom 281
D'eux 230
d'Inzeo, Raimondo 288
d'Oriola, Pierre Jonquères 288
Da Ya Ne 236
Daehlie, Bjørn 276
Dahl, Sophie 20
Dahran, Didier 92
Daimler-Benz 49
dairy farms 49
daisy chains 69
Daiwa Bank 85
Dallas 214
Dallas Cowboys 44, 262
Dallas Market Center 40
Dallol, Ethiopia 147
Dall's porpoise 118
dam bursts 203
dams: 'intelligent' 156
dance music 234-35
dancers 222; legs 98
dancing 68; tap 66
Danes, Claire 208
Danger, Doug 76
Daniels, Charles 274
Dante, Dr Ronald 53
Dantley, Adrian 268
'Dare Devils' motorcycle team 76
Dark Side Of The Moon 232
darts: reference 308
Daryni, Tamás 274
Dashwood, Gemma 267
Dassault *Mirage 4* jet 56
dasyurids 119
David Morris International 175
Davidson, Bruce Oram 289
Davidson, Owen 260
Davidson, Samuel 107

Davis, Gary 213
Davis, Geena 13, 208
Davis, Miles 242
Davis, Ross 266
Davis, Terrell 304
Davis Cup (tennis) 261
Davlin, Dave 269
Davydov, Vitaliy 278
Day, Patrick 288
Day Well Spent 223
Daytona 273
Daytona International Speedway 166
De Credd, Jacqueline 76
De Gaulle, Charles 84
De Groot, Alwin 266-67
De Niro, Robert 12
Dead Sea 150
deadlifting 285
Deadly Weapons 13
Deak, Andrea 184
Dean, James 24
Dean, Millvina 92
death: causes of 105;
    crocodile 135; disease 104-05;
    earthquakes 202; on Everest 301;
    hailstones 147; penalty 86;
    piranha 135; rock concert 233;
    scorpions 134; in siege 192
death cap fungus 143
Death Row 87
Death Valley 147
debris in space 188
Debut 228
decathlon: reference 306
Decision Hour 91
Deep Blue computer 178
deer bot-fly 131
Def Jam 236
Def Leppard 233
defence mechanisms 134
DeFoe, Ronald 89
deforestation 200
Deildartunguhver hot springs,
    Iceland 147
Dejean, Claude 60
Del Amo Fashion Center 40
Delany, Sarah and Elizabeth 216
Dell Computers 176
Delta Blipper rocket 187
Demarchelier, Patrick 138
demolition, karate 68
Dempsey, Tom 263
Denby, Robert 62
Denmark: ODA 47; open society 26
density: neutron stars 151
dentistry 109; laser 182
Dentsu Young and Rubicam 42
Denver Broncos 262, 304
Depardieu, Gerard 12
department stores 40
Departure of the Argonauts 221
Depp, Johnny 25
Des Plaines: first McDonald's 49
descendants, living 102
descents from mountains 301
Deschutes Intel P6 178
Desert Breath 220
desert locusts 130
desert survival 92
designers 20; clothes 22, 248;
    underwear 246
Desormeaux, Kent 288
Desperately Seeking Susan 19
Destriero (boat) 78, 280
destroyers 195
Detective 219
detergent advertising 45
Detroit Auto Show 158
Detroit Pistons 268
Detroit Redwings 278
Detroit Tigers 270

deuterium-tritium plasma 151
development banks 49
Deveree, Janice 100
Devil's hole pupfish 136
DeVito, Danny 13
DeWaal, Matt 79
DeVries, Colleen 38
diabetes 107, 145
Diamantides, Hélène 301
Diamond Dream bra 249
diamonds 34
Diamonds Are Forever 175
Diana, Priness of Wales 22-23, 33, 248
Dianic Wicca, USA 91
diaries 59; hoax 89
Dibiasi, Klaus 275
DiCaprio, Leonardo 208-09
Dicks, David 70
dictators: rich 32
Diddy Kong races 170
Die Entführung aus dem Serail 243
Die Meistersinger von Nürnberg 243
diesel-engined cars 158
diesel trains: speed 164
diets: Hollywood 11; koala 119; ostriches 127; polar bear 118; strange 63
digenean liver fluke 132
digital cameras 173, 197
digital printers 173
Dillon *Colossal* 166
DiMaggio, Joe 270
Dinamo Berlin football club 253
Dinka tribe 96
Dinky toys 37
dinosaur robots 180
dinosaurs 125
Dinsamo, Belayneh 302
Dion, Celine 230, 232, 241
dioxides 200
diphtheria 105
directors: earnings 53; film 210-211; youngest 70
Dirks, Rudolph 219
Discos Columbia 241
Discovery space shuttle 186
Discovery STS 51G spacecraft 23
discus: Paralympics 266; reference 306; titles 264
diseases 104-05
Disney, Celebration 156
Disney, Walt 37, 48, 215, 218
Disney company 184
Disney-Lund, Sharon 22
Disney World 184
Dityatin, Aleksandr 264, 284
diving 275; free 79; scuba 79; spying 197; stunt 299; turtles 125; whales 118
Division Bell tour (Pink Floyd) 182
divorce: oldest couple 73; settlements 33
DJs 244
DNA: fingerprints 144; fossil 144; Marilyn Monroe's 25
DNTT performers 224
Do They Know It's Christmas 28
Dobre, Aurelia 284
Dock of The Bay 237
Dockers casualwear 246
document shredders 173
Dod, Lottie 260
Dodd, Ken 98
Dodgers 270
dogs: rescues 93; stuffed 37; TV stars 138
Doherty, Hugh 260
dolls 58
Dolly (sheep) 144-45
Dollywood theme park 238

Dolman, Sisi 285
domain names 177
Domingo, Placido 242
dominoes: stacking 67; toppling 69
Domsey's Warehouse, New York 247
Dona Paz ferry 199
Donahue, Pat 60
Donkey Kong 170
Don't Speak 232
Doors 233
Dornon, Sylvain 81
Dorsett, Tony 262
doubles: nude 12; Stalin's 108
Douglas, John Sholto, Marquess of Queensberry 283
Douglas, Kirk 10
Douglas, Michael 208
Doukas, Storm 20
Dow Corning Corporation 109
Dow Jones Index 178
Dow Jones Industrial average 46
Dowdeswell, Peter 60
Dowdeswell, Tony 60
Down Under 232
Downey, Robert 12
Doyle, Paddy 303
Doyle, Sir Arthur Conan 88, 209
Dr Beat 241
Dr. Martens 246
Dr No 208
Dr. Martens 246
Dracula, Count 211
Dracula 13
dragon: dancing 68; stuffed 69
Dragon Khan roller coaster 185
draughts 75
Dream Solar car 161
dreaming 107
Dreaming Of You 241
Dreamworks 18
dressage 289; Olympics 265
dresses: expensive 22; wedding 28
Drexel Burnham Lambert 87
Drexler, Millard 52
Dreyfuss, Richard 10
Driffield, Kelly 274
Driving Miss Daisy 13
dromedary 119
Dromiceiomimus 125
Drop Kick 12
Droppo, Moose 270
droughts 147, 203
drugs: abuse 24-25; trafficking 84
Drugstore: Levi advert 45
drumming 64
drunkenness, arrests 87
Du Pont, Margaret 260
Du Prisne, George 93
Duarte, Regina 15
Dubouchet, Karine 277
Duchess Theatre, London 223
Duchovny, David 14
ductility 151
Duets II 25
Duke Nukem 170
Duly, William 86
Dumfries, Johnny 272
Dunkerque: evacuation 192
Dunlop, Joey 287
Dunn, Irene 222
Dur Dur d'Etre Bébé 70, 236
Duran Duran 231
Durante, Jimmy 98
dusky shark 134
duty-free industry 33; shops 41
Duvall, Shelley 210
dwarf caimans 124
dwarf sea horse 120
Dylan, Bob 233
Dynasty 214
Dzerzhinsk, Russia 200

E-Go Rocket car 161
e-mail 88; users 177
E.S.P. Electronics Inc. 175
E.T.: the Extra-Terrestrial 13, 71, 215
Eagles, The 232
Eagle Boys Dial-a-Pizza 81
Eappen, Matthew 176
earnings 52-53; film 210; pop stars 18; sports 16-17
ears: body art 113; grafted 112
earthquakes 202, 204; airports 156
Earthships 156
East End X Yuri 236
East Germany: informers 196
East Japan Railway Company 48
East of Eden 24
East Pakistan: cyclone 203
Easter Egg 34
Easter Egg Roll 29
Eastwood, Clint 213
Ebola fever 104-05
echiuroids 133
eclipses 148
eco-friendly cars 160
Ecureuil d'Aquitaine II 79
Edberg, Stefan 261
Eddy, Christopher 269
Ederle, Gertrude 70
Edinburgh Fringe Festival 223
Edinburgh 244
Edmonton Oilers 278
education spending 47
Edwards, Grant 64
Edwin P. Hubble space telescope 186
eels 120-21
Egea, José Manuel 283
Egerszegi, Krisztina 274
Eggington, John 162
eggs: balancing 67; eating 60; fewest 121; insects 130, 132; largest 121, 127; numerous 121; throwing 66
Eidos Interactive 171
Einstein, Albert 36
Eisman, Hy 219
Eisner, Michael 52
El Gordo lottery 38
El Niño 200
El Pais newspaper 217
Elbrus, Mt, Russia 300
electric cars 160; speed 158
electric chair 86
electric eel 121
electric frog 137
electric powerboats 280
Electrolux company 181
Electronic Arts 171
elements: short-lived 151
elephant seal 116
elephants 116: artist 138; lifted by hand 64; relocation 136
Eleutherodactylus limbatus 122
Eli Lilly company 145
Elias, Antonio 186
Eliason, Göran 76
Eliot (horse) 288
Elite New York agency 20
Elizabeth II: Queen of England 29
Elizalde, Manuel 88
Elkington, Steve 258
Elle magazine 21, 96
Elleano, Charles 224
Elliott, Bill 273

Elliott, Cheri 295
Elliott, Kathy 271
Ellis, Jim 60
Elson, Karen 21
Elton John AIDS Foundation 29
Elvebakk, Anne-Elinor 303
Elvström, Paul 264-65
Embroden, Nord 293
emerald swift lizard 125
emeralds 34
Emerson, Roy 260
Emmanuel, Elizabeth and David 22
Emmanuelle 208
emperor moth 131
Emperor of Japan 29
emperor penguin 127
emperor scorpion 128
Emperor's Cup (sumo) 282
Emporio fashion show 248
Empty Quarter, Saudi Arabia 136
En Vogue 98
Ender, Kornelia 274
endoparasites 132-33
Energiya booster 186
Energy Determination carrier 199
energy-efficiency 156
engagements: longest 73
Engel, Kaspar 266
engines: car 158; capacity 159
England v. Australia Test, 1926 291
England v. South Africa Test, 1939 291
English, John 81
Engvall, David 66
Enigma 112
Enterprise space shuttle 58
entomology 74
environmental disasters 200-01
Enza 79
epiphytic orchid 141
Epperson, Kenneth 67
Equatorial Guinea: conscription 71
ER 14, 53, 214
Erhard, Werner 59
escalators 48
escape velocity 186
escapes 92-93; prison camps 193
Esposito, Elaine 106
Essquibo River, Guyana 201
Estefan, Gloria 240
estuarine crocodile 124
Esuke, Reginald 301
Eszterhas, Joe 53
Eternity perfume 21
ethics: actors' contracts 12
Ethiopia, religious relics 90
Ethiopian Famine Relief Fund 28
ethyl mercaptan 150
Eto'o, Samuel 255
eucalyptus: koala diet 119
eucalyptus trees 141
Eurasian woodcock 126
European buzzing spider 128
European Cup: football 253
European eel 120
Eurostar 164
Eurovision Song Contest 230-31
evacuation in war 192
Evangelista, Linda 20-21
Evening magazine 44
Everest, Mt 300-301; oldest climber 72
Everson, Cory 111
Evert, Chris 261
(Everything I Do) I Do It For You 232
Evita 19, 209
Ewry, Raymond 256, 264
executions 86, 87
executives: salaries 52
Exorcist 2 128
Exorcist, The 210

explosions: at sea 199; in space 199
Exxon Valdez 201
eyes: insured 98; largest 126; spiders 129; squid 122; surgery 182; tarsiers 118
eyesight 127; defective 105
eyeworms 132

F117A Stealth Fighter 195
F22 Raptor 195
F300 Life-Jet car 161
Fabergé eggs 34
faces: insurance 98
Fahd, King of Saudi Arabia 23
Fahd, Prince Abdul Aziz Bin 32
Fairbanks, Douglas 98, 219
Faldo, Nick 17, 258
Falklands War 194
Falling In Love Again 70
falls: without parachute 92
families: acting 12; generations on Everest 300; Saddam Hussein 26
family trees 102
fan clubs 18
Fan-Yang 66
Fancy Deep Blue ring 34
Fangio, Juan-Manuel 272
fangs, spider 128; viper 134
fangtooth anoplogaster, fish 121
fans 58-59
Fantasia 218
Fantasy 228
Fanuc company 180-81
Fanuc Robotics, USA 181
Farnan, Frank 298
Farrow, Mia 25
fashion 248-49; street 246
Fashion Cafe 20
fasting: human 107; insects 132
Fat of The Land 235
Fatal Attraction 10
Fatima 90
fattest man contest 96
Favre, Brett 263
Favre, Olivier 299
fax machines 173
Faxon, Brad 258
FBI (Federal Bureau of Investigation) 177, 178
feathers: longest 126
Federal Express 177
Federov, Sergei 278
Feeney, Charles 'Chuck' 33
feet: big 99; insured 98
Felis iriomotensis 136
feminist witchcraft 91
fencing: Olympics 265
Ferrari, Eve Lolo 109
Ferrari 17, 272; Grand Prix wins 273
Ferreira, André 289
Ferrera, Hildegarde 72
Ferreras, Francisco 'Pipín' 79
Ferreri, Marco 100
Ferrigno, Lou 110
Ferry, Robert 78
ferry disasters 199
Ferté, Alain 272
fertility: mice 119
Festival International de Jazz de Montreal 243
festivals 245; Edinburgh 223
Feteris, Nicholas 298
fevers 104-05

Fiat CR42B plane 162
field mouse 119
Field of Dreams 44
Fiesta de Los Percebes 62
fighter planes 195
Fignon, Laurent 286
Filatova, Maria Yevgenyevna 284
films 208-09: animation 218-19;
    auctioned scripts 35; budget 210;
    costume 37; fans 58; hoaxes 89;
    horror 210-211; props 37;
    rights 208; scripts 208;
    sequels 211; soundtracks 234;
    stars 12-13; supermodel
    stars 20-21
Filo, Andrew 174
fin whales 119
Final Analysis 12
Final Fantasy VII 170
finance 46-47
fines 87
fingernails 101
fingerprints, DNA 144
fingers, extra 100
Finland: education budget 47
Finlandia Ski Race 277
Finney, Albert 208
fins, shark 121
fires 198, 200-01: film set 209;
    heroine 70; stuntmen 213
firearms 204
fireballs 149
Firestarter 235
fireworks: millennium 245
Firsov, Anatoliy 278
First Pacific National Bank 52
First Presleyterian Church of
    Elvis the Divine 59
Firwell, Jame 106
fish 120-21; endangered 136;
    expensive 62; ferocious 135;
    pollution 201; puffer 134;
    stonefish 135; tapeworms 132
Fisher, Carrie 10
Fisher, Harry 'Bud' 219
fishing, depletion of stocks 201
Fit TV 110
Fitaihi, Sheikh Ahmed 34
fitness: cats 138
fitness industry 110
fits: induced by film 218
Fjellerup, Eva 302
flames, hottest 151
Flaming Pie 176
flamingoes 127
flashing (juggling) 66
Flatley, Michael 98, 222
Flavr Savr™ 145
fleas 130-31, 133; rat 133
Fleischer, Max 219
Fleischer Studios 98
Fleming, Ian 197
Fleming, Peter 261
'flesh-eating bug' 104
Fletcher, Kenneth 260
Fleury Michon (IX) 78-79
Flex magazine 110
flight: birds 126; longest
    non-stop 78
Flint, Keith 235
floods 202
flotations of companies 46
flow, of river 146
flowers: bird of paradise 140;
    Diana memorial 22; largest 141;
    sculpture 220
Floyd, Raymond 258
fluorine 151
fluoro-antimonic acid 150
fly agaric 142
flying boats 162

Flying Pictures 213
Flynn, Errol 10
foetus, twin 100
Fogarty, Carl 287
Foley, Johnny Dell 66
Fôlha de Sao Paulo newspaper 217
Folklora festival 245
Folley, Zora 37
Fomitcheva, Elvira 298
Fonda, Jane 52
Fong, Denis 171
Fontaine, Just 254-55
Fonteyn, Dame Margot 222
food: companies 49; consumption of
    insects 130-31; grilled snake 124;
    strange 127
food and drink 62-63
Food and Drug Administration, 145
Food Bank 60
foot binding 113
football 252-53; clubs 252;
    earnings 16; reference 308;
    riot 198; scores 252, 262;
    stadiums 253
footprints: dinosaur 125;
    giant penguin 88
Forbes magazine 50, 52
Ford, Eileen 21
Ford, Harrison 110
Ford, Tom 249
Ford EA Falcon 77
Ford Foundation 49
Ford model agency 20
Ford Motor Co. 49, 161
Ford Mustang 76
Ford RS200 Evolution 158
Foreman, George 37
Forest Lawn Memorial Park 10
forgery 42, 85; paintings 89
Forgotten Silver 89
Formula 1 272; earnings 16
Forsythe, William 220
Fort Knox, USA 47
Fortensky, Larry 28
Fortress of Solitude, USA 185
Forvass, Anders 275
Fosset, Steve 78-79
fossil DNA 144
Foster, Jodie 111
Foster, Joy 71
Foster, Sir Norman 157
fountain pen, jewelled 35
Four Square clothing 294
Fourposter 223
Fox Broadcasting Co. 50
Fox television network 215
'Foxbat' combat jet 195
Foxwoods Resort Casino 39
Foxworthy, Jeff 238
Foyt, A. J. 272
Fradet, Eric 298
France II 165
France: show jumping 288;
    traffic jam 77
Francis, Beverley 285
Francis the Talking Mule 138
Francky (poodle) 138
Frango sweets 44
Frank Sinatra Las Vegas Celebrity
    Golf Classic 29
Frankencycle 166
Frankenjua, Germany 301
Frankenstein 211
Frankenstein Unbound 210
frankfurter eating 60
Franklin, Aretha 237
Fraser, Dawn 274
Frasier 138
fraud 85
freak waves 92
Fredriksson, Gert 297

Free Spirit (balloon) 78
freefall parachuting 298
freefalls: stunts 212
Freeman, Alfred 290
Freeman, Eric 259
freestyle skiing 277
Freewheelin' Bob Dylan 233
Frederick William I of Prussia 35
freshwater snail 133
Frick, Gary 281
Frick, Dr Mario 27
Friday the 13th 211
Friedenreich, Artur 252
Friedkin, William 210
Friends 215
Fristoe, Leonard 87
frogs 122, 133; derby 122; new
    species 137; poison-arrow 134
From Dusk Til Dawn 14
*From the Muddy Banks of the
    Wishkah* 232
Frost, Sir David 26
frostbite 106
Fruit of the Loom 246
Fu Mingxia 71
Fuchs, Gottfried 252
fuel consumption 158-59, 160
Fuji Television Network 157
Fujii, Shozo 283
Fujikyu Highland Park 185
Fujiyama, Kanmi 223
Fujiyama roller coaster 185
Full Monty 215
Fullen, Eamon 300
fund raising 28-29, 68
fundamentalists 205
funerals: Princess Diana 22;
    mourners 24; pets 139;
    in space 186-188
fungi: heaviest 140; largest 140;
    poisonous 142
Funk, Michelle 107
*Funny Thing Happened on the Way to
    the Forum, A* 212
fur trading 137
Furman, Ashrita 67, 269, 284
Furrer, Oliver 299
Furstehoff, Patrik 76
Fuzzi, Fabio 281
Fyodorov, Slava 182

G force 107; in beetles 131;
    woodpeckers 126
G-Shock US Open surfing 296
Gabelich, Gary 158
Gable, Clark 35
Gaboon viper 134
Gabor, Zsa Zsa 10-11
Gacy, John 87
Gadd, Will 295
gadgets 172-75
Gagarin, Yuri 36
Gainville, Hélène 35
Galagos 118
Galapagos fur seal 117
Galapagos tortoise 124
galaxies 148
Galbis, Juan Carlos 61
gallbladders 99
Galstyan, Robert 64
Gaman game show 215
Gambia: presidency 27
gambling 38-39
Game Boy: camera 172; jewelled 175

game shows 215
games consoles 174
gamma rays 150
Gandey, Philip 67
Ganev, Gantcho 24
Ganges river 90
gangrene 104
gangsta rap 236-37
Ganimedes Tecrent (horse) 289
Gans, Joe 283
Gansser, Franco 294
Ganster, Eva 277
Gansu province, China 202
Ganz, Victor and Sally 221
Gap company 52
Garcia, Andy 100
garden parties: Royal 29
Gardner, Ava 11
Garland, Judy 37
Gaskin, Tom 64
gastropods 123
Gates, Bill 32-33, 50, 52, 179;
    house 156
Gateway to the West arch 154
Gatto, Anthony 67
Gauguin de Lully (horse) 289
Gaultier, Jean-Paul 138
Gay and Lesbian Mardi Gras 245
Gay Pride 245
Gazamiga, Silvio 254
Gebreselassie, Haile 305
geckos 124
Gehry, Frank 156
Geidel, Paul 87
Geldof, Bob 28
Geleen, Netherlands 245
Geller, Dr Jac S. 100
Geller, Uri 225
gene sequencer 145
General Caballero 253
General Dynamics FB-111A bomber
    195
General Electric corporation 48
General Hospital 13, 241
General Motor Corporation 48-49,
    158-59
'General Sherman' sequoia 140
generations 102-03
Genetech 145
genetics engineering 144-45
Geneva Auto Show 160-61
Geninga star 151
genome, human 145
Gentry, Tom 280
Gentry Eagle 280
Geo Metro car 160
Geoghegan, Laura 79
geographer cone 135
George, Emma 297
George the giraffe 117
Gerber, Israel 57
German, Guy 65
German Shepherd dogs 196
Germany: dressage 289; show
    jumping 288; traffic jam 77;
    witch-burning 87
Germeshausen, Bernhard 294
Gerry Cottle's Circus 64
Gethin, Peter 272
Getty, John Paul 51
Getty Center 156
geysers 147, 202
Ghiggia, Alcide 255
Ghosh, Professor Bimal C. 99
ghosts: Amityville 89
Giammetti, Giancarlo 249
giant 136; Drop freefall tower 184;
    earwig of Saint Helena 136;
    elephant bird 127; hogweed 140;
    panda 136; Tasmanian crabs 122;
    Tug-of-War 69

Gibb, Barry 230
Gibshaw, Frank 175
Gibson, Bob 270
Gibson, Mel 208, 212
Gielgud, Kate 223
gigaflops 178
Gigova, Maria 285
Gila monster lizard 134
Gill, James 103
Gillard, Nick 213
Gilley's Club 244
Gimeno, Andrés 261
Gingerbread Man 12
ginrin showa coi, fish 121
ginseng 62
giraffes 117
Girault, Henri 302
girl bands 228-29
Giro d'Italia 287
Gish, Lilian 10
glaciers 147
Glastonbury Festival 225
Glay 232
Glenfiddich whisky 62
Glenn, Senator John 72
Glenn, Venice 263
gliding: reference 308
Global 45
Global Hawk aircraft 194
Global Positioning
    by Satellite (GPS) 174
Globo television
    network 214
Glomar Explorer 197
gloves: auctioned 37; of Michael
    Jackson 19
gluttony 60
gnomes and pixies:
    collection 56
GNS Spices 63
goals: soccer 252-53; World Cup
    254-55
goalkeepers 252
goby, dwarf 120
Godard, Jean-Luc 52
Goddard, Paulette 222
Godfather, Part 3 100
Godin, Noel 'Pieman' 14, 52
Godwin, Thomas 79
Godzilla, King of the Monsters 211
Goggomobil 1400 37
gold: ductility 151
Gold Cup (horse racing) 289
gold reserves 47
Gold's Gym 111
Goldberg, Whoopi 215, 218
Goldberger, Andreas 277
Golden Fleece billiard table 34
Golden Globe award 240
golden handshakes 53
golden orb-web spider 128
golden silk spider 128
Golden State Warriors 268
GoldenEye 213
Goldschmid, Isa 259
Goldstein, Dr Ronald 109
golf 258-59; charity
    tournaments 29; earnings 16-17;
    reference 308
Goliath (tortoise) 124
Goliath beetle 130
goliath bird-eating spider 128
goliath frog, African 122
Goncz, Arpad 86
Gone With The Wind 35, 208, 216
Gonzales, Delfina and Maria de Jesus
    84
Good Easter 69
Good Times virus 88
Goodson, Mark 215

Goodwin, Daniel 225
Gopalganj, Bangladesh 147
Gorbachev, Mikhail 159
Gorbous, Glen Edward 271
Gordon, Steve 166
Gore, Arthur 260
gorillas 116; silverback 134
Gotta Sweat 111
Gottschalk, Thomas 14
Governador Valadares 36
Gower, Chris 57
GPS Pioneer 174
Grable, Betty 10
Grace, Della 108
Grace, W. G. 37
Graceland 24
graduataes: youngest 70
Graf, Steffi 16
graffiti 220
Grafton Jacaranda Festival 75
Graham, Billy 91
Grammy Awards 19, 238, 242
Granada Sky Broadcasting 45
Granato, Cammi 264
Grand Enigma Reference System 174
Grand Masters: chess 70
Grand National 288
grand pianos 243
Grand Princess 165
Grand Prix 272
grand slam (tennis) 260
grandmothers: gambling 38
Grandos, Gabriel March 87
Granger, Ethel 97
Grant family 80
grapes: catching 66; eating 60
graptolite fossil 137
Grasshopper-Club football club 253
grave-robbers 24
gravedigger, longest working life 73
Gravenvoorde School, Netherlands 74
graves: celebrities 24
Great Barrier Reef 122, 146
great bustard 126
great crested newt 150
Great Five Cent Store (Woolworth) 40
Great Gatsby, The 248
Great Lakes 200
Great Moon Hoax 88
Great Trango Tower 298
great white shark 135, 205
Greatest Hits (Eagles) 232
Greece, hangings 86
Green, Andy 158
Green, David 59
Green, Jonathon 286
Green, Maurice 306
Green, Roy 263
Green Bay Packers 262
green leaf frog 122
Green Tree Financial Corporation 53
'Green Week' fair 61
Greener, Christopher 96
Greenhille, Elizabeth 103
Greenwood, Carol 301
Gregorian chant 231
Gretzky, Wayne 278
Grice, Richard 58
Griffith-Joyner, Florence 256
Griffiths, Donna 106
Grigalluniene, A. 267
Gropaiz, Fabrice 292
Grospiron, Edgar 277
Gross, Michael 274
Gross Domestic Product (GDP) 46-47
Gross National Product (GNP) 46
Grove, Andrew 53
growth rate: bamboos 140;
    trees 140; water weed 140
Grumman F8F Bearcat plane 162
grunge 20

Grunsven, Anky van 289
Guaglione 241
Gucci 249
Gudrun and Lena 61
Guelph University 68
Guernsey: cancer 105
Guerrero, Walfer 224
Gueschkova, Vesta 224
Guggenheim Museum Bilbao 156
Guidez, Yvon 40
Guilén, Octavio and Martínez,
    Adriana 73
Guinea worm 133
Guinness Book of Records 216
Guinness World Records™: Primetime
    97, 99, 224, 292, 298
guitar: most expensive 233
Gul Gul (gorilla) 117
Gulf snapping turtle 137
Gulf War 182, 192-93, 194
Gulfstream V jet 33
Gullich, Wolfgang 301
gumboot throwing 66
Gundam 218
Gunma, Japan 69
Guns 'N' Roses 231, 233
Guyana: pollution 201
gymnastics 264, 284
gyms 111

'H-span' 150
H.T.S. powerboat 281
hackers 177-78
Hackl, Georg 295
Hadrian's Wall, UK 220
hadrosaurids 125
haemophilia 106
Hagens, Professor Gunther von 98
Haggard, Merle 238
Hagman, Larry 214
hailstones 147
hailstorms 203
Hailwood, Mike 287
hair: collection 56; longest 101;
    Nelson's 99
hairballs 101
haircut: most expensive 109
haircutting: fastest 65
Haitian solenodon 134
Hakonard, Kristin 267
Hall, Andy 300
Hall, Daryl and Oates, John 228
Hall, George 252
Hall, Jerry 21
Hall, Lars 302
Hall, Layne 77
Halliwell, Geri 229
Hallyday, Johnny 183, 230
Halo Trust 23
hamadryad 134
Hamanaka, Yasuo 85
Hamash, Suham and Youssef 106
Hambleton, Kitty 158
hamburger, biggest 60
Hamel, Yvon du 286
Hamill, Mark 59
Hamill, Robert 78
Hamilton, Ian 216
Hamilton, Jeffrey 277
Hamlet 138
Hamlet 208
Hamm, Jack 259
Hammer, M. C. 236

hammer: reference 306
Hammer Films 211
Hammond, Walter 290
Hanauer, Chip 281
Hand With Thimble 221
handcuffs: collection 57
handheld computers 179
handicaps in polo 289
hands: insured 98
Haney, Lee 110
hang gliding 299, 308
hangings 86
Hansen, Ashia 306
Hansen, Rick 80
Hanson 228
Hanson-Boylen, Christilot 265
Hard Rock Cafe 233
Hargreaves, Alison 300
Haring, Keith 220, 246
Harley Davidson 76, 167
Harlin, Renny 208
Harpers and Queen 21
Harper's Bazaar 21
Harpo Productions 14
harpy eagle 127
Harris, Roy 230
Harrison, Jim 279
Harrison, Ross Granville 100
Hart to Hart 214
Hartford Whalers 279
Hartog, Jan de 223
Harvard University 144
Hasbro Inc. 174
Hashimoto, Ryutaro 26
Hasselhoff, David 214
Hatano, Kenji (Oshio) 282
Hathaway, Graham 158
Hathaway, John W. 79
Hatshepsut Temple 198
Haunted Mansion ride 185
haute-couture 41
Havel, Vaclav 26, 86
Hawaii Ironman race 302-03
hawk moths 131
Hawkster (racehorse) 288
Haworth, Pauline 301
Haworth, Steve 112
Hayes, Mark 258
Hayley, Charles 262
Haynes, Desmond 291
heads: shaping 113
health: budget 47; Boris Yeltsin 27
Healy, Ian 291
hearing: bats 119
heart: disease 105; transplants 144
heat-resistance 150
Heath, Rodney 261
heatstroke 106
Heiden, Eric 264
height: actors 13; orchids 140;
    people 96; roller coaster 185
heiresses 32-33
Heisman Trophy 262
helicopters 162-63; armed 194;
    circumnavigation 78;
    disaster 198; largest 163
Helios A and *B* spacecraft 186-87
Hellman, Walter 75
Hello! 28
Hellwig, Reinhard 56
Helm, Rüdiger 297
helmet: auctioned 37
Hemingway, Margaux 13
Hempleman-Adams, Alicia 70
Hendrix, Jimi 233
Henley, Suzanne 38
Henri IV, King of France 99
Henri-Lévy, Bernard 52
Henry, Yolanda 257
Henrys 64

hepatitis B 105
Hepburn, Katharine 13
heptathlon: reference 306
Herald Sun 217
Hercules 110
Herd, Stan 221
Herlihy, Kevin 271
Hermann, Manfred 158
Hermes 21
Hernandez, Orlando 271
Herschel, Sir John 89
Hershiser, Orel 271
Herzigova, Eva 45
Hesperiidae, butterflies 131
Hess, Beatrice 266
Hesse, Grand Duke and family 23
Heterometrus swannerdami 129
Hewlett-Packard 51
Hexactinellida sponges 123
Hey Joe 230
hi-fi: sales 41; speakers 174
Hi-Vision PlasmaX TV screen 172
hiccoughs 106
Hickey, Roger 292
Hickman, James 314
Hicks, Hugh 56
Higgins, Pinky 270
high jump 257; Paralympics 267;
    reference 306; skateboarding 293
high rollers 38
High Speed Trains (HST) 164
high-wire act 224
Highpoint 212
Hilbert, Stephen C. 52
Hillary, Sir Edmund 300
Hillary, Peter 300
Hillerich & Bradsby 270
Himmy (cat) 139
Hinault, Bernard 286
Hindenburg 299
Hinduism 90
Hindustan 'Contessa Classic' 77
Hingis, Martina 17, 261
hip hop/rap 236-37
Hirasawa, Sadamichi 87
Hiroshima 194
Hirst, Damien 51
Hislop, Steve 287
HIStory 18
hitchhiking 80
Hitler, Adolf 35
'Hitler Diaries' 89
Hits, The 238
hits: internet 176-77
HIV virus 104
HMS Otus 92
hoaxes 88-89
hockey: Australian women's team
    308; reference 308
Hoffman, Dustin 12
Hoffman, Joyce 296
Hogan, Hulk 111
Hold Me, Thrill Me, Kiss Me 241
Holding, David 266
Hole 233
Holloman Air Force Base 107
Holly, Buddy 24
Hollywood 10-11; benefits 28;
    Boulevard 10; insurance 98;
    screenwriters 53; Walk of Fame 13
Holmes, Harriet 102
Holmes, Sherlock 209
Holt, Georgia 10
Holua 92
holy goat 137
Holy Spirit Association 91
Holyfield, Evander 282
Home Alone II: Lost in New York 12
home runs, baseball 270
Honda Motors 158, 160-61, 181;
    CR500 76; TLM220R 76

honey badger 119
Hong Kong: property 33
Hong Kong Shanghai Bank 48
Honolulu, shopping centre 40
Honolulu Airport 41
Hooch, Pieter de 89
hookworms 132
Hoon Son 266
Hooper, Nellee 235
Hooper 212
Hope, Bob 13
Hope Hospital 182
hopscotch 74
Hori tribe 113
Horie, Kenichi 81
hormones: injections 108
horned sungem 126
horns: human 112
horror films 210-11
horse racing 288, 308; betting 39;
    reference 310
horseflies 131
Hörzu 216
Hoskins, Bob 45
hot-air balloons 72
hot springs 147
hotels 154; Hollywood 10;
    underwater 157
House, and sequels 211
House of Berluti, France 35
House of Style 21
Houston, Whitney 237; and Brown,
    Bobby 18
Houston Aeros 279
Houston Oilers 262
Houtsma, Alwin 267
Hovdetoppen, Mt 157
hovercraft 165; military 195
Hovhaness, Alan 242
How Do I Live 238-39
Howard, Mike 224, 298
Howe, Gordie 278
HSBC Holdings 49
HSR V1 car 160
Hu, Esther 148
Huambo, Angola 23
Huang He (Yellow River) 202
Huang Pin-jen and Chang Shu-mei 93
Huascaran 202
Huasó (horse) 289
Hudson, Walter 97
Hughes, Charlotte 72
Hughes, Gwilym 58
Hughes, Dr. H. Howard 58
Hughes, Howard 51, 163, 197
Hughes H4 Hercules flying boat 163
Hughes YOH-6A aircraft 78
Huish, Frederick 290
Huisman, Henny 14
Hull, George 88
Human Genome Project 145
human sacrifices 90
humanoid robots 181
Hume, Cronyn 223
hummingbirds 126
Humperdinck, Engelbert 56
Humulin 145
Hungary: inflation 46; World Cup
    football 254-55
Hunt, Henry 300
Hunt for Red October 217
Hunter/Killer 171
Huntington Beach 296
Hunty, Shirley de la 256
hurdling 256
Hurghada 220
Hurley, Marcus 286
hurling: reference 310
Hurlinger, Johann 81
Huron, South Dakota 203

Hurst, Geoffrey 255
Hussein, Saddam 32, 192, 194
Huston, John 208
Hutchence, Michael 25
Huxley, David 64
Hveger, Ragnhild 274
Hyatt Regency Cerromar Beach Resort 155
hydrocarbons 160
hydrofoils 165
hydroids, poisonous 135
hydroplanes 280
hyenas 119
Hylton, Steve 259
Hypercar 160
hypnotherapy lecture 53
hypothermia 106

I Believe 230
I Finally Found Someone 230
I Never Loved a Man 237
I Want You Back 228
I Will Always Love You 237
Ibiza: clubs 244
IBM computers 178
ice: physical characteristics 150; storms 202-03; thickness 146
ice climbing 295
ice cream 49; eating 60
ice hockey 278-79; women's 264
Ice Hotel 154
ice skating: reference 312
ice sledging 266
ice-yachting 295
iceberg disaster 198
Ichiokuninn no Daihitsumon 15
Icicle (ice-yacht) 295
Ickx, Jacky 273
Idaho Technology 144
If Tomorrow Never Dies 238
If You See Him 238
Iglesias, Julio 240
igloos 154
Ignatov, Sergei 67
iguanodon robot 180
I'll Be Missing You 236
I'll Make Love to You 236
illusions 224
'Illustrated Man' 112
I'm So Happy I Can't Stop Crying 239
Imagine 24
Immaculate Collection 228
immersion: longest 107
immobility 67
Impact 158
Imperial Cruiser (Star Wars) 183
Imperial Palace 154
Imperial Winter Egg 34
impersonation: Elvis 59
implants: body art 112
Imutran 144
In Search of J. D. Salinger 216
In The Box 220
In the Name of the Father 12
In The Wee Small Hours 24
in-line skating 292
Inaba, Hideaki 285
inauguration ceremonies 26
income tax: Denmark 46
Incredible Hulk, The 110
Independence Day 210, 215
India: air pollution 200; film industry 209; HIV 104; newspapers 216; Parseeism 91; presidency 26

India Today 216
Indian Botanical Garden, 141
Indian Ocean: sharks 205
Indian Railways 49
Indiana Jones and the Last Crusade 213
Indianapolis 500 272
indium gallium arsenide 182
Indonesia: duty free 41; fires 201
Indoor Boomerang Throwing Competition 67
indoor running: reference 306
Induráin, Miguel 286-87
Industrial Light and Magic 183
industrialization; Belarus 46
infections 104-05
Inferno ski race 277
Inflatable Tower Vision 183
inflation 46
influenza 104
information technology 156
Informer 236
Inglis, Nick 75
Inkatha Freedom Party 27
Inoffizielle Mitarbeiters 196
insect: games 74; robots 180
insider trading 87
installations 220-21
InstaPUMP shoes 44
insulin injections 107
insulin, synthetic 145
insurance: human body 98; legs 10; shows 222; stuntmen 212
Intel Computer Corp. 53, 178
Intel New York Music Festival 245
'intelligent' house 156; town 156
Inter Milan 16
Interbrand consultancy 42
Intercity 125 trains 164
intercontinental ballistic missiles (ICBMs) 194
International Bank for Reconstruction and Development 49
International Coastal Cleanup, 69
International Contest for Hill-Climbing Micromechanisms 180
International Mycological Institute 140
International Trans-Antarctica Expedition 79
International Ultraviolet Explorer satellite 187
International Wool Secretariat Development Centre 68
internet 176-77, 181; Blair interview 26; games 171; Mall 176; music festival 245; sites 23
Internet Explorer 179
Interstate 405 76
Intimate Revue, The 223
Into the Groove 235
Inverpolly Forest 200
invertebrates: new species 136
investment banks 49
investment consultants: fees 53
investors: earnings 53
INXS 25
Io (moon) 148
Iran, jailbreak 87
Iraq: basketball 268; nepotism 26
Ireland: Eurovision Song Contest 231
Iriomote cat 136
Irish Cap (horse) 289
iron lung 106
Irons, Jeremy 215, 218
Irving, David 89
Irwin, Hale 17, 258
islands: artificial 157; private 33
Isle of Man 287

isolation: in space 189
Issorat, Claude 267
Istana Nurul Iman, Brunei 154
It Happened One Night 35
Italian Tethered Satellite 187
Italy: CD piracy 43; crying statue 91; Mafia 84; pilgrims 91; prisoners 86
itching powder 142
It's a Mad Mad Mad Mad World 98
It's a Wonderful Life 10
Ixodida 133
Ixtoc 1 oil rig 201
Izumi, Shigeachiyo 73, 102

J. N. Nichols (Vimto) Ltd 74
J. Paul Getty Museum, 221
Jackie Chan Stuntmen Association 212
jackpots: lottery 38
Jackson, Cindy 108
Jackson, Janet 228, 234-35
Jackson, Michael 18-19, 28-29, 33, 228, 237
Jackson, Peter 89
Jackson, Reggie 270
Jackson, Stephanie 138
Jackson, T. J. Jackson 96
Jackson Five 228
Jacobs, Franklin 257
Jacobsen, Clayton 281
Jacoby, Mike 294
Jaeger, Andrea and Arias, Jimmy 261
Jagan, President 201
Jager, Tom 274
Jagged Little Pill 232
Jagger, Mick 18
Jaguar cars 158, 272
Jahre Viking 165
Jaïrzinho 255
jail sentences 87; film actors 10
jailbreak 87
James Bond: character 197; films 109, 175, 208; stuntmen 212; themes 231
James, Doris 108
James, Wayne 290
Jammeh, Lt. Yaya 27
Janet 235
Janson, Mariss 69
Janzen, Lee 258
Japan: expenditure on TV 215; eyesight 105; gymnastics 284; invasion of China 192; ODA 47; pollution 201; robots 180; royal family 23; oldest twins 73
Jaratarcha, Wichan 138
Jarre, Jean Michel 230
Javan rhinoceros 136
javelin: reference 306
jazz: clubs 243; festivals 243
jeans: Levis 43
Jefferson, Thomas 62
Jeffreys, Sir Alec 144
jellyfish, Arctic giant 122; box 135
Jerry Springer Show 103; 214
Jersey Zoo, UK 136
jet-assisted lugeing 292
jet fighters: collection 56
Jet Propulsion Laboratory 181
Jet Services 5 78
jets: fastest 162; private 33
jetskiing 281
Jewel 228
jewel robberies 85

jewellery: auctioned 34; CD player 175; mobile phone 175
Jha, Amresh Kumar 67
jig-saw puzzles: giant 74
Jimmu, Emperor of Japan 23
Jimmy the canary 139
jockeys 288
Joe Gold Cognoscenti Cues 34
Joersz, Captain Eldon W. 162
Johansson, Ivar 282
John, Elton 18, 22, 231, 248
John, Elton: and Rice, Tim 218
John Hancock Center 154
John/Joan sex change 108
John O'Groats to Land's End: drive 159
Johns, Tommy 87
Johnson, Ben 256
Johnson, F. Ross 53
Johnson, Magic 218
Johnson, Michael 305
joint replacement 99
Jones, Adrian 74
Jones, Barbara 256
Jones, Barry 252
Jones, David 74
Jones, Hamish 92
Jones, Janet 278
Jones, Jim 90
Jones, Michelle 303
Jones, Willie 106
Jordan, Michael 16-17, 42, 247, 268
Jordan, Montell 237
Jordy (Lemoine) 70, 236
Jorgensen, Christine 108
Jorrocks (racehorse) 288
Joshua 238
Joshua Tree 232
journalists 28; at risk 205
journeys: car 77; cats 138; by fish 120; skiing 277
Joyce, Joan 271
Joyner-Kersee, Jackie 257
Jr. Gemini ride 184
judges: youngest 71
judo 283
juggling 66-67
Juicy Duce cocktail 61
Jules' Undersea Lodge 157
Julia, Raul 213
Julio 240
jumble sales 41
jumbo airbus 163
jumper making 68
jumping: fleas 131; frogs 122
Jungle Book 218
junks 165
Jupiter 148, 187
Jurassic Park 53, 128, 180, 208, 215
Jussila, Jouni 65
(Just like) Starting Over 24
Juwan 16
JVC printers 173
Jyrich, Warren 106

K2, Himalaya 300
K2 Surf clothing 296
Ka-52 Alligator helicopter 194
Kable, Jeremy 269
Kabuki theatre 223
Kacsis, Sandor 255
Kaempfert, Bert 230
Kahn, Larry 74
Kaiko probe 146
Kainolaisen, Sisko 277

Kalanga tribe, Botswana 100
Kale, Duane 266
Kali Gandaki River, Nepal 297
Kali, goddess of death 90
Kaminski, George 57
Kanchenjunga 300
kangaroos 116; tree 137
Kankkunen, Juha 273
Kansai International Airport 156
Kantimathi, Sam 75
Kanto plain 202
Kapila, Navin, Bahadur, Man and Raman, Vijay 77
Kappen, Ludger 142
Kaprolaktam 200
karate 283; house demolition 68
Karelin, Aleksandr 282
Karpie, Jan 295
Kasparov, Gary 75, 178
Kassam, Firoz 22
katemfe plant 150
Kathmandu 301
Kato (cat) 139
Katrina & The Waves 231
'Katzenjammer Kids' 219
Kauai o-o 136
Kawasaki: jetskis 281; KX500 76; Steelworks 74; Z1 286
kayaking 297
Kazakhstan: nuclear weapons 194; pollution 200
Kazmaier, Bill 110
kea 127
Kearney, Michael 70
Keaton, Buster 212
kebab, longest 60
keel-scaled boa 136
Keh, Arceli 102
Keith, Toby 239
Kellie, David 81
Kempf, Bobby 60
Kenmuir, John 60
Kennedy, John 110
Kennedy, John F. 36
Kennedy, N. William 85
Kennedy Space Center 199
Kenny G 243
Kenny, Mark 64
Kensington Palace 22
Kernaghan, Marty 271
Kevlar 151
Key, Kathleen 98
Keystone Cops 98
KGB 196
Khashoggi, Soraya 33
Khomutov, Andrey 278
Khoshnaw, Dr Saladin Karl 75
Khrushchev, Nikita 36
kidnapping 204
kidney donation 106
Kilimanjaro, Mt. 292
killers: lizards 125
killer whale 118
killifish 121
Kilner, C. H. A. 106
Kim Dae Jung 86
Kim Jong Il 26
Kim Kyung-Wook 305
Kim Sung-myun 87
Kimbangu, Simon 91
Kinch, Pat 166
Kind of Blue 242
Kindar-Martin, Jade 224
King, Betsy 17
King, Billie-Jean 260
King, Denny 140
King, Stephen 211, 216, 222
king cobra 134
King Midget 159
King World 15
King World Corporation 214

King's holly 140
kipper eating 60
Kiptanui, Moses 256
Kiraly, Karch 293
Kirby, Karolyn 293
Kiribati: raft survivors 93
Kirk, Michael 10
kissing, mass 68
Kissinger, Henry 11
Kissling, Connie 277
Kittinger, Joseph 298
Kitti's hog-nosed bat 116
Klammer, Franz 276
Klaude, Manfred 57
Klees, Christian 312
Klein, Albert 159
Klein, Calvin 246
Klein, Martin 283
Klimke, Dr Reiner 289
Knaresborough Bed Race 74
Knauss, Sarah 103
Knievel, Robbie 77
Knorr, Arthur 108
Knowles, Durward 265
Knox, Taylor 296
koala 119
Kobe, Japan 204
Kobe beef 62
Kobe Ecocar 160
Kodiak bear 116
Koenig Competition cars 159
Kohl, Helmut 26
Kohlberg Kravis Roberts 49
Komi Republic 201
Komodo dragons 125
Konow, Magnus 265
Koons, Jeff 220
Kopi Luwak coffee 63
Koran, the 216
Koresh, David 90
Kori bustard 126
Koskiusko, Mt. 300
Kosolofski, Karlee 106
Kostadinova, Stefka 257
Koufax, Sandy 270
Kouna, Pasakevi 'Voula' 284
Kovacs, Charlie 77
Kraenzlein, Alvin 256
Krakatoa 201
Krausse, Stefan 265, 295
Kreml, Anni 66
Kresty Prison 86
krill 122
Kristel, Sylvia 208
Kristiansen, Ingrid 303
Krivoshlyapovy, Masha and Dasha 100
Kroc, Ray 46
Kronseil, Walter 294
Krueger, Freddy 211
'Krystyne Kolorful' 112
Kubrick, Stanley 210
Kuching 201
Kudo, Yasayuki 76
Kuhaulua, Jesse (Takamiyama) 282
Kuiper belt 149
Kujau, Konrad 89
Kumbha Mela 90
Kumite karate championships 283
Kurds 193-94
Kurri, Jari 278
Kutcher, Steve 128
Kuwait: Gulf War 192
Kuzkin, Viktor 278
Kwok, Walter, Thomas and Raymond 50
Kybartas, Ray 110
Kylie 229
Kyshtym, Russia 200
Kyusho Basho (sumo) 282

L. L. Cool J 236
La Copa de la Vida 241
La Donna Scimmia 100
La Gran Argentina 281
LA Rams 262
La Régente pearl 34
labour camps, Stalinist 92
Laboureix, Eric 277
Lacks, Henrietta 98
Lacroix, Christian 249
lacrosse: reference 310
Lacy, Major Will 72
Ladbrokes bookmakers 39
ladder climbing 69
Lady Soul 237
Lafleur, Abel 254
Lagerfeld, Karl 20, 248
Laine, Florence 72
Laine, Frankie 230
Laker, Jim 290
lakes: shrinking 201
Lakota 79
Lamazou, Titouan 79
Lambert Glacier 147
Lambrecht, Alex 112
Lammers, Jan 272
Lampard, Kim 297
Lancashire Dairies 61
Lancaster Sertoma Club 60
Lancia cars 273
Landini, Anthony 37
landmines 23, 204
Landsberg, Mark 75
landscape art 220-21
landslides 202
Lang, Tony 166
Lange, Otto 142
Langer, Bernhard 17
Langseth, Hans 100
Lanier, Michael and James 96
laptop computers 172, 174
Lara, Brian 290
Larned, William 260
Las Vegas: gambling 38-39
lasagne, biggest 60
laser-guided missiles 182
laser lights 182
laser pulses 183
laser speed traps 182
laser weapons 182
Lasker, Dr Emanuel 75
Lassa fever 104
Lassie 138
Last of the Mohicans 12
Lata, Georgia 198
Late Show, The 80
latino music 240-41
Latvia: road deaths 77
Latynina, Larisa Semyonovna 284
Laue, Ralf 60, 67
Laurel, Stan 10
Lauren, Ralph 248
Lausanne-Sports football club 253
L'Automobile 217
lava flow 147
lawnmower ride, longest 80
Lawrence Livermore National Laboratory 183
lawsuits: gypsum giant 88; tobacco 143
Lawton, Chris 285
lawyers: earnings 52
LCI company 175
Le Gavroche restaurant 62

Le Jingyi 274
Le May Doan, Catriona 312
Le Mans 272
Le-no-Hikari magazine 216
Le Petomane 101
Le Terrible destroyer 195
Leach, Reggie 278
leap-frogging 81
Leary, Timothy 186
leatherback turtle 124
Leclerc shopping centre 40
lecture fees 53
Led Zeppelin IV 232
Leden, Judy 299
Lednyev, Pavel Serafimovich 302
Lee, Ann 91
Lee, Christopher 13, 211
Lee, Harper 216
Lee, Jim 86
Lee Teng-hui 74
Leech, Wendy 212
leeches 132-33
legacies: pets 139
Legend 236
Lego 180
legs: frogs 133; Hollywood 10; insects 130; insurance 98; models 21
Leigh, Jennifer Jason 12
Leighton, Jim 255
Leino, Eino 282
Leinonen, Mikko 278
Leitch, Charlotte Pitcairn 258
Lekunze, Timothy Leku 301
L'Elisir d'Amore 242
Lelmer, William 86
Lemieux, Mario 278
lemmings 119
lemon eating 60
LeMond, Greg 286
lemurs 137
Lendl, Ivan 261
Leningrad: siege 192
Lennon, Cynthia 36
Lennon, John 18, 24, 36, 56, 230, 233
Lennon, Julian 18
Lennox, Annie 229
Lenoir, Jean 280
Lenoxbar (racehorse) 288
Leonardo da Vinci 220
Leonid meteors 149
leopard seal 135
Leppard, Tom 113
leprosy 105
leptospirosis 118, 134
Lerach, William 52
Les Noces de Pierette 221
Les Tréteaux du Cœur Volant 224
Lessing, Simon 303
Let It Ride High Roller 184
Lethal Weapon 212
letters: auctioned 35; written 59
Leucosolenia blanca 123
Levi: advertising 44-45
Levi Strauss & Co. 43, 246
Levine, Jeremy, Aylett, Mark and Arrese, Carlos 77
Lewin, Leonard 88
Lewis, Carl 256-57, 264
Lewis, Cam 78
Lewis, Daniel Day 12
Lewis, Jerry 28
Lex the Wonderdog 70
Li Hongyun 285
Li Ning 284
Li Peng 181
lichens 142
Lichtenstein, Roy 41, 232
Liebold, Dr Hans 273
Liechtenstein: prime minister 27

Life After Death 237
Life and Times of Joseph Stalin 242
Life Fellowship Bird Sanctuary 124
Life magazine covers 10
lifespan 72-73
lifespan: leeches 133; mayflies 131; portrayed by actor 12; spiders 129; tortoise 125
lift disaster 198
light: brightness 182
lightbeam, longest 182
lightbulbs: collection 56
LightCycler 144
lighting 182-83
lighting rigs 183
lightning 92, 203
Lightwater Valley themepark 185
Like a Prayer 235
Like a Virgin 19
Liles, Jeff 269
Lille Zoo 136
Lima football stadium 198
Lima, Ronaldo Luis Nazario de 16
limousines 159
Lincoln, Abraham 56
Lincoln, Evelyn 36
Lincolnshire Handicap 288
Lindstrand, Per 78
line dancing 68
liners 165; luxury 32
Ling, Sydney 70
Lion King, The 215, 218
lions 116
Lischak, Wilhelm 299
'Lison's case' 101
Lithuania: president 26
litter collecting 69
Little, Bornie 281
Little Big Man 12
Little Deuce Coupe 239
Little Girl Lost 71
Little People of America, Inc. 13
Little River Band 230
Little Shop of Horrors 143
Lituya Bay 146
Live Aid 28
Live And Let Die 231
Live at the Apollo 234
Live Through This 233
liver fluke 132-33
lizards 134; Gila monster 134; Mexican beaded 134; new species 137; Texas horned 134
loach, Tibetan 120
Lobach, Marina 285
lobster, American 122
lobsters: parasites 136
Lockheed Martin 195
Lockheed 197; SR-71 aircraft 162
locusts 130
Loebner Prize 178
Loftus, Col. Ernest 59
log rolling 74
Logan, Johnny 231
logos 42
Lombaard, Stephanus 266
London Church of Christ 68
London Metal Exchange 46
London-Sydney Rally 273
London Underground: advertising 44
London Zoo 126, 136
Lone Ranger 219
Long Haired Lover From Liverpool 228
Long, Thelma 261
long-distance running 256
long johns 36
long jump: 257; Paralympics 267; reference 306; titles 264
Long Kiss Goodnight 52, 208
Long Neck Bottle 238
long-tailed planigale 117

Longbottom, Steve 281
longevity 72-73
Longo, Jeannie 286
Lopes, Carlos 302
Lopez, Pedro 84
Lopker, Pam 50
Loraipe, Tegla 303
Lord of the Dance 98, 222
L'Oreal 20, 32
Los Alamos National Laboratory 180
Los Angeles Lakers 17, 269
Los Angeles Zoo 137
Los Del Rio 240-41
Löschner, Jürgen 57
Lost World: Jurassic Park 208
Lotito, Michel 63
lotteries 38
loudspeakers 172
Louganis, Greg 275
Louis, Joe 283
Louis Vuitton 35
Louisiana Purchase 154
Lourdes 91
Louw, Alex François 299
Love, Courtney 24-25, 233
Love, Davis Milton 258
Love Is Blue 231
Love Me Do 18
Love Parade 244
Love Shine A Light 231
Lovell, Capt. James Arthur 189
Lowe, Bobby 270
Lowe, Flying Officer P. 298
Loyola University Medical Center 97
LR Mate 100I 180
Lucas, Albert 66
Lucas, George 53, 59, 183, 210-11
Lucas, Thelma 73
Lucasfilm Ltd 211
Lucid, Shannon 188
Lucius, Natalie and Pretou, Fabien 96
Ludden, Gert Jan 75
lugeing 295; Olympics 265; street 292
luggage: most expensive 35
Luise (pig) 138
Lulu 242
Lunar City 184
lunar eclipses 148
lunar missions 188
Lunar Prospector 188
lunch table: longest 63
Luncher, Joyce 267
Lund Foundation for Children 22
lung fish 121
lung power 64
Luoma, Teppo 66
Lutz, George and Kathy 89
Luxembourg: GDP 46; pollution 200
Luyendyk, Arie 272
Luzhniki Stadium, USSR 198
Lycosa gulosa 128
Lynch, Shaun 259
Lynn, Loretta 238
Lynn, Peggy 103
Lyon, Daniel 99
Lyp Synch 218
lyrics, autographed 22

M 134 Minigun 195
M*A*S*H 214
M People 234
M & M Meatshops 60
Mabe, Joni 99
Macarena 240-41

MacDonald, Alan 65
MacDonald, Julian 248
Macedonia: health 105; president 27
machine guns 195
Mackintosh, Charles Rennie 221
MacLean, Alistair 216
MacPherson, Elle 21
Macropanesthia rhinoceros 131
Macy's department store 40
Mad Max 208
Mad Max Beyond Thunderdome 212
Madagascan red owl 136
Maddux, Greg 270
Madec, Serge 78
Madeline, Steve 74
Madonna 19, 111, 209, 228-29,
   233, 234-35
Mafia 84
Mafiya 84
magazines 216-17;
   covers 17, 20, 71
Magel, Fred 59
Magellan Systems Corporation 174
magic 224
Magic Riddle, The 209
Magical Mystery Tour 18
magicians: earnings 53
Maglioni 252
Magnusson, Magnus Ver 110
Maine University 68
Maison Jaffelin 62
Maitland, Jack 301
Maize, Joe 69
maize: genetically modified 145
majorities in elections 26
Makonouchi (sumo) 282
malaria 104
malarial parasites 133
Malayala Manorama newspaper 216
Malkin, Colin 273
mallee fowl 127
Mallory, Molla 260
malls, shopping 40-41
Malone, Joe 279
Malta, Sovereign Military Order 47
Maltese Falcon 37
Managaro, A. 266
Manchester United 252-53
Mandela, Nelson 86, 230
Mandybur, Dr 99
Mang Gorn Luang restaurant 63
manga animation 218
Manhattan 248
'Manhattan Project' 196
Manheim car auctions 50
Mannes, Annelin 257
Manoliu, Lia 256
Manor, The 11
Mansell, Nigel 272
Mantis ride 184
Mantle, Mickey 270
Manufacturers' World Championships
   273
manuscripts: auctioned 36
Maracana Municipal Stadium 253
Maradona, Diego 254
marathons 302-03
Marble Bar 147
marbles: collection 56-57
Marburg fever 104
Marciano, Rocky 283
Marcos, Ferdinand 84
Marcos, Imelda 56, 84
Marcotullio, Alain 60
Marcroix (horse) 289
Mardi Gras 245
Margarethe II, Queen of Denmark 26
Margulies, Julianna 214
Mariana Trench 79, 146
Marilyn X100 220
marine worms 123

Maris, Roger Eugene 270
Maritsa River 200
Mark of Zorro 219
market value, corporations 48
Markham, Fred 166
Marko, Dr Helmut 272
Markov, Georgi 196
Marks & Spencer 246
Marksman (racehorse) 288
Marley, Bob 236
marriages: film stars 10-11;
   longest 72-73; tallest couple 96;
   youngest couple 71
Mars 149, 181; landing 179;
   meteorite 36
marsupials 116-19
Martian rock 36
Martin, Grace 113
Martin, Patrice 296
Martin, Ricky 241
Martin XP6M-1 SeaMaster 162
Martinez, Pedro 270
Martins, Thomas and Volker 57
Masci, Thierry 283
Masek, Vaclav 255
Mason, Nicholas 64
Mason, Tom 292
Massachusetts Institute of
   Technology 180
Massey, Christopher 297
Massive Attack 176
Masson, Paul 286
Mast, Samuel S. 102
Mastandrea, Linda 266
Masterkova, Svetlana 257
Masters, Bruce 58
Mata Hari 196
Mathäser pub 63
Mathias, Robert 256
Matina, Matyus and Béla 96
mating call, frog 137
Matsushima, Akira 80
Mattel company 58
Matthäus, Lothar 254-55
Matthes, Roland 274
Mattia, Tony 56
Mattioli, Gai 248
Matzger, Eddy 292
Mauna Loa volcano 147
Max Mara 20
Maxwell, Robert 51
Maxwell Communications 51
Maybelline 21
mayflies 131
Mbutsi pygmies 96
MC Lyte 236
McArdle, Brian 68
McAuliffe, Christa 188
McCallen, Phillip 287
McCarron, Christopher 288
McCarthy-Fox, Julia and Sam 56-57
McCartney, Sir Paul 19, 36, 176,
   230, 232; Live Aid 28
McCartney, Stella 248
McCaw, Craig 33
McClellan, Gerald 283
McCormick, Patricia 275
McCoy, Millie and Christine 100
McCrary, Billy and Benny 97
McCulley, Johnston 219
McDonald, Eddie 74
McDonald, John 178
McDonald, Patrick 'Babe' 256
McDonald's 46, 49
McDonnell Douglas Corporation 49
McEnroe, John 42
McEnroe, John 261
McEntire, Reba 238
McGrory, Matthew 99
McGuire, Willa 296
McIlroy, William 101

McKay, Alan 66
McKay, Pat 283
McKenzie, Colin 89
McKinlay, Peter 66
McLaren 272; F1 6.1 159
McMahon, Richard 148
McPeak, Steve 224
meals: expensive 62
Mears, Rick Ravon 272
meat consumption 60
Meatloaf 232
Mecca 91
media empires 50
media tycoons 52
medicinal leech 132
medicine 106-07
MediEvil 170
Medved, Aleksandr 282
Meegeren, Han van 89
Meenan, David 66
Meet the Press 214
Mega-City-Pyramid 157
Megaloblatta longipennis 130
Mehlmann, Olaf 267
Mehmed (horse) 289
Mehta, Shekhar 273
Meier, Richard and Partners 157
Meilleur, Marie 102
Melbourne College of Textiles 68
Melvyn Weiss 52
memorabilia 36-37; Diana 23
Memorial Necróple Ecumênica 155
Men At Work 232
Menem, Carlos 86
Mengele, Dr Josef 144, 193
Menin, Michel 224
Men's Fitness 110
Mentis computer 174
Menuhin, Yehudi 70
Mercedes 18; speed trials 158;
   280E 273
Mercedes-Benz 161; C111-IV 273
Merckx, Eddy 286
Mercury 148
Mercury, Freddie 29
mercury pollution 201
Mercury Prize 18
Mercury-Redstone 3 spacecraft 188
Meredith, Leon 286
mergers 49
Merrill Lynch and Co. 46
'Mersenne prime' numbers 179
Messerschmitt KR 200 'Bubble Top'
   37
Messner, Reinhold 300
metal: bending 225; eating 63
meteor craters 149
meteorites 149, 204; auctioned 36
methane: emitted by cows 119
methyl isocyanate 200
Metropolitan Museum of Art 33
Metropolitan Opera House 242
Meuse River 64
Mexican beaded lizard 134
Mexican music 240-41
Mexico City 200
Mexico: scorpion deaths 205
Mezzanine 176
MGM Grand Casino 39
MGM Grand Hotel 154
Mi Tierra 241
MI6 196
Miagrammopes spiders 129
Miami Dolphins 262
Miami Super Conga 68
mice 119
Michael, George 18, 233
Michelin tyres 160
Michelle, Shelly 12
Mickey Mouse 219
Microbothus pusillus 129

microbots 180
microchips 178
microdots 197
microlight aircraft 81
microlights 299
microparasites 132
Microsoft 18, 32, 45, 50, 52, 161,
   170, 176, 179, 233
Microsoft *Office '97* 43
Microsoft *Word* 178
Middle of Nowhere 228
Midnight at the Oasis 293
midwife toad 123
MiG jet 56
Might Tango (horse) 289
migration: fish 120; insects 132-33
Miguel, Luis 240
Mihavecz, Andreas 107
Mikaie, Tabwai 93
Mikkola, Hannu 273
Mikoyan MiG-25 jet 195
Mil Mi-26 helicopter 163
Mildred Kerr (spaniel) 138
mileage, car 159
Milestones 242
Milk in Space 44
milk shake, biggest 61
Milken, Michael 87
Milky Way 148
Milla, Albert 255
millennium bug 178
millennium celebrations 32, 244-45
Millennium Falcon (*Star Wars*) 183
Miller, Edward 60
Miller, Johnny 258
Miller's Collectibles 43
Millie's Book 138
millionaires 32-33, 50-51; actors
   12-13; oldest sportsman 17;
   racing drivers 272; rock stars 232;
   supermodels 20-21; youngest
   sportswoman 17
Milstar satellite 187
Milton, Brian and Reynolds, Keith 81
Milton Keynes 40
Milwaukee Braves 270
Milwaukee Brewers 270
Mimura, Yuki 283
Mindbender 225
MindStorms 180
minelayer 162
Miner, Steve 211
Mini Night Vision scope 173
mini-robots 181
mini-series 215
minidisc recorders 173
Minimata Bay, Japan 201
Ministry of Sound 244
Minnesota Vikings 262
Minnoch, Jon 96, 108
Minogue, Kylie 229
Mir space station 187-88;
   milk advertisement 44
Miramax 210
Mischke, David 280
Misery 211
Miss Budweiser 281
Miss Sarajevo 28
Miss Universe 109, 184
Miss Venezuela Organization 109
missiles 194
Mission Impossible 213
Mississippi River swim 275
Mitchell, Margaret 216
Mitchell, Trevor 65
Mitera, Robert 259
Mitnick, Kevin 178
Mitsubishi Colt GTi-16V 76
Mitsubishi Corporation 48, 161, 172
Miyamoto, Shigeru 171
Mizushima Plant steel works 74

Mizzi, Suzanne 98
Mmmbop 228
Mobell, Sidney 35
Mobil 293
mobile phones 172; jewelled 175
mobiles, human 224
model agencies 20-21
models: insurance 98
Modes et Travaux magazine 216
Modugno, Domenico 230
Moeara Petroleum Corporation 46
Moeller, Bernie 112
Moet & Chandon 33
Mohammed, Gul 97
Mohammed, Majed Abdullah 252
moisturizers 247
Molier, Ricky 266
Mona Lisa 220
monasteries 91
Monier, Guy 62
Monkees, the 230
monkeys: heart transplant 144
monoplanes 163
Monopoly set 35
Monroe, Marilyn 25, 36
Monsanto 145
Monsieur Christophe 109
'Monsieur Mangetout' 63
monsoons 202-03
Monster Raving Loony Party 39
Mont Blanc 301
Mont Blanc freighter 199
Montagua Fault 203
Montalvo, Fernando Inchauste 71
Montanino, Dr Gennara 103
Monte Carlo Rally 273
Monte Makaya roller coaster 185
Montgomerie, Colin 17, 258
Montgomery, James 274
Montgomery, Percy 311
Monti, Eugene 294
Monteneros, guerilla group 85
Montreal Canadiens 278
monuments 154
Moon 184; crematorium 188;
   laser reflector 182; rock 36
Moon, Reverend Sung Myung 91
Moore, Archie 283
Moore, Dave 166
Moore, Demi 13
Moose (terrier) 138
Moradabad, India 203
Morales, Capt. Alberto 289
Morbidelli 850 V8 167
Morelon, Daniel 286
Morgan, Chesty 13
Morgan 4/4 159
Morgan Gardner (corgi) 11
Morgan Motor Company 159
Morgan Stanley Discover & Co. 49
Moricz, Michael 69
Morissette, Alanis 232
Morris, Reg 60
Morris (cat) 138
Morrison, Jim 24, 233
Morrow, Patrick 300
Mortanges, Charles Pahud de 289
Moser, Annemarie 276
Moses, Edwin Corley 257
Moskalenko, Aleksandr 285
mosques 155
mosquitoes 128, 133; diseases 104;
   killing 66
Moss, Kate 20, 246, 248
mothers: oldest 102; prolific 102
moths 130-31
moto-cross 286-87
Motor Mouth 65
motorbikes 166-67;
   circumnavigation 79;
   racing 286-87

motorcycles: jumping 77; miniature 166; pyramid 76; longest journey 79
Motorized Submersible Canoe 197
Motorola StarTac Lite phone 172
motoryachts 280
Moulay Ismail, Emperor of Morocco 102
Mount Athos 91
Mount Everest International Peace Climb 300
mountain beaver 130
mountain bikes 167
mountain climbing 300-301
mountain races 301
Mourik, Guus van 283
Mousetrap, The 223
mousetraps: collection 56
Moussa, Amm Atwa 102
moustaches 100
Movile Cave 136
Mozambique: GDP 47
Mozart, Wolfgang Amadeus 243
Mr Ben Vintage Clothing 56
Mr Bug Goes To Town 98
Mr Jefferson (cloned calf) 145
Mr Loverman 237
Mr Olympia 110
Mr Universe 110-11
Mrs Doubtfire 53
MS Flight Simulator 170
Ms Olympia 111
Mswati III, King of Swaziland 23
Mt. Cameroon 301
Mt. Roland 142
Mt. Wai-'ale-'ale 147
MTV Unplugged 232
Müller, Gerd 254-55
Much Ado About Nothing 223
Mudd, Jodie 258
mudslides 202
Muhammad Ali 17, 37
mules: actors 138
Mulholland Drive 10
Muller, Kal 299
multimedia 174
mummies 100; tattooed 112
Munari, Sandro 273
Munchausen's syndrome 101
Mundy, Albert E. 252
Munro, Minnie 73
murder 84, 86, 204
murders 90; rock stars 25
Murdoch, Lachlan 50
Murdoch, Rupert 50, 52
Muresan, Gheorghe 268
murine typhus 134
Murphy, Eddie 12
Murphy, Sean 259
Murray, Lenda 111
Murrie, John 66
Muscle & Fitness 110
Muscle Beach 110
Muscle Power Championships 110
Musgrave, Storey 189
Music Forever 69
musical chairs 74
musical instruments 243
musical sportsman 17
musicals 222-23
Musiol, Bogdan 294
Muslim: pilgrimage 91; pilgrims 198
mussels 62
Mussolini, Benito 288
Mustafar, Fakir 112
mustard gas 193
Musters, Pauline 96
mute swans 134
Mutt and Jeff 219
Mutton, Greg 75

My Girl 12
My Heart Will Go On 241
My Own Private Idaho 25
My Stepmother is an Alien 12
My Way 24, 230
Myers, Geoff 74-75
Myrtle Beach 298
Myst 170

Naha City Festival 69
Nakamura, Kanzaburo 223
Nakano, Koichi 286
Nakayama, Mie 283
Namba, Yasuko 72
Nanga Parbat 301
Naples 204
Napoleon Bonaparte 209; penis 98; socks 56
Narayanan, Kocheril Raman 26
Nariman, Sir Temulji and Lady 73
Narita, Mayumi 267
NASA 181, 186-87
Nashnush, Suleiman Ali 269
National Football League 214, 262-63
National Gallery 51
National Lottery 38
National Scout Jamboree 69
natural gas 160
Natural History Museum 116
Nau, Christian-Yves 293
Nauru 201
Navrátilova, Martina 16; and Shriver, Pam 260
Navstar 174
Naya, Koki (Taiho) 282
Nazi concentration camp 144
Nazi Gold 85
Nazi hanging 86
Nazir, Prem and Sheela 12
Neal, David 58
Nechisar nightjar 137
necks: extension 108; insurance 98
Necrotising fasciitis 104
Nehmer, Meinhard 294
Neiman, Leroy 53
Nekoda, Katsutoshi 293
Nekton Beta 92
Nel Blu Dipinto Di Blu 230
Nelson, Horatio 99
Nelson, John 258
Nelson, Oscar 283
Nelson, Willie 238
Nelson airship 245
nematodes 133
Nemov, Alexei 284
Nena 229
Nepenthes plants 142
Nephila senegalensis 129
Nephila spiders 129
Neptune 148
Nesser, Isaac 111
nests 127
net-casting spider 129
NetNames Ltd. 177
Network Television Marketing 61
neutron stars 148, 151
Nevada Megabucks slot jackpot 38
Nevada State Prison 87
Never Say Never Again 109
New England Whalers 279
New Kids on the Block 229
New Orleans Saints 263
New Transducers Ltd. 172
New World vulture 126

New Year parties 244
New York Cosmos 252
New York Giants 262
New York Islanders 279
New York Jets 263
New York Journal 219
New York Omnipresence 108
New York Philharmonic 242
New York Rangers 278
New York Stock Exchange 46
New York subway installation 220
New York Sun 88
New York Yankees 270
New Zealand cricket team 290
Newby-Fraser, Paula 302
Newell and Sorrell 42
NewLeaf potato 145
Newman, Fred 269
Newman, Paul S. 219
Newman, Steven 80
News Corporation Ltd. 50
News Network 52
News of the World 216
news presenters 14
newspapers 216-17
newspapers: tycoons 50
Newton, Fred 275
Newton, Sir Isaac 99
Newton-John, Olivia 230
newts 122
Nextage Shanghai 40
NFL 262-63
Ngga Pulu 300
Nguema, Francisco Macías 71
NI rocket booster 186
Niño, El 146
Nichimen Graphics, Inc. 170
Nicholas II, Russia 23
Nicholson, Jack 11-12, 208
Nickerson, Bob 269
Nicklaus, Jack 258, 308
Nielsen, Brigitte 13
Nielsen, Sofus 252
Nielsen TV ratings 44
Nietlispach, Franz 267
Nieto, Angel Roldan 287
Nigeria, prisoners 86
Night at the Opera 65
Night of the Living Dead 210
night vision scope 173
nightclubs 244
Nightmare on Elm Street 211
Niihau, Hawaii 33
Nike 16, 247, 268; advertising 44; brand name 42
Nikki Inc. 21
Nikolic, Ivan 75
Nikolo-Arkhangekskiy Crematorium 155
Nile, River 142, 146
Nimitz class aircraft carriers 164
Nimoy, Leonard 215
Nina Ricci 20
Nineteen Eighty-Four 44
Nintendo 170, 172, 174
Nippon Telegraph and Telephone Corp. 46, 49, 172
Nippon Television 215
Nirvana 24, 232
Nissan cars 160
Nissan Motor Co. 69
nitrogen, liquid 160
Nixon, Richard 35
No Doubt 232
Nobel Peace Prize 204
Nobel Prize winners 70
Noda, Uichi 59
Noll, Chuck 262
Nomad robot 181
Non-Stop Connolly Show 223
noodle making 60

Norberg, Bengt 76
Nordic skiing 276
Norman, Jessye 29
Norman, Greg 17, 258
Norman, L. 280
North African ostrich 126
North Korea: president 26
North Pole: oldest visitor 72; youngest visitor 70
Northamptonshire cricket team 290
northern pygmy mouse 117
Northwest Airlines 162
Norwegian spruce 141
Norwood Hypermarket 60
noses: flattened 113; insured 98
Notorious B.I.G. 237
Notting Hill Carnival 244
Novakov, Michael 296
novelists 216-17
Nozomi 500 trains 164
nuclear disasters 200-01
nuclear weapons 194, 196
nucleotides 145
nude acting roles 12
numbers, longest 179
Nureyev, Rudolf 222
Nurmi, Paavo 256
nut crackers 57

O. J. Simpson trial 214
Oakenfold, Paul 244
Oakland Raiders 262
Oasis 18, 232
Obayashi company 184
Oblivion roller coaster 185
O'Brien, Richard 58
oceans 146
Octave Auguste 40
octopus, blue-ringed 135
O'Dell, David 66
Odhaimbo, Joseph 269
O'Donnell, Daniel 239
Oerter, Alfred 264
office blocks 155, 157; rents 48
Official Development Assistance (ODA) 47
Ogata, Toshimitsu (Kitanoumi) 282
Ogawa, Naoya 283
Oghaby, Khalil 111
ogre-faced spider 129
Oh Carolina 237
O'Hanlan, Dr Kate 107
Ohlsdorf Cemetery 155
Ohrberg, Jay 159
oil: Gulf War 192; spillages 201; tankers 165; tycoons 50
Oil of Ulay 247
Ojedo-Guzman, Jorge 224
O'Keefe, Georgia 221
Oklahoma City 199
Oktoberfest 63
'Old Faithful' car 159
Oldman, Gary 12, 25
Oliveira, Denilson de 253
Oliver, Louis 263
Oliver Rotary Club 61
OLS hi-fi 174
Olympic Cavern Hall 157
Olympic Games 256-57, 264-65; Atlanta 271; bobsleigh 294; competitors 264; gymnastics 284; ice hockey 278; judo 283; Los Angeles 275; Melbourne 270; Seoul 285; shooting 72; show jumping 288; soccer 252;

South Korea 87; Sydney 285; volleyball 293; wrestling 282
Olympics, Special 111
omelette, biggest 61
Omnicom 42
On Her Majesty's Secret Service 231
on-line accounts 177
On My Own 216
Onassis, Aristotle 32
Oncomouse 144
One Fine Day 14
One Flew Over the Cuckoo's Nest 12
One Sweet Day 228
One Way Ticket 239
O'Neal, Jermaine 269
O'Neal, Shaquille 17
O'Neal, Steve 263
O'Neal, Tatum 12, 111
Onesi, Paul and Mary 73
onion peeling 60
Onion Roll (racehorse) 288
Open Road, The 217
opera 242-43
opera singers: earnings 53
Operation Desert Storm 192
'Operation Gold' 196
operations 106-07
ophidiids, deepest-living fish 120
ophthamology 182
opossums 119
Opportunity Village 29
Oprah Winfrey Show 14
Opuntia cactus 142
orbits: time 148
orchestras 69
orchids 140
organs: exhibited 98
Oribe, Ricardo 267
Oriental Pearl TV Tower 157
origami 69
Origin Systems Inc. 171
Orlan 108
Orphan's Benefit 218
Ortiz, Purification 267
Ortmann, Horst 66
Osborne, Charles 106
Oscars 209, 234; animation 218; auctioned 35; nominations 12, 14; special effects 183; stuntman 212; youngest winners 12
Osiier, Dr Ivan 265
Osmond, Jimmy 228
Osteogenesis imperfecta 96
Osterud, Joann 298
ostriches 126, 134
Otello 242
Ottey, Merlene 256-57
Otto, Kristin 274
Ötzi 112
Ouest-France newspaper 216
Ousland, Boerge 79
Outagamia County Fairgrounds 60
Outzen, John and Carl 80
Overacker, Leroy 70
overalls 37
Owen, Michael 255
Owens, Jesse 257
Oxenford, John 223
Oxfam shops 247
Oxford English Dictionary 246
Oxford Street 41
Oxford University cricket team 290
oxygen 150
Oymyakon, Siberia 147
oysters 123; oyster opening 60
ozone layer 200

P&O cruise line 165
P3 robot 181
Pacific crossings 78-79
Pacific giant kelp 140
Pacific Ocean 146
Packard, David 51
Packer, Kerry 38
Padaung tribe 108
Padre Pio 90
paella, biggest 61
painters: earnings 53
paintings 41; forgeries 89
Pak Yong Sung 71
Pakistan: cricket 291; presidential
    elections 26
Pal ('Lassie') 138
palaces 154; presidential 26
Paladino, Mimmo 246
Palio horse race 288
Palm Island, Australia 204
Palm, Kerstin 265
Palmer, Arnold 17, 258
Paltrow, Gwyneth 246
Pan Am skyscraper 215
Pan American Games 271
Panasonic 173
Panax quinquefolium 62
pancakes: biggest 61; races 74;
    tossing 60
Pandinus giganticus 129
Pandinus imperator 129
Pandya, Arvind 80
Pangilinan, Manual 52
Panova, Bianka 285
Pantanal, Brazil 146
Papa Don't Preach 235
Paper Moon 12
Papert, Professor 180
Papon, Maurice 193
parachuting 92, 298
parachutists: oldest 72
Paradoxurus 63
paragliding 299
Paraguay: losses in war 192
Paralympics 266-67
Paramount film company 208
paranormal hoax 89
parasites 132; malarial 133
parasitic flukes 133
parasitic wasp 130
Parent, Bernie 279
Paris Match 216
Parish, Robert 268
Park, Nick 218
Parker, Charlie 243
parking meters: collection 57
Parr, Rob 11
Parseeism 91
Parsons, Lili 102
parties 244-45
Parton, Dolly 238
Parve, Kaya 303
Pasquette, Didier 224
pass completions (football) 263
pass the parcel 74
passenger train: longest 165
Pastrana, Julia 100
Pate, Jerry 258
Patek Philippe watch 35
paternalism, toads 123
Pathfinder 179
Patrese, Ricardo 272
Patricia 241
Patriot Games 217
PATSY awards 138

Patten, Burnet 72
Patten, Neville 166
Patterson, Roger 88
Patu marplesi 128
Patzaichin, Ivan 297
Paul, Henri 22
Paul, Steven 70
Paulsen, Louis 75
Pavarotti, Luciano 28-29, 53, 242
Payton, John 71
PCD-7900 174
'Peanuts' 219
Pearl Oriental Holdings 32
pearls 34
Peck, Gregory 11
Peck, M. Scott 216
pedal-boats 81
Peel Engineering Company 159
Peel P50 159
Pegasus rocket 186, 188
Pegasus satellite launcher 186
Peintre Célèbre (horse) 310
Pektuzun, Bahattin, Bulent and Ediz
    61
Pelé 252, 254-55
Pellaton, Scott 297
Pellonpää, Henri 66
Pelsh, Valdis 15
penis: Napoleon's 98
Penn, Sean 111
pentathlon 302
Pentecost Island 299
People 230
People vs. Larry Flynt 233
People's Temple 90
Pepe Jeans 138
Pepsi 18, 42; in space 44
Percebes barnacle 62
Père Lachaise cemetery 24
peregrine falcon 126-27
Perez, Quintanilla (Selena) 240
performance art: festival 245
performing dog 139
perfumes 49, 249
Perón, Eva 209
Perrone, Tony 11
Perry, Nikki 138
personal computers 49
Peslier, Olivier 310
Pet Shop Boys 228
Peta animal rights movement 137
Peterson, Ronnie 272
Petit, Philippe 224
PetOps supercomputer 178
petroleum companies 49
Petronas Towers 155
Petrova, Maria 285
Petrovski, Albert 67
pets 138-39; richest 11
Philadelphia 76ers 96
Philadelphia Eagles 263
Philadelphia Fliers 279
philanthropists 33
Philippines: lost tribe 88
Phillips 173
Phipps, Eli Shadrack and John
    Meshak 102
phoenix fowl 126
Phoenix Zoo 138
Phoenix, River 25
phone cards: collectors' item 35
phosphate extraction 201
photographers 28
photographs: Royal Family 56
photography: aerials 58; (Diana) 22;
    fairy hoax 89
photorefractive keratectomy (PRK)
    182
photosynthesis: in lichen 142
photovoltane panels 156
Phreatobius walkeri catfish 121

Piaggio 167
pianos: grand 243
Piasecki Heli-Stat 163
Picasso, Pablo 221
Piccard, Dr Jacques 79
Pickford, Mary 98
pickled onion eating 60
Pickles (dog) 37
Pieman (social critic) 14, 52
Pierce-Arrow 159
piercings, body 112
Pietermaritzburg Msundzai Fire
    Services 69
pigs: acting 138; heart transplant
    144
pilbara ningaui 117
pilgrims 90, 91; death 198
pills 106
pilots: oldest 72-73
Piltdown Man 88
Pinda, Emmanuel 283
Pink Floyd 182, 232
pink-legged graveteiro 137
'Pink Palace', Hollywood 10
Pinkpop festival 245
Pinsent, Matthew 311
Pioneer 10 spacecraft 187
Pioneer probe 148
Piranha 173
piranhas 135
Pirelli advertisement 16
Piro, Sal 58
Pisces III 92
pitcher plants 143
pitchers, baseball 270
Pitt-Turner, Thelma 302
Pittsburgh Steelers 262
Pittsburgh Symphony Youth
    Orchestra 69
Pitzer, Piet and Erasmus, Jaco 74
Pizarro, Francisco 85
pizza, biggest 60
pizza delivery 81
Pizzarro, Malik Shabazz 67
pla buk fish 120
Place, Jonathan 106
plague: disease 104
Plainview hydrofoil 165
plane crashes 24
planets 148
plankton 121
Plante, Jacques 279
plants: dangerous 142-43; traps 142
plasma TV screens 172
Plasmodium falciparum 104
plasters: collection 57
plastic surgery 108
plastics: strongest 151
Plastination technique 98
Plateau Station 147
platinum discs 22, 228, 240
Playback Show 14
Player, Gary 258
playing card (Queen of Hearts) 23
plays 222-23
Playtex 246
Please Please Please 234
Pluto 148, 187
pneumonic plague 118
Pocket Monsters 218
Poe, Edgar Allan 89
Poetic Justice 235
poison: snakes 124
poison-arrow frogs 134
poisoning 87, 90
poisons 134; plants 142; toads 150
Poivre, Patrick 14
poker 38
Polaire, Mlle 97
polar bear 116, 118, 134

Polaroid Pocket Xiao camera 173
pole vault 256-57; reference 306
Police Story 212
politicians: earnings 52
Poliyakov, Valeriy 188-89
pollution: air 200
polo 289
Polo Sports clothing 248
Polyák, Imre 283
polymerase chain reaction 144
polyphemus moth 130
Polyus Nedostupnosti 147
Pont, Michel 56
Pont de l'Alma 22
Pontefract Sports and Leisure Centre
    285
Pontiac Silverdrome Stadium 154
poodles: models 138
Poon Lim 93
pop art 220
Pop Catalogue chart 232
pop stars 18-19
Popeye The Sailor Man 219
Popmart tour (U2) 23
Popolo di Tessaglia 243
Popov, Aleksandr 274
Porcellanaster ivanovi starfish 123
porcupine quills, body art 112
Porsche, Ferdinand 158
Porsche cars 272
Port Aventura, Spain 185
Port Richborough powerboat race
    281
Porter, Bobbie 213
Portrait of Dr Gachet 220
Portsmouth Northsea Swimming Club
    275
Portugal: religious vision 90;
    roller hockey 292
Portuguese man-of-war 135
postal stamps: Barbie 58
posters 37; most expensive 221;
    Marilyn Monroe 25
potatoes: genetically engineered
    145
Potsdamer Platz 232
Poupon, Philippe 79
Powell, David 107
power failures: ice storms 203
Power Tower roller coaster 185
Powerball Lottery 38
powerboats 280-81; jumps 213
Powerbook G3 174
powerjuggling 64
powerlifting 110, 285; reference
    310-11
Powers, Francis 196
Powitsky, Dale 92
Poyarkov, Yuriy Mikhailovich 293
PPL Therapeutics 145
Prado, Perez 231, 241
Prajapati, Radhey Shyam 67
precious stones 34-35;
    as buttons 248
predators, fish 120
pregnancy 103
prehistoric tattoos 112
Preisler, Horst 302
Presley, Elvis 18, 33, 99, 230;
    fans 59; grave 24
Presley, Lisa Marie 33
Presley, Patricia 110
press-ups 303
Prestwich, John 106
Pretty Woman 10, 12
pretzel, giant 61
Price, Nicholas 258
Price, Nick 259
Price, Vincent 185
prickly pear 142
Primagaz 78

primary cells 173
Primate Research Center 144
primates 116-17; cloned 144
prime numbers 179
Primitive Love 240
Prince 19, 229, 234
Prince Abdul Aziz yacht 33
Princess Diana 22-23
Princess of Wales memorial fund 22
Principal, Victoria 214
printers: line matrix 175;
    miniature 173
prison camps 193
prisoners 86; of conscience 87;
    on death row 87
prisons 86
Prius vehicle 160
privatization 46
Procter and Gamble 45, 247
Prodigy 234-35
producers: youngest 70
production runs: cars 158
profits 48
Project Blue (Pepsi) 43
'Project Jennifer' 197
projection screen, laser 183
Prokurorov, Aleksey 277
pronghorn antelope 118
Prost, Alain 272
Proud Mary 280
Proudfoot, Michael 92
Prudential Insurance 18
Psion Series 5 computers 179
PSV Einhoven 253
PT Sona Topas 41
publishers' advances 217
publishing companies 49
pubs 58
Puff Daddy & Faith Evans 236
puffer fish 134
Pujol, Joseph 101
Pulp 18
Pulse 8 Fitness Studio 285
Pulse Width Modulation amplifier 174
Puma car 161
Puma robot 180
Puma trainers 42
Puma Tyneside RC 257
Pumping Iron 111
Pumpkin Matthews (poodle) 139
Punjab Kesari newspaper 216
Puppy 220
purdah 91
Purkiss, Ray 281
Purley, David 107
purple nutgrass 142
Purple Rain 234
purring spider 128
Purvis, Andy 74-75
putts (golf) 259
Puya raimondii 140
pygmies 96
pygmy goby fish 120
pygmy mouse 117
pygmy mouse lemur 117
pygmy shrew 117
Pyongyang Circus 71
pythons 124

QAD software 50
Qatar: taxation 46
Quake 171
Quantum Group 53
Quarmby, Arthur 157
Québec City 245

Queen 29, 229
Queen Alexandra Stakes, Ascot, UK 288
Queen of Hearts card 23
Queensberry Rules 283
quiche lorraine, biggest 60
Quiksilver 246, 294, 296
Quinn, Alison 213, 266
Quist, Adrian 261
quiz shows 215
Quo Vadis 209

R-16 rocket explosion 199
R&B 236-37
rabies encephalitis 104
Rabotmitsa magazine 216
RAC Rally 273
racing car memorabilia 37
Racing Club de Lens 252
racing drivers 272-73
Racz, Mike 60
Radcliffe, Peter 37
radiation 150, 205
radio broadcast 88, 91
radio galaxies 148
raffia plant 141
Raffles City, Singapore 154
Rafflesia arnoldi 141
raft of canoes 297
rafting, white water 297
rafts: survival 93
Ragab, Hisham 100
Rage of Angels 216
Raging Bull 12
Ragulin, Aleksandr 278
Raiders of the Lost Ark 212
railgun 195
railway companies 48
railway wagons, pulled by teeth 64
Rainer, Adam 96
rainfall 147
rainforests 200
rallying 273
Ramli, Rohayo 225
Ramos, Richie 108
ramp jump: car 76; motorcycle 76
Rankin, William 298
Ransehousen, Anne 265
ransoms 85
Rashid, Tahir 290
Rasmussen, Poul Nyrup 26
Rastelli, Enrico 66
rat-bite fever 134
rat flea 133
ratel 119
rats 118, 134; parasites 133
rattlesnakes 124
Raudaschl, Hubert 264
Rausing, Hans and Gad 51
RAV4L-V-EV cars 160
Ray, Thomas 256
razor-toothed piranha 135
RCIN toxin 196
RD-170 rocket engine 186
Rea, Ben 139
Read, Phil 287
Read My Mind 238
Reader's Digest 216-17
Reading University 181
Reagan, Ronald 12, 35, 105
Reagan, Ron Jr 112
Real Betis 253
Rebagliati, Ross 294
Rebel Without a Cause 24
Rebel X.D. 237

Rebroff, Ivan 243
Record Breakers TV show 64-65
recycling: cans 68; cars 161
Red Bug Buckboard 159
red-billed quelea 127
red-headed woodpecker 126
red howler monkey 127
red kangaroo 116
red shift 148
Red 'Savina' Habanero 63
red tide algae 142
Redding, Otis 237
Réden pen company 35
Redgrave family 12
Redgrave, Steve 311
Redmond, Frances 101
redwood trees 140-41
Reebok 44
Reed, John 52
Reef Cat 297
reefs 147
Rees, Simon 242
Reeve, Christopher 28
Reeves, Jim 239
referees: football 253
Refsdahl, Jan Egil 106
refugee aid 33
regeneration, of sponges 123
reggae 236-37
Regina Maersk 165
Reichsbank 85
Reichstag 221
reincarnation 90
Reincarnation of Saint Orlan 108
relay running 256-57
relay swims 275
relics, religious 90
religious cults 90-91
REM sleep 107
remote control 181
Renault 160
Report From Iron Mountain 88
reproduction: lemmings 119; rats 118; snails 133
reptiles 124-25
Republic XF-84H plane 162
rescues 92-93; parachute 298
Resident Evil 2 170
Resina, Abel 252
respirators 106
restaurants: biggest 63; chains 49; dining out 63
Restsova, Anfissa 303
reticulated python 124
Reuters 46, 179
Revenge (racehorse) 288
revenues: corporation 48; film 210; fashion houses 248
reverse driving 76
Review 232
Revlon 20-21
revues 222-23
Reynolds, Michael 156
Reynolds, Peter 242
Reza, Alexander 35
Reznikoff, John 56
Rheinberger, Michael 301
Rhine, River 201
rhinoviruses 105
Rhythm is a Dancer 234
rhythmic gymnastics 285
Rice, John and Greg 96
'Rice Grain' bug 197
Richard, Joseph Henri 278
Richard, Maurice 278
Richards, Sir Gordon 288
Richards, Keith 18, 98
Richards, Mark 296
Richards, Theodore W. 70
Richards, Vincent 260
Richardson, 'The Big Bopper' 24

Richardson, Dot 271
Richer Sounds plc 41
Richie, Lionel 228
Richie Rich 12
Riddler's Revenge roller coaster 184
Ride On Time 234
riding in armour 67
Rife, Mary 280
Riffi, Gregory 298
rifles 195
Riina, Salvatore 'Toto' 84
Rimes, Leann 238-39
Rimet, Jules 254
Ringling Brothers circus 224
rings: auctioned 34
Rinspeed 161
Rio de Janeiro Carnival 244
Ripken, Cal 306
Ripley, Alexandra 215
Rite of Spring 242
Ritts, Herb 28
Ritual Entertainment 170
Riven 170
Riverdance 222
rivers 146; pollution 201
RJR Nabisco Inc. 49, 53
road accidents 77
Road Less Traveled 216
Roadstar caravan 76
Robben Island 86
robberies 85
Robbins, Leslie 38
Roberts, Clive 158
Robin Hood: Prince of Thieves 213
Robinson, Sharon 139
Robinson, Dar 212
Robinson Crusoe Island 137
Robotec 218
robotic hand: art 112
Robotics Institute 181
robots 180-81
Robson, Bryan 255
rock 232-33; benefits 28-29; concerts 29; festivals 245; festival in Rio 232; stars 24-25
rock crystal egg 34
rock debris in space 188
rocket debris in space 188
rocket engines: car 158
rocket sled 107
rockets 186-87
Rockefeller, John D. 50-51
Rocket (horse) 288
Rockwell Commander 685 162
Rocky Horror Show 58
Rocky Mountain Institute 160
Rodden, Tom 65
Roddenberry, Gene 186, 188
rodents 116-17
Röhrl, Walter 273
Rojas, Téfilo 'Sparks' 84
Rolex 16; 'Oyster Perpetual' 35
roller coasters 184
roller hockey 292
Rolling Stones 18, 98, 232, 244
Rolling Stone magazine 18, 216
Rolls-Royce: jet engines 158; John Lennon's 233
Romances 240
Romanee Conti wine 62
Romeo and Juliet 208
'Romeo' spies 196
Romero, Antonio 240
Romero, George 210
Romme, Gianni 265
Rompelberg, Fred 166
Ronaldo 308
Rookie, The 213
Rooney, Mickey 10
Roosevelt, Comm. John 295
roots, deepest 141; longest 141

ropes: rice straw 69
Rosberg, Keke 272
Rose, Pete 270
Roseanne 15
Rosenberg, Julius 70
Rosendahl, Peter 166-67
Rosewal, Kenneth 261
Rosie Lee (bulldog) 138
Roslin Institute 145
Roswell Incident 89
rotorcraft 163
Rötsch, Frank-Peter 303
Rötsch, Franz 303
Rotter, Felix 57
roundworms 132
Roussel, Athina Onassis 32
Rowan, Chad (Akebono) 282
Rowe, Denny 65
Rowe, Lazarus 73
rowing: on land 81; reference 311; transatlantic 78; youngest cox 71
Roxanne '97 239
Royal Dutch Shell Group 49
Royal Family, British 56
Royal Masonic Hospital 68
Royal Marines 301
royalties 53
Royds-Jones, Edward 72
Roye, Jerry De 73
rubies 34
Rubio, Kevin 59
Ruby (elephant) 138
Ruby, Karine 294
Rudy, Frank 247
Rueda, Fabiola 301
rugby: reference 311
Ruijter, Charles 72
Ruiz, Rafael 240
Runabout jetskis 281
running: backwards 80; reference 306
running shoes 247
Runyan, Maria 267
Rupal Face, Pakistan 301
Ruppell's vulture 126
Ruppert, Miriam 184
RuPuter computer 172
Rusedski, Greg 261
rushers 262
Rusomanno, Edidio 139
Russanova, Tatyana Mikhailovna 92
Russell, Jack 291
Russell, Ken 225
Russia: advertising market 45; air accidents 204; disease 105; *Mafiya* 84; nuclear weapons 194
Russian Revolution 23
Russian sturgeon 121
rusty-spotted cat 116
Ruth, Babe 270
Rutherford Appleton Laboratory 182
Ruud, Birger 276
Rwanda: GDP 47; prisoners 86
Ryan, Jack 11
Ryan, Lynn Nolan 271
Ryan, Montague Elizabeth 260
Ryder Cup golf 258
Ryskal, Inna Valeryevna 293
Ryujyong Hotel 154

Saab, 851-cc 273
Saatchi, Charles 51
Saatchi and Saatchi 45
Sabbathday Lake 91
Sabec, Christopher 228

saccharide 150
Sachsenhausen concentration camp 85
Saddam Hussein 26
Sadler's Wells opera company 243
Saelao, Hu 101
Safari Rally 273
safety razor shaving 65
saffron 63
saguaro cactus 141
Sailer, Toni 276
sailing: circumnavigation 79; transatlantic 78
sailing ships 165
Sain, Kalyan Ramji 100
Sakamoto, Kyu 231
Saks 249
Sakumoto, Tsuguo 283
salamander, Chinese giant 122
salami, longest 60
Salang Tunnel 77
salaries: dancers 222; prime minister of Japan 26
Salenko, Oleg 255
sales: corporations 48
Salinger, J. D. 216
Salis, Flight Lt. J. de 298
saliva, poisonous 134
Salo, Johnny 302
Salome 243
Salto Angel 146
saltwater crocodile 135
Salvadori monitor 124
Salvo, Alfonso 60
samba 244
Samdal, Anne Mette 266
sampling, albums 234
Sampras, Pete 16, 260
Samuel, Joseph 86
San Diego Chargers 262
San Diego Zoo 116
San Francisco 245
San Francisco 49ers 262
San Mateo, Peru 202
Sand, Ebbe 255
sand gazelle 136
sand mole rats 119
sand yachting 293
sandcastles 69
SanDisk Multimedia Card 172
Sanderman, David 70
Sanders, Nick 79
Sandia National Laboratories 178
Sandown, P. 280
Sandoz, Randolph 292
Sandoz factory 201
Sands of Time 242
Santa Anita racecourse 39
Sanyo-Fisher 174
Sao Paolo 253
Sao Tome and Principe: diseases 104
sapphires 34
saprophytes 140
Sara Lee 246
Sargasso Sea 120
Sarracenia leucophylla 143
Sarre, Deanne 65
satellite launchers 186
satellite navigation 174
satellites 186-87
Saturday Night Fever 37, 234
Saturn 149
Saturn 5 rocket 186
Saudi Arabia: royal family 23
sauropod dinosaurs 125
sausage, longest 60
sausage meat eating 60
Saussure, Horace-Bénédict de 301
Sauvage, Louise 266
Savage Garden 229

Savarona yacht 165
Savary, Peter de 37
Saville, Jimmy 229
Savi's white-toothed pygmy shrew 116
Savolainen, Seppo-Juhani 277
Sawchuk, Terry 279
saxitoxin 196
saxophone 243
scanners 173
scarecrows 69
Scarlett 215
scene changes 223
Schayot, Jason 66
Schemansky, Norbert 285
Scherbina, Yuri 64
Scherbo, Vitaliy 284
Schienman, Vic 180
Schiffer, Claudia 20, 249
Schindler's List 209
Schlei, Stephan 80
Schmidt, Birgit 297
Schmidt, Emil and Liliana 77
Schmitt, Dr Harrison Hagen 188
Schneider, Vreni 276
Schockemöhle, Alwin 288
Scholl, Thomas 64
schools: Hollywood 10
Schultz, Harry D. 53
Schultz-McCarthy, Brenda 261
Schulz, Charles 219
Schumacher, Michael 16, 272
Schumann, Margit 295
Schumann, Robert 70
Schwartz, Barry 246
Schwarz, Hubert 277
Schwarzenegger, Arnold 13, 110-11
sci-fi films 210; sequels 211
Scientific American 100
Scientific Industrial Corporation 186
Scioili, Daniel 281
scooters 167
scorpions 128-29, 202, 225; Tunisian fat-tailed 134
Scott, Dave 303
Scott, Ridley 44
Scott, Sir Walter 99
Scotti, James 149
Scotto, Emilio 79
Scrabble 75
Scream and Scream II 210
Screaming Lord Sutch 39
screenwriters 52
scuba-diving 79
Scud missiles 192
sculptures 37
sea horses 120
Sea-Land Commerce 78
sea star 123
sea urchins 135
Sea Wraith corvette 194
seaborgium 151
Seabrooke, Nancy 223
seals 116-17, 118; leopard seal 135
search engines 176
Sears, Richard 260
seaweed 140
second-hand clothes 18, 36-37
Second Lake Pontchartrain Causeway 155
secrecy, film 211
Secrest, Michael 166
Secret Service 197
Sedov Russian training ship 165
Seed, Huck 39
Seed, Dr Richard 144
seeds: largest 141; smallest 141
Seeler, Uwe 254
Sega Gameworks 170
Seiko 172
Seiko Epson Corporation 180

Seinfeld, Jerry 14-15
Seinfeld 14, 44, 215
Seixas, Elias 260
Seizinger, Katja 313
Sekiguchi, Yoshihiro 37
Selena (Quintanilla Perez) 240-01
Seles, Monica 261
self-sufficient houses 156
Sellers, Peter 10
Selvaratnam, Thuashni 259
Semyonovna, Larisa 264
Senna, Ayrton 37, 272
sequoias 140
Seremet WS-8 helicopter 163
Serra, Richard 156
service speed (tennis) 261
Servizia, Charles 303
SES-100B hovercraft 195
Sester, Denis 110
Seutter, Jonathan 292
seven summits 300
sex: internet 176
sex changes 108-09
sex drive: mice 118
Sex Pistols 25
sexual transformation in parasitized animals 133
Seychelles: deflation 47
Seychelles giant tortoise 136
Sgt Pepper's Lonely Hearts Club Band 228
Shabba Ranks 237
Shaggy 237
Shah Faisal Mosque 155
Shakers 91
Shakespeare, William 208, 223
Shakhlin, Boris Anfiyanovich 284
Shakur, Tupac 236
Shan Dong Acrobatic Troupe 224
Shanghai World Financial Centre 157
Shannon, Sean 65
Shape Your Body Workout 110-11
Shaq Diesel 17
shares 46
sharks 120-21, 205; dusky 134; great white 135
Shatner, William 215
Shaturia, Bangladesh 203
shaving 65
Shchennikov, Mikhail 257
She 230
Shearer, Dr D. A. 97
Sheen, Charlie 213
Sheene, Barry 286
sheep: cloned 145; Dolly 144, shearing 65, 68
Sheldon, Sidney 216
Shell Mileage Marathon 159
Shelley, Mary 211
Shelton, Lyle 162
Shepard, Cdr. Alan Bartlett 188
Sherlock, Michael 292
Sherrill, Billy 238
Shields, Brooke 14
Shilton, Peter 252
Shimantan dam 203
Shining, The 210
Shinkansen train 48
ships 165; combat 194
shipwrecks 198-99
shock absorbers: earthquakes 156
shoe shining 68
Shoemaker, Bill 288
Shoemaker, Dr Eugene 188
shoes: collecting 56; fashion 246; Nike 42; pearl-studded 35
Shoji, Yukio (Aobajo) 282
shooting: reference 311-12
Shootist, The 12
shopping 40-41; internet 176; sprees 18

shops: cost of space 41; revenue 248-49
shot put: Paralympics 266; reference 306
show jumping 288-89
showbusiness animals 138
Showcase Mall, Las Vegas 49
Showgirls 53
shredders 173
shrines, Princess Diana 22
Shula, Don 262-63
Siamese twins 100
Siberian tiger 116, 205
siblings: in pop 228
Sichuan Ribao newspaper 217
Sid and Nancy 12, 25, 233
Side Show 222
sieges: Leningrad 192
Siemens 172
Siena, Italy 288
Sigel, Jay 258
Sigmarsson, Jon Pall 110
Sign, The 229
Signals Corp, Indian Army 76
signed performances 68
Sigurósson, Oskar J. 58
Sihanouk, King Norodom of Cambodia 23
Silicon Graphics Interactive Ltd 174
Silivas, Daniela 284
silk 150
silverback gorillas 134
Silverstone 107, 272
Simon, Hugo 288
Simply Mary 214
Simpsons, The 218
sinarapan goby 120
Sinatra, Frank 11, 24, 230; letter 35
Sing Sing prison 86
Singapore: financial sector 46
Singapore Airlines 69
Singapore Food Festival 60
singers: country 238-39; dance music 234-35; earnings 53; Latin 240; pop 230-31
Singh, Vijay 258
Singh, Yajurvindra 290
Singin' in the Rain 10
Singleman, Dr Glenn 298
Sioux Indians 86
Sirens 21
Sisargas Islands 62
Sishen-Saldanha railway 164
sitting, unsupported 67
Sittler, Darryl 278
Six Flags Astroworld 185
Six Flags Magic Mountain 184
Sjölin, Lotta 57
skateboarding 292
skating: gold medals 264; waiters 63
ski-bob 294
ski-jumping 276-77
skid marks 77
skiing 276-77; Everest 301; lift disaster 198; reference 312-13
skulls: dinosaur 125; Piltdown Man 88; Swedenborg's 35
Sky Bungee Jumping 298
Skyhigh block, Hong Kong 33
Skylab 187
skyscrapers 157
skysurfing 298
Slater, Kelly 296
Slater, Richard 92
sledging 79
sleep: mammals 119
slippers 37

sloths 118
Slovenia: prisoners 86; rafting 297
Smack My Bitch Up 234
Smail, Doug 279
'smart' cars 160
'smart' weapons 195
'smartpen' 175
smell: worst 150; sense of 131, 132, 135; stinking pheasant 127
Smetanina, Raisa, Petrovna 276
SMI Motivator 158
Smith, Dave and son 224
Smith, David 74
Smith, Delia 14
Smith, Emmitt 44
Smith, Ian 291
Smith, James 'Bonecrusher' 16
Smith, Captain John 162
Smith, John 76
Smith, Keith 252
Smith, Noland 263
Smith, Sinjin 293
Smiths, The 232
smog 200-01
smog chemicals 160
Smokey and the Bandit II 213
smuggling, income 32
Smyers, Karen 303
snail, freshwater 133
snake charming 225
Snake sculpture 156
snakebites 205
snakes 124-25; endangered 136; Gaboon viper 134; king cobra 134
Snap 234
Snead, Sam 258
sneezing 106
Snetsinger, Phoebe 58
Snoopy 219
snoring 107
snow-sculpting 245
snow leopards 136
snow mountain biking 295
Snow White 218
snowboarding 294
Snowden, Wales 301
snowmobiles 80
soap operas 214
Soares, Ben 74
Sobihor Concentration Camp 193
soccer 252-53
Sochiku Shikigeki 223
SOE (Special Operations Executive) 197
soft drinks brands 42
soft tick 132
softball 271
software: millionaires 52; piracy 43
Sojourner Rover 181
solar cars 158, 161
solar eclipses 148
solar probes 186
Solar Star 158
Solberg, Magnar 303
soldiers: youngest 71
Sole, David 78
Solectrica Corporation 160
solenodons 134
solitaire 75
Solo, Fuatai 65
solo climbs 300
Solti, Sir Georg 242
somersaults 284; quadruple 71
Something (horse) 289
Somewhere Over The Rainbow 68
Somme, Battle of 192
songwriters 230
Sonny Somers (racehorse) 288
Sony 8, 173; Computer Entertainment 170; Playstation 170-71, 218

sooty tern 126
Sörenstam, Annika 17, 259
Soros, George 53
Soros Fund Management 53
Sotheby's 34-35; New York 243; London 221
Soul II Soul 235
sound: low frequency 119
sound barrier 158
Sound Bites 174
sound pollution 201
soundtracks 230-31, 234
South African bolas spider 129
South American hoatzin 127
South American teratoran 126
South Boulder Canyon 72
South China Sea: pirates 204
South Korea: arrests 87; murders 84; weddings 91
South Pacific 230
South Pole: oldest visitor 72; youngest visitor 70
Southpeak Interactive 171
Southwick, Dr Albert 86
soya: genetically modified 145
Soyuz TM15 spacecraft 188
Soyuz TM-22 rocket 187
Soyuz 11 disaster 198
Soyuz U space shuttle 187
Space pop group 230
space exploration 188-89; disasters 198-99; shuttles 72, 186
spacecraft, laser powered 182
Spacek, Sissy 211
Spaceman 44
spaghetti eating 60
Spain: civil wars 193; government lottery 38; new species 136; World Cup football 254
Spanish Miniature Motorcycling Championships 166
Spanish Song Festival 241
Spark, Rodney 68
Spartacus 10
speakers, hi-tech 172
spear throwing 66
special effects 182-83
Special Olympics 111
Special Operations Executive (SOE) 197
speckled sape tortoise 124
spectators: baseball 270
speeches: politicians 27
speed: bicycle 166; cars 76, 158; cheetah 118; dragonflies 131; helicopter 162; laser spacecraft 182; ostriches 126; parasites 132; planetary orbit 148; powerboats 280-81; racehorse 288; reptiles 125; roller coaster 184; skiing 277; snakes 125; snow mountain bike 295; in Space 189; spiders 128; trains 164
Speed-O-Motive/Spirit of 76 158
speed skating: Olympics 265
Speelman, Anthony 39
Speers family 69
Spelling, Aaron 11, 214
Spencer, Earl 22
Spencer, Terence 298
sperm whale 116, 118
Sphaerodactylus parthenopian 124
Spice 229
Spice Girls 18, 229
spices: most expensive 62; hottest 63
Spiceworld — the Movie 18, 228
spider crab, giant 122
spiders 128-29; Brazilian huntsman 134

Spielberg, Steven 53, 71, 110, 171, 180, 208-09
spin bowling 291
spiny-tailed iguana 125
Spirit of America 77
Spirit of Australia 280
spitting 66
Spitz, Mark 264, 274
Spix's macaw 136
sponges 123
sponsorship 42; surfing 296
spoon worms 133
sport bikes 281
Sportivo Ameliano 253
Sports Illustrated 17, 278
sportswear 247
Spratly Islands 80
Springbank 1919 Malt Whisky 62
Springbett, David J. 78
Springel, Herman van 286
Springer, Jerry 214
Springfield, Rick 230
Springsteen, Bruce 18, 98, 232
sprinters 256-57
sprinting on hands 64
Spruce Goose 163
Spungen, Nancy 19, 25
spying 196-97
Squaresoft 170
squash: reference 313
squat thrusts 303
squats (lifting) 285
squid, Atlantic giant 122
squirrel monkeys 119
Sri Lanka: cricket 290-91; prime minister 27; snakebites 205
SRN4 Mk III hovercraft 165
SS-18 missiles 194
SS Ben Lomond 93
SS Orient Trader 85
St Albans Weightlifting Club 285
St Bernard dogs 93
St Cyr, Henri 289
St Gotthard Tunnel 155
St James's Palace 22
St. Jean, Alan 60
St. John the Divine cathedral 155
St. Louis Cardinals 263
St. Martin, Ted 269
St Michael underwear 246
St Peter's Basilica replica 68
St. Petersburg, USA 147
St. Petersburg Times, USA 88
Stade de France 154
stadiums 154
Stafford, Col. Thomas Patten 189
stage runs 22-23
Stalin, Joseph 108
Stalingrad, Battle of 192
Stallone, Sylvester 212
Stam, Jap 253
stamina 303
Stand By Me 25
Stand By Your Man 238
Standard Oil 50
standing jumps 257
Standing Stones 176
Stanis, Stephan 252
Stanley, Lord 279
Stanley Cup 278
Stansfield, Lisa 235
Stanwyck, Barbara 222
Star Micronics 158
Star Trek 188, 215; fans 58
Star Wars 53, 210, 215; fans 59
Star Wars: Episode I 213
starfish 123
Stargene 25
Starr, Robert 163
stars 148

'Stars Across America' telethon 28
Starsky and Hutch 214
START 2 (Strategic Arms Reduction Talks) 194
Start Me Up 18
starvation 107
State Bank of India 49
State Prison, Southern Michigan 86
Statue of Liberty 224
statues, crying 91
statuettes 37
Staubli Unimation 180
steak: most expensive 62
steam cars 158
Steamboat Geyser 147
Steamboat Willie 48, 219
Steamin' Demon 158
steeplechase 256
Stegodyphus spiders 129
Stegosaurus 125
Steiff teddy bear 37
Steinfeld, Jake 110
Steinway grand piano 243
Stelarc 112
Stemmle, Brian 277
Stenmark, Ingemar 276
Stephanie, Princess of Monaco 23
Sterett, Bill 281
Stern, Ida and Simon 73
Stevens, Harry 73
Stevenson, Terry 58
Stevenson-Menchik, Vera Francevna 75
Stewart, Alec 290
Stewart, Michael 290
Stewart, Rod 232
Stewart, William 258
stick insects 130
Stickland, Jan 74
Stieglitz, Alfred 221
Stif mountain bikes 167
stigmatism 90
stilt-walking 81, 224
Sting 239
Stinger missile 194
Stits, Donald 163
Stock Exchange, Amsterdam 46
stock-market: crash 178; pop stars 18
stockbroking, computerized 179
Stokely, Scott 66
Stoker, Bram 211
Stolle, Walter 79
Stone, Sharon 208
stonefish 135
Storm model agency 20
storm prediction: computers 179
'Stormville Flyers' 89
Stradivarius violin 243
Stragauskaite, Kristina 70
Strand, Asle 295
Stratosphere Hotel Casino 39
Stratosphere Tower 184
Strauss, Richard 243
Stravinsky, Igor 242
strawberries 63
street fashion 246-47
street festivals 244
street luge 292
street magazines 217
street performers 224-25
Streisand, Barbra 230
Strenkert, Zack 103
strikeouts; softball 271
Stringer, Sharon 68
Stroebel, Pieter 288
strokes 105
Strongest Man contest 110
strutters: in revue 243
STS 67 *Endeavour* 189
STS 75 Columbia space shuttle 187

STS 76/*Atlantis* space shuttle 188
Stuart, Kenneth 301
Stubbs, Phil 78
Stück, Hans 272
Stückelberger, Christine 289
Stucke, Heinz 79
stunts 224-25; film 212-13
Sturmgewehr gun 195
Styepanova, Marina 256
submarines: disasters 199; spying 197
subsistence farming 46
Sudan: waterweed invasion 142
Suddenly Love 71
Suddenly Susan 14
sugarcane 46
Sugarcubes 228
suicides 90; failed pact 93; Japan 192; rate 204; rock stars 24-25
Suisse 4: Atlanta Olympics 264
suit 68
Sukana Park, Fiji 65
Suleimanov (Suleymanoğlü), Naim 285
Sullivan, Major James 162
Sullivan, Kathryn 189
Sullivan, Roy 92
sulphur dioxide 200
Sultan of Brunei 29, 32, 154
Sumitomo Corporation 46, 85
Summer Olympics 2000 264
Sumner, Tim 286
sumo wrestling 282
Sun 186-87
sun spiders 128
Sundarban forest, Bangladesh 205
Sunday Telegraph (Australia) 217
Sundström, Patrik 278
sunfish, ocean 121
Sung, Simon Sang Koon 60
sunglasses: John F. Kennedy's 36
Sunraycer 158
Sunrise car 160
sunshine: hours of 147
sunspots 149
Super Bowl XXVII 44
Super Bowl 262
Super Mario Bros. 171
superacid 150
Supercircuits Inc. 172; PC-51XP camera 197
supercomputers 178
Superman 28, 212
Superman The Escape roller coaster 184
supermodels 20-21; canine 138
Supramar PTS 150 Mk III hydrofoil 165
surfing 296
surfwear 246
surgery: by robot 181
surgical instruments, antique 35
SurpriseShowFin 14
surveillance by scent 196
Susan B. Anthony 93
Susann, Jacqueline 216
sushi 62
Sutro, Edward 58
Suya tribe 113
Suyderhoud, Mike 314
Suzuki 166, 286; GSXR 76
Swahn, Oscar 72
swallowing, compulsive 101
Swamp Women 210
swamps 146
Swan 20
Swan, Anna Hanen 96
Swan Lake 222
swans: mute 134

Swanson, Ernest Evar 271
Swatch 61, 246; Skin watch 173; watch collection 56
Swaziland: royal family 23
Swedenborg, Emanuel 35
Sweet Sixteen 238
swimming 274-75; gold medals 264; in 24 hours 275; Paralympics 266; reference 313-14; youngest record-breaker 70
swimming pool 155; in car 159
Switzerland: bobsleigh 294; GDP 46
sword-billed hummingbird 126
Sword of Tipu Sultan 209
sword swallowing 224
Sydney 245
Sydney Harbour Bridge 155
Symbion pandora 136
Symonds, Andrew 290
Symphony Hall 157
synagogues 155
Szewinska, Irena 256

T-Up construction 157
Tact Millennium 174
taekwondo: Olympics 264
tag wrestlers 97
Taggart, Marian 97
tails: human 100
Taisei Corporation 157
Takbulatova, R. 266
Take, Yutaka 288
Take That 229
takeover bids 49
takes, film 210
Taliban 91, 205
talin 150
talk shows 214
talking speed 65
Tally T6180 175
Talos the Mummy 211
Tambora volcano 147, 202
Tampa Bay Buccaneers 263
Tamworth, NSW 68
tandem cycles 79
Tandy, Jessica 13, 223
Tangshan, China 202
tap dancing 66, 68
tapeworms 132
Tardivel, Pierre 301
Tarrès, Jordi 287
tarsier 118
Tasadays tribe 88
taste: bitter 150; sweet 150
tattoos 112-13
Taufa'ahau Tupou, King of Tonga 245
Taupo volcano 147
Tavilla, Paul 66
taxation: exiles 51
taxi ride 77
Taylor, Billy 279
Taylor, Bob 291
Taylor, Liz 10, 28, 63, 209, 218
Taylor, Nikki 20
Taylor, Vince 110
Taz's Texas Tornado ride 185
teabag labels: collection 57
Teague, Al 158
Tebeitabu, Arenta 93
teddy bears 37
teenager: richest 32
teeth: auctioned 99; bleaching 109; extra sets 101; fish 121; insured 98; weightlifting 64
Teflon 151

Télé 7 Jours magazine 216
telecommunications companies 49
telegrams 36
telenovelas (soap operas) 15, 214
telephones: cellular 172
Teleprogramma magazine 217
telescope, space 186
telethons 28
television: audiences 22, 214, 262; contracts 214; moonwalk 188; networks 214; programmes 214; rights 215; sets 215; stars 14-15; stations 50; Vietnam War 192; 360° 175
Teltronics Inc. 174
Temujin 171
temperatures 147; dry-air 107; highest artificial 151; lowest artificial 151; planets 148; sub-zero 92
Temple, Shirley 12
Temple Emanu-El 155
temples 155
Temptations 237
Tenerife 198
Tennessee River 238
tennis 260-61; earnings 16-17; Paralympics 266; youngest international player 71
Tenochtitlan 90
Tenove, Glen 285
Tenzing, Tashi Wangchuk 300
Tenzing Norgay 300
Teodorescu, Radu 110
Tergat, Paul 302
Terminator 111
termites 130
Terra Encantada 185
Terra Firma Islands 142
terrorist attacks 198-99
Terry, Ellen 223
Terry family 223
Test Match scores 290-91
test tubes 150
Tetra-Pak company 51
tetrachlorodibenzo-p-dioxin 150
tetrodoxin 134
Texaco petroleum 49
Texas horned lizard 134
TF1 20hrs TV show 14
TGV 164; *Atlantique* 164
Thailand: cremation 105; GNP 47
Thames, River 224
Thames Video Collection 215
Thatcher, Noel 266
That's The Way Love Goes 234
The 12 Year Old Genius 237
The Sun 216
The Times 45, 89; correspondence 59
Théâtre des Champs-Elysées 242
theatre-goers 58
theatrical flops 222
theatrical runs 222-23
theft 85; World Cup 37, 254-55
theme parks 184-85
Theodorescu, Monica 289
Theory of Relativity 36
Theridion sisyphium 128
therizinosaurids 125
thermometers: natural 151
thermonuclear devices 194
Thessman, Terry 166
Thieme, Johann Heinrich Karl 73
Think Big company 97
Things to Do in Denver When You're Dead 100
Thipyaso, Chimoy 87
This Is How We Do It 237
This Is Your Life 15
Thomas, Keith 66

Thomke, Dr. Ernest 246
Thomson, Jeffrey 290
Thornton, Kathryn 189
thread snake 124
Three Musketeers 213
Three Tenors in Concert 242
three-toed sloth 118
thresher shark 121
Thresher submarine 199
Thriller 19, 228
Thrupp, Darren 267
Thrust SSC 158
Thubten Teshe 90
Thuggees 84, 90
Thurston, Kat 299
tickets: World Cup 1998 254
ticks 133
tidal waves 203
tiddlywinks 74-75
tigers 116, 134, 205
Tight Roaring Circle 220
tightrope walking 72, 224, 298
tights 246
Tijuana Brass 231
Tikhonov, Aleksandr 303
Tilden, William 260
Tillekeratne, Hashan Prasantha 290
Time magazine 217
Time Warner Inc. 52
Times Square: millennium party 244
Timm, Robert 162
Timm, Thomas 270
Timmis, John Henry IV 209
Timperley, Simon 167
Tirkkonen, Sari 66
Tissot, Jane 288
Titan rocket 186
Titania 182
Titanic 198
Titanic (film) 92, 208-09, 241;
   soundtrack 231; stunts 213
Tiwi sculpture 37
TLC 236
To Kill a Mockingbird 216
toads 122; poisonous 150
tobacco plant 143
tobacco spitting 66
tobacco tin 36
tobogganing 72
Toby (poodle) 139
Todos Santos, Mexico 296
toes, extra 100
Tokai fault 204
Tokoro, George 15
Tokyo: air accident 198;
   office rents 48
Tokyo Car Show 161
Tokyo Disneyland 184
tomatoes: genetically modified 145
Tomb Raider 170
Tomorrow Never Dies 208, 212
Tomorrow's World 67
Tong, Mark 79
Tonga: millennium party 245
tools: chimpanzees 119
Top of the Pops 229
top spinning 74
Toppan, Jane 84
torch juggling 67
tornado cluster 203
tornadoes 147, 203
Torokichi, Tameemon (Raiden) 282
Toronto Blue Jays 270
Toronto Maple Leafs 279
Toronto Underground 40
Torosaurus 125
torpedoes 195
Torres, Osel Hita 90
Torres Trois, Francisco 75
tortoises 124; Abingdon Island giant
   136; Seychelles 136

Toto (dog) 37
toupee 109
Tour de France 286
tourists, most killed 198
tower blocks 154
Tower Records 18
Townsend, Pete 28
toxins 134-35; artificial 150
toy brick pyramid 74
Toyota 160; Landcruiser 77
Toys 'R' Us 41
toyshops 41
tracheostomies 106
track events: Paralympics 266
tracking by scent 196
Tracy, Spenser 12
trademarks 43
Trader Vic's 60
traffic: California 76; jam 77
Tragis, Jack 304
trainers: collector's items 42
trainers, personal 110
trains 164-65; accidents 198;
   countries in 24 hours 81;
   Japan 48; pulled by hand 64
trainspotters 58
Trammps, the 234
trampolining 285; Olympics 264
Trango Towers 300
Transat des Sables 293
transatlantic crossings 78;
   flights 78; youngest person 70
transfers: football 253
translations, of novels 216
Transylvania, murders 84
trapeze acts 224
travelling pets 139
Travolta, John 22, 37, 234
Treaux, Tamara de 13
tree-dwelling 67
tree shrews 117
tree topping 65
trees: growth rate 140; largest 140
Trett, Elmer 166
Tretyak, Vladislav 278
Triads 84
trials: court 214; internet verdict
   176; war 193
triathlon 303; Olympics 264
tribes, primitive 88
tricycles 166
Trieste 79
Trieste II bathyscaphe 199
trillionaires 50
triple jump: reference 306
triplets 102
Tripp, Ryan 80
Triton (moon) 148
Trojan 200 37
Troops 59
tropical emperor scorpion 129
Trottier, Bryan 279
truffles 62
Trump, Donald 51
truth serum 196
Tsai Wan-lin 50
Tschach-Wlezcek, Petra 294
Tsibliyev, Vasily 44
tsunami 92, 146
Tsutsumi, Yoshiaki 52
TT motorbike race 287
Tu-95/142 plane 162
Tuber magmatum pico 62
tuberculosis 104
Tucker, Tony 16
Tudor, Larry 299
tug-of-war 69
Tui Malila (tortoise) 125
tumours 107
Tunisian fat-tailed scorpion 134
tunnels 155

Tupolev Tu-22M bomber 195
Tupolev Tu-144 163
Turkey: counterfeit brands 42;
   education budget 47
Turkish Delight 61
Turkmenistan, prisons 86
Turlington, Christy 20, 246
Turner, Eddie 298
Turner, Lana 10
Turner, Ted 33, 51-52
Turner, Tina 232
Turpin, Professor Tom 74
Turpin, Ben 98
turtles 124-25; dives 125;
   new species 137
Tutsi tribe 96
Tvervaag, Arne 257
TWA airline 51
Twain, Shania 238
Twigge, Stephen 75
Twins 13
twins 102, 103; heaviest 97; oldest
   73; sex change 108; shortest 96;
   Siamese 100; tallest 96
Twism record label 17
Twist, The 229
Twitty, Conway 238
Two-Headed Boy of Bengal 100
Two Little Boys 230
Two Pina Coladas 238
tycoons 50-51
Type 65 torpedo 195
typhoons 203
tyrannosaurus rex robot 180
Tyson, Mike 16, 282

U2 232, 244
UB40 236
Ueno Zoo 117
UFOs 89
Ugly Dog Contest 139
Uguday Melodiyu (Guess the Melody)
   15
Ullrich, Frank 303
Ultima Online 171
Ultimate In-line Challenge 292
Ultimate roller coaster 185
Ultra Hightech Starlite 150
Ultra Quiz 215
ultraviolet laser 182
Ulysses spacecraft 186
Umbilicaria aprina 142
Umbrellas, The 220
(Un, Dos, Tres) Maria 241
underground houses 157
underground shopping centres 40
underground trains 198
Underhill, UK 157
underpants: collection 56
understudies 223
underwater hotel 157
underwater rescue 92
underwear: collection 56;
   designer 246; JFK's long johns 36
Unforgettable 237
Unger, Stu 38
unicycles 80, 224, 166-67;
   speed 166
unicycling, backwards 67
Unilever N.V. 49
Union Carbide 200
United East India Company 46
United Nations: 50th anniversary 26;
   peacekeeping force 193
Universal film company 208-09

Unser, Al 272-73
Untitled (Breakers) 220
Uphoff, Nicole 289
Ure, Midge 28
Urner, Steve 66
US Customs 43
US Justice Department 179
US Major Soccer League 253
US Masters golf 258
US Open (golf) 258
US PGA golf 258
US Postal Service 49
US soccer federation 42
US Treasury 47
USA: advertising 45; Alzheimer's
   disease 105; America's Cup 315;
   armed robbery 85; basketball 268;
   clothing industry 247; firearms
   204; genetically-modified crops
   145; GNP 46; internet users 177;
   murder rate 84; pollution 200;
   prisoners 86-87; sex changes 109;
   shopping malls 40; space budget
   188; video recorders 215
Use Your Illusion 233
USSR: basketball 268; chess 75;
   diphtheria 105; gymnastics 284;
   ice hockey medals 278; nuclear
   explosions 194; pentathlon
   medals 302; volleyball 293
Ust Kamenogorsk, Kazakhstan 200
Utricularia plants 142

Vaal Reefs 198
Välbe, Yelena 276
Valens, Ritchie 24
Valentino 249
Valentino, Rudolph 98
Valetta, Amber 21
Valle, Renato della 281
Valles Marineris 149
Valley of the Dolls 216
Vampire jet 56
Vampire's Kiss 12
Van clothing 294
Van Berg, Jack 288
Van Berg, Marion 288
Van Gogh, Vincent 220
Van Horn, Dr Bruce 39
Van Lennep, Gees 272
Van Lierde, Luc 303
Vangen, Klas 295
Vanguard 1 satellite 187
vanity case, Cartier 34
Vanity Fair 20
Vare Trophy golf 259
Variety Club of Ontario 39
Vasaloppet ski race 277
Vasco da Gama bridge 63
Vassilyev, Feodor, wife of 102
Vava 255
Veja magazine 217
Velstra, Tjeerd 289
Venera probe 148
Venezuela: beauty queens 109;
   presidency 27; religious vision 90
Venice Beach 110
Venoil tanker 199
Venpet tanker 199
Ventura, Frantisek 288
Ventura, Sergie 293
Venus 148
Venus fly trap 143
Verhoeven, Paul 208
Verity, Hedley 290

Vermeer 89
Vermuelen, Nick 57
Verri, Francisco 286
Versace, Gianni 20, 248
vertebrae: most valuable 99
vertebrate, lightest 120
vervain hummingbird 127
Vespa ET4 167
Vesuvius 204
Viacom 48
Vibroplant team 74
Vicious, Sid 19, 25, 233
Victor tanker 199
Victoria cricket team 290
Victoria, Queen of England 56, 99
Victoria and Albert Museum London
   20
Victoria's Secret 249
VID1 video transmitter 172
video cameras, pinhole 172
video game arcades 170-71
Video Reality 171
video recorders 173, 215
video transmitters 172
videos 215; fitness 111;
   libraries 215; piracy 42
Vietnam War: televised 192
Vietnamese warty pig 136
Village Vanguard club, 243
Villwock, Dave 281
Vincent, Troy 263
Viner, Brian 57
vinyl chlorine 200
violins 243
Virgin Atlantic Challenger 11 78
Virgin Global Challenger 78
Virgin Group 52
Virgin Mary 90-91
Virgo 148
virus, computer hoax 88
viruses 104, 132
Vlaeminck, Eric De 286
vocal range 243
Vogue 20-21, 235
voices: insurance 98
volcanoes 147, 202, 204; noise 201;
   in Space 148
Volcom clothing 294
Volkswagen 'Beetles' 158-59
volleyball 293; beach 293
Volvo 850 Turbo 76
Vorhees, Jason 211
Vosper Thornycroft 194
Vostok, Antarctica 147
Voyager 1 space probe 149, 179, 187
Vu Quang ox 137
Vulovic, Vesna 92
Vyse, Thomas 139

Wadlow, Robert 96
Wadomo tribe 100
Wagner, Richard 243
Wai Man Chung, Paul 303
Waimangu geyser 147, 202
Waimea Beach 296
waist measurement 97
Wal-Mart Corporation 50
Wal-Mart Stores, Inc. 40
Walker Cup golf 258
Walker, John 196
Walkert, Kare 107
walking: athletics 256;
   backwards 80; on hands 81;
   on water 81; with a cross 80

Walkman 180
Wall, The 232
Wall, Wendy 67
wall of death riding 76;
    oldest rider 73
Wall Street 46, 53
Wall Street Journal 217
Wallace, Bill 87
wallets, longest 41
Walsh, Courtney 290
Walt Disney Company 48, 52;
    films 218
Walter, Steffi 295
Walton, Keith 34
Walton, Sam 50
wandering albatross 127
Wang Yan 256
Wang, Nina 52
war 192-93; booty 35; crimes 193;
    criminals, DNA identification
    of 144; necessity of, hoax 88;
    trials 193
War and Remembrance 215
War Child charity 28
War of the Worlds 88
Warby, Kenneth 280
Wardas, Roman 24
Wardle, Lucy 299
Warelius, Bo 281
Warhol, Andy 220, 232
Warne, Shane 291
Warnecke, Mark 313
Warner Bros. 209
Warren, Mike 92
warts: famous 99
Warwick Rex (horse) 288
washing cars 68
Washington Redskins 262
Washington University 160
wasps 130
watches: collecting 56;
    thinnest 173; most valuable 35
water: physical characteristics 150
water hyacinth 142
water-melon seed spitting 66
water weeds 140, 142
waterfalls 146
Watergate tapes 35
Waterloo 231
Waters, Benny 243
waterskiing 296-97; reference 314
waterskis, walking on 81
Waterworld 210
waves: surfing 296
Wayne, John 12
We Are The Champions 29
We Have All The Time In The World 231
wealth 32-33, 52-53; Saudi royal
    family 23; tycoons 50-51
weasels 119; dancing 133
weather research 179
Weaver, Dennis 156
Weaver, Sigourney 13, 213
Webb, Chloe 25
Webber, Andrew Lloyd 222
Webber, Molly 73
Weber, Bruce 138
Weber, Sharon 296
webs: spiders 128-29
websites 176-77, 215; British
    monarchy 23; Star Trek 58;
    Troops 59
Wedding Singer, The 71
weddings 91; auctioned cake 35;
    dresses 22, 35, 248; Liz Taylor 28;
    Las Vegas 39; oldest participants
    73; pets 138; Prince Charles and
    Diana 22; theme park 184
weeds 142
weevil fossil 144
Wegrath, Vivian 299

Weider Corporation 110
weight: actors 12; cats 139;
    human 96, 108; insects 130-31;
    spiders 128
weightlifting 110-11, 285;
    reference 314-15
Weil's disease 134
Weiler, William 253
Weiner, Bruce 37
Weirdo the rooster 139
Weiskopf, Tom 258
Wek, Alek 96
Welles, Orson 10, 88
Wells, H. G. 88
Welsh mountain sheep 145
Wembley Stadium 28-29, 228
Wendel, Ella 139
Weng Weng 13
West, Lawrence 67
West Beach clothing 294
West Bengal 202
West Edmonton Mall 41
West Japan Building 156
West Side Story 208, 230
Westergren, Carl 282
Westgate, Richard and Guy 299
Westin Stamford Hotel 154
Westland Lynx 162
Westwood Studios 171
whale shark 121
whales 118; skull 137; stranded 133
'whales' (gamblers) 38
Whales of August 10
What a Wonderful World 72
wheelbarrow races 74
wheelchair journey 80
wheelchair sports 266-67
Wheeler, Ken 'Flex' 110
wheelies: bicycle 76; motorcycle 76
When Doves Cry 234
Whetu, Mark 301
whisky: expensive 62
White, Reverend Roy 75
White Elephant Sale 41
white-fronted falconet 126
White House 29; staff 27
White Sands missile base 182, 187
white sharks 120
White Sully chickens 139
white water sports 297
Whiteside, Norman 255
Whittaker, James 300
Whittal, Robby 299
Whitworth, Alan 220
Whitworth, Kathy 258
Who's Who 70
wholesalers 40
whooper swans 126
Whybrew, Victoria 106
Wiatt, Carrie Latt 11
Wichita Falls 147
Wickheim, Jubiel 74
Wickwire, Norma 99
wife-carrying 65
wigs 109
Wild Aster (racehorse) 288
wild box huckleberry 140
wild fig tree 141
Wilhelm, James Hoyt 271
Wiliam Goldberg Diamond
    Corporation 34
Wilkes Land 146
William Hill bookmakers 39
Williams, Clive 167
Williams, Robin 12, 53
Williams, Sean 269
Williams, Susan Montgomery 66
Williams racing cars 272
Willis, Bruce 13
Willis, James 263
Wills, Judy 285

Wilshaw, Sylvia 74
Wilson, Michael 112, 269
Wilson, Richard 36
Wilson, Robert 242
Wimbledon 260-61
wind breaking 101
Windows '95 18, 179; advertising 45
Windsor, Duke and Duchess 34-35
Windsor, Jane 21
wines: most expensive 62;
    tasting 60
Winfrey, Oprah 14, 214
Wing, Brett 297
wing-beat: birds 126
wing-span: aircraft 163;
    birds 126-27
Wingo, Plennie L. 80
Wings of Desire 12
Winkler, Hans 288
Winnetka Congregational Church 41
Winnipeg festival 245
Winnipeg Jets 279
Winooski One Hydroelectric Dam 156
Winslett, Kate 209
Winston, Harry 249
winter rye 141
winter carnivals 245
Winter Olympics 264-65, 294-95;
    Norway 157; skiing 276
Winter X Games 295
Wisden, John 290
Wise, Robert 211
witches 87, 91
Without Remorse 217
Wizard of Oz 37, 68
Wöckel, Barbel 256
Wolf, Eddy 224
Wolf, Markus 196
Wolfe, Tom 216
Wolverhampton Orchestra 69
Woman 24
Woman In Me, The 238
Wonder, Stevie 237
Wonderbra ad 45, 246
Wong Kwan 32
woodcock 126
Woodmore, Steve 65
Woods, Tiger 16, 42, 44
Woodstock fair, 1969 245
Woodward, Karl 259
Woodward, Louise 176
wool sponge 123
Woolworth Corporation 40
Worden, Alfred 189
Words of Love 24
working life, longest 73
World Advertising Trends 45
World Alpine Championships:
    skiing 276
World Bank 49
World Barefoot Championship
    (waterskiing) 297
World Championships: gymnastics
    284; ice hockey 278;
    softball 271; swimming 274
World Cup: football 154, 241-42,
    254-55; golf 258; replica 37;
    snowboarding 294; trophy 254
World Drivers' Championships 273
World Health Organisation (WHO)
    104-05, 200
World Indoor Championships 257
World Nordic Championships:
    skiing 276
World of Residensea 32
World Poker Series 38
World Snail Racing Championships 74
World Solar Challenge Race 161
World Trade Center 224-25
World War I: avalanches 202;
    chemicals used 192

World War II 86, 196; cost 192;
    death by crocodiles 135
World Wide Web 177
World Wife-Carrying Championship 65
World Wildlife Fund (WWF) 136
Wou Bom-kon 84
Wozniak, Steve 245
wrestling 282-83; with pigs 110
Wright, Alison 301
Wright, Elsie 89
wristwatch computer 172
writers: earnings 53; film scripts 211
Wulff, Graham 247
Wunderland Bei Nacht 230
Wyndham, Western Australia 147
Wynette, Tammy 238
Wynn, Ed 74

X-Files, The 112
X-Seed 4000 157
Xarate, Lucia 97
xenotransplantation 144-45
Xu Nannan 276

yachting: Olympics 264;
    reference 315
yachts 165; most expensive 33
Yahoo: internet 176
Yamaha XS 400 76
Yamamoto, Yohjii 248
Yamashita, Yasuhiro 283
Yarawala 37
yard of ale 60
Yarnold, Hugo 290
Yates, Dorian 110
Yates, Sarah and Adelaide 100
Year of Living Dangerously, The 13
Yekaterinburg 23
yellow fever 104
Yellow Pages 44
Yellowstone National Park 147
Yeltsin, Boris 26
Yeoh, Michele 212
Yersinia pestis 104
Yes Sir I Can Boogie 241
Yim, Benjamin and Amanda 35
yo-yo: biggest 74; most loops 74
yodelling 64
yohimbine tree 150
Yokokura, Akira 130
yokozuna (sumo) 282
Yomiuri Shimbun newspaper 216
Yoo, June 67
Yordanidis, Dimitrion 302
You Ain't Woman Enough 238
You Might Be A Redneck If 238
You Were Meant For Me 228
Young, Clara Kimball 98
Young, Capt. John Watts 189
Yuasa Exide 173
Yugoslavia (former): war 192
Yuma, USA 147
Yungay, Peru 202

Z0 concept car 160
Zamba, Frieda 296
Zeeff, Jon 176
Zehnder's Hotel, USA 59
Zeitung, Die 216
Zelle, Margaretha 196
Zeng Jinlian 96
Zenit space shuttle 187
zero-emission cars 160
Zeus 181
Zhan Xugang 315
Zheng He junk 165
Ziegfeld's Follies 222
Zil-41047 159
Zin, Serge 299
ZLEV (Zero Low Emission Vehicle) 160
Zmuda, Wladyslaw 254
Zobel, Judge Hiller 176
Zoff, Dino 252
Zorro 219

PHOTO CREDITS

ADVERTISING ARCHIVES: 44, 45 (x2), 246. **ALLSPORT:** 284 Simon Bruty, 303 Bob Martin. **ALPHA:** 57 Angeli, 73 Angeli. **ASSOCIATED PRESS:** 6 Itsuo Inouye, 6 Kevorn Djansezian, 7 Mark Fallander, 12 Michel Euler, 12&13 Reed Saxon, 15 Nelson Machin/ABC, 16 Fred Jewel, 16 Antonio Calanni, 17 Jytte Nielsen, 17 Steve Stevett, 23 Giovanni Diffidenti, 23 Jacqueline Arzt, 26 Max Nash, 27 Alexander Zemlianichenko, 27 Ron Edmonds, 28 Damian Dovarganes, 32 Mike Fiala, 33 Jonathan Exley/ABC, 35 Anatoly Maltsev, 35 Emil Wamsteker, 36 Stuart Ramson, 37 Sotheby's, 37 Gino Domenico, 38 Lennox McLendon (x2), 38 EFE, 40 Lionel Cironneau, 42 Sakchai Lalit, 44, 46 John Moore, 48 Katsumi Kasahara, 49 David J. Coulson, 49 Jack Dempsey, 50, 51 Ed Reinke, 53 Green Tree Financial Corp, 53 Noemi Bruzak, 58 Susan Goldman, 60 Michael Lipchitz, 61 Sven Kaestner, 62 Michel Lipchitz, 67 Mark Lennihan, 69 Marty Lederhandler, 72 Bill Waugh, 73 Bill Sikes (x2), 76 Lennox McLendon, 77 Jeff Scheid, 78 Chris Brandis, 78 Jalil Bounhar, 79 Rob Orchiston, 79 David Thompson, 81, 80 A.F. Singer/CBS, 84 Pat Roque, 85, 86, 87 Adam Stoltman, 88 Farmers Museum (x2), 89 Eric Draper, 90 Saurabh Das, 91 Joan Esteve/EFE, 92 Barry Sweet, 96 Jean-Marc Bouju, 97 Liu Hong Shing, 98 Bernhard Kunz, 101 Tassanee Vejpongsa, 102 Mohamed El-Dakhakhny, 103 Michael Kardis, 106 Lacy Atkins, 109 Long Photography, 112 Damon Winter, 117 Ueno Zoo, 118 Sherwin Crasto, 122 Barry Sweet, 128 Michael Caulfield, 132 Minnesota Pollution Control Agency, 133 Craig Line, 134 LM Otero, 136 Lou Krasky, 136 Michel Springler, 137 Pierre Thielemans, 137 Tad Motoyama, 138 Charles Dharapak, 138 Susan Ragan, 143, 144 Jack Smith, 144 Mata Kokkali, 156 Eric Draper, 156 Santiago Lyon, 158 Dusan Vranic, 160 Marty Lederhandler, 161 Chrysler Corp, 161 Donald Stampfli, 163 Sergei Karpukhin, 165 Murad Sezer, 166 Peter Cosgrove, 166 Mauel Podio/EFE, 167 Guilo Broglio, 173 Katsumi Kasahara, 174 Michael Schmelling, 175 Lennox McLendon, 177, 177 Michael Probst, 178 Adam Nadel, 178 IBM, 180 Katsumi Kasahara, 181 Itsuo Inouye, 181 Michael Tweed, 184 Lennox McLendon (x2), 184 Jim Tuten/Busch Gardens, 186 NASA, 186 EFE, 186 Silvina Frydlewsky, 187 White Sands Missile Range, 187, 193 Win McNamee, 194 Denis Poroy, 194, 195 Manuel Chavez, 196 Lionel Cironneau, 196 Heinz Ducklau, 197 Dimitar Deinov, 198 Peter Lauth/Keystone, 198 Undersea Imaging Intl, 199 Ajit Kumar, 199 David Longstreath, 201 Bernama, 202 Martin Mejia, 203 Doug Dreyer, 204 Jonathan Hayward/CP, 205, 205 Zaheeruddin Abdullah, 211, 214, 216 Katsumi Kasahara, 216 Susan Goldman, 220 Richard Drew, 220-21 Whitney Museum of Modern Art, 224 Joan Marcus, 224 Nigel Teare, 224 John Parkin, 225 Mark Fallander, 225, 235 Kevorn Djansezian, 238, 239 Michael Caulfield, 240 Jose Caruci, 241 Diego Giudice, 241 Thomas Kienzle, 244 Sven Kaestner, 244 Jan Bauer, 247 Kathy Willens, 248 Laurent Rebours, 248 Michel Euler, 249 Michel Lipchitz, 250-51 Kirthmon Dozier, 254/255 & 256 Remy de la Mauviniere, 256 Denis Paquin, 257 Keystone, 257 News Ltd, 258 Susan Sterner, 258 Laurent Rebours, 259 David Longstreath, 260 Brian K. Diggs, 260 Thomas Kienzle, 261 Kevork Djansezian, 261 Steve Holland, 262 (x3), 263 Doug Mills, 264 Eric Draper, 264 Alexander Zemlianichenko, 265 Beth A. Keiser, 265 Lynne Sladky, 266 John Bazemore, 266 Tsugufumi Matsumoto, 267 Denis Paquin, 268 Michael Conroy, 268 Tannen Maury, 269 Mark J. Terrill, 270 Frank Gunn, 270 Drew Murphy, 271 John Bazemore, 271 Bill Sikes, 272 Laurent Rebours, 272 Lionel Cironneau, 273 Luca Bruno, 273 David Graham, 274 Tom Strattman, 274 David Longstreath, 276 Paul Sakuma (x2), 277 Claudio Scaccini, 277 Luca Bruno, 278 Tom Pidgeon, 278 *Sports Illustrated*, 280 Andy Newman, 282 Itsuo Inouye, 282 Jack Smith, 284 Chitose Suzuki, 285 Fabrice Coffrini, 285, 286 Jozef Klamar, 288 Pietro Cinotti, 289 Louisa Buller, 289 Vincent Yu, 290 Pavel Rahman, 291 Rick Rycroft, 293 Chien-Min Chung, 293 Kevork Djansezian, 294 Robert F. Bukaty (x2), 295 Robert F. Bukaty, 296, 300 Bonod Joshi, 302 Peter Dejong, 302 Tony Cheng, 302 Denis Paquin, 304, 305 (x2), 306 (x2), 307 (x2), 308 (x2), 309 (x2), 310 (x2), 311, 312 (x2), 314, 315. **BILDERBERG ARCHIVE:** 221. **BOOMERANG:** 112 Steve Haworth/Zuma. **COMSTOCK:** 221 Dr G. Gerster. **CORBIS:** 10, 18, 18 Mitchell Gerber, 24 Bettmann, 24 Tim Page, 28 & 29 Neal Preston, 41 James Marshall, 47 Nevada Wier, 47 Gina Glover, 48 Kelly Mooney, 59 Kevin Fleming, 63 Kelly Mooney, 66 The Purcell Team, 66 Arne Hodalic, 71 Mitchell Gerber, 72 Hulton-Deutsch Collection, 74 Chris Taylor, 75 Gunter Marx, 76 Reinhard Eisele, 86 Tim Wright, 88 Christopher Cormack, 90 UPI, 93 UPI/Bettmann, 93 Wolfgang Kaehler, 98-99 Science Pictures, 99 Mary Clark/Cordaiy, 106/107 Science Pictures, 110 Dave G. Houser, 111, 132 Anthony Bannister/ABPL, 132/133 Steve Austin/Papilio, 150 Bob Rowan, 150 Kit Kittle, 151 Owen Franken, 154 Earl Kowall, 155 Eye Ubiquitous, 156 Roger Ressmeyer, 162 George Hall, 163 Museum of Flight, 164 George Hall, 179 NASA, 182 Neal Preston, 192 Bettmann, 192 US Department of Defense, 192-93 U.S. Department of Energy, 193 US Department of Defense, 197 Gianni Dagli Orti, 200 Eva Miessler/Ecoscene, 201 Tim Wright, 202-03 Roger Ressmeyer, 203 The Purcell Team, 217 Kevin Fleming, 234 David Reed, 239 Neal Preston, 239 Pat O'Hara, 240 Neal Preston, 242 Erich Auerbach, 242 UPI/Bettmann, 243 Hulton-Deutsch Collection, 244 Stephanie Maze, 245 Richard Glover, 245 Peter Finger, 254 Christian Liewig, 275 Neal Preston (x3), 281 Michelle Chaplow, 292, 296 Tony Arruza, 297 Patrick Ward, 301 Robert Holmes, 300&301 Galen Rowell, 314, 315, 336 Hulton-Deutsch Collection. **EMPICS:** 252, 252, 253, 253 Leo Vogelzang, 254 Tony Marshall, 255 Michael Steele, 259, 286 Mathew Ashton, 287 Presse Sport, 291, 311, 313, 313 Steve Mitchell. **FSP:** 70 David Atlan, 71 Ponomareff, 91 Pete Souza/Gamma/Liason, 97 Ferry/Gamma/Liason, 101 Kumar Ajit/Gamma/Liason. **GARDEN PICTURE LIBRARY:** 142 JS Sira, 142 C. Fairweather, 143 John Glover, 143 JS Sira. **IDOLS:** 19 George Bodnar, 228 Barry Marsden, 229 William Rutten, 232 Barry Marsden, 233 Gene Kirkland, 235 Sergey Sergeyev, 236 Y. Lenquette/Vision. **IMAGE BANK:** 8-9 Daniel Arsenault, 30 Henry Sims, 30-31 Derek Berwin, 32-33 Andy Caulfield, 38-39 C. Van Der Lende, 39 Mitchell Funk, 46 Andy Caulfield, 61 D. Roundtree, 62 Anthony Johnson, 65 D. W. Hamilton, 73 Larry Keenan, 80 Flip Chalfant, 82-83 Tomek Sikora, 85 Bardos&Bardos, 86 Mahaux, 98 Derek Berwin, 106 Garry Gay, 107 Benn Mitchell, 107, 114-15 Derek Berwin, 116 & 118 Joseph Van Os, 123 Derek Berwin, 125 James Carmichael, 125 Joseph van Os, 126 Derek Berwin, 127, 127 Grant V. Faint, 128 Luis Castaneda, 129 P. Goetgeluck, 130 Alain Chambon, 130-31 Luis Castaneda, 140 Grant V. Faint, 135 A. Boccaccio, 145 F. Ruggeri, 146 Steve Bronstein, 147 Andre Gallant, 151 White/Packert, 154 Pete Turner, 154-55 Frans Lemmens, 157, 164 Pete Turner, 167 Terje Rakke, 168 Steve Dunwell, 168-69 T. Anderson, 180-81 Stephen Marks, 182, 190-91 H. De Lespinasse, 212-13 Gary Russ, 226-27 Tomek Sikora, 262-63 Yellow Dog Prds, 278 Terje Rakke, 279 M. Tcherevkoff, 282-83 Jay Silverman, 297 Tom King, 299, 299 Terje Rakke, 304-05 Peter Holst, 306-07 Steve Satshek, 308-09 Terje Rakke, 310-11 David Madison, 312-13 Stephen Marks, 314-15 John Banagan. **IMAGES:** 118 & 119 *National Geographic*, 122 & 124 *National Geographic*. **JOHN CONNOR PRESS:** 57. **KATZ:** 15 Mark Selinger/Outline, 20 Dana Lixenberg/Outline, 21 Andrew Eccles/Outline, 21 Darryl Estrine. **KOBAL:** 25, 210 (x2), 211 (x2), 212, 213 (x2). **LFI:** 228 David Fisher, 230, 230 Ted Hawes, 236, 236 Nick Elgar, 237 Gregg De Guire, 240 David Fisher. **NASA:** Cover, endpapers, 146, 148 (x2), 149 (x3), 188 (x2), 189 (x2). **NETWORK:** 204 Mike Goldwater. **OXFORD SCIENTIFIC FILMS:** 116 Keren Su, 117 Richard Packwood, 120 & 121 Norbet Wu, 129 Mantis, 141 Kjell Sandved. **PA NEWS:** 20 Neil Munns, 22 (x2), 22 Michael Stephens, 23, 45 Sean Dempsey, 51, 63 Manuel Moura/EPA, 78 Chas Breton/Western Daily Press, 81, 105, 124 Hoang Dinh Nam/AFP, 139 EPA, 145 Roslin Institute, 160 Renault, 161 Honda, 162, 163, 185 Rui Vieira, 194, 225, 229 Lousia Buller, 231 Neil Munns (x2), 234 Sean Dempsey, 290 Rebecca Naden. **PLANET EARTH:** 121 James D Watt, 123 Paulo De Oliveira, 134 Chris Huxley, 141 Robert A. Jureit. **POPPERFOTO:** 131 Reuters. **PPCM:** 176. **RETNA:** 232 King Collection, 232 David Atlas, 233 Baron Wolman, 233 Andy Earl. **REX FEATURES:** 11 (x2), 24 Kirk Weddle/Sipa Press, 25 Brian Rasic, 39 Sipa Press, 41 Ralph Merlino, 52 Terry Richards/Sun/Sipa Press, 52 Sipa Press, 63 Nils Jorgenson, 100 Shakhverdiev/Sipa Press, 108 Sipa Press, 108 Ben Simmons/Sipa Press, 109 Dave Hogan, 113 Ian Waldie, 175 Charles Ommanney (x2), 298 MAMP/Sipa Press. **SCIENCE PHOTO LIBRARY:** 104 NIBSC, 105 A. Gragera/Latin Stock. **SOLO:** 20 (x5). **SPLASH:** 10 Rupert Thorpe. **SYGMA:** 68 Alberto Pizzoli, 74 Steve Liss, 103. **TONY STONE:** 30 Tony Garcia, 152-53 Susan Werner, 243 Jon Riley. **WELLCOME TRUST:** 104, 132 (x2). **OTHER:** 6 & 246 Baush & Lomb, 217 *The Big Issue*, 64 Kevin Brown, 77 Saloo Choudhury, 42 Coca-Cola Corporation, 159 Combidrive Ltd, 336 Diageo PLC, 218 Disney, 69 Herb Ferguson, 58 Kevin Rubio & Shant Jordan/Pat Perez of TheForce.net (x3), 7 & 54-55 Ron Tom/Fox Television, 99 Prof. Brimal C. Ghosh, 266 Gordon Gillespie, 170 GT Interactive, 14 Harpo Inc, 28 *Hello!* magazine, 157 Ian Lambot/Foster and Partners, 180 Lego, 43 Levi Strauss & Co, 136 Peter Lomas, 113 Grace Martin, 159 McLaren Cars Ltd, 197 MGM, 172 NEC, 172 Nintendo Corporation, 68 Garry Norman, 173 Panasonic, 43 Pepsi Corporation, 280 & 281 Dag Pike, 32 Residensea, 139 Sharon Robinson, 298 Rudolf Rupperath, 70 Robert Schumann, 65 Sean Shannon, 34 The Collection of Mr & Mrs Bernard C. Solomon, 11 Spelling Productions, 173 Swatch, 172 Transducers Inc, 14 20th Century Fox, 183 20th Century Fox, 208 & 209 20th Century Fox, 219 Matt Groenig/20th Century Fox, 249 Victoria's Secret, 176 Virgin Records, 158 Volkswagen, 209 Warner Bros, 19 Mario Testino/Wea.

ACKNOWLEDGEMENTS

Founder Editor: Norris McWhirter • Guinness Publishing Ltd would like to thank the following organizations and individuals: Andrew Adams • Duncan Anderson • Sarah Angliss • John Arblaster • Belinda Archer • Richard Balkwill • Howard Bass • BBC • Dennis Bird • Paul Boyd • Richard Braddish • Ben Brandstätter • Robert Brook • Christie's • Hilary Curtis at The World • Andrea Davies at the Tate Gallery, London • Peter Dredge at the Royal Yachting Association • Clive Everton • Adrian Firth • Michael Flynn • Foreign and Commonwealth Office • Paulette Foyle • Tim Furniss • Max Glaskin • Dr Martin Godfrey • Simon Gold • Dave Golder • Stan Greenberg • Guinness *Rockopedia®* Team • Capt. Elwyn Hartley Edwards • Ron Hildebrant • Ron Hill • Duncan Hislop • Sir Peter Johnson • Ove Karlsson • Matthew Keating at *The Guardian* • Nicky King • Tara King • Fiona Leahy • Caroline Lucas • Vincent Lucas • Dave McAleer • Chris McHugh • Chris Mason • Keith Melton • Andrzej Michalski • Andy Milroy • The Natural History Museum • Barry Norman • Antonio Pasolini • Natalie Pecht • John Randall • Jo Renshaw • Chris Rhys • Ellen Root • Irvin Saxton • Dr Karl Shuker • Tony Shuker • David Singmaster • Karen Smith • Sotheby's • Gerry Spencer • Kurt Steffick • Martin Stone • Sian Stott at *Hello!* • Jackie Swanson • Steve Trew • Juhani Virola • Jonathan Wall • Professor Kevin Warwick at Reading University • John Watson • Lt. Col. Digby Willoughby • Hugh Wrampling •

getting into *the book*

COLLECTIONS

Interest in big collections, such as the world's biggest collection of Barbie dolls, seen right, is evident from the many requests from collectors received by the *Guinness Book of Records*. To be considered for inclusion, collections should be clearly 'themed' or contain broadly similar, but different, items. Duplicates do not count.

OPEN TO THE PUBLIC

Ashrita Furman, one of the most prolific record-breakers, is pictured here breaking the record for balancing glasses in front of an audience. Most record attempts, particularly those staged to raise money for charity, are widely publicized and attract large numbers of spectators. Few challenges could be as public as those on the *Guinness World Records™: Primetime* TV shows, but all attempts should, where possible, be open to public scrutiny.

SPORTS RECORDS

The *Guinness Book of Records* is the final arbiter for all the records in this book. However, in the case of sporting (and certain similar) records, verification lies with the official world governing body of each sport. For example, records in track and field athletic events, such as the javelin, are provided by the International Amateur Athletic Federation (IAAF).

GETTING INTO THE BOOK

The *Guinness Book of Records* features many people who have accomplished extraordinary feats. Do you think you have what it takes to become one of those extraordinary people? If you think you would like to break, or establish, a record, you are on the way to getting into the book.

I CAN DO THAT

Not everyone can break the 100-m track record, walk the high wire at a record altitude or become the world's youngest supermodel. But everyone can break or set a record, as an individual or as part of a team.

One option might be to start a large and unusual collection. This need not entail great expense: among current record-breaking collections are four-leaf clovers and lightbulbs. Nor would you have to be a professional dancer to take part in an attempt on the world line dance record. Even the most sedentary could participate in a record-breaking event — by joining in the biggest gathering of couples kissing simultaneously, for instance. Another way of getting into the book could be to devise your own record category.

DOCUMENTATION

Each and every record claim must be accompanied by detailed documentation. Two independent witness statements are the minimum requirement, and your witnesses should be people of some standing in the local community: a doctor, lawyer, councillor, police officer or an official of a professional or sporting body, for example. Certain records may also require the judgement of an expert, such as a surveyor or a public health official. Neither witness can be related to you. Witnesses should not only be able to confirm that they have seen the successful progress and completion of the record attempt, but also that the guidelines have been followed. *The Guinness Book of Records* is

BIGGEST AND SMALLEST

The smallest road-worthy car pictured here is one of many tiny items that hold world records. All minuscule and gigantic items should be perfectly scaled-down or scaled-up versions of the real thing. They must be made from the correct materials and be fully functioning.

unable to supply personnel to invigilate attempts but reserves the right to do so.

Many record attempts also require a log book or some form of similar documentation. The requirements are specified in the guidelines. Good quality photographs taken on a 35 mm camera are usually required. Newspaper cuttings, usually local, are useful additional evidence. It is a good idea to get your local newspaper interested in your record challenge and persuade a reporter to be present.

APPLY EARLY

Whatever record category you decide to attempt, it is important to contact us early. If your proposal is accepted as a new category, we may have to draw up new guidelines with the assistance of experts. So please allow both us and you plenty of time for preparation. You should also check with us shortly before the attempt in order to make sure that the record has not recently been broken.

GUIDELINES

Specific guidelines have been drawn up for almost all human achievement challenges, from window cleaning and bed making to stamp licking and custard pie throwing. The six categories for which the most requests are received are ladder climbing, longest paper chain, longest paper clip chain, human centipede, darts and line dancing. The following guidelines for the longest paper clip chain give a flavour of the regulations and standards that record-challengers can expect:

1. The maximum length of each paper clip used is 4 cm ($1\frac{1}{2}$ in).
2. The maximum number of people who may make the chain is 60, and the time limit is 24 hours (in one 24-hour period — not, for example, eight hours one day, eight the next and eight on a third day).
3. The chain must be one single chain, with each clip hooked into one end of another clip.

The current world record for the longest paper clip chain is 27.189 km (16 miles 978 yd). It was made by 60 members of Nanyang Technological University, Hall of Residence 8, Singapore, in 24 hours from 25 to 26 July 1997.

MARATHONS

Marathons, from unicycling to musical feats, are traditionally identified with the *Guinness Book of Records*. Continuous challenges of more than 24 hours operate under strict safety guidelines. Expert advice as well as consultation with the *Guinness Book of Records* should be sought before trying them.

PHOTOGRAPHIC EVIDENCE

Susan Montgomery is pictured below breaking the record for blowing the biggest bubble gum bubble. Detailed documentation is necessary to establish any record claim. For almost all categories, photographic evidence — of a reproducible standard — is required, and a video of the event as well is even better.

WILL IT BE IN THE BOOK?

Not all new records appear in the book. With many thousands of records on the *Guinness Book of Records* database, the book is a selection of the subjects and categories that we believe are of the most interest to our readers. More records will be available on our website.

TAKING CARE

Safety precautions are an important factor in record guidelines. All record attempts are undertaken at the sole risk of the competitor. Guinness Publishing Ltd. cannot be held responsible for any (potential) liability whatsoever arising out of any such attempt, whether to the claimant or any third party.

GUIDELINES

For most human endeavour categories the *Guinness Book of Records* has specific guidelines to ensure that all contestants are attempting a record under exactly the same conditions as previous and subsequent challengers. Only in this way can we compare achievements.

NEW CATEGORIES

Every post brings us a host of wacky suggestions for new record categories, and we try to find ways of encouraging and accepting as many of these ideas as possible. What we are looking for in a new category is a challenge that is interesting, requires skill, is safe and — most importantly — is likely to attract subsequent challenges from other people.

GETTING IN TOUCH

To contact the *Guinness Book of Records*, call 0891 517607* (++ 44 891 517607 if calling from abroad). Alternatively, you can find our website/e-mail us at infouk@guinnessrecords.com, fax us on 0171 891 4504 (++ 44 171 891 4504 if dialling from abroad) or write to us at:
Guinness Publishing Ltd.,
338 Euston Road,
London NW1 3BD,
United Kingdom
* Calls cost no more than 50p per minute.

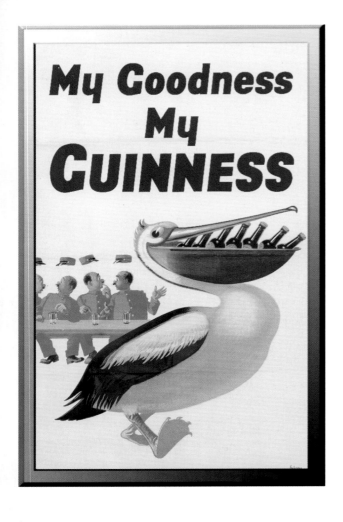

house, yet Guinness did not actually own any of the pubs — except for the Castle Inn on its hop farms at Bodiam, Sussex. Thus the company was always on the look-out for promotional ideas.

Whilst at a shooting party in Co. Wexford, Ireland, in 1951, Sir Hugh Beaver, the company's managing director, was involved in a dispute as to whether the golden plover was Europe's fastest game bird. Again in 1954, an argument arose as to whether grouse were faster than golden plover. Sir Hugh realized that such questions could arise among people in pubs and a book that provided answers for debates such as these would be of great use to licensees.

Chris Chataway, the record-breaking athlete, was then an underbrewer at Guinness' Park Royal Brewery. He recommended the ideal people to produce the book — the twins Norris and Ross McWhirter, whom he had met through athletics events, both having won their blues for sprinting at Oxford. The McWhirters were then running a fact-finding agency in Fleet Street.

They were commissioned to compile what became *The Guinness Book of Records* and, after a busy year of research, the first copy of the 198-page book was bound on 27 August 1955. It was an instant success and became Britain's No. 1 best-seller before Christmas.

In 1759 Arthur Guinness founded the Guinness Brewery at St James' Gate, Dublin, and by 1833 the brewery was the largest in Ireland. Arthur Guinness Son & Co. Ltd became a limited liability company in London in 1886, and by the 1930s Guinness had two breweries in Britain producing its special porter stout. The slogans 'Guinness is good for you', 'Guinness for strength' and 'My Goodness, My Guinness' appeared everywhere. Guinness was the only beer on sale in every public

The Guinness Book of Records English edition is now published in 40 different countries with another 37 editions in foreign languages. Sales of all editions passed 50 million in 1984, 75 million in 1994 and will reach the 100 million mark early in the next millennium.